CW01096213

Front Cover
Martin Söderqvist enjoys the powder in Zermatt.
Photo by Jimmy Petterson.

w w w . s k i i n g a r o u n d t h e w o r l d . n e t

Author
Jimmy Petterson

Primary Photographer
All photos, unless otherwise noted,
are by Jimmy Petterson.

Additional Photographers
Kristoffer Erickson
Ari Heinilä
Keoki Flagg
Igge Holm
Fred Lindholm
Caspar Möller
Ronald Naar
Erik Petterson Sjöqvist
Tom Plofchan
Felix St. Clair-Renard
Martin Söderqvist
Lars Thulin
Papi Tuomala

Graphic Design
Peter Nordgren
Alvaro Susena

Copy-editing and Proofreading
George Koch
Gina Schaar
Patrick Thorne

Image Scanning
Mesán System AB

Produced by
Zetterqvist Publishing Company
Amalia Jönssons gata 16
SE-421 31 Göteborg
Sweden

Printed by
SG Zetterqvist AB, Göteborg, Sweden 2005
Arctic The Silk 130 g

Design/Layout © Zetterqvist Publishing Company 2005
Text/Photo © Jimmy Petterson 2005

ISBN 91-6317-101-5

Below is an incomplete list of the friends, acquaintances and other people who appear among the photos in this book. I have shared some fun in the snow with many of the people on this list, and I extend my thanks to all of them.

Christer Ahlund	Christy Curtis	Anders Hagman	Petri Lehikoinen	Pontus Nordahl	Mika Salokangas	Satuki Takasaka
Antti-Pekka Auvinen	Paul Curtis	Thomas Heisig	Tatu Lehmuskallio	Jazze Noren	Peter Sandberg	Hermann Taxer
Kåre Banke	Ryan Curtis	Christer Henning	Levi Levisen	Kristin Näsman	Kristin Sandven	Andreas Thelander
Simon Bastelica	Marco Degani	Matti Honkanen	Fredrik Liljeberg	Helmut Obermoser	Sylvain Saudan	Papi Tuomala
Uwe Bauer	Jonas Delogne	Simon Jacomet	Pelle Lindh	Pia Oldenburg Vilstrup	Gina Schaar	Tuomas Uotila
Rafael Betschart	John Dorsey	Ken Jensen	Christer Lindgren	Trond Olssen	Leslie Schaar Bowser	Bruno Visconti
Leif Betten	Ortwin Eckert	Keith Johnston	Magnus Loo	Liza Pahl	Charlotte Schager	Henrik Westelius
Christoph Bichsel	Stig Emmanuelsen	Steffan Jossen	Adam Lyberth	Kalle Persson	Rupert Scheiner	Paul White
Alexandre Blanc	Alf Engen	Anders Karlsson	Johan Löfstedt	Erik Petterson Sjöqvist	Florian Schuchter	Jocko Wikström
Maxim Blanc	Andrea Enzio	Mohammed Karraoui	Jason Mack	Jean Michel Pons	Reinhard Senoner	Scott Wolf
Max Boholm	Niclas Fagerlund	Pascal Keller	Emil Magnusson	Glen Plake	Ketil Singstad	
Arne Bredow	Daniel Gardtman	George Koch	Julien Maingault	Kevin Quinn	Eva Sjöqvist Wenzer	
Pierrick Colin	Sergio Gabbi	Kent Kreitler	Carl Mårtensson	Tom Reichert	Felix St. Clair-Renard	
Dean Collins	Alexander Giacomelli	Ludvig Kreutzmann	Anders Nilsson	Bernd Ritschel	Doug Stoup	
Hermann Comploj	Minna Gynther	Espen Laurendz	Jonas Nilsson	Bert Romani	Einar Sund	
Michele Cucchi	Charlie Haggem	Phil Le Roux	Jörgen Nilsson	Antti Salmensuu	Martin Söderqvist	

Jimmy Petterson

SKIING AROUND THE WORLD

Over 30 years in search of the ultimate ski descent

Contents

Rafael Betschart plummets down toward Engelberg on the off-piste descent known as Laub—arguably the best off-piste run in the world.

About the Author

Jimmy Petterson is an American, educated at the University of Southern California and graduated *cum laude* with a bachelor's degree in history, a teaching credential and a master's degree in Instruction and Curriculum. He could have spent his life as a teacher, molding young minds and preparing the next generation to take over our world. Instead, to his father's great disappointment, he has spent most of the last 30 years as a ski bum.

Jimmy's obsessive pursuit of the ultimate ski run and the perfect powder dump has led him to take jobs including ski instructor, off-piste guide, travel guide, slopeside singer-entertainer, bar owner, hotelkeeper, travel arranger and most recently ski writer and photographer. He has skied in 48 countries during his search for ski nirvana, and his work has been published in fifteen of those nations.

Among Jimmy's journalistic accomplishments are 30 magazine covers and more than 300 published ski features. His articles describe his visits and experiences in such far-flung ski destinations as Bolivia, Iceland, Turkey, Greece, Lebanon, Kazakhstan, Uzbekistan, China, Soviet Georgia, Morocco, Greenland, India, Slovakia and Poland. He has also written about and photographed many of the more conventional ski areas of the Alps and the Rockies. Nevertheless, he has built a reputation for his coverage of the more unusual destinations.

Jimmy has described how he came to develop this particular niche.

"During my early childhood in the 1950s, many ski areas in the United States still had a pioneer spirit about them. In the years that followed I have seen the sport grow from the crawling stage into the multi-billion-dollar mega-industry it is today. Naturally, I embrace the progress of the industry and the access it has given me to a myriad of mountains and slopes that were unattainable by lift a generation earlier. At the same time, I also sometimes miss the simplicity, the sense of pioneering and the familiarity that existed among the early patrons of the sport.

"Over the years that my career has afforded me the opportunity to go almost anywhere in the world, my roots have often been evident in my choice of location. Interspersed with reporting on some of the biggest and best ski resorts in the world, I often sought tiny, remote and even underdeveloped areas at which to ski. In the likes of Antuco, Chile or Kashka-Suu, Kyrgyzstan, most of the skiers on the hill were on a first-name basis, and a pioneer atmosphere was still the order of the day."

In the pages that follow, Jimmy has combined the many legs of his ski odyssey into this unique book.

"It has been a tough job," laments Jimmy, his tongue pressed hard into his cheek as he wipes mock sweat from his brow, "but somebody had to do it!"

Acknowledgement and Dedication

As a child, one of my favorite stories was that of Peter Pan. He and all his friends never grew old, and I, too, have tried diligently to avoid progressing to the next stage after childhood. Peter Pan lived on a magic island where aging didn't take place. I, on the other hand, have used the simplest of means—avoiding responsibility.

As I watched many of my contemporaries graduate from prestigious Beverly Hills High School, go on to collect degrees and diplomas from various institutions of higher learning and begin to climb the corporate ladder, I opted for the simple life of a ski bum. This lifestyle included no pressure of corporate decision-making, no entrapments of serious relationships and a pleasant, superficial, day-to-day philosophy of living.

I can't really take all the blame or all the credit for pursuing this hedonistic line of non-work, for it actually lies deep-rooted in my family. My mother, born in Austria, and my father, a Norwegian by birth, were both already avid skiers by the time they immigrated to the United States during World War II. My mother became the first female certified ski instructor in California, and both my parents worked in small ski areas during the 1940s. Skiing, in other words, was their lifestyle too. The only difference between us is that they were able to shift gears into a "normal" pattern of life when I came into the world—well, almost normal.

People speak figuratively of "being born on skis", but I suppose that I came as close to that reality as is literally possible. My mother attempted to ski in her eighth month of pregnancy, an overzealous act which resulted in my being born two weeks prematurely.

"Watch out for those moguls, mom!"

A couple of years later, at the age of two-and-a-half, mom and dad put me on my first pair of skis in the local San Gabriel Mountains, outside Los Angeles. Thus began my long journey through the world of snow.

The family connection to the mountains actually goes one generation further back, to my great-uncle, Paul Preuss. During my formative years, my mother often spoke of her famous Uncle Paul, whom she told me had been a well-known mountain climber back in Austria in the years preceding World War I. Growing up in Los Angeles a half-century later, where fame was equated with movie stars and baseball heroes, I had no proper frame of reference to gauge my late uncle's prowess. Even when a book came out about the life of Uncle Paul, it was written in Italian, by an Italian climber–author, and it all still seemed rather obscure and distant.

Much later, in the mid-1980s, Reinhold Messner, renowned as the greatest climber in the world by virtue of his oxygen-free ascents of Everest and other 8000-meter-high peaks, wrote another book about Uncle Paul. It was only then that I realized that my mother had not really exaggerated. Messner described Paul Preuss as his idol and as the father of free climbing. I began to realize that our family truly has a tradition as mountain pioneers.

In discussing our family's mountain heritage, I do not want to leave out my uncle, Edi Schaar. While Paul Preuss died long before I was born, my mother's brother Edi, who skied from 1913-2000, was an inspiration to all of us in the family. Edi was the link between Paul Preuss and my generation. Born in 1905 into an entirely different world than the one we now live in, Edi was an alpine climber and a ski pioneer whose long life mirrored the development of nearly a century of skiing.

Edi was a participant on countless ski tours in the Alps at a time when you could count the number of ski lifts in the world on the fingers of one hand, and ski touring was synonymous with skiing. He was one of the first people to try metal edges, as Rudolph Lettner, the inventor of the ski edge, mounted edges on my uncle's skis free of charge in exchange for an endorsement. Edi escaped Nazi Austria by hiking over the Alps, and a year later, he began teaching this very European sport to the inhabitants of his new homeland, America.

Kristin Näsman pauses on the Bernkogel in Saalbach, Austria to enjoy the day's last rays of sunshine.

Perhaps most important, Uncle Edi had an undying passion for the mountains and for skiing, which kept him gliding over the snow into his 96th year of life. To see an old man's enthusiasm for and devotion to this demanding young-person's sport has been a major influence on me. Perhaps, having seen Edi ski and hike in the mountains in his eighties and nineties has been the pixie dust for my own belief in Peter Pan.

At the same time as I acknowledge and thank the previous generations of my family for their part in helping lead and guide me down this happy mountain slope of life, I must also give thanks and credit to another person who has inspired me—my son, Erik.

As we get older, we sometimes have trouble gleaning the same enjoyment from a pursuit as we did in our youth. This is only natural. One cannot expect a person who is experiencing powder snow for the one-thousandth time to get precisely the same exhilaration and thrill that he felt 50 years earlier. Despite my drinking as much water from the fountain of youth as I could get my hands on, the law of diminishing returns has affected me, no matter how hard I have fought against it.

Since 1989, I have had the good fortune of holding down the first steady job of my life—that of being a daddy. I didn't really apply for the job, but it was nevertheless foisted upon me, and it has been a great pleasure ever since.

Like any job, fatherhood has its positive and negative aspects, but one of the great fringe benefits is the infusion of youth into one's own life. All of a sudden, bouncing through the powder for the one-thousand-and-first time becomes a new experience all over again, as one is teaching, watching and enjoying it with a loved one for whom the experience is truly new. Erik has been a great and patient learner, with a father who has certainly tried to push him too far, too fast.

There have been a number of long-suffering girlfriends who have had to endure my passion for skiing, and they too deserve thanks for their ability to put up with my misappropriated priorities on so many occasions. In addition, they have had to suffer through a series of courses in off-piste and powder skiing which they never chose to take of their own free will. These instructional sessions became a nerve-wracking, pressure-filled test of each one's worthiness as a girlfriend.

As if that was not enough, they were also forced to go against all normal female nesting instincts, and live an insecure and financially unstable seasonal existence, so as to have any chance to maintain a semblance of a relationship with me. So, Eva, Minna and Aynur deserve many thanks and much credit for their perseverance, in each case, for much longer than could have been expected.

Over the years, I have also had the good fortune to meet and share powder turns and ideas with a number of other ski photographers. Some of them have been kind enough to donate a few photos to

this book, and I am honored and flattered that they are a part of this project. Many thanks go to Kristoffer Erickson, Keoki Flagg, Ari Heinilä, Igge Holm, Fred Lindholm, Caspar Möller, Ronald Naar, Tom Plofchan, Felix St. Clair-Renard, Martin Söderqvist, Lars Thulin and Papi Tuomala for their generous contributions.

Finally, I would like to thank the many ski friends, cronies, buddies and pals who have made this odyssey through the ski world so much fun. Happiness shared is happiness doubled, and this is certainly so in skiing.

From my early ski days in Alta, Utah with my childhood friend, Johnny DeStrakosch, to my most recent seasons, it would not have been half the fun without the friends. We have shared a love of skiing that created enormous amounts of positive energy. Sharing with friends has turned many run-of-the-mill ski days into memories for life.

In between Johnny and the present day is an almost endless list of wonderful people with whom I have shared a run, a day, a vacation, a season and sometimes a lot more. While it is impossible to name them all here, I would like to mention a few people who have been great ski partners and who have also played a roll as ski models for my lens. Among those people who deserve mention in this category are Christy, Paul and Ryan Curtis, Daniel Gardtman, Minna Gynther, Christer Henning, Keith Johnston, Anders Karlsson, George Koch, Caspar Möller, Jonas Nilsson, Rupert Scheiner, Marja and Mika Salokangas, Martin Söderqvist and Papi Tuomala. (A more complete list of friends and acquaintances who appear as ski models appears at the front of the book.)

During the years of my work as a ski journalist, these friends and many more have been kind enough to ski for my camera. The task of being a ski model has sometimes been a difficult sacrifice, as minutes and hours have been eaten away from some of the best powder days. Therefore, my ski friends also deserve a great deal of thanks.

There is very important work that goes on behind the scenes in the task of creating a book of this nature. I am very grateful to Patrick Thorne, Gina Schaar and George Koch whose work with copy-editing and proofreading has been invaluable to me.

Another person who deserves thanks for his brilliant work on this project is Peter Nordgren, the man responsible for the layout of this book. Peter has had to put up with my persistent meddling with his work, but he has dealt with my constant presence in his office with remarkable patience and understanding.

My great hope is that the future will bring more of the same joy of skiing that has already encompassed my life for so many years. I hope that I, along with Erik and my many ski buddies, will continue to frequent the slopes as long as Uncle Edi did.

Bring on a little more pixie dust please.

7

A strong beam of light shines up toward the heavens from the other side of the range
to create a bizarre and beautiful sunset in the Milky Way region of Italy.

Introduction

Most everything begins with an idea. Despite the light bulb picture that has come to symbolize the idea, ideas do not often just click into our brain as one turns on a light switch. More often, they develop over time, from a primitive, rough thought into a more refined concept, before eventually becoming reality.

So it was with the idea for *Skiing Around the World*. This idea began as a game, taught to me by my friend Papi Tuomala. In 1985, the same year I began my career as a ski journalist, Papi told me of a competition that he had with his friends. It was quite simple. One got a plus point for each land one skied in, one got a minus point for each visited country that offered skiing and where one had not skied, and the person with the most points was the leader.

Because of my new profession as a ski writer, I became very successful at this game, rapidly overtaking Papi and other friends. Somewhere along the way, I began to realize that I had actually skied more countries than most people had ever visited. This odyssey has not only provided some very interesting and sometimes unusual ski experiences, but it has been a fascinating journey through a cultural smorgasbord.

As a ski writer, I am often in need of reference material, and I became well acquainted with ski books. In searching through many such volumes, I noticed that a certain kind of book that would interest me very much did not seem to exist. Because I was so bent on visiting odd and unusual ski destinations, I sought a book that would tell me about such places, as well as show me pictures so that I could visualize whether skiing in such a spot would be interesting or not. I could not find such an animal.

There were zillions of books on ski technique, many guide books to the top resorts in America, the Alps or even the world, and volumes on the history of skiing. None of the literature, however, focused on the different ski and cultural experiences that one could find by traversing the globe to the outer limits of the ski galaxy.

Many guidebooks told me the best runs and restaurants in Chamonix, Aspen or St. Anton, but nowhere could I find the number of lifts in Dizin, Iran, the vertical drop in Isafjördur, Iceland, or the parameters of the ski season in Cedars, Lebanon. I could find no photos of the skiing in Bansko, Bulgaria; Nozawa Onsen, Japan; or Vasilitsa, Greece; so I did not know if the slopes were tree-lined runs or open bowls, and I had no idea if they would provide good off-piste skiing or not. Some obscure spots on the skiers' map could be diamonds in the rough, and others would certainly not be worth a visit even if I were staying an hour away. How was I to know which areas were best suited to my needs?

There was really only one way to find out—go to the source. And so, I did, time and time again. I did not make these trips with professional models but rather with friends who were good skiers.

This book is the product of these many journeys. It is my hope that it will help others decide the most suitable destination for them to ski and inspire them to venture into an ever wider range of countries to mix a ski holiday with an interesting cultural experience. I hope my readers will glean the knowledge to find the best skiing in the developed ski world and to embark on adventures in the underdeveloped sections of the planet as well.

Finally, I hope that today's generation of skiers can, with the help of this book, find their way to one or two of the wonderful locations, lost in a time warp, where skiing is still a pastime and not an industry. There are various countries where the sport is still in its infancy. It is at a stage of development equivalent to that in the United States or the Alps in the 1940s. I think that many people would enjoy, in an odd sort of way, the experience of skiing as it once was—a hobby for a small fraternity of friends who wanted to get away from the city and sought both exercise and solitude in the mountains.

With regard to the developed ski countries of the world, it is not my intention to describe all the ski areas nor is it my plan to even choose, necessarily, the best ski resorts. Rather, I wish to describe a carefully chosen handful of ski areas that are representative of each particular country. The chosen spots will include some of the largest, most famous and best ski areas, some smaller, lesser known but worthwhile areas, and some that are picked simply because of their beauty or some unusual characteristic.

Regardless of whether you want tips on the best off-piste skiing in top resorts, suggestions of powder pearls that have not yet been discovered by the masses, or locations at the outer limits of the ski world, you will be able to find the information here. Welcome to *Skiing Around the World*.

Jimmy Petterson
writer, photographer and ski bum

South America in a Nutshell																
LOCATION	NEAREST TOWN	NEAREST AIRPORT	SEASON	PEAK ELEVATION	VERTICAL DROP	SIZE	SNOW	BEAUTY	VILLAGE	NOVICE	INTERMEDIATE	ADVANCED	OFF-PISTE	NIGHTLIFE	RATING AVERAGE	WEB SITE
ARGENTINA																
Copahue	Caviahue	Neuquén	July-September	2151 m	405 m	2	1	2	4	2	4	3	1	2	1	2.2	www.caviahue.com
Cerro Bayo	Villa La Angostura	Bariloche	July-September	1752 m	732 m	2	2	2	5	3	2	3	2	2	2	2.5	www.cerrobayoweb.com
Cerro Castor	...huaia	...	June-October	967 m	792 m	2	1	3	4	3	2	3	3	4	2	2.7	...rocastor.com
Ce...			July-September		970 m	3						3	3	2			...tanatago-
														2		

Nutshell Guide

Each geographical section of this book finishes with a chart entitled, "In a Nutshell". This chart needs some explanation to get the most use out of it.

Some of the categories, like vertical drop and size of the resort, are quantitative and simple to understand, while many of the other categories are the subjective opinion of the author, based on personal experience and extensive research.

RATING SCALE
1. Poor
2. Fair
3. Good
4. Very good to excellent
5. This score indicates that the area is exceptional in this particular category.

NEAREST TOWN   This category is to help the reader locate the ski resort on the map, in case the resort is small and not so well-known. In many cases, this category is unnecessary, as the ski resort is also the nearest town. Most resorts in the Alps and North America fall into this category. In other cases the nearest town and the nearest airport could well be the same refer to the same place. In certain cases, however, the ski resort is not a town. In other cases, the ski resort and the town, although they are more or less at the same location, have different names.

NEAREST AIRPORT   This category generally indicates the closest international airport. Nevertheless, that airport is not always the most practical location to fly to. The best airport to fly to is dependent on whether there are direct flights from one's embarkation point to the relevant international airport. For example, some Austrian resorts are closest to the international airport in Salzburg. Nevertheless, if one is flying from a location that does not have direct flights to Salzburg, it is generally more practical to fly to Munich and continue by ground transport than to wait for a connecting flight.

SEASON   The season indicates the normal opening and closing times of the ski resort. This often changes from year to year depending on the amount of snow that falls that season. Nowadays, the calendar also plays a part in the length of the season. Many ski areas stay open for one week after Easter and then close. Therefore, in a year when Easter falls early, their lifts will cease operation earlier than in a season with a late Easter. The best way to stay abreast of the exact opening and closing dates is by checking their web site.

PEAK ELEVATION   This figure indicates the highest point in the lift system. It has nothing to do with the highest mountain in the area. This figure is given in meters. There are advantages to high altitude resorts and other advantages to ski areas that are lower, and therefore, no rating points have been assessed on the basis of peak elevation.

VERTICAL DROP   This is given in meters and a rating is also indicated in this category. The vertical drop is measured as the vertical difference between the top and bottom of the longest uninterrupted run in the lift system. This figure can sometimes differ from the information on the ski resort's home page. The resorts sometimes measure vertical drop as the difference between the highest point in the lift system and the base of the lowest lift.

Ski areas with less than 400 vertical meters of skiing, are assessed one point. A resort with 400-799 meters of vertical receives two points. One with 800-1199 meters rates three points, 1200-1599 meters earn a resort four points, and all ski areas with 1600 vertical meters or more receive five points.

While ski resorts with big vertical typically offer much more diversity, they also usually attract many more skiers. I, personally, have had some of my most memorable ski days in tiny ski areas where the vertical drop is minimal, but the number of skiers on the slopes is far fewer than the vertical meters. This equation can often make for a great day of skiing with the right conditions.

SIZE   This quantitative category is based on the number of ski lifts. It awards one point to ski areas with fewer than ten lifts, two points to resorts with 10-19 lifts, three points to those with 20-29 lifts, four points to areas with 30-39 ski lifts, and five points to resorts with 40 lifts or more.

SNOW   This is a category based on both snow quality and quantity. Quality is, of course, a very subjective category. It can be negatively affected by proximity to the sea or a large body of water that would make for a higher frequency of wet snow. In addition, some ski resorts are victims of particular winds that play havoc with the snow conditions on a regular basis. This fact also plays a role in the qualitative part of this score.

The elevation of the resort is also a factor in calculating snow quality, with higher resorts generally offering better quality. Finally, the direction of the slopes is factored into this equation as well. North-facing slopes in the Northern Hemisphere, and south-facing pistes below the equator are most likely to preserve snow quality between storms. Of course even with all these factors being taken into consideration, the snow may be better or worse than expected on the day that you choose to visit!

BEAUTY   Beauty is in the eye of the beholder, so this is one of the most subjective categories. I personally find jagged peaks and cliffs to be more beautiful than rolling hills. I also find the dramatic features of volcanoes and glaciers to add an extra dimension to the beauty of a resort. Finally, ski areas that offer panoramas over the ocean or other bodies of water score highly on my personal beauty scale.

VILLAGE   This is a category that rates the charm/ambiance of a ski village or town. It also takes the visual beauty of the town into consideration. It does not have anything to do with practicality, or the quality of the hotels, restaurants, and other services. Older, authentic villages that predate the ski industry rate much higher on my scale than purpose-built villages, even if they are state of the art.

NOVICE   This category simply rates the area for beginners. It reflects how suitable the slopes are for skiers who are in the first week or two of their skiing life.

INTERMEDIATE   This category rates the resort for intermediate terrain. Resorts which had poor grooming or lots of moguls when I visited do not rate very highly, while lift systems that offer good cruising terrain score well. A large ski area with good intermediate terrain will score more highly than a small ski area with similar terrain because the large area offers more variation.

ADVANCED   This section is based on the number of pistes that are rated black and on the variety offered by the more difficult runs. A ski area that has some steep pistes with moguls and other tough runs that are groomed will rate more highly because of this diversity.

This score only applies to the pistes, as off-piste skiing is a separate category. Many ski areas that receive a high score for advanced skiers get an equally high rating for their off-piste skiing, but it is not always so. Some ski resorts, like Saalbach-Hinterglemm for example, have very few steep slopes and nary a mogul, but have many good off-piste descents.

OFF-PISTE   This is a section which is close to my heart. It is my favorite sort of skiing. It takes many factors into consideration including average snowfall, normal quality of snow, amount of open terrain, availability of tree-skiing and even the number of powder freaks who generally frequent the mountain. Certain areas in the world which are famous for their off-piste skiing do not score as well as other areas simply because there are too many good skiers at those locations on a seasonal basis. The plethora of powder hounds that frequent Chamonix, for example, causes Chamonix to receive a lower rating than lesser-known Andermatt.

The United States and Canada are most famous in the world for their snow quality, but they generally do not score as highly in this category as the Alpine resorts. The reason for this is the higher tree line in North America, the smaller size of the North American ski areas, and the often restrictive policy toward off-piste skiing that exists in the U.S. and Canada.

NIGHTLIFE   This section gives a score that considers both the après-ski scene and the nightlife available after dinner. In some cases the ambiance of the resort's after-ski scene could give it a good rating, even if the nightlife is not as exuberant as in other locations. Telluride, for example, scores well here because of the originality of many of the old Western bars that date back to the 1800s.

In more unconventional ski areas, such as heliski operations, I use a different scale. In such cases, the nightlife category is more indicative of interesting options after the ski day is finished, but it is not comparable to the traditional après-ski in a conventional resort. Canadian Mountain Holidays' resort in the Bobby Burns region, for example, is isolated in the wilderness and therefore scores low on the nightlife rating. Himachal Heliski, by comparison, based in the fascinating Indian village of Manali, offers skiers a fantastic cultural experience once the chopper blades have come to rest. It therefore scores well in this category.

RATING AVERAGE   This is a total average score of the other categories. This can often be a misleading figure. If one has a specific reason for visiting a ski resort, the rating average is not a good way of finding the best resort for you. For example, a resort may be very suitable for off-piste skiing, but has received low scores for its suitability for novices, intermediates, and disco-dancers, thus giving it a poor overall rating. This section gives the best scores to large resorts that are extremely well-rounded, while it is rather unfair to small, cozy resorts that excel in one or two categories.

WEB SITE   This category is rather cut and dried. Often, the web site given is the official web site of the resort, if that exists. Some of the official web sites are only in the local language. As this kind of thing is being updated regularly, I have not specified which web sites are in English and which are only offered in the native language of the resort.

ABOVE: Einar Sund leaps out over the fjord in Narvik, Norway.

Warning: Don´t Try This at Home

When people first began strapping boards to their feet and sliding down mountains in this peculiar fashion, there were, of course, no pistes. Nowadays, for skiers to enjoy and appreciate the same sense of freedom and excitement that their forefathers got from skiing, they must seek experiences outside the marked trails. Although this is quite natural, unfortunately the number of casualties from avalanches has been on the rise in recent years.

In this day and age the use of transceivers, shovels and avalanche probes is becoming increasingly common among off-piste enthusiasts, and the equipment is more sophisticated than ever before. But the number of backcountry skiers is on the rise, and one reason for the increase in fatalities can probably be attributed to a lack of adequate understanding of the issues involved in off-piste skiing. A second contributing factor can be that a rider's love and addiction to the powder experience

causes him to take foolish risks. Without some knowledge to allow his intellect to do battle with his emotion in the decision-making process, he is almost certain to take too many chances.

It cannot be emphasized enough how important it is that off-piste skiers are equipped with the three aforementioned pieces of potentially life-saving equipment every time they venture past the perimeter of the secured ski area. But this alone is not enough. Without a reasonable amount of avalanche knowledge and education, this equipment may serve no better purpose than to help a skier's next of kin locate his corpse.

Enlisting the services of a mountain guide is also a step in the right direction, but that is no guarantee of safety from the white death. Guides often make mistakes and overstep the boundaries of prudence in their desire to satisfy their clients. A number of the largest

LEFT PAGE
Avalanche as seen from the Tasman Glacier in New Zealand.

THIS PAGE
UPPER: Avalanche rescue dog.
LOWER: It's important to pay attention to the signs.

brought even more snow on top of the unstable base, our leaders decided that on our final day, we would still make an attempt to ski in the highly wind-sensitive regions above 5000 meters.

I was silent throughout breakfast. The food seemed tasteless, and nothing slid down easily past the lump in my throat. I thought about my instincts, which I had ignored two years earlier. I conjured up a picture in my mind of my young son. I also visualized staying behind and meeting a triumphant group of skiers later that afternoon, returning from a successful conquest of the peak that we had come to ski. All my many experiences created a tumultuous kaleidoscope in my brain, as I wrestled with the decision that would have to be made momentarily.

Fifteen minutes after breakfast, I walked out to the helicopter. Many surprised looks and questions greeted me, when the rest of our party saw me arrive in tennis shoes and blue jeans. I wished them well, and returned to my tent at our base camp, as the whir of helicopter blades slowly faded into the distance.

For the next six hours I worried about the group. Then finally, the helicopter reappeared, a speck on the horizon, and soon after, the group disembarked all smiles. The first ones out of the chopper quickly related the day's events for me. Our lead guide had once again set an avalanche into motion high up on Mt. Semanyov. This slide fortunately did not take him along for the ride, and the plan was then aborted. They had spent the rest of the day skiing on safer slopes.

My emotions were justifiably mixed—relief, for the group had all arrived back safely; justification, for my fears proved to be correct; and envy, for I had missed a great powder day in a spot where I would certainly get few chances to revisit. Perhaps, my strongest feeling, however, was one of satisfaction, for after over 20 years of struggle, I had been able, at least for this one time, to say no.

Keeping all of this in mind, PLEASE DO NOT USE THIS BOOK AS A GUIDE. Use it for inspiration and information. Add to it the proper equipment, practice in the use of that equipment, a local guide, and an education in avalanche science. Then, enjoy the wide and wonderful world of skiing.

avalanches with which I personally have come in contact during my many off-piste adventures have occurred in the accompaniment of a mountain guide.

In the aftermath of a very close brush with death, while skiing with a guide some years ago, I felt compelled to ponder my fate, consider my mistakes, and discern what I should have done differently. The case was clear. I had ignored my own instincts and knowledge, and allowed the fact that I had a guide to lull me into a false sense of security. I had turned off my own intellect and allowed myself to be led astray.

Had I been a less experienced skier, I could perhaps have laid the blame on our guide, but that was not the case. By that time, I had accumulated enough experience to be responsible for my own decisions, even if my ideas might have differed from those of my guide. I hoped the lesson would be internalized properly.

It did not take too long before this "learning experience" was put to the test. Two years later, I was on a high-altitude heliskiing adventure in Kazakhstan. On the fourth day of our six-day adventure, our lead guide was swept away but survived a large slab avalanche. After a day that

NORTH AMERICA I

PREVIOUS PAGES: The author ponders life amidst the glassy waters of Valdez Arm, Alaska. Photo by Caspar Möller.
THIS PAGE: Charlie Haggem shows off some of the steep terrain of Mt. Baker, Washington.
RIGHT PAGE: The snow-capped peaks of the San Gabriel Mountains seem close enough to touch behind the palm trees of Los Angeles.

Chapter 1. UNITED STATES

It is altogether fitting that I begin my story in the United States, for it is here that my odyssey began more than 50 years ago. Believe it or not, ski areas exist in 41 of the 50 states, including such unlikely ones as Indiana and Iowa in the flatlands of the nation, Alabama and Georgia in the Deep South, and even Hawaii.

Nevertheless, the best skiing in the United States is found in the West, and I have chosen to describe a range of western U.S. destinations to represent American skiing.

This trip begins in the San Gabriel Mountains outside Los Angeles, where I first affixed my wobbly two-year-old legs onto a pair of boards. This is an area where one can easily ski in the mountains and swim in the Pacific Ocean on the same day. The travelogue also visits the Sierra Nevada Mountains of California, the Cascades of the Pacific Northwest, and various destinations in the Rocky Mountains. The final stop of this chapter is America's last frontier—Alaska.

Many ski areas in the American West have some unique quality. In the Sierra Nevada Mountains, Lake Tahoe provides one of the world's most beautiful backdrops for skiing. Taos, New Mexico lies in the middle of Indian Territory, amidst spectacular desert scenery. There, the dry, desert air makes for some of the best snow in the country.

The Wasatch Range and other sub-ranges of the Rocky Mountains are also famous for their dry, light powder. In Utah, Alta offers arguably the greatest powder skiing in the world. Colorado's tiny Wolf Creek, a little-known ski area, gets more snow than anywhere else in the state, and historic Telluride is not only one of the best ski mountains in the Rockies but is also a fascinating, old mining town.

Then, in the Pacific Northwest, one skis on volcanoes, and the likes of Mt. Bachelor, Mt. Hood and Mt. Baker show a different aspect of nature that also stands out for its unusual beauty.

While very few skiers ever make it to the remote state of Alaska, it has had extensive press coverage in recent years, with good reason. Many skiers love to push their limits and experience something exotic and extreme. Alaska is certainly the place to do it.

SAN GABRIEL MOUNTAINS — EARLY BEGINNINGS

I remember it as if it were yesterday, although over 50 years have passed since our family ski vacations were initiated. Those early excursions are among the strongest recollections I have of my childhood.

My mother was a saint and my father was a martyr. Time has given me that insight, to which I was, of course, oblivious, when those early weekend ski trips transpired.

Our home was about a two-and-a-half-hour drive from the local mountains. More accurately speaking, two-and-a-half hours of driving got us to our destination when we left the house early on Sunday morning. The return trip was at least a three-and-a-half-hour ordeal of weekend drivers in a slow and steady procession, winding their way down the San Gabriel and San Bernardino mountain roads until they all funneled into the clogged L.A. freeway system.

Add to this scenario the fact that my mother's best friend, Ini DeStrakosch, would gab and gossip nonstop with my mom for the entire journey. Meanwhile, her children, Johnny and Peggy, joined my sister and I to create a purgatory of shrill screams, sudden bursts of laughter and loud arguments all the way home, while dad was trying to weave his way through merciless Sunday evening traffic.

I HAVE ANOTHER VERY DISTINCT RECOLLECTION of my early ski days. In this case, my memory has been enhanced by the many times my father, in later years, detailed the story for different friends. It was probably not the only incident of my premature retirement from skiing, but it was, no doubt, the most volatile.

This particular outburst of childish rage occurred at the local area of Blue Ridge (today part of a ski area called Mountain High). It occurred on an occasion when the powder was very deep and a blizzard raged throughout the day, rendering visibility close to nil. My parents loved to ski powder, and this day provided a rare opportunity to try and pass on that heritage to their offspring.

The hitch was that it is not so easy to learn to ski powder, and nine-year-old Jimmy was becoming extremely frustrated with his lack of success in this new type of snow. By the afternoon, fatigue was added to frustration after my umpteenth fall and the usual struggle to try to get back up out of my self-created hole. Finally, I removed both of my skis and began struggling down through the heavy snow on foot. I stumbled through the storm, casting my skis down the mountain, one after another in front of me. All the while, tears were streaming down my face, and

I screamed at the top of my lungs that I was never again in my life going to ski.

I added a number of epithets about how much I hated skiing, and basically did everything in my power to evoke a sense of guilt in my poor father. Of course, my father's only sin was that he had been generously giving his time to try to instruct me in the fine art of powder skiing, while he most certainly would have rather been making powder turns with my mother on the steeper slopes.

Despite his efforts to laugh off my temper tantrum, I am sure that seeds of doubt must have crept into his fatherly conscience. He must have wondered whether he had made the right decision to take me on that particular run.

The ski areas around Los Angeles were typical family hills in the 1950s and still are today. Such locals' areas exist, in fact, all over the United States and around the world and are the grass-roots backbone of the ski industry. Today, with so much emphasis on freeride skiing, it can sometimes be these small, simple family resorts that provide wonderful opportunities for finding good powder, because the regular patrons are busy teaching their children to ski on the bunny slopes.

The mountains around Southern California have a handful of ski areas all situated 70 to 160 kilometers from Los Angeles. One can choose among Bear Mountain, Kratka Ridge, Mountain High, Mt. Baldy,

Mt. Waterman, Snow Valley and Snow Summit. There are about 70 lifts among these areas, and although one cannot compare the San Gabriel and San Bernardino Mountains with the Rockies, they do offer some fairly good skiing from mid-November into April.

During a recent trip to L.A., my friend Caspar Möller and I decided to visit Mt. Waterman, which along with Mt. Baldy has some of the best off-piste skiing in Southern California. It had been raining for a few days in the city, and we awoke to a Los Angeles morning right out of the 1930s—the pre-smog era when Angelinos awoke on most winter mornings with a view from the snow to the sea.

As we headed northeast out of the city, the snow-covered range looked close enough to touch. We could already see the possibilities as we approached Mt. Waterman along the Angeles Crest Highway. Off to our right was a whole array of steep ridges and ravines scattered with widely spaced pines. Whichever route through the trees that an off-piste skier would choose took him right down to the road, just a short hitchhike away from the lower lift.

Mt. Waterman, with only three lifts, is one of the smaller areas in Southern California, but we needed no more. The powder was superb, and we were all alone in the trees. Thumbing a ride was easy at first but became increasingly difficult as the day wore on. Something had to be done.

Usually, powder hounds are ecstatic to have their slopes exclusively, but

THIS PAGE
LEFT: A teenaged Jimmy Petterson breaks through the Alta powder in the 1960s. This is really where the seed was planted. I spent the next 35 years trying continually to recapture this feeling all over the world. Photo by Tom Plofchan.
RIGHT: Baldy Chutes.

RIGHT PAGE
Alta powder is world-famous for its low water content.

we needed a third skier now, so that two of us could ski and the last person could pick the others up. We combed the lunch cafeteria, observing people's garb and trying to discern who might be a likely candidate for off-piste skiing. There was nobody.

We took one run on the piste and saw a lone skier doing some serious mogul bashing, and we knew we had our man. Our recruit was only too willing to be shown some powder gullies, and for the rest of the day, we took turns—first skiing down two runs of powder and then running a shuttle bus service for the other two.

Our return to L.A. took us through the downtown freeway interchange at exactly the worst time of the evening. The traffic was at a dead standstill and a number of horns were honking impatiently. Caspar and I were passive. Our dinner might have to wait an extra hour, but we were returning to the city with a better understanding of why millions of people were willing to put up with this kind of inconvenience on a regular basis.

ALTA — SENTIMENTAL JOURNEY

Most of us have a special place, very dear to our heart, where we spent many vacations with our family as children. It is a picturesque and timeless spot where family tradition took us back time and time again during those youthful years of endless summers and white winters.

For some of us, this special place is grandma's summerhouse by the lake, full of funny old furniture, vinyl records, a stack of ancient Donald Duck comics from when Carl Barks still drew the characters, and those bunk beds that were so much fun to sleep in. For others, this childhood tradition brought us to an Alpine ski resort, where we would always stay in little Pension *Herzlich*, and Frau and Herr Hasenbichler would welcome us each winter as if we were their own long-lost children. The down comforters were so soft and billowy that we kids could get lost in them for hours, and we knew every tree stump and mogul in the resort as we knew our own backyard. For all of us, our special place is a location as secure as our own bedroom, where nothing changed from year to year, and where the whole family, even dad, had time to play together.

Alta, Utah, is for me such a place. My parents, my sister, Christy, and I began going to Alta in the early 1960s, when I was twelve. For the next ten years, we spent every Christmas and Easter vacation in this small ski resort which already then had a reputation for the deepest and lightest powder in the world.

As I look back through rose-tinted glasses, it seems that it invariably

snowed four days out of every seven. On the first night, the lodge staff often dusted off some vintage 16-millimeter footage of ski school boss Alf Engen and his staff bobbing up and down deftly in a sea of white, and we would all get in the mood for the week to come. They would show this stuff in slo-mo, of course, so we would literally drool as we saw Alf's chest breaking through the powder like a snowplow in front of a locomotive—and that was in his *up* motion! Then he would drop back down and submerge entirely before reappearing, mouth agape, gasping for air.

All the while we watched, it was snowing buckets outside. It was a wonderful feeling, watching Alf do what he did best, knowing that the next morning we too would be enshrouded in powder.

There was a certain status to being first on the mountain and last off the hill, and when it was snowing, we almost always got to the lift while they were still digging it out. We were never alone. There were always dozens of people waiting for the Wildcat Lift to creak into motion on a snowy morning. Sometimes we were first and very proud, but it didn't really matter. There was always enough for everybody.

Care was needed when skiing powder in Alta, especially for us kids. The snow was so deep and light that I would often completely disappear when I fell. And watch out not to breath in those situations. If you sucked those light snowflakes into your lungs, you could literally drown. Getting back up again—forget it. There was no way. Try to push yourself up with

your hands and you got no resistance. Try a ski pole and it would just disappear. Even the adults had problems—believe me.

The ski patrol usually got the mountain open pretty quickly, but in stages. Early in the morning, just a few of the easier runs like Mambo and Main Street would be open...maybe even Spruce. After a couple of runs—just about when the open runs were getting skied out—we would notice that they had opened West Ballroom and perhaps Race Course. On it went like that throughout the day.

Alta did not have many lifts and the lift lines could get kind of long, even on stormy days, since Alta skiers loved snowy days. If we were lucky, avalanche danger from Mt. Superior would threaten the access road, and the people from Salt Lake City couldn't come up. Then, those few of us who stayed in Alta itself had our own private mountain.

At the end of the ski day, we always tried to time it so we got our last ride up at 3:58. That way, we would be last off the mountain. I often succeeded in this endeavor, and yet, there was one person who, I suspect, was even more successful than me—my mother!

One of my most vivid memories of my childhood was a blustery, snowy day in Alta. My teenager's pride got the better of me, and I ignored my icy fingers and frozen toes and pumped powder until the bitter end. I was thawing out in the lobby, the circulation slowly returning to my extremities, when the door from the ski room pushed open. There stood mom. It was a full 20 minutes after I had returned, so she had clearly managed to sneak in one more run than I had.

Her clothes were covered with snow that drifted to the floor with a shrug of her shoulders. Her cheeks were a ruddy red from the wind, her dark hair was white—a tangle of icicles, and she wore a grin from ear to ear. Not only had she had a great powder day, but she had also held out longer than her gung-ho teenager had. It was a moment to make any mother proud of herself. Yes, first tracks and last-one-off-the-mountain were all part of the Alta tradition.

For ten years—ten formative years—Alta was an integral part of my life. We may only have been there for 15–20 days a year, but we spent the other 350 days looking forward to those holidays. I learned to ski in Alta, and more importantly, I learned to ski powder there. I spent years trying to prove myself worthy of the resort's motto, "Alta is for skiers". The fur coat and après-ski crowd went to Sun Valley or Aspen, whilst those who could endure the hardiest climate that Mother Nature could dish out returned to Alta each winter.

Since those idyllic family holidays, much has happened. Growing up has intervened. I stopped having vacations with the family and went skiing with my friends. We wanted adventure and tried many new places to ski. I moved to Europe, and my skiing took me primarily to the Alps. And my mother, whom I still think of as an Alta snow gremlin, passed away. Alta has a safe spot in my memory, frozen forever in space and time, somewhere in the 1960s, but my reality is a lifetime away.

NOT SO LONG AGO, I WAS in Utah and I could not resist the temptation to return to this place that had meant so much to me as a child.

My emotions were very mixed and I pondered the conflicts. Is it better to leave your childhood cocooned in your memory, or risk shattering that protective shield with the realities of change and modern-

» The snow was so deep and light that I would often completely disappear when I fell.«

ization? Do you wish to see your old childhood park asphalted over for a new parking lot? I understood the risks, but the urge to revisit my boyhood haunt was overbearing.

Caspar and I drove up from Salt Lake City, and I was filled with curiosity, my neck craning with every curve in the road. Finally, I caught a glimpse of Alf's High Rustler, the 45-degree slope that looms above Alta like a giant trophy to Alf Engen's legendary swoops down her powder-filled face. I had come home.

continued on page 22

ALF ENGEN — THE KING OF POWDER

Alf Engen was, perhaps, the greatest all-round skier who ever lived, but more important to those of us who religiously worship deep powder snow, he was the father of powder skiing. Powder hounds ought to begin every ski day by getting into their powder crouch, genuflecting with an up-and-down pumping motion and saying a short prayer of thanks to the round-faced Norwegian elf who made it all possible. Alf was to powder what Thomas Edison was to electricity. He didn't invent it; he merely figured out how to use it.

The Alf Engen story is the classic American immigrant fairytale. His father died young, things were tough in Norway, and Alf's mother used her entire savings to put her nineteen-year-old son on a ship bound for the "Promised Land".

Even before Alf left Norway, he had out-jumped the entire Norwegian jumping team that won Olympic gold in 1928. He broke the world ski-jumping record in 1931 and won the national title eight times between 1931 and 1946. He also took national championships in the slalom and downhill and twice won the National Four-way Championships that included jumping, slalom, downhill and cross-country. A trophy case that houses over 500 awards is additional proof that Alf truly was a consummate all-round skier.

This man had a lifelong love affair with skiing. He was a walking, talking, carving, pole-planting dictionary, textbook, history book and encyclopedia of skiing, all packed neatly into one book cover. Incidentally, he also loved his family, Alta, people and life in general. This was one happy man. He did not speak; he bubbled. Ask him a question about skiing, and his eyes twinkled like Santa Claus on Christmas Eve. I reckon that Alf Engen started out, like all of us, as a kid, but he just never got any older.

In 1948, Alf took over the ski school in Alta and began experimenting with powder technique. He originated the method of weighting the skis evenly, the core of powder style to this very day. From that moment on, Alf Engen continued to alter and add to his new "double dipsy".

As skis became shorter and more flexible, he was constantly redefining the state of the art, refining powder style to the smoothest, most fluid motions that each generation of skis would allow. He toned down the upper body motion long before the rotation method fell out of vogue. He developed pole-planting technique tailored for powder, and he invented the "Alta start" of digging the heels of the skis into the snow and facing down the fall line, to help initiate the first turn in powder.

If Alf did not teach you to ski powder, the chances are better than average that he taught your dad or perhaps he taught the instructor who taught your dad. Maybe Alf taught the instructor who taught the instructor who taught your dad. It's a little like the old Adam-and-Eve thing—if you can trace your powder lineage back far enough, Alf Engen stands tall as the trunk of the tree.

By the time I skied with Alf, he was already well into his eighties. He had had over 60 years to learn the language of his new country, and of course he had done so, but his accent was strictly North Pole. As we rode up the lift, he related for me the tale of when he broke the world jumping record with a leap of 231 feet at Ecker's Hill in the early 1930s.

"I von $500," explained Alf, "and dat vas a lot of money in da Depression, by golly! Denn, dis promoter offer me $250 more if I could go up again and break my own record. Vell, I knew I could do dat, no problem. I tought dis vas a good vay to earn some extra money. I figured I could yump 233, string it out, and break dat record a few more times. Da problem vas, I couldn't remember vhere I started da run-off down da ramp. So, I started much too high vit my next yump and floo out 247 feet."

Alf also spoke with reverence about High Rustler, Alta's test of manhood—350 vertical meters of ski run that rises precipitously from the Little Cottonwood Canyon. "In da old days ve vould have figure-eights on High Rustler for a month, if a snowstorm didn't cover dem first, because almost nobody could ski her. I alvays skied vit at least 220-centimeter skis. I vouldn't dare go onto anything shorter because I vas used to yumping skis, vhich vere 245 centimeters long.

"So, 220s—dey ver short for me. Vit dose planks, I had to ski 50 meters before my first turn. Ve had to ski much faster to get enough speed to float in da powder. By golly, ve vould ski High Rustler in six or seven turns!"

Alf's technique from those long gone days was really not so far removed from the big-mountain powder turns that are so in vogue among today's freeriders.

I asked Alf if he had ever been injured skiing.

"Ya sure. I cracked my ankle six or seven times in yumping competitions. Vun time, I remember I made a yump and felt something go in da landing. I didn't vant to see da doctor, for den I vould miss da finals da next day. So, I yust taped da ankle and yumped da following day as vell. After dat I vent to da doctor, and he confirmed dat my ankle vas cracked."

"How did you come out in the competition?" I asked with great curiosity.

"I come in second place. By golly, dat vas da only time my younger brudder Sverre beat me."

Alf compared his two different lives in skiing. "As a competitor, you are a loner. People say hello as you are on your vay up da yump, and you don't even hear dem. Teaching, on da udder hand, is a people yob—more suitable to my nature."

By now, we had reached the top and we began to ski. Part way down the mountain, the irresistible urge to teach and share began to come over him once again.

"I vant you to try somting vi used to do in da 1950s," Alf called to me. "It's called a reverse-shoulder lazy-mambo style," he said, and went on to describe it. "And yust for fun, try it on da outside edge. Dat is alvays a good exercise," he added.

I tried my best to impress the old master. I don't believe I was very successful, but it really didn't matter.

Alf hollered, "Very good, Yimmy," and other words of encouragement as he had to so many skiers before me.

He smiled from ear to ear of his impish face, savoring once more what he had enjoyed for so many years—the simple satisfaction of sharing.

Alf Engen passed away in 1997 at the age of 88. He skied into his 86th year, even after suffering a massive stroke the year before, which left him almost totally paralyzed.

During his life on the snow, Alf accomplished a great deal more than the 500-plus awards and trophies that he had won. He had coached the United States Olympic Team, had helped with the planning and development of many ski resorts, had taught uncountable numbers of people how to ski, and had made other contributions to skiing too numerous to mention.

It would be difficult for anybody to pick out any one achievement that stood out above the others. Nevertheless, I have the feeling that had we the chance to ask Alf what he was most proud of, he would answer swiftly, without batting an eye. He would merely point to some almost invisible skier, submerged in powder, and say, "Dere goes von of my students!"

The last time I had visited Alta with my family, in 1972, there were five lodges and six lifts, and Alf Engen was the head of the ski school. I now learned that Alta has five lodges and *seven* ski lifts, and Alf Engen's son, Alan, had taken over the duties that his father had performed so admirably for well over 40 years.

I stopped in for a short chat with Alan Engen. I was a flurry of questions, and he tried to keep up.

"Yes, the patrol still gets the mountain open pretty darn quickly... yes, Superior still closes the road quite often in a big storm...yes, we still get a lot of the same families back every year. Why, about 70 percent of our guests are return customers. Sure, there have been some changes over the years, but not too many," answered Alan. "Look at all the moguls on High Rustler. There are so many good skiers nowadays. But, I still think Alta is the greatest place to ski, because it has stayed small and friendly."

» The walls are big and steep. It's like skiing a steep alley between brick buildings. «

We skied down a couple of runs together and Alan was off to a meeting.

"Have a great time. I hope to see you around during the next days," he called.

I SKIED ONTO THE COLLINS CHAIR. THE ORIGINAL Collins Lift became America's fifth chair lift in 1939, after it had been transformed from an aerial tram which had hauled ore in the mining days.

At the top, I basked in the radiance of April's sun and looked around. Down to my right was the High Traverse that accesses such Alta classics as Stone Crusher, Lone Pine, High Rustler and Greeley Bowl. Down to my left was Ballroom. It was there that my mother had taught me my earliest powder technique. That picture of her walking into the lobby on that long gone snowy day popped back into my head and my eyes welled up with tears.

Then I gazed up at the steep couloirs that seemed to rise vertically to the summit. Baldy Chutes are the epitome of the precipitous off-piste skiing that Alta is famous for. Each chute is over 40 degrees. The chutes are invariably topped by large cornices, and avalanche danger keeps them closed almost all the time. During more than twenty visits to Alta in my youth, they had never been open.

"Now, with spring snow," I thought, "maybe..."

I started along the High Traverse. Ten minutes later, I was looking down the nefarious face of High Rustler. Once again, I paused to survey the area. Some stratocumulus clouds were visible in the distance, and I thought about the weather pattern that has made Alta the powder Mecca.

The weather blows in off the Gulf of Alaska and moves southeast, drying out over the deserts of Nevada and Utah to give Alta powder that wonderful dry quality that renders it as light and fluffy as a French soufflé. The clouds then move over the Great Salt Lake, picking up moisture, and finally drop the mother lode at the end of the Little Cottonwood Canyon, leaving Alta with an average snowfall of about 13 meters per year. Somewhere in Alta must lie a snow magnet, because, strangely

enough, neighboring ski areas such as Park City, Brighton and Solitude average 2–4 meters less snowfall per season.

My mind was enjoying my daydreams atop High Rustler, but the hour was late and my legs would still have to negotiate me between the steep, soft moguls. Time to go. I pumped, hopped, jumped, grunted, huffed and puffed my way down. Once, I got tripped up by a mogul, which threw me to the ground. By the time I was safely back at the Rustler Lodge, my legs were like rubber but had just enough left in them to drag me to the Jacuzzi. From there, I could gaze out at my conquest (or was it High Rustler's victory?) from a safe and comfortable distance.

CASPAR AND I AWOKE the following morning to a cloudless sky. I looked out at Baldy Chutes—very tempting, but that would just have to wait. We had decided to ski part of the Utah Interconnect Tour, an off-piste excursion among Alta, Snowbird, Solitude, Brighton and Park City. This was something new for me.

We began with a short walk from the top of Alta's Supreme Lift. That took us to a lovely corn-snow descent that meandered past a frozen lake and ultimately brought us down to Brighton. We skied there for the rest of the morning. After a cheeseburger, we completed the next stage of the Interconnect, taking us over a ridge into Solitude. A few runs in Solitude took us to the top of the Summit Chair Lift and a short traverse known as the Highway to Heaven. Once again, we stood perched atop a picturesque off-piste tour, which leads back into the Little Cottonwood Canyon. Back in Alta we still had time for a few more runs before the Jacuzzi beckoned.

The following morning was sparkling once again. This must be a safe time to ski Baldy Chutes, I thought. The sign at the base of the Sugarloaf Lift read "Closed". Caspar and I went to the patrol shack, and chatted with the ski patrol. We told them our story, made our request, and without much ado, we were given permission to ski the run that had tantalized my imagination for the past 30 years. I almost fell down the stairs of the shack, as I was in such a hurry to get started.

"Hurry up, Caspar. Let's not give them time to change their minds," I whispered, as I untangled my feet.

Soon, we were making the 30-minute hike to the top of Mt. Baldy. I was froth with anticipation. Finally, I was going to ski the perpetually closed run.

Brad Asmus, in his book, *The Powder Hound's Guide to Skiing Alta*, has written the following about Baldy Chutes: "The crowning achievement of many powder hounds' careers is a run down one of the Baldy Chutes... a symbol of ability, commitment, and courage that serve as a right of passage...rarely opened...uncontrolled falls in Main and Little Chutes can have serious consequences."

Caspar and I arrived at the top around midday and decided to ski Main Chute, which Asmus describes thus: "Having dropped in, you're in. The walls are big and steep. It's like skiing a steep alley between brick buildings."

BY APRIL, THE CORNICE ABOVE the chute has had all winter to build up and is an ominous sight. We opted to circumvent it by skiing the ridge for 50 meters, and then cutting into Main Chute below the cornice. We may be stupid, but we ain't crazy!

Even our chosen route was no piece of cake. The snow on the ridge was tricky, changeable stuff which the wind and sun had played with, and no less steep than the couloir itself. Caspar made his turns one at a time, and the unpredictable snow on the landings of each jump turn often threw his body into a position between precarious and ugly. He did manage to stay upright throughout in a textbook example of survival technique on extreme slopes.

Once in the corridor, the snow was better. We could choose between soft spring snow along the northeast-facing perimeter of the gully and wind-packed powder on the opposite side of Alta's ultimate elevator shaft. We alternated between our options for the sake of variety. We took our time. After waiting so many years to ski this run, I found myself savoring every moment. I tried to cling to each turn a little longer, indelibly printing a photo of it all in my mind's eye, for I didn't know if I would ever get another chance.

All too soon we found ourselves close to the bottom. I pointed out to Caspar a large rock at the base of the chute known to all as McConk's Rock. I explained that the rock was named for Jim McConkey, the

THIS PAGE: Powder days like this remain within a skier's soul forever.
RIGHT PAGE: Taos, New Mexico offers excellent tree-skiing.

legendary Canadian wild man and father to freeride hero Shane McConkey. Jim McConkey, who added much color to Alf Engen's ski school in the '50s and '60s, is purported to have added a *coup de grâce* to many a descent down Main Chute by doing a *Geländesprung* off the rock and landing upright halfway down Ballroom.

Caspar could not resist. It was nothing to make Mr. McConkey fear for his place in ski folklore, but Caspar capped our run with a flourish, and made a small jump from McConk's Rock back into the realm of the everyday skier.

That evening, I called my dad. "Hey, I miss you, dad. Alta isn't the same without you."

"That's kind of you to say, son," he replied. "It's nice of you to think of me."

"...And you know what, dad? We skied Baldy Chutes today!" I told him excitedly.

"Well, good for you," answered my father. "I never got to do that myself."

Then I called my sister, as well, and told her the news. And my mom... I have the feeling that she already knew.

TAOS — INDIAN TERRITORY

While Alta is a must stop on anybody's American ski itinerary because of its unrivaled powder, it is certainly not the only U.S. resort with a reputation. Many ski areas of the American West are famous and it is hard to avoid the hype. One undoubtedly arrives at a ski center here with an image in mind.

The marketing people lead us to believe that the powder is so light that one is rendered weightless—moon skiing, whilst the moguls are as large as igloos. The girls are all snow-bunny versions of Beach Boy heroines, and the guys are crazed-out cliff jumpers like Scott Schmidt and Glen Plake. They all mix together on this wild playground where the pre-Hollywood Americans used to play "cowboys and Indians" for real.

Caspar Möller was again my companion on this trip, and we set out to discover the truth about skiing in this land of legend, the great American West. We began a road-trip around the southwestern United States, a sort of snowy version of Easy Rider or Jack Kerouac on skis.

Our first destination was Taos, New Mexico. Before departing Los Angeles, we made one short and unfortunate stop on Hollywood Boulevard, where Caspar purchased a battery-operated Fender mini-amplifier to be able to practice his guitar in the car. This torture appara-

tus produced such a distorted sound that Caspar's Stratocaster sounded more like a Greek bouzouki than a guitar.

As we drove, the batteries began to weaken, and soft static mixed with the other "sounds" from Caspar's amp. Nevertheless, he continued his methodical repetitions of "Hotel California" and "Sweet Home Alabama". As we crossed the border into Arizona, I suggested to Caspar that I was a bit tired. He took over the driving, and the rest of the afternoon was rather pleasant.

We did not ski every day on our trip, but rather, we took some time along our way to enjoy the amazing scenery in this part of the country. En route to Taos, we saw the sunrise over the Grand Canyon, and that same afternoon, we passed through Monument Valley. This is one of those strange places in the middle of the prairie, where huge sandstone monoliths stretch skyward out of the desert. Numerous classic Hollywood Westerns were filmed here.

By midnight, we approached the Indian pueblo of Taos. Under the light of the moon, we could see the prairie give way to the Sangre de Cristo Mountains that rise above the plains to an elevation of 3700 meters.

Through the years, Taos has been home to Indians, cowboys, artists, and more recently, skiers. Frontiersman Kit Carson and writer D.H. Lawrence, both former Taos residents, are long gone, but the 800-year-old pueblo still houses a large community of Indians. In addition, over 80 art galleries adorn the streets of Taos today. Ernie Blake, the eccentric German who brought skiing to the valley, is also no longer around, but his mountain is very much alive.

OUR FIRST MORNING IN TAOS, Caspar and I were met by Caspar's buddy, Charlie. He would be our guide to the Taos Ski Valley. It did not take long to realize that Taos is definitely a mountain for good skiers, especially mogul freaks. Chair One rises sharply over a cut in the woods known as Al's Run, generally the first piece of real estate that a skier sees in Taos. Al's Run is a steep, continuous pitch of bunker-sized moguls, which seems long as you inspect it from the lift and endless as you try to ski it.

"This'll make a good warmup," said Charlie with the sly grin of someone who has secret information.

It was closer to a burnout than a warmup for me. In any case, by the time we were one-third of the way down, my thighs were definitely more than warm, and I was up to my eyeballs in bumps, even when I stood right-side up.

"Al's Run was rated as a 'most difficult' run back in the '60s, but it has been downgraded," explained Charlie. "It's only a single diamond today. Now that we're all warm, I'll show you guys some of our double-diamond terrain," he chirped happily.

Single-diamond runs are listed in the legend of the Taos trail map as "Most Difficult–Experts Only", whereas double-diamond runs are described as "Extremely Difficult–Use Extra Caution–Experts Only".

We headed up to the top of the mountain to what is known as the High Traverse.

"Ah, it's nice to get all the fluids moving in the old joints," said Charlie cheerfully.

The only fluid running on my body was sweat, but I kept that to myself and followed our host.

The High Traverse is a treacherous series of pointy moguls laced with rocks, tree roots and other obstacles. Every so often, a double-diamond sign nailed to a tree identified various so-called runs. The "runs" differed from Al's Run in that they were even steeper and narrower. Some were chutes between rocks, while others were not really runs at all but tight tree-skiing. In most ski areas these chutes and gullies would have been untouched. Here, one had the additional difficulty of moguls amongst all the other obstructions.

Charlie suddenly peeled off the traverse into an elevator shaft called Stauffenberg and snaked down through the vertical obstacle course like a man who had done years of practice in this kind of terrain. Caspar and I were not as fortunate. The "mogul mouse" was hiding all over Stauffenberg, grabbing at my ski tip, pulling at my pole, and general just

tripping me up. I tried an unbecoming, wide-stanced survival technique in an effort to stay on my feet. When that method also failed, I resorted to attempting to direct the lines of my falls, so as to avoid large pine trees. In the words of the trail map's legend, this was my way to "use extra caution".

By day's end, I stumbled into the Hotel St. Bernard bar at the base of the lifts, badly in need of something to help me forget the drubbing my self-confidence had received during the day. Caspar and I each downed three or four salt-rimmed margaritas (what else would you drink in New Mexico?), and I was suddenly ready for whatever tomorrow could dish out. Apparently, the next day's menu would at least include softer moguls, for it had begun to snow.

FOR THE NEXT FEW DAYS, we followed Charlie through most of the nooks and crannies of Taos, while the powder continued to accumulate. The new snow did not get rid of the moguls—it merely disguised them. On our first day I had wondered what could possibly be more difficult than skiing down steep, narrow chutes amidst tight trees and moguls. Now, I knew—skiing down steep, narrow chutes amidst tight trees and *hidden* moguls…in poor visibility! It didn't matter. It was a challenge, and at least my rather frequent four-point landings were getting softer as the snow kept falling.

Charlie had one evening off from work, and he showed us around in the village of Taos, a half-hour's drive down the mountain. We began with margaritas and nachos at the Taos Inn, a historic adobe structure brimming with New Mexican flavor and style. A portion of nachos is meant to be an appetizer, but when we ogled the mountain of chips, beans, jalapenos, salsa, melted cheese, guacamole and sour cream, we understood immediately that dinner would be redundant.

Our après-ski graduated into evening entertainment, and we moved on to the Sagebrush Inn. This is a local cowboy hangout a few miles out of the center of town, fitted with a rocking country band, and patronized by more ten-gallon hats and cowboy boots than I had ever seen in one place. For the next five hours, I attempted to learn the Texas two-step. It went about as well as my mogul bashing. I realized that my repertoire of giant slalom turns, powder technique, and conventional dance steps were no match for what Taos had to dish out, and I was ready to hit the road again.

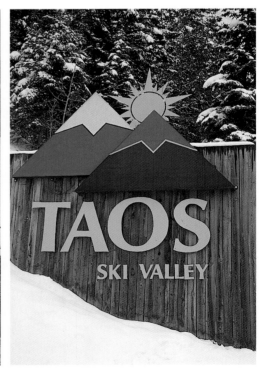

WOLF CREEK — MOST SNOW IN COLORADO

I drove north into Colorado. Caspar had barely gotten through his fifth rendition of "The House of the Rising Sun" at distortion level ten, when I saw a road sign pointing to Great Sand Dunes National Monument. This was not on the itinerary, but I couldn't resist.

A half-hour later we were gazing out over a very strange sight. Right between the prairie and the snow-covered Rockies stood a nice-sized chunk of the Sahara—quite a few miles of large rolling hills of sand. The only thing missing was a herd of camels. The skiing was not as deep as in Taos, but who cared. A 40-minute hike gave us an unusual introduction to Colorado skiing. The sun began to set over our final few turns on the sand, and we motored on to the town of Del Norte, the last town east of Wolf Creek Pass.

If Colorado has an armpit, it could well be Del Norte, but on the other hand, the prices were not exactly Aspen either. We checked into the El Rancho Motel, which was cheap and basic. Then, we looked for a place to eat—no luck. It was 8:15 in the evening, and all the eateries were already closed. This was real small-town America.

A local pointed us to the Antique Bar, where, it was suggested, we could get a drink and perhaps some popcorn. The Antique Bar was a rough, low-lit saloon, filled with a few pool tables, a half-dozen customers and a bearded, wizened old cowboy named Panda tending bar.

We ordered Bloody Marys. Panda filled two beer glasses with a few ice cubes, poured vodka two-thirds of the way up, and threw in a bit of tomato juice for color. I was pretty sure that if I had ordered a second he would have just placed the bottle on the bar and said, "He'p yo'sef!" I mean, this place was right out of Dodge City. Caspar needed a cup of coffee after his not-so-bloody Mary, and I opted for a beer. We paid next to nothing for our evening's consumption, then headed off to bed.

The following morning we awoke early full of anticipation, knowing that we were only about an hour from our next destination, Wolf Creek. What? You haven't heard of Wolf Creek? Well, neither has anyone else and therein lies the key to this little powder hole—no people. Lack of skiers is not enough by itself to make for a great ski area, but taking into account the fact that Wolf Creek also gets the most snowfall of any place in Colorado, it has a pretty potent combination.

You still don't believe me? You can look it up. Steamboat Springs averages eight meters of snow per season—peanuts! Aspen gets seven-and-a-half meters—chicken feed! Copper Mountain? Breckenridge? They get about six-and-a-half meters—boring! Wolf Creek, situated almost directly atop the Continental Divide, averages a robust eleven-and-a-half meters of snowfall per season.

WOLF CREEK IS A REAL LOCALS' ski area with no trace of a town—not even a hotel. There are five lifts, a base lodge with some of the best lunches either side of the Divide, and those eleven-and-a-half meters of powder. What more does a skier need?

Well, there was one more thing we needed—tire chains. Snow chains are not exactly standard equipment when renting a car in Los Angeles. We had not given that fact much thought whilst touring around the Rockies in late March. But the further we got up Wolf Creek Pass, the harder the snow was falling. We guessed that we couldn't be too far from the top, but the snow on the road was about 5 centimeters deep.

"Just keep driving, don't brake and don't slow down," encouraged Caspar. "Otherwise we'll have to drive back to Del Norte to get a running start again."

I tried to keep my pressure on the gas pedal even. My palms were getting a bit sweaty. I really wanted a crack at first tracks. The road seemed to wind interminably but finally we spied the turn-off sign. One kilometer

Wolfie guides us through the trees of the Waterfall section of Wolf Creek.

further, I slid our carriage slowly into a snowdrift right next to the lift.

Over a cup of coffee, we met a local who introduced himself as Scott Wolf, "But my friends call me Wolfie," he added.

"I don't believe this! Are you serious? Wolfie from Wolf Creek!" I exclaimed.

I was beginning to think I had mysteriously driven our Buick right into a Walt Disney fantasy. I was about to ask where the three little pigs lived, but I didn't want to offend Wolfie.

"So what?" I thought. If this was a fantasy, I was ready to fantasize for a while.

Wolfie was a potato farmer in summer and a ski instructor in winter. Luckily for us, as in any good fantasy, he had the morning off and was happy to show us around. We rode up the Treasure Chair Lift surveying the pines, which looked like a scene from a fairytale. They were perfectly spaced for tree-skiing, and their branches were heavily laden with snow.

I watched Wolfie as he pointed his skis between two trees and disappeared in a swirling cloud of white. I followed. The snow was bottomless—a different fantasy feeling from childhood—that of flying and tumbling in the clouds. Only the series of ice-cold face shots brought me back to reality. After leaving our squiggles of abstract expressionism on the soft white canvas all morning, Wolfie said, "Now I'm gonna show you guys the Waterfall."

Instead of heading back toward the lifts after skiing Boundary Bowl, we continued in a long schuss over the flats, arriving in a very steep, cliff-laden area where a waterfall exists in summer. Both sides of the falls were full of tantalizing ridges, gullies, knolls, and of course, more trees.

"Aren't we gonna end up way below the lifts here, with a long walk back?" I asked.

"Don't worry. Just follow me," Wolfie replied simply, and once again disappeared in a galaxy of Rocky Mountain stardust.

TELLURIDE
COWBOYS AND POWDER SNOW

I drove our Buick onto the main street of Telluride, Colorado, but the town looked as if a stagecoach would have been more appropriate transportation for our arrival. By now, we had left Indian Territory behind and entered the land of the cowboy. Many resort towns like Aspen, Park City and Breckenridge, began as mining towns in the Old West, but none captures the bygone days of that Victorian era better than Telluride.

The resort is an odd combination of Hollywood glitter and old cowboy town. It is where the rich and famous go to be everyday people for a week, but they do not quite succeed. This is a place where you might run into what appeared to be a bunch of dusty old cowpokes, but under the Stetson hats, you see that it really is Sylvester Stallone, Tom Cruise and Robin Williams. They, along with Clint Eastwood, Sting, Daryl Hannah and a host of other Hollywood stars, are regular visitors or own homes here. Nevertheless, the atmosphere has managed to remain closer to Dodge City than Beverly Hills.

This is where Butch Cassidy robbed his first bank in 1889 and the town center has not changed much since then. The main street is a living, breathing museum of the roaring mining days, and the side streets are lined with picturesque Victorian houses. Everywhere you walk in Telluride, you expect the Cartwright brothers to come riding around the corner.

You can still eat dinner at the Athenian Senate, a Greek restaurant which was one of 26 bordellos in the mining days, and where Jack Dempsey once worked as a dishwasher and bouncer, before becoming heavyweight champion of the world. Alternatively, you can down whiskey shooters in the Moon Saloon or the Last Dollar Saloon, which do not look much different from when they were the second home to hundreds of silver miners. To top it all off, this monument to the Wild West is nestled in a small river valley of the San Juan Mountains, with spectacular Alp-like peaks rising to about 4000 meters all around.

CASPAR AND I DID NOT get long into our first morning in "cowboy town" before deciding that we were going to be outlaws. We had arrived a day late in Telluride. That is to say that we started skiing on the second sunny day after a snowstorm. Now, it does not take a genius to figure out that in a resort like Telluride, you have a better chance of stealing the sheriff's horse than finding powder two days after a snowfall—except, of course, if you are an outlaw.

Let me explain. When it comes to skiing, the U.S. is not really the "land of the free", as it is purported to be. In the Alps, you can ski powder more or less wherever you find it. American ski areas, however, have more rules, regulations and restrictions than a British boarding school. Just as the cattlemen fenced in the open range 100 years earlier, American ski resorts have roped off the mountains today. Most ski hills across the United States are encircled entirely by rope and many are rife with signs proclaiming: "Area Boundary–Out of Area Skiing is Prohibited".

In this place that Butch Cassidy had put on the map, Caspar and I had but one solution—becoming powder bandits. On the mountain so aptly named Gold Hill, there was a rich bounty of deep powder just the other side of all the ropes. We passed the morning like a couple of cattle rustlers, staying hidden in the trees, and stealing the best that Gold Hill had to offer.

We spent the next day on Telluride Face. Runs like Bushwhacker, North Chute and Spiral Stairs have moguls that will throw you around like a bucking bronco, and then, there is the Telluride classic—the Plunge. The Plunge is 1000 vertical meters of excellent advanced skiing. Half the run is left ungroomed for the mogul maniacs, while the other half is like a classic downhill course, prepared with the aid of a winch cat, a special piste machine that pulls itself along a cable to groom steep terrain.

All afternoon, Caspar and I practiced for the Hahnenkamm on the Plunge, and finished close to the bottom of the run at an après-ski bar called the West End Tavern. It was there that I met Bob, a 23-year-old graduate of Harvard and a local ski bum. Bob invited me to join him for a ski tour the following day, and it was on that excursion with a local that I began to understand the essence of Colorado.

In the few days since arriving in Telluride, I had already come to realize that mandatory standard equipment in this part of the world included an SUV, a pair of pins and some smoke. (In case you do not speak fluent

When the snow finally settled, and the world again came into focus —wonder of wonders—a shiny orange snow cat stood before us, waiting to take us back to the lifts at no extra charge. It was just part of the friendly service of Wolf Creek, Colorado. (The Alberta Chair Lift has now replaced the snow-cat service.)

WE SPENT THE NIGHT with Wolfie in his home in Monte Vista, west of Wolf Creek, and we repeated the whole story the following day. That afternoon we bid a fond *adios* to our host. I packed the skis on the rack, Caspar unpacked the Stratocaster and torture box from the trunk, and we were off to Telluride.

We made a short detour to see the amazing cliff dwellings built by the Anasazi Indians in the 1200s. As we watched the sunset from high atop Mesa Verde National Park, I realized that the American West is truly a wonderful combination of ski resorts, history and natural beauty.

THIS PAGE
An odyssey among the ski areas of the western U.S. provides much interesting scenery along the way. UPPER LEFT: a slot canyon in Arizona. Photo by Erik Petterson Sjöqvist. UPPER RIGHT: Dusk over Telluride, Colorado. MIDDLE: Monument Valley, Arizona. LOWER: Mt. Hood, Oregon at sunrise.

RIGHT PAGE
UPPER LEFT: Rainbow in Arches National Park, Utah. UPPER RIGHT: Wave crashes high onto the cliffs in Oregon. LOWER LEFT: The author admires the view in Canyonlands National Park, Utah. Photo by Caspar Möller. MIDDLE: Sunset over the Minarets, near Mammoth Mountain, California. LOWER RIGHT: The Buffalo roam again in Colorado.

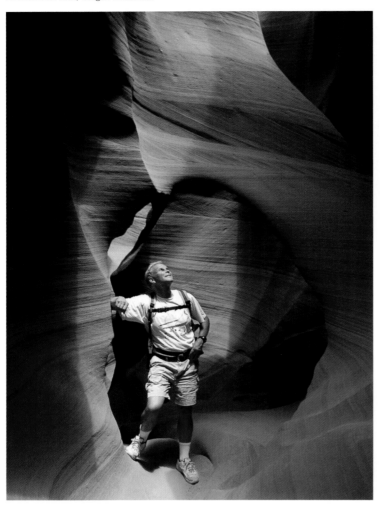

"American", this translates as a sports utility vehicle, telemark skis and some marijuana.)

Bob did not let me down. He picked me up at 8:30 a.m. in a Chevy Blazer and placed my touring skis in the back, next to his telemark equipment. We drove half an hour out of Telluride and climbed a few hours up a south-facing slope called Black Face. When we reached the summit, I was ready to glide down onto the awaiting corn snow. Bob, however, apparently trying to reach a higher peak, pulled out a large joint.

"Drugs are all part of the Telluride experience," he explained succinctly, as he offered me a drag.

As I cruised down, carving wide arcs in the April corn snow, everything suddenly became mystically clear. The acorn had really not fallen far from the tree. Nothing much had really changed at all. Life out west in the mid-1800s was all about escape, freedom and self-reliance, and here in Colorado 150 years later, it was no different.

The Indians escaped the day's harsh realities with their peyote, and the Colorado skiers still smoke a local weed. Kit Carson and his peers derived their mobility and independence from their horse and six-shooter, and today's American has his SUV and a pair of pins. A backpack is just a modern day saddlebag, and the locals here have merely traded picks and shovels for ski poles.

The soul and spirit of the West are the same as they always were. Three hundred million dollars worth of silver later, the mountains around Telluride are devoid of minerals, but modern-day Americans are still hiking high into those same hills, searching and seeking. They pursue the perfect corn-snow descent glistening in the late morning sun, or they hunt for the untouched powder, pristinely sparkling on some distant north face. In a sense, they are in quest of their roots—looking for a last refuge where they can still exercise the pioneer spirit of their forefathers.

TIMBERLINE — AMERICA'S LONGEST SKI SEASON

Among the many mountain ranges within the United States, none is more spectacular and interesting than the Cascades. This range primarily consists of rolling green mountains rising to elevations of around 2000 meters and covered with thick vegetation akin to rain forest. A weak line in the Earth's crust runs through the range, resulting in a string of volcanoes which rise dramatically out of the Cascades every 100 kilometers or so, all the way from Washington to northern California.

In northern Oregon, a gargantuan white pyramid rises out of the Cascades, dwarfing the surrounding mountains with the majesty of the Pharaohs. It is Mt. Hood, home to Timberline, the ski area with the longest ski season in North America, staying open for skiing until early September each year.

At the base of the lifts is Timberline Lodge, an epic piece of Americana. The lodge is a celebration of the American West in both function and style. It is one of Uncle Sam's answers to the great, palatial spa hotels in St. Moritz, Bad Gastein and similar old European resorts.

The exterior was used as a backdrop to Stanley Kubrick's horror movie, *The Shining*. It is an impressive sight with its steep-pitched roof that seems to be modeled after the mountain itself. Built during the Depression as a government-funded project, the hotel was constructed in the spirit of the mountain and surrounding nature. In the center of the lodge is the foundation of the 28-meter-high hexagonal chimney. It is built of gray boulders and has three walk-in fireplaces in the lobby and an additional three in the upstairs dining room.

Gigantic wooden beams and pillars make up the framework of the lodge. Perhaps most impressive are the five logs which seemingly support the structure. They are each about 10 meters high and over a meter in diameter, and like everything else in the hotel, they are hand-hewn.

Upstairs, in the dining area, huge wrought-iron chandeliers hang from the three-story-high ceiling. The furniture, the watercolors and the draperies are other hand-made products of the proud artisans of the Depression. From the detail put into all the work, one can see that the lodge was built by highly skilled carpenters. Amazingly, the lodge, with all its trimmings and trappings, was completed in only eighteen months.

OF COURSE, THERE IS MORE to Timberline than just the lodge. The slopes are not difficult but are an absolute delight for spring skiing. Almost 800 vertical meters of skiing are above the tree line, and in May, the south-facing slopes create a giant ballroom of corn snow.

Mt. Hood is also the most-climbed glaciated peak in North America, and second only to Mt. Fuji, Japan, in the entire world. There is a good reason for this. The views afforded climbers are memorable. In spring, the rolling ridges of the Cascades create an undulating sea of green stretching to the horizon. Due south of Mt. Hood, still more of the snow-covered Cascade volcanoes lord triumphantly over the surroundings. Mt. Jefferson, the second-highest peak in Oregon, looks close enough to touch. Beyond her pointy top, one can see three more volcanoes known as the Three Sisters.

Mt. Hood has something to offer everybody. Many racers come here to train during Timberline's summer season. Its terrain park makes Timberline a popular destination among snowboarders as well, especially during their summer camps.

The gentle slopes make the area a good fit for both beginners and intermediates of all snowsports disciplines. Off-piste enthusiasts should also not be disappointed. Most riders seem to stay on the pistes, leaving much of the wide, open terrain untouched. In addition, the cone shape of Mt. Hood lends itself well to off-piste skiing, as it is so easy to understand the lay of the land. A short traverse at the top gives a skier the possibility to ski down many different lines. When the run is finished, of course, he has a simple, but longer traverse back to the lifts.

MT. BACHELOR — 360 DEGREES OF SKIING

Not far from Mt. Hood is another little-known volcanic ski resort, Mt. Bachelor, which offers an impressive 1000 vertical meters of skiing. Here, there is no on-mountain lodging, and skiers generally stay in the village of Bend, 30 kilometers away.

Like Mt. Hood, Mt. Bachelor offers fantastic scenery. The rime-covered rocks that decorate the double-diamond terrain of the Cirque area are spectacular to look at, and they also provide some interesting jumps for skiers and boarders.

On a clear day, one can gaze out across the entire state of Oregon and into Washington and California on either side. The 360-degree panorama looks out over Diamond Peak to the south, while to the north, near-by Brokentop can be seen, as well as the cone-shaped peaks of the Three Sisters and Mt. Jefferson. In addition to its full-circle view, Mt. Bachelor offers 360 degrees of skiing as well, if all the lifts are open.

Bachelor's season is not quite as long as that on Mt. Hood, as it has no glacier. Nevertheless, it also has one of the longest seasons in the United States, opening its lifts in November and generally offering skiing until the American national day, the Fourth of July.

While the winter months can provide some good powder here, the proximity of the Cascades to the Pacific often makes for heavy, wet snow. This mountain's real forte is spring skiing. The full-circle of terrain is ideal for allowing a skier to follow the clock to ski the correct sun

LEFT PAGE
LEFT: Timberline Lodge on Mt. Hood is a tribute to the workmanship of the Depression years.
RIGHT: The interior of Timberline Lodge.

THIS PAGE
Tom Reichert leaps over rime-covered rocks atop Mt. Bachelor.

exposure and find perfectly softened spring snow almost all day long.

The entire back side of the mountain is off-piste. Skiing this unpisted section is made easy by a "catch line", a line of rope that has been placed all around the lower perimeter of the hind side of the ski area. The cord warns off-piste skiers how far they can ski down before they must begin traversing back to the lifts.

Nothing comes without a drawback or two. The best skiing on Mt. Bachelor is dependent on the Summit Lift, which takes skiers to the upper mountain, and the Northwest Express Lift, which accesses the large freeride area on the back. The Summit Lift is very susceptible to wind, often keeping it out of commission, while the Northwest Express is frequently a victim of the chronic locals'-mountain syndrome of being closed on weekdays for lack of skiers.

BUT TAKE SOLACE. THIS AREA is extremely rich in alternative sports, including great mountain-biking possibilities, three top golf courses, horseback riding, and fly-fishing. River rafting and kayaking are popular on the nearby Deschutes River, and the Gorge, the premiere windsurfing paradise in the continental United States, is also close by. If the critical lifts are closed, there is always an alternative. If all else fails, Bend has three microbreweries that produce a good selection of tasty ales. That is always a viable option on a rainy day in the Pacific Northwest.

MT. BAKER — THE BEST GIFTS COME IN SMALL PACKAGES

Another ski area in the Cascades that proves that good things come in small packages is Mt. Baker, in northwestern Washington. Many ski resorts around the world take pride in the amount of sunshine they receive during the winter season, and the marketing department boasts about their sunny-day statistics in no uncertain terms. Mt. Baker is not among them—quite the contrary. The locals from in and around Bellingham, who are the patrons of this little resort, are extremely proud of the fact that their snowsports playground gets about the least amount of sun of any ski resort in the world.

Sun and snow often have a reciprocal relationship and the lack of sun in this region means that the snow flies in great abundance. Mt. Baker receives an average annual snowfall of around 13 meters, and in the record-breaking winter of 1998-99, over 28 meters of fluff fell on the resort!

My friends, Rupert Scheiner, Vince Deluca and I drove along the beautiful Washington coastline from Seattle to Bellingham en route to this major snow hole. The scenery was like that in Norway. Bays of all shapes and sizes and long arms of the sea, like fjords, filled with thickly forested islands, decorated the coastline. West of Bellingham, an archipelago called the San Juans spreads seaward. This is killer-whale territory, and tourist boats regularly guide people through the labyrinth of islands to see these huge mammals on their annual north–south sojourns.

In Bellingham, we turned our car inland onto historic Highway 542 for the last hour of our journey. We drove past the casino on the Nooksack Indian Reservation, past rural houses, farms and ranches, and into an amazing rain forest. It looked like a primeval world. Ferns covered the muddy ground, and light green moss coated the tree trunks and hung from the branches. Parts of this forest have never been logged, and mammoth-sized redwoods towered high above the rest of the trees. I half-expected a group of amphibious dinosaurs to come tromping through the woods.

In the small hamlet of Glacier, about 35 kilometers from the mountain, we passed over Glacier Creek. Here, a break in the thick vegetation that surrounds the ancient volcano revealed Mount Baker's glaciated peak glistening in the morning sunlight. I parked the car, grabbed my camera, and walked back to the bridge, but by the time I got there, the mountain was again shrouded by a cloud. As I stood there disappointed, another man arrived with his camera, looked through his lens, and also let his camera drop without clicking the shutter.

"Don't be too disappointed," the stranger said to me. "I *live* up here, and I never get that photo either!"

Soon we arrived at the ski resort, a small eight-lift, family-run area that rises no more than 457 vertical meters up two peaks known as the Panorama Dome and Hemisphere. These two tops are both approximately 1500 meters high. To the south, Mount Baker (3277 m) is the second-most active volcano in the Cascades, but is not actually part of the ski area. Not quite as high, but looming dramatically over the resort on the eastern flank, is Mt. Shuksan. Dominated by a huge, hanging glacier, it is a stunning, jagged peak that looks like an import from Alaska. The locals claim Shuksan to be the second-most-photographed mountain in the world, trailing only Mt. Fuji in this category.

It was Good Friday, and any Friday in April is a good day to ski at Mt. Baker. Like many small locals' areas in the world, Baker does not have the population base to stay open all week late in the season, and hence, it only operates Friday through Monday during April. With the heavy snowfall that often hits this ski area, Friday mornings frequently offer a stockpile of new snow that has not been touched for the past three days. Such was the case on this particular Friday.

The atmosphere at Baker was just what one would expect of a friendly, family-run resort. The small staff was up early planting 2000 Easter eggs around the pistes for a morning hunt. Almost everybody on the mountain seemed to know each other, and the pace was as slow and friendly as a Fourth of July barbecue on the village green.

At the White Salmon Lodge, Rupert, Vince and I were met by Charlie Haggem, a young marketing assistant for the mountain, who had promised to show us around. Charlie was not the kind of marketing man you would meet in Vail or Deer Valley. He did his marketing on the mountain and not in the office, and his tools were his helmet and boards more often than his phone and computer.

It soon became apparent that Charlie was also an escapee from the suicide clinic of the local insane asylum. We took a warmup run in the terrain park, where he did his eagle imitation and I doubted he was ever going to touch down again. As it turned out, this was just a sample of things to come.

Charlie introduced us to his buddy, Dean Collins. Together, these two were like the "Flying Wallendas". I have never seen anyone so high off the ground before without a hang glider or a trapeze to hang onto. In fact, Dean was not that far removed from the whole trapeze and big top scene. He had worked for the world-famous Ringling Brothers and Barnum & Bailey circus for a number of years, doing a complete act of freestyle jumps, tricks, and flips. At 39, he had not slowed down one iota from his circus days.

For the next few days, Charlie and Dean showed us around their little mountain playground. While the park here had some huge ramps that propelled skiers and boarders into the stratosphere, Charlie and Dean were happier out-of-bounds, and they saw the whole mountain as their terrain park. In fact, Baker is a bit like one big natural terrain park—full of cliffs, cornices, and short lines that are close to vertical. Charlie and Dean knew them all.

CHARLIE LED US OUT-OF-BOUNDS onto the Chair Eight Elbow Traverse. Mt. Baker's policy is to allow freeriders unlimited access beyond the area boundary, provided that they have an avalanche transceiver, a shovel and the knowledge how to use them.

The new snow was heavy but quite skiable on the upper mountain. The lower half of the run was cut up and had the consistency of porridge. That was of no concern to Charlie. While Rupert, Vince and I thrashed around like flies in a vat of molasses, Charlie shifted into overdrive and powered through the sludge like a downhill racer on a salted course.

Now we were ready for some more serious out-of-bounds skiing, so I went to the rental shop to get some fatter skis. Nowadays, there is hardly a snow condition that cannot be skied with the right width of ski. I chose a pair of boards with a 99-millimeter waist.

Again, we left from the top of Chair Eight, and began a steep 10-minute hike up Hemisphere. We continued to the east onto Shuksan Arm, alternately traversing and hiking for close to an hour. Charlie, who used to ride mountain bikes professionally, usually does this jaunt in a 15-minute trot, but he was kind enough to keep a pace which was comfortable for mere mortals.

Ultimately, we arrived at a descent that the locals call "Heli", as it gives freeriders a heliski experience without the chopper. It was snowing

Dean Collins leaps off a cornice at the Mt. Baker ski area, with glaciated Mt. Shukstan in the background.

lightly and the fog rolled in and out. Bad weather or poor visibility does not deter the locals from doing the most radical lines on the mountain. Mt. Baker is not a place for fair-weather skiers.

Our first line was a ridge that rolled over to about 40 degrees at its steepest. It would have made a good photo. I thought about stopping to snap a few shots, but it was just too sweet. My fat skis floated perfectly, giving me a good solid ride down to the flats. Rupert and Vince were on skinnier race-carve skis, and bounced down in a series of short turns, and "New School" Charlie hit Mach speed as he deviated only slightly from the fall line.

We arrived at tree line and continued down into some beautiful glades. It looked as if the sun might peek through for a moment, and I wanted to wait for better light to take a few photos. Our marketing man nixed the idea.

"Hey Jimmy," said Charlie, "It's no idea to wait for the sun. It probably won't happen, and anyway, we don't want to give people any false illusions of what to expect here. Just take the photos in the fog and the snow. That's what Mt. Baker is about."

It was a refreshing, honest attitude, especially coming from a marketing man. Then again, as I said before, Charlie was not exactly your run-of-the-mill, hand-shaking, back-slapping PR guy. For that matter, Mt. Baker turned out to be a far cry from your everyday mom-and-pop, family-operated, locals' resort.

LAKE TAHOE
SKIING WITH A VIEW

In the 1860s, Mark Twain described Lake Tahoe thus: "...a sea, whose royal seclusion is guarded by a cordon of sentinel peaks that lift their frosty fronts nine thousand feet above the level world; a sea whose every aspect is impressive. To obtain the air the angels breath, you must go to Tahoe."

Today, the air is still a pleasure to breath, and the lake looks as clean as it was when the local Paiute and Washoe Indians bathed in it 150 years ago. Lake Tahoe is without doubt and without prejudice, one of the most beautiful spots on Earth. Driving along the shore of this large body of water, which has a circumference of 116 kilometers, there is a new, breathtaking panorama around almost every bend in the road.

In addition, over a dozen ski resorts are today located among those "sentinel peaks" that Mark Twain described, including Squaw Valley, Heavenly, Alpine Meadows, Homewood, Kirkwood, Northstar-at-Tahoe, Sierra-at-Tahoe, Sugar Bowl, Diamond Peak, Boreal, Tahoe Donner and Mount Rose. Squaw Valley, which hosted the Winter Olympics in 1960, along with Heavenly, are the largest and most famous of the areas, but many of the smaller resorts are also well worth a visit.

A number of these centers have a view of Lake Tahoe, and that is reason enough to come here. While Homewood and Kirkwood have superb views, none of the Tahoe resorts has a more stunning panorama than Heavenly. Here, the lifts rise up almost from the lakeshore, and from many spots on the mountain, it seems as if a skier might disappear directly into the shimmering blue-green waters below. Some of the best off-piste skiing at Heavenly is down the back side, from where skiers can enjoy an alternative remarkable view over the Nevada desert to the South. The nightlife in Heavenly revolves around the nearby casinos, which offer world-class nightclub acts as well as gaming.

On the opposite side of the lake, the North Shore, lies Alpine Meadows, another area that offers excellent off-piste possibilities after a snowfall. While there is also a lot of challenging terrain at Alpine, the laid-back atmosphere here makes it a particular favorite among families.

THROUGHOUT HISTORY, CALIFORNIA HAS BEEN a region where one could find some of the most interesting, weird, and often extreme personality types, and this is just as true of the Sierra skiers as of the Hollywood stars.

As far back as the 1850s, Snowshoe Thompson (born in Norway as Jon Torsteinson-Rue) pioneered skiing in the Tahoe region on a pair of homemade, 3-meter-long, 11-kilo skis. For twenty years, Snowshoe

THIS PAGE
UPPER: Snow-covered mountains on the shore of Lake Tahoe as seen from Sand Harbor.
LOWER: Emerald Bay, Lake Tahoe.

RIGHT PAGE
UPPER: Glen Plake. Photo by Keoki Flagg.
LOWER: Jason Mack leaves a wake of powder behind him on Jake's Peak, near Lake Tahoe's South shore. Photo by Keoki Flagg.

delivered the mail to isolated miners on a 3-day, 145-kilometer route across the Sierras. He was the first of many legendary skiers to hail from the Tahoe region.

Today, some of the most radical local skiers spend much of their time among the steep slopes and cliffs of Squaw Valley. A few years after Sylvain Saudan and Patrick Vallençant began pushing the limits of steep-skiing in Chamonix, Scott Schmidt began to establish the American version of extreme skiing by dropping 30-meter cliffs on KT-22, Squaw Valley's radical freeride mountain. Ever since then, Squaw has been a hotbed for extreme freeriders, with the likes of Kent Kreitler and Shane McConkey included among the local heroes.

Of all Tahoe's ski legends, the most colorful in a figurative and literal sense must be Heavenly's Glen Plake. While Schmidt brought notoriety to Squaw Valley through his appearance in a whole slew of Warren Miller films, Glen put his skills on display for filmmaker Greg Stump, beginning in the mid-1980s.

IN THE ENSUING YEARS, PLAKE'S ACCOMPLISHMENTS and his multi-colored extreme Mohawk hairstyle have certainly made him the world's most recognizable skier. The early part of his career was checkered, as numerous arrests and jail time were interspersed with spectacular ski-film performances and a couple of world-championship titles in hot-dog skiing.

At the start of the '90s, Glen swore off both drugs and booze, and his passion for skiing has, since then, carried him on a steady upward climb. Today his outrageous punk hairdo, which offended many people twenty years ago, is a nostalgic retro symbol of the glory days of the hot-dog era. True to his roots, Glen has not only kept his Mohawk intact, he has also continued to ski on 215-centimeter-long downhill skis—even in the moguls!

When it comes to off-piste skiing, Glen is also a traditionalist.

"Skiing is turning to me," says the Mohawk man, and he prefers to ski powder with many turns and face shots as opposed to high-speed straight-lining on super-fat skis.

Glen also has a passion for the grassroots of skiing. In 1992, he

embarked on a 68-day, 21,000-kilometer road-trip through 33 states and 50 small ski resorts. On that trip, he spent time skiing and rubbing elbows with locals, giving them free instruction and inspiration. Today, Glen continues to have this grassroots road-trip as part of his annual schedule, having morphed from the bad boy of skiing to one of its foremost ambassadors.

Perhaps Glen's most important contribution to skiing has been the manner in which he has changed the sport. Through his unusual skiing skills, his emblematic hairstyle, and his love of skiing and people, Glen became one of the first sponsored skiers who did not come from the ranks of the racing circuit. That simple fact has changed the whole manner in which skiing has been marketed. Today, top freeride skiers are as visible to the public as racers, and the top freeriders can earn a living from skiing. Simply put, Glen Plake was the first professional ski bum!

Today, Glen is back at Heavenly, where it all started for him as a young racer. He is involved with public relations for the ski resort as well as heading up the Gunbarrel 25 event. This is a competition perfectly suited to his roots in mogul skiing as well as his passion for the extreme and the bizarre. Begun in 2004, the event involves skiers attempting to complete 25 runs down Heavenly's heavily moguled black-diamond Gunbarrel run.

Whether one wants to ski bumps along side Glen in Heavenly, jump cliffs with the "rock stars" of Squaw Valley, or ski with the family in Alpine Meadows, the Tahoe Basin offers a great variety of resorts within close proximity of one another. Add to that an inordinate amount of sunshine and a season that stretches from mid-November until the end of May and you have the makings of one of the real ski paradises of North America.

MT. ALYESKA — SEWARD'S REDEMPTION

When United States Secretary of State William Seward purchased Alaska from the Russians, in 1867 for $7.2 million, he became the butt of more political jokes than former President Clinton and Monica Lewinsky. The press and the public called the deal "Seward's Folly" and referred to the territory as "Seward's Icebox".

In the many years that have intervened since Seward became the laughingstock of America, countless billions of dollars in gold and oil have been extracted from Alaska. It is a shame that he was never able to grin out at the critical public from a 21st century TV screen and say, "I told you so!"

As a skier, the many snow-poor winters of recent years got me thinking back to my old history lessons about "Seward's Icebox." While almost every major ski area in the world, from Japan to Austria, has invested millions of dollars in snowmaking equipment during the past decade, Alaska is also a super-power in the increasingly rare natural resources of ice and snow. This is a landmass that includes over 75,000 square kilometers of glacier—a rather soothing statistic for a snow junkie.

During one of the recent "greenhouse winters" in the Alps, my frustration with artificial snow got the better of me. My sister Christy, her husband Paul and I invested in three air tickets to Anchorage. Sixty kilometers from Anchorage, overlooking a beautiful narrow bay called Turnagain Arm, is the biggest ski resort in Alaska, Mt. Alyeska. With a base at a mere 76 meters above sea level, it is also one of the lowest ski resorts in the world.

UPON OUR ARRIVAL on April 9, the word was that the mountain had received over 3 meters of snow—so far that month! We were saved! This was not the only stat worth jotting down. The resort averages 15 meters of snowfall per season, and during this particular year it had already recorded about 22 meters of white stuff with the added precipitation brought on by the El Niño effect.

On our first ride up the tram, there were only seven other skiers going up, but three of them were Reg Crist, former U.S. Ski Team downhiller, Daron Rahlves, also of U.S. Ski Team fame, and Kim Reichhelm, two-time female World Extreme Skiing Champion. The movie stars may go to Aspen or Telluride, but the people at the forefront of the ski world can often be found in Alaska nowadays.

The April powder was heavy, and we were all grateful for the invention of fat skis. Day two added 60 centimeters of snow to the base, and by our third day, the continued snowfall closed the lifts. In such circumstances, Alaska offers plenty of alternatives. For the next few days, we had a full menu of activities, including a wildlife cruise into Prince William Sound, where we observed sea otters, bald eagles, sea lions, mountain goats, dolphin and whales. Another day we tried our hand at a bit of kayaking.

UPON OUR RETURN to Mt. Alyeska, the storm had vanished and 80 centimeters of chaste powder was waiting to be violated. Just outside the Alyeska Prince Hotel rests the helicopter of the Chugach Powder Guides, and if ever there was an ideal day to have a chopper at one's disposal, this was it. While the extreme heliskiing near Valdez has copped the ski magazine headlines for many years, the heliskiing in the Western Chugach near Alyeska is probably safer and more suitable to the general ski public. The area has less wind, and the emphasis is on good deep-snow skiing rather than radical descents.

The chopper dropped our group atop a peak just behind the Alyeska Resort. North of us lay a whole range of powder-drenched tops as far as the eye could see. They had that typical Alaska look of a ruffled potato

LEFT PAGE: Paul Curtis enjoying a day of heliskiing near Mt. Alyeska.
THIS PAGE: Kevin Quinn appears as a mere speck on a pink ridge in the Chugach Mountains near Cordova. In springtime, the lingering evening sunlight allows heliskiers to ski until about 10 p.m., which is when this photo was taken. Photo by Keoki Flagg/PNH.

chip standing on edge, with a series of almost vertical ridges and couloirs lined up side by side.

One of the co-owners of the operation, American Olympic downhill gold-medal winner Tommy Moe, was one of our guides. By the time the snow dust had settled behind us, we had all put 6000-7000 vertical meters of heaven under our skis, and we settled into some old sofas in the helicopter hangar for a small celebratory party.

A score of happy riders beamed from ear to ear, as they quenched a long day's powder frenzy with iced beer. Moe displayed the same huge smile that decorated his face the day that he showed up all his European detractors in the Olympics. He told anyone who cared to listen that this had, perhaps, been his best powder day ever, and nobody doubted his word.

This was the last day for Christy, Paul and me, and I recapped our visit in my mind. Alaska, with its trillions of tons of ice and snow, is certainly a bastion where skiing will be safe from any further greenhouse damage for millenniums to come. With conventional skiing at Mt. Alyeska, some of the best heliskiing in the world and unrivaled scenery, America's largest state is truly a skier's paradise. Add to all that a list of extracurricular attractions that include kayaking, dog-sledding and magnificent wildlife, and a ski vacation in Alaska is bound to be a unique and memorable experience. I only wondered if the U.S. government might want to send one of Seward's descendants over to Moscow as a special emissary to discuss a deal for Siberia.

VALDEZ — THE PRICE OF FREEDOM

Sir Edmund Hillary was not only the first man to see the view from 8848 meters, he was also an adventurer who traversed the globe from the Himalayas to Antarctica. During his odyssey, he visited Alaska in 1962, passing through the fjord lands of Prince William Sound, gazing upon the Chugach Mountains that stretch across the northern flank of that magnificent watery land, and traveling up the long fjord known as Valdez Arm to the village of Valdez. Hillary told his guide, Mike Lopez, that Prince William Sound and Valdez were the most beautiful areas he had ever been.

Valdez has had a remarkable history since it was originally put on the map by the Klondike gold rush of the 1890s, but it was not so often its awe-inspiring scenery that attracted visitors. At the time of the gold rush, a tent city sprung up, but once the gold fever had subsided, only about 500 hardy people stayed on.

The population was no greater by Good Friday, 1964, when the third-largest earthquake ever recorded rocked and rolled the village longer and harder than Elvis's recording of "All Shook Up". Situated only 65 kilometers from the epicenter, Valdez shook for more than 4 minutes, and the Richter hit 9.2. By the time an enormous tidal wave had receded, 32 people had perished, and the entire town had to be rebuilt on more stable ground.

IT WAS OIL RATHER THAN gold that stimulated Valdez's next major influx of visitors. Valdez is the northernmost ice-free port in North America. Hence, the rebuilt town was chosen to be the terminus of the Trans Alaska Pipeline, which was built in the early 1970s to transport oil from the rich oil fields of Prudhoe Bay in Northern Alaska. The town's size multiplied 20-fold during the building phase of the pipeline.

Don't blame an Alaskan if he sacrilegiously refers to Good Friday as "Bad Friday". Twenty-five years after the great earthquake, again on this holy day, in 1989, the town was back in the news, when the oil tanker Exxon Valdez hit a reef, creating the greatest oil-spill disaster in North American history.

It was in the 1990s that the area's natural beauty created a new kind of boom around this Alaskan hamlet. Ski mania became the latest craze to replace gold and oil in the boom-or-bust cyclical existence of Valdez. Every spring, quite a few of the world's gnarliest ski bums arrive here from Squaw Valley, Jackson Hole, Crested Butte, Alta and other sundry steep mountain areas.

A small company called Alaska Backcountry Adventures (ABA) is largely responsible for that development. In 1991, ABA began an unusual "no-rules" brand of heliskiing from atop Thompson Pass, about 40 kilometers out of Valdez. The lack of regulations and controls was particularly odd in the United States, considering the proliferation of ski lawsuits that abound in this litigation-happy country. Nevertheless, befitting Alaska's license plate logo of "The Last Frontier", ABA took a Wild West approach to heliskiing.

ABA began dropping a handful of borderline-lunatic extreme skiers, without guides, on basically any spot that their customers pointed to, whether it was suitable for landing or not. Valdez became the last bastion of total ski freedom in the United States. While most American resorts had, by this time, roped-off and restricted out-of-bounds skiing, here in Alaska, the only limits were a skier's ability and intestinal fortitude. That fact, needless to say, began to attract a very special group of skiers and riders, not to mention pilots.

Chopper pilots were thrilled at the chance of testing their skills at dropping skiers onto landing zones that no other heliski operation in the world would dream of using. The world elite of extreme skiing and boarding began to arrive in droves to test their skills on a never-ending array of sick first descents.

The World Extreme Ski Competition made Valdez its venue in 1991, and the notoriety of this Alaskan village began to spread like a prairie fire among serious backcountry and off-piste skiers. Soon, an ever increasing number of gunslingers were arriving in town to rub elbows with the rock stars or perhaps, even try to outshoot them.

By now, ABA has added guides to their service, and other heliski

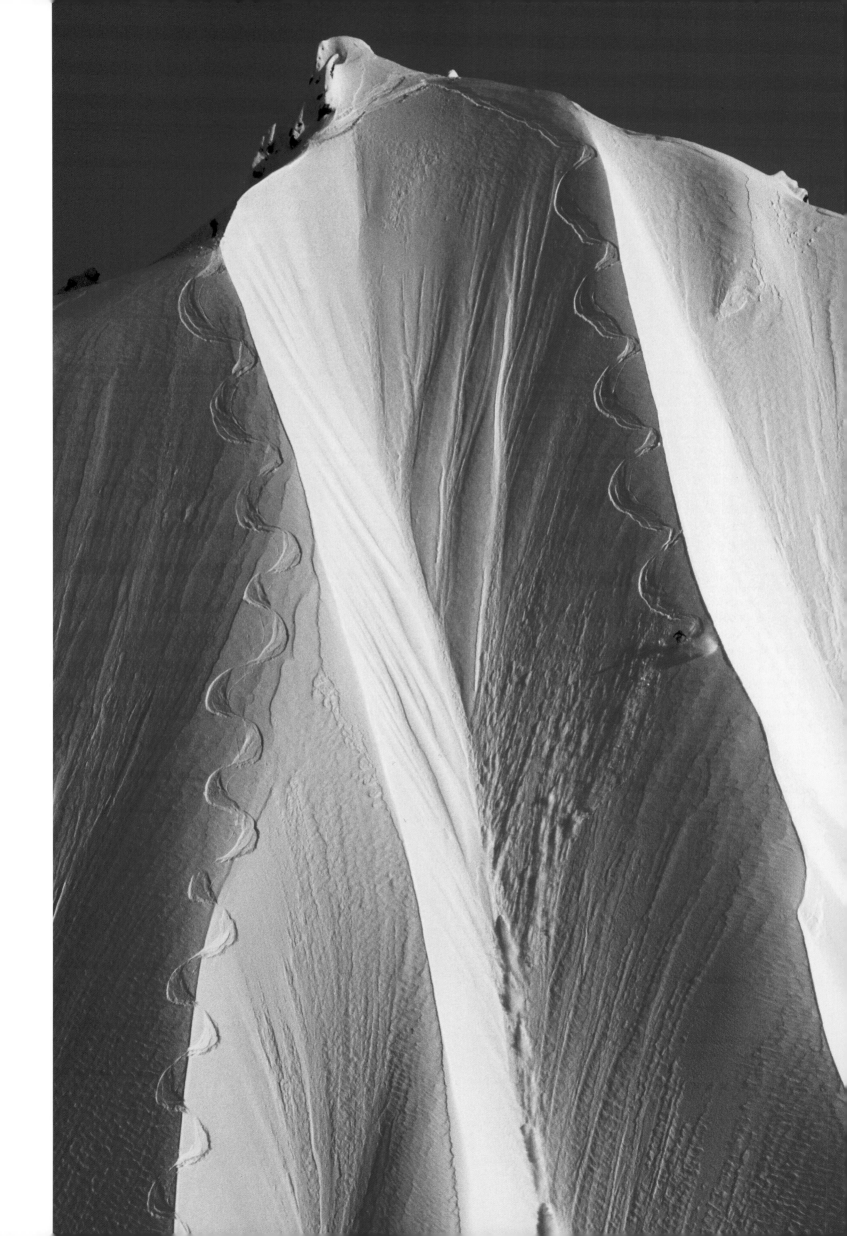

LEFT PAGE: Kent Kreitler skis the Fin in the Chugach Mountains, near Cordova, Alaska. He is skiing with Points North Heli-Adventures. Photo by Keoki Flagg.
THIS PAGE: Snow cat takes skiers up to the Berlin Wall atop Thompson Pass, near Valdez.
NEXT TWO PAGES: The last rays of sun light up the Books Range, near Valdez.

operations have sprung up to deal with the growing numbers of customers. In spite of the addition of guides and the increase of activity, the heliskiing in Valdez has remained unique. Elsewhere in the ski world, the chopper is the domain of the rich and famous, a powder playground for the globetrotter set who have the bucks to blow $5,000 or more on a week of fun. That crowd goes heliskiing to ski powder.

With ABA, one doesn't have to book for a week—not even a day! With ABA, one can buy heliskiing by the run. Here, ski bums skimp on meals and buy adrenaline rushes one at a time. In addition, most Valdez skiers do not really seem to come for the powder but rather for the extremely steep terrain.

The maritime storms which blow in off the Bering Sea and the Gulf of Alaska leave a snowpack that is more stable and less avalanche-prone than snow in many other parts of the world, allowing the possibility for skiing such daunting terrain. This does not mean, by any stretch of the imagination, that the descents are safe. Rather, the maritime snow affords skiers here the possibility to attempt steeper slopes, so that extreme gradient and exposure must be added to avalanche danger among the risks involved in Valdez heliskiing.

I PULLED INTO THE PARKING LOT OF ABA on a foggy day in mid-April. The scene was a caricature of American ski-bum life. The whole lot looked like a tailgate party for skiers and boarders. The headquarters of ABA is an old dilapidated trailer. Alongside this less than auspicious structure were parked nine or ten large motor homes. Divided among four or five ski bums, the motor home fulfills both transport and housing needs, and is one of the cheapest ways to ski bum in Alaska.

A handful of riders sat in each motor home, playing cards, swilling beer, and/or swapping tall tales of life in the "big leagues". In between these large vehicles were all kinds of RVs, converted vans, and crashed-in ski-bum wrecks. Alongside the parking lot, a number of tents completed the scene of ski-bum housing.

Rastas and clean-cut jocks milled about in the lot, occasionally glancing up when a patch of blue appeared. The only thing their appearance had in common was the presence of climbing harnesses strapped around their waists. This is mandatory equipment in Valdez, in case one has to be hauled out of one of the zillion crevasses in the area.

Harnesses are not obligatory dress on down days, of course. It never became completely clear to me whether the bums merely wanted to be in a state of readiness in case the skies suddenly cleared, or if it gave their Rambo hormones an extra kick to have a few carabiners permanently dangling from their waist. Either way, many of the residents of the lot acted as if they had been injected with an overdose of testosterone before they arrived. Even the girls here had hair on their chests.

I tried to find the least macho-looking specimen in the vicinity, and I eventually struck up a conversation with a soft-spoken telemark skier who introduced himself as John. John was a Valdez regular, who came here every spring, when the season was on the wane in Utah. He was in a non-macho Ford Fiesta, which he laughingly referred to as his "microvan". It was full to the hilt with ski gear. Since he had also been sleeping in this cramped vehicle for the past two weeks, it could have been more aptly called a "Ford Siesta". John soon introduced me to Kevin, Josh and Ian, who were, like me, rookies to the Valdez scene.

FOG HAD PLAGUED VALDEZ for three days, and the natives were getting restless. John suggested that we fill out the time with a few hours of free "road-shots". On the Valdez side of Thompson Pass is a huge hairpin curve. On "weather days", John explained, one could pass the time by skiing about 400 vertical meters from the upper to the lower section of road that made up the hairpin.

We played a quick challenge round of "scissors, rock, paper". Ian was the loser and became the first driver, while the rest of us made turns in the late-afternoon spring slush. John led the way through a series of stairsteps of short, steep pitches followed by flat run-outs. There were a few rock faces and small cornices where one could get air and practice one's technique for the challenges that lay ahead. We played three more rounds of "scissors, rock, paper", until all but Josh had taken a turn as our

chauffeur. Josh was named the day's winner, and we all headed back to Valdez for a meal at the Totem Inn and an early night's sleep. It was best to be prepared. The next day could be bluebird.

A 7:30 wake-up call proved our hopes to be overly optimistic—a fourth consecutive day of fog and snow was in store for the inmates of the parking lot. We headed for ABA's headquarters anyway. Sometimes the weather is better on the other side of the pass, and we wanted to be ready, in case the sun broke through. As we drove over the summit, we passed a few boarders beating the boredom by rolling

»...and elated ski bums started popping out of their nests and bustling around like busy ants.«

down the west flank of Thompson Pass on oversized skateboards. We checked out the Tsaina Lodge, headquarters for Doug Coombs' heliski operation. A few of the guides were shooting pool, and a handful of skiers strutted around, showing off their harnesses to anyone who was interested. We were not and headed back to tailgate heaven.

I was definitely in need of some activity. "What about a cat ride?" I suggested to John and the others.

Just then, a hole opened up above us. The clouds parted suddenly like Moses doing his magic on the Red Sea, and elated ski bums started popping out of their nests and bustling around like busy ants. Avalanche transceivers were being strapped around people's waists, helmets appeared, avalanche shovels, water canteens and alternate clothing options were being busily stuffed into backpacks, and the sleepy encampment was abruptly buzzing as if the enemy had just been sited on the horizon.

John, the veteran, remained calm. "Probably, just a 'sucker hole'," he said succinctly.

Then addressing the quizzical looks on his band of rookie followers, he went on to explain that a "sucker hole" was an opening in the clouds which suckered people into believing the weather would clear—the gods playing games with the easily excitable minds of young ski bums.

He was right. Twenty minutes into the bustle of activity, the one-dimensional, bleak gray returned to cover the camp. Like a geyser that had run its course, all activity ceased once again, and the encampment soon returned to an atmosphere of listless monotony.

MY SNOW-CAT SUGGESTION WAS NOW considered seriously, and a half-hour later, we were winding our way up Mt. Odyssey in a bright yellow, enclosed piste-machine. Mt. Odyssey is a piece of granite to be reckoned with, having been the site of many of the extreme-skiing competitions, and I was happy to have John, who knew the mountain, with us for my real inauguration to Valdez.

The cat had barely started rolling when a small plastic bag of marijuana popped out of someone's pocket. American ski bums have numerous idiosyncrasies, not the least of which is their penchant for smoking dope. The song "Rocky Mountain High", John Denver's ode to the natural high, notwithstanding, many American ski bums seem to be more into a

drug-induced high. The sweet smell of the illegal weed permeated the snow cat for the next 30 minutes. This all seemed particularly odd to me, considering the extremeness of the terrain and the importance of clear judgment in choosing a line to ski in Valdez.

Soon, we were at our point of disembarkation. A dozen ski bums and a small cloud of smoke emerged quickly through the open back door. There are all kinds of routes, from safe, open bowls to steep, exposed couloirs, that are available on Mt. Odyssey. We waited a few minutes for visibility, and we were in luck—another brief opening in the clouds appeared. A "sucker hole" does not last long enough to start a day's heliski operation, but it is certainly a blessing when one is standing atop 1000 vertical meters of powder.

I dove into an open field of powder with nothing dangerous in sight. Fifty turns down, I glanced back long enough to see that everybody had followed my lead, and a dozen shapely snake-like impressions were imprinted on what had been a virgin mountain just moments before. The snow was quite light at the top and got gradually heavier the further down we got. It didn't matter much, as the entire group was equipped with fat skis, which we maneuvered effortlessly even through the heavier snow. We skied for long stretches with the help of the "fatties", pausing only long enough to admire our tracks, which were quite visible thanks to the "sucker hole".

Back at the road, my comrades hitched back to the ABA lot, once again

suckered into the idea that flying might be possible, but I opted, instead, for another cat ride that was a sure thing. My second run was not as fortuitous. The visibility was like the inside of a Ping-Pong ball in a glass of milk. Directly below, in the middle of the slope, I could barely make out a dark image—a vague form that I knew to be rocks.

The light was so bad that I could really not discern the grade of the slope. I had to make short jump turns and get an impression of the angle by feel. It was skiing by Braille. Fortunately, 30 or 40 turns down, the light got slightly better, and I could see that I had already navigated the steepest section of mountain. Giving out an inaudible sigh of relief, I began to relax and skied the rest of the run in longer bursts of turns.

It was not late, but the visibility was getting worse instead of better, and I opted to drive back to Valdez and research more bad-weather alternatives. El Niño had been blowing one storm after another over the coastal mountains all season long, and there was no sign of a change. I took a long drive for a short visit to Mt. McKinley, or Denali, as it is known in Alaska. At 6194 meters, Mt. McKinley is the highest point on the North American continent and well worth a visit.

THE DRIVE BACK FROM DENALI PARK boded change. Halfway back to Valdez, I drove out of the cloud cover and began to cruise under a vast carpet of stars. The night was cold and crisp, always a good sign, and when, around midnight, veils of light began to undulate and shimmer

» Man has come with ropes and ice axes, with masks and oxygen tanks and with skis and poles, and the whims of Mother Nature have determined who has perished and who has survived. «

in the distance, I felt confident that there would be sun the next day. I pulled the car onto the shoulder four or five times during my drive and gazed up with fascination as the northern lights flashed their mysterious magic above the endless Alaskan horizon.

The next morning, I awoke to a bluebird day. At nine o'clock, I arrived at the parking lot to a scene of chaos and pandemonium. There were more vehicles there than ever. Naturally, after all the bad weather, everybody wanted to heliski that day. Around 150 people were milling around the muddy ski-bum encampment in various states of confusion. I rushed into the rental shop to rent a harness.

"We're all out," said Phil, the Australian operator of the rental shop.

"What about some fat skis?" I pleaded.

"All we have left is one pair of 165s, which I don't believe is your preference," he drawled with a touch of Australian understated sarcasm. I was ready to scream when he added, "I don't think it will matter anyway, because there are a lot of problems today."

What the hell does that mean, I thought to myself, slowly working my way into the kind of frenzied state of mind that most of the bums were in when I had arrived that morning. I hurried into the ABA "office" and inquired about the flying situation.

Shannon, the girl in charge of operations, broke the bad news to me. "One chopper has been leased by a film crew today, and one pilot is sick. That means we're down to only one helicopter for all those people out there. Jeff, Ian and those guys are lined up to go out in 20 minutes, but they filled out their group with someone else as their fifth person when you left for Denali. Maybe, I can fix you up with a group and get you out around four o'clock, but that's no promise. There are 22 groups I gotta get up there now with only one chopper."

Near the helicopter, I ran into my group of buddies. John was going to be flying in 15 minutes, but he was not much happier than I was.

"They're just flying road-runs because they're overbooked," he lamented. "I want to go deep. You can hop in for me after one run if you want."

Road-runs are the descents closest to the highway, allowing skiers to be picked up by bus, cutting the flying time necessary for the helicopter. Having already been here a number of times, John had skied virtually all of the road-runs, and was only interested in paying his hard-earned cash for a run deep into the backcountry.

I thanked him for the offer, but the entire affair seemed so disorganized that I decided to go back to the snow cat. With the good weather, the cat would be taking people up to the even steeper and longer run known as the Berlin Wall, and I figured this would be as good a chance as any to explore that run as well.

The ride up to the Wall cost a few dollars more than our earlier ascent and took an additional 10 minutes. The last section of mountain, however, was much too steep for a snow cat, and we were required to hike the final 20 minutes or so.

As I caught my breath at the top, I surveyed the possibilities. There was really no route that didn't leave a lump in my throat. The easiest lines with the least danger from exposure to rocks were about 45 degrees and still left me with the uneasy feeling that I definitely did not want to fall. On the other hand, there were quite a few tracks all over the Wall, so that I did not feel quite so fearful of avalanches.

SOME PEOPLE HIKED MUCH FURTHER along the ridge to try to get a virgin ride, but under the circumstances, I was more than happy to take my chances where some others had already been the guinea pigs. Even if the conditions seemed safe from a major slide, this certainly did not preclude the eventuality of sloughing, an ever present hazard on steep, exposed slopes. At 45 degrees, a skier's turns in powder will invariably set some surface snow into motion. As this surface slough gathers more snow and picks up speed, it can catch up to the skier five or six turns down, and be more than enough to knock him off balance if he is not careful.

I skied down the Wall tentatively, cutting out of the fall line regularly to avoid the sloughs. Following the long, steep section, which is a continous adrenaline rush, one arrives on a plateau from where one can descend directly or traverse out for a long ways, before continuing down.

» There's no more skiing today. Two people fell off a cornice, and one of them is dead.«

There exist limitless possibilities and they all empty out onto the highway. One can be quite assured of virgin snow for the whole latter half of the run.

In this case, the second half of the descent was a potpourri of snow conditions—powder, corn snow and the usual spring nemesis, breakable crust. I broke a good sweat working the crust, but I was in no hurry.

The run was enjoyable and I went back to the cat for an encore. Just at the bottom of the steep section, John appeared, moving quickly uphill on his telemark skis and skins. He had left the heliskiing after one run as planned, and we skied a run together, taking our time, photographing and enjoying the unique Alaskan scenery.

Four o'clock had arrived, and it was time to check in with Shannon to see if I could get a run with the helicopter. What I got, instead, was an icy slap in the face. Shannon had looked harrowed and stressed that morning, but she looked much worse now. Her eyes were red and it looked as if she had been crying.

Her words came out slowly, with long pauses between each short sentence. "There's no more skiing today. We shut down about an hour ago. Two people fell off a cornice, and one of them is dead. He was in Kevin's group—a guy named Ian."

I suddenly felt numb. I walked like a zombie back into the lot and began querying others for more information. Soon, I was able to piece a more complete story together.

The group had landed atop a run called Cracked Ice. The helicopter had left, and the guide had walked a few steps away to relieve his bladder. Ian and the person who had replaced me in their group had walked about fifteen steps up from the landing spot to look down the other side. Unbeknownst to them, they had been hiking on a cornice. The weight of two people was too much for the cornice, and it gave way. Ian had hit his head on a rock and died instantly, while the other skier had survived with not much more than major lacerations.

WHILE I WAS GATHERING information, John wandered back into the lot, and I shared the tragic news with him. We got into his car and drove to the top of the pass where he opened a whisky bottle. There, as we sipped, we looked out over what is probably the most stunning set of peaks in this part of the Chugach Range. Southeast of us, the section of mountains known as the Books stood proudly, daring the best of the best to ski her forbidding ridges and couloirs.

This jagged set of peaks got their name because they somewhat resemble books lined up on a shelf—that is how vertical their ridges and ravines look. They appeared to be totally unskiable, but some of the rock stars have been there and violated the Books in their ever present quest for first descents.

We were parked close to the spot where we had skied the road-runs with Ian on the day we had met. The shadows were getting longer. It was almost nine o'clock, the sun was sending its last rays of light onto the Books and they were turning crimson.

Unfortunately, we could not really enjoy this most beautiful of sunsets juxtaposed with the death that had blotted the day. Yet somehow, the stunning mountains and the death of a skier were not unrelated. As the Lorelei tempted sailors, the wonders of nature have always lured man closer and closer to her raw core, as he has sought a communion with her. Man has come with ropes and ice axes, with masks and oxygen tanks and with skis and poles, and the whims of Mother Nature have determined who has perished and who has survived.

The sun disappeared from the Books, the last of our whiskey had long ago been swallowed, and John and I returned to Valdez. I had, however, not reached any sense of mental closure to the long day's events.

THE FOLLOWING MORNING, I AWOKE to another sparkling bluebird sky, all three choppers were back in service, but I did not feel like going up. Instead, I packed a hearty lunch, dropped a kayak into the deep blue waters of Valdez Arm and took my lunch and my contemplation out to sea.

I thought about the tragedy that had occurred on Mt. Everest some years earlier. It was largely attributed to the many amateurs who were being guided up the highest mountain in the world. That incident had a relationship to what was happening in Valdez. Valdez is today for skiers what Mt. Everest has been for climbers ever since Sir Edmund and Tenzing Norgay first set foot on her lofty summit. It is the ultimate challenge—the location where the top people in their field come to test their limits. While Doug Coombs, Dean Cummings and company are off in their spare time pushing the envelope of what is humanly possible on skis, they are financing their adventures by guiding amateurs in an extreme environment.

The infatuation with extreme sports, which had once been the realm of the professional, had now infiltrated a lower stratum of sportsmen, and more deaths would be inevitable. The sport of skiing was moving in an ever more dangerous direction, and I was having trouble reconciling the negative aspects of this development with my own love of adventure.

Just then, a small group of sea otters distracted me from my reflections. About 50 meters portside of my kayak, they played, carefree in the sunshine, and peered with curiosity at me.

My thoughts turned now to the Russians who were the first foreigners to come to this wild, free land in pursuit of sea-otter furs. It had always been adventurers who had led the way to Alaska, whether they were chasing furs, gold or snow. In each wave of newcomers, there had certainly been brave and skilled amateurs along with professionals. Similarly, in each group that had passed this way, some survived and others perished. They had known the risks. Freedom does not come without a price, and that price is danger. The otters could live out their days in the secure, predator-free environment of a zoo, but would they make that choice?

I pulled my kayak into a sweeping turn and paddled past the playful otters. I had found the answer to my dilemma. I arrived back in Valdez at sunset with a more peaceful mind.

THE NEXT MORNING, I BOARDED AN ABA chopper at 9:30 with four snowboarders and no misgivings. We landed atop a 40-45 degree pitch, which our guide, Ty, called an intermediate run. Two of the boarders were definitely not convinced and clearly had some reservations. It was not their idea of a warmup run to let our leader determine how skilled they were. Ty asked if everybody was comfortable with the run. It was a free choice. Our air taxi could return and pick anyone up. Everybody decided to descend on boards.

Our second lift took us to a peak which began with an even steeper slope—45-plus degrees. From the top, we gazed out over a gargantuan river of ice. The glacier below us stretched about 3 kilometers across the valley floor and appeared to be about 25 kilometers long. Scores of other glaciers emptied into the ice flow.

LEFT PAGE
John Dorsey cruising on his telemark skis amidst the glacial beauty near Thompson Pass.

THIS PAGE
UPPER: All over Alaska, monster glaciers wind their way down toward the sea.
ABOVE LEFT: Eagles are much more plentiful than skiers in this part of the world.
ABOVE RIGHT: Large ship in Valdez Arm.

The initial pitch we were to ski was about 500 vertical meters. The boarders sliced it in six or seven turns and stayed far ahead of any potential sloughs. I like to make many turns in powder in spite of the trend toward big-mountain turns, and I felt free to descend at my pace—the freedom to go slowly.

I made 150 turns—maybe more—nobody was counting. I traversed out of the fall line to let sloughs go past, I paused to catch my breath and I stopped to enjoy the view. Sir Hillary most probably had never stood atop this particular peak, but I am quite sure he would have agreed that it was one of the most beautiful spots on Earth.

THIS PAGE
If you're unlucky, you could find yourself face-to-face with a giant grizzly while heliskiing in Canada. Just ask Canadian Mountain Holiday founder Hans Gmoser, who has experienced it himself.
RIGHT PAGE
Rupert Scheiner testing some of the double-diamond terrain in the Blackcomb Glacier Zone.

Chapter 2. CANADA

There is no doubt that Canada possesses a bounty of mountains. The Canadian Rockies and the numerous other ranges running throughout British Columbia are stunningly beautiful and include an almost endless array of peaks. The list of ranges includes the Purcells, Cariboos, Selkirks, Monashees and Coast Mountains and is longer than a seven-year-old child's Christmas wishing list. It will therefore come as a surprise to most people that the ski industry in western Canada was at the level of a Third World country as recently as the early 1970s!

Eastern Canada, on the other hand, blessed by a larger population base, already boasted well-known resorts like Mont-Sainte-Anne and Mt. Tremblant as early as the 1940s, matching the development of early U.S. destination resorts such as Sun Valley and Stowe.

A few developments in the '60s and '70s began a major metamorphosis in Canadian skiing. To begin with, Hans Gmoser, a transplanted Austrian, came up with a new and innovative way for skiers to access the wild and untamed peaks of British Columbia—the helicopter. Fellow pioneers Mike Wiegele and Herb Bleuer were not far behind with the inception of their own heliskiing operations.

This innovation captured the fantasy of skiers worldwide. Although only a small percentage of those skiers could afford such an extravagant method of reaching virgin slopes, the concept was so inspirational and exciting that before long, the Bugaboos, the first range to be explored with Hans's helicopter, became a household word among skiers in the know. Canada's mountains were now on the skier's map and in the skier's mind—a white dream of endless powder fields.

Then, in 1966, came the early beginnings of the Whistler/Blackcomb Resort in western BC. This fledgling endeavor had many difficulties at the outset, and Blackcomb almost went into receivership in the early 1980s. By the late '80s, it had turned the corner. By that time, the building of new lifts had given the area the longest vertical drop in North America (1600 vertical meters), and Whistler began getting annual recognition as one of the top five most-popular resorts on the continent in reader polls of American ski magazines.

Simultaneously, resorts in the national park area around Banff and Lake Louise, which had over the years attracted huge numbers of summer guests to visit their pristine lakes and forests, decided to try their hand in the international ski industry. The historic Banff Springs Hotel, which had always gone into hibernation during the winter, opened its doors to skiers in 1969.

Nine years later, the three small locals' areas of Norquay, Sunshine and Lake Louise began a cooperation on interchangeable lift tickets in an attempt to create a region that could begin to be internationally competitive. Still, while their facilities were substantially modernized, the overall number of lifts offered by the three combined areas was not very large. Over the next two decades, with success came expansion, and the region slowly grew into a destination resort.

Despite the improvements, Whistler Blackcomb and the Banff/Lake Louise ski regions were still small by comparison with top Alpine areas, and their new-fallen powder snow was most often skied out within a day. Nevertheless, European skiers somehow blurred the distinction between the endless supplies of deep powder available to Hans Gmoser's heliski guests and the limited amount available to visitors of the Canadian ski resorts, and a myth was born—go to Canada to ski endless laps of stardust!

The late 1990s and the early years of the 21st century in Canada have seen a fair number of resorts in western Canada rise from relative obscurity into regional resorts and in some cases low-volume destination resorts. Fernie, Kimberley, Kicking Horse, Sun Peaks, Big White, Panorama, Silver Star and Castle Mountain all fall into this category. In some cases, expansion and development have helped these smaller resorts gain recognition, while the Canadian powder myth and some major marketing have also played a part in helping these ski areas blossom in recent years.

BANFF, LAKE LOUISE, SUNSHINE
MOGULS, WILDLIFE AND THE BANFF SPRINGS HOTEL

My friend Rupert Scheiner and I met up with Canadian ski journalist George Koch in spring to experience Canadian skiing. Both Rupert and I have spent most of our skiing lives in the Alps, and within hours of our landing in Calgary airport, we were in the throes of "ski culture shock". The differences between the sport as it exists in most of the Alps and in Canada are profound.

We rode for about two hours from Calgary to Banff in George's Dodge Dakota and watched the dry, flat prairie of Alberta give way to a glorious skyline of peaks, as we approached the Rockies from the east. We were soon cruising at full speed amidst those peaks, and the distinctive features of the mountains immediately told us that we were not in the Alps.

The mixed layers of sandstone and limestone create peaks with sheer cliffs divided by small layers of slightly less-steep rock. Those layers were covered with snow, giving many of the mountains the appearance of a giant layer cake. We passed hundreds of snowfields and a number of hanging glaciers that rest spectacularly above the cliffs.

Our drive also differed from what we have experienced in the Alps. Instead of the windy mountain roads with interminable hairpin curves that I am accustomed to in France and Switzerland, the Trans Canada Highway to Banff was almost a straight line of pavement.

BANFF IS A LOVELY TOWN featuring a long, wide main street, lined with an array of restaurants, hotels and high-end shops. It looks like a town in the North American West should look. Many exposed logs and much natural rock are used here in the construction of the buildings, while faux-aboriginal rugs and patterns abound on the furniture upholstery. In addition, almost every hotel and restaurant has its walls lined with

photos depicting the historic "cowboy and Indian" days of the not so distant past.

A visitor to the French Alps generally gets a choice of French cuisine or French cuisine, and Austria, Italy and Switzerland similarly give tourists little variety from their local fare. The diversity of restaurants in Banff, however, provides a whole range of foods. Canadian steakhouses offer such local specialties as buffalo and elk steaks. Chinese restaurants stand alongside Italian pasta houses, numerous sushi bars, a Greek restaurant, many Mexican eateries and other places where one can get a Swiss fondue.

ON OUR FIRST SKI DAY, we drove 20 minutes to Sunshine Village. The lift attendants politely wished us good morning, took the skis from our hands and inserted them into the proper slot on the gondola. At the top station, the lift personnel repeated the procedure in reverse. This was true service—it couldn't be the Alps! As we proceeded from lift to lift, lines were a rarity. If there was a short wait, it was orderly—nobody to trample on your skis and elbow their way past you in the queue. This was a new world of skiing!

In recent years, Sunshine has added a new mountain, catering to advanced skiers, to its terrain. Originally a family resort of easy and intermediate slopes, Sunshine now has a more universal appeal as a result of the Goat's Eye Mountain project. Despite this major expansion, it remains a small ski area. A good skier can easily sample all of the twelve lifts and most of the terrain in a day.

Similar to most other North American resorts, Sunshine's smallness is accentuated by the fact that it is "decorated" with more rope than a

LEFT PAGE
Rupert Scheiner cuts up the powder in Lake Louise.

THIS PAGE
LEFT: World-famous Banff Springs Hotel.
RIGHT: To ski Delirium Dive in Sunshine Village, one must pass through this special gate, where an operating avalanche transceiver acts as a key.

rodeo's lasso competition. The boundary of the entire ski area is cordoned off. Within the ski area, rope is also used to keep skiers out of numerous closed areas. Whereas the Europeans would put up a "Closed" sign every kilometer or so, here in Canada, there can be no mistaking which areas a skier may or may not enter.

The policy regarding off-piste skiing in Canada is actually the same as in much of the Alps. In Canada, as in the Alps, skiing beyond the boundary ropes is perfectly permissible at the skier's own risk, with the knowledge that the area has not been secured for avalanches and is not patrolled. Going beyond a rope that closes off a section of the mountain within the existing ski area, however, is strictly prohibited. This policy is also followed in much of the Alps although it is not as strictly enforced.

In addition to the abundance of rope, there is also no shortage of signs in Canada. Innumerable placards to warn skiers of rocks, areas with minimal snow, slow-skiing zones and avalanche danger augment dozens of "Closed" and "Area Boundary" signs. This is a country that has clearly become fixated with safety and risk-reduction.

GEORGE, RUPERT AND I HAD BEEN looking forward to skiing Sunshine's only extreme route, Delirium Dive, but poor visibility caused it to be closed when we arrived. According to George, this extreme skier's playground is closed quite regularly. Avalanche danger and poor snow cover are other reasons why it is often off-limits.

We warmed up with some easy cruising on some of the "family runs" and worked our way over to Goat's Eye, where we skied down Cleavage, a mogul run between two large rocks.

After lunch, the sun made inroads, and Delirium opened. Just entering this much-touted descent was a true experience in the differences between European and Canadian skiing. The entrance was the rope and sign epicenter of Sunshine. One sign proclaimed that skiers were only allowed to ski in this area if they had both an avalanche transceiver and a shovel with them. A narrow corridor for hiking to Delirium was roped off and a locked door barred entry to the walkway. Another sign explained that one must place one's transceiver against the door lock. This functioned as a key to allow passage for those who were properly equipped for the backcountry.

The snow cover at the top of the Dive was a bit sparse, and we gingerly entered, trying to avoid the rocks. The run, a rock-lined group of gullies in an amphitheater-like mountain cirque, was steep and good, and the few centimeters of snow that had fallen in the morning made the descent extra pleasant. Nevertheless, we had skied in steeper, more difficult terrain hundreds of times in the Alps without any hoopla. It did cross my mind to wonder what all the commotion was about.

The commotion was, pure and simply, about the difference between the Alpine and North American attitude toward safety. In the Alps, the policy is more *laissez faire*. Enter at your own risk, and be responsible for the consequences. In North America, by comparison, the consumer is protected from his own ignorance and poor judgment, by an endless set of rules, regulations and ropes.

The difference in the practice and enforcement of mountain law is, perhaps, related to the difference between the mentalities of the skiing populations on these two continents. North Americans are, by nature, extremely ambitious, often beyond all realistic expectations, and many of them need to be protected from themselves in their quest for ski accomplishments in the highly visible extreme genre that exists in today's ski world. Most Europeans, by contrast, are generally recreational skiers, and enjoy the sport without the necessity to challenge the absolute limits of their capabilities in life-threatening circumstances.

DAY TWO BROUGHT US to Lake Louise, 45 minutes' drive from Banff, the largest and most well-known of the ski resorts in the area. Once again, we were immediately exposed to one of the major differences between Canadian and European skiing. A few of the easy pistes on the front of the mountain were groomed, but most of the 17 square kilometers of ski area were riddled with

»Here, you have to learn to ski moguls or die.«

moguls. Most European resorts have a fleet of snow cats grooming almost all the runs every night in resorts that have 20 times the ski terrain of Lake Louise. Here, you have to learn to ski moguls or die.

George took us down some of his favorite descents. Eagle 6 was narrow and steep, with a few too many small rocks on the upper section to trip skiers, and a few too many large ones below to receive tripped-up skiers. I skied cautiously. George likes those kinds of runs. He also led us down Out of Bounds Bowl, which is actually in bounds, and Ptarmigan, which is in tight trees, with moguls in between. This was an obstacle course where even Hermann Maier would have to turn his tempo down a notch.

I am not used to moguls, and by closing time, my knees were in need of a full service. The solution was an après-ski in the spa of the famous Banff Springs Hotel. The Banff Springs was built in 1888 on the site where hot mineral springs had been discovered five years earlier.

To call this building a hotel is like referring to the Queen Mary as a boat or calling the White House a house. The Banff Springs is a 770-room 19th century castle. It is home to a dozen restaurants and lounges from where one can indulge in everything from afternoon tea with a view to die for in the Rundle Lounge to dinners fit for royalty in the vaulted-ceiling atmosphere of the Banffshire Club. In addition to all this, it has the first million-dollar golf course in the world (built in 1924), a host of designer shops, a world-class spa, a 25-meter-long indoor swimming pool and an outdoor pool heated to about 36 degrees. The

outdoor pool is just the ticket for those who want to enjoy a fresh-air Rocky Mountain sunset with a margarita in their hand without getting cold. Rupert and I fell into this category. We soaked lazily and sucked on our straws until we were immersed in total darkness.

The Banff Springs was the brainchild of Cornelius Van Horne, president of the Canadian Pacific Railway, who can also be credited with building comparable stately hotels in Lake Louise and Jasper, as well as virtually starting the Canadian tourist industry with the construction of these hotels.

"If we can't export the scenery, we will import the tourists," said Van Horne, and his Scottish castle certainly did the trick.

On our third day in Banff, we visited the local ski resort, Mt. Norquay, situated in the outskirts of the city. With only five lifts, this is the smallest of the three ski areas, but it is a convenient and picturesque alternative to Lake Louise or Sunshine, especially if one is looking to ski for a few hours or half the day. The whole gamut of beginner, intermediate and advanced slopes all lie on the lower section of a mountain whose spectacular cliffs and couloirs rise high above the pistes.

From the top of the North American Chair, Rupert, George and I gazed out over Banff, the meandering, turquoise Bow River and the Banff Springs Castle far below. More immediately below was another black run froth with treacherous moguls. Fortunately, the bumps had been softened by the spring weather, and my knees survived the ordeal. Nevertheless, I opted for cruisers after that.

As we drove the short distance back to town, we had to stop to allow

a group of mountain goats to pass across the road. Just a few minutes later, in one of the residential areas of Banff, a small herd of elk rested on somebody's front lawn. The wild animals that we saw every day were constant reminders that this entire region is just a small part of Banff National Park.

The atmosphere created by the national park was ever present. In the Alps, I am used to passing farms and villages every few kilometers wherever I drive, but we were in Canada. Vast expanses of virgin forest stretched as far as the eye could see. This was home to the deer, caribou, elk and bear, and there was very little of man's intrusion into the wilds to disturb their habitat. Solitude prevailed.

The next day at Lake Louise, spring had gone back into hibernation. Snow floated out of the heavens, and the three of us cut as many tracks into the new fallen snow as our time allowed. We stayed on the front side of the mountain, where the judiciously spaced pines gave us a bit of perspective in the poor light. It was the best skiing of our visit, and the poor visibility readied us for our next destination, Whistler Mountain, which is renowned for bad weather.

WHISTLER BLACKCOMB — SELLING THE EXTREME

Situated in the Coast Mountains about two hours' drive northeast of Vancouver, Whistler Blackcomb is subject to innumerable storms that blow in off the Pacific Ocean all winter long. This is a ski resort where you can definitely save money on sun-protection cream. I was still traveling with Rupert, and we arrived on Blackcomb Mountain to a mixed diet of low fog, high clouds and intermittent snow flurries.

This is not a place where you sleep in on a gray day and wait for bluebird. Lake Louise receives an average of 3.8 meters of snow per season while Whistler Blackcomb is the beneficiary of more than 9 meters. The fair-weather skier becomes the non-skier in this part of Canada. Two local ski patrolmen, whom I met at lunch the first day, estimated that the ski area was blessed with an average of one sunny day a week.

Don't expect that because of the inclement weather, you will have the mountain to yourself. The locals are used to the climate, and they are busy skiing lines in the most extreme spots on the mountain in the worst of conditions. They shed rainwater like ducks, have built-in bat radar to combat fog and are as sure-footed among the rocky couloirs as the most agile mountain goats.

This is not the Alps, where the first sunny day after a storm reveals

a virgin mountain. Whistler Blackcomb is the largest ski area in North America, but the skiers who know the mountain shred every square centimeter of it while the snow is flying.

Rupert and I tried our best to act like locals. We started our day by immediately climbing up the few steps known as Spanky's Ladder, which gives access to the double-black-diamond terrain around Blackcomb Glacier. We chose Ruby Bowl for our first descent. The upper bowl had a pitch in excess of 40 degrees and the snow on top was powdery. Many skiers had been there the day before, so we jump-turned our way through the cut-up snow. About halfway down, the going got heavy.

Peaking at 2284 meters, Blackcomb is a relatively low mountain and the humidity-laden storms that blow off the Pacific do not generally make for dry powder. We battled our way through the thick snow until we met up with the blue piste called Blackcomb Glacier Road, and cruised the 5 kilometers back to the lifts. As the day progressed, we added Jersey Cream Bowl, another steep section of mountain with a treacherous entry, to our list of double-diamond accomplishments.

Blackcomb and Whistler have some of the most exciting terrain anywhere in North America for the helmet and transceiver set. Cliff

jumps, cornice leaps into narrow chutes and steep tree-skiing are all part of the everyday world here. Best of all, it is all secured against avalanches.

The double-diamond descents at Blackcomb and Whistler are not really what a mere mortal would call a ski run. Wherever a 2-meter wide patch of snow exists between two cliffs, a double-diamond sign goes up and a black line is placed on the trail map. It matters not that this narrow slit might plummet away at 50 degrees below you or that the average skier would call it a cliff rather than a run. In the Alps, such terrain would never be labeled or charted, nor would it be blasted for avalanches each morning. It would be left to the imagination and bravado of the most balls-to-the-wall freeriders

» Wherever a 2-meter-wide patch of snow exists between two cliffs, a double-diamond sign goes up...«

to discover and dare. Here, however, the most death-defying lines are all part of the marketing strategy.

Alexandra Gill, a writer for the Globe and Mail, one of Canada's two national newspapers, has written that Whistler Blackcomb "is a monument to wretched excess, built on the twin passions of extreme sports and rampant commercialism." Marking and marketing every cornice and couloir as a run is exactly where those two passions meet.

RUPERT AND I ARE JUST LIKE every other freeride gunslinger in the West, and we wanted to notch up as many single- and double-diamond runs on our gun belt as the next guy. The following day, we tried Whistler Mountain. It was snowing again (so, what else is new?) and the powder was lighter than the day before.

We skied Horseshoe 5, where we maneuvered our way into the run with a not-so-glorious "ass-side-slip" to avoid jumping the cornice. It was worth it. A couple of lines of untouched powder rewarded our efforts. We skied McConkey's, found some more powder in Sun Bowl and then skied Whistler Bowl, Doom and Gloom and Stefan's Chute, all off the Peak Chair. Many places were tracked, but sometimes we found a fresh line. It hardly mattered. It was all the same in the fog anyway, and we often *sought out* a track to help us in the low visibility.

Our third day brought even more powder and the temperature was still dropping. All bets were off on seeing the sun during our stay, but

powder in mid-April was nothing to complain about. Other people were definitely giving up on sunshine. I watched one man trying to film his family in the pea-soup fog—a video that will certainly turn out to be as colorful and exciting as a film of a polar bear hibernating during an Arctic snowstorm.

It was late in the season and the long vertical that Whistler offers gave Rupert and me the full gamut of snow conditions between the top of the Peak Chair and the small village of Creekside, about 1500 meters below. We began in 5 centimeters of good powder, which eventually gave way to heavier snow. Then, we continued in spring corn, and when our calves and thighs were most tired, we finally plowed through the lowest section in sticky mashed potatoes.

OUR FINAL DAY WAS upon us. The weather had not really changed much. The Blackcomb Glacier was covered with 8–10 centimeters of new snow, and Rupert and I snaked 300 turns into the fresh snow of the upper mountain before the snow got too wet.

Late in the day, we again entered the realm of double-diamond danger through Big Bang into Jersey Cream Bowl. To our left was an even more treacherous entry into the bowl called Extreme Couloir, and in between was a section of cliffs and rock faces.

About halfway down, our attention was drawn upward by the sound of skis chaffing against stone. We were shocked to see three French Canadians working their way along narrow shelves of snow between the cliffs. The first two jumped successfully into the bowl, avoiding a long series of exposed rocks below their landing.

Their comrade's entry was not so fortuitous. His leap of faith sent him cart-wheeling down like a rag doll in what was one of the worst falls I have ever seen. Rupert and I watched, mouths agape in horror, as he careened helplessly over three sets of rocks and cliffs. Only sheer luck or divine intervention saved him from a broken neck or worse. This terrifying film clip from an extreme ski video was set to a soundtrack of hilarious laughter from his two friends.

This grotesque vignette seemed to personify Whistler Blackcomb. The "excess of extreme sports and commercialism" mentioned by Ms. Gill in her article came back to my mind. The area already suffers from over-development, over-indulgence, and prices that are much higher than any other ski resort in the country. All the while, Whistler Blackcomb has avidly pursued and won a bid for the Winter Olympics

LEFT PAGE
Rupert Scheiner is happy for a few seconds of visibility on Blackcomb before the sun disappears for a few more days.

THIS PAGE
UPPER LEFT: Day Lodge at Lake Louise.
UPPER RIGHT: Whistler Blackcomb offers plenty of cornice jumps for those who dare.
LOWER: The flat plains of Alberta give way to the Canadian Rockies as one heads toward British Columbia.

Canadian skiing has come a long way in a short time. Whistler Blackcomb and Banff have developed into world-class resorts, where the guy riding up the chair with you might well be North American, but he could just as easily be Japanese, Mexican, German, British or Australian. Many new Canadian ski areas are one or two steps behind these two big-name resorts in their developmental chain.

AS THE LIKES OF FERNIE, KICKING HORSE, RED MOUNTAIN and others watch the industry leaders, seeking direction for their next move, one can only hope that they remember that bigger is not always best, and that new is not necessarily synonymous with quality. As future visits might bring me back to Canada to discover the relative merits of many of these budding ski areas, I hope that their development is in keeping with an aesthetic and level-headed growth pattern. In a day and age when more and more people head to the mountains to escape the fast-paced excess of big-city life, there is a definite need for small, low-key mountains where one can still get the back-to-nature experience that is at the very root of skiing.

in 2010. The situation seems to me to be quite similar to the French Canadians whose laughter revealed their blindness to the dangers of their excess.

Whistler Blackcomb, with its big-name, big-mountain status, its high-profile, high-roller clientele and its penchant for extravagance and excess, is the Las Vegas of Canadian skiing. Banff, with its untouched forests and wildlife, exemplifies the solitude and virgin nature that draw a completely different type of skier to Canada. There is a place for both these models in a large land like Canada, and each will continue to draw the type of guest who equates best with each type of resort.

LEFT PAGE: The view of a helicopter against a stark, blue sky is enough to get any powder skier drooling.
THIS PAGE: Skiers are willing to part with big money for this kind of powder experience.

CANADIAN MOUNTAIN HOLIDAYS — THE GRANDFATHER OF HELISKIING

Skiing has always been about freedom. The first mountaineers and climbers who pioneered the sport used it as a way of extending their hiking and climbing season into the winter. By clamping skis onto their feet, they could now get away from the crowds of the city into the boundless mountains for an additional four to five months every year. From those days until the mid-1930s, there were almost no ski lifts to help people up the mountains, and skiing was a full-blown adventure sport. Those early mountaineers glided down through untouched powder, establishing first descents with great frequency.

As the more famous regions of the Alps and the Rockies became ever more populated with lifts and skiers, some of the remaining adventurers and mountaineers among skiers began retreating from the mainstream of a sport that was developing into an industry. They sought the ultimate freedom that they had once felt in the years before hangar-like cafeterias and large cable cars transformed the solitary and tranquil mountains into a bustling white playground.

ONE OF THE PEOPLE who tried to put the sense of freedom and adventure back into skiing was Hans Gmoser. In the mid-1960s, he began organizing heliski trips to the Bugaboos, taking skiing in a new direction, one that has in the ensuing years grown into a whole separate industry.

In those early days of Canadian Mountain Holidays (CMH), the skiers slept in an abandoned lumber camp, and one was much more likely to see a bear than another human being in this deserted corner of the world. Many years later, at the onset of the new millennium, Hans is an occasional guest instead of an owner-operator of CMH, and the accommodation has improved dramatically. The adventure and freedom of heliskiing, however, have not been lost along the way.

My friend Jari Tuomala and I decided to experience the ultimate skier's adrenaline rush, and headed to CMH's haven for off-piste enthusiasts. Canadian Mountain Holidays now has eleven areas to ski amidst the rugged mountains of western Canada, and we chose to visit a region called the Bobby Burns, near Parson, British Columbia.

In late April, we drove to the end of a deserted dirt road in the Canadian wilderness—deserted, that is, except for 42 other off-piste freaks from various corners of the world, who shared our powder dream of Canadian heliskiing. As there was no winter access by road into the Bobby Burns Lodge, an eleven-passenger Bell 212 chopper soon whisked us off to our destination. The rather luxurious ski lodge was a far cry from the old lumber camp, but just as remote. We would get the adventure without the hardships.

As I walked around my new surroundings, I noticed a framed typewritten letter hanging in a place of prominence in the lodge. Dated 1936 and signed by flight pioneer Orville Wright, the letter concluded with the statement:

" The helicopter type of aeroplane offers several insurmountable difficulties...Experiments with this kind of machine are so costly, and the chance of developing anything having a commercial value so remote, I do not think any individual can afford to undertake this as a business proposition."

This was certainly a letter belonging to Hans Gmoser. I chuckled to myself at his sense of humor, and wished that I could one day meet the man who had owned and operated CMH for more than 25 years before selling the company some years ago.

I CRACKED OPEN MY CURTAINS early the following morning to view a crystal-clear blue sky and the spring sun already blazing down on the fields of white surrounding the lodge. If our anticipatory adrenaline and a robust breakfast were not enough to insure that everybody was wide awake, the intrusive roar of the helicopter was certain to bring any lethargic participants to full alertness.

We carefully bowed low under the whirring blades and clambered aboard our vehicle of total ski freedom. Perfect visibility afforded us the chance to see for a couple hundred kilometers in each direction, and yet, we knew full well that this was just a tiny corner of Canada's mountainous real estate. Our guide, Bernard, conferred with the pilot, exercising the God-like liberty of choosing which peak our chauffeur should deposit us upon.

Bernard made his choice, and soon he pushed gently off into 15 centimeters of untouched powder. We all gleefully followed. Dry angel dust sprayed into the air and seemed to turn into vapor before it ever touched back down. Swoosh, swoosh, swoosh...20 turns...effortless...40 turns...60 turns...doesn't Bernard ever stop...80...100...it didn't matter...one didn't get tired...120 turns...140...stop. Well, okay, maybe I did get a little tired. After all it was our first day!

We had met Mother Nature at her annual crossroads between winter and spring. About halfway down the slope, the snow suddenly transformed to corn snow. Another 150 turns in this easy-spread margarine brought us back to the helicopter, waiting patiently to give us our next lift. The rest of the day followed the same pattern, and by the time our weary group tumbled into the sauna, we had logged more than 12,000 vertical meters, more than I had ever skied in one day.

BY MIDWEEK, MY EARLIER WISH became reality—we were joined by Mr. Heliski, himself. In speaking with Hans, he likened heliskiing's inception to an illegitimate birth. Hans is the first to admit that, rather than heliskiing being born of some master plan, his offspring was more an accident than anything else.

Hans immigrated to Canada from his native Austria in the 1950s and fast found a home guiding people on touring skis

»One week cost \$260 and I didn't see that people would pay that much money to go skiing.«

among the remote mountains of British Columbia. In 1963, he guided a few weekends of heliskiing which were arranged by Art Patterson, but nothing much came of it then. But two years later, Hans was asked by some of his ski-touring customers to organize a helicopter for some tours, and he complied. The idea of heliskiing was born out of that simple request, and the rest is history. CMH's fiefdom now includes 22,000 square kilometers of terrain.

In between runs on Wednesday, Hans reminisced about the early days. "The idea of heliskiing was hatched out of a spirit and philosophy of adventure," he explained. "With touring, you had to ski back the same way you hiked up. At the top, we saw all these tantalizing places where we couldn't go. The use of the whirlybird, of course, opened up the possibility of descending down a limitless array of alluring slopes.

"The 45-kilometer road to our base camp was in such poor shape, it took nine hours to bring the first group in. Everything was a real adventure," related Hans. "Because our first helicopters took only two

passengers, it took 45 minutes to an hour to assemble a group at the top. And we sometimes skied some awful snow conditions in the old days," Hans laughed. "We didn't even consider picking people up halfway down, if the snow was bad. We always skied to the bottom."

Hans described the accommodations in the abandoned lumber camp that housed his earliest guests. "We had an outhouse, and the shower was a plywood shack with a small tub suspended from the rafter. The water was emitted from a garden hose and disappeared through the floorboards of the shack. The guests slept in bunk beds, six or eight to a room."

Seventy skiers braved these conditions during CMH's initial season in 1966.

The development of heliskiing came as a bit of a surprise to, of all people, its originator, admitted Hans. "One week cost $260 in those days," he explained, "and I really didn't see that people would pay that much money to go skiing."

In between anecdotes and fragments of conversation with Hans, we were corn-snow cruising. Some superb terrain—runs with names like Puff, Malachite, and Serac—whooshed by us.

I asked Hans about any unusual memories, and he pondered a moment.

"Well, we knew very little about landing in flat light, at first," he explained. "So, Jim Davies, our pilot, and I decided that he should hover close to the ground, and I should jump out so he could see me and use me as a reference point. I pulled open the door to try this method. I was ready to jump, but Jim said, 'Be careful, throw your pack out first.' I did, and the rucksack fell over 60 meters..."

We skied down another run, a north face with about 10 centimeters

» You can out-ski a grizzly behind you, but they are very fast going uphill or in the flats.«

of powder. About half way down, we crossed some grizzly tracks in the new snow, which reminded Hans of another experience from his early days in Canada.

"We were touring one day," began Hans, "when we came across a young grizzly bear below us. He was a fair distance away at first, and we waited, hoping he would leave. But instead, he began to come closer. You can out-ski a grizzly behind you, but they are very fast going uphill or in the flats. Well, we finally had to begin skiing down, and that brought us even closer to our friend. He wasn't about to be scared away, either, and he continued to approach.

"By now, we were coming into the flats at the end of the run, and as the grizzly drew even nearer, pandemonium broke out in our group, and it was every man for himself. One guest fell and got tangled up in some bushes. Sure enough, the bear came sniffing right up to the guy, close enough to touch. The skier screamed, of course, and the scream was what it finally took to scare the grizzly away."

FRIDAY MORNING WAS ONE OF THOSE storybook days from Never-Never Land—fresh snow from the light snowfall over the past couple of days and not a hint of a cloud. It was the kind of weather that makes it possible to fly past the perimeter of the Bobby Burns area, and into an entirely separate range of mountains, the Selkirks.

Heliskiing is already a unique experience, and doing it in the Selkirks is the *crème de la crème*. There is nothing too special about the Selkirks, other than a bunch of runs that plunge 1700 or 1800 vertical meters through spectacular landscapes, beginning on wide glaciers and finishing in the forest.

Our first run was "only" 1200 vertical meters—"a warmup" according to Bernard. Eight minutes later we were at the bottom. One could amass some pretty impressive mileage skiing at this pace, I thought to myself. Then, our chopper lifted us onto Porpoise, 1800 meters above the valley, followed by Lobster Claw. At about the same elevation in each run, the powder turned to corn snow, and the glacier gave way to steep, open tree-skiing. The slopes gradually funneled into avalanche gullies—where most of the trees in the middle had been cleared by annual snow slides. The skiing became steeper and narrower as we got further down.

Each run was something new. XTC was 1700 meters of vertical, and it was followed by Swiss Fighting Cows. I lost count of the meters, but Bernard didn't. By the end of the day, we had pumped out around 16,000 vertical meters of turns—talk about lactic acid overdose.

AT DINNERTIME, I GLANCED AT a wooden plaque in the dining room. On the top was the simple inscription: "Bobby Burns 200,000 feet" (approximately 60,000 meters). Engraved below were the names of all the people who had reached this milestone during their week at Bobby Burns. That year, four people had accomplished the feat up until our visit. By the end of skiing on Saturday, more than a dozen of us had also joined the club.

As our luggage was being packed onto the helicopter for our return to civilization, I signed the guest book in the hotel lobby. I saw where someone had written: "This week has been the best adventure of my life."

I thought back about something Hans had said earlier in the week. "I enjoyed this backcountry skiing so much myself that I wanted to show off and share all these great places," he had explained. "The greatest reward was the gratification of seeing the enthusiasm of the people."

Canadian Mountain Holidays has come a long way since Hans's original two-seater flights up the Bugaboo Glacier. The raw adventure has been tempered somewhat with a blend of emphasis on comfort and safety, but the end result is more or less the same. More than 40 years after its

LEFT PAGE: Even in April, one can usually find plenty of powder on the north faces.
THIS PAGE: The sauna at the Bobby Burns Lodge.

inception, Canadian Mountain Holidays is still opening a gigantic wilderness area in the many mountain ranges of British Columbia to be shared by an ever increasing number of clients. Hans merely has to browse through his old guest books any time he wishes to reap the reward of what he started so long ago.

If he ever does have time to reminisce through those volumes, he might come across this entry: "April 25—Thanks ever so much to Hans Gmoser for the successful attempt to prove Orville Wright wrong. Thanks to CMH for an unforgettable week. Jimmy Petterson."

North America in a Nutshell

LOCATION	NEAREST TOWN	NEAREST AIRPORT	SEASON	PEAK ELEVATION	VERTICAL DROP	SIZE	SNOW	BEAUTY	VILLAGE	NOVICE	INTERMEDIATE	ADVANCED	EXPERT	OFF-PISTE	NIGHTLIFE	RATING AVERAGE	WEB SITE
CANADA																	
Banff Region																	
A. Lake Louise	Banff	Calgary	early Nov.–early May	2637 m	991 m	3	2	3	5	2	5	5	5	3	2	3.5	www.skilouise.com
B. Mt. Norquay	Banff	Calgary	mid December–April	2133 m	503 m	2	1	2	4	5	3	2	3	1	3	2.6	www.banffnorquay.com
C. Sunshine Village	Banff	Calgary	mid November–May	2730 m	1070 m	3	2	3	3	2	5	4	3	3	2	3.0	www.sunshinevillage.com
Bobby Burns–CMH	Golden	Calgary	late Dec.–early May	3050 m	1800 m	5	5 [1]	5	5	2	1	2	5	5	2	3.7	www.cmhski.com/areas/bobbie_burns_ski
Whistler Blackcomb	Whistler Blackcomb	Vancouver	October–May [2]	2284 m	1609 m	5	4	4	3	2	5	5	5	3	4	4.0	www.whistlerblackcomb.com
UNITED STATES																	
Alta	Salt Lake City	Salt Lake City	November–April	3246 m	640 m	2	2	5	3	2	3	3	5	5	2	3.2	www.alta.com
Lake Tahoe Region																	
A. Alpine Meadows	Tahoe City	Reno	mid Nov.–late May	2631 m	549 m	2	2	4	4	4	2	4	5	4	3	3.4	www.skialpine.com
B. Heavenly	South Lake Tahoe	Reno	mid Nov.–late April	3060 m	1067 m	3	4	4	5	3	3	4	5	3	5	3.9	www.skiheavenly.com
C. Kirkwood Meadows	South Lake Tahoe	Reno	November–May	2987 m	609 m	2	2	4	5	3	3	4	3	4	2	3.2	www.kirkwood.com
D. Squaw Valley	Tahoe City	Reno	November–late May	2759 m	869 m	3	4	4	4	3	4	5	5	4	3	3.9	www.squaw.com
Mt. Alyeska	Girdwood	Anchorage	mid Nov.–mid April	838 m	762 m	2	1	3	4	2	2	4	3	2	2	2.6	www.alyeskaresort.com
Mt. Bachelor	Bend	Redmond	late Nov.–late May	2763 m	1025 m	3	2	4	5	3	4	4	4	3	2	3.4	www.mtbachelor.com
Mt. Baker	Glacier	Bellingham	November–April	1550 m	455 m	2	1	3	4	2	3	3	3	4	2	2.7	www.mtbakerskiarea.com
San Gabriel and San Bernardino Mountains																	
A. Mt. Baldy	Los Angeles	Los Angeles	mid Nov.–mid April	2619 m	640 m	2	1	3	3	1	2	2	2	2	1	1.9	www.mtbaldy.com
B. Mt. Waterman	Los Angeles	Los Angeles	mid Nov.–mid April	2437 m	365 m [3]	1	1	3	3	1	1	2	2	3	1	1.8	www.mtwatermanpatrol.org
C. Mountain High	Wrightwood	Los Angeles	mid Nov.–mid April	2497 m	426 m	2	2	3	2	1	3	2	2	1	1	1.9	www.mthigh.com
D. Snow Summit	Big Bear City	Los Angeles	mid Nov.–mid April	2497 m	365 m	1	2	3	3	2	3	2	1	1	2	2.0	www.bigbearmountainresorts.com
Taos	Taos	Albuquerque	late November–April	3408 m	796 m [4]	2	2	5	3	5	1	3	5	3	3	3.3	www.skitaos.org
Telluride	Telluride	Telluride	November–April	3735 m	1074 m	3	2	5	5	5	5	5	5	3	5	4.3	www.telluride.com
Timberline	Government Camp	Portland	year-round [5]	2591 m	1090 m	3	1	3	5	2	3	2	3	3	1	2.6	www.timberlinelodge.com
Valdez Heliskiing	Valdez	Anchorage	late Feb.–early May	varied [6]	1500 m	4	5 [1]	5	5	2	1	1	5	5	1	3.4	www.valdezalaska.org/activities/winteroperators.html
Wolf Creek	Pagosa Springs/South Fork	Durango	early Nov.–early April	3625 m	488 m	2	1	5	3	1	3	3	4	4	1	2.7	www.wolfcreekski.com

(1) Although there are no lifts, having a helicopter at your disposal is worth five points.
(2) Summer skiing on Blackcomb Glacier is also available from June–September.
(3) Runs to the road as described in the book have appreciably more vertical.
(4) Taos offers 998 meters of vertical including the hike to Kachina Peak.
(5) Closed a few days in September for maintenance.
(6) Different heliski operations have different landing altitudes.

EUROPE – ALPINE COUNTRIES

II

PREVIOUS PAGES: Martin Söderqvist and the Matterhorn try to impress each other in Zermatt, Switzerland.
THIS PAGE: *Kasnock'n*, a specialty of the Pinzgau region of Austria, is generally eaten directly out of the frying pan.
RIGHT PAGE: Rupert Scheiner puts a lone track into the powder on his way down into the Hörndlingergraben from Hinterglemm.

Chapter 3. AUSTRIA

As I have Austrian roots, it is only natural that my discovery of the wonderful world of the Alps began in that quaint and cozy country. Debate will always exist as to which of the Alpine countries offers the best vacation opportunities. Some people prefer to visit destinations in the western Alps of France and Switzerland, where much of the skiing is above tree line. Here, the landscape consists of many large open bowls, chutes and slopes. Others prefer the tamer terrain prevalent in much of Austria, with its tree skiing, meadows and glens. Still others return with regularity to the stunning limestone monoliths of the Dolomites, whose beauty is hard to deny. Most people agree, however, that the ambiance and *Gemütlichkeit* in Austria are unparalleled.

Again, it is an almost impossible task to choose but a handful of ski resorts to represent this major ski country. With many hundreds of ski villages dotting the map of western and central Austria, only the flat provinces of Vienna and Burgenland got left behind as this small Alpine nation transposed itself from a provincial farming land into a ski industry giant over the last half-century. In fact, a tourist driving through Austria could easily get the impression that one could traverse most of the country merely transporting oneself with lifts and skis—and maybe one could.

Numerous ski regions not specifically dealt with in this chapter deserve an honorable mention. Kitzbühel was one of the first major ski resorts in Austria and still today is one of the country's most popular destinations. The resort is also famous for the Hahnenkamm Downhill, one of the most difficult races on the circuit, held here every January. Although Kitzbühel is quite a bit lower than most ski resorts in the world, it boasts more than 60 lifts and its long tradition, historic town center and famous après-ski make it well worth a visit for skiers of all abilities.

Sportwelt Amadé includes over a dozen villages, among which are Zauchensee, Altenmarkt, Flachau, Wagrain and St. Johann im Pongau. It is one of the largest ski areas in Austria with around 140 lifts and over 350 kilometers of pistes. The resort is a perfect location for families with young children, but it has little to offer advanced and expert skiers.

Another large region is Ski Welt, featuring Ellmau, Westendorf, Scheffau and Söll, among others. It is not quite as large as Sportwelt Amadé, but its approximately 250 kilometers of pistes will also keep intermediate skiers busy seeing new terrain for weeks. Ski Welt, too, is primarily below the tree line, and lacks the variety of terrain to be popular with advanced skiers.

The Hochkönig Schischaukel is yet a third such area. The likes of Maria Alm, Dienten, Mühlbach, Hintertal, Reith and Hintermoos will save families quite a few Euros in comparison to nearby Saalbach and Kitzbühel, but the Hochkönig area does not have the variety of pistes nor the après-ski to compare with its up-market neighbors.

Of the seven ski provinces in Austria, Tyrol stands head and shoulders above the rest. Historically speaking, our modern style of skiing all started in St. Anton and the Arlberg region of Tyrol, where Hannes Schneider developed the stem turn in the 1920s, pushing the Norwegian telemark technique into the background. This region has stayed at the forefront of Austrian skiing ever since, with the prestigious Dr. Stefan Kruckenhauser developing the *Wedeln* technique from his base at the Bundessportheim in St. Christoph. Later, in the '60s and '70s, local St. Anton skier Karl Schranz became the marquee idol of the Austrian ski team for a generation. Today, nothing much has changed. The rugged mountains that flank the Arlberg Pass still make up one of the most visited ski areas in the world.

There are numerous other top resorts in Tyrol besides St. Anton. Innsbruck twice hosted the Olympic Games, and Sölden is one of the higher Austrian resorts, with two glaciers and near year-round skiing. Then there is Ischgl, a key resort in another large region with more than 250 kilometers of pistes and an après-ski scene that is at least as good as the skiing.

Not far away is the Zillertal, a valley boasting perhaps the best glacier skiing in the world and which, nowadays, links fifteen villages from Tyrol into Land Salzburg. I have also chosen to write about the Pitztal, a lesser-known ski region despite its ranking as the highest ski resort in Austria and Nauders, another little-known village worth visiting.

While Tyrol grabs most of the glory in Austria, the rounded, more hilly peaks of Land Salzburg also deserve a visit. Here, the Gastein Valley, with its regal old hotels dating back to the heyday of its prominence as a spa, has much to offer. The lift pass includes the villages of Badgastein, Dorf Gastein, Grossarl, Bad Hofgastein and Sport Gastein, the latter being one of the best off-piste mountains in the Alps.

Another area of note in Land Salzburg is the province's only summer and winter ski area, Kaprun. Towering over the village like a giant pyramid is the Kitzsteinhorn Glacier. This 3000-meter peak gives a high alpine atmosphere to this province, which is mostly covered by heavily forested mountains that rarely rise above 2500 meters. A few different off-piste routes down the west side of the "Horn" to Niedernsill each give well over 2000 vertical meters of skiing, among the ten greatest vertical descents in the world.

Perhaps the best skiing in Land Salzburg can be found in Saalbach-Hinterglemm. This ski area is not only worth visiting for its well-rounded array of pistes, but also for its excellent après-ski and nightlife, which exemplify the *Gemütlichkeit* that Austria is known for. My personal love affair with the Alps has been most influenced by Saalbach-Hinterglemm, and it is there that this chapter on Austria, fittingly, begins.

SAALBACH — GEMÜTLICHKEIT AND HIDDEN POWDER

I was fresh out of university, finally a teacher after five hard years of study, and I was working as a substitute in the Los Angeles ghetto. It was the last day of school before Christmas vacation, and education was the furthest thing from the minds of my teenaged malcontents. The day seemed interminable, but finally, the three o'clock bell released my young charges and myself from our mutual purgatory. They all sprinted out of the classroom like Carl Lewis with a hotfoot, while I slowly gathered my belongings and marched dejectedly through the untidy halls of Crenshaw High School.

Many locals half-jokingly call this school Fort Crenshaw, and it definitely looked as if the fort had come under siege. It was a depressing sight. Many of the students had cleared out their lockers before the vacation and left their refuse on the floor. The halls were strewn with crumpled papers, torn books, apple cores, soda cans and half-eaten lunches. Gangland graffiti and obscenities were visible on lockers and walls, and the pungent odor of marijuana seemed to linger in the air whenever I walked past a restroom.

"Is this really what the future holds for me?" I wondered.

I pushed open the door to the faculty parking lot and read the spray-painted words, "TEACHERS FUCK OFF", and at that very moment, I decided to do just that. Paul Simon wrote, "The words of the prophets are written on the subway walls and tenement halls", and it seemed time for me to heed one of those prophetic directives.

BY FEBRUARY, I HAD TRADED the smell of marijuana for the fragrance of pine needles, and the ugly eyesore of dirty classrooms had been exchanged for a panorama of snow-covered Alps. Instead of teaching history to the illiterate under-class of Blacks and Mexicans in L.A., I was instructing skiing to uncoordinated upper-class Danes and Englishmen in the Hinterglemm Ski School.

That was 1973. I had meant to take a short break from the depressing conditions of inner-city school life. This past January, I arrived in Saalbach-Hinterglemm to begin my thirty-first season in the Alps. I tried one more time for a few years to teach school, but it was to no avail. For most of the intervening years, I have worked at various ski-related jobs in Saalbach and done whatever was necessary to maintain my hedonistic lifestyle. The L.A. ghetto is light years away, just a faint impression from another millennium. What can I say about a place that has changed my whole life?

For many avid skiers, Saalbach-Hinterglemm is just one stop on a long list of Alpine winter vacation spots, and they never really get to know this area very well. They visit the Glemmtal somewhere on the list between Zell am See and St. Anton, an early stop on their ski odyssey, before graduating to the tougher, more rugged French Alps. There, they live out their final years in glory, slaloming playfully between glacial seracs, leaping over crevasses and swapping tales with other ski bums about death-defying avalanches.

But wait! Stop! Let us backtrack a moment to Saalbach-Hinterglemm, a resort which has one of the largest interconnected lift systems in Austria and which hosted the World Championships of Skiing in 1991. Is this cozy village just an intermediate way station on the skier's map, or does it deserve a return visit and closer inspection? The answer to this question, of course, depends upon what a person looks for in a ski resort.

I have continued to return to Saalbach each season, partly because I prefer the intimate quality of staying in a small *Frühstückspension* to the impersonal and ugly apartment complexes so common in the French Alps. Here, in the Glemmtal, Frau Breitfuss will greet you by your first name

Christer Lindgren and Pia Oldenburg Vilstrup making the 20-minute hike to ski the Amsel in Saalbach.

upon your return, and her husband, Toni, will immediately sit you down in the kitchen to drink a welcome-schnapps. Saalbach-Hinterglemm epitomizes this personal aspect of Austria, and even in the large hotels, the owner usually knows and personally greets his return guests.

MANY OF SAALBACH'S REPEAT CUSTOMERS do not come back year after year merely because of its friendliness. For beginners and intermediates, there is no doubt that this area is an excellent choice for a holiday. The terrain is well-suited to intermediate skiers, and even a beginner will often have the ability to ski from village to village among Saalbach, Hinterglemm and Leogang within a week or two of having first put on a pair of skis.

Among good skiers, the Glemmtal will not attract mogul enthusiasts, as the staff who prepare the pistes often spend half the night flattening moguls into oblivion with a vengeance. Black pistes are also not in great abundance, and the black runs of the Schattberg Nord, the Zwölferkogel

Nord and the Zwölferkogel Ostseite are some of the only places one will find moguls of any magnitude. The well groomed slopes, on the other hand, are very appealing to good skiers who like high-speed cruising. There is another major perk for experts—powder. Saalbach-Hinterglemm as a powder paradise is one of the best-kept secrets in the Alps. There are a few reasons for the Glemmtal's high rating in the powder category. First of all, the lift system has very little down-time in stormy weather. During the heavy snowfalls that riddle the Alps periodically each winter, many of the lifts in the higher resorts must be closed due to avalanche danger. The steep, exposed slopes at high elevations are often too dangerous to ski during a major storm, and the lack of visibility above the tree line renders the slopes useless to a skier who does not have built-in radar.

In Saalbach-Hinterglemm, however, the Schattbergbahn and other main arteries of the lift system are almost never closed. The best time to ski powder is during a snowstorm, when the snow is the lightest, the

softest and the deepest. In Saalbach, the lifts stay open, allowing powder hounds to take advantage of these top conditions.

SECONDLY, THE GLEMMTAL OFFERS some excellent tree-skiing. At 2100 meters, even the highest point in the lift system is only a few hundred meters above the tree line. In bad weather with low visibility, the skier in the know just darts into the woods, where the trees give protection from the wind, visual perspective and a relatively safe haven from avalanches. What could possibly be more exhilarating to a freerider than creating his own slalom course among the heavily snow-laden pines in waist-deep powder. Here, in the trees of the Schattberg Westgipfel, the Reiterkogel, the Zwölferkogel and the Bernkogel, as well as the back bowls a short walk behind the Westgipfel, a skier can often find powder long after a snowfall.

A final reason why the Glemmtal rates very high for off-piste skiing is

THIS PAGE
UPPER: Kristin Näsman enjoys Saalbach's excellent tree-skiing.
LOWER LEFT: The Spielberghaus with the off-piste slopes of the Amsel in the background.
LOWER RIGHT: The onion-domed church and the Turmhaus, now home to the Zum Turm bar, are the two oldest buildings in town.
RIGHT PAGE
A lone skier has left his signature on the north face of the Stemmerkogel.

the lack of good skiers. Saalbach-Hinterglemm's reputation as a destination for intermediates and partygoers has kept the powder freaks here to a minimum.

In the Glemmtal, the scene after a snowfall is quite mellow. The Germans are busy keeping their per capita beer drinking rating at the top of the world rankings. The families from Scandinavia, Holland and the United Kingdom are busily cruising around and stuffing their guts with *Apfelstrudel*. Meanwhile, the powder snow is lying quietly in the shade, waiting sometimes for days for some appreciative freeride enthusiast to put it to good use before it becomes relegated to a subsidiary role under a new layer of fresh snow.

Even advanced skiers enjoy a good après-ski after a long hard day of pumping powder. In this category, Saalbach certainly lives up to its reputation. While various spots in the village offer a lively scene after the lifts are closed, most guests begin their après-ski in one of the many mountain huts on the slopes.

The Panorama Alm near the top of the Kohlmais Lift has a sunny verandah and a beautiful view of the valley. It is a popular after-ski stop for the fur and diamond set, who begin their after-ski right after lunch. As the afternoon air begins to cool, many people head down to a whole community of bars that have sprung up around the beginners Turmwiese. Bauer's Schialm, Spitzbub and the famous Hinterhagalm are among the attractions here.

While the Panorama Alm is a rather mellow place to watch the sun drop behind the end of the valley, the Hinterhagalm has a different atmosphere entirely. It is a United Nations meeting in a steam bath. Most of the customers are too drunk to stand up, but it is impossible to fall down in this room of wall-to-wall people.

The dance floor is a throbbing mass of humanity, bumping and grinding in their ski boots to a steady stream of "evergreens" played by a band situated under the eaves of the hut. All the while, the rafters are full of people dripping sweat and spilling brew onto the dancers below, and an amazing group of waiters bob and weave through the crowd, balancing trays of beverages miraculously above the throng without spilling a drop.

IF ONE PREFERS A COZY après-ski atmosphere to the organized chaos of the Hinterhagalm, the Turneralm or the Pfefferalm are just the ticket. In these dimly lit huts, one can drink a *Glühwein* or two by candlelight, and finish the last ski run of the day by moonlight.

Perhaps the nicest thing to do in Saalbach is to combine the powder skiing in the trees with the *Gemütlichkeit* of the mountain huts, for even while skiing off-piste, one often happens upon one of the Glemmtal's rustic retreats when one least expects it.

A skier can weave through the forests of the Stegeralm for example, and finish the run at the Grabenhütte. Another alternative is to descend one of the numerous unmarked routes down the powder-laden north faces behind the Hochalm into the Hörndlingergraben. A 40-minute glide along the valley floor brings an off-piste enthusiast to the Eisene Hand, a restaurant situated literally in the middle of nowhere. There, a Wiener schnitzel or a *Kaiserschmarrn* (Austrian chopped up pancakes) and a pint of beer is the perfect *coup de grâce* to a great run, before a taxi ride to Leogang brings skiers back to the lift system.

Perhaps my favorite outing in Saalbach is an off-piste run down the Amsel to the Spielberghaus. This is a wonderful tour to do at lunchtime to feast on the best *Kasnock'n* (Austrian pasta covered with melted cheese and fried onions and eaten directly from the black frying pan in which it is cooked) in the valley. Alternatively, it is also pleasant to take this route at the end of the day and reward oneself with their homemade apricot schnapps.

Imagine this scenario. Picture yourself bobbing up and down rhythmically in knee deep powder, picking your way among trees that are right out of Bing Crosby's "White Christmas". The branches are bowed to about 30 degrees from the trunk, and they literally creak under the weight of so much snow.

Each time you drop to the low point of your turn, a burst of powder splashes up against your goggles, blinding you momentarily. Then, you rise to the apex of your arc and must make a split-second decision between which two pines to place your next turn. You explode into an opening, and ten more virgin turns lie in front of you before the next clump of trees awaits your approach. You nudge a branch as you pick your way down and are nearly buried by snow avalanching off the tree.

"Brrrrrr! A warm *Jägertee* would go down nicely right about now," you say to yourself.

There is no time to daydream...your eyes comb the area for the best line...here comes the next group of obstacles. Before you know it, you have completed another tight powder slalom through some thick, hundred-year-old "slalom poles", and you are sitting comfortably in the Spielberghaus with that *Jägertee* steaming in front of you.

Perhaps, as you are savoring your hot and potent tea with rum, another skier will trudge in, powder snow clinging to his ski clothes from head to foot and a big grin on his face. He calls out, "*Servus*", and one of the waiters answers, "*Grüss dich*, Jimmy!" It is not really an unlikely scenario.

IF THIS SHOULD HAPPEN, call me over to your table, please. Let's drink an apricot schnapps together, and you can tell me about some of *your* favorite powder places. When the *Jägertee* and the schnapps have done their job and we again feel warm from within, we'll go back outside. We'll ski the rest of the day together, and I'll show you some secret powder nooks and crannies that even the local forest fairies and trolls are not quite sure how to find.

LEFT PAGE: The author skiing down through the meadows on the lower slopes of the Schattberg. Photo by Caspar Möller.
THIS PAGE: St. Anton has for many years been one of the most popular Alpine destinations for powder skiers.

ST. ANTON — A SKIBUM TURNS 40

St. Anton is another Austrian ski resort that has not only enjoyed a long and glorious history, but has also played a large role in my own ski story. We all have special spots on this planet to which we repeatedly return, and for me, St. Anton is one of those locations. A combination of love, memories and nostalgia act as a magnetic force to pull me forever back to this historic village nestled in the shadow of the mighty Valluga.

A few years ago, I organized just such a return visit. Again, I was meeting up with fellow ski writer, George Koch. This would be a special reunion for us, however, for George and I had met in St. Anton in March 1980. Now, George, St. Anton and I would all reunite for the first time in very many years. George and I decided to meet at a preordained date and time in the *Bahnhof* (train station) restaurant, our headquarters from our early ski bumming days.

As I wound along the curvy mountain road toward the Arlberg, the inevitable nostalgia began to consume my thoughts. I reminisced back to my first visit to St. Anton.

It was January 1970 and I was studying history for a term in Heidelberg, Germany. During that week, I skied the renowned Valluga, spent a day in the famous St. Anton Ski School, ate a lunch on the lovely terrace of the Arlberghöhe in St. Christoph and danced with a bevy of beautiful Swedish girls at the Klause discotheque. I was a tourist—a first timer.

Like many visitors to St. Anton, I returned...not just once...not twice... but forever. A second-time visitor becomes a return guest. Later, returning skiers graduate to the rank of "regulars"...and ultimately, a handful of the most devoted become St. Anton ski bums.

During Easter week 1970, I became a return guest. In 1974, three visits later, I would have considered myself a regular. By 1976, when I started getting singing jobs in various places around town, I suppose I had graduated to the status of a ski bum.

It did not take long during those early visits to discover that the most special place in St. Anton was the first place in town that I ever saw—the *Bahnhof*. Situated directly in the middle of town, a stone's throw from the old Hotel Post, and looking out over the tram tracks that carry skiers up the Gampen, the bar and restaurant of the *Bahnhof* was in those days the heart and soul of St. Anton. It was not only central but also sold the cheapest beer in town—Fohrenburger—the only beer in town according to *Bahnhof* devotees. The east room was the watering hole for the *Einheimisch* or locals, while the west room, I soon discovered, was the *Stammlokal* for regulars and ski bums.

IT WAS IN THE WEST ROOM during that first winter that I first met Kelly from Canada, Joan from Australia, Gunnar Mönthe from Sweden and the infamous Eddie from South Africa. I do not really know if they were ski bums in 1970 or only regulars. Gunnar Mönthe, I suspect, was a mere tourist. No matter. Over the years to come they became institutions.

"Bahnhof" Eddie, an irascible, obnoxious, gruff, but somehow, likable character, who already then drank more than he skied, became a permanent fixture in the *Bahnhof*. The original table where we had met became known as "Eddie's table". There, Eddie brought a generation of St. Anton regulars to their knees with laughter with his course humor, his constant profanities and his lewd, drunken, off-key version of Alouette, which usually ended with Eddie mooning the *Bahnhof* congregation. Kelly became one of the best skiers ever to pump Arlberg powder and was the telegraph operator of the ski-bum underground communication system. He always knew where a new arrival might find inexpensive accommodations or from whom one could procure a used season pass for a minimum investment.

Joan had already established the Underground Restaurant in Pettneu in 1968, which is still famous throughout the Alps for its all-you-can-eat ribs and chicken-wings dinners. Since those long ago days, she has moved

the establishment into the heart of town. Gunnar was soon to buy the Krazy Kanguruh and turn it into one of the best-known after-ski bars in the Alps.

Perhaps the most wonderful thing about the *Bahnhof* is that friendships were born there—so many friendships. They were not born overnight, mind you, but over time…over the course of a season…perhaps a few seasons. The *Bahnhof* was where we lived. We all had a room where we slept, of course, but we lived in the *Bahnhof*.

We discussed the ski day, ate meals, swilled beer and gulped down shots of Jägermeister. We had discussions here, long into the winter nights… about avalanche danger…or the relative merits of slalom or giant slalom skis…our favorite runs…our favorite girls…and everything else that could possibly pop into the mind of a bunch of ski bums in their twenties. We brought guitars to the *Bahnhof* and sang together, and of course, sometimes we got drunk together. Simply put, we bonded in the *Bahnhof*.

It was also in the *Bahnhof* that I first met George Koch in 1980, a seventeen-year-old Canadian, the youngest ski bum and thirteen years my junior. But age made not much difference. We both loved skiing, and during that winter, we became lifelong friends and ski partners.

My mind was still in a misty, rose-colored past somewhere, but it was 7:50 p.m. and my car was fast approaching the *Bahnhof* of today. George was waiting as I walked in. We gave each other a big hug.

"*Zwei Bier, bitte.*"

WE BECAME SO ENGROSSED in our mutual nostalgia trip that we had not even noticed a middle-aged man with shortly cropped gray hair at one of the neighboring tables. As I approached the bar to buy a second round of Fohrenburger, a voice floated quizzically across the room, calling my name.

I turned to look more closely at the gray-haired man. "Kelly? Kelly… I don't believe it! Don't tell me you're still here?" We sat down with Kelly.

"No, no. I live in London with my family. I renovate houses there," he answered, "but, I still get over here now and then for a visit of a few weeks. It's strange that you and George are here just now. There are a few other guys from the old days who happen to be here this week."

Just then, "New Zealand Al" and "Sport Resor Anders" walked in, and another round of surprised greetings for old friends was exchanged.

"What about Eddie, Kelly?" I inquired. "You knew him best. Do you know what became of him?"

Kelly's soft eyes turned sad. "Not for sure," he said slowly. "I do know that he was in an institution for alcoholics down in Innsbruck for a while." He looked down. "Nobody's heard from him for a few years now. He was in pretty bad shape. Some people suspect that he's dead. But, I think the Austrians probably deported him back to South Africa," he added with a glimmer of hope.

George and I downed one more round, reminisced for another half-hour with Kelly and the others and headed for bed. We definitely wanted to get an early start on the slopes the next day. We just had to ski all our old favorite runs, and especially some of the off-piste descents that have made St. Anton and the Arlberg such a popular destination among good skiers through the years.

We began our first morning with a ride up the Schindlergratbahn. At the top, a group of skiers all clad in identical ski parkas were embarking down a steep couloir that descends between rock cliffs and emerges into the Ulmerhütte run. We were told that they were the Dutch Interski (a ski instructor organization) Demonstration Team, a fact that they probably would have preferred to keep secret by virtue of the exhibition they put on. They were certainly no match for the difficult off-piste terrain that St. Anton has to dish out. By the time they were halfway down the corridor, they looked as if they had been in a rugby match, and ski equipment lay on display all around.

George and I waited until the obstacles all gradually removed themselves, and we also took a plunge down this off-piste ravine. That accomplished, we decided to ski down the Schindlerkar descent. As we rode up the Valluga, again I recollected the past.

It was here in St. Anton that I developed as a skier, and I added a vast amount to my mountain knowledge. I learned how to follow the sun to find the best corn snow. In spring, we began in the early morning with runs down the south-facing slopes of Mattun and Schindlerkar between 9:30 and 11 a.m. Then around noon, we moved over to the steep gullies and southwest slopes above St. Christoph, and after lunch, we skied down the steep west-facing ridges and chutes of the Rendl.

> » We all had a room where we slept, of course, but we lived in the *Bahnhof*. «

George and I began now to pick our way between the bunker-sized moguls that filled Schindlerkar from one side to the other. It was a real test of our lactic acid endurance. This run was very different from the 1970s. Before the Schindlergratbahn began to bring skiers up here en masse, one rarely saw any moguls on this steep run. I thought for a moment about the pluses and minuses of "progress" but had to quickly return my attention to my skiing so as not to be eaten up by the monster bumps.

In the afternoon, we found some excellent corn snow on the Rendl. While the Schindlerkar will probably forevermore be a mogul run, the Rendl did not seem to have changed so much. A short traverse from the top of the Riffelbahn Chairlift got us quickly to a wide choice of open corn-snow fields, which tighten into rather sheer corridors lower down. Ultimately, we ended each such run in the Moostal, about a 10-minute hike from the piste.

By 2:30, the corn snow was too soft, and we settled into a couple of sun chairs at the middle station. This had not changed much either. This area, known to locals as Rendl Beach, still seemed to be the late-afternoon hangout for the ski bums in spring.

I LEANED BACK IN MY CHAIR, closed my eyes and drifted back to 1974. That was the year the Rendl side of St. Anton was opened, making available one of the best powder slopes in the world—and nobody skied there! All the tourists did battle for a reservation on the famous Valluga, while we skied through thigh-deep powder day after day on the Rendl, rarely crossing a track.

Then there was March 10, 1980, maybe the best powder day I have ever experienced. My God! Was it so long ago? I could still almost feel the fluff in my face. By 1980, a fair number of powder-hungry regulars were wise to the Rendl, but on that day a low fog shrouded the village

and kept most everyone in bed. For 8 hours we bounced up and down the Wannele route and the North Face. By the time the fog had burnt off enough to stimulate the majority of the skiers into action, we already had skied over 10,000 vertical meters and were ready for a hot bath.

I suddenly shivered in my chair, blinked my eyes open and noticed that the sun had fallen behind the mountains. It was time to ski down.

That evening, George and I had an excellent venison dinner followed by blueberry *Palatschinken* (Austrian crepes) in the Fahrner Stub'n, and we went back to the *Bahnhof* for a nightcap.

It had been a prototypical spring day, and back in our old haunt, I thought about love. It was also here in the *Bahnhof* almost twenty years earlier that I had met and fallen in love with Andrea, a beautiful and innocent nineteen-year-old dental student from Freiburg, Germany. She and I had had one of those rare, mad, love-at-first-sight experiences. Our infatuation had taken us on a wonderful, spontaneous, month-long trip from St. Anton, through the Italian and French Alps, and up through Germany, Holland and Norway, before it burnt out as fast as it had ignited.

George interrupted my daydreams to plan the next day's skiing, and we decided to do one of the classic off-piste runs in the Alps, the Pazieltal, from the Vallugagrat down to Zürs.

OUR SKI DAY BEGAN with a 30-minute hike and a precipitous entry, after which the Pazieltal opens up, offering slopes of almost all exposures. Unless one skis down right after a snowfall, this route can, and usually does, include the whole gamut of snow conditions, from old powder to wind pack, crud, crust and even corn snow. The snow was pretty tracked out and the visibility was poor, but we enjoyed ourselves. This run was for old time's sake, and George and I had enough memories from here to imagine we were thrashing through light powder.

We arrived in Zürs and stood in the lift line, when a voice once again called my name. I turned and was literally overwhelmed. Her hair was longer, and she was a woman now instead of a girl, but Andrea's natu-

ral smile and sparkling eyes were just the same. We rode up the chair lift together, trying to catch up with all that had happened in each other's lives since we last had met. Suddenly, tears began to stream down Andrea's face.

"It was such a special, wonderful time..." she whispered, as she took out a handkerchief. I could only mumble an affirmation as I too became misty-eyed. Later, we met her children, ate a nostalgic lunch and exchanged addresses, before George and I headed off.

IN THE AFTERNOON, WE SKIED the White Ring, the Zürs-Lech circuit, skiing the Madloch down to the tiny village of Zug, continuing from Zug to Lech and finally up the Rüfikopf in Lech to return to Zürs.

We went to the Underground for dinner. Gone were the days of sneaking two extra baskets of the all-you-can-eat ribs in a plastic bag out to the car, but the meal was still on the menu and as scrumptious as ever. In addition, the live music was good, making the Underground one of the most happening places on the Arlberg.

Having skied St. Anton, Zürs and Lech, it was a must to take a day in Stuben. Actually, it had been hard to wait *that* long. The Albonagrat, which rises 1000 meters above the tiny village of Stuben has some of the choicest skiing anywhere in the Alps. With only 100 permanent residents, 630 tourist beds and three lifts, Stuben probably does not sound too impressive, but do not be fooled.

Stuben is a powder hole, where the storms, which invariably blow in from the West, get stuck as they attempt to cross the Arlberg Pass. Here, each storm is compelled to drop the mother lode to lighten its burden enough so that it can rise above the pass and escape eastward. Hence, this little snow magnet pulls down an average of 12 meters of snowfall per year. In addition, most of the skiing on the Albona is on an open north-facing wall of snow a few kilometers wide, which seems always to have space for just one more set of powder tracks.

George and I began our day by skiing down the Rauz run from the

LEFT PAGE
The author enjoying one of the best powder days of his life on the Rendl in St. Anton, March 10, 1980. Photo by Igge Holm.
THIS PAGE
UPPER: The Albonagrad in Stuben, with its wide open north face, is one of the best powder mountains in the world.
LOWER LEFT: The exterior of the old *Bahnhof* in St. Anton.
LOWER RIGHT: The *Bahnhof* restaurant was always a place where a ski bum could bring his guitar—or even his didgeridoo—to entertain the other guests.

Valluga to Stuben. Today, we were here seeking corn snow, but as we rode up the double chair lift on this warm spring morning, my thoughts once again meandered back in time. They took me to the years when Stuben only had an old single chair in two stages up to the Albonagrat. It was mid-winter. The wind howled, we were wrapped in blankets that they still dole out to help warm up the patrons of the Albona, and 60 centimeters of powder lay under our dangling skis. There had been so many days like that.

I THOUGHT ABOUT A PARTICULAR DAY when we had hiked to the Maroiköpfle and had skied the renowned powder run to the village of Langen. We then hitched a ride back to Stuben and celebrated the day by eating and drinking a kingly meal in the Hotel Post. By the time we had finished, there were no more buses, but the innkeeper closed up and drove us back over the pass to St. Anton. Now that was true Austrian *Gemütlichkeit*.

I was again startled back to the present by the top station, and George and I began a run down to the Maroi Valley. The morning sun had prepared the corn snow to perfection, and we glided almost effortlessly to the valley below without stopping.

Soon we were on the road in the forest, transporting us to the isolated Rasthaus Ferwall, a cozy little restaurant in the middle of nowhere, seemingly placed in this location by God just to suit the off-piste skiers of the Maroi Valley. A tasty *Kaiserschmarrn*, a taxi ride back to St. Anton, one more afternoon of corn snow on the Rendl and another day on the Arlberg had passed into my personal history.

Something new had been added to the Arlberg since my previous visit. The Sonnenkopf ski area of Klösterle was now part of the Arlberg ski pass, and that seemed worth an investigation on our last day. The pistes here were generally easy or intermediate in nature, so George and I cruised leisurely for most of the day.

We did discover an area off the Obermoos Lift that looked to be a good place to be after a snowfall. And then there was the back side into

the Nenzigasttal. This is an off-piste route that deposits a skier between the Klösterle and Langen. The conditions were not right to allow us to try this descent, but that was all right, too. For over twenty years, I had been coming back to the Arlberg, and there had always been something new to allure me along with the tried and true. It felt good to again have a new route to explore on my next visit.

IT WAS OUR LAST NIGHT, and we wandered down to the *Bahnhof* for a final beer. This time, nobody I knew was there. At one table sat eight or ten locals, probably exchanging jokes in their almost indecipherable dialect, for every few minutes a hearty laugh filled the smoky room. At another table sat a group of young skiers just about to down a round of Jägermeister.

"Were they tourists who had just stumbled in here by accident," I wondered to myself, "or did they belong to a new generation of ski bums, each living an early chapter in his or her own St. Anton story?"

I sucked on my beer. The *Bahnhof* had changed too, I thought. A new train station had been built on the other side of town, and the former ski bum room had been torn down. The skiers and locals now shared the same room...and Eddie will probably nevermore swill back a beer and wail a raucous rendition of Alouette within these four walls.

Yet, the changes did not really matter. It was somehow the same anyway. The place was full of old locals, remembering their youth, perhaps, over a few beers, and young skiers building memories that would inevitably bring them back to this special place. And I, in the middle of my life—somewhere in between—sat with a tear in my eye for the past, a dream in my heart for the future and a nagging thought in my brain of where Eddie might be.

SÖLDEN AND THE WIZARD OF ÖTZ

How many times have you picked up a ski magazine and questioned the validity of the content. The photos always depict meter-deep powder, the sky is invariably blue, and the text reads like something the marketing department of the resort has thrown together. Does it all seem very unlikely? You know from real-life experience that when you spend your hard-earned cash on a ski holiday, fog and ice are often your fate.

I have read such fantasy accounts from ski journalists on numerous occasions, and my reaction is invariably the same. "Bull____!" I say to myself. "These pretenders have been paid off by the local chamber of commerce, wined and dined with a few seven-course dinners, and offered the virginity of a couple of local alm-Heidis," I mutter under my breath. I imagine that the ski photos that complement the article were taken three years earlier in an entirely different country, and I doubt the entire journalistic industry.

It is, therefore, with great reluctance, that I put my own credibility to the test with this fairy tale description of my experience in the Ötztal. In early March, Phil Le Roux, Jonas Nilsson and I drove along the Inn Valley from Innsbruck and hung a left where the arrow pointed toward Sölden.

THE DRIVING WAS SLOW as a blizzard whirled around us. Outside my Jeep, the road was slippery and white, the visibility was close to nil, and I began to get hypnotized by the snowflakes dancing in the light of our headlights. I turned the wheel over to Jonas and fell into a magical white dream in the back seat. I remember nothing of the dream but that it transferred me to some enchanted land, and when I awoke we had arrived in Sölden.

The next thing I recall of any significance to this tale is shaking hands the following morning with Alexander Giacomelli, a mountain guide with whom I had arranged to ski. Alex soon proved to be more than just a guide. He is the third generation in his family to assume the task of leading people to the best possible snow in his beloved Ötztal Alps. At the age of six, he already accompanied his father on an excursion from Vent (1900 m) to the peak of Austria's second-highest mountain, the glaciated Wildspitze (3774 m). Later, when he was 20, Alex became the youngest *Bergführer* in Austria.

Still many years my junior, but with years of guiding under his belt, Alex combined youthful exuberance and enthusiasm with experience and the wisdom of his forefathers to make him part guide, part mountain goat and part wizard. He could not magically make perfect powder appear or turn breakable crust into pristine corn snow like some medieval alchemist, but if there was any good snow in the valley, Alex would certainly sniff it out and lead his guests to it.

Our first morning, the problem was not to find the powder, but rather to be able to see it. Fresh snow continued to pour out of a thick cloud that encompassed the entire lift system. Most of the skiing in Sölden is above the tree line, including two glaciers, which each rise up to 3250 meters.

Only the lowest 400–500 vertical meters of ski terrain is made up of forest, and that seemed much too tight to ski without a defoliant in one's rucksack—not so. Alex first led us to a secret cut in the woods slightly below the Gaislachkogel middle station. When he saw how much we enjoyed a powder romp in the forest, he guided us over some avalanche barriers into a steep glen in the trees.

The visibility was much better in the lower elevations with the perspective one gained from skiing in the woods. We now looked down over a varied landscape of steeps and hollows sprinkled with enough small trees, ravines, knolls and small rock faces to make for a highly interesting obstacle course.

ALEX WAS SOMEWHAT RETICENT WITH WORDS but I soon learned that it was worthwhile to take heed of the few words he imparted. As we observed the landscape below, we carefully tried to choose a line. Alex mumbled something about staying to the right and proceeded to disappear out of sight in a trail of powder exhaust.

Rather than follow his words or tracks, I saw what appeared to be a good line further to the left. It was a good line, too, at least for a dozen turns, until I hurtled over an unseen rock face, gasped for air, and uttered a split second prayer in free fall. I made a soft, white touchdown just centimeters away from a second granite outcrop, and from that point on, I listened intently to Alex's every utterance.

We worked our way down through the glen to a road that could have deposited us easily back onto the piste, but our ski sorcerer had other plans. He dipped back off the road into even thicker forest. Now, only a short distance above the village, the 60 centimeters of new snow had a consistency akin to porridge.

Alex cut and swerved, adroitly avoiding the woodwork, while we sweated, kick-turned and used a variety of survival turns to negotiate our way through this lowest level of trees. Our leader was having so much fun, he probably didn't even notice that he was leaving us winded in his wake, or perhaps this was his subtle way of letting us know that he was in fact the sorcerer and we were but would-be apprentices.

WHILE WE TRIED TO REENERGIZE with a well-earned lunch at a cozy hut called 'S Pfandl, the clouds magically began to dissipate and the dramatic landscape of the Ötztal suddenly became a reality to us. Steep, jagged peaks line both sides of the village. One could easily see that Sölden was not really one village, but a group of hamlets, both on the valley floor and on the low and high alms. In fact, the community is made up of small clusters of houses which all have names in their own right, such as Rechenau, Rainstadl, Grünwald, Mapuit, Rettenbach, Innerwald, Ausserwald, Unterwald, Wohlfahrt, Platte and at least a dozen more. Winding through the scattered hamlets is a stream called the Ötztaler Ache.

Up the valley, the lifts of Obergurl and Hochgurgl could be seen amidst white fields of powder. Near the end of the Ötztal stood the Hauslabjoch, where a few years ago the preserved remains of the 5200-year-old Bronze Age man called Ötzi was found in the eternal ice near the Similaunhütte.

» **Where virgin white meets infinite blue, a boundless valley lies stretched out before you, and the only thing that stands between you and paradise is your ability to believe.«**

THIS PAGE
LEFT: All over Austria, the old mountain huts provide a cozy lunch atmosphere.
CENTER: Phil Le Roux dives into the Krumme Rinne.
RIGHT: Minna Gynther finds a line of sunshine high on one of Sölden's two glaciers.

RIGHT PAGE
Phil Le Roux on the front face of Gaislachkogel.

We could also see that the east face of the Rettenbachtal, just a couple of chair lift rides away, had just enough perfectly formed tracks on its face to tantalize any powder skier. We quickly gobbled up the last few bites of lunch and made our way to the top of the Gampebahn. From there, Alex led us on three or four merry romps, and for the rest of the day, we never had to cross a ski track.

Alex was not only revealing himself to be a great guide, but he was also showing us another endearing attribute. His eyes twinkled and a broad, toothy grin stretched across his face whenever he stopped to wait for us between long stretches of linked powder turns. This was a young man who not only knew what he was doing, but loved what he was doing as well.

Alexander had told us that his absolute favorite skiing was on the various faces and couloirs off the top of the Gaislachkogel. On our second day, he made us clearly understand why. We awoke that morning to a cloudless blue, and our guru wasted no time in leading us down the front face under the gondola, known as Die Rinne. This face is entirely off-piste—1000 vertical meters of mountain dressed in an 80-centimeter-thick white winter coat. The upper slopes are 35 degrees and then some, mellowing out to gentler gradients. Crossing other ski tracks was once again not obligatory. That proved more and more to be the case on almost every run behind the Wizard of Ötz.

Our early morning wakeup run was followed by a 40-degree chute down the back side of Gaislachkogel to Gaislachsee. Once we passed the snow-covered lake, we swung around to the east flank of the mountain and continued this 1600-vertical-meter descent to a small hamlet called Bodenegg. The width of the slopes here had to be measured in kilometers. The morning sun was strong, and we found a verandah to drink in

the warmth of the sun and an ice-cold beer. It was not even midday, and Phil, a veteran of six full ski seasons in various destinations in the Alps and Australia, was already proclaiming this the "best ski day of his life"!

Now, with full visibility at our disposal, Phil, Jonas and I were bubbling over with ideas, pointing to various tempting slopes in all directions and asking Alex about the possibilities. In some cases, he advised that we must wait another day for the snow to settle. In other instances, he retorted with a phrase that gradually became his trademark.

"Okay, let's have a look," he would suggest, as he glided into position to inspect the route more closely.

The front face of the Gaislachkogl has couloirs lined up neatly in a row, all easily accessible for anyone who dares. They vary in difficulty from extremely difficult to impossible, and Alex now chose one that was half-way in between. He told us to wait while he "had a look". Forty turns later, he motioned with a wave of his hand and called out, "Next."

I used the excuse of being the photographer as an explanation of why I should go next. This was, however, an exaggeration of the truth—no—it was an outright lie. I could see full well that this chute was so narrow that two sets of tracks would decimate the virgin, leaving no more good lines and no good photos either. I dove in before any objections could be made. In spite of the steep incline of the gully, the extremely deep snow kept my speed in control, and I pulled up next to Alex 40 face shots later, to watch the others.

WE FINISHED OUR DAY with a couloir of a different nature, one that Alex called the Krumme Rinne. This was a long ravine with an elbow curve that extended four or five times the length of the day's earlier endeavors. Whereas rocky outcrops separated the earlier chutes from one another, this was a deep ravine between two major ridges, giving it a more dramatic appearance. Looking down the gun barrel of the couloir prompted our hearts up into our throats. By the time the ravine spit us back out into the Rettenbachtal, we were again ready for some R&R and the nearby Hühnersteign Hut was situated conveniently a short schuss away.

Alex now wanted to show us the glacial skiing on the Rettenbach and Tiefenbach Glaciers. The Ötztal Alps includes 86 glaciers, two of which

provide both summer skiing and snow security for poor winters. Now, in a bountiful winter with excellent conditions all over, only the Rettenbach Glacier was open.

Some of the pistes here are relatively easy cruisers, typical of glacier skiing, but the front face is rather steep with some good mogul runs. In addition, there was still untouched powder along the periphery of the pistes, and our sorcerer led us on a few frolics in freshies to the side of the Rettenbachjoch Chair. With a grin, he pointed out where, on some future visit, he could lead us over some wild terrain into the neighboring Pitztal. Then we followed Alex between a few rocks below the glacier lifts, and we finished the day by skiing massive stretches of totally untouched north faces that feed into the Rettenbachtal.

DAY FOUR'S MENU OFFERED a short ski tour from the top of the Schwartzkopf into the Pollestal. This was a backward ski tour, in which one skis first and hikes out afterwards. The snow on the first pitches was less than perfect, for the wind had played with it the night before, leaving us to struggle with a long string of jump turns on 35–40-degree slopes of wind crust.

The dimensions of the valley were mind-boggling, however, and the solitude was magnificent. The more protected lower regions again offered the same type of light powder we had skied all week, a much appreciated reward before we trudged out the valley for a couple of hours to the village of Huben.

The next day saw us back on Alex's beloved Gaislachkogl. We spent seven full hours yo-yoing up and down between the peak and the Rettenbachtal, still skiing virgin north faces until the lifts closed. I was amazed. It was now the fourth full day since the last snowfall. In many of the top ski resorts in the Alps, such slopes would have been history in two hours. Yet here in Sölden, the masses of powder on all sides of the Gaislachkogl seemed to be the exclusive domain of "Alexander the Great" and whoever his lucky followers happened to be.

Our magician had one last card up his sleeve. We still had hardly touched the most popular part of the lift system, the huge Giggijoch area, and Alex told us to meet there on our last day. The upper moun-

tain here is made up of wide highways of corduroy divided into blue and red pistes, where the majority of Sölden's guests cruise around to their heart's content.

With the consecutive days of warm weather, the south and east sides of the Giggijoch had had time to transform into corn snow by now. We traversed high off the top of the Hainbachjoch and slithered a smooth, silky trail into the spring corn. If one traversed far enough, these slopes also were unblemished by ski tracks.

Soon, we moved over to the east faces where we had laid first tracks almost a week earlier. Here, too, the corn snow glistened provocatively in the sun. Our old powder tracks were still etched in the mountainside, but they could be avoided. Where we had earlier in our visit linked tight powder turns, we now swooped down the mountain in wide sweeping arcs, spraying corn kernels off our skis in a hailstorm of ball bearings.

We had, by now, come full circle. Our pathfinder had led us from one end of the Ötztal Arena to the other. We had skied in the trees, the chutes and the wide, open spaces, and we had experienced waist deep powder and sparkling corn.

MY TALE HAS NOW COME to an end. I am quite sure I have lost some disbelievers along the way. Other readers have perhaps read this far, but categorize these pages as pure fantasy. But, before passing final judgment on the viability, reliability and credence of this story, do yourself a favor. Book a week of skiing with the "Wizard of Ötz" for next season through Sölden's tourist office.

Go to Sölden and meet the wizard in the flesh, in his fiefdom, where reality and fantasy meet in a surrealistic fusion of fact and fiction. Let him lead you to where the snow is so deep and fluffy, you seem to be skiing on clouds. Permit him to show you an endless dance floor of pristine corn kernels that allow your skis to take on the characteristics of Gene Kelly's tap shoes. Let him guide you to that distant spot on the horizon where virgin white meets infinite blue, a boundless valley lies stretched out before you, and the only thing that stands between you and paradise is your ability to believe.

INNSBRUCK — THE WORLD'S STEEPEST PISTE

February 8 was a black morning for me. I was staying with my buddy, Keith Johnston, near Saalbach, and one of the winter's big storms had been dumping on the surrounding landscape for days. The morning of the eighth was cold and clear without a whisper of wind. It was a postcard day, but my schedule necessitated that I drive all the way across the Alps to pick up my son the next morning in Lyon.

I was something between frustrated and furious. This would be arguably the best powder day of the season and I would miss it. Keith was teasing me as he packed his boards onto his car to head the 14 kilometers up to Saalbach, while I fumed.

I stopped for a few minutes in Lofer to take photos of the picturesque village with the buildings and trees all clad in their heaviest coat of winter white. Shortly before noon, I arrived in Innsbruck.

In town, I couldn't resist stopping for a short wander around the center to take a few more pictures. Innsbruck is not only one of the few locations to twice host the Winter Olympics, it is a beautiful university town. The

»From the top, the possibilities are extremely steep or even steeper.«

city is crammed tightly into the narrow Inn Valley, with the river bearing the same name snaking its way through the center.

Innsbruck is steeped in Austrian history as well as ski history. Franz Klammer's immortal 1976 downhill run here can be revisited on video, and visitors will also enjoy a walk through the narrow streets and picturesque houses of the old town. History drips off the rooftops like snowmelt in a spring thaw, and one can almost expect to meet Empress Maria Theresa and her entourage as one passes through this charming quarter.

In the city center is the famous Goldenes Dachl, a court box for Emperor Maximilian I (1494-96), which is covered by a roof of more than 2600 gilded tiles. Around each corner of the cobblestone streets of the Old City awaits another chapter of Renaissance Europe.

In Innsbruck, one can even sleep in historic surroundings. Around the corner from the Goldenes Dachl, for example, lies the 600-year-old Goldener Adler Hotel. I am not sure whether Franz Klammer ever rested his weary legs on a bed here after a tough downhill, but many notable people have done just that. Here, you might well lay your head down in the same quarters that gave shelter to Wolfgang Mozart, Chancellor Metternich, Wolfgang Goethe or Heinrich Heine in centuries gone by.

South of town, the mountains rise gradually skyward. The famous Axamer Lizum, which hosted the ski events during the Olympics, is visible to the southwest. In the opposite direction, the dramatic peaks of the Nordkette jut virtually straight up into the heavens directly behind the rooftops, like a canvas backdrop at some old theater. The view of the old town with the snow-decked Nordkette looming behind, was so often photographed during the two Olympic years, that Innsbruck became a cliché of the archetypal ski town.

THE NORDKETTE IS A STUNNING ARRAY of precipitous peaks, the picture perfect background for a ski town, but hardly a likely place to actually ski. It is too raw, too steep, too unfriendly and too difficult. Perhaps only a town with such a tough ski reputation as Innsbruck would dare to build ski lifts in the Nordkette, but that is exactly what they have done.

It was the Nordkette at which I, too, pointed my camera lens. I was still very upset with fate's mishandling of my schedule.

All of a sudden, it occurred to me. I had passed through Innsbruck

innumerable times, as it is a major crossroads in the Alps, but I had always been in a hurry to get somewhere. I had never taken the time to discover the skiing around this two-time Olympic host. My situation had generally been exactly like today—except for one thing. Today, I was upset, pissed off, irritated and agitated enough to change my fate.

After a few clicks of the camera, I got back into the car, wound my way through the narrow streets of town and pulled up to the Nordpark ski area. Nordpark is home to a piste which is reputed to be one of the steepest bona fide runs in the world, and a run or two would not upset my schedule that much.

Lifts rise out of Innsbruck in three stages, bringing riders almost 1800 vertical meters above the city. The trip finishes atop the Hafelekar Cable Car, from where one can enjoy some breathtaking views of the town. One can only enjoy the panorama for a short time before one realizes that there is no easy way back down from here unless one is willing to go through the humiliation of taking the cable car in the wrong direction.

FROM THE TOP, THE POSSIBILITIES are extremely steep or even steeper. The various descents include the Karrinne, Direttissima and two variations of the Seilbahnrinne, which are all between 40 and 50 degrees. I was lucky enough to meet a few locals who promised to show me the Karrinne, the official route and arguably, the steepest official piste in the world. Between 40 and 45 degrees, this predator has taken the lives of numerous skiers who were not up to the challenge, according to one of my newly found guides, a slightly crazed local kamikaze named Florian Schuchter.

"How did they die?" I asked Florian, gazing up at the ominous looking elevator shaft. "Avalanches or hitting their head against rocks?"

"No, no," he answered quickly, "just skiing—and falling, of course! Often the Karrinne is hard and rather icy, with very big moguls. A skier who falls at the top cannot arrest his fall. He slides down very quickly, bouncing from mogul to mogul..."

"...And by the time he gets to the bottom, he has had a ride like a Ping-Pong ball in a washing machine, and his internal organs are minced meat," I finished.

"Yes, something like that," Florian concluded.

Fortunately, this was not such a day. The fresh snow was soft and the moguls were still manageable, as I went to the top with Florian and his friends, Martin and Gary.

To get to the Karrinne requires a few minutes of walking around the back of the lift station. To the right, the mountain falls away steeply, and I was glad that there was no ice along the promenade. The run is flanked on one side by a windblown ridge, and below, Innsbruck looks close enough to spit on—or crash into, whichever the case may be.

I looked around. Outside the periphery of the two marked routes were hundreds of tracks, descending down every off-piste route imaginable. Ordinarily, I would have been happy to try one of these alternatives but not on a day with a level-four avalanche warning. Even my three local friends agreed that it was too dangerous.

THE SKI WORLD is changing. Snowboards, fat skis, and freeride skis are making it ever-easier to ski difficult off-piste terrain. Unfortunately, it is not possible for snowsports enthusiasts to acquire the mountain knowledge necessary to assess avalanche danger in the short time that it now takes to attain the ability to descend off-piste.

We were ready for our descent, and that revealed a different aspect of the equipment changes. Florian was equipped with wide-bodied freeride skis—the kind of boards you sit back on after a big dump of powder and ski the entire slope in eight to ten turns. Gary was on his snowboard. He needed no more than four or five turns. Martin and I had more traditional skis and worked our legs to ski down. Florian and Gary waited for us.

Below the middle station, the locals skied off-piste among dwarf larch trees. I tried to follow, but with no success. With close to two meters of new snow, tree wells next to the larches created a virtual mine field of peril. Many of the miniature trees were completely buried inches below the snow, creating deep, invisible holes into which one could easily fall.

"Just ski fast," called Florian.

I had a different idea—cut back to the piste.

The lowest section of the mountain is a narrow road with a long series of switchbacks.

"Here, we usually play our own version of boardercross," called Martin, but again I was reluctant. This was their home mountain and it was my first time skiing here. They took off on a bump-and-run race, while I cruised down at my own speed. I guess I wasn't too far off the pace, because my pals had not yet ordered their first beer by the time I made it to the bottom.

I had no time for a beer. I felt very satisfied with my decision to ski for the afternoon, but I had lost a few hours and had to hurry on my way across the Alps. Little did I know that my short indulgence would have a chain reaction of consequences.

AS I DROVE ACROSS from Austria to Switzerland, I noticed that I had blown a fuse and my dashboard light did not work. But my afternoon of skiing put me behind schedule, and I could not afford the time to test fuses and fix this right away. I won't need to see the dashboard this one night, I thought. After all, I can feel approximately how fast I am driving.

One hour outside of Lyon, the car engine began smoking. I turned on the interior light and looked at the dashboard that had been darkened by my fuse failure. The control panel showed that the engine was overheated in a major way. Had the dashboard light been working, I would have noticed this much sooner and added coolant.

Now, it was too late. The head gasket was badly damaged, among other things, and before I got my car back from the mechanic in Lyon, I was € 2000 poorer! That price tag, if nothing else, made my run in the Karrinne the most expensive descent of my life—an epic run with a commensurate price tag.

BAD GASTEIN — AN UNFINISHED STORY

Bad Gastein has a very different look and feel than most of the other ski towns and villages in Austria, and for good reason. The history of the valley has also differed radically from its neighbors. Gastein has, for thousands of years, been blessed with radon thermal springs whose waters have been bathed in for their healing qualities. While most of Austria's ski resorts have developed from agrarian peasant villages, Bad Gastein has been attracting the aristocracy of central Europe since the Middle Ages. While the other now prominent ski resorts of Austria were previously made up of small wooden farmhouses, Bad Gastein was amassing a large number of grandiose and luxurious Jugendstihl spa hotels to cater to their upper-class summer visitors.

Gastein has streets and hotels named after figures from its glorious past, like the Kaiser Wilhelm Promenade and the Minotel Mozart. After all, everybody who was anybody came here in the 19th century. Indeed, a list of spa visitors from Gastein's glory days reads like a guest list for a Hapsburg wedding: Emperor Frans Joseph I, Archduke Maximilian, Chancellor Bismarck, waltz king Johann Strauss, philosopher Arthur Schopenhauer, King George of Greece, King Carol I of Romania…the list goes on and on.

The Gastein ski region is made up of various separate lift systems. A 21st century visitor driving into the valley will first reach the ski resort of Dorfgastein, a more traditional Austrian village whose lifts link it with Grossarl, a town in the next valley. Next comes Bad Hofgastein, a more modern village featuring the longest ski run in the area, an 8-kilometer, 1460-vertical-meter descent called the Hohe Scharte Nord.

Finally, built right into a steep hillside, the congregation of huge hotels known as Bad Gastein comes into view. The historic splendor of such edifices as the Hotel Salzburgerhof, the old casino and the Arcotel Elisabethpark set the town apart from most other ski towns, but there are dozens of other old hotels as well. A closer look reveals that many of them are dilapidated, and in fact, some have had their doors closed for years.

Despite some very good skiing in the valley, Gastein's winter business has never been able to attract as many visitors as the spa brought to the valley a century ago. This fact, of course, is good news for skiers, who won't have to worry about long lift queues and slopes that are too crowded.

ON MY FIRST DAY in Gastein, I skied from the Stubnerkogel to Bad Hofgastein. There, I found some lovely powder by traversing out from the Hohe Scharte Nord run. I also spent a day at Dorfgastein, where I skied some prime corn snow on the faces down to Grossarl.

That evening, I met Niclas Fagerlund. Niclas is a snowboarder who had spent about five seasons in Gastein. He assured me that whatever I had discovered in Bad Gastein, Dorfgastein or Bad Hofgastein would pale by comparison to the skiing at Sportgastein. This was, according to Niclas, the only place to ski in the entire lift system. Niclas worked in a disco, and the more beer he served me, the more enticing Sportgastein became. Early the next morning, the previous night's beers made my bed also very enticing, but I resisted the temptation and joined Niclas on the rugged mountain at the end of the valley known as the Kreuzkogel.

There are many great ski resorts in the world, but strangely enough, there are not as many great ski mountains. This is not so odd perhaps, as most of the larger ski centers are comprised of various mountains, some offering shady, powder-filled slopes, while others are full of sun-drenched pistes with the obligatory verandahs for skiers to enjoy long lunches and late afternoon *Glühwein*. Some mountains are full of open slopes, others

have trails cut out of the forest, and still others have glades that are perfect for tree-skiing. It is often a combination of the characteristics of a ski area's mountains that gives the resort its versatility.

A FEW OF THE WORLD'S RESORTS offer a single, great ski mountain. These include the Albonagrat in Stuben, the Gemsstock in Andermatt, the Grands Montets in Argentière and the Monte Rosa on the Swiss–Italian border. In the case of the Albona, the endless expanse of powdery north faces is the key to its greatness, while the south-facing corn snow slopes that take off-piste skiers to Rasthaus Ferwall add a degree of versatility. While the Albona summit accesses such a huge amount of north-facing terrain, from the top of the Gemsstock, a skier can reach even more slopes and with a variety of exposures.

The Grands Montets' claim to greatness comes from its beautiful rugged terrain of glaciers and precipices as well as the fact that there are various descents of over 2000 vertical meters. Add to all that a versatility of open upper slopes and steep tree-skiing on the lower mountain, and it would be hard to argue its prominence among good skiers.

The Monte Rosa rises high above the lifts of Alagna Valsesia. While Alagna's lack of pistes render it less versatile than the other two, good

skiers can also find descents of over 2000 vertical meters amidst a sea of glacial ice on the slopes from Forcella Bors (3550 m).

The Kreuzkogel at Sportgastein is also among the great ski mountains of the world. While its 1065 vertical meters does not hold a candle to the Grands Montets, the Monte Rosa or even the Gemsstock, it can make up for that in versatility. The various pistes on the mountain face west and are blue and red cruisers. As with my other highly rated mountains, it is the off-piste terrain, however, that gives the Kreuzkogel its claim to stardom.

The mountain is best-known among freeriders for its vast north face, which is a so-called *Schiroute*—a marked route that is ungroomed and unpatrolled. Niclas knew a dozen routes down the *Schiroute* and he was ready to show me as many as I dared try. The western aspects of the Kreuzkogel also have lots of territory between and outside the marked trails, but I found the eastern flank of the mountain to be most intriguing.

One could get to the east faces by two paths. First, we entered through a rather treacherous slope near the top station, where exposed rocks awaited the falling bodies of skiers who misplaced an edge on the first or second turn. Later in the day, we traversed and hiked for 20 minutes along the back to reach an entrance much further into the backcountry. Either way, the whole mountainside emptied into the Weissenbachtal, a long valley that is home to the cross-country ski track of the resort. The

possibilities were only limited by one's energy to walk back around the mountain at the bottom to return to the lifts.

HERE, MY FRIEND NICLAS HAD somewhat of a handicap. Snowboards are not nearly as adaptable as skis to walking on flat ground. We explored a few routes with limited walking. We found powder on the upper slopes and corn lower down.

On the way down, Niclas surprised me. "This is not really my favorite mountain," he suddenly said. "It's the best one in the lift system, but my favorite is that one over there," he continued, pointing to a cone-shaped peak across the valley.

Schareck, 3122 meters of man-eating mountain, stared me in the face. Part way down the steep north face were some evil looking rocks.

"It's about 45 degrees at the top," added Niclas.

I was relieved that it wasn't steeper, for from where I stood, the face was ominously shady and looked almost vertical. Niclas went on to explain that as often as conditions allowed, he took the morning train through the tunnel to the Mölltaler Glacier, where he rode the lifts up the other side of Schareck. There are various descents back to the Weissenbachtal, all of which are difficult, but Niclas always rides the most challenging one.

Saalbach, where I spend a reasonable amount of time every winter, is

THIS PAGE
UPPER: Bad Gastein, with its many large Jugendstihl spa hotels, has a different look than other Austrian ski resorts.
LOWER: Through most of the history of Bad Gastein's famous thermal baths, it was mandatory for both males and females to wear bathing caps. This policy is no longer in effect.

RIGHT PAGE
Daniel Gardtman in a cloud of angel dust on the north face at Sportgastein.

only an hour's drive from Gastein, and I determined that I would join Niclas some time for a ride down Schareck. The right time to ski such a face does not really come that often, however. I would want good weather for optimal visibility. I would not want to do it too soon after a snowfall, when the snow has not yet settled completely. On the other hand, I could also not afford to wait too long. Otherwise, Niclas would put tracks on it with somebody else. After all, the descent is not that wide, and snowboarders use up a lot of space.

One season passed since Niclas first pointed Schareck out to me, and my plan did not get fulfilled. Another season came and went. I got to Bad Gastein and skied some good powder, but the right opportunity did not arise. A third season and a fourth became history. Again I visited Gastein. It was too early in the season, and there was not enough snow on Schareck.

A skier's dreams are no different than other plans and ideas that we all have for the future. Some of our dreams get realized quite soon after they are born, others live in the back of our mind for many years before they reach fruition and still others are never fulfilled.

Sometimes ski stories seem to have a ready-made formula—something like I came, I saw, I conquered—but life is not really like that. Articles often follow that pattern because the many ski plans that never reach fruition due to weather, injury or other circumstances do not become stories. A tale usually craves a climax, and when we do not fulfill our plan, a potential story ends up in the wastebasket. In that sense, reality is not served.

I have waited for five years now to finish this short narrative on Bad Gastein…and I haven't done so. I wanted the climax. The story was useless without the last page. But the end of the story has been there all along, staring me in the face.

A skier lives on dreams. As soon as or even before he has completed a great run or settled behind a beer at the end of a powder day, he already has plans for some-

» Bad Gastein was amassing a large number of grandiose and luxurious Jugendstihl spa hotels…«

thing new—a descent to try the next day or a resort to visit the following year. That is part of what addicts many of us to skiing—the fact that no matter how many mountains and slopes we have skied, there is virtually an infinite number of new experiences still awaiting us.

One day, I will conquer Schareck…or maybe I won't, but it really makes no difference. Schareck symbolizes the dream of adventure, and at the end of the story the dream will live on.

PITZTAL — THE HIGHEST SKI RESORT IN AUSTRIA

It is often great fun to get off the beaten path to discover and explore some of the lesser-known ski areas, and Tyrol, with more than 100 ski villages, is a great place to do this. The best method to accomplish this task is by car. By automobile, one is free to wind up the myriad of side valleys that permeate the Alps and uncover some of the small gems, known only to the locals, which do not appear in any charter travel brochure.

Somehow, the misconception has evolved among skiers that to find good skiing late in the season, one must go to the *higher*, more rugged western Alps of France and Switzerland. The *lower*, hilly ski areas of Austria are all but forgotten in the April rush to the Haute Savoie region of France or the Swiss canton of Wallis.

Pitztal is one of the Austrian ski areas that dispels that myth. The top of the Pitztal Gletscherbahn, at 3440 meters, is higher than any point in the Trois Vallées, the Portes du Soleil, Verbier, Val d'Isère, La Plagne or Les Arcs.

One becomes immediately aware of the rugged nature of the area as one drives among the small villages of the Innerpitztal. Small enclaves of houses are spaced sporadically throughout the valley, each followed by an empty piece of road, devoid of buildings, where long, steep avalanche paths stretch up toward the heavens.

The snow was falling heavily as George Koch, Iain MacMillan, Anders Karlsson, Minna Gynther and I arrived in the little hamlet of Plangeross. With fresh powder and an area laden with glaciers, my friends and I decidedly wanted the services of a mountain guide to help us find the best skiing. We were lucky enough to have Ernst Eiter, the head of the ski school, meet us early the following morning. Ernst, who had previously won a world ski championship for mountain guides, was a local product, and had skied this valley since when it had been one of the poorest pockets of Austria. In the early 1980s, the ski facilities of the valley consisted of merely four lifts.

The sky was steel blue, the temperature was –23 degrees centigrade at the top, and 20–30 centimeters of fresh powder awaited us. Ernst first took us up the Rifflsee ski area, a small system composed of a cable car, a chair lift, and three T-bars. Everywhere we looked on the Rifflsee, steep ravines and ridges, covered in last night's bounty, were beckoning temptingly.

"Ernst, can we ski there?" "Ernst, what about that gully behind you?" "Hey, Ernst, it's not too dangerous to take that steep off-piste couloir, is it?" Our questions bubbled out.

Ernst was an amiable, easy-going character who seemed to take our exuberance well in stride. "Yes, I suppose." "Sure we can ski that gully, if you like." "The couloir? Well, if we're careful, it should be all right," he answered us in order.

MOST OF THE MORNING, Ernest led us down various unmarked routes through small, well-spaced pines and shrubs. We would have been happy yo-yoing up and down the Rifflsee all day, but Ernst had more ambitious plans.

"Come, I must show you our glacier ski area," he said with a sweep of his hand. "We are very proud of the possibilities there. You know, many of the top ski teams in the world train here during the fall."

With that, Ernst led us to the pride of the Pitztal, an underground funicular railway that bores 3 kilometers and 1100 vertical meters through Austrian rock in a mere 5 minutes. Soon, we were atop the Hinterer Brunnenkogel at 3440 meters. It may not be the top of Europe, but you can see most of the continent from here, or so it seemed. Ernst pointed out a nearby sea of glaciers called the Wildspitze, Austria's second-highest peak at 3771 meters.

"We have a reasonably nice view from here," Ernst chirped modestly. With that, he also directed his finger to indicate various peaks in the

Dolomites of Italy to the South, the Zugspitze in Germany to the North, and various summits in Switzerland to the West.

"What about Everest?" queried George, tongue in cheek.

"Yes, it is to the east, but the Wildspitze blocks the view," retorted Ernst, without missing a beat. "But come, it is still –15 degrees, and you get cold standing still. Enough of this sightseeing…you came here to ski, no?" With that remark, he was off with the three of us in happy pursuit.

All of the pistes on the glacier are within a 700-vertical-meter area encompassing two glacial cirques. Ernst led us a merry chase through spectacular seracs, among deep crevasses and down steep powder faces between cliffs that divide the two cirques. Each turn shot a crescent of powder upward, where it seemed to merely evaporate in the cold, dry air.

WE EVEN DID A FEW RUNS on the pistes—wide boulevards of perfectly groomed powder. There were not many tourists here at the little-known Pitztal Glacier, so we were able to scream down these autobahns without endangering the slower traffic. Before we knew it, the sun was low in the sky and it was time to call it quits.

"Do we take the train back down?" Iain asked our leader.

"Oh, no," replied Ernst, with a touch of hurt in his voice. "There are many nice off-piste tours that lead us down into the valley."

We then began a beautiful 1700-vertical-meter tour that led us over the tongue of one of the glaciers, back to the valley floor.

Before we knew it, we were sitting in a cozy hut with a cold beer and a huge *Brettljause* of Austrian cold cuts in front of us. As we devoured all the food in our path, Ernst made us promise that we would come back sometime soon, so that he could show us some of the other routes from the glacier down to the village. This was not a hard promise to make. We thanked our guide profusely and pointed our car toward yet another village that we had never before heard of. We wondered what kind of surprises Nauders might hold in store.

NAUDERS — POACHING POWDER

Nauders (1400-2750 meters) lies two valleys over from the Pitztal, in the Obere Inntal, an international corner 3 kilometers from the Reschenpass into Italy and 4 kilometers as the crow flies from the Swiss border. Our first surprise was not long in coming. After our perfect sunny day in the Pitztal, we had not gotten far on our way before we drove face-on into the next polar front. By the time we pulled into Nauders, we had to maneuver our car into 20 centimeters of cold powder that had already settled on the parking lot.

We pondered the trail map during an excellent dinner of rabbit stew smothered in mushroom sauce. Our discovery journey was revealing itself to be very enlightening. In fact, the further we got, the more we understood how little we knew.

We now learned from our local map that Nauders is part of the greater Ortler Ski Arena, which includes over 70 lifts and 250 kilometers of pistes spread over twelve villages in Austria and Italy. There are Sulden am Ortler, former racer Gustav Thöni's home, with skiing up to 3150 meters, and Schnals, whose skiing peaks at 3212 meters, not to mention Latsch, Trafoi, Watles, Meran and a half dozen more villages included in the system.

ON OUR AGENDA WAS only Nauders, and that kept us plenty busy for the next two days. In the morning, our car was almost buried, and the mercury showed –15 and holding. It was not the weather we had expected to find in April. When we arrived at the lifts, we saw that the two highest ones, the Tscheyeck (2700 m) and the Panorama Lift (2750 m) were closed. The fact that these two lifts were essential to reaching most of the off-piste skiing in the area made little difference. We rode up into the storm atop the Almlift, where we were virtually alone, and the snow was waist deep right on the piste! When we wanted a bit of variation, we opted for the 80 centimeters of powder next to the Zirmlift or the Geisslochlift.

With literally nobody to compete for fresh tracks, and the piste machines apparently immobilized by lack of interest, we took on their usual duties, and spent the day ski-packing the powder. It was, alas, to no avail. The storm was dumping new snow faster than the few of us could pack it down. By mid-afternoon, the Almlift attendant was shutting off the lift while we skied, for we were indeed his only guests.

At 3:45, we became the victims of a fortunate mistake. The lift operator, who looked to be one of the local valley incest products, gave up his post early, thinking that nobody in his right mind would still be skiing. The result of his miscalculation was that the lift was locked up when we arrived for our final ascent. Hence, we were forced to make our way back to the village through the forest.

With understandable apprehension, we forged off into unmarked territory. The wind swirled around us, and the visibility was close to nil. Our trepidation soon turned to glee, as the woods provided shelter from the storm, and were filled with open glades and great skiing lines.

The following morning, the Tscheyeck area was still closed, and the storm showed no sign of abating. When we found that the wind had also made a mess of things on the upper slopes, we knew exactly where to go—our recently discovered forest. The trees in Nauders grow up to 2300 meters, the highest of any place in the eastern Alps. This gave us 600 vertical meters of tree-skiing in a wide expanse of real estate between the Almlift and the two Lärchenhang lifts.

ON OUR THIRD OR FOURTH RUN, a lift attendant observed us diving into the larches, and began ranting something in German about young trees. He kept punctuating his sentences with "*Verboten! Verboten!*" but we were quite sure that he was not ready to leave the cozy confines of his hut to chase some crazy foreigners into the woods. Besides, we were well prepared with the all-purpose excuse for all foreign indiscretions. Sometimes on the lift we rehearsed our well-oiled phrase, "*Nix verstehe!* No understand!"

We had, however, begun to *verstehe* quite a few things by this last day of our April adventure in a couple of the lesser-known ski areas of Austria. We understood that for each village we had visited, there were ten more waiting to be discovered. We also comprehended that skiing obscure ski villages in low season meant cheap prices, few people and tons of powder for ourselves. Lastly, we understood, intuitively, that this would definitely not be our last April in Austria.

LEFT PAGE
Minna Gynther finds a path between some of the stunning seracs high up in the Pitztal ski area.

THIS PAGE
Anders Karlsson making illegal powder-turns in the trees of Nauders.

THE OLD MEETS THE NEW IN THE ZILLERTAL

Very often in life's sojourn, it is the people one meets, even more than the interesting locations, that add the spice to life's meal. Hermann Taxer is one of those people.

Not so long ago, I found myself sitting in a square room paneled almost entirely with wood. The low ceiling was also pine, with darkened knotholes and a large crossbeam. Almost two centuries of age was worn into the walls and ceiling. In one corner of the room was a wood-burning oven of brown tile, flanked on two sides by a wide bench covered with 8-centimeter-thick cushions. Hermann Taxer had leaned two pillows against the wall, and was sitting cozily with a thick historical novel in one hand and a glass of red wine in the other, as the wood in the oven beside him crackled.

To my left was an intricate nativity scene made up of about 40 small figures and featuring the three kings bringing gifts to the Christ child. Across the room, was a unique Christmas tree no more that 70 centimeters high. It was shaped like a dwarf pine, and was actually created from branches of different sorts of pine trees, holly, and other assorted mountain vegetation, all placed in a vase. Gerda, Hermann's wife, had hung dried orange slices, walnuts, tangerines and tiny star-shaped cookies from the branches and called it her Christmas bouquet. A strong smell of pine incense filled the room.

Gerda had just taken a large canister of fresh milk, left by the neighbors, in off the front porch and placed some on the breakfast table beside the freshly squeezed blood-orange juice, the sliced peasant bread and the bacon and eggs. To my right was a plate full of *Vanille-kipferl*—a crescent-shaped vanilla-flavored cookie which I hadn't tasted since my own mother last baked them for me more than twenty years earlier.

The house is an old peasant house, built in 1814, which Hermann and Gerda began leasing in 1965, and the location is the little Austrian ski village of Gerlos. How I got placed in the midst of this magical setting is not the whole story but certainly the best part of this tale.

It started as a press junket. Yet again, Canadian ski journalist and old friend, George Koch, was with me. George, Jonas Delogne, Martin Söderqvist, Pelle Lindh and I had all been invited for a week of skiing in the Zillertal. We were set up for a few nights in the cozy Hotel Maria Theresia in Mayrhofen and for some days in the four-star Sonnenhof in Zell am Ziller.

Mayrhofen and Zell am Ziller are probably the most famous of the ski villages in the Zillertal. The likes of Hochfügen, Kaltenbach, Finkenberg, Gerlos, Königsleiten, Lanersbach and Vorderlanersbach are probably no more recognizable, even to knowledgeable skiers, than a list of Siberian military outposts. However, they too make up a part of what has become, in the last couple of years, an ever more integrated ski area. By adding new lifts linking the villages, the Zillertal has made vast improvements in the last few years and can now compete very competently with the best lift systems in Austria.

We began our visit in Mayrhofen and rode the new 150er Tux Cable Car up the Wanglspitz. This mountain would make Alaskans proud. It is freeride heaven, but it is for experts only—mandatory transceiver and

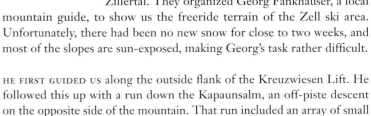

shovel terrain. Pressing our faces up against the windows of the huge cable car, we could see couloir after couloir covering the face of this newly accessible peak. No descent was less than 35 degrees, and most routes included pitches of 40–45 degrees.

On this day, the avalanche danger was virtually nil, and we skied the main couloir, which had been skier-packed. We could enjoy the adrenaline rush that accompanies a steep descent without feeling any uneasiness about the powers of nature that are beyond our control. Nevertheless, the chute was narrow in places, the snow was firm and a lost edge seemed very ill-advised.

ONCE WE SAFELY ARRIVED back at ground zero, I felt I had accomplished the day's hard-core challenge. I was quite happy to cruise the pistes for a while, allowing my eyes to scan the mountains for future off-piste endeavors. Old tracks from the Schafskopf entered the same valley from the other side, telling the story that people had enjoyed some great powder a week or so earlier. A little later, a ride up the Rastkogelbahn brought a huge open bowl into view—a bowl that would make for a fantastic corn snow descent to Lanersbach sometime in the spring.

The days that followed exposed the versatility of the Zillertal. With lifts that go as high as 3250 meters, much of the skiing is of a high alpine nature, with huge, open bowls and valleys. However, there are also many places to seek refuge in a storm, with trails below the tree line where one can dive into hidden powder stashes in the forest.

The final and ultimate ingredient to the Zillertal's versatility is the Hintertux Glacier. Rising like the crown jewel that oversees the entire region, Hintertux offers, arguably, the best glacier skiing in the world. The glacier ski area not only adds a dimension of snow security to the region, it also offers excellent skiing for all ability groups, a rarity among glaciers. On a powder day, the Seegrube Schiroute will have freeriders drooling like Pavlov's dog, and the 1750 meters of vertical are enough to put even Hermann Maier's quadriceps to the test.

We partook of the Zillertal's entire gamut. After our couloir skiing on Mayrhofen's Wanglspitz, we enjoyed some cruising in Königsleiten, found a bit of old powder in the trees in Lanersbach, and skied some steeps in the glacier area.

The tourist office didn't miss a bet when it came to showing their foreign visitors the best of the Zillertal. They organized Georg Fankhauser, a local mountain guide, to show us the freeride terrain of the Zell ski area. Unfortunately, there had been no new snow for close to two weeks, and most of the slopes are sun-exposed, making Georg's task rather difficult.

HE FIRST GUIDED US along the outside flank of the Kreuzwiesen Lift. He followed this up with a run down the Kapaunsalm, an off-piste descent on the opposite side of the mountain. That run included an array of small ridges and gullies, a smorgasbord of rocky outcrops, which Jonas, our jumping specialist, enjoyed, and some widely spaced tree-skiing.

Finally, we capped the day with a short hike along the ridge of the Kreuzjoch, at 2559 meters, the highest peak in the Zell area. This

THIS PAGE
UPPER: Martin finds a stash of powder in the trees of the Eggalm.
MIDDLE LEFT: Pelle Lindh follows Martin up the Kreuzjoch.
MIDDLE RIGHT: Minna Gynther high up on the Hintertuxer Glacier.
LOWER: Martin skiing on the back side of the Hintertuxer Glacier.

RIGHT PAGE
UPPER LEFT: Hermann Taxer relaxing in his living room in Gerlos.
UPPER RIGHT: Our ski boots dry out by the wood-burning stove in Hermann and Gerda's kitchen.
LOWER LEFT: Peasant woman on the slopes of the Zillertal.
LOWER RIGHT: Local children celebrate an Austrian holiday by donning costumes and masks.

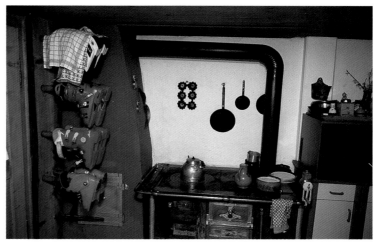

descent, which our guide referred to as the Kreuzjochhütte run, began with a steep, sun drenched slope of "educational snow", a.k.a. breakable crust.

Our wide-bodied skis, an extra amount of toil and sweat, and a few obligatory kick turns helped us survive the difficult snow. Once we had passed the steepest section, however, we were greeted by some long stretches of legitimate powder. We were now in the middle of a large bowl between Zell and Gerlos, and it was easy to imagine what the skiing would be like with fresh snow.

WE HAD NOT YET seen much of Gerlos, and that was on tap for our second-to-last day. We were cruising down from the Isskogel, when Martin stopped short, eyeing a couple of lone tracks snaking down the shaded north flank of the mountain.

"Come on," I said. "Don't be stupid! I saw them too, but we have no idea where they go. They could easily have been made by people with touring skis and skins."

Martin gazed longingly for another moment at the alluring ski tracks, and dejectedly turned his attention back to the piste. We skied on for no more than a couple hundred meters, when a handful of rucksack-clad skiers caught my eye. I stopped to give the group more careful scrutiny. There were six people, all wearing touring skis, and they were standing on the ridge with their skis pointing toward the powder stash we had just been eyeing.

I approached one of the men, and asked in German whether he was familiar with the area. Hermann Taxer sized me up quickly, and answered with an understated, "Quite familiar." He invited us to join them.

Hermann is a 62-year-old Bavarian man with a 25-year-old's body— either that or there is a big red "S" on the chest of his long under- wear. He was clearly the leader, and he swooped into the knee-deep powder with his old-fashioned, narrow touring skis churning out

effortless turns as if he were Jeremy Nobis on a pair of state-of-the-art freeride boards. Okay, his style was more Stein Eriksson than Jeremy Nobis. His knees were glued together. He could have easily set a match- book between his knees at the top of the run and pried it out again at the bottom.

HIS BAVARIAN BUDDIES and the rest of us followed in breathless pursuit. Hermann would always pause long enough to see that everybody was still with, and then, as we huffed and puffed to catch our breath, he would again slither into high gear.

Soon, the open slopes gave way to the forest, but Hermann knew every tree and stump in the woods and continued to glide smoothly amidst what was becoming an ever more difficult obstacle course. Gerda now hung back to bring up the rear, as Hermann was beginning to outpace everybody by an ever increasing margin.

Finally, we emerged from the forest at a cozy hut called the Krummbachrast, where a cool beer and a goulash soup were just what I needed to replace lost sweat and energy. I tried repeatedly to buy Hermann's meal in compensation for his kind and excellent guiding, but he would not hear of it. Somewhere in his rejection of my offer was a message, but I was not sure what it was.

My offer to buy lunch was turned down and met, instead, by a counter- offer. Would we like to join Hermann and Gerda for another day of ski- ing? Would we ever! The next morning, at ten o'clock, we showed up at the Taxer winter home. Soon thereafter, Hermann led us up the ancient Fürstalm Double Chair, followed by the Kirchspitz T-bar.

With all of the tourist bureau hoopla about new, express, six-seat chair lifts, huge cable cars, comfortable gondolas, and inter-linked ski areas, the Fürstalm was definitely an isolated dinosaur which time had forgotten. It is made up of only three lifts, and they are not linked with anything else. Somehow, I could immediately see a parallel between Hermann and this

little, old-fashioned ski hill. Perhaps, they were both dinosaurs amidst the modern-day Super Zillertal.

It did not surprise me, considering Hermann's guiding prowess, that most of the Fürstalm terrain was in the shade, and there were still numerous pockets of untouched powder in plain sight. Hermann abstained from all the visible goodies, and dropped off the back of the Kirchspitz Lift, and we dutifully followed.

Martin yelped gleefully as he swooped down in a series of wide, arcing freeride turns in the still excellent powder. The open upper slope gave way to some lovely, gentle glades. Steep, tree-skiing followed, and finally, we emerged into some meadows. The two-week-old powder was, amazingly, still good, even on the lower slopes, and there were very few old tracks. One does not spend close to 40 seasons in a ski area without learning a few tricks, and Hermann had clearly learned them all.

The descent finished with a steep pitch, covered in natural moguls, that ultimately spit us out onto the cross-country track in the serene midday sun of the Schönachtal. Again I wanted to invite Hermann and Gerda for a lunch, but again he declined my offer. I thought once more about the hidden message between the lines of his refusal to be compensated, but it still evaded me.

"We have no time for lunch," retorted our local Superman. "We got a late start, and I want to show you the 'full' run from the Kreuzjoch. Your guide in Zell showed you a variation back to the Ziller lifts, but I want to take you right from the cross at the peak back down to my house!"

WE WORKED OUR WAY through the lift system, and made a half-hour hike to the peak. As on the day with our *Bergführer*, the entry was steep and the snow was difficult. While we were skiing, in principle, the same side of the same mountain that we descended two days earlier, this was actually a completely different valley, even larger than the previous one. There were no other tracks on the upper mountain. Hermann admitted that this was almost his own private run.

By the end of the run, Hermann was still bouncing like a jackrabbit despite some vicious crust on the lower mountain. I, however, was exhausted and sweating blood. Darkness was quickly falling on the landscape by the time I dragged myself into Hermann and Gerda's rustic home.

Our leader plopped some extra-strong Bavarian beer onto the table, while Gerda placed a host of different sausages and cheeses along with homemade bread in front of us. We were famished and it seemed like we

Jonas Delogne tears down the Hintertuxer Glacier.

ate and drank for hours, as we rehashed the details of the last couple of days with our new friends.

It was the perfect ending to a classic day. Somehow, the table full of cold cuts tasted even better than the great pepper steak I had eaten a few days earlier in Zell. As an après-ski, this totally outclassed the laughter of pretty *Fräuleins*, the gay music and the clinking of glasses of the many after-ski bars in Mayrhofen.

It was my last day in the Zillertal, and my plan had been to drive an hour to my next destination, Saalbach. The Taxers plied me with more German beer and then lamented that I had better not drive to Saalbach after having consumed so much alcohol! They insisted that I spend the night at their home.

Why not? Gerda's food and the traditional après-ski suited my style. In addition, a long evening of good discussion with new friends, leaning against the warmth of the tile oven, also outshone a sauna and a game of Ping-Pong in a four-star hotel.

AT BEDTIME, GERDA STOKED a fire in the oven of the kitchen, and I lay my weary muscles onto the kitchen sofa, under an old Austrian quilt that must have weighed 5 kilos. My head rested on a huge pillow of eider-

down. The ponderous weight of the quilt gave me a sense of security that reminded me of my childhood, and I lay back and once again began to ponder the hidden message in Hermann's repeated rejection of compensation.

At first, the meaning of it all was still hazy, but as I listened to the crackling fire, lucidity began to come. "We are mountain men," began the message. "We are true skiers, in the traditional sense of the word. We tour, we ski the backcountry, we know and respect the mountains and we take responsibility for ourselves. We share a love of skiing and mountains, and hence, we share our knowledge and our most treasured secret descents with kindred spirits. This sharing of what we both love comes naturally and requires no compensation."

I slipped into a deep sleep with that message in my mind. The next morning, over the delicious bacon and eggs, I made Hermann and Gerda a new proposal.

"I have spent many seasons in Saalbach," I told them. "I know a few interesting hideaways in the Glemmtal that rarely get skied, where the virgin powder waits for weeks on end to get violated. Why don't you visit me there and let me show you around?"

My offer was accepted without hesitation.

Chapter 4. FRANCE

Many people consider France to be the land with the best skiing in the world. Whether this is true or not, it is certainly among the top countries to visit for snowsports. With over 300 ski resorts, a skier could certainly spend a few winter seasons in France skiing new runs every day, and he would still need the rest of the decade to explore all the off-piste territory.

That being the case, France becomes an extremely difficult country from which to choose a mere handful of ski areas representative of what this nation has to offer to a skier. Over a score of France's ski areas are in the Pyrénées, including major resorts like Les Angles, Peyragudes, and Piau Engaly, all of which have at least 750 vertical meters of skiing. Nevertheless, France's top *stations de ski* are clearly in the Alps.

France is the home of the world's largest lift-accessed vertical drop and longest run—the Vallée Blanche in Chamonix. In addition to that, Les Trois Vallées, Paradiski (made up of La Plagne and Les Arcs) and the Portes du Soleil, which lies in both France and Switzerland, are the three largest lift-linked ski regions in the world.

France has thrice hosted the Winter Olympic Games. The first-ever Winter Games were held in Chamonix in 1924, while the 1968 Games took place in Grenoble and the 1992 Olympics were centered in Albertville.

Chamonix, situated in the Haute-Savoie region, is to France what St. Anton is to Austria. It is one of the world's foremost mountaineering centers and the home of Mont Blanc, the highest mountain in the Alps. Its status is legendary, and despite the thousands of ski resorts which have been conceived and created since

Chamonix's days as a pioneer ski village, it still ranks as one of the most visited, most beautiful and most interesting ski areas in the world.

Also in the Haute-Savoie is part of the Portes du Soleil, made up of such villages as Avoriaz, Morzine and Les Gets, offering 650 kilometers of pistes in conjunction with a number of Swiss villages.

Moving south from the Haute-Savoie, one comes to the Savoie region and Albertville, a town used as a base for the Winter Olympics, whose skiing events took place in various ski resorts in the neighborhood. Near Albertville are some of the superlatives of French skiing, including Tignes–Val d'Isère, Les Trois Vallées, La Plagne and Les Arcs.

Southeast of Albertville lies Grenoble, a major town situated in the midst of the Dauphiné-Isère region. Like Albertville, Grenoble is not itself a ski resort, but is situated in the midst of many fine ski villages. Among the ski areas near Grenoble is Alpe d'Huez, another resort dating back

to the early days of skiing. It boasts the longest black run in the world, a 16-kilometer descent. Also close to Grenoble is Les Deux Alpes, a top resort whose pistes go up to 3568 meters, making it one of the Alps' highest ski areas.

Travelling even further south, one comes to the Hautes-Alpes featuring Briançon, Serre Chevalier and La Grave, the legendary off-piste ski area on the back of Les Deux Alpes.

Finally, as one moves towards the Mediterranean, one arrives in the Alpes du Sud, made up of such resorts as Isola 2000, Vars and Pra Loup.

The French Alps are generally more rugged than their Austrian counterparts, and for the most part, the skiing is higher. Virtually all the top ski areas have lifts that surpass 3000 meters. These high resorts translate into more terrain above the tree line and more open slopes. This can be both good and bad. The open slopes of the high French Alps make for excellent off-piste possibilities but also are more avalanche-prone and difficult to make use of in poor weather.

The northern ski resorts in France are covered on their lower slopes with the same kind of pine and spruce forests that are prevalent in the Austrian Alps, but as one travels further south in France, the woods consist more and more of larch trees, which drop their needles in winter. The larches allow better visibility and make for better tree-skiing than pine forests.

Further down the mountain, the ski towns of the French Alps often leave something to be desired in comparison with the villages in the rest of the Alps. Many so-called *stations de ski* were developed from scratch in the '50s and '60s, whereas the ski resorts in Switzerland, Austria and Italy have invariably sprung up around existing farming villages.

To their credit, the French *stations* were often built with ski-in and ski-out access between the apartments and the lifts, but they were also often created without the forethought required to allow these resorts to fit aesthetically into their surroundings. Some of the French resorts, therefore, lack the charm and coziness inherent in ski villages in the other Alpine countries.

These modern-looking cement and steel ski-ghettos, however, are not the case everywhere. Quite a number of French resorts like Chamonix, La Grave and Briançon are charming medieval towns that are every bit as picturesque as their counterparts to the east.

Max Boholm carving corn snow in Meribel.

Chamonix's dramatic nature, featuring jagged rocks and glacial ice, has made this legendary resort very popular among ski photographers. In this photo, the Grands Montets and the Mer de Glace provide a spectacular background as Magnus Loo jumps from a cliff on the opposite side of the valley. Photo by Felix St. Clair-Renard.

"THE TIMES THEY ARE A'CHANGIN'"

In 1970, I was studying German language and history at Schiller College in Heidelberg, Germany. During a spring break, four other students and I packed my Volkswagen Passat to the gills with gear and pointed it toward France. We stayed in youth hostels and the like, dined on *baguettes* and beer, and lived as cheaply as we could. A few days after our departure, I made my first ski descent in the French Alps—Chamonix's Vallée Blanche.

Since then, I have visited different parts of the French Alps almost every winter, and during a recent spring, once again, I drove around the French Alps with three companions. This time, I drove a Jeep Cherokee, but it was packed just as full as on that very first trip. The roof rack carried five pairs of skis and a ski box full of other gear. The car's interior was fitted like a jigsaw puzzle with six backpacks, three hockey bags, a suitcase, my guitar, and a half-dozen other small bags with photography equipment and other odds and ends.

Part of the time, we still traveled in the same style as so many years earlier. One morning, we stopped in a wonderful *boulangerie* in Bourg St. Maurice, bought a *baguette* and some pastries and ate breakfast in the town square. Two nights were spent in a 9-square-meter room in a Formula 1 hotel (a chain of cheap and basic hotels) in Albertville. It was actually a room for three, but we sneaked Max in and he shared a *single* upper bunk bed with Carl. The bill was €6 per person per night.

There is something about the ski bum life style that gives me a good feeling. Maybe it keeps me feeling young, or perhaps it gives me the sense of security that some things never change. There is something else that never changes—nature. A revisit to the Mer du Glace on the

Vallée Blanche proved it to be every bit as spectacular as it had been in my youth. Even after having seen so many interesting sights the world over during the intervening years, the power and majesty of Chamonix's glaciers overwhelmed me still.

NOT EVERYTHING STAYS THE SAME, however, and the ingredient that has transformed the most during the many years of my visits to the French Alps is the skiing itself. First of all, skiing has grown immensely in popularity during that span of time. It has metamorphosed from a pastime into a huge industry. The skis have changed many times, as has the focus of the sport. The trend has gone from long skis to compact, mid-length and hot dog skis, back to long skis and on to carving and freeride skis.

Thirty-five years ago, nothing on the mountains was groomed. After a snowfall, one skied the powder, which after some time became skier-groomed. After some days, moguls developed. They grew and grew until the next snowfall flattened them out again. Nowadays, even the toughest ski areas of the French Alps groom large sections of the mountain to perfection every night. In addition, summers are used to manicure the ski slopes. Rocks and other obstacles are removed to create a smoother surface. In Tignes, earth has been added to some slopes to lessen their grade and grass has been planted during the summer.

Snowmaking equipment has been added to lower slopes all over France as well. This country that has always had the most laissez faire attitude towards all aspects of skiing has become increasingly proactive. The snow cannons allow for a longer season during which skiers can ski all the way to the valley, and they also help create easier descents without the

hazards of skiers having to slalom between rocks and grass on the lower slopes in spring.

All these changes have made piste skiing much easier, and the ever increasing number of skiers that frequent the slopes is the result. Off-piste skiing has also become much easier in recent years with the advent of the snowboard and ever wider freeride skis. As a result, many of the gigantic ski resorts of the French Alps, which used to provide many days of powder skiing after a snowfall, are getting skied out in a day or sometimes even half a day.

This trend toward the powder being consumed and devoured ever more quickly exists in all the major ski countries these days, but nowhere is it more prevalent than in France. It is also somewhat surprising in France because of the large size of many of the resorts, but even their huge acreage does not help the most famous ski resorts preserve their new snow for more than a few hours.

There is one fact, however, that allows France to remain among the great locations to find powder snow. With such a plethora of ski resorts, each time a Sainte Foy or a La Grave gets discovered by too many powder hounds, there seems to be another small, unknown village waiting in the wings to provide for the needs of a new generation of ski bums.

CHAMONIX — THE GRAVEYARD TELLS THE STORY

Chamonix is the Manhattan of the ski world in more ways than one. Its jagged peaks and towers of granite create a skyline similar to the man-made skyscrapers of the Big Apple. Like the hub of New York, Chamonix has its share of movers and shakers, but it is often hard to sort out who they are amidst the plethora of pretenders and wannabes. They are also both melting pots of many nationalities. In the case of Chamonix, the stew in the pot includes extreme skiers, ski bums, sightseers, mountain climbers, photographers and charter tourists from all over the world. Oh, yeah, there is one more analogy with Manhattan—only the strong survive!

Chamonix is a place where ski reputations are made and legends are created but also where the mountains often stand taller than the men who challenge their sanctity. One small mistake is all that stands between the immortality of ski fame and the stark mortality that one finds at the bottom of an avalanche or a crevasse.

Gunslingers come here from all around the globe to face off with some of the most hair-raising ski terrain on Earth. It often comes to pass that Mont Blanc, the Grands Montets or one of the other giants that tower over this famed mountain village turns out to be the last one standing after a shoot-out. Ashes to ashes, dust to dust, and all that jazz.

Chamonix is *The Good, the Bad, and the Ugly* and *Beauty and the Beast* rolled into one. While the killer peaks around the town can act like untamed beasts, the village with its surroundings is possibly the most beautiful in the world. It is full of Old World charm including a car-free center, cobblestone streets, cozy bars and bistros and lovely old Victorian hotels and houses. All around the town is a panorama of steep cliffs and massive seas of glacial seracs, all lorded over by the dome of the Alps, Mont Blanc (4808 m), as well as the spectacular Aiguille du Midi and the Grands Montets. These features give Chamonix the wild beauty that has attracted skiers and climbers the world over for many generations.

91

While its stupendous nature is Chamonix's greatest asset, it has become its downfall to some degree as well. The stunning scenery here has made Chamonix the world's largest ski resort, with over 60,000 visitors on an average day in the high season. That is most definitely a drawback. Many parts of the lift system are inadequate to take care of this number of people. Granted, only half of the visitors are actual skiers. Nevertheless, peak periods like Easter week can be a nightmare of lift lines, and many of the lower sections of the mountains must be descended by aerial tram, creating a long queue to get home at the end of the ski day.

The lift queues are not the only negative aspect of Chamonix's beauty and fame. All season long over 500 ski bums do battle for the privilege of first tracks on some of the favorite off-piste routes. The morning after a heavy snowfall, the unloading area of the Grands Montets resembles something between a Friday evening rush hour on the Hollywood Freeway and a cattle stampede on the Texas prairie. Hence, the resort that built its reputation on fantastic off-piste possibilities is nowadays one of the least likely locations to make a set of first tracks. Even randonnée routes that require a few hours' hike before the first turn is made must be done on the first morning after a snowstorm to ensure a virgin run.

An additional drawback is the spread-out nature of the lift system. Only the Aiguille du Midi and the Brévent ski areas begin directly from the town, while the Les Houches, Le Tour, La Flégère and Grands Montets lifts must be accessed by bus.

The Grands Montets, the most popular mountain in Chamonix, is in Argentière, 12 kilometers from town. Directly after a snowfall, there are stupendous off-piste tours among the seracs of the glacier off the back side, tree-skiing in powder down to the village of Le Lavancher, and classic off-piste tours such as Pas de Chèvre and Rectiligne. Descents from the top are about 2000 vertical meters long, so begin your ski conditioning a few months before visiting, if you don't want to risk death due to lactic acid overdose!

TWO DAYS AFTER A SNOWFALL, mogul lovers can ski bumps to their heart's content all over the front face in Argentière. That face is about the size of Texas, so despite the large number of visitors, the mogul fields are not at all crowded.

The pistes can be a different story. The Grands Montets does not have many pistes, and despite Chamonix's tough reputation, most of the visitors are cruisers who can tend to create a bit of a traffic jam on some of the more popular runs.

One solution to this is to try the pistes of La Flégère or Brévent, which are much less frequented than those of the Grands Montets. These mountains face south, and are particularly to be recommended on sunny mornings during March and April. The corn snow sparkles and beckons, and one can shift into fifth gear and fly, for the crowds are somewhere else. By 11:30, the snow is too soft and it is time to move on.

Then there is the classic run from the Aiguille du Midi (3842 m) over the Mer de Glace, a record-setting 22-kilometer descent. It takes skiers an amazing 2800 vertical meters back to Chamonix and passes over and through an icy, crevasse-filled landscape that cannot be equaled in beauty anywhere in Europe. Best of all, there are routes which are not too difficult, so most skiers have the opportunity to experience the so-called Vallée Blanche with the aid of a guide.

Novice skiers in Chamonix will be most at home either at Le Tour or Les Houches, at opposite ends of the valley. Both these areas provide mellow skiing with almost the same stunning views as the other mountains.

Chamonix's skiing, at the right moment, can be as good as it gets, but you must be lucky. The high elevation of the mountains can provide excellent powder on the best of days, but the extreme nature of the terrain puts the upper part of the Grands Montets and the Mer de Glace very much at the mercy of the elements. They can be closed for long periods due to high winds, snowstorms or avalanche danger.

Chamonix is more of a happening than a ski resort. It is where skiers come to see and be seen. Many skiers wander around town and sit on the sunny verandahs decked out in helmets, harnesses hung heavy with carabiners and mountaineering rucksacks with ropes and ice axes attached. A handful of these people can actually ski as well, but if you wait long enough for one of them to leave his deck chair and beer, you might well see him stem-turn his way down the slope.

Some skiers come to watch and observe the most outrageous and extreme the Alps have to offer, while others come to be seen and stake their claim on Alpine history. Some just come to mingle and rub shoulders with the rope and ice ax crowd.

Whatever reason one has for coming to Chamonix, however, all skiers should visit this Alpine Mecca at least once. They will not leave without having formed a strong opinion. Most people love or hate Chamonix, and some people actually adore and despise her at the same time, but few are ambivalent.

THIS HISTORIC SKI TOWN is defined to a large degree by its residents and visitors. One of the institutions of the valley is Swedish-born Felix St. Clair-Renard, one of the most prodigious ski photographers in the world, who has been a winter resident of Argentière since 1980. He is as original and unique as Chamonix, so in some way, they are very well suited to each other. As Chamonix is one of the oldest ski resorts in the world, Felix, now past 60, is also a veteran who is still going strong.

After wandering the Alps with his camera for

» **The couloirs, cliffs, and glaciers are indiscriminate about whose lives they snuff out...**«

about five seasons, Felix found that the extreme nature around Chamonix provided the most interesting backdrops for his photos. In addition, it was in Chamonix that Felix could pick and choose models from among the best skiers in the world.

During a recent visit to Chamonix, I pulled up to Felix's chalet in Argentière, situated conveniently about 100 meters from the Grands Montets lift station. It was ten in the morning on a cloudy day, and Felix was dressed in his ski clothes, ready for action in case the sun would break through. We sat over tea and my host spoke of his longtime second home. Even a Chamonix-lover like Felix was not completely positive.

"I must admit," said Felix, "that it becomes more and more difficult to get the right conditions for perfect photos in Chamonix today." A wistful look filled his eyes. "In the old days, we could lay down fresh tracks in Le Lavancher for a week after a snowfall. Now, the fresh snow is absolutely all gone in a few hours.

"But I still have a few secret places that I am surprised that none of the many new photographers seem to have found yet," my host quickly added with a twinkle in his eye.

Felix went outside briefly to check the weather and returned with two beers and the comment, "It might be a long breakfast—it has started raining."

Under the eaves of his house is a blue sign with "Felix" inscribed in white lettering. Also hanging on the outer wall is a triangular white sign with a red border that has the single word "Avalanche" written on it. The father of ski photography takes both of these words very seriously. If the former is to survive, he must remain forever vigilant for the latter.

Before I ever skied a turn with Felix, he took me on a short walk through the Argentière cemetery. Glancing at the tombstones, I became immediately aware of the fact that many of the people resting there did not live out a full life. I am unsure of how many of them died as a result

of the many occupational hazards of working in Chamonix. These dangers include crevasses and cliffs in addition to avalanches.

Felix pointed to a grave and asked if I had known J.F. Causse. I had not.

"He was a photographer who didn't heed the advice of his guide. He died along with two models in an avalanche back in the '80s," explained Felix.

In a different aisle was the headstone of a family grave—mother, father and a small child.

"He was an excellent *pisteur*," explained Felix, "and a very nice man. A huge avalanche took out his house in 1999. There is another graveyard in Chamonix, of course, and it is much bigger than this one," he added somberly.

THE COULOIRS, CLIFFS AND GLACIERS on and around the Mont Blanc massif are indiscriminate about whose lives they snuff out, sending old friends to rest alongside complete strangers. Canadian extreme skier Trevor Petersen, who loved Chamonix, ended his life here under an avalanche. French extreme snowboarder Bruno Gouvy died at the bottom of a crevasse, and fellow boarder Alain Moroni pressed his luck a little too far on a "you fall, you die" descent in Chamonix some years back. The list of victims is long but that only adds to the mystique of the world's most famous mountaineering town.

It was a sober saunter through the memorials to the deceased, and I realized that Felix had not survived the hazards here by being careless. This became clear again on the following day, when I joined the master on a short photo session with his friend and model, Jocko Wikström. As my host guided us over the glacier on the back side of the Grands Montets, he pointed to a group of skiers carving up the powder far below a huge hanging glacier.

"One should never ski there," pointed out the old pro. "A few times every season, a huge block of ice breaks off that glacier and crushes everything in its path."

As Felix explained to Jocko where he should turn for the camera, he painstakingly made sure that his model was aware of whatever potential dangers might be lurking. After "working" for an hour or so, we skied back down to Felix's house for lunch. I couldn't keep up. Maybe he was merely conserving his old knees by minimizing his turns, but Felix was doing a pretty good Franz Klammer imitation as he downhilled the lower section of the Grands Montets.

WHEN I FINALLY CAUGHT UP, the explanation was simple. "I don't usually ski down to the bottom at this time of day when that piste is empty, and it is so nice to do some power cruising when the slope is well-manicured.

"One generally finishes the day on that piste between four and five o'clock and one takes one's life into one's hands. Almost every skier on the Grands Montets empties out onto that one trail. When I ski with my children there, I have them ski in front of me, and I keep a very short distance behind them, holding my ski poles far out at an angle to try and ward off the many out-of-control skiers."

THIS PAGE
LOWER LEFT: A run down the famous Vallée Blanche begins with an obligatory walk down this ridge from the cable car.
LOWER RIGHT: The crevasses and seracs of Chamonix's glaciers fascinate the many tourists who visit here. Here, Charlotte Schager takes in the scenery.
RIGHT PAGE
The Grands Montets Cable Car rises high above the piste.

Nobody was in a hurry to rush back onto the slopes after lunch. Shirts got stripped off on Felix's sun-drenched porch, so I decided to cruise around the Le Tour region for a few hours. The atmosphere was relaxed. Wide, intermediate slopes above tree line fill the front side of the mountain. The shady back side begins with open slopes followed by a handful of pretty trails that wind through the forest. I could see at a glance that on a powder day with low visibility, this could well be the right place to be.

Après-ski was another happening. I had arranged to meet Felix at one of the local bars, where another ski legend and long time Chamonix resident was rocking and rolling. Gary Bigham had a new band, the Crevasse Holes.

"No," said Gary with his American country singer accent, "we are called 'Gary Bigham and the Crev-Assholes'! *They* are the Crev-Assholes," he added, pointing to his drummer and bass player with a smirk.

This was the umpteenth band that Gary has been involved with as well as doing many solo gigs throughout his long stay in Chamonix, but that is hardly his only claim to fame. Gary is an idiosyncratic nonconformist who first arrived here in the 1970s as an aerial ski specialist in the days when hot-dog skiing ruled the slopes. Pictures of Gary appeared in numerous publications, but after a while, he switched to the other side of the lens, taking still photos and making films. Throughout the years he has entertained various generations of Chamonix visitors with any one of his many talents, always accompanied by his quick wit and his "Fear and Loathing in Las Vegas" type of humor.

Felix and I, and a bar full of ski bums swilled back pitchers of beer, as Gary and the Crevasse Holes wailed through covers of Johnny Cash, Elvis, Patsy Cline and Simon and Garfunkel, interwoven with a mix of newer music to keep the younger generation happy as well.

IT WAS NOT LONG BEFORE another American, extreme skier and big-wall climber Craig Calonica, sat down at our table. Fresh back from skiing in the Himalayas, Craig has also called Chamonix home for quite a few years. Craig has numerous visits to Mt. Everest, where he also has skied, on his list of achievements, and he now runs the first-ever heliski operation in Nepal. Then Arnaud Adam, a former winner of the World Extreme competition in Valdez, came by to greet everybody.

The "rock stars" of the ski world from virtually every decade and generation can be found in Chamonix. I wandered back into the center of town to rendezvous with one of the first men to put Chamonix on the map as the extreme-skiing capital—Sylvain Saudan. In 1967, Sylvain made a first descent of the Couloir Spencer, and the following year, he added two more of Chamonix's climbing routes, the Whymper Couloir

THIS PAGE
UPPER: The majestic and mythical Aiguille du Midi.
LOWER LEFT: The sun's last rays light up the sheer walls of Le Grand Drus.
MIDDLE RIGHT: Some of the massive spires that surround Chamonix provide a postcard background for the local train station.
LOWER RIGHT: Anyone for a picnic?

RIGHT PAGE
LEFT: Papi Tuomala glides through La Grave powder in the shadow of La Meije.
RIGHT: One can ski off-piste from La Grave to the village of St. Christoph.

and the Gervasutti Couloir, to his list of ski conquests. The latter descent has an average gradient of about 60 degrees, enough to put his name into the Guinness Book of Records for the steepest run of all time.

The father of *ski extrème*, now past 70, was still looking good. His shock of longish hair was now graying but just as thick as ever, his boyish smile was intact, and his eyes still twinkled as he spoke. Sylvain reiterated some of Felix's sentiments as he discussed his long time home.

"I am starting up my heliskiing operation in the Himalayas again," he told me with enthusiasm. "I must go there to get the kind of skiing we used to have here in Chamonix in the '60s and '70s. Look at a route like Pas de Chèvre nowadays. That was a great off-piste descent some years ago. Now it is a piste! It has moguls!"

And so it is with progress! What once was the exclusive playground of the world's best skiers has become another victim of mass tourism. And yet, like the twinkle in Sylvain's eyes, Chamonix still has a beauty, a charm and an aura that are hard to resist.

Felix may complain that it is now more difficult to get good photos than before and Craig Colonica and Sylvain may guide clients to the distant Himalayas, but they all seem to come back. Ultimately, this, too, is part of the irresistible charm of Chamonix, for after all, what is more important to a town than its inhabitants? Walk around "Cham" long enough and you will cross paths with a whole skiers' hall of fame. If you can't meet them live and in person, you can always take a short walk through the cemetery.

LA GRAVE — MACHO MOUNTAIN

Some ski bums who got fed up with the ever increasing numbers of skiers tracking out the Chamonix powder began migrating some years ago to the unique village of La Grave. One of them was Pelle Lang, a Swede, who spent a number of seasons in Chamonix as a top model for photographer Mats Lindgren. He sought whiter pastures in La Grave and opened Skier's Lodge.

I first read about his project in a small ad on page 181 of Powder Magazine. It read: "Looking for UNTOUCHED snow on UNCROWDED slopes??? UNEQUALED 7054 ft. of vertical in UNSPOILED, UNCOMMERCIALIZED alpine village. UNWIND overlooking UNRIVALED scenery at UNBEATABLE prices. SKIER'S LODGE, LA GRAVE, FRANCE."

The tiny ad amused and interested me, so I decided to check out this little off-piste retreat.

The tiny 12th century village of La Grave, the spectacular mountain, La Meije and the skiing on the Dome de la Lauze make up one of the most unusual ski resorts in the world. Situated part way between Grenoble and Briançon, La Grave offers 2150 vertical meters of relentless, uncompromising, high alpine skiing. Every hazard known to skiers is here, blatantly staring you in the face.

La Grave's alluring fresh powder is like the forbidden treasure in an

Indiana Jones film, but the treasure is surrounded by perilous seracs, crevasses, cliffs, precipices, and steep, avalanche-prone couloirs. Concealed logs, rocks and tree stumps lurk under the snow of nearly every powder turn. In the small, humorous book about "real men" that was popular some years ago, it said, "Real men don't ski; they go avalanche surfing." The toughest of the "real men" probably do their avalanche surfing in La Grave. This is a macho mountain.

To ski the Dome de la Lauze in deep powder conditions not only requires the bravado and daring inherent in "real men", but a true mountaineer's knowledge of snow, mountains and avalanche science. La Grave is not really a ski resort. It is, rather, an Alpine experience direct out of the 1930s. In an age when skiers are generally coddled and protected from their own ineptitude by a host of paternalistic lift companies, La Grave maintains a laissez faire philosophy with regard to mountain safety that is a throwback to a bygone era of skiing.

The fact is that for the final 1750 vertical meters of skiing, La Grave has no pistes whatsoever. There are no ropes or signs to warn skiers of cliffs, crevasses and other veiled dangers, and avalanche control consists of not much more than one large sign that informs the skier each morning of the level of risk on that day.

France formerly used a scale of one to eight to describe the degree of

avalanche danger. Condition one is about as nefarious as a hard-packed bunny slope, while condition eight translates to, "Go play golf, because today you don't want to be anywhere near this mountain."

I arrived in La Grave on Easter Sunday. It was mid-April and the avalanche danger was level six. This usually indicates that a lot of powder has come, and you want to be skiing—but you also want to be sure of what you are doing. I was very happy, under the circumstances, to be skiing with Pelle. We were joined by Chip and Casey, two more ski bum refugees from Chamonix.

"La Grave kinda resembles the way Chamonix must have been in around 1950—very laid back. You know what I mean?" said Casey.

I gazed around the mostly empty parking lot at about a dozen cars and nodded. "Yeah, I know what you mean."

It had snowed all day Saturday and was still coming down in buckets as we walked up the steps of the valley lift station. We stepped into one of a group of five interconnected six-person cabins, an odd contraption that is the backbone of La Grave's lift system. The cabins climbed slowly from the village (1450 m) to the Col des Ruillans (3290 m), making stops at two intermediary stations along the way. From the Col de Ruillans, there are two T-bars, the longer of which takes a skier to the Dome de la Lauze (3564 m).

THE UPPER MOUNTAIN offers intermediate skiing on the glacier and has La Grave's only piste, whereas from the Col des Ruillans downward, one is in the domain of mountaineers and mountain goats. On this day the lift was, quite understandably, open only to the second tower, at 2400 meters.

As we emerged from our cabin, I was surprised and happy to see that we were just above the tree line. While much of the Alps have no trees above 1800 meters, here, the indigenous larch trees provide an extra 500 vertical meters of visibility and wind protection, a very positive factor on a snowy day.

We spent the next few hours yo-yoing up and down the 600 vertical meters between the first and second towers, savoring about 70 centimeters of French soufflé, Mother Nature's Easter-egg surprise. We saw other tracks hither and yon among the larches, but rarely crossed paths with another human being.

On about our fourth run, a lone skier emerged from the woods and climbed into the cabin in front of us. He was an odd sight. Dressed in an old blue and gray down parka with a fur-lined hood, he mimicked the cawing of a crow as he pumped through the larches. He carried a rather large backpack and a snorkel protruded from his mouth. He looked like an Eskimo on a diving expedition.

"Kind of odd to be out skiing alone on a day like this," I commented to nobody in particular.

"Oh, he's all right," said Casey. "That's Vermont Bill. He's one of the 'Crud Brothers'," he continued, as if that were an explanation.

"Well, he certainly didn't learn to ski like that on the boilerplate in Vermont," I said. "Why are they called the 'Crud Brothers', Casey?"

"I guess 'cuz they like to ski anyplace where it's real gnarly. He's been a ski bum in Chamonix, Taos and a bunch of other places, and this seems to be his new home."

THIS PAGE
La Grave's legendary off-piste terrain is accessed almost entirely from this unusual lift.

RIGHT PAGE
Glacial ice high up in La Grave's ski area provides a dramatic background for this lone skier.

When four happy but tired skiers finally returned to town, I inquired at the valley station how many skiers had been on the mountain that day.

"About 100," I was told.

How can a ski area that draws only 100 skiers on Easter Sunday be financially viable? The answer is that it cannot. The rugged nature of the mountain determines that during bad weather, La Grave will rarely attract the 300 skiers necessary to break even for the day. On such days, most people prefer to drive 30 minutes to ski in nearby Serre Chevalier or Les Deux Alpes on the back side of the resort.

Not only are the weather and the rugged nature of the mountain a hindrance to the winter profitability of La Grave, but the overriding philosophy of the locals plays a large part as well. Conservative, environmentalist, and extremely concerned with preserving the small-town charm of the village and the austere solitude of the skiing experience, the villagers are not inclined to make the kind of changes necessary to attract mass tourism.

Many of the local people have, of course, a financial stake in tourism, and yet they are unwilling to forsake their values and transform their mountain Shangri-la into a big-time ski circus for the mere reward of a few more Euros in the till. From this philosophy evolves the laissez faire policies of the lift system, which assure that La Grave will remain a haven for purists and recluses.

My first day in La Grave was capped at the Skier's Lodge by a very nice four-course dinner that I devoured with a fervor approaching gluttony. A cozy guitar session by the fireplace made a perfect finish to our day. I stepped out onto the verandah for a breath of fresh air, and the surprising view of a few million stars told me that I should go to bed, for tomorrow would be a day I wouldn't want to miss.

We began skiing on Easter Monday in the open terrain east of the cable car, often struggling to make turns in snow that was almost too deep to ski. We were surrounded by a world of blue ice, as the five spectacular glaciers of La Meije created a dazzling backdrop to every turn. By the third descent, we were ready for something a little more daring. Somebody led us over to the Couloir de la Banane: 35-40 degrees of white, nestled between jagged rocks on one side and a sheer cliff on its other flank. I would not want to be the one who tested la Banane for avalanches on the first day after a heavy snowfall, but one lone track preceded us. I thought to myself that it had been nice of Vermont Bill to be our guinea pig.

THERE WAS ENOUGH POWDER LEFT in the forest to keep us busy all afternoon. We were a rather tired but very satisfied group of skiers as we sat with our Kronenbourgs on the sun-drenched verandah of the Hotel Castillan, watching the shadows gradually creep down the face of La Meije.

Casey looked at me with concern. "How much do you usually get paid for an article, Jimmy?"

"It's different. Why?"

"Oh, I was just wondering how much I'd have to pay you to trash the article. It doesn't matter. I just want you to realize how lucky you've been to hit La Grave with these conditions. I mean, during the season, we get tons of days with brutal wind crust. Just make sure you put that in your article."

"Okay, Casey, I promise!"

* * * * * * * *

That first visit to La Grave took place in 1991. What Casey had told me was true, of course. La Grave has days when the skiing is as good as it gets, but the lack of pistes is also a handicap when the conditions are wrong.

It really didn't make any difference what I wrote about La Grave, however. The word eventually got out. In the ensuing years, it has become a kind of cultist powder Mecca.

Today, La Grave is not quite what it was in the early '90s, but it is still rather laid back. The nightlife consists of swapping lies with other ski bums over a couple of beers or extra hours of sleep, which most people need after a full day on the mountain. Pelle Lang has moved his hotel from one old building to a different old house, has become a qualified mountain guide, and knows even more terrain than he did when we met. A mid-week, bad weather day might now see a full 25 skiers on La Meije instead of three or four, and on a powder day, one can still hear the lone "Caw, caw!" of Vermont Bill in the larch forests.

THIS PAGE: Sundials on the walls of houses are common around Serre Chevalier.
RIGHT PAGE: Serre Chevalier ski bum Kåre Banke leaps from a cornice above Briançon.

SERRE CHEVALIER — THE "BORDER-PASS GAME"

Whether a skier is in search of powder or sunshine, he can increase the odds of finding his favorite conditions by carefully choosing a ski location that is close to a border between two regional climate zones. These climate zones often change precisely at the top of some of the major mountain passes in the Alps, which often coincide quite closely with the borders between the Alpine countries.

The northern and southern sides of the Alps frequently have drastically different weather conditions from one another, but one can find this phenomenon among the resorts on opposite sides of east–west passes as well. By choosing a ski destination close to the dividing line, one has the possibility to drive a short distance over a pass in search of either snow or sunshine. I have given the name "border-pass game" to the strategies of choosing and using such resorts to one's best advantage.

On the French–Italian border, not far from La Grave, is a ski area that lends itself perfectly to the "border-pass game". It is a group of thirteen hamlets known most commonly as Serre Chevalier. There are two routes to get there. One can come from Grenoble, winding one's way past Alpe d'Huez, Les Deux Alpes and La Grave. Then, one drives over the Col du Lautaret and enters from the French side at Monetier Les Bains, on the western end of what the locals call Le Grand Serre Che. Alternatively, one can approach the resort from Italy, crossing the frontier at the border ski village of Montgenèvre, situated atop the pass of the same name. From there, one descends the serpentine road to Briançon, the easternmost outpost of the Serre Chevalier lift system.

ONE OF THE FIRST THINGS one might notice upon entering Briançon is a sign boasting an average of 300 sunny days a year. I did not think so much about that sign upon my arrival in the hamlet of Chantemerle, writing it off as French bragging or exaggerated marketing. Two weeks later, however, after one partly cloudy day, and 13 days of pure sunshine, the grain of salt was removed from my mind and I had gained a new respect for that initial welcome sign. I also understood why most of the 250 kilometers of pistes faced north.

If one has traveled in both directions from Serre Chevalier, over the Lautaret and the Montgenèvre Passes, one begins to understand that Le Grand Serre Che is situated in a microclimate zone, protected by the passes on either side. To some people in France, this region is known as the "blue hole". When the weather comes from the south, Serre Chevalier gets coated in white, and her neighbors on both flanks often get left out. When a storm comes from the east, however, it is the ski areas of the Via Lattea (Milky Way) in nearby Italy that get dumped on, while La Grave is the beneficiary of western snowstorms.

The local microclimates leave a skier situated in Serre Chevalier with a lot of options, as we were soon to find out. I was on a family holiday on this trip, joined by my son Erik, my sister Christy, her husband Paul and their son Ryan. It was only natural that we began our stay by exploring the possibilities that Le Grand Serre Che had to offer before moving further afield.

Upon our arrival, there was still some powder left from a snowstorm a few days earlier. The mountains here are covered with larch trees, spaced perfectly for an adventurous skier. Above the tree line, Serre Chevalier is full of large bowls, open slopes and a good choice of couloirs, many of which require just a long enough hike to leave some untouched lines a couple of days after a snowfall.

Some of the steepest and best runs for off-piste powder skiing are in the western part of the system near Le Grand Serre Che's highest point, the top of the Télésiège de l'Yret (2830 m). From there, we dropped into La Montagnolle, a steep off-piste bowl. Many powder-turns later, we emerged into the Tabuc Valley, ultimately arriving in Le Monetier les Bains.

After lunch, we rode up the Cibouit Lift and traversed out to a ridge that looks back into the Tabuc Valley. This time we found ourselves staring straight down some 40-degree shafts of snow between rocky outcrops. The Couloir de la Crete was more than enough to get everybody's adrenaline flowing on day one of our visit.

OVER THE NEXT FEW DAYS of sunshine, while the last remnants of powder got skied out, the surface on the southern faces was slowly baking into a tasty offering of corn snow. The pistes down toward Briançon were maturing nicely, and near the pistes, some short, steep pitches of corn snow between the rocks spiced up these descents.

As we gazed down past the unusual offering of February spring snow to the snowless valley below, the old town of Briançon, dominated by the Fort du Chateau, could hardly go unnoticed. Built on a cliff-laden hillside, the old town and its medieval walls stood out in marked juxtaposition to the modern lifts, snowboarders and freeriders that I watched in the foreground. I was certain that it deserved further investigation.

Each of the villages that make up Le Grand Serre Che has atmospheric medieval sections, but some of them are, unfortunately, hidden behind modern structures built to house the many skiers who visit this region every season. Le Bez, for example, a lovely old village of narrow streets with a handful of cute and cozy restaurants, is obscured by the modern ski area of Villeneuve in such a way that one could quite easily spend a week in Villeneuve without discovering it.

Briançon, by contrast, which is more of a town than a ski village, has managed to maintain a harmony between its older and newer sections. It is a rare location where one can combine a ski vacation with a historical and cultural experience, and we took advantage of the possibility with a late-afternoon visit.

The steep, cobblestone main street of the old town is lined with picturesque shops, *crêperies*, small restaurants and the like, enough to keep a visitor occupied for an entire afternoon. Leaving the old town by way of the upper Pignerol Gate, we were immediately brought back to the here and now by the sight of a small Poma lift, a field of artificial snow and a snowboard fun park situated literally in the shadow of the walls of the fort. This incongruous sight brought our minds back to skiing and we headed back to get a good night's sleep.

BY NOW, WE HAD BECOME well-acquainted with the pistes and some of the off-piste possibilities of Serre Chevalier, and we were ready to be a bit more adventurous. Looking at the map, it appeared that, from various spots behind the mountain known as Serre Chevalier (2491 m), one could drop into some fields of corn snow and descend a back valley to some other mountain villages. It was about this time that I became acquainted with Christophe Trombert, who worked at the Ski Complice rental shop just next to our apartment. Over the next week or so, Christophe was to become the guardian angel of our stay in Le Grand Serre Che.

Unfortunately, Christophe, who was in the midst of his education to become a *guide de montagne*, was busy working everyday. He was, however, not only a wealth of information about the skiing in this region, but he was also extremely generous with sharing his knowledge.

Upon my inquiry about skiing down to the little villages of Les Combes and Puy Chalvin, Christophe assured me that one could certainly follow the route I had seen on the map, and he described the way in enough detail so that I could hardly go wrong. He added that it was a picturesque trip, but the route did not really offer much vertical before ending up on a snow-covered road.

"Come see me again after zee excursion, and I can geeve you some better suggestions," he added.

Our trip was just as our friend had described. After a few easy slopes of corn snow, we were at the end of the real skiing. We followed the val-

THIS PAGE
LEFT: With his rucksack packed for a picnic, Paul Curtis leads his family down the back side of Serre Chevalier's Téte de la Balme toward the little ski resort of Pelvoux.
RIGHT: Couloirs of Serre Chevalier.

RIGHT PAGE
Family picnic by a small chapel en route to Pelvoux.

ley floor for a while, until we began to ski on the road to Les Combes, a small enclave of buildings used only in the summer. The path continued, and just as the snow ran out, it deposited us in Puy Chalvin. This is a village that does not seem to have anything that even vaguely resembles tourism. It is not a bad place to have a lunch at the end of a small excursion, but there are no restaurants. It is definitely a bring-your-own-picnic kind of place. From here, we had the option of a taxi, a bus or hitchhiking back to Briançon.

The next morning, we went back for a chat with Christophe. "Have you heard of Pelvoux?" he asked. "Eet ees a leetle ski village about 25-keelometers from here. I seenk only the locals know about eet. There ees only a few lifts, but you can ski quite good off-piste, and there are no people. You know, now, when Paree and Marseilles have zee school vacation, eet is quite crowded here in Serre Chevalier, but you weel not find zee same situation in Pelvoux."

Half an hour later, we were winding our way to this unknown French ski village, and an hour later, we were diving into a field of ripe spring snow down the southern flank of the mountain. The open upper slopes gradually poured into a few soft gullies and natural halfpipes. The snow was so enticing that it was virtually impossible to stop.

When we finally came to a halt to get our bearings, I realized that we could have made use of Christophe's physical guiding skills instead of only his verbal advice. In our exuberance, we had descended a fair way beyond a good exit, and we found ourselves walking, pushing and poling for the next 45 minutes to get back to civilization. I rationalized that a few simple mistakes like that go with the territory of adventures in new ski areas, but my son was not quite as easy to convince.

» Entering Briançon is a sign boasting an average of 300 sunny days a year.«

On the opposite side of the lift was another off-piste valley, this one offering both north-facing powder slopes and east-facing corn snow. This was also a place where many locals rode the lifts to the top, and then mounted their touring skis to access the powder slopes above and beyond the lifts.

As I gazed around me to take in the spectacular panorama, one of Serre Chevalier's lifts in the distance caught my eye. It looked as if one could ski off-piste from there to Pelvoux. That afternoon, I checked with our senior advisor, who confirmed my analysis of the Vallon de Chambran.

The following morning was consistent with the whole past week—just another sunny day in the "blue hole". It was optimal weather for putting our plan into action. We got an early start, stuffing our rucksacks with wine, water, baguettes, liver paté, goat cheese, prosciutto ham from nearby Italy and local salamis.

We worked our way through part of Serre Chevalier's lift system from Chantemerle to the Téte de la Balme, and began descending the back side at around 11:30. This descent, apparently, was nothing the local ski bums had discovered, as there were no signs of old tracks. The kernels of corn sprayed off our ski edges like so much buckshot and preceded us down the mountain.

We were all grins as we emerged in a wide flat valley that sloped just enough to keep us from pushing. We glided up to the old stone houses of a summer settlement and unpacked our picnic next to a small chapel. Somehow, a bottle of cheap local wine and some simple bread and cold cuts have an exquisite taste after such a classic Alpine back-valley descent.

AFTER LUNCH, THE FINAL LEG of our Serre Chevalier-to-Pelvoux run was a little more difficult. The snow cover was rather meager on these sun-drenched lower slopes. Nevertheless, with a bit of bushwhacking, we picked our way down to a residential area of vacation homes just above the village, where a local was kind enough to drive us into the center. We were really too large a group to hitchhike, but we split up and all managed to get lifts quite quickly back to our starting point.

The baguettes that were such an integral part of our picnic are actually an important part of daily life in France. Most tourists, us included, get into the French habit of picking up some fresh bread every morning. This practice led, in fact, to the next part of our story.

As I was picking up our breakfast ration the next morning, admiring a particularly lovely pink sunrise, I noticed that all the cars approaching from the east had about twenty centimeters of snow on their roofs. Not entirely trusting my instincts without conferring with Christophe, I stopped on the way back to our flat for a consultation. He assured me that it was quite possible that a lot of snow could have fallen 40 minutes away, while Serre Chevalier had remained sunny and warm.

Our morning drive was a real eye opener. Chantemerle had not received an iota of snow. The black Luc Alphand piste, named after the famous local downhiller, looked in perfect firm condition to host just such a race. A few kilometers down the road, the roofs of Briancon's Old Town had received a light dusting. After another 20 minutes of driving, however, the border town of Montgenèvre had received about 30 centimeters of fluff.

Montgenèvre, the only French member of the large Milky Way lift system, is a pearl, and yet it has gotten lost in the shuffle of large, famous resorts around it. For French skiers, Montgenèvre is further afield from the population centers of the country than the popular ski destinations of Les Deux Alpes, Alpe d'Huez and Serre Chevalier. The Italians, on the other side, have a shorter drive to nearby Sestriere and Sauze d'Oulx, and after all, they would rather ski in Italy than in France.

Historically, this area did not always go unnoticed, as people came from far afield to cross through the strategic Monginevro Pass, traveling through the town of Montgenèvre on their way. In 53 B.C., Julius Caesar came this way, and Hannibal took his army on its famous elephant ride along this route as well. Nowadays, Montgenèvre is ignored, except among locals, despite superb credentials that any ski resort would be proud of.

The village is high (1850 m), giving it good-quality snow and a long season. It has a respectable vertical of over 800 meters, 24 lifts, 8000 tourist beds and good skiing for all ability groups. In addition, it is part of the Milky Way lift system, with 400 kilometers of pistes. Heliskiing, outlawed in France, is also available here because of its proximity to Italy.

THE EAST-FACING SLOPES on the Aigle side of the village are primarily covered with easy, open runs, where most of the locals cruise around in between long pauses to bronze their skins. All the while, the La Crete and Rocher de l'Aigle areas are full of powder-drenched valleys, gullies, and couloirs. In addition, one can also traverse or hike in various directions from the top of the Rocher Lift to reach interesting off-piste routes, such as the steep north face of Mont La Plane.

We found some nice fresh powder that day by crossing the Colleto Verde Pass into Italy and skiing the black Durance descent down to the village of Claviere. On the opposite side of the valley was another great off-piste descent to Claviere from atop the Col de l'Apet. By the time we returned to Serre Chevalier that evening, we were really beginning to understand the advantages of the local microclimate zones.

There was still more to come. Some days passed. Then, the west wind began blowing a front in from the Atlantic, and it was time to traverse the Col du Lauteret, and play the "border-pass game" in the other direction—to the renowned off-piste slopes of La Grave.

The "border-pass game" lends itself perfectly to La Grave. This piste-less paradise can be horrible after an extended period without new snow, when its unprepared terrain is a potpourri of wind-pack, crust and crud.

One ideal way of getting the best of this unusual ski resort is to stay in Serre Chevalier, and pick and choose the right day or days to visit La Grave. We chose just such a day. Half a meter of fluff had fallen, and we swayed and swerved among the well-spaced larches, as carefree as a family of mountain hares.

In the village of Le Grand Serre Che known as Monetier les Bains (Monetier at the Baths), we stopped at the newly reopened thermal baths to soothe our powder-ravaged muscles. The thermal springs here have been used for bathing by the local people as far back as the first century A.D., but they were closed down in 1950 because of poor maintenance. Then, for the 1999–2000 season, they were finally refurbished and reopened. A thermal bath is a great après-ski, and we floated around lazily under the stars.

Soaking in the soothing water, I thought back over our stay in Serre Chevalier. It definitely was a top ski resort, with good skiing for all ability groups, lots of variety and various hamlets and towns dripping with atmosphere and history.

I realized that there exist, of course, many ski areas that have a healthy combination of ski terrain, lift facilities and atmosphere. Nevertheless, the success or failure of most ski holidays hinges on the one factor that has always been out of our control—weather. The success of this vacation had been a combination of the special microclimate zones in and around Serre Chevalier, our mobility, and a lot of good advice from our local friend, Christophe.

For people planning to visit here, one of the sunniest ski resorts in the Alps, there are but a few tips that I can offer. First, if you don't have a car, get a bus schedule. Second, check the latest snow conditions of all the nearby ski areas regularly. Third, learn the rules and strategies of the "border-pass game". And finally, ask around in Chantemerle for the whereabouts of Christophe Trombert. He may well have become a full-fledged mountain guide by then and could give visitors the benefit of his knowledge of the local mountains in person.

VARS & PRA LOUP — MAMA, DON´T LET YOUR BABIES GROW UP TO BE SPEED SKIERS

If one wants to go for a ski holiday in the real France, forget about Chamonix, La Grave, Serre Chevalier and about two dozen other tourist traps where you will meet more Englishman, Swedes, Dutch and Americans than Frenchmen. These are all great resorts—don't get me wrong. But during my many ski travels, I went in search of a true French experience. Where do the locals go for a ski holiday?

Many of the French go to the Maritime Alps, the southwestern-most section of this great range of mountains—the last of the high peaks before the range peters out into the foothills of the French Riviera. Many of the resorts in this region, such as Vars, Risoul, Pra Loup and La Foux d'Allos are totally unknown beyond the borders of France. While these ski resorts have very little international recognition, they are quite large. The combined Vars-Risoul ski pass, for example, includes 55 lifts, but despite its size, a daily lift pass is quite a bit cheaper than at more famous resorts of a similar size.

Vars is made up of four small settlements—Saint Marcellin, Sainte Marie, Sainte Catherine and Les Claux. A few lifts rise up out of Sainte Marie while the hub of the skiing is in Les Claux.

HIGH ABOVE THE RESORT is the magnificent Crête de l'Eyssina (2837 m), a couloir-riddled mountain that is very reminiscent of the Canadian Rockies in its striated appearance. The gullies and chutes under the peak stretch high above the top lifts of the resort, and I could see that reaching the summit required anywhere from a 30-minute to a 2-hour hike, depending on the distance of the couloir from the Crevoux Lift. It had not snowed in a week or more, and I could just make out the traces of old tracks coming down through some of the ravines. A local explained

to me that in the past few years, numerous extreme skiing competitions had been held in these chutes.

While recent years have seen many ski venues adopt extreme skiing into their program of activities, Vars has been a hotbed of sorts for a different breed of adrenaline junky since the early 1990s, when it became one of the main locations for speed-skiing competitions. This, as one can imagine, can be a grave problem for local mothers.

Most healthy boys grow up enjoying sports. They play soccer, tennis or ice hockey in their free time. Kids who grow up in ski resorts often start racing at a young age and spend many hours of their free time on the slalom course. If they are very daring, they might even opt for the downhill. It is different in Vars.

Here, young children grow up wanting to emulate those skiers in bizarre "Star Wars" outfits that defy death on their beloved local Chabrières slope. Children as young as five start speed skiing here in competitions that may ultimately lead them toward immortality—or perhaps terminate their mortality.

It is a horrific thought. Five-year-olds have skied up to speeds of 90 kilometers per hour! Don't ask me what kind of mother allows her infant to start speed skiing, but Vars is where it happens.

PART OF OUR ENTOURAGE WAS STAYING at the Caribou Hotel, and coincidentally, the 21-year-old son of the owners was among those young men of Vars who had gone astray at an early age. In fact, at age fifteen, Julien Maingault set the world record for *cadets* (in the fourteen-to-sixteen age group) when he blazed down the Chabrières run at a speed of almost 218 kilometers per hour. Of course, that was way back in 1998. Now that

LEFT PAGE
Julian Maingault shows off his freeride style.

THIS PAGE
UPPER LEFT: The Crête de l'Eyssina rises dramatically above the village of Vars.
UPPER RIGHT: Serre-Ponçon Lake, as seen from high up in the Vars ski area.
LOWER: Julien poses with his speed skis.

he had come of age, Julien had his sights set on the adult world record, which is over 250 kilometers per hour!

I met Julien one afternoon at his parents' hotel. He offered to show me around a few of the slopes one day, but I was hesitant until I found out that he doesn't always roam the slopes at Mach speed on his 240-centimeter-long speed skis. In fact, Julien is very comfortable on a snowboard as well, is an avid freeride skier and does about everything one can do on snow. During most of the winter, while he waits for the speed skiing season to begin in the spring, he earns money instructing both skiing and snowboarding in the local ski school, while he also helps his parents with some of the hotel chores in the evenings.

"Well, as long as we're skiing normal skis, and I don't need any Darth Vader face gear to protect me from death, I might join you for a few runs," I said to Julien.

"Ohhh! Za ski school is so-o-o-o boring," Julien moaned to me. "I must do something that gets the adrenaline flowing!"

"Adrenaline flowing," I muttered under my breath. "Julien is lucky if his favorite sport doesn't get the adrenaline flowing all over the snow."

I was visiting this region with my son Erik, a teenager, who was listening with rabbit ears to every enthusiastic word that spilled out of Julien's mouth. When Erik tried on Julien's headgear, I felt the time had come to break off my interesting conversation with the young speedster and get Erik directed onto the conventional ski slopes. He wanted to try the speed skiing venue, which is almost 50 degrees at its steepest point, but that got nixed by dad.

Erik and I rode the lifts up to the top of the system, at Pic de Chabrières. On the way, a beautiful panorama of Serre-Ponçon Lake unfolded. We sampled the relatively easy red and blue runs around Risoul. Then we skied down some steep off-piste descents off the Pointe de Razis. I had to keep Erik interested with some challenging stuff to keep his mind off the speed skiing. Young teenagers are so impressionable, and I would face the death sentence from Erik's mom the day after returning from our holiday if he came home focused on speed skiing as his new hobby.

JULIEN WAS A POLITE young man, but I had to avoid him when I was with Erik. There is a country-western song which warns, "Mama, don't let your babies grow up to be cowboys." With some minor paraphrasing,

I could see this song could be applicable here. In many ways, our children are influenced by a myriad of factors that are beyond our ability to control. But I did not want to mess up in one of the few places where I have a strong influence. I did not want to introduce my son to the mortal dangers of speed skiing.

There was no real way to avoid the speed skiing hoopla in Vars. There were posters all over, advertising speed sportsmen films and events featuring these daredevils of the snow. I refer to sportsmen rather than skiers because the sport has proliferated in recent years to encompass snowboarders, monoskiers and even mountain bikers. Julien's buddy, Eric Barone, had recently set a new speed bike record, for example, descending the Chabrières run at 217 kilometers per hour!

Skiing is an addiction. Speed is a different obsession. I, an admitted addict of the former category, had personally introduced my son to skiing and its hypnotic partner, powder. I was not going to do the same with the additional drug of speed. The time had come to say *Au revoir*.

JUST A SHORT DRIVE OVER the Col de Vars is the ski resort of Pra Loup. Rather than staying in the ski center, we opted to get a room in the charming village of Barcelonnette, situated in the Ubaye Valley a few kilometers down the mountain. We checked into the Hotel du Cheval Blanc, a small inn dating back to the 17th century, which had been owned by the same family for over 100 years.

The village has an odd and interesting history. From 1850 to 1950, more than 7000 people from this area migrated to Mexico. Most of those people were entrepreneurs and merchants and many made small fortunes in their new home across the Atlantic. Some of the most successful of these immigrants returned to Barcelonnette to build beautiful villas, which are visible all over town.

The 60 old vacation homes of the Barcelonnette immigrants are not the only evidence of the village's longstanding connection with Mexico. All over town, the hotels and restaurants boast names like Villa Durango, L'Hacienda, La Mexicaine, and Hotel Azteca.

There are a number of different ski resorts all around Barcelonnette, and like Vars, they cater to French families in and around nearby Marseilles. Their prices are very family-friendly, with the small ski area of Sainte-Anne offering a day pass for about €15, while Super Sauze's system of over 20 lifts can be skied for €22.

The largest and by far the most interesting ski areas in this section of the Southern Alps are Pra Loup and its sister resort of La Foux d'Allos. They offer 50 lifts and 167 kilometers of pistes, but what is perhaps most interesting is the huge area of off-piste terrain in between the two resorts.

We were lucky enough to have Gilles Frankel, at one time the youngest ski school director in the entire École du Ski Français, to show us around Pra Loup for a few hours. A member of the French national team as a teenager, Gilles later snowboarded professionally as well and spent many hours on telemark skis, before directing his skills into teaching at the ripe old age of 27.

He guided us into the gigantic freeride domain—four big valleys

THIS PAGE
UPPER LEFT: Pra Loup lunch hut.
UPPER RIGHT: Pra Loup gondola.
LOWER: Panorama of the Pra Loup ski area.

RIGHT PAGE
Pra Loup has large expanses of open freeride terrain.

between the two resorts. The largest of these is the Vallon de Seregnier, which can be entered from opposite sides, from Le Lac, atop the Pra Loup section of lifts, or from Tête du Sestrière to the east. This valley alone could keep a freerider satiated for days. There was no doubt that over here I could get Erik's thoughts away from speed skiing, suicidal mountain biking and other such diversions.

Gilles glided, hopped, skipped and jumped amidst this natural terrain park like a bunny on Easter Sunday. While he spoke of his love and enjoyment of teaching, I could see that he had a lot of ski energy that had not had an outlet for some time. He swooped down through the cut up powder in a series of long New School turns, throwing in a back scratch or two off a small cornice or rock here and there.

Gilles played with the terrain like only a kid in his own backyard can do. He pointed his skis into a narrow ravine and used it like a natural halfpipe. Then he did a powder slalom through a small grove of trees.

We could hardly keep up. He bounced out of the pines onto a long steep pitch and raced down through the open slope as if he were on his way to a fire.

In fact, he was in a hurry. Unfortunately, Gilles had to get back to the ski school and he was late. We followed in hot pursuit as he sped down the pistes back to town. He took a moment here and there to point out other areas of freeride heaven within his domain of the South Alps.

There was much more. The lifts that connected Pra Loup with La Foux d'Allos seemed to be designed and engineered by a powder skier. Each lift deposited us at the perfect spot from where one could traverse along ridges extending out in both directions from the top. Each ridge, in turn, gave access to both sides of the mountain. In essence, each lift station, therefore, provided easy access to numerous entries to four mountainsides. One could hardly do better with a helicopter.

For the next few days, Erik and I experimented as much as we could without a guide. All the guides were fully booked, as this was the French school holiday. There is a large valley to the east of Pra Loup's Fau Lift. I had asked Gilles about Le Bois du Fau, and he had described it as best he could.

The next morning, Erik followed me into this large section of uncharted terrain. It began with easy open slopes above the tree line. Soon, the skiing became more interesting as we entered some glades in amongst the trees. Gradually, the valley narrowed into a series of steep avalanche gullies. I had been following some snowboard tracks. A seasoned veteran like myself ought to have known better. After a while, the tracks ended abruptly, and I didn't need to be Daniel Boone to see that the boarder had turned around and started to walk back up.

THE HIKE UP WAS STEEP, the snow was deep and Erik was not happy with his guide. I don't blame him. We trudged on for a ways and crossed over a number of ravines, looking for a safe exit. I was beginning to think Erik might have been safer with Julien on the Chabrières speed skiing run in

Vars. We eventually extricated ourselves from Le Bois du Fau and moved on to other adventures.

We skied to the far end of the ski area. From the Tête de Vescal, we traversed past the eastern boundary of the resort. Here, the trees were not so dense and the lines were more obvious. In addition, I had been able to surmise from my maps that we would reemerge on the road which carries summer visitors over the Col d'Allos and down to Nice, about 90 minutes away. The road was heavily laden with snow at this time of year and gave us an easy glide back to the lifts.

On our way back to Pra Loup, we again found ourselves atop Le Lac. I gazed down a gargantuan out-of-bounds valley to the west. There were no tracks. It was tempting, but after losing my way in the forest, I was no longer in a mood for the trial-and-error

» After losing my way in the forest, I was no longer in a mood for the trial-and-error method...«

method—at least, not when I had my loyal son in tow. We skied on the piste back to the village, where I again consulted with Gilles.

"Ahhh! Yes. Ze Vallon des Thuiles—it ees a very nice route—about a 15-kilometer descent, but you need a car to come back."

Gilles had hit the nail on the head. "Come back," he had said. Yes, I would come back. I must come back. The Vallon des Thuiles mandated that fact. We had only touched the tip of the iceberg here in the Maritime Alps. I would return at a time of year when the French schools were in session. Then Gilles would have time to show me the Vallon des Thuiles, the correct route through Le Bois du Fau, and a lot more.

I could not bear to leave this region with so many virgin routes still undiscovered, unless I had, at least, a *plan* to return. Yes, I was truly a helpless addict. I was no different from Julien and his speed-skiing habit. Mama, don't let your babies grow up to be powder skiers!

107

TIGNES–VAL D'ISERE — THE COULOIR CRAZIES OF VAL CLARET

On my most recent visit to France, Carl Mårtensson and I visited Val Claret, the highest village in the Tignes–Val d'Isère lift system. Here, Jazze Noren, who hails from the flat southern part of Sweden known as Skåne, was our host. Since the late 1980s, Jazze has made Tignes his home, while operating a bar, formerly called La Poutrerie, and now named the Mover Cafe.

To meet a resident of Skåne who can negotiate a slope any steeper than a frozen lake is a rarity in itself. Here in Val Claret, however, you will often find Jazze and one or two of his employees from the flatlands making turns in places so steep and narrow that mere mortals have to straight-line sections of the couloir.

To begin our first morning, Jazze guided us over to the Couloirs du Chardonnet. These are his favorite chutes—north facing, where the powder stays good for days. That is, the snow is protected from the sun—but not from the ever growing population of freeride enthusiasts. Chardonnet was riddled with tracks. It was not always so. I thought back to so many days in the 1980s when I joined Jazze in these chutes. In those days it was almost only he, his friends and his employees who frequented this part of the mountain.

Jazze was not satisfied, of course, and he led us to the other side of the valley, where a quick 15-minute walk took us to the top of a peak known to the locals as "Mickey Mouse's Ears". From here, a series of steep couloirs are spread out along the shady back side of the mountain. We stood peering with a certain degree of trepidation down a slender half-cylinder which seemed to narrow away to nothing.

"This is one of our favorites," proclaimed Jazze. "But it is the tightest of all the chutes from up here."

And tight it was. The ski run began with a coin toss, and the loser had to go first. This is a rather odd system among good skiers, especially those who like to ski off-piste. Making first tracks in fresh snow is usually an honor and a thrill bestowed upon winners, but the avalanche danger inherent in making first tracks in such steep chutes reverses the usual winner–loser perception here.

The task of the first skier is to test for avalanches every step of the way, by jumping hard in the snow, trying to induce any poorly bonded snow to break loose and slide down before he and the others begin the real skiing. Hence, this "lucky" precursor gets the honor of skiing the virgin along with the accompanying danger involved.

The second skier, on the other hand, feels safer from being swept away by a snow slide, but there is often no powder left for him to ski in the narrow sections of the chute. Everyone who makes it to the bottom in one piece is presumed to be a winner, and the intensive care unit of the local hospital claims the losers.

After a short series of jump turns, we were almost immediately upon the narrowest part. As I tried to side step this needle-thin section, my boards were getting caught on the rocks on both sides. Jazze was chuckling from below as he watched me sweating, trying to punch my ski poles as firmly as possible into the nearby snow, and negotiate my skis beyond this trapdoor.

Why ski such places that are so narrow and steep? In the case of some chutes like the "Mickey Mouse's Ears" couloir, it is a means to an end. Once we had passed through the most difficult point, the corridor opened up somewhat. At first, there was only space for a few skiers to make tight powder turns, but later we reached broad open powder fields. All of these excellent slopes are only accessible by skiing the couloir.

Jazze explained that other corridors are skied mainly for the challenge. Many good skiers, especially those ski bums who have spent many full

seasons skiing, no longer get the same thrill out of their favorite pastime, if it is only to ski some crowded piste. Therefore they search out a more extreme descent for the sake of adventure.

The Pramcou is a good example of such a descent. It is so steep—close to 50 degrees at the top—that it hardly holds snow. The first couple of turns invariably start a slough that rids the slope of most of the fresh snow. Therefore, skiers hardly choose this route for the sake of the powder.

The challenge is really the only motive. The entry necessitates a few very exposed turns above some rock cliffs before a traverse to the skier's right makes the rest of the descent somewhat safer. That is to say that after the traverse, a poorly planted edge or the loss of balance due to a slough will probably only result in a long ignominious slide, but not in being sent cascading over a pile of granite.

During the '70s and early '80s, before Jazze and his band of couloir fanatics showed up, the local French mountain guides and ski patrol were almost the only skiers climbing into these narrow couloirs so characteristic of the terrain in this area. In fact, one of the classic chutes in Val d'Isère is appropriately named the Couloir des Pisteurs. After the arrival of Jazze and his friends, there was about a ten-year period when they reigned supreme in the local chutes. Nowadays, however, as skiers have gotten increasingly better, even these difficult places get skied more and more.

LEFT PAGE: Jazze enjoys an après-ski beer in the spring sunshine.
THIS PAGE: George Koch makes a leap of faith into the "Mickey Mouse's Ears" couloir.

Jazze pointed at a nefarious-looking passage between the rocks high above Val Claret and exclaimed, "Look at the Couloir de la Grande Balme. Ten years ago that place would hardly ever get skied. One has to hike to get into it, and the skiing is quite treacherous. Now it looks like a piste."

Jazze hates moguls, and ascribes to the theory that "If God had wanted man to ski moguls, he would have let snow come down in piles." In these death-defying couloirs, Jazze reasons that he is sure to avoid any trace of a mogul. As the number of snowsports enthusiasts entering the couloirs increases, however, Jazze has found himself seeking *even* more difficult terrain. He sometimes takes mountaineering equipment with him to access some spots where one can only enter with rope.

The Couloir de Face Nord d'Aiguille Noir de Pramcou is such a steep chute that one needs crampons to hike up the narrow chute, which one later descends on skis. This has become Jazze's last haven from today's large number of off-piste skiers. In fact, in the fifteen years or so since Jazze first skied this ravine, it has come to be known among the French ski patrol and other locals as the Couloir Suédois (the Swedish Couloir).

I took one look at Jazze's personal couloir and realized that he is even crazier than I thought. Jazze laughed at my reaction.

"One thing is for sure," he said. "If I don't pee directly before I make my first turn up there, I certainly will wet my pants on the way down!"

We all seek different solutions to the same problem, and we must seek remedies that suit our own circumstances. I am every bit as intent as Jazze on avoiding the ever more crowded pistes and increasingly busy off-piste terrain of the French Alps. I do it by skiing in the likes of Iran, Russia or Kazakhstan.

Jazze, on the other hand, is tied to Tignes by his restaurant. It is the most natural solution for him just to move up one more notch on the extreme scale, and once again, he is alone, heart in his throat, amidst the solitude that partially defines skiing for him.

Jazze has changed somewhat from the early years, when he was out skiing every day. He has mellowed a bit with age and experience, and he has other interests and pursuits besides skiing. In addition, the administration and management of the Mover Cafe takes quite a bit of time. But when the weather and conditions are right for some steep skiing, comb the most unskiable-looking spots above Val Claret. If you see a small speck high up in a forbidding couloir and the speck has too much color to be a rock, there is a better-than-average chance that Jazze is once again proving to nobody in particular that flatlanders can ski with the best of them.

THIS PAGE
UPPER LEFT
The well-known Aiguille Percée (Eye of the Needle) rock formation in Tignes.
MIDDLE LEFT
Daniel Gardtman contemplating his testament as he stands at the point of no return in the "Mickey Mouse's Ears" couloir. Jazze calls this couloir the "Fourteen-Year-Old"—because it is so tight!
RIGHT
Karl Mårtensson enters one of Tignes-Val d'Isère's many couloirs, with Lac de Tignes in the background.
LOWER
Fredrik Liljeberg leaps toward an uncertain fate from the Pointe de Foglietta (2930 m) in Sainte-Foy. Mont Blanc is visible in the background.

RIGHT PAGE
Karl Mårtensson checks out the terrain in Meribel.

SAINTE-FOY AND POINTE DE FOGLIETTA

Carl and I drove a short distance down the valley from Tignes–Val d'Isère to the small and relatively little-known ski resort of Sainte-Foy. Before the 1990s, Sainte-Foy was merely a poor hamlet, but at the beginning of the decade, three lifts were built a few kilometers away from this little French village. The lifts succeed one another to bring a skier from an elevation of 1550 meters up to 2670 meters. The top station affords off-piste skiers the option of traversing quite far out on either side to reach untracked snow or to ski a rather easy off-piste route down to the abandoned village of Le Monal.

During our short visit, the powder had already been obliterated on these easily accessible areas, so we opted for a 45-minute hike up to the Pointe de Foglietta (2930 m). From there, a long ridge extends around the periphery of a huge bowl. Most entries into the bowl require mandatory air, but I managed to find a location that allowed me to remain on terra firma. The initial slopes are steep, gradually planing out, and finally ending, after close to 10 kilometers of skiing, in the little town of Le Miroir. We found some fresh lines, but like so many places nowadays, even little Sainte-Foy had changed from its early years.

Sainte-Foy is on the main artery between Bourg Saint Maurice and Val d'Isère, and ski journalists and film crews discovered this new powder hole shortly after it had been built. By the mid-1990s, Sainte-Foy had received enough notoriety to have a mini-cult following.

Its nearness to Val d'Isère also makes it easy for ski bums and mountain guides with groups from that major resort to head down the road when the best conditions prevail. Nevertheless, Sainte-Foy is still a good bet for finding a stash of powder on the right days, and a trek up the Pointe de Foglietta should pay off even days after the last snowflakes have fallen on the region.

LES TROIS VALLEES — 600 KILOMETERS OF PISTES

Again it was time to move on—to Les Trois Vallées. This was one of the first ski regions where the resorts recognized the benefit of linking their lift systems together in an effort to offer their guests more variety, having done so back in the early 1970s. By now, the original three valleys have added a fourth by linking up with Orelle a few years ago. While Val Thorens, Méribel and Courchevel are the most famous stations, the resorts of Les Menuires, Saint Martin de Belleville, La Tania and Brides-les-Bains are also connected in what is one of the two largest lift-linked ski areas in the world.

This is a resort with unending superlatives—200 lifts, 600 kilometers of pistes, 1500 snow cannons and a lift capacity that can move 260,000 people per hour. The list of impressive statistics goes on and on.

The various villages have quite different atmospheres. Courchevel is the most up-market of the resorts. While there are some rather challenging black routes from atop the Saulire, most of the terrain is not so difficult.

Méribel and Les Menuires benefit from being in the center of the lift system, but Les Menuires is an eyesore of cement and steel, while Meribel, with many chalets in addition to its hotels, is more in harmony with the surroundings. Val Thorens, at 2300 meters, is the highest ski resort in Europe and usually attracts the hard-core off-piste skiers.

Carl and I opted for still another choice—Saint Martin de Belleville—a traditional village in marked contrast to the larger areas, which are purpose-built resorts. While St. Martin shares with Méribel and Les Menuires the advantage of being central in the lift system, here the traditional elements of slate, stone and wood give the village an ambiance that one cannot find in the large ski centers of Les Trois Vallées.

THIS IS PROVINCIAL FRANCE, WITH small houses invariably clustered around a Baroque church. Saint Martin is the largest of a few hamlets that are all situated down the valley from Les Menuires, and best of all, one can ski off-piste to any of them. The west-facing slopes of the Belleville Valley are made up of gentle, open terrain, where off-piste enthusiasts can ski to St. Marcel, Praranger or back to St. Martin. St. Marcel makes a particularly nice destination for such an endeavor, as one can relax and reenergize with a lunch at the well-known La Bouitte, a lovely restaurant that recently earned a *Guide Michelin* star.

For freeriders with a palate for more challenging terrain, there are also some interesting possibilities from the La Masse side of the valley that end up close to these same hamlets. The Col de la Fenêtre and the Vallée des Encombres descents finish near the hamlet of Le Châtelard, while the Les Crêtes route comes down near St. Marcel.

The weather was spring-like during our visit and it had been a while since the last snowfall. Whether we stayed on the trails or opted for off-piste terrain, corn snow was to be the *plat du jour*. Carl and I decided to spend our first day primarily in the Méribel region, where the east-west orientation of the slopes is well suited to spring conditions.

We spent the morning on the east-facing slopes of Roc de Fer, Roc des Trois Marches and Mt. de la Challe. By eleven o'clock, these areas were getting too soft, but the sun had not yet softened the crust on the west faces. We kept active in the meantime in the steep mogul fields under the Saulire cable car from Courchevel. By early afternoon, the west faces of Saulire and Mont du Vallon had softened to perfection, providing a nice dessert to the day's menu.

La Masse has some of the best skiing of any single mountain in Les Trois Vallées and versatility to boot. It was the target of our second

morning's activities. Again we spent the early hours playing in some off-piste spring snow on the east faces. Later, we descended one of Les Trois Vallées classics—the Lac de Lou descent from La Masse.

We had hoped to spend the afternoon in Val Thorens, but it was not to be. Despite the spring conditions, there were strong winds in the highest elevations. The upper lifts of Val Thorens are quite wind-sensitive, and the access to both the Cime de Caron and the Col de Pierre Lory were closed. Instead, we did a Lac du Lou run from the Boismint Lift and worked our way back to St. Martin.

CARL AND I SAT ON A VERANDAH and reminisced together over an après-ski Kronenbourg. With the upper section of Val Thorens closed, we would have to live vicariously through our past experiences. Carl had spent two ski bum seasons in Val Thorens and told me about some great runs in the St. Pères Couloirs high up on the Aiguille de Péclet. I, too, had skied one of those couloirs, and that run was just a small part of one of my favorite ski bum experiences.

It was April 1982, and I was finishing a long season of ski bumming with my first-ever visit to Les Trois Vallées. I dragged my gear off the

train in Moûtiers and asked a young man where I could find a bus to Val Thorens.

"Zere are no more buses at zis time of zee evening," he replied, "but if you wait a few minutes, I can give you a lift. I am just picking up my girlfriend on zees train."

Patrick Berthon not only gave me a lift, he also put me up in his apartment in Val Thorens, where he and his brother Eric were both ski instructing. Eric had a couple of days free from the ski school, and within a few hours of my arrival in Les Trois Vallées, I had a free bed and guide. This, of course, was long before one could print "Couloir St. Pères" onto the Google web site and have a few thousand entries pop up on the screen. It was a time when only the locals knew the special runs in Les Trois Vallées.

Eric led me on a 40-minute hike over the Glacier de Chavière and down this beautiful ravine on my second day in Val Thorens. It was apparently a test of my abilities—and fortunately I passed.

The next day, I was again behind Eric and a couple of his friends, as we followed a similar route but hiked even higher up the mountain. After about 90 minutes, I found myself staring down one of the steepest and most nefarious slopes I have ever, to this very day, skied. It is simply called North Face.

The descent is about 50 degrees at the top and the snow was very firm, wind-packed powder. Worst of all, the convex nature of North Face makes it impossible to see all the way down, but Eric was quick to inform us that a crevasse at the bottom of the slope swallows skiers who make mistakes. Only after one has negotiated the steep upper section can one traverse out to the side and continue the run beyond the grasp of the crevasse.

Eric tied a 50-meter-long rope around my waist and looped the other end around his skis, which he pushed firmly into the snow. This allowed me to make my first few turns without danger, but soon I was on my own. It was the first time I had ever used a climbing rope.

I survived the North Face intact, and for the next few days, Eric continued to show me his favorite off-piste runs interspersed with some mogul bashing. If Eric was fearless in the face of off-piste dangers, he was a maniac of the moguls. In the bumps, I had not the slightest chance of following him.

Eric's considerate guiding was one of my early experiences with the ski bum code of sharing. Whereas surfers, for example, are extremely territorial and would rather kill a stranger than share a wave, real skiers are very magnanimous.

Little did I know that Eric was practicing for his future profession. Some years after, in 1986, I read a name in a ski magazine that I recognized very well. Eric Berthon had become the world champion of mogul skiing. In 2002, I again came across his name. He was the freestyle coach of the French Olympic team at the Salt Lake City Winter Games.

Carl and I finished our beers and our nostalgia session. This was the end of our short stay, but reacquainting myself with Les Trois Vallées had reopened a door that had been closed for too long. When I got home and had a bit more time, I tried to find Eric on the Internet, and it did not take long to locate his web site.

Moments later, I was involved in another nostalgic conversation—this one on the telephone. Eric was now raising a family, teaching his two young children to ski, instructing at a few freestyle camps and guiding people off-piste in Val d'Isère. As I had seen his name now and then through the years because of his exploits in the ski world, he had also seen mine.

"I have thought on many occasions about those few days we spent together," said Eric. "I would be reminded of that time whenever I came across one of your articles in *Ski Français* or one of the other ski magazines."

Ski bumming is a youthful pastime. Of the many avid skiers who spend a season or two devoted to their love of the sport, most of them are ultimately swallowed up by the mainstream. In the words of songwriter George Thorogood, they "get a haircut and get a real job." It was a reassuring moment to get on the phone with Eric Berthon over twenty years later and realize that he, like I, was a chronic ski bum.

AVORIAZ, MORZINE AND THE PORTES DU SOLEIL BORDER CROSSINGS

The stiffest competition with Les Trois Vallées for the title of largest lift-linked ski area in the world comes from the Portes du Soleil, which is made up of fourteen villages on the French–Swiss border. Courchevel and company have a larger hourly uphill capacity, while the Portes du Soleil has a few more lifts and trails. As in Les Trois Vallées, there is a dif-ference of atmosphere among the various villages of the Portes du Soleil. Some, like Avoriaz and Torgon, are modern-style ski centers while the likes of Morzine, Châtel and Champéry are traditional villages.

While there are certainly pistes to keep skiers of all ability groups interested, the Portes du Soleil is really a paradise for intermediate

skiers. Avoriaz has some of the most advanced terrain including a number of black pistes that descend to Les Prodains and the infamous Swiss Wall at Chavanette. The Wall is a steep east-facing slope with gargantuan moguls. It is enough to strike fear into the heart of most any skier, especially when the snow is firm. The faint of heart can take the chair lift down and even that might make some individuals queasy.

For freeriders, close to the top of the Fornet Lift in Avoriaz, one can enter into the Mines d'Or descent, one of the best off-piste areas in this gigantic lift system. This run drops into the Vallée de la Manche, passing the very pleasant Mines d'Or restaurant on the way—not a bad place for a lunch or an après-ski. Alternatively, there are some interesting runs in the trees on various aspects of Mont Chéry in Les Gets.

The Portes du Soleil was one of the first ski regions to come up with the idea of linking many small ski villages together into one massive area. Olympic gold medalist and sunglass king Jean Vuarnet was one of the main brains behind creating a huge cross-border ski region with the development of Avoriaz as the centerpiece.

SIMILAR TO SOME OF THE OTHER humongous lift systems that have slowly developed in the Alps over the past 50 years, there are also some drawbacks to the large size of the Portes du Soleil. While the many square kilometers of terrain give both versatility and variety to the area, a skier cannot use even half of this large region without carrying a sleeping bag and pajamas in his backpack. A person staying in Les Gets who has a favorite slope in Châtel needs half the day to transport himself there and the rest of the day to return home.

There is often an associated problem. Many of the pistes that connect villages of such large lift systems are glorified roads that do not provide quality skiing. In addition, these very pistes are among the most crowded on the mountain, because the local marketing department has

LEFT PAGE
The Swiss Wall from Avoriaz down into Switzerland is famous for its bunker-sized moguls.

THIS PAGE
Anders Karlsson enjoys the view of Les Dents du Midi on route to Champéry, Switzerland in the huge Portes du Soleil ski area.

brainwashed most of the tourists into thinking that the whole point of coming to their enormous lift system is to ski among as many different villages as possible. The Portes du Soleil suffers to some degree from this syndrome.

Size does not have to be a problem. Stay in Avoriaz or Morzine one season and ski among the nearby lifts of Les Gets, Champéry, Les Crosets and Champoussin. Don't beat yourself up and try to do it all. On a subsequent visit, stay in Châtel. From there you can ski among Torgon, Morgins and La Chapelle d'Abondance without too much hassle.

VAL CENIS AND THE MAURIENNE VALLEY
HEREDITY OR ENVIRONMENT — THE AGE-OLD QUESTION

While there are about a dozen world-famous ski resorts in the Savoie and Haute Savoie, these regions are home to approximately 100 more obscure ski centers. Many of them are extremely pleasant areas—smaller, of course, than the renowned ski-venues but with a price tag that is also more affordable. These resorts often cater to families but are also good value for skiers looking for uncrowded slopes and untracked freeride terrain, as long as they don't mind an evening atmosphere that is rather sedate. Val Cenis is such a location.

Nestled in the Maurienne Valley, Val Cenis is actually the *most* famous of a large handful of ski resorts in this valley, including Bonneval-sur-Arc, La Norma, Aussois, Val Fréjus, Termignon-la-Vanoise and Bessans. The resort is made up of the two villages of Lanslebourg and Lanslevillard, both of which are cozy, authentic French mountain enclaves rather than the modern *stations de ski* that are typical of many of the largest French ski resorts.

If the villages of the Maurienne Valley are not household names among skiers, it is certainly not for lack of beauty. This is part of the Vanoise National Park, a spectacular little corner of France situated along the Italian border. The isolated valley is boxed in between two mountain passes that are closed all winter. To the south is the Col du Mont Cenis (2083 m), and on the northern end of the valley is the Col de l'Isèran (2764 m), Europe's highest mountain pass, which separates the region from Val d'Isère and does not usually open until early June.

I HAVE ALWAYS JOKED OR HALF-JOKED with my friends about the inhabitants of many such isolated valleys in the Alps. When one sees or speaks with some of the cross-eyed local lift attendants, one becomes quite certain that inbreeding is no myth. One can be sure that many of the locals have, through the years, become more than mere "kissing cousins". This thought was far from my mind as we began our stay in Val Cenis, but it was to emerge strongly into my consciousness later on.

Driving up the valley, my friend Rupert, my son Erik and I enjoyed passing through the string of mountain hamlets. Each was built up around a baroque church, and most of the houses were built entirely of

stone, covered by slate roofs. Many homes dated back to previous centuries. The views upward, however, were shrouded by thick fog.

It is fortunate that the trees in this section of the Alps grow to an elevation of about 2100 meters. They were our saviors on our first day, during which the clouds lay heavy over the valley and snow spewed from the heavens. We spent most of our time on the middle section of the mountain, skiing off the Arcellins II Lift, where the larches and pines are spread out, and there is plenty of space to lay powder tracks.

THE SECOND DAY, IT CONTINUED to snow, albeit not as heavily, and at times the visibility improved greatly. In the morning we found a virgin west face off the top of the Mont Cenis Poma Lift, and for the next few hours, we methodically used up all the powder that slope had to offer. Nobody else followed us to share our stash. The visibility had improved by this time, so I can only imagine that the French, Belgian and Eastern European tourists who make up much of the local clientele were satisfied confining themselves to the pistes.

For the next few days we sampled a few of the other offerings of the Maurienne Valley. Each of the ski resorts here faces north, except for Aussois, which gives the valley a south-facing option. Even in mid-April, there was plenty of snow left here, allowing for some early morning corn snow. The lifts of Aussois also give access to one of the finest tours in the area. An hour's hike from the top of the Bellecôte Poma Lift is a 1700-vertical-meter descent called La Faculta.

Val Fréjus is different from most of the other ski centers in the valley. It is a relatively new resort, with both the village and the lifts having been constructed in 1984. With only eleven lifts, Val Fréjus nevertheless offers a good variety of options for both piste skiers and freeriders. Whether one prefers steep, black moguled runs like Punta Bagna or blue and red cruisers like Le Lac or Le Pas du Roc, one can find them here. Then there is the picturesque blue Le Jeu descent, which swings deep into the end of the valley and exits along the valley floor.

Off-piste fans can drop off the upper section of the Le Jeu trail almost anywhere. They then can ski open north-facing slopes that drop into the

LEFT PAGE
Simon Bastelica flies through the air on his home mountain in Val Cenis.

THIS PAGE
The Haute Maurianne Valley is full of hamlets like this.

forest before spitting a skier back out on the lower part of the piste again. We tried the so-called Pra-Dieu descent in heavy powder—good exercise, but four days after the last snowfall in April, we decided that searching out the corn snow might be a better option.

We skied the spring snow in a few short couloirs between the Le Lac and La Combe pistes. Then we traversed high above the Punta Bagna Lift where a series of west facing 35–40-degree slopes and ravines were still untracked—more corn snow. There was much more of interest, but time and snow conditions were against us. The local proof of manhood, the Couloir d'Arrondaz, had slid a few days earlier. The long north-facing back valley, Le Grand Vallon, was tempting, and the steep Petit Vallon had only a few tracks on it, but it was too late in the day for such endeavors. They would simply have to wait for some other opportunity.

La Norma is another more modern village one valley over from Val Fréjus and linked by a common lift pass and a shuttle service. The lower slopes are wooded, with lots of open slopes above the tree line. We enjoyed a few runs in the Combe à Simon area, a virtual playground for freeriders with many ridges, valleys, ravines and slopes of all shapes and sizes interspersed with small clusters of trees. Many challenging off-piste routes can also be found off the top of the La Norma peak (2917 m) with three couloirs heading the list of the most difficult descents.

ON SUNDAY, WE WERE BACK in Val Cenis, and we awoke to one of those days that one remembers and still talks about over a few beers twenty years after the powder has become snowmelt. Cloudless azure skies and 40 centimeters of heaven waited patiently for us to reach the summit.

We were lucky enough to have Philippe Roger, a local mountain guide, at our disposal. There was certainly no place in the shadow of Pointe du Grand Mont Cenis (3377 m), Pointe du Lamet (3684 m) or Pointe de Ronce (3611 m) with which Philippe was not acquainted. For that matter, Philippe's terrain knowledge certainly spread further up and down the valley than these three peaks that lord over Val Cenis.

To the west, the skyline was dominated by La Dent Parrachée. Way back in the late 1970s, Philippe celebrated his eighteenth birthday by climbing the peak and making the first descent of the 55-degree east face.

He is a former freestyle skier, who, at 45, still enjoyed punctuating his piste descents with a few pirouettes and helicopters, but one could see that he enjoyed the freeride world even more. He had spent a fair number of seasons guiding in Val Thorens, Méribel, Courchevel and La Plagne, but had now returned to the cozy confines of Val Cenis, where he had spent his winter holidays with his parents since his childhood.

"Za beeg stations are not for me," explained Philippe. "I prefer za familiarity and friendliness of Val Cenis. Zees are za real villages, where people live all year around. Za local people ski in za winter and zey are farmers in za summer. We have about ten *fromageries* here, and we have not only za good ski but also za good cheese. Zis is my paradise."

Without further ado, Philippe began showing us around his utopia. The uppermost La Met Chair Lift had been closed for two days, and it didn't take a genius to understand that this was the best place to begin the day. Even here, however, Philippe was of invaluable service.

I traversed out past the furthest track, and was about to point my skis into the fall line, when he merely warned, "Attention! Ski a little further; too many rocks under the snow there."

After a rock-free descent, Philippe led us on a 10-minute walk along a ridge to the peak of L'Ouillon de la Tomba. We were joined by Simon Bastelica, one of Philippe's buddies, a local who had been a downhill racer for the French national team. Simon skis powder as if he were tucking the Hahnenkamm. We made another set of first tracks, this time into the north face of La Tomba. Simon expended energy for about four turns, while the rest of us took our time, pumped about 100 turns and had already burned enough calories to earn us a three-course lunch. But we were by no means ready for that yet.

We arrived at the summit just in time to see two more local lunatics pursuing a suicidal line that ended in a 15-meter huck over granite. The most amazing part was that they both nailed the landing!

"Hey, Jimmy, would you like to get a few 'big air' photos?" asked Philippe.

I am not one to look a gift horse in the mouth. Before you could utter, "Jump or die," our group had expanded by two 16-year-old cousins, Maxim and Alexandre Blanc.

Philippe was quick to point out again that everybody knew everybody in little Val Cenis. "We are like one beeg family."

We now traversed high to the east until we came to the steepest pitch of the day, a 40-degree virgin. On the way, the three local lads hurled themselves over a few more tons of rock, just for the

» Simon skis powder as if he were tucking the Hahnenkamm. «

fun of it, and I noticed that none of them wore helmets. It was then that I began to think about those mountain-valley incest victims that I had so often joked about in the past. Our three new acquaintances were very kind, polite and friendly, not to mention excellent freeriders, but they were clearly not playing with a full deck!

The powder was superb. Erik, Rupert and I easily got our quota of face-shots, while our new friends continued their death-defying circus act until midday, when the cousins disappeared, with a polite *adieu*, to go home for lunch.

Our lunch consisted of a *tartiflette*, a local potato and cheese specialty, and I gazed out over the green valley below. I thought about what a wonderful spot the French Alps are for an April visit, when spring meets winter in a harmonious feast of blooming fruit trees and green meadows alongside jagged peaks still decked out in winter white.

I had little time for my contemplation, as we still had a full afternoon program ahead of us. We did the Lake Run down to Lac du Mont Cenis, skied a few untracked faces into the Col du Loup and added some tree skiing on the lower slopes.

Soon it was five o'clock and time to trade adrenaline for an après-ski beer. We sat on the verandah of the Bar des Rochers, next to the ski school. Philippe pointed out that this establishment was owned by the parents of Alexandre, one of the youths who had skied with us in the morning.

I WAS STILL CURIOUS ABOUT one thing. I asked Alexandre's father why his son doesn't wear a helmet when he spends almost more time in the stratosphere than on the snow.

My French is not very good, but the answer seemed to be that helmets were all sold out when they wanted to buy one a while back, so maybe they would purchase him one next year! He was quick to point out, however, that his son does wear a back protector.

"Oh well," I thought to myself, "What's the big deal about a little extra equipment? Most of the locals probably ought to wear straitjackets as well, and that equipment also seems to be missing from the region!"

At the end of the valley, just before the road over the Col de l'Isèran

disappears under snow, is the village of Bonneval-sur-Arc. Philippe had told us that we should definitively visit Bonneval during our stay, for the terrain is gnarly, and the people…well, let's just say that the people suit the terrain.

Bonneval's extreme terrain had taken its toll on the local population, according to Philippe. In the early 1980s, this was the scene of one of the major ski avalanche tragedies in modern history, when about a dozen people, all locals, met their fate at the hands of the white death. This disaster, however, had little effect on the attitude of the local residents, Philippe told us, who saw avalanches merely as one of the many innate hazards of the mountains. After the dust had cleared, the villagers continued to challenge the mountain with the same derring-do that they always had.

I could see what Philippe meant even before we arrived. Driving along the last piece of road approaching the village, we observed tracks emerging from a few couloirs that looked unskiable. All that was still visible of the tracks were the last few turns, because snow sloughs and small avalanches had obscured the rest. The scenery above Bonneval was spectacular as well. Hanging glaciers interspersed with jagged peaks dominated the landscape above the village.

» This line was sicker than anything I had ever seen in an extreme competition. «

The Bonneval tourist brochure also concurred with Philippe's assessment of the locals. It states, "…the people of Bonneval…have always loved this harsh but magnificent land. They are said to be hard mountain people and this is true."

I AM ALWAYS A KEEN OBSERVER of my surroundings in the mountains, and particularly so when I am visiting an area which is new to me. My observations added further proof to the tough reputation of the locals.

I noticed a snowboarder riding off-piste from the top of the Pointe d'Andagne. "This could be interesting," I thought, until his line ended in a long series of high cliffs. They were much too extensive to jump. But this character was either Spiderman or another mountain-valley incest victim. This line was sicker than anything I had ever seen in an extreme competition. He used rocks as trampolines, and suddenly

he was cruising out, unscathed, below the cliffs. Later in the day, I noticed that he had done an encore performance, as if to point out that the crazy line was no mere accident.

I understood that this was *not* a location where one should follow a stray set of tracks willy-nilly wherever they might lead. Surprisingly, there was still plenty of powder left over from the day before in locations that were skiable for mere mortals and men of sound mind. We found good powder on the north face of the mountain all day, and interspersed that with some cruising on the well-manicured and empty pistes.

AT THE END OF THE DAY, I WENT to the ski school to get more information for my story and met instructor Paul Blanc, a young man in his thirties. He named for me the various couloirs that descend to the road—Couloir de la Fontaine, Senail Coupé, Tchou, Midi, Trois Mentons and Andagne.

Then, I asked him about the avalanche in the early '80s. There are times when one wishes that one could suck the words back into one's mouth, and this was one of those times.

"Yes, it was in 1982," Paul answered matter-of-factly, "My father and my sister were two of the eleven victims."

I am generally a rather talkative person but I was speechless. I put down my pen and stopped taking notes.

After a moment, I half-mumbled, "I'm sorry."

"Of course, it was a bad time for our village, but it is a long time ago," said Paul, without batting an eye. The accident clearly had not deterred Paul from a life of mountains and skiing. He pointed on the map to where the accident had happened, and it was the same place where a local girl had been caught in a small slide just the day before!

I couldn't help but think again about my theory of inbreeding. "These people are missing some gene which relates to rational thinking," I thought to myself.

"Do you have quite a few relatives here in town?" I asked, trying not to betray the reason for my question.

"Oh, yes," shot back the answer quickly, "I have about 40 cousins in the village!" The entire village has no more than 240 inhabitants.

"Aha," I thought to myself, "theory vindicated!" I felt like Einstein having just jotted down his theory of relativity. In retrospect, however, I must admit that my conclusion was somewhat premature.

LEFT PAGE
Val Fréjus has lots of open terrain.

THIS PAGE
UPPER LEFT: Simon Bastelica shows that he prefers flying to skiing.
LOWER LEFT: The local youths of Val Cenis have apparently not yet discovered helmets.
RIGHT: Simon Bastelica flies through the air once again. Are these guys really playing with a full deck?

That evening, the Lombarde wind blew another storm in from the south. By morning, the upper slopes were decked out in half a meter of new snow, and it was still coming down. The cloud cover handicapped us in the early hours, but after lunch the visibility improved somewhat, and we began a series of fifteen laps on the 30–35-degree slopes west of the La Tomba Poma Lift. The Met Chair at the top was closed, and the lower runs were porridge, but we had found our little piece of heaven for the day. Anything more would have been superfluous.

As I rode up the Poma that afternoon, a group of local seven- and eight-year-olds skied playfully through the powder in a steep ravine beside the lift. They were waist deep in snow and seemed to love every minute of it. Suddenly, I was forced to rethink my position. "These little guys will be the cliff-jumping maniacs of the next decade," I thought to myself, and why not? If they are already so fluid on their boards in all terrain at this early age, it is the natural progression of things.

I suddenly saw the true light. Environment rather than inbreeding was the true determining factor in the Maurienne Valley, just as it is everywhere else. Some kids who grow up on the south side of Chicago are junkies and pushers by the time they are teenagers, and children from Calcutta are often pickpockets and beggars. Many of the kids with whom I grew up in Beverly Hills are now doctors and lawyers, driving their Beemers and Benzes through traffic every day to and from their large estates and villas.

HERE IN THE ISOLATED MOUNTAIN VALLEYS of southern France, the young people are exposed to other heroes and other dangers. All things considered, I think I will try to steer my Erik clear of South Chicago, Calcutta and even Beverly Hills. In fact, I see no reason why I shouldn't return with him next season to the rugged environment of the Maurianne Valley. If I have any influence at all, however, he will take an avalanche course and wear a helmet.

Chapter 5. ITALY

Like its neighbors to the north, Italy is a major ski country. It shares the Alps' highest peak with France, although in Italy, the mountain is known as Monte Bianco. Courmayeur, like its French counterpart, Chamonix, is a mountaineering center with rather extreme off-piste skiing on the Heilbronner Glacier as well as some ideal freeride terrain accessible from the Cresta d'Arp on the other side of the valley.

While the majority of the 400-plus ski areas in the country are situated in the provinces along the northern border, skiing exists in virtually all sections of Italy. There are a number of ski resorts in Tuscany, various ski villages close to Rome, and even the province of Basilicata, in the far south, offers skiing. In addition, there are lifts on the islands of Sardinia and Sicily!

Perhaps the ski region most representative of Italian skiing is that which encompasses the stunning Dolomite Mountains. With over 460 ski lifts, this is one of the largest (non-connected) ski areas in the world. That, in conjunction with the spectacular scenery, is reason enough for all skiers to make a pilgrimage here sometime in their lives. The Dolomite ski region has been of historical significance as well, as one if its towns, Cortina d'Ampezzo, hosted the Winter Olympics in 1956.

Another of Italy's most noteworthy ski areas is the Via Lattea (Milky Way) region in the province of Piedmont near the French border. This lift system, host to the 2006 Olympics, has more than 90 lifts and 400 kilometers of pistes, counting it too among the world's largest ski areas.

While Sestriere is the Via Lattea's most famous ski resort, I have chosen to focus on Sauze d'Oulx, the lesser-known back side of Sestriere. Sauze is not only a more picturesque town, it is also situated closer to the center of the ski region.

To fill out my section on Italy, I have chosen two ski resorts that are not at all as large or famous as the Dolomite and Via Lattea ski areas. Alagna Valsesia cannot compete with its neighbors in number of lifts, but it does have a 2069-meter lift-served vertical drop, placing it among the top ten in the world in that category. It is a picturesque village, built in the shadow of Monte Rosa and linked with the villages of Gressoney and Champoluc. Alagna is an unusual ski area with almost no pistes and very steep terrain, quite in keeping with the most recent direction of the ski world toward extremism. It is just one of many excellent resorts for off-piste skiing in the Aosta Valley.

The furthest south that one can ski in Italy is on Mt. Etna, on the island of Sicily. This is an experience at least as unusual as skiing the totally unprepared mountains of Alagna. Mt. Etna's ski terrain is not extreme, but the nature is just as radical in a different sense. Here, one skis under a plume of smoke, as Etna is the most active volcano in Europe. As recently as 2002, a major eruption destroyed one of the two ski areas on the mountain, and lava came within a stone's throw of the village of Linguaglossa. That is extreme enough for me.

THE MAGICAL DOLOMITES

The late Patrick Vallençant, the legendary French extreme skier, had a favorite refuge, away from his native Chamonix, for skiing radical couloirs. Ever since Patrick, many years ago, first told me of his partiality for steep skiing amidst the craggy pinnacles and towers of the Dolomites of Northern Italy, I had longed to explore them myself. My desire finally came to fruition.

My friend Caspar was again my companion on this trip, and we cruised over the Brenner Pass and wound our way into Val Gardena close to midnight. A full moon illuminated the jagged Langkofel group of peaks, and it looked a bit like the floodlights on Notre Dame Cathedral. I could hear the hunchback and a thousand other Gothic gremlins and banshees lurking around amongst the rocks. We grabbed a quick pizza (Of course, what else? This was Italy after all.) and nestled in under warm quilts in the village of Selva.

Selva dates back to the 13th century, and as the morning sun brought some of the other peaks of the Dolomites into a clearer perspective, they, too, conjured up visions of medieval times. Their limestone spires and steeples filled the skyline like a community of feudal castles and churches. The light calcium rock that makes up this range gave the sheer faces distinct shadings of yellow and orange, and the soft stone was formed into thousands of pinnacles and gargoyles.

The steep, narrow gullies and couloirs that abound here are juxtaposed with large areas of open, intermediate terrain, dropping eventually into forested trails leading back to the many villages surrounding the Dolomites.

It became immediately clear that we would need a guide to find our way into the skiable couloirs, amidst the maze of ornate obelisks. For that purpose, we enlisted the services of Hermann Comploj, a sturdy, compact, confident man, who, it turned out, was not too far descended from a chamois. Hermann was born and raised in Val Gardena and spoke the local language of Ladino, a bastardization of Latin native to four mountain villages deep in the Dolomites and vaguely related to

Rhaeto-Romansch, the equally obscure tongue of the Engadine Valley of Switzerland.

Hermann also spoke Italian, German and English and seemed, as many mountain men, to part with words in any of the languages with equal reluctance. Hermann's taciturn nature was of no great concern. We told him that we wished to be guided into some steep, narrow and rarely skied chutes, and he assured us that he could fulfill that task.

We started our first day skiing half of the famous tourist circus known as the Sella Ronda, until we arrived at Passo Pordoi. Here, in the least likely spot on Earth to build a lift of any kind, a cable car took us more than 700 vertical meters up a perpendicular rock wall. From the top, one can ski the famous Val Mezdi (Midday Valley) descent, so named because only around noon does the sun manage to send a few rays of light between the vertical walls on either side.

The tour began with a flat 45-minute walk to the Rifugio Boe. There, we entered the relatively steep throat of the valley. Officially, this route is off-piste, but it is very well-known and not extreme. Hence, the gully was a field of moguls. We bounced through the bumps in the narrow entry and eventually the valley widened.

Standing in the shadows of the cliffs that rise toward the heavens, I felt like John Wayne on a solo ride through Arizona's Monument Valley in mid-winter. I expected at any moment that the entire Apache nation would appear along the cliff-top in full headdress.

We skied out of the Val Mezdi before any Apaches or avalanches could block our retreat. The tour had been visually stunning albeit not the kind of difficult couloir we had imagined skiing during our stay here. I mentioned to Hermann that I hoped he trusted our skiing ability enough to guide us into some more formidable gorges and canyons.

"We cannot do everything in one day," he retorted, without a trace of a smile, and I wondered what tomorrow would bring.

Hermann picked us up early the following morning and drove us to the Marmolada Glacier. The lift here resembled an implement of torture

Descending from the Passo Pordoi, Martin Söderqvist shoots through a narrow crack in the dramatic limestone cliffs of the Dolomites.

from the Spanish Inquisition, but we were assured that it was specifically built for transporting skiers, as recently as 1974.

The lift was a narrow basket for two passengers, who must perform a pony-express entry while the garbage can-shaped apparatus moves quickly past. Meanwhile, the lift attendant lunges after the basket, depositing the skis, hopefully without knocking out either of the passengers' teeth in the process. With a little luck, two skiers and two pairs of skis then stand tightly pressed together up to the top station, where the entire procedure is reversed.

This would be an opportune lift line to search out a partner with the endowments of Pamela Anderson, I mused, but I ended up pressed chest to chest with Caspar. He must have eaten garlic pasta for breakfast. My thoughts returned to strange methods of torture, but I survived the ride intact.

HERMANN HAD TOLD US TO BRING our touring skis, so we knew we had a bit of work awaiting us this morning. We began with a few lines of powder turns. Then, without a word, Hermann altered his bindings into the walking mode. He pointed to a narrow corridor in the distance and we began to hike. About two hours later, we placed our skis on our shoulders and began to kick small toeholds into the snow of a 40-degree couloir. It was clear that we were to ski down the opposite side.

As I approached the top, I expected a small ledge or flat shelf where we could sit, rest and leisurely step into our skis for the descent. No such luck! I swallowed hard and my heart lurched into my throat as I reached the notch between the rocks. No ledge, no shelf, no place to rest, no comfortable spot to put on the skis and about 50 degrees steep and even narrower down the opposite side.

Hermann was already unpacking his rope, and as he saw the fear in my eyes, a wide smile crossed his face.

"This is f_cking skiing, guys!" he grinned, and I realized, with mixed emotions, that he had not underestimated our abilities after all.

Caspar, who has some climbing experience, nonchalantly roped himself in and rappelled down the back door of the Forcella Marmolada. With much trepidation, I took the rope around my waist for security, put my skis and poles in my right hand, and slowly worked my way downward. Hermann hollered encouragement from above and Caspar laughed from below. I felt like the court jester.

Once I was safely beside Caspar, Hermann threw down the rope and shouted, "Okay, I ski it down."

With that, our Merlin the magician of the mountains hopped into the couloir, which was hardly wide enough for his skis at the top. One cannot really side slip wind crust, but Hermann sidehopped the first 20 meters, jabbing his poles into the snow on his way down as a sort of braking system. Then, he made three or four double-pole-plant jump turns, and he was at our side.

The difficult part of the day's tour accomplished, we looked across broad fields of virgin corn snow stretching out below us, which ended in the wide Contrin Valley. The valley was a picture of springtime, far removed from the ominous castle ramparts and parapets above, and we finished our tour cross-country skiing along a stream and winding our way down a forest trail to the village of Alba.

A COUPLE OF BEERS and a short hitchhike later, we were back on the Marmolada. One of the great joys of skiing in spring is a day when one can ski corn snow in the morning and powder in the afternoon. This was just such a day. A 20-minute hike from the top of the "garbage can lift" took us to fields of January powder—in April, no less. This day had everything—corn snow, powder, pristine skies and adventure. In addition, Hermann had begun to loosen up and enjoy his assignment of guiding a couple of foreigners from the modern world through his medieval

domain of dungeons and dragons. The only remaining question was what did Hermann have in store for us tomorrow to top this?

Again our host picked us up early and told us to bring our touring skis. We soon were marching the same 45-minute route that we walked the first day toward the Val Mezdi. This time, we took a left turn at the Rifugio Boe and continued our hike. Soon Caspar, who much prefers skiing downhill to walking uphill on skis, was grumbling.

"I can't believe this. They comp us with a free Super Dolomiti lift pass, with 460 lifts at our disposal, and we spend our whole vacation walking."

"Shhh, Caspar," I whispered. "Don't antagonize Hermann. His humor may change and he could leave us at the mercy of the Gothic beasts that rule this domain."

SURE ENOUGH, WE WERE FAST approaching an area that was certainly swarming with spirits, specters and phantoms from the Dark Ages. It was a scene directly from a Spielberg film. Obelisks and minarets surrounded us. Certainly, the area had been booby-trapped to stop Indiana Jones or any other would-be intruders of this sacred cathedral. One false move and the flying buttresses that held up the walls of this temple were sure to fold up, and the towers of stone would come tumbling down upon us. Only one escape route was apparent—a sheer face of wind-packed powder between the turrets. We followed our intrepid leader exactly so as not to unleash any booby-traps.

As the slope began to plane out into a valley, Hermann began to traverse to the left rather than following the obvious path down the valley to the right.

"Of course," I said to myself. "They want us to go right. It looks like a clear path, but it's certainly blocked by a fire-breathing serpent."

I whispered to Caspar, "I think Hermann's on our side after all!"

"I'm not so sure," retorted Caspar, as Hermann placed his skis once again on his shoulder and began to zigzag up another perilous-looking corridor between the cliffs.

I normally would have suspected the sun-drenched, soft snow of this south-exposed slope to be an avalanche trap, but I was becoming ever more confident that Hermann represented the forces of good.

This time, there was a comfortable ledge at the top, which overlooked our path back to civilization—a precipitous powder-filled gorge, which narrowed into an 8-meter-wide elevator shaft. We could see the serpentine road about 900 meters directly below us. We tried not to let the view disturb our lunch. I began to wolf down a sandwich while Hermann opened his thermos.

"Have some tea, guys," offered Hermann. "This is called 'magical rhum'. It's a homemade blend from my teahouse down in town."

"You're kidding, right? I mean, I can picture you owning a bar in some dungeon-like local cellar, or even running a small alpine and climbing shop...but a teahouse? Come on!" I said.

"Really, guys. You'll have to stop by this afternoon and have some of my wife's carrot cake."

One sip of his tea assured me of Hermann's earnestness. It was an enchanted blend of rose petals, wild mountain berries and some 14th century aphrodisiac. One swallow brought incandescent visions of young nubile nymphs frolicking half-naked in lush carpets of mayflowers. All horrible visions of forked-tongued creatures who lived among the gargoyles here in the belfry of the Dolomites were purged from my mind, and I now felt certain that this magic potion would keep us safe from all evil.

After lunch, Hermann took out his shovel and excavated a small hole to check for avalanche booby-traps.

"All clear!" He finally called.

Powder turns in the initial corridor were followed by jump turns to fight off the crust in the elevator shaft. Nothing could thwart our efforts after our magic elixir. We definitely felt that we had earned a reward after negotiating to completion what Hermann called the Forcella Piz da Lec.

That afternoon we took our guide up on his invitation and we made a visit to his teahouse. We watched with wonder as Hermann plucked

THIS PAGE: LEFT: The Dolomites are characterized by pinnacles of limestone like this one in the background as Martin Söderqvist whizzes past. UPPER RIGHT: Hermann Comploj leads us amidst some of the stunning cliffs near his home in Val Gardena. LOWER RIGHT: Similar to Austria, the Dolomite ski region is also characterized by many cozy huts like this one in front of the Sass Pordoi.
RIGHT PAGE: Many pistes in the Dolomites are relatively gentle, but the off-piste fare will challenge the best skiers. Here, Reinhard Senoner skis down a steep pitch from atop the Sass Pordoi.

ingredients from a dozen bags to create another batch of "magical rhum" tea. We each devoured a moist slice of carrot cake as well and felt well fortified against any potential evil that might await us on the morrow.

Wednesday morning, we drove to Cortina d'Ampezzo. In Val Gardena, one sees some fur on the local ladies, but in Cortina, the foxes wear mink, the bunnies wear ermine and the wolves abound. This is Italy's winter answer to Monte Carlo. Of course, the local garb is beside the point, which, in our case, was to ski the Bus de Tofana.

WE BEGAN WITH A RIDE UP the cable car at the Tofana di Mezzo and then hiked 20 minutes further. (No touring skis were necessary and Caspar was ecstatic.) *Bus* is Italian for hole, and we now found ourselves standing in front of a window in the rocks, prepared to climb through and ski whatever we found on the other side. We stepped through the portal and looked down.

The back side was steep, as usual. Apparently, a recent invasion of Huns had been thwarted by hurling huge white cannon balls at the intruders. The Huns seemed to have abandoned the site, but the siege had left its scars. We skied down the first section very careful-

» This is f_cking skiing, guys!" he grinned... «

ly, trying to avoid the frozen trenches and snowballs of this long forgotten struggle. Finally, we emerged from the battlefield and could dance blithely over wide expanses of ripe corn snow the rest of the way down.

The weather was changing, and the S-shaped imprints we left shimmering like snail tracks in the corn snow above Cortina proved to be our last glimpse of spring in the Dolomites. By the following day, low clouds shrouded the peaks, and we were confined to the lower slopes, where there was some visibility.

We spent the morning skiing about 50 centimeters of "April powder", a euphemism for slogging through sticky gobs of overcooked cannelloni.

We were skiing in the Falzarego area, scenically one of the most beautiful parts of the Dolomites according to Hermann, but we would have to return on another occasion to enjoy the views.

AFTER A MORNING OF EXERCISE in the heavy powder, we brushed off our armor outside the Rifugio Scotoni. *Rifugio* is the Italian word for refuge, and conjures up an image of a primitive shack where one can warm up and purchase a plate of frankfurters and baked beans. Italy's *rifugios* are sometimes more developed than that.

Here, two cooks sweated over a large, indoor, open grill in the middle of the dining room of this rustic restaurant. We ordered a mixed grill and received an oversized wooden plate covered with ribs, a pork chop, a cut of beef, bacon, a garlicky Italian sausage, grilled vegetables and a baked potato. A bottle of *vino tinto*, a few *grappas* (Italian schnapps) and two hours later, we rolled out the door and back onto our skis.

Friday morning looked even gloomier than the day before. The mist and fog had settled lower on the spires and towers of our medieval playground. It was an appropriate time to finish our adventure in the Dolomites. We stopped off at the wizard's teahouse, purchased a two-year supply of "magical rhum", "strawberry-kiwi", "peach-apricot" and "forest fruit" teas to ward off modern-day evil spirits and bade Hermann and his wife a fond farewell.

In our short stay, we had only scraped the surface of the hundreds of skiable chasms and ravines in the Dolomites, and we promised Hermann that we would be back. We hopped in our time machine, which looked remarkably similar to a rusty, old Volvo station wagon, and headed north, out of the 1300s and back over the Brenner Pass into the 21st century.

All looked normal again—no Gothic spires or medieval castles towering overhead and no wizards, witches or dragons—just ordinary cows grazing lazily. Had it all been a dream? I wrenched my right arm back into my rucksack and pulled out a tin of "magical rhum" tea. No, it had indeed been real. On the bottom of the tea tin was a sticker with Hermann's telephone number, our time machine's code back to the land of Camelot.

SAUZE D'OULX AND THE VIA LATTEA
A SKI BUM'S BEST FRIEND IS HIS PHONE BOOK

The first time I heard of Sauze d'Oulx was long ago, when a British friend who knew of my fondness for off-piste skiing suggested that this might be the ideal ski area for me. He described a resort with many red, blue and green runs where his countrymen flailed and floundered like a thousand Keystone Cops, while millions of tons of powder lay untouched in the forest, being tracked only by the resident deer and mountain goats. I made a mental note and went on with my life.

The next time Sauze d'Oulx came to my attention, it was a Swedish friend who told me of skiing powder with a mountain guide among the large larch forests that cover the mountains above the village. As they were skiing, the guide suddenly spotted a deer in the woods. He let out with a kind of war whoop and schussed straight toward the startled animal.

Now, a deer can ordinarily outrun a man 100 times out of 100, even if the man is Ben Johnson. In this case, however, the man was equipped with skis, which the deer was not, and the snow was so deep that our four-footed friend had virtually no chance against a powder skier. While the deer tried in vain to leap away in a meter of bottomless fluff, the ski guide spread his legs like a bowlegged cowboy and skied right up onto the frightened animal's back. An addendum was added to my mental note.

The third time Sauze entered my awareness was when my friend Rupert Scheiner and I drove past the "Welcome to Sauze d'Oulx" sign. What met our eyes upon arrival in Sauze pretty closely matched my friend's description of twenty years prior. Around every corner of the windy streets were signs heralding the Scotch Bar, the Andy Capp Pub, the Cotton Club, McGinnity's Irish Pub and a dozen other establish-

one invariably, without too much effort, finds other skiers of a similar ilk. This would prove to be a large part of our story in Sauze.

During our first day of skiing, it was snowing, the visibility was poor and Rupert and I tried to find our way around a small section of the lift system. We were about as successful as a couple of blind, retarded rats in a labyrinth. We gave up our mission a bit early and went to the Sporting Club wine bar for après-ski. There, over a glass of *vino tinto*, we began chatting with Rob Raymond. He was English (naturally) and had spent many winters in Sauze. He had first come here in his early twenties, no different from the thousands of other Brits who made up a good part of Sauze's work force, planning to spend the proverbial season in the Alps before getting serious about life.

I imagine that his skiing ability at the time was no better than that of hundreds of his countrymen whom we saw sprawled out into all kinds of contortions during our first day on the pistes. But, a broken back, broken nose, two broken cheekbones, one cracked skull and twenty years later, Rob Raymond was still in Sauze. In the interim, he had moved on from his first job in a ski shop to seven years on the ski patrol, many years organizing tourist races and a myriad of other odd jobs necessary for ski-bum survival. In the process, he had also become a very accomplished skier.

> **» The ski guide spread his legs and skied right up onto the frightened animal's back.«**

Rob very kindly offered to show us around. He also introduced us to Marco Degani, a local ski guide who, Rob explained, knew the region even better than he did and might have some free time. As Rob was no ordinary ski bum, Marco was not your run-of-the-mill mountain guide. He was the president of the Piedmont Guide Association and had been skiing and guiding people all over the world.

Marco not only knew the Milky Way area blindfolded, but the list of other experiences under his belt was longer than a pair of speed skis. Marco had climbed and telemark-skied couloirs near Boda in the north of Norway, guided numerous trekking excursions in Nepal, led a group through the deserts of Yemen and skied from an elevation of 7500 meters in China.

THE FOLLOWING MORNING, Marco and Rob began showing us around their backyard. The sun was shining on about 20 centimeters of newly fallen snow on the upper mountain. We began by skiing some of the easily visible off-piste runs that would probably soon be tracked up by the handful of competent skiers in Sauze.

Around eleven o'clock, we laid first tracks down the back side of Mt. Fraiteve to the village of Borgata. After quickly downing a pasta lunch, we remounted Fraiteve, and Marco directed us to a series of lovely couloirs. They all lay untouched, even now after lunch.

We leapt into the central couloir and wove our way between the jagged cliffs on either side until we emerged atop a huge open bowl. A hundred-odd turns later we arrived directly at the middle station of the gondola that links Sestriere to Sauze. We finished the day back on the north-facing slopes of Sauze, with Rob leading us on three or four tree-slaloms among the widely spaced larch forests that cover much of the southern Alps.

While we had no problem finding many good lines of powder, Rob pointed out that if his fellow countrymen would attempt to ski the forests here, the hospitals would be full from Milano to Sicily. The Torino crowd, on the other hand, had a style that would leave most of them dead on impact if they ever ventured into the woods. Either way, he indicated that we would be able to find chaste snow in the forest for days to come.

San Sicario also has a run amongst the trees that is well worth a visit. Beginning on the open upper slopes far to the west of the Fraiteve T-bar is a long descent that eventually drops into some beautiful trees, full of glades, ridges, gullies and whatever else a perfect skier's playground

ments to cater to the strong British contingent of tourists. Apparently, hordes of English guests share the slopes with Italian kamikaze weekenders from nearby Turin, while most of the rest of the ski world has yet to discover this pearl of the southern Alps.

Sauze's lack of recognition in much of the ski world is rather strange, as it is part of the Milky Way lift system, one of Italy's largest ski regions. Directly connected with Sauze is world famous Sestriere, one of the dinosaurs of the ski industry, built by the Fiat family in the 1930s. In addition, one can also cavort on skis among the villages of Grangesises, Borgata, Cesana Torinese, Claviere, Jouvenceaux, San Sicario and the French village of Montgenèvre.

THE ENJOYMENT OF SKIING often goes beyond the carving of turns on freshly groomed corduroy or face shots in a meter of eiderdown. It extends to the ambience of a ski resort, and even more importantly to the people one meets and the friendships that are born of shared experiences on the slopes. Whether one is a charter-holiday guest or a career ski bum,

LEFT PAGE
Guide Marco Degani enjoys a morning of heliskiing in the backcountry behind Sestriere.

THIS PAGE
LEFT: Rupert Scheiner about to drop out of sight in the Via Lattia backcountry.
RIGHT: Sestriere, site of most of the ski events in the 2006 Winter Olympics.

should include. The run begins at 2700 meters and ends on a long, roller-coaster traverse that continues almost interminably before spitting free-riders back out onto the blue run close to the bottom, 1000 vertical meters below.

The Milky Way system is one of the few areas in the Alps that offers heliskiing right at its doorstep and for relatively little money. Here was a place where a ski bum could save his tips from waiting tables and splurge on a chopper run. For the next two days, we drove in convoy with a bunch of local ski and board bums to the nearby helipad. I imagine the chopper service is used to catering to groups of wealthy Milanese, and some jaws certainly dropped when our entourage of ski bum-mobiles pulled up.

Darroch Simon, a New Zealander, led the convoy in twenty-year-old, orange Mercedes diesel mini-van. A couple of Italians followed close behind in an old VW Golf, spewing exhaust fumes thick enough to start a full-scale smog alert. Rupert and I followed the Italians in my rusty Volvo, headlights ablaze to cut through the smoke, and bringing up the rear was a young English snowboarder named Spencer Grundy, in an ancient converted van, decorated with a multi-colored sunrise, half a dozen snowboard decals, and a smashed headlight and turn indicator. The pilot certainly thought that we had missed the turn-off to the city dump, but once we showed him some cold hard cash, he figured we had come to the right place after all.

In spite of over 90 lifts around the Milky Way, there are plenty of near-by peaks that are inaccessible from the lift system and yet, no more than a few minutes away by air. We skied down a couple of brilliant runs in the mountains behind Sestriere.

IT BECAME CLEAR THAT EVEN the heliskiers in this corner of the ski world were not very experienced, because we chose a descent that Marco had never before skied, as his patrons invariably were only capable of the easier runs. Marco grinned from ear to ear at the chance to ski a new and challenging route. The chute that we chose was a direct north face, and despite the bright sun, the powder was well protected from the ill effects of spring warmth. Twenty centimeters of airy, weightless moon dust swirled about our legs as we christened this unnamed corridor.

Marco followed this up with another north face that began with a narrow passage between the rocks and continued into a series of steep, open slopes. The group was all smiles when we sat down to the obligatory noontime pasta. After lunch, Rob led us back among the larches until it was time for some après-ski Chianti at the Sporting Club.

The next morning, we were flown to the opposite end of the Milky Way, beginning atop the Chalanche Ronde, across the valley from San Sicario. The altimeter showed that we were around 3000 meters high as we all clattered down from the chopper and sank to our knees in powder. Thirteen-hundred vertical meters of swooping and whooping later, we were ready for our second flight of the day, to an even longer descent from atop the Rochers Charniers into the Vallone delle Baisses and the village of Claviere.

FOR THE NEXT FEW DAYS, we explored the big north-facing bowl atop the Sauze system and left many fresh tracks near the uppermost lift in Sestriere, the La Motta T-bar (2823 m). Eventually, the powder began growing thin, if only from all of our own tracks.

Something that Rob had mentioned helped us decide where to ski on our final day. Rob had never skied in Bardonecchia, an old ski village just 30 minutes away but not a part of the Milky Way. A nearby ski system with 23 lifts and 1460 vertical meters of skiing that had not been discovered by a twenty-year veteran of the area seemed worth a visit.

Once again, Rupert and I were not disappointed, and Rob proved that you *can* teach an old ski bum a new trick or two. We found corn snow in the morning on Mt. Jafferau and powder in the afternoon on the opposite side of the valley near Punta della Mulattiera. As in Sauze, thousands of larches adorned the slopes, but here there were almost no people to be seen on the lifts, in the pistes or anywhere else. In between tours in amongst the trees, we could not help but take advantage of the empty, well groomed slopes and tear down a few of the intermediate pistes in full-blown GS turns.

At the bottom of the last run it was time to part ways. We all took out our phone books and exchanged addresses. I told Rob that he was welcome to sleep on my floor in Saalbach anytime, and I would be more than happy to return the favor and show him around our favorite powder haunts. Rupert added that Rob had a standing invitation to Sydney, if he ever wanted to go Down Under to ski in the Australian Alps. Rob, for his part, thanked us for stimulating him to try skiing in Bardonecchia after twenty seasons and invited us back for a return visit.

Thus ended a typical week in the life of three ski bums. We were a few hundred Euros poorer, a bounty of fresh tracks wealthier and our most valuable asset—our address book—had been enriched. We each had an additional name and telephone number as well as one more standing invitation to sleep on somebody's floor in the Alps. The Lord knows we ski bums work hard, but we *do* have a great retirement plan!

THE ALAGNA OFF-PISTE CULT

In 1956, in a back valley of the poor Piedmont region of northwestern Italy, a low-capacity cable car was constructed in three stages to take skiers from the farming village of Alagna Valsesia, at 1191 meters, up to Punta Indren at 3260 meters. That descent beneath the towering Monte Rosa massif became one of the longest lift-accessed descents in the world, but very few people knew. Perhaps more importantly, nobody seemed to care.

Nearby, Zermatt and Chamonix were fast becoming household names in the ski world, while most skiers remained oblivious to Alagna.

Time passed. Courmayeur and Cervinia flourished on the Italian side of Mont Blanc and the Matterhorn, respectively. In Alagna, the wood of the picturesque old Walliser houses was a shade or two darker for age and the lift company had a few more years of financial difficulty under its belt. Otherwise, nothing much had changed. Alagna's terrain was just too challenging for most skiers.

Even in the early 1990s, it was not at all uncommon for the Monrosa Lift Company that operated Alagna to sell no more than twenty tickets on a weekday—to one of the classic ski runs in the world! But like the dawn that creeps tentatively into Alagna's narrow valley, the ski resort was about to begin emerging from its decades of obscurity.

The skier of today is a different beast than his forebears. Powder freaks and freeriders are forever on the lookout for their next adventure. Alagna was perfectly suited. The only task was to get the word out—and out it got, like a genie being released by the accidental rubbing of an old lamp.

Alagna's transformation began in the mid-'90s. One day, without warning, the cult phenomenon began to engulf Alagna with its magic and mystic. Like its predecessor, La Grave, Alagna quite suddenly became tinged with an aura that had been absent for close to 40 years.

The cult effect works in strange ways. It moves magically and evasively throughout the world, like the aurora borealis. It suddenly touches a religious sect in San Francisco, then vanishes, only to reappear in Hollywood to transform some fledgling film star into an instant cult figure. Then, the cult effect drifts out of sight, only to pop up again, perhaps in a dying ski village, casting a spell over some decrepit relic of a ski lift from a bygone age.

Cults have rewritten history, as they have picked up momentum and move into the mainstream. Christianity started as a small cult; so did communism.

IT WAS, THEN, WITH A THOUGHT to history that I felt an uncontrollable urge to research the origins of the new Alagna cult by traveling to the source. Accompanying me on this mission was ski-sociologist Minna Gynther and powder-cult investigator George Koch. Past research to off-piste cult hideaways has revealed a pattern. Certain ingredients are always in the location, latent and waiting for a catalyst to begin the chain reaction that leads to worldwide fame.

First, the location must be virtually unknown to ski industry people. The skiing is the exclusive domain of the local villagers and weekend warriors from a few nearby towns. Second, the place must have an inordinate amount of off-piste territory or be blessed with copious dumps of powder snow—preferably both.

Third, cultists disdain the entrapments of modern-day ski centers, including mega-people-movers such as high-speed quads and efficient high-capacity gondolas. They also loathe expensive luxury hotels, which they generally cannot afford. Like ancient religious sects that would worship secretly in caves and live in catacombs, cult members prefer primitive accommodations. Cultists seek surroundings that are not likely to attract ordinary tourists. Most suitable are old-fashioned villages that look like they are from another century and lifts akin to museum pieces.

A helpful though not crucial final ingredient is some singular fact or statistic that gives the area bragging rights. Cult members love to whisper things like, "Can you believe it's got one of the longest vertical drops in the world, and nobody knows about it? Shhhh!"

AS WE PULLED INTO ALAGNA, we immediately began to see that it suited the profile. For five centuries, the people of the Valsesia Valley had searched for gold around here. Most of the buildings not only looked like but also were from one of those previous centuries. The ancient wooden houses with slate roofs created a postcard-perfect foreground to beautiful Monte Rosa.

We drove into the parking lot of the Alagna cable car at 9:30 in the morning and parked amidst a mere half-dozen other vehicles. Our task was to locate the catalyst for the cult phenomenon—the leader of this sect if there, in fact, was a leader.

As it happened, we did not have to find the source of the cult. The source found us. We had not even walked from the car to the lift, when we were intercepted by a darkly tanned middle-aged gentleman with flowing gray hair and an impish smile. I had heard of Sergio Gabbi, for he had figured prominently in various write-ups that I had read about Alagna. He had apparently been informed of our arrival.

"Jimmy Petterson?" he inquired. I nodded and Sergio continued, "You will ski with Michele Cucchi today. He is one of the top guides in Alagna. I can meet you at six o'clock to discuss the plans for the week. I'm sorry, no powder," he added with a shrug, "but I think we can show you some interesting skiing anyway!"

Michele led us into the first stage of the cable car, where 40 years worth of spilled diesel rose to our nostrils. (Since the time of my visit,

an eight-passenger gondola and a double chair lift have replaced the two lower legs of the old cable car.) We shared the cable car with three other skiers and about 700 liters of water. At the middle station, we helped the lift attendants carry the 25-liter containers onto the next cable car—the price of a prompt continuation.

Michele Cucchi, a charming, lanky man in his thirties, had just come down from an early morning warmup run on Canale Longhez. This is a 45–50-degree north-facing chute with an extremely rocky entry. It was covered with wind-rutted, uneven snow, packed so hard by the wind that one would have needed a razor blade to get an edge into it. He looked disappointed when we suggested that for our first day, we might prefer to get an overview of the region by cruising around the pistes of Alagna and the neighboring villages of Gressoney and Champoluc.

Alagna itself has almost no pistes, so we skied off-piste into the Gressoney lift system and then cruised on perfectly groomed corn snow to Champoluc and back. At about four o'clock, our group arrived at Paso del Salati, where the Gabiet Gondola from Gressoney deposits skiers to put them into position to plunge back down toward Alagna. Near the top, we paused at the 100-year-old Guglielmina Hotel for some refreshments.

THIS PICTURESQUE ANTIQUE, WITH PAINT peeling off its walls, is situated at close to 3000 meters. It evokes a distant memory of Alagna's golden age. At the turn of the 19th century, Alagna had been a summer mountain retreat for the crème de la crème of Italian high society. The queen of Italy stayed regularly at the Hotel Monte Rosa, in the heart of the village, and the Guglielmina boasted 80 beds that were full all summer. In this pre-lift era, guests rode up on mules.

We soon left the Guglielmina, slid over vast fields of corn snow in the gargantuan Olen Valley and arrived back in town just in time for my meeting with Sergio. As we discussed, it became increasingly clear

LEFT PAGE
Lunatic guide Andrea Enzio about to enter Vittoria. With its 60-degree entry, Vittoria is Alagna's ultimate proof of manhood.

THIS PAGE
UPPER LEFT: Chopper landing to bring us up onto the Monte Rosa.
LOWER LEFT: Minna glances down as Andrea Enzio lowers her into an Alagna *canalino*.
RIGHT: Michele Cucchi finds that a small waterfall is in his way near the bottom of one of Alagna's chutes.

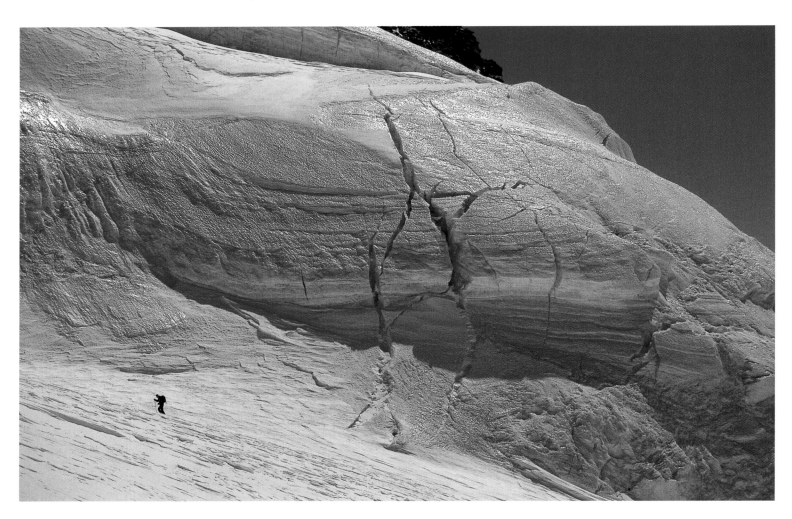

that he was the guru of the Alagna cult, and that he had almost single-handedly put the processes into motion to bring international recognition to his back-valley hideaway.

Among other things, Sergio had schemed to bring Swedish ski journalist Gunnar Andersson here in 1992. Gunnar became Sergio's original mouthpiece to spread the gospel of Alagna. Not too long thereafter, the first Swedish ski bum, Patrik Jonsson, arrived. So did the Swedish Down Film crew, led by Niclas Allestig. Their footage about Alagna increased the number of ski bums to about twenty by the following season and enhanced the legend of Alagna, upon which the cult is based.

IN THE MEANTIME, SERGIO WAS NOT resting. In his quest to spread the religion, he contacted *Powder Magazine*, the bible of off-piste skiing. In 1995, editor Steve Casimiro, photographer Scott Markowitz and a team of top models arrived to savor the delights of Valsesian powder. They soon spread the saga of this forgotten ski village to an even larger segment of the population. Powder worshippers began the long pilgrimage from all corners of the skiing world.

Because the cult was growing quickly, Sergio began to accumulate an elite core of guides. At our after-ski meeting, disciples Michele, Roberto Vazler and Andrea Enzio were also present to help plan our adventures.

Sergio was helping some scientists high on Monte Rosa the following day, and he suggested that we join in the helicopter. He got no argument from me. The next morning, we landed in the shadow of the Rifugio Margherita, at 4554 meters, the world's highest mountain refuge. The Matterhorn, Mont Blanc and Monte Rosa rose above a sea of clouds that obscured the valleys below. Roberto led us among towering walls of ice and over harsh, exposed, wind-swept slopes to the top of a long, steep pitch known as Canalino Gnifetti.

» Entry at 60 degrees, slope 50 degrees. Any error won't be forgiven. Guide advisable.«

At this point, it is important to explain the difference between *canalino* and cannelloni. *Canalino* is an Italian word for couloir or gully, while cannelloni is a pasta. Sergio Gabbi and his disciples eat cannelloni for dinner, but they devour *canalini* (plural of *canalino*) for breakfast and spit out the stones. They wash this all down with a few swallows of glacial ice water, which then runs in their veins for the rest of the day, while they coolly negotiate ski terrain that would make Superman tremble.

Minna, George and I now gazed down—straight down—Canalino Gnifetti, more of a wall than a couloir, with rocks and cliffs in the middle. Roberto pointed out a large crevasse at the base of the slope's left side. He suggested casually that this particular obstacle would make it advisable to ski to the right of the rocks.

The top of the wall was a convex 50-degree slope, which we began to ski just above the rocks. That is enough to give anyone wobbly legs, disciples excluded. The snow was excellent corn snow, but Minna stood nervously at the top, wondering why there isn't a helicopter around when you really need one. She apprehensively alternated between side slips and hesitant jump turns, as Roberto tried to coax her down by calling out, *"No problemo!"* and *"Normalo!"*

After eight to ten turns, we traversed to the right, alleviating the "you fall—you die" feeling. At this point, the angle mellowed out to between 40 and 45 degrees, which seemed like a piece of cake by comparison.

Soon, we were down below the Gnifetti Canalino, gliding effortlessly over glistening spring snow, leaving long sets of symmetrical tracks in the midday sun. By the time we arrived at the middle station of the cable car, we had skied about 2700 vertical meters. Earlier in the season, we could have amassed another 650 meters of vertical right into the village. By this time in spring, however, the crocuses were in full bloom lower down. The lift would eventually have to take us down the last leg of our journey.

THAT EVENING, DINNER AT the Restaurante Unione, a charming stone building that used to be the village's union hall, was almost like necessary first aid to replenish our energy. Prosciutto ham, fettucini with asparagus, *polenta* (a cornmeal-based specialty) smothered in a cheese sauce, and *crème brûlé* with wild berries were all heaved back and washed down with a few pitchers of sparkling Italian wine. Now, we felt ready to take on tomorrow's disciple, Osvaldo Antonetti.

Osvaldo brought his wife along to translate for us, as he spoke no English. He did, however, ski fluently in any language. Our warmup run down the Eagle Couloir (35 degrees) was like a Sunday walk in the park. After lunch, a 15-minute hike from Passo del Salati brought us to a variation of the Gran Canale Stolenberg, a somewhat wider route that once again made me feel tiny and extremely vulnerable at the top, wishing for a short communion with God, mother or the good fairy.

Fifty fearful turns later, I looked back up and felt like a macho skier, but I knew that sensation to be very transitory. The feeling would possibly last until the next time one of Alagna's guides deposited me atop some death-defying *canalino* and said with a smile, *"No problemo! Normalo!"*, while my pulse rate doubled, and I gravely questioned my chosen profession.

This happened the next morning, when I stood with my eyes transfixed downward and felt that same gnawing doubt once again, courtesy of our newest leader, Andrea Enzio. If Sergio is the Christ figure of this perverse sect that worships the deep, the steep and the nearly impossible, then Andrea Enzio is John the Baptist.

Andrea, a master of all kinds of downhill transport over snow, belongs to the third generation of mountain guides from his family, and he is trying hard to be the last. He skis places that would make a kamikaze cringe. If he reaches middle age without needing a wheelchair, I will be convinced that he has a direct line to God. Jesus could walk on water, a horizontal feat of no small doing, but Andrea is just as impressive in the vertical world.

WE CLIMBED BEHIND ANDREA into a glacial basin known as the Bors and skied over to look at Alagna's ultimate proof of manhood—the initiation to the cult—a *canalino*, amidst a virtual torture chamber of killer cliffs, called Vittoria. Sergio had been the first maniac to make this descent.

Vittoria is described in *The Alagna Guide Book*, written by Marco Rizzi, as: "Extremely difficult. Entry at 60 degrees, slope 50 degrees. Any error won't be forgiven. Guide advisable. Ski extreme, only for ski mountaineers."

When the guru or one of his disciples takes a mere mortal into Vittoria, he ropes the skier in, at least for the upper section. Andrea, however, first skied down this cliff at the age of fifteen, alone, with no rope or climbing aids. He made the first ever snowboard descent of Vittoria in 1988, and on this particular day, he was guiding us on telemark skis, hoping to talk us into the leap of faith. George said he had read about too many suicide

sects in recent years, and I had forgotten to go to church the previous Sunday. Therefore, we opted for an alternate route.

Andrea's second choice was the Canalino de la Miniere, where he had to lower us into the chute with rope as well. The snow was soft corn snow, but the many snowballs that run down such a steep passage in the spring had rendered the surface uneven. Our route was completely pockmarked with sun-cups, deep ruts, and small stones from the cliffs above. What seemed like an eternity of survival skiing later, this *canalino* emptied into smoother, wider slopes and Andrea grinned at us with approval. Having survived our daily Italian machismo test, we were rewarded by an afternoon of relaxing cruising.

On our final day, Paulo Paglino was our host. Minna skipped the first run, probably fearing that if she skied any more such *canalini*, she would start growing hair on her chest. Paolo took us back into the Bors Valley from the Punta Indren, on a run that he promised would be an easy warmup. Suddenly, he asked if we wouldn't like to try an "interesting variation" to the normal route.

"What the hell does that mean?" I muttered.

"No problemo," retorted Paolo, in what, by now, had become a familiar anthem. "A small passage between the rocks—not so steep."

"What means small passage?" asked George, in his best Italian.

"It is at least as wide as the ski length. *No problemo.* You will like it! I check if it's okay," answered Paolo, and off he skied.

"I knew I skied too well on the first slope," lamented George. "If I only would have side slipped a little, snowplowed, and done a head plant on that initial pitch, he never would have suggested this!"

By now, Paolo was waving us down, calling "It's okay," punctuated on both ends by *"No problemo!"*

We skied down to Paolo, and stood at the throat of what was definitely the narrowest *canalino* yet.

"Just as I suspected. 'It's okay,' means nothing more than that there is snow," said George, as we looked down the 4-meter wide elevator shaft known as Canalino del Pilone.

THIS PAGE
UPPER: The old Walliser houses of Alagna bask in spring sunshine in front of the imposing Monte Rosa massif. LOWER LEFT: Minna uses a jump-turn technique to negotiate the wind-packed snow on Monte Rosa. LOWER RIGHT: The paint peeling off the walls of the old Guglielmina Hotel merely adds to its character.

RIGHT PAGE
UPPER: Etna periodically blows out amazing smoke rings.
LOWER: Majestic Mt. Etna is the most active volcano in Europe.

"Yeah, this is no cannelloni. This is more like a string of spaghetti," I answered.

I conjured up a mental picture of a film I'd once seen of Sylvain Saudan double-pole-planting his way down some extreme slope, and I vaulted into my "Saudan mode". It worked quite well, and soon I was at the bottom, gazing up through my camera lens at George. He was bounding from side to side, enclosed by two orange rock walls that forced him to keep his skiing as precise as possible. Watching George's descent was a pretty sight to see, and we all had a good feeling at the end of our final day, after having skied all these special places with the assistance of the "disciples".

When it was time to bid *arrivederci* to our new friends, Michele said, "You must come back so we can show you Alagna in powder."

"Yes, and all the places we could not ski because there was not enough snow down in the valley," added Paulo.

"And don't forget that we do Vittoria next time!" Andrea chimed in with a wink.

We all answered with a sincere promise to return in the near future, and I suddenly realized that the cult had gained three more followers.

*   *   *   *   *   *   *   *

Cults are a living phenomenon, and since the time of our visit, the Alagna cult has continued to grow, augmented by the growth of the freeride revolution. The days when a mere handful of cars would stand in the parking lot on a sunny morning are, for all intents and purposes, gone, and many other changes have also taken place.

A public corporation has taken over the ski lifts from the financially overmatched Monrosa Company, building new lifts, removing old ones and planning future projects.

Instead of the 2069 vertical meters that Alagna offers today, it formerly had a full 2359-vertical-meter descent thanks to the now defunct Roccette T-bar that took skiers onto the glacier above Punta Indren.

There is a project, however, in the planning stage that may take skiers in the future to Cresta Rossa (3670 m). Were this to happen, Alagna's vertical drop would increase to 2479 meters, giving Alagna a third-place ranking in the world, behind only Chamonix's Vallée Blanche and the descent from Mont Fort in Verbier to the village of Le Châble.

MOUNT ETNA — FIRE AND ICE

Skiing combines the act of negotiating one's way down a mountain face on two boards with a nature experience. Sometimes, on a day of light, deep powder snow, for example, the skiing itself is the main attraction, while on other occasions, the beauty, serenity or power of the surroundings can be the dominant aspect of the day's proceedings.

The quiet stillness of gliding over meadows of virgin corn snow while songbirds chirp a spring melody takes a skier far beyond the actual mechanics of making turns. Skiing in the shadow of the steep, craggy limestone cliffs of the Dolomites, to take another example, creates an entirely different atmosphere. The nature that surrounds a skier can emit an aura of tranquility, of foreboding or of enormous strength, and it is the sheer power of nature that most often stirs my soul when I am skiing. I often stand on a slope in awe of my environment, dwarfed by a dark granite cliff or a blue wall of glacial ice, and I can almost feel the unharnessed energy that created those physical features.

NOT SO LONG AGO, MY SKIS introduced me to another compelling force of nature, similar in age to the most ancient glacier and yet more powerful still. My friend Rupert and I skied down a mountain that could meet any glacier head-on and force her into a weak submission. She is more dangerous that the most nefarious glacier, whose deep crevasses might swallow up human beings in the blink of an eye. Her pent-up energy is as unpredictable as the persistent movement of glacial ice is foreseeable. Her volatile temper, irrational behavior and random actions are as difficult to chart as the movements and activities of a scorned woman on the first of April.

Mt. Etna has towered head and shoulders over the island of Sicily for over 600,000 years. She has instilled more fear and wreaked more havoc

than the Mafia. She has been the source of terror, catastrophe, mystery, inspiration and fascination throughout her long and fiery history. Homer and Virgil have written accounts about Etna in ancient times, while Goethe and Guy de Maupassant are but a few among many writers during the last few centuries who have been intrigued by Europe's highest volcano.

There is no rhyme nor reason, no pattern and no predictability with Mt. Etna. Some eruptions have been short, like the week-long outburst of 1979, while others have seemed endless, like the ten-year eruption between 1614 and 1624.

The mountain is pockmarked by literally hundreds of craters, each representing a unique eruption, and each with an individual history all its own. Some of the explosions were cataclysmic, like the devastating one that began on March 8, 1669. Before the dust and cinders had settled 122 days later, a 14-kilometer-long cleft in the mountain had opened up. During that eruption, a billion cubic meters of lava flowed out of Etna's belly, destroying much of Catania and numerous neighboring villages and snuffing out the lives of over 20,000 people.

The eruption of 1886 gave rise to a miracle, when Cardinal Dusmet brought the veil of Saint Agatha to the endangered city of Nicolosi. The cardinal stood but 100 meters outside the village hoping the veil would

THIS PAGE
The wind has blown the ashes from Mt. Etna to the south, covering Etna Sud in black, while the Etna Nord ski area is covered with white.

RIGHT PAGE
Rupert Scheiner skis down into one of Mt. Etna's many craters.

ward off the fast approaching lava. Indeed, the cardinal and the veil succeeded in doing what no glacier could ever have done, and the lava ceased its forward movement at the feet of the devout cardinal.

Since then, there have been eruptions that have destroyed villages, devastated woodlands and destroyed ski lifts. The Sicilians, however, have learned to live within their unpredictable environment, and they answer Etna's insults and abuses by rebuilding what she breaks. It is, therefore, perhaps not so surprising that the local people have built not only one, but two ski centers on the slopes of this beast.

Etna has her positive sides as well, helping to fertilize the land and attracting hundreds of thousands of tourists. The Sicilians seem to have a good relationship with the sometimes tyrannical, yet often benevolent matriarch of their island. The local people admire her beauty, are grateful for her generosity, and respect, but do not fear her omnipotence. They overlook her excesses and transgressions as we might forgive the tempestuous outbursts of a loved one. Nobody has a stronger sense of family than a Sicilian and Etna, after all, is family.

» The lava ceased its forward movement at the feet of the devout cardinal.«

My Etna adventure began with a simple phone call to the ski area of Etna Sud, a group of four lifts with 500 vertical meters of skiing, situated near the village of Nicolosi. My Italian is limited, but the person on the other end of the line seemed to be saying that the lifts were closed due to a volcanic eruption. He then advised that I call, instead, to Etna Nord. This, of course, did not make sense to a non-Sicilian. It must be a language problem, I figured. If my understanding was correct, that Etna was undergoing some major volcanic activity, why should I call the ski resort on the other side of the mountain? Surely, people are staying as far away from the explosions as possible.

I WANTED TO GET TO the bottom of this mystery, so I called the tourist office in Linguaglossa, a short drive from the five lifts on Etna's northeast face. This time, a lady assured me that I had not been misinformed. Etna Sud was closed, as much of the snow was buried in volcanic ash; but the wind blows consistently from the north and west, and at Etna Nord, everything was business as usual.

A couple of weeks later, Rupert and I were flying past Mt. Etna, headed for Catania. The views from the plane were stupendous. We looked out over the rugged coastline of Sicily bordered by the blue-green waters of the Ionian Sea. The vegetation back from the coast was green, as it certainly always is in these latitudes. Jutting out of the surrounding green was the imposing white presence of the volcano, lording over the surroundings like an albino dragon, spewing plumes of smoke from her gaping mouth.

The mountain looked even more imposing from below than from the plane, smoke still pealing relentlessly from this 3350-meter-high chimney as we wound our way toward the ski center the next morning. The juxta-

position of cactus and brightly blooming flowers with the winter white in the background gave a surrealistic quality to the scene.

It was early March, and the snow was spring-like. The slopes were firm in the morning, but even here on the north side of the mountain, they eventually warmed up into corn snow. The lower slopes had a few trees, which grow, in this region, up to about 2000 meters. Above that elevation, the landscape was barren. From the upper runs we looked out over the ocean, reflecting the deep blue of the Mediterranean sky. Long ridges of lava divided the terrain into natural ski runs, and the cones formed by previous blowups were an ever present reminder of where we were.

One could traverse far out to either side of the upper lift to reach quite a large area of off-piste skiing. The ski runs ranged from gentle to intermediate in ability, and the off-piste terrain was similar, allowing us to cruise around the mountain at will.

AFTER TWO DAYS OF CRUISING on the corn snow of Etna Nord, Rupert and I drove around to the south side of the volcano. In Etna Sud, while the ski runs were rendered rather useless, the gondola to the middle station was open for sightseers. Our initial surprise and shock over the Sicilians' fearless and fatalistic approach to a volcanic eruption had mellowed by now, and we were curious to get as near as possible to the core of power.

One does not get the opportunity to experience volcanic activity very often, and the hypnotic qualities of Mt. Etna, which had intrigued and fascinated men throughout history, were luring Rupert and me ever closer to the source.

Riding up the gondola, we suddenly beheld a most unusual sight. Glancing up, I noticed that our host mountain had just blown a perfect smoke ring into the sky. I have watched many smokers exhale a series of rings from their mouth, but I must admit that this was the largest one I had ever seen.

From the top of the gondola (2500 m), I looked up at a patchwork of snow and ash and decided to attach my touring equipment to my feet and skin up a short ways to a small stone *rifugio*. Rupert hiked. From the hut, I also had to continue on foot, and that method became trickier by the minute.

A short walk past the *rifugio* brought us to great furrows of lava, which upon close observation were moving almost imperceptibly forward. The outer shell was hardened volcanic rock, but underneath that layer, the lava was a glowing red. Periodically, one of the outer stones would tumble down exposing us to a blast of volcanic heat. Lava reaches temperatures of 700–1000 degrees centigrade, and this liquid heat was warming up the chill mountain air like a sauna. Further above us, the lava was flowing out of one of the craters like a golden river, but we could not proceed any higher.

At this spot, we met a young British cinematographer who told us that he had been right here during a burst of Stromboli activity just two weeks previous. On that occasion, a hailstorm of red-hot rock spewed from the crater like a giant fireworks-show on New Year's Eve. We suddenly realized that we had been somehow lulled into a false sense of security by the Sicilians' apparent harmonious coexistence with Etna. We should never have ruled out the possibility of a sudden and dramatic outburst of temperament from our host.

IT WAS GETTING LATE, AND we still had our descent in front of us. The lift had closed a couple of hours earlier, and the last strains of a golden sunset were upon us. For the next half-hour, we picked our way down the lower mountain on skis, finally arriving at the bottom in utter darkness. As we drove back to Linguaglossa along the eastern flank of Etna, we could see small rivers of golden lava against the pitch-black background.

We were now ready for some beach and culture. The following morning, Rupert and I took a scenic tour through parts of the western coast of Sicily stretching from Syracuse to Taormina. Syracuse is a living museum of antiquity, where Greek and Roman ruins can be found almost everywhere amidst the modern-day city. The ruins of the Temple of Apollo and the amphitheater built during the reign of Dionysius the Elder are

just a couple of the remnants of what once was one of the strongest of the Greek city-states.

Catania, by contrast, is a baroque city. While some signs of antiquity are also visible here, like the amphitheater from the second century AD, much of Catania was destroyed in a massive earthquake in 1693. Therefore, most of the landmarks of Catania, such as the Fontana dell'Elefante, the Church of Santa Maria dell'Indirizzo, the Arco di San Benedetto, the San Giuliano Church and many others, are products of the baroque style so popular in the period following the earthquake.

The natural beauty of this region can match the manmade architectural splendor of Sicily. The Rocks of the Cyclops jut out of the ocean near Aci Trezza like the long necks of sea serpents. The Alcantara Gorge, quite close to Linguaglossa, is another spot worth visiting. Flanked by basalt walls that clearly show their volcanic heritage, the Alcantara River winds a narrow path through the rocks here.

Perhaps the most beautiful spot along the coast is the village of Taormina. It is here that the creations of God and man form a most harmonious union. The village is built on the hillside overlooking a beautiful turquoise bay. The narrow cobblestone streets of Taormina seem to defy modern-day cars to transgress their sanctity, as they wind among old stone houses. Five minutes' walk from the central square lie the superbly preserved remains of a Greco-Roman theater. All the while, Etna broods over the whole scene like an omnipotent white goddess who has observed various cultures and civilizations come and go without ever relinquishing her power.

Etna rises a full 1000 vertical meters above the highest lift on Etna Nord, making ski touring very popular here. The area of the mountain, which has a diameter of approximately 40 kilometers, is immense, and ski touring is the best way to avail oneself of many of those square kilometers of snow. I had already done a tour of sorts on Etna Sud and felt no guilt about the fact that Maurizio Barone, the head of the ski school at Etna Nord, had organized a snow cat to transport us to the higher reaches of the mountain.

Our driver took us to the Observatory of Volcanology di Pizza Deneri

(2800 m). With the usual language barrier to impede communication, we tried to convince him to take us even higher. Amiable and accommodating, as most Italians, our chauffeur was nevertheless, reluctant. The word *pericolo* (danger) crept into almost every sentence he uttered. After a little more convincing, our friend, with obvious reservations, drove us up another 300 vertical meters or so. He motioned for us to get out quickly, and with a skeptical shake of his head, he directed the snow cat downhill—double time.

RUPERT AND I WERE VERY grateful for the extra altitude but still not entirely satisfied. We slung the skis on our shoulders and slowly started ascending the northeast crater. The wall of the cone was steep, and it was imperative to plant each step carefully. The snow layer was very thin by now because of the warmth of the cone. Sometimes my carefully planted foot broke through the snow, with my full weight coming down onto an uncertain landing among the loose stones underneath. It was a condition that was inviting a sprained ankle.

About 50 vertical meters from the top, I noticed that we were not alone ascending Mt Etna. Below us, gaining altitude more quickly than we, was a thick layer of cumulus clouds. I glanced regularly over my shoulder as I advanced upward. The clouds were gaining on us.

Etna is a very big mountain on which to be lost in the fog, and caution finally took over from the hypnotic lock which Etna's smokestack had had on me. We turned around and cautiously skied over hard wind crust back toward the observatory.

Below the building, a long, steep ridge with a smooth surface awaited us, and we were still relatively high above a sea of clouds. We tap-danced a series of short jump turns onto the ridge with an airy sense of being on top of the world. Our euphoria was temporary, as it always is, and soon we dove headfirst into the fog. We had our bearings and skied without problem back to the base of the mountain.

Rupert and I still cruised a few of the pistes that afternoon, and before the lifts closed, the fog and clouds had dissipated as quickly as they had materialized. We drove down the road through the thick pine forests that

LEFT: At Etna Sud, Rupert pushes some dried lava out of the way with his ski pole to expose the glowing red lava moving slowly underneath.
UPPER: Which of these kindly looking gentlemen is the "Godfather"?
LOWER: Carnival decorations adorn the town square of Linguaglossa.

ABOVE: One can enjoy pretty views of the Ionian Sea while snowboarding or skiing at Etna Nord.

fill the area between the ski center and Linguaglossa and then turned east. There were still so many angles and aspects of the mountain that we had not yet seen, and we began to drive around Etna's perimeter.

The view was forever changing. We left the pines and passed all kinds of other vegetation, including oaks, larches, poplars, beeches, birch trees and even orange groves. The eastern flank of the mountain is void of most vegetation, for it is along this side that the lava usually flows down. Here, one drives through a veritable sea of volcanic rock. Then the southeastern aspects of the mountain came into view, quite void of snow because of all the ash, and the pyramid changed color from white to black, like a chameleon.

After a while, we had again turned the corner to face the western side of the mountain. From this view Etna was once more decked in snow, but her chameleon-like nature was again apparent. Sunset was upon us, and her snowy slopes had turned pink in the last rays of light.

I PONDERED THE INFINITE NUMBER of faces of this mountain. The volcano's multi-faceted nature, however, went far beyond her superficial appearance, for Etna meant something different to everybody she touched. To some people, she was a killer and a destroyer, while to others, she was a place of eternal beauty. To the geologist, she was a case study; to the farmer, she was a provider; to the writer, she was a story; and to the poet, she was an inspiration.

Rupert and I are skiers, and to us, Mt. Etna was something else again. She was a rare skiing experience, one that we had never come close to having anywhere else. She provided the platform upon which I understood better than ever that my love of skiing transcended the actual sport and was rooted in my communion with nature.

Over 400 years ago, historian Tommaso Fazello wrote that Etna was "wonderful because it does not allow the fire to be extinguished by the snows nor the snows to be dissolved in the fire." That same balance between fire and ice that fascinated Fazello gave us a unique experience on skis.

By the time Etna faded into the distance outside the porthole of the plane flying me home, I was certain of one thing. In one short week, we had gotten to know many of the faces and aspects of this unusual mountain, and yet, no matter how much we had learned, she remained a fascinating mystery. Mt. Etna is many different things to many different people, but to all she is an enigma. She will remain so forever.

* * * * * * * *

Postscript: About ten weeks after my return from Sicily, I phoned down to the tourist office to verify a few facts. During the conversation, I became aware that but a few weeks after Rupert and I had hiked to the *rifugio* and beyond it to observe the lava on Etna Sud, the lava had inundated that very hut and covered it entirely. As we spoke, a new intensive outburst of temperament from Etna was spitting out so much ash that even as far away as Catania, the residents were forced to walk the streets with umbrellas.

Since then, another eruption destroyed all the lifts and ski runs on the south side of the mountain. At the present time, the 6-person gondola that takes skiers from 1900 meters to 2500 meters has been rebuilt, and plans are in the works to rebuild more lifts in the near future.

Etna Nord has also been affected by recent volcanic activity. Three of the five lifts have been destroyed, leaving only two lifts currently in operation.

The situation will most certainly change again. Lifts will be rebuilt and the mountain will again take them away. While planning a trip to Mt. Etna, it is advisable to stay in constant touch with the latest news and the local tourist office—and just in case, bring your touring equipment!

A sea of clouds obscures the valley en route off-piste from Arosa to Lenzerheide.

Chapter 6. SWITZERLAND

An Austrian friend once asked me, "What is the difference between an evening in Zurich and a night in a Vienna cemetery?" He paused a moment, and when I had no quick response to his riddle, he answered, "Zurich has more people, but the cemetery in Vienna is lots more fun."

I must admit that I chuckled at this derogatory humor, for it fit some preconceived notions I held about the Swiss. They rolled up the sidewalks in Zurich at 10 p.m., didn't they?

It is true that Switzerland is full of small, cute mountain villages, but I had been of the impression that Austria had managed to preserve its well-known *Gemütlichkeit*, while the more businesslike nature of the Swiss had robbed the tourist sector of that cozy sort of atmosphere. It is, after all, a country of conservative bankers and stiff-collared industrialists, isn't it? I figured that if I wanted to organize a peace conference, Switzerland could well be the right location, but if I were planning a ski holiday with ambiance, Austria would be the best bet.

My aversion to Switzerland had also been price-related. I had visited the likes of Zermatt, Gstaad and St. Moritz, but that had been when Daddy was still footing my bills. Those days are, unfortunately, long gone. For many years thereafter, I had made a conscious effort to avoid Switzerland on my ski holidays. I still have memories of walking in and out of the King's Club disco in St. Moritz as a young man. I could not even afford a glass of orange juice, let alone the vodka to mix it with.

A couple of years ago, however, I tightened my belt buckle, locked my prejudices in the closet at home and drove across the Austrian border with my friend Martin Söderqvist. I was going to see firsthand if the myths about the Swiss had any validity or not.

It did not take me very long to realize the error of my ways—to learn that this country, so rich in ski history, is still an extremely relevant place to ski today. Along the way, many of the myths and prejudices that had built up in my mind also fell by the wayside.

It is astounding that such a small country has made such a large impact on a sport that has become popular all over the world. Switzerland was where ski tourism really began in the mid-1800s. The Swiss were looking for some way of expanding on their rather popular summer tourism, and winter sports seemed like it might do the trick. They haven't looked back since.

The second Winter Olympics were held in St. Moritz in 1928, and soon after, many majestic summer resorts, like Andermatt, Engelberg and Zermatt, began directing their focus toward winter sports. A century later, the Swiss are looking to try to fill their hotels in the *summer*.

Many of the original resorts are still going strong, while of course, scores of new lift systems have sprung up all over the country. Nowadays, one can almost ski across the entire land by merely gliding from one ski village to the next. As in many countries with a long winter-sports tradition, the best skiing can be found both in the old classic ski resorts as well as in some smaller, lesser-known ski villages.

There are numerous Swiss resorts with a long history, excellent skiing or both, but space does not allow me to focus on all of them. Among those resorts that deserve better than a mere honorable mention are Davos, Flims, Laax, Saas-Fee, Grindelwald and Wengen. In this chapter, I visit the world-famous ski villages of St. Moritz, Zermatt and Verbier, and the excellent freeride destinations of Andermatt, Engelberg, Disentis and Val d'Anniviers.

ENGELBERG — MYTHS AND MOUNTAINS

Engelberg is a beautiful old village at the foot of Mt. Titlis, placed in one of the most picturesque valleys in the Alps. It is a place where man-made edifices are juxtaposed in fluid harmony with the spectacular scenery of Mt. Titlis, Reissend Nollen, the Grosse and Kleine Spannort, the Wendenstöcke and a host of other dramatic peaks that surround the old spa village.

Man's contribution to the area began as long ago as 1120, when a Benedictine monastery was established. Still active today, the monastery is a huge complex that nowadays includes a boarding school, a cheese factory and an enormous cathedral with Europe's largest organ.

About 100 years ago, magnificent ornate buildings of a different nature began springing up in Engelberg. A sanatorium and medical center were established, and they in turn gave rise to a number of extravagant spa hotels. The Terrace Palace (built 1904), the Hotel Europäischerhof (1902) and the Bellevue-Terminus (1898), among others, were built to coddle the rich and famous of the turn of the last century. These regal buildings had gargantuan dining salons, pillared lobbies with high ceilings, ballrooms, ice skating rinks and virtually every luxury their guests might possibly fancy.

These huge hotels soon found that they needed to create some winter activity to keep their rooms and personnel occupied during the colder months of the year. In 1913, Switzerland's first aerial cable car was constructed here, and Engelberg began attracting skiers from all around Europe.

MARTIN AND I CRUISED into Engelberg to the majestic sight of the pompous old hotels and wondered how long our ski-bum budget would keep us in bread and water. The most centrally located of these grand old relics is the Bellevue-Terminus, situated at the end of the railroad line, as its name suggests. We went to the reception desk to inquire where we might find an inexpensive pension suitable to our budget. It was right here at the very onset of our stay that my stubborn prejudices about high-priced Switzerland began to collapse like a house of cards.

The girl at the desk informed us that, while the Bellevue had some regal chambers that command a kingly ransom, it also had some clean, modern rooms without private toilets and showers that were quite inexpensive. We were in shock at the low prices and checked in immediately, before they had the chance to change their minds. This was one of the cheapest rooms I had found in the Alps in many years, and in Switzerland no less.

OUR FIRST MORNING, MARTIN AND I made another very nice discovery. Engelberg, with its long international skiing history, had over the years transformed into a kind of large locals' resort for the inhabitants of Lucerne. Hence, the mountain was not very busy on weekdays. Despite clear skies and 20 centimeters of fresh snow that first morning, the Jochstock (2564 m) was virtually empty. About 75 percent of the ski terrain in Engelberg is left ungroomed, and most of the Jochstock area falls into that category.

We spent the entire day putting first tracks into such off-piste routes as Steintäli, Grosses Suzli, Kleines Suzli and Sommerweg. Every now and then a stray snowboarder passed by, but we were almost alone. It was late March and the sun was warm, but the predominantly north faces of the Jochstock preserved the powder all day.

At five o'clock, we entered the Yucatan, a Mexican restaurant alongside the Bellevue and the most happening après-ski bar in town. It was happy hour with two-for-the-price-of-one drinks, and at that rate, they offered about the cheapest drinks in the Alps. I began to wonder why I had shunned Switzerland for so many years.

The next day, Martin and I went up the mountain into a raging blizzard. Almost all the skiing in Engelberg is above tree line, and that fact did not help our chances of finding our way in the storm. We began to ski under the Jochstock Express Lift. We needed radar. The snow was getting so deep that perhaps we would have been better off with sonar. The scene around us was whiter than an albino bride. We saw no contours, and we could not tell where the groomed slope met the virgin snow. We were skiing by Braille without a Seeing Eye dog.

After a couple of runs in the pea soup, I noticed a lone figure gliding silkily through the blizzard as if it had been a bright sunny day. Who could be so crazy as to be skiing off-piste in deep powder in these conditions—and alone?

I had to find out who this phantom of the fog was! And more importantly, could we join him? Would he be our eyes so that we could also enjoy the powder? Martin and I waited on top for the mysterious lunatic and asked if he minded if we teamed up together. Rafael Betschart accepted us under his wing. Without much further ado, he traversed out into the mist, with the two of us in tow. By now, about 60 centimeters of fresh snow lay all around us.

Rafi's legs began pumping up and down like well-oiled shock absorbers, and I tried to keep abreast of him. Only by keeping him in view could I gauge how steep the slope was. My efforts were in vain. He disappeared in a cloud of snow dust faster than the Lone Ranger on a mission of mercy. I was on my own.

Rafi told us to follow him onto a ridge but warned us that it was narrow in one place. Perfect! Five turns later, our leader was out of sight, and I dropped off the ridge like falling through a trap door. The landing was soft, but I concluded that I must stay closer.

I could not even see Rafi's track in the flat light of the blizzard, but once we got off the ridge, it did not matter. Now there were few irregularities in the slope. With Rafael to guide us to the right starting point, the snow was so deep that we could actually ski blind.

Riding up the lift, our new powder pal told us that he was a ski instructor enjoying his day off. Most of the ski instructors I had ever known made use of their free days by sleeping off a hangover or schussing between the sheets with some nubile snow bunny. They would never be out in such a blizzard on their day off unless somebody was paying black money straight into their pocket for a private lesson.

ANOTHER ONE OF MY SWISS MYTHS began to crumble. I would have suspected that even the Swiss bankers and watchmakers would have stayed home from work on a day like this. Rafael was not at all the conservative kind of skier I had expected to find here.

After many similar runs, our Seeing Eye dog took us to a tiny, self-service cable car that runs between Untertrübsee and Obertrübsee. The visibility was better here in the lower elevations, and Rafael led us into a short, untracked couloir under the lift. This was a suitable climax to our day, and soon we were thanking our guide over a pitcher of margaritas in the friendly confines of the Yucatan. The day's conditions had only been suitable for yetis and Rafaels, and we hoped that the morrow would be kinder to us mere mortals.

Our wish was granted. The following morning we awoke to a blue sky and a full meter of fresh snow atop Mt. Titlis. Our newfound leader met us at the base of the lifts, and we ascended to Stand (2428 m). The top of the mountain was not yet open and we followed Rafael to the entry to Laub.

We now looked down upon perhaps the most perfect powder slope I have ever seen. Laub is a wide, north face of about 1000 vertical meters. It slopes at a consistent 35 degrees or so for almost the entire duration of the run, so that one must hardly make any adjustments for terrain irregularities. Laub is proof positive that God is a skier.

It was almost too easy. Turn into the fall line, put your body into cruise

THIS PAGE
The Titlis Rotair was the first rotating cable car in the world.

THIS PAGE
The Titlis Rotair was the first rotating cable car in the world.

RIGHT PAGE
If Martin Söderqvist tells you that the powder was waist deep on Mt. Titlis that day, you better believe him—he has proof.

control and bounce gently up and down a few hundred times without even thinking. *Voila*, you are at the bottom again, ready for round two. The powder on Laub was feather light and the perfect depth so that the 35-degree slope could be skied effortlessly. With somewhat less snow, one would have had to expend some energy to dampen one's speed, and any more snow would have necessitated a more exaggerated up-down motion to unweight and power through. With the perfect snow depth to suit the angle of the slope, however, we bounced down without expending any energy. It was truly a dream run.

BY THE TIME WE ARRIVED BACK in Engelberg, we saw that the mountain was now open to the top. We rode up the gondola to Trübsee and the cable car to Stand. Then we entered the Rotair, which transports people to Klein Titlis (3028 m). The Rotair, completed in 1995, was the world's first rotating cable car. As we stood at the window of the circular aerial tram, we got a 360-degree panorama, as the outer section of the tram revolved around the center. All the while, a well rehearsed guide spewed out information about the Rotair and the surrounding mountains as if we were riding some Disneyland attraction.

The crowd in the Rotair was also more Disneyland than Alpine powder bum. That was perhaps the most amazing aspect of the entire experience. We were surrounded by a swarm of Asian sightseers, all in street shoes, their little Nikons and Canons clicking away to an indecipherable background chatter of Thai, Korean and Japanese. There were first tracks to be cut in about one meter of powder all over Mt. Titlis, and we were sharing the cable car with a crowd, many of whom were seeing snow for the first time!

The experience was almost surrealistic. It seemed as if we had walked into a Salvador Dali painting; or perhaps we had fallen down Alice's rabbit hole and emerged on some package excursion to see the Great Wall of China.

Anywhere else in the ski world, we would have been surrounded by the hard core—weather-beaten mountaineers with rucksacks full of climbing gear and young snowboarders with their mirrored Oakley shades gleaming in the sun. Here in Engelberg, however, powder skiing would be the privilege of but a few of us, while the remainder of the guests were satisfied to throw a few snowballs. (Rafi reports that today, Engelberg has become the winter headquarters for a fair number of Swedish ski bums. Hence, there is more competition for first tracks today than there was at the time of our visit a few years ago.)

THE ROTAIR FINALLY STOPPED its slow spin and we disembarked. A few tourists from Bangkok asked me to take a photograph of them in the snow. The camera clicked along with many others, the videos whirred, the Asians shivered and a small handful of freeriders headed into the virgin snow of an area know to the locals as Steinberg.

Once more, Martin and I tried to follow Rafael, which again was not easy. We had the advantage of visibility, but so did Rafi, and he was gliding left and right over the powder fields to find the best lines, faster than I could change direction.

"Be careful," warned our leader before disappearing. "You are on a glacier now."

It certainly did not seem so, what with a meter of snow blanketing everything. I stopped for a moment to reconnoiter, while Rafael and Martin traversed out to the left. I opened my pack and took out my camera. In the process, I glanced down and was suddenly horrified. Between my skis was a black abyss. Waist deep in snow, I was, nevertheless, staring directly into a crevasse! "Conservative Swiss, my ass," I thought out loud. "Rafi is a lunatic!"

I immediately pushed forward off the crevasse and made sure I was on solid snow before repacking my camera. By this time, Rafael and Martin were way down below me, and I stood atop a steep slope, presumably still on the glacier. There were a number of tracks on this section, so I chose a line to the right of the cut-up snow. Below, Rafael was waving his arms and gesturing, but I could not decipher his meaning. Two turns into my descent, I heard the rasping sound of my ski edges gnashing against

glacial ice. I had discovered what my friend's gesticulating was about, but it was too late.

The seductive powder had again lured me astray. It had concealed a section of steep blue ice and my skis lost their grip. For a moment, I tumbled in what seemed like free fall, performing cartwheels toward an uncertain fate. By the time the dust had cleared, I looked back up to find that I had been very lucky not to have skied 10 meters further to the side, for a giant, blue serac was adjacent to my track, staring me in the face. I cursed my careless stupidity. I should have known better than to ski wide of the tracks on an unfamiliar glacier.

The remainder of our run down Steinberg went smoothly. The snow was so deep that, in some instances, our chests were breaking the snow line, pushing a small wave of snow continuously in front of us. We enjoyed numerous sets of turns in which we saw literally nothing but pure white until we ground to a halt in order to regain our bearings.

AT LUNCH, OUR LITTLE GROUP was joined by one of Rafael's colleagues, a mountain guide named Alessandro. It was decided that the day's coup de grâce would be a 2000-vertical-meter run from the top of the Rotair down the Galtiberg, a tricky and treacherous route in which one often needs either a guide or the morgue—sometimes both. We opted for the former and hoped we would not need the latter.

The entry into Galtiberg was deceivingly simple. The snow was a meter deep here as well, as we now followed our two leaders on a wide, rolling pitch. We glided back into motion with Engelberg basking in the sunshine directly below us. For quite some time we enjoyed the same conditions we had skied all day. This slope, however, was convex, and it steepened as we continued down.

Alessandro began mumbling something about there being a lot more snow than he had expected. He then explained that the usual route is to traverse a narrow shelf above some cliffs, but the amount of snow made this route too dangerous today. A small snow slide would be enough to push a skier over the cliff, and even Shane McConkey and his companions would not jump this cliff for fun. This was a "you fall, you die" sort of precipice, explained Alessandro, and he advised that we descend by way of an alternate route.

Plan B, the "safer" route, was less dangerous, however, because it was a steep, natural avalanche ravine. Therefore, by this time of year, it had already been the scene of a major slide or two. At first, we could avoid the old avalanche path, but as the couloir narrowed, we had to pick our way for a couple of kilometers through huge mounds of avalanche rubble. Alessandro cautioned us to stay away from the left side, a granite wall many hundreds of meters high, from where loose rocks often fall, creating an additional hazard. He was clearly not too comfortable with plan B either, and he gently coaxed us to keep moving quickly while trying not to panic the group.

I was no happier than Alessandro. Four o'clock on a spring afternoon after a heavy snowfall is not the best time to be halfway down an avalanche gully. To negotiate such a steep canyon filled with the remains of a heavy spring avalanche, however, does not proceed quickly. We were in the lower elevations by now, and I was sweating profusely. In addition, the sunshine had disappeared, and we were under a heavy layer of fog, rendering our efforts even more difficult. I certainly burned more calories on that one run than during the entire rest of our stay in Engelberg.

When we finally got below the fog, we could see the corridor

THIS PAGE
LOWER LEFT: The interior of the monastery's chapel.
LOWER RIGHT: The old buildings of Engelberg add to the charm of the village.

RIGHT PAGE
UPPER: The Glacier Express might be the most beautiful way to cross through Switzerland, but it doesn't stop for hitchhikers.
LOWER: Martin Söderqvist enjoying the corn snow of the Nätschen area of Andermatt.

emptying out onto some flat farmland. I was like a football player with the goal in sight. I now scrambled from side to side, picking the best path, as I crunched over, between or through huge clumps of snow-slide debris. I had only one thought in mind—reaching a completely safe spot away from this avalanche trough as soon as possible.

Soon, Martin, Rafael and I were back once more in the familiar surroundings of the Yucatan, replenishing our dehydrated bodies with half-priced pitchers of margaritas. It was Friday and the weekend crowd from Lucerne was beginning to pack the bar. They had not been around in time to partake of the day's powder orgy, but they clearly did not care whether this was "after ski" or "after work". They were ready to party.

I mulled over our experiences of the past few days through the kaleidoscope of too many margaritas. We were staying in a stately old hotel for less than the cost of a small pension in Austria. We had been led around Engelberg's off-piste territory for two days by a crazy Swiss character who would make Mao Zedong look conservative. Now we sat in a happening Mexican après-ski bar (the Austrians or the French would be too traditional or conservative to have a Mexican bar in a ski resort) that was becoming more energetic by the minute. I realized that all my prejudices and preconceived notions about Switzerland had dissolved faster than a headache tablet in a glass of water.

I was wrong. One more of my prejudices was still to fall. A couple of weeks later, fortified by my positive experience in Engelberg, I returned to Switzerland, this time to the posh resort of Davos. Two friends and I skied off-piste down the Jakobshorn. The sun was warm, the run was long and we all had become very thirsty by the time we approached an old farmhouse near the bottom of the descent. I knocked on the door to inquire whether we might buy some liquid refreshment.

A large man answered my knock and invited us all onto his verandah, while his wife fetched something for us. She reemerged with a pitcher of homemade apple juice as well as a few beers. The couple stayed and chatted with us, as we downed everything placed in front of us. When it came time to pay and depart, the couple absolutely refused to accept any financial remuneration for their favor. We warned them to be careful with that kind of hospitality, for we might well return for more. They laughed and said we were welcome to return.

WE BID OUR HOSTS FAREWELL and continued down, only to find a small restaurant below. The farmers could easily have directed us to that guesthouse, I thought, but they opted to show us some genuine Swiss hospitality instead. This was real *Gemütlichkeit*—not the made-for-tourists variety. It had been a small gesture of friendliness but the sort that I had not often experienced in the Alps.

Now the last of my forgone conclusions about the Swiss had also been proved wrong. My visits to this little insulated land had been a good trade-off. I had gained a rich experience and a new friend in Rafael, and all I had had to give up were a few long-held prejudices and a bad joke about the Swiss nightlife.

ANDERMATT — SECRET SWISS SNOW ACCOUNT

Powder skiers and off-piste fanatics are always searching to discover some new hideaway that is not yet overcrowded with their brethren. They are on a constant watch for a location that gives them salvation from the plethora of popular powder havens where the fresh snow gets skied out in the course of a few hours. This diligent and vigilant search carried on by the world's powder hounds has uncovered new gems every few years, including La Grave, St. Foy and Alagna.

Throughout the '90s, the burgeoning snowboard population, the advent of carving and all-terrain skis, and the reinvention of off-piste skiing under the new label of "freeriding" have created ever-increasing pressure to find good new territory for skiing powder. Nevertheless, in spite of all the hyperbole of the freeride movement, a little pearl of powder in the epicenter of the Alps has managed to maintain its anonymity—but it was not always so.

In fact, 130 years ago, quite a while before the Swiss knew much about how to utilize their abundant natural resource of snow, the little village of Andermatt began to build up quite a following of international tourists for both summer and winter fun. Similar to Engelberg's development, but some years earlier, a handful of grandiose hotels, including the Hotel Bellevue (1872), the Grand Hotel Danioth (1880) and the Hotel Gotthard (1890) sprang up on the strategic Gotthard Pass at the foot of a mountain called Gemsstock.

In 1904, the community imported four Norwegians to impart their knowledge of telemark skiing, and Andermatt quickly transformed itself into one of the world's first ski resorts. At the time when motorized uphill transport was beginning to reshape the skiing world, Andermatt was again at the forefront, and the second ski lift in all of Switzerland was constructed here in 1937.

World War II, however, drastically changed Andermatt's destiny. Tourism disappeared from Europe and the luxurious hotels of this mountain spa were relegated to the ignominious task of housing Swiss mountain troops, a national duty from which they never recovered. Half a decade of misuse left the once grand hotels in need of renovation, and this once proud and grand ski village drifted slowly into ski obscurity.

Today, the ski terrain in Andermatt consists of three mountains which offer just eleven lifts and 56 kilometers of pistes but a staggering 300 square kilometers of skiable terrain. (This last figure is predicated on one's willingness to include up to 2 hours of hiking in one's activities.) The area of off-piste terrain is ten times greater than the area of prepared pistes. As the snowboard and freeride revolutions coincide with the inception of a new century in Andermatt's long history as a winter sports center, it may just be the right time for this picturesque Swiss village to regain the exalted status it once held.

Martin Söderqvist and I wound our way through the dramatic Schöllenen Gorge to reach the high plateau that houses Andermatt. We were certainly not the first travelers to be impressed by the dramatic entry to the village. Almost 300 years ago, one of the first tunnels ever built for road travel was carved out of the granite here. Known as the Urnerloch, it was a forbidding hole in the mountain measuring just slightly over 2 meters wide.

Goethe was impressed by the view during his visit here in 1707. Then, almost a century later, poet and playwright Friedrich von Schiller, whose

In Andermatt, the area of off-piste terrain is ten times larger than the area of prepared pistes.

drama immortalized the legendary William Tell, also passed through the Urnerloch.

Schiller described it thus: "You believe yourself to be in the kingdom of the shadow, then opens a black and horrible door, unto a smiling landscape where autumn and spring are wed. I would like to flee from life's exertion and eternal pain, into this happy valley."

MARTIN AND I HEADED UP the 2963-meter-high Gemsstock, whose cable car accesses more skiable off-piste terrain than many other ski areas with twenty lifts or more. We had the good luck of asking Carlo Danioth's advice about the ski area. It turned out that some years earlier, Carlo had become the youngest head *pisteur* in Switzerland, and he offered to show us one of his favorite descents.

We followed Carlo and two of his friends intrepidly for no more than a minute before I became doubtful whether our chance meeting had, in fact, been fortuitous or not. The Gemsstock is fraught with precipitous and perilous routes, and we found ourselves now edging our way along a death-defying traverse. I had no wish to end up as hamburger meat, and moved slowly and timidly along the mountainside, while the Swiss waited patiently.

Suddenly, it all became worthwhile. After but a few minutes of sweat and fear, we stood above a long, virgin couloir—a full week after the last snowfall! My feeling was akin to escaping from an abyss into the radiance of the sun, and I could not help but think of Schiller's description of emerging from the blackness of the Urnerloch to the welcome warmth of the Ursern Valley. It felt as if we had passed along the narrow path of purgatory and evaded the clutches of Satan to reach the gates of St. Peter.

The Charlie Couloir is no stroll in the park, mind you. It is a long, 45-degree chute brimmed by a dramatic wind cornice. Peering down this elevator shaft is enough to make any skier's heart accelerate its rhythm. Now, however, there were no visible rocks in our path to imperil life and limb, and I felt a great sense of relief and exhilaration. After all, this is what we had come for.

Carlos and one of his cohorts leapt off the cornice into Charlie like Swiss mountain troops on the assault. Moments later, they were waving at us from a couple hundred meters below. The corridor had old powder on the right side, corn snow on the left and breakable crust in between— a veritable snow smorgasbord, all within 20 meters' width. Martin and I alternated among the snow conditions, preferring to avoid the crust but not always succeeding. If we kept our turns tight, we had consistent snow, but each time we failed to keep our turning radius to a minimum, we ended up in no-man's-land.

Charlie eventually opened up into wide fields of powder and finally funneled into another narrow shaft known as Giraffe. Here, we jump-turned another 500 vertical meters until we ended up along a creek in the vast Unteralp Valley.

ULTIMATELY, OUR EARLY MORNING ADVENTURE brought us to the base of the Nätschen area, a small cluster of four lifts that rise 900 vertical meters up the Gütsch Mountain. The slopes were drenched in early morning sunlight, and billions of corn crystals glistened in the sun. Who were we to resist?

Arriving atop the Grossboden Lift, vast, treeless fields of spring snow lay below. We easily traversed up-valley to a spot beyond all tracks. Suddenly, an ear-piercing boom reverberated across the valley, shattering the serenity of the morning.

"Do you think somebody's trying to send us a message?" Martin asked jokingly.

"Yeah, maybe the locals want this virgin corn snow all to themselves," I retorted.

We pushed off into the fall line and had just begun snaking tracks upon the shiny surface when another blast shook the valley. We guessed that the military was practicing with some of their "toys", but it was rather

disconcerting, nevertheless, as the loud intrusions continued at regular intervals for the next hour or so.

The sun had cooked the corn to perfection. A wafer-thin layer of ice crushed under the weight of our skis with each turn, and small crunchy bits of the sherbet cascaded down the mountain with us. The ice kernels created a beautiful "shhh, shhh, shhh" sound that put the ideal audio soundtrack onto our spring morning. Martin and I followed this procedure two more times. We tested different short couloirs with each run until the spring snow became too soft to hold our weight properly, and we spent the remainder of the day on the pistes.

Over an après-ski beer, Martin and I wondered how Andermatt had avoided discovery by the new generation of freeriders. Was it sloppy research on the part of today's powder sleuths, or were the Swiss conspiring to keep this place under wraps? It could have been an oversight of the entire freeride community, but somehow I felt there was more to this than met the eye.

As a journalist, I am suspicious by nature, and I began to think about the exceedingly lukewarm reception our coming had inspired. I am accustomed to the tourist bureaus of various Alpine resorts bending over backwards to please visiting journalists, but in the case of Andermatt, my request for a complimentary room had been turned down. Even a day of free off-piste guiding was nixed.

Alex Clapasson, the manager of the lifts, gave us an explanation. Andermatt is a poor village without the resources to splurge on such public relations, claimed Alex. Could that be true, or were the Swiss protecting some long-guarded native secret? I was beginning to suspect the latter. Carlo had been the only chink in the armor of the plot to keep us in the dark on the true identity of Andermatt as an off-piste paradise.

It was now time to discover the Andermatt nightlife, and we discovered that there was not much to discover—not for a man, in any case. The military has maintained their presence in Andermatt after the end of World War II, and they still train their mountain troops here. In every bar in town, we found more soldiers than civilians, and a peek into the Dancing Gotthard, the town's major discotheque, revealed two women, twenty male tourists and about 80 soldiers. Oh well, an early night is good for the health.

THE NEXT MORNING, MARTIN AND I opted for an off-piste descent into the Guspis Valley on the west-facing side of the Gemsstock. This was yet another valley with various entries, and it too was devoid of people. Clapasson had told us that there were twice as many off-piste skiers on the slopes of Andermatt now, compared with ten years earlier. I was beginning to understand that a decade ago, he was alone in the powder. We again worked our way down 1500 vertical meters with only a few old tracks as proof that other humans do sometimes frequent this valley.

We soon arrived at the base of the third portion of Andermatt's ski system, the Winterhorn. Little did we know that our surprise at the vastness of this freeride paradise had only just begun. The Winterhorn is a classic off-piste mountain, as good as any I have ever seen. It is reminiscent of the endless powder faces of the Albonagrat above Stuben.

Two old lifts take riders 1000 vertical meters up the Winterhorn from Hospental. As we rode the upper lift, my thoughts returned to my conspiracy theory. The girl at the tourist office had clearly stated, "If you are good skiers, the Gemsstock is the only interesting area for you."

The further we got up toward the summit of the Winterhorn, the clearer it became that this statement was the result of total incompetence or part of a disinformation campaign. A 2-minute walk from the top station gave us a view out over the back side. The possibilities were immense and again we were alone. It was too good to be true.

"Where the hell is everybody?" I asked Martin. "Doesn't anybody know about this place—or doesn't anyone care?"

We rode ridges, banked off both sides of some gullies, kept our turns tight on a few steep faces and cruised through the open terrain near the bottom. Then we glided along the snow-covered St. Gotthard Pass highway (closed in winter) until we were back at the parking lot. It was mid-March and there were a dozen cars. I thought about some of the famous off-piste havens and the masses of skiers who do battle for every square inch of virgin turf there, and I could well understand the reason behind this Swiss conspiracy. Only one thing still puzzled me. Where, in God's name, were the Swiss?

Next, we traversed in a westerly direction on the Winterhorn's north side. We followed a handful of tracks. Soon they peeled off down the mountain, and we followed, leaving our own tracks in about 10 centimeters of old powder. We made turns until our legs rebelled.

Near the bottom, a couple of stone structures came into view. We had magically arrived at a small, isolated sun-terrace and restaurant between Hospental and the next village of Realp. A large beer and a plate of *Rösti* later, we hitchhiked back to the lifts and repeated our procedure for the rest of the day. We experimented with new routes each time and did not see another skier all afternoon.

> **» The leader of the conspiracy was somebody who knew in advance that we were coming here.«**

Something just didn't seem to fit, but I could not figure out what it was. Perhaps the Swiss mountain troops were using this area for target practice. Or even worse—maybe they were in on the conspiracy to protect the secrecy of this off-piste Mecca. I thought again about the blasts we had heard on the Gütsch the previous morning. Maybe they shoot or imprison all people trying to leave the valley to spread the word to the outside world.

As journalists, that would put us in the utmost danger. I knew my imagination was working overtime but I couldn't help it. This was a mystery and it was necessary to contemplate every possibility.

I WENT BACK TO CHAT with Alex Clapasson the next morning to see if he might be able to shed any light on the enigma. He was not only the manager of the lifts, he was also an exceptionally well-traveled mountain guide. He had accomplished major climbing conquests all over the world including peaks in Alaska, Russia, Patagonia, Yosemite, Africa and the Himalayas. He knew Andermatt perhaps better than anyone.

We asked Alex if he might have time to ski us around a bit, but he said that he was unfortunately too busy. Clapasson kindly apologized again for the lack of support that Andermatt had given us with regard to hotel and guiding, but he offered that he could personally organize a free journalistic trip to little-known Val d'Anniviers for the following winter, if we were interested. We thanked him and headed back up the mountain.

For the next few days, we followed a pattern similar to our first two

THIS PAGE
LEFT: Martin in the Giraffe Couloir.
RIGHT: Martin skis down to the road from the Winterhorn.

RIGHT PAGE
The Matterhorn is visible from most of Zermatt's skiing terrain. Martin Söderqvist is the skier.

days in Andermatt. We saw few people on the pistes and nary a soul when we left the beaten track. Evenings, we looked into every conceivable place where there might be a bit of nightlife, but to no avail. Nocturnal activity was quite nonexistent. Maybe that was part of the master scheme—a ski resort with no nightlife is certainly not apt to attract visitors, and hence, this freerider's dream resort would remain unknown.

We kept a close eye on the military just in case my conspiracy theory was correct, but they seemed to be oblivious to us. We skied wherever we wanted, gathered information unhindered and in the end, departed Andermatt as easily as we had arrived. There were no unpleasant searches and seizures, and nobody tried to confiscate my film, which of course was proof of the outstanding off-piste possibilities in Andermatt. In fact, we were treated well in all respects.

The police files are full of unsolved mysteries. Some lack a motive. Others lack a suspect. We had both. The motive was clear. Keep the secret of the Andermatt off-piste paradise intact. The suspect was obviously anybody and everybody who stood to gain from that secret—namely the local freeriders. But we could not place the suspect at the scene of the crime. In four full days of skiing exclusively off-piste, we had seen no other skiers with the exception of Carlo and his friends, and they had guided us.

Then it finally occurred to me. The leader of the conspiracy was somebody who knew in advance that we were coming here. He had therefore consciously stayed out of our way during our visit. If we had detected but one other person enjoying the empty miles of corn snow and powder, we would have recognized him to be the culprit.

Suddenly, like the fog lifting off the mountains in the early morning sunlight, everything became clear. Of course! Why hadn't I thought of it before? Alex Clapasson was one of the only ones who knew of our visit beforehand. He is himself a mountain guide, and yet, he had invited to organize for us a free stay in a ski area halfway across Switzerland rather than guiding us in Andermatt. Certainly, nobody loved the vast virgin slopes of Andermatt more than Alex. Instantly, everything crystallized in my mind.

At the same time as I concluded Alex to be behind the "Andermatt anonymity plot", I could hardly view him as a villain. On the contrary, I empathized with Alex. Would I, in fact, have done things any differently, had I been in his place? My answer, of course, was a resounding "No!" Alex, a mountain man of the highest repute, was merely trying to protect the privacy and sanctity of his home. After all, for some people, a man's home is his mountain.

ZERMATT — WHERE LEGENDS MEET

When it comes to skiing, Zermatt was there at the forefront, having built the world-famous Gornergrat Railway in 1898 and opening its first ski school in 1902. It is the classic ski resort. It is difficult to describe Zermatt without using as many superlatives as a Mercedes advertisement. It is a legendary venue for skiing and well-deserving of legend status.

Zermatt has the largest number of high-capacity lifts in the world. It is in the top ten worldwide in vertical drop with 2200 meters of skiing top to bottom. It also has one of the ten longest runs in the world, a 15-kilometer journey from the top of the Klein Matterhorn to the village.

For those who prefer après-ski, Zermatt also ranks among the top ten ski resorts worldwide, with eight nightclubs and well over 100 eateries. To top it all off, it has the highest lift in the Alps, which takes visitors to 3899 meters, and some of the most stunning mountain vistas anywhere. One can view from here no fewer than 38 peaks that exceed 4000 meters, and the imposing ice of glacial seracs and huge crevasses add an additional intensity to the surrounding nature that can be replicated in very few ski areas.

Zermatt has all that, and then there's the Matterhorn. It stands alone at the end of the valley like a giant citadel. It is gorgeous, stunning, staggering, stupendous, spectacular, magnificent, awesome and inspirational, but that entire description doesn't really do it justice. It is the perfect mountain! The mere sight of the Matterhorn towering over the end of the valley is enough to make a devout atheist drop to his knees, genuflect and pray. God must have apprenticed and practiced mountain building with the other million-odd peaks and precipices in the world; then, I imagine that once he was an accomplished master, he created the Matterhorn as his final work.

The legendary mountain naturally creates additional legends that bask in its aura and feed off its notoriety. Edward Whymper was the first to be touched by Matterhorn glory, following his triumph over the peak in 1865. Ulrich Inderbinen has probably shared the spotlight with the 'Horn most often. Ulrich was a local lad who became a mountain guide early in the 20th century, climbed the Matterhorn over 350 times, and still put his footprints on the peak after his 90th birthday.

Despite the 'Horn's apparent impregnability, novice climbers can climb its east face with relative ease, while the north wall has probably conquered more climbers than the other way around. French extreme skier Jean-Marc Boivin has even made a descent of the east side, but I was very content to just glide around in the shadow of this Swiss giant.

KEITH JOHNSTON AND MARTIN SÖDERQVIST WERE MY companions on a spring visit to Zermatt. With the five days we had at our disposal, we could only scratch the surface of the skiing possibilities. Zermatt, together with neighboring Cervinia and Valtournenche, has almost 400 kilometers of pistes and enough off-piste descents in between the marked runs to keep experts discovering routes for years.

Nevertheless, it is easy to come to some general conclusions. To begin with, Zermatt has great skiing for all ability groups. Nowhere in the world can beginners and intermediates cruise along wide boulevards of snow with more beautiful backdrops and vistas than here in Zermatt. The elevation almost guarantees perfect packed powder on the easy upper slopes of the mountains, even late in the season.

Experts will also not be disappointed. Despite its renown, there are plenty of uncrowded trails where advanced skiers can get into fifth gear. The terrain is extremely varied. Off-piste enthusiasts can lay tracks among the seracs high on the glaciers of the upper mountain or weave their way through the trees on 40–45-degree slopes in the glades of the Schwarzsee area. Narrow couloirs and gullies that would be permanently forbidden terrain in many ski areas are marked pistes in Zermatt.

Martin Söderqvist sweeps down toward Zermatt from the Klein Matterhorn section of the ski area.

The ski area can be divided into six general regions: the Sunegga, the Gornergrat, the Schwarzsee and the Klein Matterhorn on the Zermatt side of the ski area, plus Cervinia and Valtournenche on the south side. Generally speaking, the upper mountain of the Klein Matterhorn and the Cervinia side provide easier skiing, while all the other areas have a more mixed offering.

On our first day, we were looking for good freeride terrain and Zermatt has an abundance of that. We warmed up with a couple of runs down the National piste, which has served in the past as a venue for FIS giant slalom races. All the while, we hungrily eyed the vast kilometers of steep, north-facing slopes off the back of the Gornergrat. We could not hold out for long, as the call of the powder was too strong. Before much time

had passed, we found ourselves diving off the top of the Rote Nase, the last stop above the Gornergrat. We circumvented a few crevasses and swooped down through soft virgin snow.

EVEN THE RIDE UP IS AN EXPERIENCE on the Gornergrat, a cogwheel train that is, for all intents and purposes, a functioning museum piece. If one rides the train from the bottom, one should try, at all costs, to get a seat. If you are one of the unlucky standing-room passengers, prepare yourself for a full 40 minutes of standing in your ski boots, with your arm outstretched to hold onto a ceiling strap for support. You might not get the blood circulation back into that arm until lunchtime.

Sitting comfortably in one of the seats, however, is one of the most

ski etiquette, we stood no chance. A traffic light signaled the imminent approach of the old train by first changing from red to orange and then turning green, as a metal gate simultaneously began to slowly withdraw to allow us to board.

"Even before the amber lamp lit up, the train came into view and people began clambering over the restraining gate. They used their ski poles adroitly to assure themselves a clear path to the train. The men bullied their way ahead of their families, threw down gloves, ski caps, rucksacks and parkas on every seat within arms length and firmly bellowed, '*Besetzt!* (occupied) *Besetzt! Besetzt! Besetzt!*' Their hoarse hollers and a belligerent stare were generally enough to ward off any attempt by the meek to wrest away one of the half-dozen seats which each of these people was saving for his family and friends."

I chuckled to myself at this old tale and thought how much had changed through the years. The

> **» The Matterhorn is gorgeous, stunning, staggering, stupendous, spectacular, magnificent, awesome and inspirational, but that entire description doesn't really do it justice.«**

Gornergrat still had all its old charm, but Zermatt's lift capacity has increased greatly over the years and most of the time, one can nowadays avoid Walter Braun's trauma.

THE GORNERGRAT AFFORDS STUPENDOUS VIEWS of the Monte Rosa (4634 m) and the Gorner Glacier, and the pistes are simple enough so that cruisers can keep one eye on the piste and the other on the wondrous surrounding nature. There is even plenty of easy terrain beside the piste for would-be powder skiers to practice in the fluff between the top station and the Riffelberg stop, about 500 vertical meters further down.

Below the beautiful Riffelberg Hotel, however, those who veer off the piste need full focus on where they are going, and even that may not be enough. Steep pitches and couloirs are situated perilously close to sheer cliffs, and skiers who venture too far to the south might find that their options are the last cliff jump of their life or a long hike back up. We miscalculated our line but realized our mistake in enough time that a mere half-hour hike got us rerouted into the couloirs rather than over the cliffs.

The north side of the mountain from the top of the Gornergrat is the home of the Kelle Piste and various steep powder descents between the rocks. This time, we scouted the territory carefully from the opposite side before venturing into no-man's-land. There was more than enough of interest to keep us busy for the rest of the day.

Our second day was devoted to the massive amount of territory on both the Swiss and Italian sides of the Klein Matterhorn region. This is an impressive experience before one even mounts one's boards. Our third cable car of the morning took us smack into the cliff face of the Klein Matterhorn. Swiss mountain engineering never ceases to amaze me, and this is one of the better examples of the remarkable Swiss mastery over their jagged habitat.

Shortly after one walks through a long tunnel and emerges on the south side of the peak, a sign beckons visitors to visit the Gletschergrotte (glacier cave). This is a worthwhile side excursion for everybody and a must if one has children. A visit does not take much more than 20 minutes, and one can see a number of displays of ice carvings. In addition, one can view crevasses from the unusual underside, looking up.

The Swiss side of the upper mountain is a fabulous place for inexperienced skiers to hone their skills in a high alpine milieu. Skiing here will have them gawking and gaping in all directions. In this environment of ice and granite cliffs, gaping crevasses and the omnipresent Matterhorn, visitors can hardly help but feel close to the Creator.

The Italian side of the mountain down to Breuil-Cervinia and Valtournenche is a wide, open playground for intermediates. Most

pleasant ways to ride up a mountain. Bring a beer and a sandwich, enjoy the Swiss scenery unfolding outside your window and imagine what skiing was like a hundred years ago.

As I sat comfortably watching the Swiss Alps go by, I could not help but think about a cocktail party story from long ago. My parents' friend, Walter Braun, described the Gornergrat experience of the 1950s, a time when the skiing public had grown much more quickly than the industry's ability to increase lift capacity.

Walter's description went something like this: "We stood packed so close together that the smell of yesterday's evening meal emanated strongly from the mouths of most of the surrounding skiers. We knew about the long ride up the Gornergrat, but as a skier weaned on American

We are not talking about threading the tightrope between life and death for a handful of turns, arcing into a tuck and taking the last couple hundred meters in a schuss! Saudan's run down the Marinelli couloir was not only a case of maintaining his balance on a deadly face, it was a feat of endurance that makes most of today's extreme exploits in the short chutes around Valdez pale by comparison. Then, take into consideration the difference between Sylvain's 1960s equipment and today's gear, and his accomplishments are akin to Hermann Maier gunning down the Hahnenkamm on a pair of cross-country boards.

skiers with even a few weeks of experience are able to ski much of this terrain unhindered.

We were looking for something more difficult, so we dropped off the Ventina Ghiacciaio piste and into the untracked snow under the uppermost cable car of the Cervinia lift system. The snow had seen too much sun, and definitely provided a formidable challenge. We jump-turned through the crusty fare until we finally met back up with the piste. By this time, we were quite happy to relax and enjoy the cruising territory that makes up most of this region. We replenished our carbohydrates with some Italian pasta before working our way back to Switzerland.

At dinnertime we met up with another class act and legend who has had a long association with this area, Sylvain Saudan. Sylvain's connection with Zermatt dates back to one of his early steep-skiing expeditions, a memorable conquest of the Marinelli Couloir from Zermatt down into Italy. The descent has an average gradient of between 50 and 55 degrees, an inclination that may not sound that devastating by today's standards unless one knows that the couloir dives down a full 2300 vertical meters!

THE 21ST-CENTURY VERSION of skiing—which spotlights extreme skiing as a competitive sport and has seen "off-piste" skiing reinvented, expanded and marketed as "freeride" skiing—owes a lot to Saudan, who started it all back in the mid-1960s.

His descent of Mt. McKinley in Alaska from an elevation of 6200 meters down to 1900 meters was, at that time, the longest descent ever made. The father of extreme skiing was still at it in 1982, when his plunge from Hidden Peak in Pakistan was man's first run from an 8000-meter peak.

Sylvain joined us for a *raclette* dinner and brought us up to date on what he is involved with now. Today, Sylvain no longer puts his life on the line in the pursuit of the extreme, but he also has no thoughts of putting his skis in mothballs.

"I am not ready for zee retirement," Sylvain said. "How can one retire when one 'as only been having fun zee whole life."

Among other things, he usually spends November and December on

the Zermatt glaciers, advising, instructing and imparting knowledge and ski philosophy to skiers eager to improve their technique. He can take pleasure in the fact that he has been among a few extreme skiers who have survived to tell their stories to a younger generation. During his early years, Sylvain basked in the sunshine of his accomplishments, but in recent times he gets his greatest enjoyment from sharing.

Unfortunately, Sylvain was on his way back to Chamonix, and we did not have the opportunity to ski with the old master. We were lucky enough, however, to have the head of the Stoked Ski School, Üli Bärfuss, to give us tips and guide us around the following day.

AS THE CROWDS HEADED *en masse* up the route toward Italy that we had tried the previous day, Üli guided us to the Schwarzsee section of the ski area, a region which offers transport on the new Matterhorn Express gondola and two old T-bars. As is so often the case, a meager offering of uphill transport disguised the fact that the downhill possibilities were disproportionately large.

Most skiers in this area putter around a couple of blue pistes that connect Schwarzsee with Furi. In between those unspectacular routes, however, are the Aroleid, Tiefbach and Momatt pistes, plus a wide expanse of steep tree-skiing. Most ski resorts would deem these Zermatt runs as avalanche gullies and rope them off. In fact, one of them, the Momatt descent, cannot be opened early in the season, as the frozen waterfall in the guts of the gully must first be covered with enough snow to render it skiable. When Üli led us into these chutes five days after the last snowfall, the runs were still untouched.

For the next three days, we were certainly the most regular patrons of this prime Zermatt real estate, as we skied laps among these virgin forest routes. It was almost too easy, requiring no traversing and no walking. We merely dropped off the main trail partway down the run and laid a long series of turns around well spaced trees, stumps and bushes. At the

bottom, one long schuss brought us back to the lift.

We would have been quite content to continue this pattern run after run, but Üli apparently thought we required a bit of variety for our last day. He led us on the trail toward the Hörnlihütte, used by climbers ascending the east face of the Matterhorn. I got a good set of sweaty palms at one passage, as the path followed a narrow ledge above a sheer cliff. Once past this obstacle, the rest of the hike was a cakewalk.

Soon, we were carving up the powder, closer to the Matterhorn than ever. We felt tiny and humble so near the base of this grand peak. The run was a fitting climax to our short stay in Zermatt.

For skiers who wish to be humbled by Mother Nature's grandeur, Zermatt and the Matterhorn should definitely be paid a visit. If you happen to visit in the late fall, it could also be fun to ski a few turns with the other local legend, Sylvain.

If you happen to stand near the Matterhorn with Sylvain in the late afternoon, ask him to relate a couple of tales of his adventures. He is one of the greatest storytellers that I have ever met. As the sun drops low in the sky, you may notice that the towering peak and the short Swiss skier cast a shadow of equal length. As Sylvain's story paints you a picture, you might just ponder if the Matterhorn isn't listening as well, with just a touch of admiration, for it is normal for both parties to stand up and take notice when legends meet.

VERBIER AND THE FOUR VALLEYS – NEW YEAR'S RESOLUTION

Verbier has the name. It is the largest individual ski area in Switzerland, by virtue of its 205 kilometers of pistes and its 46 lifts. It is a five-star resort for any and all kinds of skiers. Gnarly ski bums are here, looking for monster moguls and death-defying couloirs. The mink-and-diamond crowd from Geneva and Paris are present as well, partying in their million-dollar chalets, cruising the pistes, showing off their latest toys and partaking of the village's gourmet restaurants.

Fewer people have heard of La Tzoumaz, Nendaz, Veysonnaz, Bruson, Les Collons or Thyon, some of the other villages that make up the huge, lift-linked region called the Four Valleys. These are some of the poor stepsisters that, together with Verbier, bring the statistical totals of the entire region to an extremely impressive 400 kilometers of pistes and 96 lifts.

If one goes even a little further afield, all within about an hour's drive are a myriad of little family resorts such as Vichères, Champex-Lac, Super St.-Bernard and Crévacol. These are some of the second cousins to the poor stepsisters. Just like ragged stepsister Cinderella, however, Verbier's poorer relatives, who are not ordinarily dressed up for a gala, should not be underestimated. They have their own qualities that might win the heart of a skier.

Each of these ski villages has its own charm and individuality, and together, the entire area becomes more than just a composite of its separate parts. It offers everything from Verbier's exclusive, up-market selection of *haute cuisine* and luxurious chalet living, to the charm of medieval villages like Bourg-St.-Pierre and Bruson. The skiing here also covers the gamut between the predominantly blue and red pistes of Thyon and Les Collons and the vast, off-piste territory of Verbier.

AMONG THE SKIING ELITE who feel at home here are three-time freeride world champion Francine Moreillon, famous Finnish freerider Pette Halme, Bond stuntman John Falkner and legendary extreme skier Dominique Perret. However, you are not so likely to meet any of this crowd on the mountain. They have been tearing up powder in Verbier for so long that they are more familiar with this area than their own living rooms and are rarely visible where mere mortals ski.

Perhaps one might get a glimpse of one of these super skiers taking a warmup run between the bunker-sized moguls of Mont Fort, before they disappear down some back side or into the deep forest. It was some of this off-the-beaten-path terrain that Anders Karlsson, Pontus Nordahl and I were interested in when we enlisted the services of one of Verbier's top guides, François Perraudin, to point us in the right direction.

François explained immediately that it was no longer as easy as it had been some years ago to find untracked powder in Verbier, as there were today so many good riders. In addition, Mont Gelé, a great freeride mountain with no pistes at all, was nowadays rarely open, as a reaction to the increased avalanche danger posed by so many new freeriders with so little knowledge.

François went on to tell us that longtime Verbier off-piste classics like the route from Mont Fort to Tortin, the Stairway to Heaven and the back side of the Mont Fort are invariably tracked-out almost immediately. One must hike if one is seeking first tracks on the second day after a snowfall. His words rang loud and clear, so we packed our skins and touring inserts into our packs and followed our leader to the Lac des Vaux area.

A SWEATY CLIMB ULTIMATELY BROUGHT US atop some scrumptious couloirs looking down at Tortin. We gazed down, surveying the terrain, which widened below the chute into an open but uneven field of powder.

"I test za snow," said François, as he leapt eagerly into the guts of one of the gullies. He bounced a few turns mirthfully in the light snow and called back over his shoulder, as an afterthought, "By za vay, be careful! Za bumps are rocks!"

"Better late than never," I thought to myself upon hearing his warning, as I directed my skis carefully between the bumps. We were only part way down and there was plenty more, but François stopped and began remounting his touring gear.

"I vant to show you za Champs Ferret. It is not so much furzer to walk," said our leader.

Our extra walk was very worthwhile. A long valley of powder awaited us. The slopes were steep, and despite the trees, which provided some safety from avalanches, I reckoned that this was not a place I would like to visit before the new snow had had a chance to settle and bond. The upper slopes were open and we glided through the old powder in large, sweeping arcs. Lower down, we tightened our turning radius drastically to weave among the judiciously spaced pines. At the bottom, we once again had a hike to get back to the lifts at Prarion.

By this time, we were famished, and settled into a restaurant to replenish our lost fluids, whilst gorging ourselves on a local specialty called *croute aû fromage*. This treat, made up of toast drenched in melted cheese and often covered with mushrooms, ham and/or a fried egg, fit the bill admirably.

After lunch, there was little time to do much more than cruise back to the village, but François gave us a few tips before we parted. According

THIS PAGE
LEFT: It is advisable to head up the mountain early, if you want to get any fresh powder in Verbier.
RIGHT: The Pub Mont Fort has been an après-ski institution in Verbier for many years.

RIGHT PAGE
First tracks down to Verbier from Savoleyres was like a black-and-white photograph from a bygone era—a time before so many skiers were here to cut up the morning powder. Johan Löfstedt is the skier.

THIS PAGE
UPPER: This map depicts the unusual layout of the pistes at the Champex-Lac ski area.
LOWER LEFT: Jonas Delogne in the powder snow of Crévacol.
LOWER RIGHT: The village of Crévacol.

RIGHT PAGE
Pontus Nordahl flies through the powder in Verbier.

to our leader, a short hike off to the left of the Col des Gentianes Lift would lead us into some devastating descents down to Lac de Cleuson. He also recommended the Vallon d'Arbi, one valley over from where we had skied down together.

It was, however, high season, and the tempo in Verbier was akin to the day before Christmas at Macy's. I was ready to go further afield in search of something a little more laid back—and I found it in spades! In fact, there were enough quiet little corners of powder in the near vicinity to justify a separate vacation.

After a snowfall in Verbier, the ski bums battle for first tracks in earnest, like a bunch of Wall Street brokers chasing a hot initial public offering. In the likes of Bruson, Vichéres, Champex-Lac, Super St.-Bernard and Crévacol, my biggest problem was having a set of tracks to follow! I knew that many freeride pearls existed, but without any tracks to show me the way, I was not always sure how to get in and out of them.

THESE ARE ALL TINY FAMILY RESORTS with two to five lifts. A statistic like that may not compare very favorably to Verbier proper, but when the number of off-piste skiers on any given day is less than the number of lifts, it bodes well for anyone looking for powder.

Champex-Lac was a good example of this scenario. I was joined on a visit to this little ski area by Swedish snowboarder Lisa Mörtberg, and we seemed to be the only freeriders on the premises.

Champex-Lac is perhaps the most bizarre ski area that I have ever seen. The uphill transport here consists of two inconsequential beginner's lifts, one short T-bar on the upper mountain and one of the steepest chair lifts in the world, which takes skiers up a heavily forested mountain for more than 700 vertical meters.

The downhill possibilities are even more unusual. The upper T-bar offers a couple of red pistes and a whole lot of intriguing tree-skiing. The main lift services one very black, unprepared ski run to the skier's left of the chair and a long, red descent, which is no more than a road with one giant hairpin curve. In between the uncompromising black route and the westernmost point of the reclining "V" was a virtual cornucopia of ultra-steep tree descents, but without a path to follow, Lisa and I did not dare dive below the base of the upper lift.

IT WAS SNOWING HEAVILY and we satisfied ourselves gobbling up lines in the trees under the short Breya 2 Lift, which we could survey on the ride up. Curiosity, however, has been the downfall of many a powder junkie, and I couldn't quite put the long, steep forest out of my mind. Close to closing time, I noticed a large man and his eight-year-old son. Wearing a rucksack and with powder clinging to his beard, he looked the part of a true Swiss mountain man. I struck up a conversation.

I had pegged him correctly. He was a local who had literally learned to ski on this small, unique mountain. When I asked him about the off-piste possibilities in the lower forest, his teeth became visible and a broad smile peeked through his thick beard. His eyes twinkled as he began to describe the many options, all of which he seemed to know down to the finest detail. After all, this forest had been his playground for his entire childhood and had left a permanent imprint.

As I began to see the possibility of a guided tour to satisfy my indefatigable curiosity, Erik Papilloud saw his chance to have somebody bring up the rear behind his son, an absolute necessity for skiing off-piste with a child. The chemistry between us was excellent, like the chance meeting of two old fur traders in the mountains of the pre-Gold Rush American West. We exchanged stories on the lift, and the pact was sealed that we would finish the day with a run through the forest.

WHAT WE FOUND ON OUR FINAL DESCENT was more than any of us had bargained for. The moment we dropped below the upper lift, the snow depth more than doubled from 40 centimeters to about a meter. It was early in the season and there was no base under the powder, creating a certain danger of getting tripped up by hidden obstacles.

Erik seemed oblivious to that possibility and dove into the thicket like Robin Hood in pursuit of the sheriff's gold. It was clear that he knew this labyrinth of trees, stubs, glades, glens and gullies, and I had no problem being one of "Robin's merry men"—not at first.

On each pitch, Lisa and I waited for Erik's little boy to work his way down to Papa, and then, we too filled our mouths with face shots. Erik was a gentleman. After leading for a while, he said he would take over as rear guard, giving Lisa and me a chance at first tracks.

I found a good line and each time I thought it had petered out, I rounded one last tree, only to find another opening. By the time I finally found myself boxed-in by trunks and stubs, we were about halfway down.

Now, I could see that the fun was over. It was too early in the season and the snow cover further down was downright poor. Tree roots and

rocks were in full view now. In addition, the area was so steep that avalanches from the previous spring had changed the landscape by downing a number of trees, which now lay helter-skelter across the slopes below us.

"Oh, za forest looks quite deeferent from ven I skied it last season," lamented Erik, in an attempt to ward off any possible criticism of his guiding abilities.

I could imagine that a month from now, with an additional meter or two of snow, this tree run could have been a dream from top to bottom, but that was no solace right now. We clambered over obstacles, ducked under others, took off our skis on a few occasions, made a few dozen kick turns and sweated an awful lot. Finally, at the bottom, Erik invited us for a *Glühwein* to close out our little adventure on a pleasant note.

Champex-Lac was not the only small area in this region where we had the off-piste skiing more or less to ourselves. Lisa and I found a similar lack of skiers on the little four-lift mountain of Vichères. Here, there was much more open terrain on the lower mountain than in Champex-Lac, but we found no Erik to guide us and stormy weather kept us pretty close to the marked trails.

THE CLOSEST SMALL SKI AREA to Verbier, which is even included on the Four Valleys lift ticket, is Bruson. Getting there is a simple matter of riding the gondola from Verbier down to Le Châble and taking a short bus ride to this little medieval village. Unpretentious and uncrowded, the four lifts here offer both tree-skiing and open terrain for powder fans. Bruson is popular with Verbier veterans, who often ski here when stormy weather keeps much of the Verbier system closed.

Anders joined me in Bruson, and we were lucky enough to be there one afternoon when the first beams of sunlight caressed the virgin snow after a snowfall. We dove into the open meadows of the back side, adjacent to the Grand-Tsai Lift. The descent was short, but we were virtually alone and had our pick of every line on the mountain.

Following a hefty lunch, we followed a tip from one of the local lift attendants and began a hike above the upper lift to Six Blanc. This endeavor opened up a large bowl of powder below us. By the time we reached the tree line, I was high on powder, and there was a great temptation to continue straight down into the unknown. Anders' more sober mind prevailed, and we traversed back to the piste.

Perhaps the best of the small ski areas in this part of Switzerland is Super-St.-Bernard. The last village before the Grand St. Bernard Tunnel is an obscure little community of medieval homes and buildings called Bourg-St.-Pierre. During my visit a few years ago, the tourist office was no more than a corner of the living room of one of the hamlet's more public-minded citizens!

The ski location is equally petit, but only if you count lifts—one beginners tow and one gondola. It is immense, however, if you consider accessible terrain. I have rarely seen one lift that accesses as much skiing as the Menouve Gondola. Situated adjacent to the Grand St. Bernard Tunnel that connects Switzerland to Italy, this 750-vertical-meter antique, built in 1963, is a true classic.

There is a red run—very dark red—that goes under the lift back to the base. Alternatively, one can ski through a long, snow-filled tunnel and emerge on a black run, which is not really a run at all, but a wide valley of almost limitless off-piste possibilities. Wherever one comes down here, one alights on the hiking trail that once was the main thoroughfare over the St. Bernard Pass. This route, while no longer necessary to trans-Alpine travel, is still a well-worn path, as hosts of touring skiers trek from the base of the lift station to the Grand St.-Bernard Hospice.

Still an active monastery, the Hospice has for hundreds of years been a place where a weary traveler can find a bed and a warm meal. Long before ski lifts and tunnels, the monks at this large retreat atop the St. Bernard Pass raised and bred the first St. Bernard dogs to be used for snow rescue.

Not much has changed since those early beginnings. A touring skier

is welcome to use the monastery as a base for making day tours, and he will surely share the premises with some large, furry canines. A visit, even if only for lunch, is worthwhile just to see the monastery, and if one has time for a few days of touring, all the better, for one could hardly find a more unusual and authentic base for such activities.

THESE INTERESTING OPTIONS would seem to be more than enough to make for a rewarding visit to little Super-St.-Bernard, but there is even more. From the peak, one can also ski a long, off-piste valley down into Italy. The top of the lift marks the virtual dividing line between the northern and southern flanks of the Alps, a fact that often produces totally different weather or snow conditions on the two sides.

Anders, two other friends, Jonas and Per, and I took advantage of a perfect, cloudless day to dive down the south-facing valley into Italy on the morning of New Year's Eve. The north-facing pistes back to the base of the lifts were well packed powder, but with no new snow. The moment we traversed out into Italy, however, 30 centimeters of powder began to spray up from our skis. The contrast was amazing. Although I had often heard that storms coming from the south or north can get hung up

atop the Alps and do not share their bounty with both sides, this kind of graphic proof was rather astounding.

We swished silently through a valley that seemed to go on and on. We finally worked our way onto a road that wound around for so long that I thought we could end up in Spain, but we finished our excursion in the Italian village of Crévacol. The run was certainly 10 kilometers long, if not more. We knocked on the door of the nearest house to inquire if we could buy something to drink and call a taxi.

"*Si, si, taxi, no problemo,*" replied a warm, happy woman. "*Vino blanco? Vino tinto?*" she then asked.

Before the taxi arrived, four thirsty skiers made short work of two carafes of *vino tinto* and an assortment of Italian sausages. In spite of our repeated offers, our Italian benefactor refused any payment, and we were well on our way to a memorable New Year's Eve.

OUR DAY OF SURPRISES was still half full. Crévacol is yet another small local ski area. Even arriving at lunchtime, we found that the 30 centimeters of powder that was all around had gone virtually untouched all morning. The sun terraces were full of Italian families working on their tans, the

pistes were sparsely populated and the powder—well, by 12:30, four foreigners were beginning to leave their mark on it.

On the front side of Crévacol, broad areas of fresh snow lay rotting in the noonday heat, certain to be wasted by the sun due to the lack of customers. A peek down the north-facing back side revealed more open spaces, even fewer tracks and the great powder preservative—shade. There was no time to waste, and we pushed off, discovering a large expanse of broad, open bowls and slopes that eventually gave way to ravines, gullies and ridges scattered with trees.

At the bottom, we skied directly on the tunnel, winding our way back to still another village that time had forgotten. Our day finished with a hitchhike through the tunnel into Switzerland and a satisfied drive back to a New Year's Eve celebration of revelry and fireworks. Bustling Verbier seemed light-years away from where we had been just a few hours earlier.

We had all performed a sacrilegious act that day. Although strongly forbidden by the ski bum credo, we had left vast spaces of powder untouched. Tons of virgin snow could have been ours for the asking, and we had just driven away, leaving it unmolested. It had hurt to leave, but there was so damned much! We just couldn't do it alone. We couldn't

ABOVE: Jonas Delogne skis powder from atop the tiny Super-St.-Bernard ski area into Italy. There is still room for a few more fresh tracks.

use it all up. The worst part was that our visit to the Four Valleys was coming to an end. There was no tomorrow to return and begin putting down more lines where we had left off the day before. Yes, it truly was a waste.

We sat in the Pub Mont Fort, one of Verbier's most active nightspots, awaiting the New Year to be hailed in. Some Brits were wailing a rather drunken version of Auld Lang Syne. I had mixed feelings about our last day—a great swirl of powder and discovery tempered by having to leave much untracked snow to waste away at the mercy of the wind and sun.

My sentiment was quite appropriate for the bittersweet occasion of New Year's Eve, but soon the champagne corks began to pop. I made a New Year's resolution to return to the Four Valleys. There would be more back sides and hidden ravines to be discovered, and with a little luck, we would again receive a fall of fresh snow. I was warmed by a comforting thought. Despite the virgin slopes that got left behind, snow is after all a renewable resource. Happy New Year!

ST MORITZ — THE WORLD'S FIRST SKI RESORT

Johannes Badrutt, the legendary St. Moritz hotelier of the 1800s, is given singular credit for starting winter tourism in the Alps. In 1864, he made an unusual bet with four of his regular summer clients from Great Britain. Badrutt suggested that they should visit his hotel the following year during the winter. If they were unhappy with their holiday, he would pay their round-trip travel expenses, whereas if they were satisfied, they were invited to stay as long as they wanted on his tab!

This win–win proposition was hard for the Brits to turn down, and as it turned out, they found their winter vacation so enjoyable that they remained in St. Moritz from Christmas until Easter. Naturally, the satisfied visitors returned to England with marvelous stories for their friends and acquaintances in the British high society, and before long, Badrutt's Palace Hotel was filling up its rooms in what had previously been a dead season. Thus was the Alpine winter tourist industry born, and I suppose, considering the financial arrangements of their long visitation, that the four Englishmen were perhaps the first ski bums.

In the 21st century, winter tourists to St. Moritz need a somewhat heftier bank account to finance a season in the capital of winter glitz and glamour. Today, a double room in the Palace during the high season costs anywhere between €800 and €1350 per night—and dinner is extra! The high cost of living in the birthplace of winter tourism has turned the ski bum into an endangered species.

IN THE ENSUING YEARS since that long-ago bet, St. Moritz has hardly rested on its laurels. It has continually been at the forefront of winter sports, keeping the famous resort always in the spotlight. The town has twice been the venue for the Olympic Games and four more times been the site of the Skiing World Championships. No other ski resort in the world can come close to St. Moritz's record for hosting prestigious ski events.

The hotel standard of the village goes hand in hand with the high level of ski events that St. Moritz has become used to holding. Amazingly, 3400 hotel beds in town are situated in four- or five-star hotels. Badrutt's Palace, along with the Kulm Hotel, the Kempinski Grand Hotel des Bains, the Carlton and the Suvretta House, all provide five-star accommodations.

If you like fine cuisine, your palate will also be well serviced in the Engadine Valley. This Alpine cleavage of the rich and famous, which in addition to St. Moritz includes the villages of Sils Maria, Sils Baselgia, Silvaplana, Champfèr, Celerina and Pontresina, boasts seven Michelin stars and 341 Gault Millau (another French restaurant rating system) points.

Many visitors may come to St. Moritz for the good food, the ultra-high hotel standard or merely to mingle with high society, but Rupert Scheiner, my son Erik and I entered the Engadine in quest of a good pizza and first tracks. We found both. As it turned out, a pizza was about the classiest meal we could afford, but we had rarely skied anywhere where it was easier to make first tracks.

The ski area accessible directly from town is known as Corviglia. This is the most frequented of the local mountains and an excellent location for intermediate skiers. Here, one begins by riding the famous Corviglia cogwheel train up the first section of the mountain, before a variety of lifts spread skiers out in all directions. We enjoyed a warmup day cruising the perfectly groomed boulevards and also had time for a few advanced couloirs on the back side of the Piz Nair.

A 30-minute drive from town, directly across the valley from one another, are the Diavolezza and Lagalb ski areas. Diavolezza has a beginners tow, a chair lift and a cable car, while Lagalb has only a small tow and a cable car, but these facts are misleading. There are few lifts and few skiers, but a hell of a lot of mountain in both cases.

The Diavolezza ski area offers a rather easy but picturesque and worthwhile ungroomed route over the Diavolezza-Morteratsch Glacier. While this attracts the tourists, hardly anybody skis the much more challenging off-piste route down the Val Arias on the other side of the cable car. Rupert, Erik and I were alone on the corn snow in this back valley and were still alone as we skied the Tour la Rösa down to the road far behind Piz Lagalb.

The wealthy guests of St. Moritz might have been sleeping in, enjoying a lounge chair on some verandah or puttering around on the pistes, but they seemed to have absolutely no interest in venturing off the beaten track. As it turned out, this was not entirely true. One St. Moritz guest did indeed indulge in off-piste skiing—and we met him the next day.

THE OTHER MAJOR LIFT SYSTEM serving St. Moritz, closer to town than Diavolezza and Lagalb, is the Corvatsch-Furtschellas area. The Corvatsch is not only the highest of St. Moritz's ski venues, it is also the most challenging.

We skied a few runs to reconnoiter the mountain, but we needed some expert advice. I scrutinized the passengers who shared our cable car. Many skiers were dressed for show, but I noticed one man whose equipment and clothing were functional rather than flashy. I guessed right.

Battesta Albin was not merely a local who knew his way around, he was a mountain guide. I asked him if it was possible to ski a particular back valley I had seen. Then he gave Erik, Rupert and me an even more careful examination than I had given him, and he exchanged a few mumbled words with a gentleman next to him.

"You could ski it," he answered, "but it will not be good. My client, Karl, here, has given me the okay to invite the three of you to join us. That way, I can show you some much better places."

We followed Battesta and Karl in fresh powder over the 40-degree tongue of the Corvatsch Glacier. It was only a test, he explained, to make sure we were solid skiers. We passed the test and tailed our guide down the even more challenging Furtschellas Couloir. Ultimately, we finished the day with an off-piste variation of the black Hahnensee descent back to St. Moritz Bad.

We had originally come to St. Moritz thinking that the high prices would translate into a lack of ski bums and lots of fresh tracks for us. This theory proved to be correct. Little could we know, however, that we would be led to the best skiing thanks to the benevolence of a German industrialist and his private guide.

Perhaps Battesta had pulled out a page from Johannes Badrutt's strategy book. Mr. Badrutt had been the benefactor for those first British "ski bums" in an effort to stimulate future winter business. It worked, and many English tourists soon followed those first winter guests to St. Moritz.

Now, more than 140 years later, Battesta Albin was conceivably also attempting to drum up some future business by donating some gratis guiding. If Battesta's generosity was a marketing strategy to attract more ski bums to St. Moritz, I have only one comment. I hope it doesn't work.

DISENTIS
FREERIDING AND FREETHINKING
WITH SIMON JACOMET

Disentis is a Swiss ski village also known as Mustér in the local language of Rhaeto-Romanic. If you haven't heard of it in either language, you are not alone. Disentis certainly is known to the handful of monks who inhabit the 1300-year-old monastery that dominates the village. Otherwise, no more than a handful of local powder fanatics are aware of this resort, and they have managed to keep it one of the whispered secrets of the Central Alps. Situated in the canton of Graubünden, near the Oberalp Pass, Disentis is a powder hole that gets snow when the storm fronts come from the north as well as from the south.

There are also points of interest in and around Disentis that go beyond the realm of skiing. Just a few kilometers away from the village is the source of the Rhine River, a much-visited destination during the summer months. If that does not suit your fancy, what about going underground in search of semi-precious stones? The region around Disentis is a virtual Mecca for semi-precious and even some precious stones. Lots of the locals are avid rock hounds, and many homes are decorated with beautiful crystals of all shapes, sizes and colors.

Alternatively, one can forego the shelf decorations and go directly for the valuables. The 1980s and 1990s saw a kind of minor gold rush begin in precisely this valley, and numerous times during the last few years, nuggets large enough to break the all-time Swiss record have been found just a "nugget's throw" from the lifts. In 2001, a man with a simple pan plucked a nugget out of the local river that was worth 250,000 Swiss francs. We, however, came in search of white gold.

BERT ROMANI, EDITOR OF THE DUTCH publication *Ski Magazine*, had tipped me about Disentis and had also recommended that I get in touch with a local skier named Simon Jacomet.

"He was an influential supporter of the carving ski in its early days," explained Bert, "and he's an interesting character."

I sent an e-mail to Mr. Jacomet and soon received an unusual reply—a photo of Simon in full ski garb on his freeride skis...underwater!

Under the photo, referring to the poor winter we had been having, Simon had written, "Don't be fed up, just look for alternatives! The one I'm trying out on the picture is no real compensation—and the problem is that I never find the right wax."

Interesting character, indeed! Of course, I became even more curious to meet this unusual personality. In his e-mail, Simon had also promised to show us around the ski area for a few days.

Simon was out of town on the day I arrived in Disentis with my friends Martin Söderqvist and Emil Magnusson, but there was no shortage of his image, which appeared on a number of billboards in the valley lift station. Simon had spent a few winters on the Salomon Demo Team, and his photo in free flight, up to his neck in powder or in carving stance has certainly been seen by most skiers, whether they know it is Simon Jacomet or not. One shot of Simon in a jumping tuck, shooting straight up at the moon, was almost the defining marketing image for Salomon's AK Rocket in the late '90s.

It was March, the weather was warm and without Simon to guide us, we skied the corn snow on the pistes and explored the mountain as best we could. The ski area works its way from the village, at 1150 meters, up Péz Ault, to an elevation of 2850, offering a hefty 1700 meters of vertical.

The lifts are built in four stages. A cable car takes visitors up the first 700 vertical meters from the village to the Berg Restaurant at Caischavedra. The ski possibilities from here back to town include one piste, which is primarily a transport road, and a plethora of steep, narrow chutes in the trees.

The second stage of the lift system is a long high-speed quad that is relatively flat—good intermediate skiing. Next comes a short, steep quad, which goes from 2200 meters to 2500 meters. It provided us with much of our skiing during our visit. Finally, another long, flat lift takes skiers

Emil Magnusson has to ski by radar during a dump of spring powder in Disentis.

the final leg to the top. One valley west of the mountain are two additional lifts that run parallel to the upper two lifts.

The entire ski resort has no more than thirteen pistes, and a good skier could easily ski every one in half a day. The off-piste area accessed by these few lifts, however, is enormous, and one could spend many weeks exploring the various possibilities. We kept ourselves pretty much to the pistes, practiced some cliff jumps and waited for Mr. Jacomet to show us some of the freeride terrain.

Simon's return coincided with 30 centimeters of fresh powder, as if he had God's own weather almanac in his back pocket. Thick fog shrouded the landscape, but this was Simon's backyard. He just turned on his radar and bounced into the barely visible oblivion with vigor. Once he had laid a track to give us some perspective, it was just for us to follow and enjoy. We moved counterclockwise from the second lift, laying first tracks on every slope. Once other people followed us off the piste, we just moved further west to etch in a new set of first tracks. The day culminated with a 10-minute hike up the razor-backed ridge of a mountain called La Muota and a brilliant run back to the Caischavedra station.

BETWEEN RUNS, WHILE RIDING the lifts, I tried to get a better handle on who our leader really was, but that was no easy task. I asked Simon numerous times what he actually did for a living, and each time I got a different evasive answer. He wouldn't let me pin him down to a specific job title, but I was quickly learning that he was a rebel who did not like to be labeled, pigeonholed or categorized.

I also found out that Simon had not only modeled for Salomon, he had also been involved with design and product development. In that capacity, he had given vision and direction to the whole carving revolution.

Simon originally studied art. During his years of involvement with skiing, he has used his right-brain artist's mentality to infuse some soul and inspiration into an industry dominated by engineers and technicians.

"Skiing should be fun and should be less confined by rules and definitions," Simon explained. "I did not want carving to be bound by the same regimentation that limits conventional skiing. Carving gives the opportunity for all skiers to have more fun and express themselves emotionally on skis more easily. It also allows beginners to learn the sport more quickly," he added.

By 1997, Simon's philosophical influence on the nature and direction of carving had many people calling him the "carving guru". It did not take long for him to rebel against the whole idea of being labeled. Such a title,

as flattering as it might have been, collided with Simon's sense of freedom and his artistic nature. The quick-thinking, fast-changing and impatient Mr. Jacomet had no time to be anchored by somebody else's definition trying to cage his ever-evolving nature.

Meanwhile, we had trouble keeping up with his fast-moving skis in the here and now, but it was an enjoyable challenge and we did our best all day.

The next morning, Simon and his brother, Ervin, were waiting for us at the parking lot, and by now, more than 60 centimeters of new snow blanketed the mountain. The cable car was almost empty. Five or six skiers and an equal number of sightseers in street shoes accompanied us. God only knows what the sightseers were planning to do in the storm. There was certainly nothing to see.

We desperately wanted to taste one or two of the mega-runs, but the old slush from a few days earlier was still isothermal at the lower elevations, making for a high level of avalanche danger. The previous day's tracks were of course completely covered, and we began the day with a repeat performance.

Around noon, a few soft sunbeams managed to negotiate their way through the thick layer of cumulus clouds. Simon and Ervin must have interpreted this as a sign from God, for they immediately began babbling in indecipherable Rhaeto-Romanic. Before we could so much as buckle our boots, they had decided that we should dive off the back of La Muota into the Val Pintga.

It could be that our guides had reassessed the avalanche danger in those 30 seconds, or it is possible that the translation of their native tongue would have read, "Avalanches be damned—let's go for it!" I did not really want to know. They explained that Val Pintga means "small valley", but even though we were entering it about 400 vertical meters below the top lift, it was neither small nor short. We swooped in like birds of prey for yet another set of first tracks.

Inspired by our descent, the Jacomet brothers got completely carried away. We followed our leaders to one of their favorite runs in the steep, tree-laden pitches on the lower front side of the ski area. This proved to be overly optimistic. After all, this whole part of the mountain had been devoid of snow a few days earlier.

The first 150 meters of vertical were fine. I could imagine the spectacular skiing in these glades in the heart of winter—with a proper base—but that was not the case today. The remaining 600 vertical meters consisted of a thrash through 2-meter-high bushes. Traversing was not really an option, and kick turns got you as tangled up in the bushes as a person trying to dance the jitterbug with an octopus.

Simon, who skied here with a technique that was half-snake and half-jackrabbit, could have negotiated this obstacle course without any heavy breathing, but he was kind enough to stay back and make sure that the old man of the group was surviving. I was grateful. I was forced to quaff a number of beers at the local billiard pub that evening in an attempt to replenish my depleted fluids.

An evening session of beer and billiards afforded me the chance to learn more about our new friend. Philosophical differences ultimately caused Simon and Salomon to part ways. Like any huge concern, Salomon did not move with the swiftness that an impetuous artist like Simon demanded. Therefore, he became involved with a few old friends to design the first Rhaeto-Romanic ski for the Swiss company RTC. He guided us during the day on a prototype pair of Billaballa skis. (Today Simon is the brain behind the development and design of the Zai ski.)

Not only does Simon use skis of his own design, but the enigmatic artist lives in a self-designed home, one that might just be the strangest house in Switzerland. Some people say the house looks like a container from the outside, and there is no debate that there is not one wall of the home that is 90 degrees to the ground. Basically, Simon designed and lives in a crooked house.

Simon's skiing on our final day, however, was anything but crooked. Again, despite weather that was very similar to the previous two days, our host managed to direct us to some fantastic lines all over the mountain.

I was beginning to notice a pattern in the behavior of the Jacomet brothers. Just around the time that the relatively safe off-piste skiing got skied out each day, the Jacomets invariably did a positive reassessment of the avalanche danger that allowed them (and us) to continue in untracked powder for the rest of the day.

To be fair, I must add that the local freeriders shared information generously, speaking with each other all day long to find out where the others had been and which descents might or might not be safe. Simon and Ervin made constant use of this Old-World "ski-buddy" system to keep us in fresh lines. It was just such a tip from one of Ervin's pals that gave us the last glorious powder orgasm of our stay.

During our last descent, Simon pointed out that we had merely skied the tip of the iceberg.

With a sincere smile, he said, "This means you will have to come back soon. There is so much more we can show you!"

The various 1700-vertical-meter descents from the top had been unavailable. That menu includes, among others, numerous variations of the Val Gronda (the Big Valley) and a fabulous descent all the way to the neighboring village of Sedrun, to name just a few.

We were not suffering from these omissions. We bounced merrily through a series of face shots on our last run and I watched Simon closely. His skiing style resembled his lifestyle, I thought to myself.

He fought to let the new carving ski be a different answer for different skiers. He did not want the new ski to be associated with a "must-learn" new technique, but rather that this great advancement in ski design should be all things to all skiers. His attitude was the same when it came to powder skiing.

One moment, he could pump out traditional-style powder turns and the next minute he might scream down in a series of big-mountain freeride turns. He is as comfortable in the air as he is on terra firma, and judging by the initial photo he sent me, being submerged under water on skis is also not a problem for Simon. He thrives on variety because the larger his repertoire, the freer man he is, and freedom is his home.

This free and open style is the way Simon wants to live, and he accords others the same respect. He may personally prefer shooting down a mountain at Mach speed in a series of big turns and living in a crooked house, but he would never tell his neighbor that a traditional turn or a conventional home is the wrong way to go.

François Voltaire once said, "I disapprove of what you say, but I will defend to the death your right to say it." Were Voltaire still alive, François and Simon might have made suitable ski partners, and I am quite sure that Simon would not have tampered one iota with Voltaire's skiing technique.

VAL D'ANNIVIERS — FAT SKIS AND SECRET VALLEYS

The Rhône Valley cuts through a portion of southwestern Switzerland like a giant green snake. Even during the winter, the valley often maintains its summer colors, in marked contrast to the snow-covered mountains that line both sides of the narrow plain. The placid farmland is juxtaposed with the rugged Berner Alps to the north and the towering Pennine Alps to the south. Every few kilometers along the freeway through the valley, signposts mark side roads that wind their way up to small mountain villages and ski resorts of various shapes and sizes.

Some of the ski areas are well-known mega-resorts like Verbier and Crans Montana, while others are tiny destinations, known primarily to the locals of the various towns along the Rhône River. One of the side valleys is Val d'Anniviers, home to the villages of Vercorin, Chandolin, Saint-Luc, Grimentz and Zinal.

Jonas Nilsson and I traveled up a road that consisted of a long series of hairpin curves. So tight were the turns that the local buses often had to shift into reverse and drive around the bend in two stages.

As we slowly gained altitude, we found that the setting magically transformed from the modern-day Switzerland of the Rhône Valley into a high-mountain valley of villages that time seemed to have forgotten. Along both flanks of Val d'Anniviers, ancient houses with hundreds of years of sunshine burnt into the wood dotted the landscape. It looked like a spot where, any moment, Heidi would come skipping around the corner with a pail of fresh milk.

Ultimately, we arrived at our destination, Grimentz. This is a village where skiing is not so much a business as it is a pastime, and tradition is of more value than commerce. The big summer events of Grimentz are still the local competition for the windowsill decorated with the most beautiful geraniums and the annual cow-fighting contest.

To stroll through the village is to wander into the 13th century. Narrow streets wind among antique chalets, barns, cow sheds and storage build-ings called *Raccards*. The *Raccards* are the most amazing structures. They are generally separated from the foundation by eight large, flat stones, each of which rests on a narrow piece of carved wood, creating a meter or so of empty air space between the ground and the building. This building technique was a method of insulation as well as a way of keeping mice and rats out of the food stocks.

We had arranged to ski with mountain guide Stefan Jossen, but we reached the valley a day early. This gave us some time to explore on our own before Stefan and the rest of the group would arrive. We opted for the slopes of Zinal, a short drive up the narrow valley from Grimentz. As we began to ascend through the small lift system, the Imperial Crown, five peaks which all top 4000 meters, began to come into view. Soon, the Weisshorn (4505 m), the Zinalrothorn (4221 m), the Obergabelhorn (4063 m), the Dent Blanche (4357 m) and the Matterhorn (4476 m) filled the near horizon. I was so caught up in the panorama that it took me a while to notice that all around us, just beyond the marked pistes, were plenty of fresh lines of powder from a recent snowfall.

It was mid-January, the depth of low season, and the resort was almost devoid of guests. We gobbled up powder lines right alongside the Combe Durand Lift, with no fear that anyone else would poach them from us.

Then we went up the Corne de Sorebois, and found some open slopes that were completely untouched. We could see that there was much more virgin snow covering various back sides of the mountain, but at this point, they were totally superfluous. We could wait for Stefan to lead us into the backcountry.

AFTER A VERY SATISFYING warmup day, Jonas and I arrived back at the Hotel A la Marenda to meet Stefan and the rest of our group. Among the others who would follow Stefan for the next six days were a group of German freeride fanatics who call themselves the "German Bulls". The

"Bulls" were Stefan's annual customers right here in Grimentz, and for good reason.

Stefan Jossen might well be the most qualified person in the world to guide skiers in the Val d'Anniviers. Born in the nearby Berner Alps, he has been exploring the off-piste possibilities of this region since 1992.

At first glance, Stefan fit the stereotype of what I have come to expect of a guide. He was physically fit of course, and he was quite serious, a necessary trait in a job that holds such responsibility. He displayed a pleasant sense of humor but did not speak too much more than what was absolutely necessary. He was self-confident about his skiing and his guiding, but also very cautious.

"It is quite easy to recognize which guides are good," he told me dryly. "They are those who are still alive."

Stefan, as it turned out, was no ordinary guide. In 1985, at the age of 21, he had been in a climbing party that conquered Mt. Fitzroy, in Argentina, one of fewer than 50 groups who have achieved that feat. Four years later, another climbing group in which he participated made one of only about twenty conquests of Cerro Torre, also in Patagonia.

That same year, Stefan was one of three others who joined world-famous mountaineer Hans Kammerlander on a Nanga Parbat expedition. While Kammerlander's fame and ambition compelled him to attempt and succeed to reach the peak despite almost suicidal conditions, prudence prevailed among the rest of the party, and Stefan and the others satisfied themselves with a shorter descent from "only" 7500 meters. Suffice it to say that Jonas and I felt ourselves relatively secure under the supervision of our leader.

STEFAN ASKED JONAS AND I if we had fat skis. I told him that I figured that fat boys were aids for the handicapped and the elderly, while Jonas reckoned that his all-mountain skis were plenty wide enough. (The anatomy of skis has changed very quickly in recent years. Basically, however, skis whose width under the boot is below 68 millimeters are designed for piste skiing, while a 68–80-millimeter waist designates an all-mountain ski. The even wider skis are known as big-mountain skis or fat boys. Fat skis, in the true sense of the word, however, are the widest of all, with a waist width of 105 millimeters or more.) Stefan tried once more to convince us that it might be a wise idea to rent a pair of big-mountain skis, but his suggestion fell on deaf ears and he apparently gave up—or so I thought. I was mistaken.

The next morning, 30 centimeters of new snow from the night before covered the slopes, it was snowing heavily and the visibility was nil—a day when one feels most grateful to have a guide. It was the kind of day when even the most grizzled veteran of powder skiing does not want the honor of making first tracks.

» **The others satisfied themselves with a shorter descent from 'only' 7500 meters.**«

At best, the lead skier is likely to be skiing with his weight adjusted for a 35-degree slope when it suddenly planes out, and he finds himself kissing his ski tips. At worst, he may ski face-first into a boulder or plummet into free fall over some invisible cliff.

In the face of this kind of weather, Stefan found routes in the white-out that we would not have found on a *clear* day. He also did us the favor of setting down a first track to follow. With somebody to lead us, we all could bounce blithely through the powder with our worries at a minimum.

By the afternoon, I had forgotten about the fat-ski discussion of the previous day, but Stefan apparently had not. We had so far been doing short runs on the upper mountain. Now, however, our pathfinder began to lead us down below the tree line, testing the lower slopes, which had not yet received much snow this early in the season. He knew what to expect. I did not.

As we skied down into the lower elevations, the new powder was somewhat heavier and rested on a thin crust. Under the crust was a layer of depth hoar right next to the bare ground. The crust held for Stefan and the "German Bulls", gliding on their wide-bodied skis. Jonas, on his all-terrain skis, was a borderline case, breaking through every so often.

Meanwhile, uncompromising Jimmy Petterson, on his carving skis, sank below the crust into the bushes under the snow like an anchor mired in seaweed. I could not make a turn to save my life.

The "Bulls" started dancing through the trees like ballerinas, while I kick-turned my way to the bottom of the mountain. I may be stubborn but I am not completely stupid. Directly after skiing, I went to the ski shop and rented a pair of big-mountain skis. I knew that once the skies cleared and we started getting into the out-of-bounds skiing, we would often be following routes that would take us to the base of the mountain. I was beginning to understand that fat skis were a bit more multi-purpose than merely being a crutch for the geriatric crowd!

THE NEXT MORNING, THE SUN WAS BACK, and a half-meter of powder glistened and sparkled under her light caress. Zinal was on today's agenda, and Stefan began the morning on the Combe Durand, where Jonas and I had skied alone on our first day. On this morning, however, we proceeded further on the high traverse, beyond a sign that said "*Domaine Freeride*" and another one that told us that we were leaving the controlled and secured ski area. Just like two days earlier, we did not even need to go that far afield. There was plenty of untouched snow closer at hand, but after all, we had a guide and it was exciting to try something new.

The "*Domaine Freeride*" offered a little of everything. There were steep pitches between rocky outcrops, and more gentle slopes decorated with huge boulders every now and then. Two days earlier, Jonas and I had skied a few short runs in this area and cut back to the middle station. Now we followed Stefan off-piste all the way down, enjoying a run that was twice as long. We eventually joined up with the black piste back to town.

As usual, Stefan saved the best for last. One can ski back to Grimentz from Zinal by way of what is perhaps the best freeride area in the valley—the Piste du Chamois. This is a long and aptly named north face beginning atop the Corne de Sorebois Lift.

As we stood at the top, we saw no sign that either man or beast had been here recently—but that would soon change. Whoever would be the next freerider or chamois in the area after us would certainly see eleven squiggly tracks. We skied over steep faces and gentle meadows and finally disappeared into the forest. We arrived back in Grimentz in time for a hearty lunch and a few more adventures before time and sunshine ran out.

THAT EVENING, ANOTHER TREAT was in store for me. I was invited into the cellar of the Burgesses House, where the most extensive selection of glacier wines is kept, some of which are over 100 years old.

A village as old as Grimentz has more traditions than the Vatican, and one of these long-standing customs revolves around the local wine, known as the Vin du Glacier. The annual ritual involving this wine began about 400 years ago, when the Anniviards bought a vineyard in nearby Sierre and started producing wine. The newly fermented wine was always brought up to the mountains and placed in huge larch barrels in the local cellars to age close to the glaciers.

Today the oldest barrels are 250 years old, and there are still over 100 houses in Grimentz with wine maturing in their cellars. The tartar on the inside of the barrels is often up to 5 centimeters thick, and the wine is generally aged for at least 25 years, giving it a peculiar taste, unlike any other wine in the world. Each June, the new wine is added to the top of the 500-liter barrels, mixing in with harvests from previous years.

The wine is only used for the private consumption of the locals, and the wine cellars are the gathering places for the villagers to discuss both political and private affairs. Today's gathering under the House of Burgesses was in honor of a ski race that was being held over the weekend, and I was lucky enough to be allowed to tag along.

THE KNOWLEDGE OF THE GLACIER-WINE TRADITION is a good enough reason to stimulate any visitor to try to get to know one of the local inhabitants, for how else can one gain the opportunity to taste this rare and unique wine? After all, following a day of Val d'Anniviers champagne powder, tasting some local glacier wine is the perfect après-ski.

The following days were full of surprises. Every time that Jonas and I thought that we had now seen it all, Stefan pulled still another rabbit out of his ski cap. With each day, we became more amazed at the extent of off-piste terrain in this secret valley.

There were many more highlights. One day, we skied a few variations of a back valley from the top of the Orzival Lift in Grimentz, which ended up conveniently with an après-ski at a restaurant in the tiny hamlet of St.-Jean. A fabulous powder run on the wide west faces behind the lifts of Zinal climaxed another day. This route ended at the Lac de Moiry, where we crossed a monstrous dam and still skied a few eastern slopes before following a trail back to Grimentz.

ALL THE WHILE, AS A MEMBER of the fat-ski gang, I was no longer huffing and puffing to keep up with the "German Bulls" on the lower slopes. Meanwhile, Jonas gritted his teeth and battled his way down the final pitches of each descent with pure survival technique. We continued to etch first tracks into some new valley or face every day, but all too soon, we found ourselves saying our farewells in front of the hotel.

It had all gone by too fast, and I suddenly realized that while we still had not come close to running out of powder in Grimentz and Zinal, we had not even been to the Saint-Luc/Chandolin ski area, the lift system with the most lifts in Val d'Anniviers. I asked Stefan if he had left that area out of the program because it did not offer any off-piste possibilities, but as we were exchanging adieus, he put that thought to rest.

"Oh no," answered Stefan directly. "Saint-Luc has some very interesting terrain as well, but we must leave surprises for next year, no? You do plan to come back, don't you?"

As my Jeep began its slow, hairpin-curve descent, I glanced across the valley at the mountains above Saint-Luc. I felt like a man who was leaving a party early—while the clinking of champagne glasses and the laughter of bevies of slim, young ladies were still ringing in his ears. I understood why the "German Bulls", who had skied in almost every known powder

hole on the planet, had chosen Val d'Anniviers as the one location where they made an annual pilgrimage.

I figured that we would meet again somewhere between Zinal and Grimentz. I would walk back into the party, and the festivities would still be going on, as if I had never left. Stefan and the "Bulls" would be there, and we would all clink our ski tips together under the virgin champagne powder. We would gaze back up at our tracks from below and see more beautiful curves than one could find at a gathering of Hollywood starlets. I mused at my metaphor. I thought the comparison was good, but there was a flaw. I suspected that there would always be more virgins on the slopes of tiny Val d'Anniviers than in all of Hollywood and Beverly Hills combined.

Chapter 7. LIECHTENSTEIN
THE WORLD'S SMALLEST SKI COUNTRY

Martin Söderqvist and I were returning from the Swiss Alps to Austria, and as one invariably does when traveling this route, we drove through Liechtenstein. Many people don't even notice when they pass through this tiny principality. After all, if you happen to sneeze, you basically miss this miniscule land of 34,000 people. There are ski resorts like Innsbruck, Sarajevo or Bariloche that have a larger population than the entire nation!

In the middle of this little land, however, is the small ski resort of Malbun. It is Liechtenstein's only ski venue. In some nations, it would take a good skier a number of years to ski all the lifts. In Liechtenstein, half a day will suffice. Malbun has seven lifts and a vertical drop of 396 meters.

Our timing was good, however, as we arrived early in the day, and it was snowing even down in Vaduz, 17 kilometers away. In Malbun, the snow was coming down hard and we first rode to the top of the Sareiserjoch. There, the resort personnel immediately admonished us for skiing off-piste.

The Sareiserjoch consists mostly of open terrain, while the Hocheck, on the other side of the valley, has both open slopes and glades in the forest. The solution to our situation was simple. For the rest of the day, we poached powder in the forest and drove on into Austria with our reputations intact.

On the next occasion that I find myself passing through Liechtenstein, I will make sure to again have some time in case the conditions are right. An important principle of skiing is that it is always better to be in a small ski area with good snow than in a large ski resort with bad snow. In skiing, as in life, timing is everything.

Chapter 8. GERMANY

When skiers discuss the Alpine countries, they usually analyze and compare ski resorts in Switzerland, Austria, France and Italy. Some knowledgeable people might even mention Slovenia in passing, but Germany is often lost in the shuffle. Germany, which is normally too large and strong to be left out of any conversation on European politics, economics or the like, has a very important position in the ski world as well. Somewhere in the neighborhood of twelve million Germans are full- or part-time skiers, and that has a major impact on the entire ski world, especially in the German-speaking countries.

Hundreds of small ski areas can be found all over the German countryside. All the best areas are in Germany's Alps, but ski resorts also exist in the Bayerische Wald, the Schwarzwald and various other sections of the country.

The non-Alpine ski areas of Germany all suffer from low elevation and minimal vertical. Winterberg, near Kassel, is a good example. The resort has about 30 lifts, but the vertical drop is a meager 165 meters, and the lift system peaks at just a hair over 800 meters. This kind of ski resort is not going to attract a wide range of clients from the international ski set.

On the other hand, a number of the German resorts do have a lot to offer. The infrastructure is usually very efficient in German ski areas, and many of the villages are even more quaint and picturesque than their counterparts in Austria, if that is possible. Among the better resorts are Reit im Winkl, Berchtesgaden, Bayrischzell, Oberstdorf, Lenggries and Feldberg.

These villages, all situated along Germany's southern flank, each boast more than twenty ski lifts and over 500 vertical meters of skiing. The one negative aspect of these ski areas is that they are still relatively low in comparison with most of the world's ski resorts. Oberstdorf's lifts rise to a respectable 2200 meters, but the other areas are almost entirely below the tree line.

One ski area in Germany is, without doubt, the *crème de la crème*—Garmisch-Partenkirchen. Hitler's pride and joy when it was the host of the 1936 Winter Olympic Games, Garmisch today has close to 40 lifts transporting skiers around on Germany's highest peak, the Zugspitze. Not only can you ski 1350 vertical meters on the slopes of Garmisch, most of the skiing is above the tree line, as the ski lifts rise up to 2830 meters. The open bowls and faces of the Zugspitze make Garmisch a favorite among freeriders.

In the realm of off-piste skiing, a peculiar sidekick to Garmisch is the little village of Mittenwald and specifically the bizarre descent from the Dammkar. Only a short distance away from Garmisch, the Dammkar cable car rises up to a stunning, cliff-ridden peak and offers over 1300 vertical meters of skiing, but in this case, there is not a single prepared piste!

LEFT PAGE
Bernd finds a nice line of powder on the Zugspitze in Garmisch.

THIS PAGE
UPPER: Bernd Ritschel is one of the top mountain photographers in the world.
LOWER LEFT: The downhill race that used to be held regularly on the steep slopes of the
Dammkar. Photo courtesy of the Karwendelbahn.
LOWER RIGHT: Mittenwald is a Hansel and Gretel village pulled right out of a 17th-century
fairy tale.

BERND RITSCHEL AND THE BAVARIAN ALPS

I pulled off the Garmisch-Partenkirchen Autobahn and pointed my Jeep toward the Bavarian village of Kochel am See, the home of Bernd Ritschel. Bernd is a colleague—a fellow photographer—and he had promised to show me around on skis in his little corner of the world. To have Bernd Ritschel as a guide in the Bavarian Alps is like having Winston Churchill show you around 10 Downing Street or Beethoven give you music lessons.

Bernd's early connection with the mountains of his native Germany and many other ranges came from his climbing. Climbing is still his first love, but he has also spent the last fifteen years or so photographing most of the mountains of the world. He and his camera have visited 65 different nations, almost always with the purpose of photographing the most prodigious peaks of those lands. But, there is no part of the world with which he is more familiar than the Alps around his hometown. Who can photograph them from more different, unusual and odd angles than a climber? Nobody! So, it was with no small amount of anticipation that I pulled up to the home of Bernd and his wife, Ela.

A quick tour around Bernd's home left no doubt about his vocation and his avocation. His cellar served as his mountain-equipment warehouse. One wall was home to a dozen pairs of downhill skis, one pair of telemark skis, two pairs of cross-country boards and an odd set of 130-centimeter-long skis used for winter mountaineering. This gear was complemented by fifteen pairs of ski poles, twelve backpacks of various shapes and sizes, 25 pairs of ski boots, eight pairs of snowshoes, four sets of crampons and five ice axes.

Whereas his large cellar was adequate for all of Bernd's mountain equipment, it took two full rooms of his house to accommodate his photography gear. Bernd's family includes thirteen cameras, 29 lenses, and nineteen camera bags and rucksacks. By the time you read this book, it will certainly have grown beyond that. Alongside all his equipment are 140,000 slides—neat and well-ordered.

Ela is not left out of the loop. She keeps very busy working on layouts for much of Bernd's work, which so far has included 23 books composed solely of his own photos and 50 books to which he has contributed photos. Keeping track of the number of magazines, newspapers, advertising brochures and other publications in which Bernd's work has appeared is beyond his computing skills. Suffice it to say that there are few photographers in the world who have been more industrious and productive in the field of mountain photography than my host, and I felt honored to be his guest.

When I first contacted Bernd, asking him for advice about skiing in Germany, he merely said, "Come down to me—I will show you the best skiing my country has to offer."

Our first day, Bernd drove us to nearby Garmisch-Partenkirchen, his favorite German ski resort. Garmisch is the German equivalent of Chamonix in France, St. Anton in Austria or Cortina in Italy. It is the grandfather of German skiing, a ski location treated with reverence by even the most atheistic wing of the New Age snowsports culture. Besides having hosted the Winter Olympic Games in Hitler's day, Garmisch is the annual venue for the famous New Year's Day ski-jumping competition, still held on the same jumping hill that was built for those Olympic games.

The ski areas that make up the Garmisch region include the Hausberg, Kreuzeck, Eckbauer, Wank and Zugspitze. While all five of these lift systems provide reasonably good skiing, the Zugspitze, Germany's highest mountain, rises head and shoulders above its neighbors in elevation as well as stature. It was not surprising, then, that Bernd chose to show me this spectacular peak.

It is hard to avoid all the historical aspects of the Zugspitze. One can access the mountain by three different means, and two of the three are

THIS PAGE: Panorama from the Zugspitze.
RIGHT PAGE: If Bernd Ritschel is a photographer first and a climber second, where did he get the time to learn how to ski so well?

historic. The Tiroler Zugspitzbahn, which ascends from the Austrian side, was the first method of reaching the Zugspitze, having been originally constructed in 1926.

Shortly thereafter, in 1930, a cogwheel train through the mountain was completed from the German side, and in 1963, the 46-passenger Eibsee Seilbahn gave a third option for ascending Germany's highest peak.

Garmisch, however, has not attempted to rest on its laurels and be satisfied to serve as a ski-history museum. It has definitely kept up with the times, offering one of the best halfpipes and terrain parks in the Alps. With the help of one of Germany's three glaciers, the Schneeferner, the season here ordinarily lasts until the end of June, and the end of the season is nowadays well-known for its large snowboard camps.

WE RODE UP THE SPECTACULAR Eibsee Cable Car, which rises 1950 meters up the ominous-looking north face of the mountain. From the top, I took a few minutes to admire the scenery from the large lookout platform. Directly below, the Eibsee lay frozen in the morning shade. Beyond the lake to the north, the Alps peter out into flat farmland, while the Zugspitze rises dramatically above its pastoral surroundings.

Bernd and I turned toward the ski area and scouted the slopes with our eyes. Most of the region is comprised of blue and red pistes that are perfectly suited to high-speed cruising, but we also noticed a nice slope of powder with plenty of lines still available. This was surprising to me because there had been no new snow for the past five days.

We traversed high from the Weisses Tal Lift. If one dared to peer over the cliffs on the back side of the mountain, one was afforded a view straight down onto the Seefeld ski region of Austria. We skied the old powder and cruised some runs on the well prepared pistes to warm up.

Riding on the lift in between runs, Bernd told me more about his life as a photographer. He shoots between 1000 and 1500 rolls of film in an average year, and keeps only 25–30 percent of the images. His photos cover the gamut of mountain activities including skiing, touring, snow-

shoeing, mountain biking, ice climbing, rock climbing and mountaineering. Although the mountaineering photos have the lowest marketability, it is that endeavor that Bernd prefers over all others.

"I could earn twice as much money shooting golf and keep my fingers warm to boot, but that is not where my heart is," explained Bernd. "As a fashion photographer, I could earn three times the money but the mountains are my world."

Despite the fact that he could earn even more money in other branches of photography, he has received as much as €4000 for a photo—not too bad for doing what one enjoys.

As we arrived at the top of the lift, the mountain goat emerged in Bernd. He had seen a few tracks snaked into the snow high above us. He led me over to a staircase of boot notches etched into the snow and began to ascend. There was nothing for me to do but follow.

The hike was no more than a few hundred meters long, but most of it was very steep. It was more of a ladder than a staircase. While the snow we were heading toward for our descent was soft and powdery, the route up had a somewhat different exposure, and was rather firm. A misstep here would be equivalent to an ignominious and potentially painful tumble back to our starting point. To make matters worse, whoever had created this stepladder had a much larger leg span than I, so the steps were spaced too far apart for me. I found myself having to kick a fair number of new toeholds into the snow pack.

While I struggled around the halfway mark, my companion had almost reached the top. For Bernd, of course, this was a walk in the park, while it looked like the last leg of Everest to my unfit body.

Finally, we both arrived at the top, traversed into the sun and were ready to match the nice pair of tracks that had lured us onto this slope. On the way down, I was also no match for Bernd. He laid a set of tracks into the snow that one could look back at and admire. I, on the other hand, was doing my first real skiing of the winter, and had not yet found my "ski legs". I would have liked to have an eraser to delete my tracks from the landscape, but that would have to wait for the next dump of snow.

Bernd pointed out the start of the Gatterl descent, a south-facing route that finishes in the village of Ehrwald, more than 1800 vertical meters of skiing. He also spoke of the Fenster Riffelriss, a seldom-skied run from the middle station of the cogwheel train back to the village.

"Oh, and over there is where one begins the Neue Welt (New World) descent," Bernd added, pointing to the west. "Now that run is really interesting," he said with a twinkle in his eye. "It includes a mandatory rappel and has numerous sections of 45 degrees or more, but it is too dangerous at this time of year. Normally, one only skis Neue Welt during the spring, in corn snow."

Such excursions and endeavors would have to wait for another time, and considering my current condition, I was relieved. Bernd, however, still had an ace up his sleeve for the following day. On tap was a visit to the village of Mittenwald and the Dammkar run, where Bernd and I were joined by one of his buddies, mountain guide Christof Schellhammer.

Both Mittenwald and the Dammkar are strange places that exist in a bizarre time warp. They are anachronisms, and although they lie side by side, they are rooted in different centuries.

Mittenwald is a Hansel and Gretel village pulled right out of a 17th-century fairy tale. Narrow, cobblestone streets wind their way among ancient houses, most of which have murals depicting medieval life. Johann Wolfgang von Goethe, Germany's most prolific writer, referred to Mittenwald as a "living picture book" way back in 1786, and the village has not lost any of its charm since then.

The town is home to a lovely baroque church, and it has been famous for its violins ever since Matthias Klotz started a violin-building tradition way back in the 1600s. In the following century, Klotz's nephew is said to have made Mozart's concert violin here. Still today, one can see the craftsmen in their little workshops and at Mittenwald's 140-year-old violin-builders school, turning out beautiful stringed instruments of all sizes.

The Dammkar is also a relic of a bygone era, but its ski history goes back only as far as the last century. After World War II, it became

ABOVE: I know Bernd is not planning to ski down that way. Is he checking out a climbing route?

extremely popular among the Bavarians to hike up the Dammkar and ski back down. It is hard to imagine why this particular mountain became the goal of the local skiers, as it is extremely steep and does not lend itself very well to touring. A Sunday outing on the Dammkar was definitely no stroll in the park.

Be that as it may, skiing the Dammkar became so popular that on given days as many as 500 skiers hiked up the 1300 vertical meters. The long snake of people known as the Dammkar Wurm (Dammkar worm) zig-zagged back and forth up the mountain on a regular basis every winter for about twenty years. Then, in 1966, the worm died a merciful death, as the Karwendelbahn was completed, rendering the hike no longer necessary.

For the rest of the century, the Dammkar attempted to compete head-to-head with the growing number of ski resorts in the Alps, without much success. After all, a mountain offering one steep and difficult descent is no match for the many larger resorts that abound in the Alps. What had flourished as a unique mountaineers' peak had transformed itself into a lift-accessed mountain with very little to offer ordinary skiers.

At the outset of the new century, however, the Dammkar took a step backward to move into the future. It trashed its winch-drawn piste machine that had attempted, with great difficulty, to keep a vague sem-blance of a piste prepared on this rather extreme mountain, and turned the area into a freeride mountain. Similar to La Grave in France and Alagna in Italy, the Dammkar would henceforth offer a skiing experience imported from a previous era.

It was early in the season, and the rocky mountain had not accumulat-ed enough of a base on the lower regions to open for the season, but my local friends had the connections to get us up the mountain in spite of

the minimum snow cover. As we emerged from the cable car at the top, we proceeded for a ways through a long tunnel. This feature had been added to the top station in 1977, after numerous people had plummet-ed to their death on the initial traverse during the first years of the cable car's operation.

The current entry and beginning of the descent was also no piece of cake, but at least it avoided the treacherous traverse above exposed cliffs that had sealed the fate of a number of skiers in the '60s and '70s. There was no shortage of snow at 2244 meters, where we began trying to nego-tiate some difficult wind crust.

Soon, we dropped below the wind-exposed section of mountain and were greeted by fresh powder. Our bodies shifted into a smooth, rhyth-mic, bouncing motion. The scenery was stunning. The mountain was reminiscent of the Dolomites, as dramatic, sheer rock faces stretched upward from the rather narrow valley in which we skied. I could under-stand what had drawn enthusiasts from all over Bavaria to make this ardu-ous ascent so many winters ago.

I CAME AWAY FROM my Bavarian weekend having experienced two new mountains and having made one new friend. Bernd and I had found much common ground in our few days together—skiing, mountains and pho-tography. Bernd had shared his favorite slice of the Bavarian Alps with me, and I came away with a clear comprehension of why my new friend photographs mountain activities and leaves the more profitable golf pho-tography to someone else.

That someone else would not be me. I may never earn anything close to €4000 for one of my ski photos, but there is no higher salary than the mere opportunity to work with something you love.

Europe – Alpine Countries in a Nutshell

LOCATION	NEAREST TOWN	NEAREST AIRPORT	SEASON	PEAK ELEVATION	VERTICAL DROP	SIZE	SNOW	BEAUTY	VILLAGE	NOVICE	INTERMEDIATE	ADVANCED	OFF-PISTE	NIGHTLIFE	RATING AVERAGE	WEB SITE
AUSTRIA																
Bad Gastein	Bad Gastein	Salzburg	December–April	2686 m	1450 m	4	5	3	3	4	2	5	2	4	3.5	www.gastein.com
Innsbruck Nordpark (1)	Innsbruck	Innsbruck	December–April	2334 m	1478 m	4	1	4	4	4	2	3	3	3	3.1	www.nordpark.com
Nauders	Nauders	Innsbruck	December–April	2850 m	1450 m	4	3	4	3	3	4	4	3	3	3.4	www.nauders.info
Pitztal	Plangeross	Innsbruck	mid Sept.–late May	3440 m	1700 m	5	3	5	4	2	3	4	5	5	3.8	www.pitztal.com
Saalbach-Hinterglemm	Saalbach-Hinterglemm	Salzburg	December–April	2096 m	1093 m	3	5	4	3	4	5	5	3	5	4.2	www.saalbach.com
St. Anton & the Arlberg	St. Anton	Innsbruck	December–April	2811 m (2)	1507 m (2)	4	5	5	3	3	3	4	5	4	4.1	www.stantonamarlberg.com
Sölden	Sölden	Innsbruck	late June–mid May	3250 m	1880 m	5	4	4	3	3	4	4	3	5	3.9	www.soelden.com
Zillertal	Mayrhofen, Gerlos, etc.	Innsbruck	year-round (3)	3250 m	1750 m	5	5	5	3	3	4	4	4	4	4.0	www.mayrhofen.at
FRANCE																
Chamonix	Chamonix	Geneva	December–April	3842 m	2807 m	5	5	4	5	3	2	3	5	4	4.3	www.chamonix.com
La Grave	La Grave	Grenoble	December–early May	3550 m	2150 m	5	1	4	4	4	1	2	3	5	3.0	www.la-grave.com
Portes du Soleil	Avoriaz, Morzine, etc.	Geneva	December–end of April	2470 m	1470 m	4	5	4	3	2	4	5	3	4	3.4	www.avoriaz.com
Pra Loup	Pra Loup	Marseilles	December–April	2500 m	1000 m	3	5	3	3	1 (4)	4	5	3	4	3.3	www.praloup.com
Sainte Foy	Sainte Foy	Geneva	December–April	2620 m	970 m	3	1	4	3	3	1	3	3	4	2.6	www.ski-savoie.com/sainte-foy
Serre Chevalier	Serre Chevalier	Turin	December–April	2830 m	1430 m	4	5	3	3	2	4	4	4	4	3.5	www.serre-chevalier.com
Tignes-Val d'Isère	Tignes-Val d'Isère	Geneva	Dec.–May, June–Sept.	3456 m	1900 m	5	5	5	4	2 (5)	5	5	5	5	4.5	www.tignes.net or www.valdisere.com
Les Trois Valleés	Courchevel, Méribel, Val Thorens, etc.	Geneva	early Nov.–early May (6)	3200 m	1552 m	4	5	4	4	1	5	5	5	4	3 (7)	4.1	www.les3vallees.com
Val Cenis	Lanslebourg/Lanslevillard	Turin	December–April	2800 m	1400 m	4	2	4	4	2	4	4	3	3	3.1	www.valcenis.com
Vars	Vars	Marseilles	December–April	2750 m	1100 m	3	5	3	4	3	3	4	2	2	3.1	www.vars-ski.com
GERMANY																
Garmisch-Partenkirchen	Garmisch-Partenkirchen	Munich	October–June	2830 m (8)	1300 m	4	4	4	4	4	4	4	3	3	3.9	www.garmisch-partenkirchen.de
Mittenwald	Mittenwald	Munich	December–April	2244 m	1311 m	4	1	3	4	5	4	1	2	3	2.9	www.mittenwald.com
ITALY																
Alagna	Alagna	Milano	November–April	3260 m	2069 m	5	4	4	5	5	1	1	5	5	3.6	www.alagnal.it
Dolomites	Canazei, Cortina, Selva, etc.	varies (9)	December–April	3243 m	2019 m	5	5	3	5	4 (10)	5	5	4	5	4.3	www.superdolomiti.com
Milky Way	Sauze d'Oulx, Sestriere, etc.	Turin	December–April	2823 m	1473 m	4	5	4	3	3 (10)	5	5	4	4	4.2	www.vialattea.it
Mt. Etna Nord	Linguaglossa	Catania	December–March	2300 m	500 m	2	1	3	5	5	3	3	2	3	2.8	www.etnasci.it/linguaglossa.htm
Mt. Etna Sud	Nicolosi	Catania	December–March	2500 m	600 m	2	1	2	5	5	2	2	1	2	2.3	www.etnasci.it/nicolosi.htm
LIECHTENSTEIN																
Malbun	Vaduz	Zurich	December–April	2000 m	700 m	2	1	3	3	3	3	3	1	2	2.2	www.malbun.li
SWITZERLAND																
Andermatt	Andermatt	Zurich	December-April	2963 m	1527 m	4	2	4	4	4	1	2	3	5	2.9	www.andermatt.ch
Disentis/Sedrun	Disentis/Sedrun	Zurich	December–May	2833 m	1594 m	4	3	4	3	3	2	2	2	4	2.8	www.disentis-sedrun.ch
Engelberg	Engelberg	Zurich	mid Nov.–late May (11)	3020 m	1970 m	5	3	4	4	4	2	3	3	5	3.6	www.engelberg.ch
St. Moritz	St. Moritz	Zurich	late November–May 1	3303 m	1505 m	4	5	4	4	3	3	5	4	5	4.0	www.stmoritz.ch
Verbier	Verbier	Geneva	November–late April	3330 m	2509 m	5	4	4	4	3	2	4	5	4	4.2	www.verbier.ch
Val d'Anniviers	Grimentz, Zinal, Saint-Luc, etc.	Geneva	December–April	3000 m	1593 m	4	5	4	4	5	4	4	5	5	4.3	www.sierre-anniviers.ch
Zermatt	Zermatt	Geneva	year-round	3899 m	2200 m	5	5	5	5	5	5	5	5	5	4.9	www.zermatt.ch

(1) This chart only gives info about Innsbruck's Nordpark ski area. There are many more lifts and ski resorts which are part of the greater, non-lift-linked ski area.
(2) The highest lift in the system, to the Valuga Grat, is only accessible with skis when accompanied by a guide.
(3) Most of the villages of the Zillertal have a season from December to April, while Zell im Zillertal's season goes to the end of March and the Hintertux Glacier is open all year round.
(4) Pra Loup itself has no ambiance, while the nearby village of Barcelonnette is quaint and atmospheric.
(5) Val d'Isère actually rates three points for village ambiance, while Tignes rates only one point.
(6) Summer skiing is also possible on the glacier in July and August.
(7) The nightlife varies from village to village here, with Courcheval rating highest, Les Menuires rating lowest, and Val Thorens and Méribel somewhere in between.
(8) The highest lift actually goes to 2962 meters, but it is necessary to descend with another lift to 2830 meters. It is at this elevation that the skiing begins.
(9) Depending on the actual resort, the nearest airport could be in Bolzano, Milano, Innsbruck, Verona or even Venice.
(10) The ambiance of the villages varies somewhat, so this score is an average.
(11) There is also limited skiing and boarding available on the glacier during the rest of the year.

175

EUROPE – THE MEDITERRANEAN   III

PREVIOUS PAGES: The undulating ridges of the Pyrenees as seen from Boí Taüll, Spain.
THIS PAGE: The Pyrenees as seen from the air. RIGHT PAGE: Bert Romani heads down toward the road in the backcountry near the Baqueira ski resort.

Chapter 9. SPAIN

Spain is a nation blessed with mountain ranges and ski resorts in almost all sectors of the country. Many of the ski destinations are modern, purpose-built resorts, but the option often exists to live in a more traditional mountain village, not too far removed from the ski area.

Thirty ski areas dot the Spanish landscape, from the Sierra Nevada Mountains, which overlook the Mediterranean Sea in the far south, to a whole slew of resorts throughout the Pyrenees, along the northern border of the country. While these two ranges provide the best skiing in Spain, there are even ski resorts in the Basque country and in central Spain, just outside Madrid.

The skiing in the Pyrenees offers the most diversity of any of the regions in Spain, as close to half of the Spanish resorts call this area home. On the other hand, the highest skiing is in the Sierra Nevada resort, which boasts snow well into April.

SIERRA NEVADA — SNOW, SAND AND CULTURE

Easter vacation is approaching, the winter back home has been long and hard and it is finally time for a family vacation. Your wife wants to go to Tenerife and work on her tan, your kids are screaming for Euro Disney and you had hoped to get in some spring skiing in Austria. Ah—the joys of family life. You pause a moment in the midst of this chaos and disharmony and ponder your options.

You can: (A) be a pussy, capitulate to your spouse and be utterly bored for seven days on the beach; (B) go along with your kids' suggestion, and be sure your wife will spend 80 percent of your next year's income doing her spring shopping on the Champs Élysées; (C) make a stand on behalf of your own wishes, discuss reasonably and ensure that the family will be on unfriendly terms during the whole vacation, no matter where you go; (D) take separate vacations; (E) finally get that divorce that you have been contemplating for the last five years; (F) consult Jimmy Petterson's handy book, *Skiing Around the World*, to find a suitable compromise option.

Perhaps the wife would be satisfied with the beaches of the Costa del Sol in Spain, while you cavort in the spring snow of nearby Sierra Nevada. You would be able to ski, the little woman gets to relax at the beach, and the kids have alternate options. In the Andalusia section of Spain, only a couple of hours' drive from the Mediterranean, lies one of Spain's top ski destinations, the 3300-meter peak of Mt. Valeta and the Sierra Nevada Mountains.

It was with a combined ski, beach and cultural vacation in mind that my friend, Arne Bredow, and I packed a suitcase full of ski paraphernalia along with a couple of bathing trunks, and boarded a plane for Málaga in mid-April. I must admit that we got some cross-eyed stares from lobster-red British tourists and bewildered Scandinavian sun worshippers as we carried our skis and boots through the streets of Torremolinos to our rental car. We didn't care—we knew what we were doing.

Arne and I bought some *empanadas*, a bag of pistachio nuts and some coconut juice for the ride, and we headed north to Granada. A 45-minute drive from the ski area, the magnificent old city of Granada is ample proof that a vacation to this region can combine culture with snow and sand, but that would have to wait. We wound our way up the highest road in Europe past blooming apple trees and acres of olive groves. Soon the pastoral green scenes of springtime passed away into the valley and the landscape transformed into a winter white.

The road, known as Los Neveros, goes up to 3100 meters, but for skiers there is no necessity to surpass the elevation of 2100 meters, the level of the base of the lift system. We could see at a glance that the village here was not going to compete very strongly with Austria for coziness. The buildings were primarily high-rise apartments reminiscent of many of the French ski stations. Thrown into the mix were just enough chalet-like structures to make the whole scenario totally incongruous.

In historic and picturesque Granada, just a stone's throw away, the cost of accommodation is, generally speaking, less than half of that in the ski resort. This fact left no doubt as to where we would settle in after the ski day was finished.

THE SKIING IN THE SIERRA NEVADA is serviced by over twenty lifts, and most of the terrain is best suited for beginner and intermediate skiers. We immediately made our way over toward the Laguna Chair Lift, the highest lift, which takes a skier up to just under the peak of Mt. Veleta. It accesses 700 vertical meters of mountain, including a fair amount of off-piste terrain. We spent most of the morning discovering various routes between the rocks of this section of the mountain, known as Tajos de la Virgen.

At midday, we stopped at the middle station for a large plate of *paella*

(a typical Spanish dish consisting of saffron rice cooked with chicken, pork, shrimps and mussels) and a bottle of Rioja wine.

"Quite civilized," I thought to myself as I leaned back into a deck chair to let the meal digest.

After lunch, we cruised around the rest of the lift system. In Tormelinos, I had taken a dip in the Mediterranean, and the air temperature had been 32 degrees centigrade. But here in the mountains, it was –3, and we skied on firm winter snow rather than the spring snow that I had expected.

After the ski day was finished, we still had time to wander around in Granada for a few hours. In the city, the snow-capped Sierras provided a picture-postcard backdrop behind the orange walls of the world-famous Moorish Palace, the Alhambra. We circumambulated the old citadel, visited the gargantuan Catholic cathedral in the city center and began to meander through the crooked cobblestone streets of the old town in search of a restaurant.

One could easily spend many hours exploring the nooks and crannies of the old town, where the streets are so narrow that a motorcyclist would probably scrape his knees on both sides attempting to ride around. We finally found an appropriate bistro, where a plateful of mixed fresh fish and two carafes of sangria sent us very satiated to lullaby land.

During the following days we alternated among sightseeing visits to nearby Gibraltar and the picturesque village of Rondo, beach time in

Torremolinos and Marbella, cultural visits to Malaga and Granada, and of course, more skiing in Sierra Nevada. Our week in the Andalusia section of Spain did, indeed, provide us with the balance of snow, sand and culture that we had initially sought.

I do hope the suggestion provided here will prove adequate to save a few marriages. If Andalusia does not meet the approval of the rest of the family, please check out other "ski and beach" solutions in the book. You might try Mt. Parnassos in Greece, Saklikent in Turkey, Faraya in Lebanon, Mt. Troodos in Cyprus or the San Gabriel Mountains, near Los Angeles.

If none of these proposals of "ski and beach" solutions are successful in resolving the problems of the family vacation, I have one additional idea. Book a ski vacation in America's divorce capital—Nevada. Just send two shreds of a torn up wedding certificate and $5 in care of this publication, and within three weeks, you will receive our special "Ski and Divorce Guide", featuring information on every ski resort in Nevada.

THE SPANISH PYRENEES — ROAD-TRIP AND ROAD-SHOTS

road-shot (rohd-shot) *n. accessing off-piste lines by skiing down to the road, from where one can alternatively be picked up by a ski partner or hitchhike back to the lifts.*

I have skied road-shots long before I ever heard that term, and probably long before it was coined. In Austria, there are many routes from St. Anton, Stuben, St. Christoph and Zurs down to the Arlberg Pass or the Flexen Pass, where taxis patrol regularly to bring freeriders back to the lifts. We also did them on Mt. Waterman near my home in Los Angeles. Even as a child, I skied deep powder from Alta down the Peruvian Gulch with my parents, years before the Snowbird resort existed, and we hitchhiked back to the Wildcat Lift.

The first time I heard the expression was in the late '90s, when John, a ski bum from Utah, guided a group of us on road-shots on the big hairpin curve on the way to Thompson Pass, near Valdez, Alaska. Of all the places where I have taken advantage of the local highway to ski some great lines, however, I don't know that I have ever found a more suitable location than the Pyrenees of Spain.

This beautiful range that marks the division between Spain and France is also perfectly suited for a road-trip, as one can drive from resort to resort with rarely more than an hour's driving time between areas. I was joined on this tour by Bert Romani, the editor of the Dutch publication *Ski Magazine*, and my buddies Martin Söderqvist and Steve Langkamp.

Every ski road-trip takes on its own personality—a unique entity which develops out of the combined personalities of its participants, molded by the joint experiences which gradually bond them together. A typical men's road-trip involves a plethora of good-natured insults, which get gradually more vulgar as time passes, a lot of talk about skiing and sex, a lot of skiing and no sex. This was, then, a typical road-trip.

Everyone complained about the smell of Martin's boots, in which he was apparently cultivating a new species of mold. He suggested that the malodor merely counterbalanced the stench of my socks. Steve got ridiculed after he forgot his board in Port Ainé, and nobody said anything too mean to Bert, as he was paying the bills.

BOÍ TAÜLL

Our entourage began in the little-known, purpose-built area of Boí Taüll. This family resort offers about 700 vertical meters of skiing and the highest ski lift in the Spanish Pyrenees, the Puig Falcó Lift, which rises to 2751 meters.

I often fantasize how a ski region should be before arriving at the destination. Rarely do my fantasies get fulfilled. Chamonix should be full of deep powder, and the granite cliffs should be plastered with frozen, windblown snow. I arrive, instead, to rain and fog. Greek skiing should be sunny slopes, bikini-clad girls basking on the ski hut verandah, and glistening corn snow. I arrive to a blizzard that does not abate for the entire week. Alta should be ice-cold with the deepest powder anyone has ever seen, and I get 20 degrees centigrade and corn snow. You get the picture—there is often a great chasm between fantasy and reality.

In the Pyrenees, however, our experiences lived up to my preconceived notions. Spain should be deep azure-blue skies and shirtsleeve weather. While Spanish *madres* and *padres* keep their *niños* in tow on the blue pistes, pristine fields of corn kernels wait patiently to be skied for the first time. In Boí Taüll, reality met fantasy in peaceful harmony.

Most of Boí Taüll is a big north-facing bowl with east- and west-facing sides to the semicircle. In addition, the Puig Falcó Lift gains skiers access to a huge side valley to the northeast of the main ski area.

We began our day with a few warmup runs to get the juices flowing and get a feel for the off-piste conditions. It became immediately clear that there was corn snow in abundance.

The Puig Falcó Lift was broken, and this proved, perhaps, to be the blessing of the day. A 20-minute hike gained us enough elevation that we could traverse into the next valley, which was virtually untouched because of the broken lift. A steep face of ripe corn snow, which ordinarily was a piste, was as pure as the Virgin Mary. Martin swooped down in about four New School turns. I took my time, with old-school jump turns, and Bert did something in between.

At 4:30, with the lifts closing, the corn snow was still good, and I noticed that it was possible to ski off-piste to the road from the top of the Vaques Lift. Bert generously volunteered to be the designated driver, and Martin and I skied our first road-shot of the journey. Thus was born a major personality trait of our tour.

PORT AINÉ

The next day we moved on to Port Ainé. We drove through a picturesque gorge before the serpentine road climbed a steep mountainside to the lone hotel at the base of the lifts.

"Hey! What meathead put this place on our itinerary?" bellowed Steve, as the last hairpin curve brought the mountain into view.

"I guess the Spanish Tourist Office thought this would be the perfect ski venue for the flatland Dutch," I said, ribbing Bert.

One flat, low hill, forested about halfway up, stood in front of us. The little resort with a half-dozen lifts was a fine place for Spanish families learning to ski, but unlike many other family resorts, we could see little to offer for advanced skiers. The 790 vertical meters listed in Port Ainé's marketing brochure was also misleading, as half of the vertical resulted from one trail cut out of the trees that dropped below the actual resort. The rest of the mountain rose only about 400 vertical meters above the hotel.

We tried to make the best of the day. We first tried one of the "black runs", a rather narrow piste in the trees, which couldn't have been more than 20 degrees.

"I'd hate to see their blue runs," said Martin. "They're probably uphill."

There were some nicely spaced trees on the western side of the resort, and we darted into the forest for a run. Unfortunately, the shade of the trees had prevented the development of corn snow, and the resultant condition was breakable crust. That was no problem for Steve, on a snowboard, or Martin, who weighs no more than 60 kilos, but Bert and I found ourselves off-balance, out of control and trying to avoid waltzing with a pine on every other turn.

Fortunately, as in most Spanish ski resorts, we could indulge in a long lunch to fill out the day. Spaniards typically love to eat, and this is also Bert's special talent. A skier's meal in this very civilized land is not the usual hamburger one would buy in Aspen or *Gulaschsuppe* that would comprise lunch in Austria. Here, one can sit down to a table with a white table cloth, a bottle of wine and three courses, and we did—noodle soup, salad, large prawns fried in olive oil and blueberry cheesecake! After lunch, we indulged in some large shots of *aguardiente*, an extremely potent Spanish brandy distilled from potatoes. It tasted like a mixture of Italian grappa and snow-cat fuel. Now, I was really ready for a siesta, and Port Ainé's easy cruisers were suddenly perfect for me.

BAQUEIRA BERET

Day three stood in marked contrast to our experience in Port Ainé. We woke up early and drove over the Bonaigua Pass to Spain's most famous resort, Baqueira Beret. The drive was beautiful, and here we saw that the Pyrenees truly had lots of steep and spectacular terrain. In places, 4–5 meters of snow along the road dwarfed our car, as we wound our way to the resort. During the last few kilometers, the damage of a dozen big avalanches could be witnessed, as the guardrail alongside the road was either mangled or crushed under snow and tree debris.

Again the sky was a deep blue, and the corn snow glistened in the hot spring sunshine. Baqueira Beret offers the full gamut of terrain for all ability groups. We cruised easy rolling hills between the pistes at full speed, spraying spring snow left and right. Then we moved to steeper slopes and some couloirs.

BY NOON, WE WERE READY FOR our first road-shot of the day—a steep southeast-facing slope, which landed us about half a kilometer down the road from the Bonaigua Lift. The steepest pitch was already too soft for my 85 kilos, but the rest of the descent was perfect.

Steve was the designated driver on this run. He boarded down on the piste to pick up the car and was waiting for us at the preordained location as we finished our virgin tour at the highway.

After this run, we went to discover the rest of the ski area. It was huge. Baqueira Beret has only about 94 kilometers of pistes, but

THIS PAGE: So many off-piste routes in the Spanish Pyrenees were just a short hitchhike back to the lift.
RIGHT PAGE: Most of the skiing in the Spanish Pyrenees is above the tree line, but in Port Ainé, one can do some tree-skiing as Martin Söderqvist demonstrates.

they are spread over a gigantic area, and the primarily treeless terrain can be skied almost anywhere with the help of a bit of traversing.

We found our way to the black double-diamond Escornacrabes run, which begins with a spectacular couloir that truly lives up to its double-diamond classification. So many black pistes in Spain seem mislabeled, but this so-called piste was definitely not for the faint of heart. The center of the couloir, pitched at about 40 degrees, was the easiest entry, but the north and south flanks had entries that were closer to 50 degrees. Soon the chute spit us out into some meandering terrain of ridges and valleys decorated with small trees, where almost nobody had skied. We cruised through this section and ultimately arrived in the Beret sector of the lift system.

A few spanish style tortillas readied us for a few more road-shots. The south- and east-facing slopes coming down from the relatively new Blanhiblar Lift allow a skier to descend literally anywhere and arrive at the road that connects Baqueira with Beret. By now our car was too far away, so this would be a hitchhiking road-shot.

Ordinarily, south- and east-facing corn snow descents are optimally skied around 10 a.m. if they are steep, and can still be skied until about 11:30 or noon, if they have a very low gradient. It was now close to three o'clock, but surprisingly, the corn snow was still perfectly ripe, as long as one avoided the steepest sections. Martin went into fifth gear and began cranking out big turns at full throttle, sending crescendos of corn kernels flying in all directions, and we followed in close pursuit, each of us choosing our own line.

We needed a quick hitch back to the lifts, because we still had one big descent left on our agenda. We were lucky. The first passing car—a big jeep—picked us all up and brought us directly back to the lift.

Our last run of the day was a road-shot of a more ambitious nature, a gargantuan bowl dropping down to the hamlet of Begergue on the back side of the Blanhiblar Lift. This was so far off the beaten path that we really needed a designated driver. Bert raced back through the lift system to pick up his Audi, while the rest of us enjoyed the best run of the day.

This last run was primarily north-facing, with east and west aspects, but corn snow had even developed on the northern slopes under the intense heat of the Spanish sun. The descent had the variety of a Spanish *tapas* menu—steep faces, couloirs, ridges, gullies and rolling hills—take your pick. It all ended by picking our way through a patchwork of bare spots and spring brooks of snowmelt, and before we knew it, we were enjoying a beer on the verandah of one of the stone buildings in the village, waiting for our chauffeur.

BEGERGUE TURNED OUT TO HAVE four rustic Spanish restaurants, and we decided to dine at the Casa Peru. The meal began with the staple of every Spanish dinner, the obligatory *pan con tomata*, which consists of toasted Spanish white bread scraped with raw garlic and tomatoes, and drenched in olive oil. The second course was made up of various *tapas* (starters) including an excellent vegetable *empanada*.

Then came the soups—large portions that were meals in themselves. I had cream of pumpkin, Martin and Steve gorged themselves on garlic soup, and Bert tried onion soup, crusted over with melted cheese. The main courses specialized in game, including venison and rabbit. We washed this all down with some excellent Rioja wine, and by the time I squeezed in a blackberry-and-lemon sorbet, I was ready to be carted back to the hotel in a wheelbarrow. I would need another ambitious day of skiing to work off that meal.

I got it. Day two in Baqueira began with—what do you expect—a roadshot. A short traverse from the top of the Tuc de la Llanca Lift brought us to a saddle, and we again dropped into a nameless, virgin valley. It was ten o'clock, and we stayed on the eastern slopes of the valley, which were perfect, with a couple of centimeters of spring snow scraping off the surface with every turn. Our route dropped onto the other side of the Bonaigua Pass, and conveniently met the road at a rustic tavern. Bert hitched back to the car to pick us up, while the rest of us refreshed ourselves with a cool drink in the morning sun.

THIS PAGE
UPPER AND LOWER: On a road trip through the Pyrenees, one gets the opportunity to see many beautiful views.

RIGHT PAGE
Martin carves up virgin corn high in Boí Taüll.

We had begun our day at the eastern end of the lift system, and now we raced across the pistes, to the point furthest west—the Dossau Lift in Beret. Like everywhere else in Baqueira Beret, this lift accesses some pistes where the Spaniards cruised around happily with their families, while large sections of the mountain lie untouched. In this case, it was the steep eastern slope that lay waiting to be caressed and massaged by our skis.

It was afternoon, but the conventional wisdom that a steep eastern or southern slope would be too soft to ski at this hour did not hold true. The spring snow was still the right firmness, and we dove into the 40-degree face, carving big mountain turns at high speed. Partway down, we cut back toward the lift and entered a forest of widely spaced trees, where we had to alter our turning radius drastically.

The run was too good to be left and forgotten. We returned to the peak to explore some more. Further from the lift system than the route we had just taken was an 800-vertical-meter avalanche ravine, even a bit steeper than our most recent descent. A helpful ski patrolman advised us that this descent would terminate on a road to a small enclave of 17th century stone houses. A couple of them had been recently restored and were now used as refuges. That was all we needed to know.

We dove back into the corn like famished children at Thanksgiving dinner. Millions of ice pellets raced us down the steep gully, giving off the familiar "Shhhh, shhhh, shhhh" sound to add an audio track to our rhythmic turns.

The snow had been so good all day that we had not even taken time for lunch. Now it was 4:30, we had run out of ski time and we settled down in the sun in front of Refugi Amics de Montgarri with a cold beer and a full three-course meal, highlighted by a roast duck breast that could have been from a *Guide Michelin* restaurant. It was the perfect ending to another classic day, but in fact, the day's adventures were not yet over.

We still had to get back to the car. This kind of road-run, to a snow covered road, was not as easy a proposition as the ones we had so far

experienced. The *refugi* was 5 or 6 kilometers from the lifts, and was primarily used by people who were walking with snowshoes or riding snowmobiles. Bert and Steve managed to hitch a ride with a couple of snowmobiles and skijored back to civilization.

Martin and I were not as lucky. We would have to work off our meal with an evening promenade. The road was quite flat and most of the time we walked on our skis. It was already six o'clock and pitch dark at the start of our little hike, and by the time I finally trudged the last few steps to the car more than an hour later, I was exhausted.

The day was still not over. This was a road-trip, after all, and it was time to move on to our next destination. I was sound asleep in the car by the time Bert pulled up to our hotel near the ski resort of La Molina.

LA MOLINA AND MASELLA

La Molina established itself as a center for skiing way back in 1911, and began adding lifts in 1947. It is Spain's oldest ski resort. In the late '90s, however, it built a gondola to join up with the neighboring resort of Masella, and together they have created a much more versatile ski region.

While Molina has some steep terrain, its forte is long, gentle pistes. Masella's lift system, on the other hand, is built amidst sheer cliffs and rocky ridges, interspersed with an array of difficult but skiable couloirs, known in Spanish as *tubs*. Views from the top are stunning, as skiers can look out over a vista of the broad, green Vall du Segre flanked by more snow-capped peaks on the opposite side of the valley.

We began our skiing with what now was becoming an almost obligatory part of our daily itinerary—a road-run. This time, it was a gentle rolling route from the top of Molina's Torrent Negre Lift down to the south of the resort.

Most of our previous road-shots involved a designated driver. Our one hitchhiking endeavor in Beret resulted in us being picked up by the

first passing car. Here, we even improved on that! After no more than a 5-minute wait, a car driving in the opposite direction turned around and took us back to the lifts!

The rest of the day, we skipped the road-runs and focused on *tub* skiing. Most of the best *tubs* were marked on the map as areas forbidden to skiers. That made them easy to find! It was understandable, however, that they were closed to the general public, as the average Spanish skier exhibited more bravado than skill. I could easily imagine a rush on local hospital beds if this terrain were officially open. Nevertheless, the ski patrol had given names to many of the local *tubs*, indicating that certain people in the know did ski them when the conditions were right. We skied one nicknamed "the Funnel" and another appropriately known as "the C___" because it was such a narrow opening!

Late in the day, we traversed out to the west from the Tosa Vermella Lift only to feast our eyes on an enormous, steep valley. The spring snow on the western flank was very tempting, and two lone tracks gave evidence to the fact that there probably was a road that could be reached somewhere long below. There was nobody to ask, and it was too late in the day. Masella had too much interesting terrain for a mere one-day stop.

EL FORMIGAL

Steve returned to his family after our day in La Molina and Masella, and our group was down to three skiers. Another night drive, another sunny morning and more spring snow awaited us, this time in El Formigal. This budget-priced, purpose-built resort, situated in the western Pyrenees, is rich in broad, open terrain, perfectly suitable for novices and intermediates.

The skiing here is divided into three areas, Zona Crestas, Zona Sarrios and Zona Anayet. For us, the best skiing was in the wide off-piste area between the latter two zones. A short hike from the top of the Collado

Chair Lift accessed every possible kind of terrain. There were, once again, some X-rated *tubs* between jagged ridges, a big, steep, northerly face and rolling hills and valleys facing east. All the alternatives took us right to the road. Is the pattern becoming familiar?

It certainly was beginning to become a routine for us, but with each road-run, we were more and more impressed with the Spaniards' attitude toward hitchhiking. We did two more such descents, and on both occasions, the first passing car picked us up. This is no easy trick, with three fully equipped skiers!

CANDANCHÚ AND ASTÚN

When we were children, we always wanted to save the best for last. Our favorite candy we would eat last, our favorite attraction at Disneyland we would ride last, and so on. And so it was, that as we three overgrown kids were finishing our road-trip, we ultimately landed in Candanchú and Astún, two neighboring ski resorts a couple of kilometers apart at the far west end of the Pyrenees.

It was no mere quirk of fate that we had left these two jewels as the dessert of our journey. Candanchú is one of the few ski resorts in the world that has more black pistes than any other category of run. To be exact, it has twenty descents that are black pistes or marked off-piste routes, compared with eighteen red runs, eleven blues and ten greens.

We knew this information before we started our journey. What we didn't know was that Candanchú also offers some of the most magnificent views in the ski world. We were left gaping in awe at the extreme nature of the large cliffs and sheer rock faces in and around the resort. It looked like a cross between the Canadian Rockies and the Dolomites of Italy. And in between many of the limestone walls were steep ribbons of white, which started our adrenaline flowing at a mere glance.

As luck would have it, we started our day by following a few off-piste tracks down a glorious horseshoe-shaped canyon, walled-in by vertical rock on the opposite side, and ended up—wouldn't you know it—at the road.

The highlight of this day, however, came with our afternoon descent down the Tubo la Zapatilla. This is no ordinary couloir, nor is it an ordinary run. Many ski resorts, I am sure, would have such a chute permanently closed. Other resorts with a more *laissez-faire* attitude might try to ignore the existence of such a tempting killer couloir in the midst of their ski area, and leave it to those who dare to discover and try it for themselves.

Candanchú, however, marks this descent clearly on its ski map and leaves the rest to providence. At the entrance to this giant elevator shaft hangs a large bag with rescue equipment. I trust it comes in handy quite often!

» The Zapatilla Couloir could easily vie as the steepest official piste in the world.«

I would estimate the Zapatilla Couloir to have a gradient of about 45 degrees. It could easily vie with such runs as the Karrinne in Innsbruck, Baldy Chutes in Alta and a handful of others as the steepest official piste in the world.

We waited until after 2 p.m. to allow the snow in this passage, where the sun rarely shines, to soften up. A 45-degree slope which is icy seems like 60 degrees and then some. Even at two o'clock, I felt as if a carelessly set edge would be very ill-advised.

Martin put it succinctly, as he mumbled to nobody in particular, "A fall here is gonna translate into a very long slide."

"Did you have to say that?" I answered.

Martin laughed, but it was a nervous laugh.

Bert apparently wanted to get it over with as quickly as possible, and said, "I'm getting out of here." With that, he shot down without even a glance back up for the sake of nostalgia.

I enjoy steep skiing, especially when it is in such regal surroundings. This well could have been God's staircase, or more likely the elevator shaft to Hades, but there was no doubt that it was a location laden with a large supply of nature's energy. I lingered a while in the shadow of the massive rock face on the west flank, and Martin and I took a few photos. Then we began to ski—slowly. Our deliberate descent was not merely to take care in this difficult couloir, but to savor the moment of a great run.

After skiing the Tubo la Zapatilla, I thought our final day would be anticlimactic. This was not true. Astún and Candanchú had, up until recently, sold a joint lift ticket. In fact, the Candanchú trail maps still depicted the Astún lifts and descents. To our surprise, four runs marked on the map ended on the highway that divides the two resorts! We had arrived in "road-run heaven".

From the highest point in Astún's lift system, atop La Raca (2300 m), long, steep slopes, ridges and ravines stretched all the way around the mountain from due south to northwest. Four of these possibilities were noted on the map as ski routes (unprepared and uncontrolled descents). Besides those four were a hundred more, and many of them were virgin—at least before *we* arrived.

At 10:30, we skied a south-facing route, at 1:30, we descended a west face and at 2:30, we chose a northwest-facing ravine—perfect corn snow, perfect corn snow and perfect corn snow.

"Ohhh! Not again another perfect sunny day with virgin spring snow," wailed Bert in mock agony after our first road-shot. "It's getting so boring."

In between road-runs, we skied a few pistes, sat in the sun with yet another three-course lunch, and wondered how they get so much snow in the Pyrenees, when it's always sunny.

By the time darkness came to Astún, we had run out of time and our road-trip was drawing to a close. I had also run out of clean ski socks, and all my socks would have to ride home with Martin's foul smelling ski boots in the ski box. In addition to that, after eight days on the road, we had exhausted our supply of bawdy tales about damsels whom we had relieved of stress or put into distress during the wild days of our youth.

The only thing we had not yet run out of was sunshine and corn snow. The Spanish Pyrenees had impressed us right down to our final run. A good entertainer leaves the audience wanting more, and so it is with a good ski vacation as well. We would end our stay with an *hasta la vista* instead of *adios*.

LEFT PAGE: The author on a road-run from Astún down toward the village of Candanchú. Photo by Martin Söderqvist.

THIS PAGE
UPPER LEFT: Modern architecture characterizes Astún. MIDDLE LEFT: Bert admires the snow depth near the top of the pass en route to Baqueira. UPPER RIGHT: Martin sprays up corn snow in Masella, with the green Vall du Segre in the background. LOWER: Bert and Martin ski in synch in the trees of Port Ainé.

Chapter 10. ANDORRA

SKI AND SHOP

The April sun was beaming through our window, warming the hotel room, and I woke up and walked onto my verandah. I gazed out over a village of stone houses with slate roofs flanking cobblestone streets. Some buildings dated back to the Middle Ages, while others were built in the 1990s, yet they meshed together in a seamless architectural scheme. Perhaps this sounds like a description of La Grave or another of the medieval villages of the French Haute Savoie, but that is not where we spent this holiday.

As we walked through the village to the lifts, we were impressed by the fact that the streets were immaculate and looked as if the cobblestones had been scrubbed with a toothbrush. Litter does not seem to be part of the vocabulary in this country. Wrong again—it is not Switzerland.

My then-girlfriend, Minna, and I reconnoitered the area, and found that some of the lifts here were Doppelmayr high-speed chair lifts. No, we are also not in Austria.

The black pistes here are what most experienced skiers would rate as red, the red pistes are like blue ones elsewhere, the blue ones are green and the green trails are horizontal or slightly uphill, but we are not in the Dolomites or elsewhere in Italy.

After our first ski day was finished, I discovered that an après-ski beer was very inexpensive, but I was not in Jasna or anywhere else in the Slovak Republic.

My beer was not the only thing that was relatively cheap here. Upon our return to the hotel, a small shop waylaid me. A liter of vodka was obtainable for a giveaway price and I couldn't resist. You think I am on a ski holiday at Mt. Elbrus, perhaps, or elsewhere in Russia? Not so!

Even the gasoline for our rental car was very economically priced, but we were not in the Rocky Mountains or anywhere else in the United States.

After filling gas, we drove down to look around the capital of the country. It is situated less than half an hour's drive from the ski slopes we had just descended. We were, however, not in Vitosha, the ski resort that overlooks Sofia, Bulgaria.

Helicopter skiing is also possible in this country, and the mountains here lend themselves very well to both heliskiing and touring. There are many exposures and routes down most of the peaks. I must add, however, that we were not in the Bugaboos or elsewhere in the Canadian Rockies.

For those who have not yet solved the mystery, Minna and I were visiting Andorra, a tiny land of 464 square kilometers (about half the size of New York City) and 70,000 inhabitants, nestled into a little corner of the Pyrenees between Spain and France. Mountains cover every square centimeter of this minuscule princedom, and 60 of those peaks are over 2500 meters high.

According to legend, the country was founded by Charlemagne in the year 784, and since then, Andorrans have enjoyed living in peace and harmony, avoiding war for over 1200 years. Nowadays, Andorra is a modern and wealthy country, although the Andorrans did not confer the right to vote to women until 1970 and first created a constitution in 1993. (Draw your own conclusion on the relationship between 1200 years of peace and the late advent of women's suffrage.)

FOR MANY YEARS, TOBACCO WAS the main product of the country, and it was primarily smuggled out of Andorra and sold in France. Smuggling is actually legal here. Later, because of Andorra's tax-free status, shopping gradually became the national sport, national flower and national anthem. Tourists began to flock here from all over Europe each year to partake in spree shopping for liquor, cigarettes, perfumes, optics, electronics and even cars. All the while, in the past few years, skiing has sneaked past shopping as the number one industry in Andorra, and that says a lot!

Snowsports can be enjoyed here from November into late April, and nowadays, Andorra attracts about nine million tourists annually, with many of those visitors coming for the skiing. Skiers can stay in the capital, Andorra la Vella, or in one of the small mountain villages, as everyplace is close to everyplace else in Andorra.

LEFT PAGE
Andorra has rather inexpensive heliskiing, allowing skiers to get away from the crowds.
THIS PAGE
UPPER: Spring is in full bloom in the picturesque village of Ordino, while there is plenty of

snow left on the nearby slopes.
LOWER LEFT: The exterior of the Caldea aquatic center.
LOWER MIDDLE: Inside the Caldea.
LOWER RIGHT: Locals load tobacco onto a truck.

We stayed in Ordino, perhaps the most picturesque of the mountainside hamlets, and also conveniently situated only a short drive from each of the ski resorts in the country.

Our first day, we drove about 7 kilometers to the nearest ski area, Arinsal, a cute but spread-out little village. There are about a dozen lifts, all contained in a wide, open area with almost no trees. In addition, it is linked by cable car to nearby Pal and is half of what is called the Vallnord ski region. This resort boasts 1092 vertical meters of skiing, but this statistic can be misleading as there is often too little snow to ski to the village. (The vertical drop to the middle station is 642 meters.)

WE ASCENDED FOUR CONSECUTIVE lifts, which brought us to an elevation of 2560 meters. Most of the ski terrain is relatively easy, and a short black piste is situated to the side of the La Capa Lift, near the top. Most interesting for advanced skiers, however, is an off-piste descent known as El

Cubil. A 5-minute traverse from the top took us to the entry of this long, steep slope.

We looked down an imposing east face of corn snow, which narrows into a ravine and ultimately ends on the serpentine road that leads to the middle station of the resort. Ordinarily, this would be an avalanche trap—a place one would be loath to ski on all but the safest occasions. But here, the road is the off-piste skier's best friend. The safety of the road necessitates that this long avalanche funnel must always be blasted and secured. Hence, if the road is open, one can be rather sure that the ravine is safe for skiing.

We leapt into action with the gusto that accompanies this kind of security. A few centimeters of new powder scraped off the corn snow under our skis and sent hundreds of small snowballs into motion. About halfway down, it is possible to cross over to the northern flank of the ravine. Here, 10 centimeters of powder lay untouched in the shade, changing our

run from a spring experience to a short winter orgasm. Near the bottom, the April snow cover was sparse, and we picked our way between rocks, shrubs and a small, cascading brook until we were on the asphalt.

After our run down El Cubil, we moved over to the sister resort of Pal. It offers 585 vertical meters of skiing and is similar in size to Arinsal, but in Pal the runs are tree-lined. Some pistes have moguls, while many are groomed, but there is virtually no off-piste skiing. We enjoyed an afternoon of cruising and headed down to Andorra de Vella for the evening.

The capital city is dominated by the Caldea, an ultra-modern, futuristic-looking swimming and aquatic center. The mirrored facades of its pyramid-shaped tower reflected the late afternoon sun, and the thought of relaxing in this center's labyrinth of saunas, Jacuzzis and steam baths was hard to resist after a long day of skiing.

We dove into the main lagoon, a huge body of thermal water that connects with outdoor pools by way of narrow channels. We popped in and out of various Jacuzzis, both indoor and outdoor, and then tried the Indo-Roman baths, which include both hot and cold pools of water, all in a regal setting. This is the kind of place one would expect to find Nero being fawned over by a bevy of naked water nymphs. It required a few hours to explore the many nooks and crannies of this unique spa.

The following day, we visited the resorts of Pas de la Casa, Grau Roig, Soldeu and El Tarter. The four areas make up what is called Grandvalira, a lift-linked region that includes over 60 lifts, well over 100 pistes and 850 vertical meters of skiing from atop Tossal de la Llosada (2560 m). Nevertheless, none of these locations can compete with Ordino or Arinsal for atmosphere, and Pas de la Casa, situated literally on the French border, exemplifies all of the worst attributes of '70s French ski-town architecture.

WE ENLISTED THE SERVICES of a guide to show us around this large area. Augustin led us away from the lift system on a 20-minute walk up to Pic d'Encampadana. He explained that during the high season, the ski resort provides snow cat service for off-piste skiers to reach this area, but now the season was winding down and the service had been discontinued.

We did not mind. A short walk in the spring sunshine was just what we needed to get our blood circulating. From the summit, Augustin pointed out off-piste routes to a couple of neighboring villages, but it was now too late in the season for these descents. Instead, he chose to lead us down a wide, medium-steep gully, which headed back toward the lifts. The gully was filled with spring snow, and we glided rather effortlessly down.

The pistes were more impressive than the off-piste terrain in these resorts, and we spent our afternoon testing as many cruisers as we had time for. Grandvalira is an intermediate utopia. The trails were well-groomed and the snow guns even extended to the top of the north-facing slopes. I didn't see a lift line all day.

Dinner is also an event in Andorra. In the various villages that surround the capital are many old *bordes*, chimneyless cottages used for keep-

ing cows and hay. This country, which once relied on agriculture for its livelihood, has, however, changed directions in recent years, and many *bordes* have been converted into cozy restaurants. While the main courses, particularly the grilled meats, are excellent, the *tapas* are the real specialty of the meals here. Each evening, by the time we had finished a sampling of a half-dozen such starters, we were so full that most of the main course had to be given to the dogs.

WE HAD ONE SKI RESORT yet to visit, Arcalis, which has the most varied skiing of Andorra's resorts. It offers excellent pistes and cruising terrain for lower ability skiers, but also has some quite challenging pistes and off-piste options. In addition, the heliskiing is excellent and, like everything else in Andorra, very reasonably priced.

We warmed up with a few runs on the corn snow, which was just beginning to soften. Then, we skied a moguled north face that descends among large rocks and small cliffs. One of the lift attendants pointed out a rather wide gully called the Couloir of Death. That name is a gross exaggeration and gives the chute a much more ominous air than it deserves. It looked quite tempting, and Minna and I embarked on 5-minute walk to the entry. A sugar coating of a few centimeters of powder gave our edges something soft to grip, and we glided easily down this not-so-deadly passage between the cliffs.

Now, we were ready for the heliskiing. Our guide, Mark, gave us a choice among a few descents, and we chose an intimidating ravine. It was 35–40 degrees and rather narrow in the upper section, after which the slope fell away, rendering the lower part of the run unobservable.

We plunged in with a degree of trepidation. The warmth of the April morning had taken its toll. The 20 centimeters of powder were somewhat heavy, and we found ourselves huffing and puffing with each turn. Once we got through the throat of the couloir, the slope widened out and we angled across to a better exposure. Now we were down to about 10 centimeters of fresh snow, but it was lighter, and a layer of firm corn snow underneath the loose snow made an excellent foundation for us to turn on.

Suddenly, we could breeze through 50 turns without overexerting ourselves. Ultimately, we emptied into a huge open canyon, where there was space for scores of skiers to lay tracks; but we enjoyed the privilege of solitude that characterizes heliskiing. About 900 vertical meters below our starting point, we ran out of snow, and by then, we had also run out of time on this ski vacation.

OUR HOLIDAY HAD BEEN an excellent combination of good skiing, excellent food and picturesque villages, rich with ambiance. For me, it had had the added bonus of adventure, what with our helicopter run, and for Minna, it had been a shopper's dream. Best of all, the vacation had a price tag that could hardly be beaten anywhere in the Western world. I just wonder what to do with the 50 liters of liquor and 5 liters of perfume that we smuggled home.

LEFT PAGE
LEFT: Arinsal and Pal make up the Vallnord ski area. This photo depicts the trails of the Pal section of the resort. UPPER RIGHT: Minna Gynther on the El Cubil descent from Arinsal down to the road. LOWER RIGHT: Lunch restaurant in Arinsal.

THIS PAGE
Greece is one of the countries where one can have a ski and beach holiday. This church is on Korfu.

Chapter 11. GREECE

SKI ODYSSEY

It was late March when Christer Henning, Minna Gynther and I boarded a southbound plane en route to Greece. As I entered the aircraft with my ski boots as hand baggage, the stewardess gave me a curious glance, and asked if I was on the right plane. Few people outside Greece know that there are around twenty ski areas in this Mediterranean country, more famous for her beaches. Although we knew full well of the skiing opportunities in Greece, even we ended up being surprised at what the ancient gods had planned for us.

We quickly organized a rental car in Athens and pointed it northwest toward Mt. Parnassos, Greece's largest ski resort, situated 180 kilometers from the capital. Lower down on the same broad mountain that is home to the ski resort lie the ruins of Delphi, one of the most significant locations of ancient Greek times. It was here that people would come to the temple of Apollo to listen to the oracle's predictions between 1000 and 300 B.C.

We paused for a couple of hours to rummage through the fascinating remains of the stadium, temple and amphitheater, but we needed no oracle to enlighten us about the coming days. The ominous dark clouds closing in quickly from the west spoke a thousand words—and the future was not at all what we had expected. Arriving in Greece on March 28, we had anticipated a week of spring skiing, but that was not at all in the oracle's crystal ball.

By the time Christer, Minna and I reached Arahova (940 m), the picturesque mountain village that services Mt. Parnassos, snow was falling heavily. The red tile roofs were turning white, and the locals were busily pulling their wares off the displays along the main street and back into their old stone houses. Arahova is the mountain equivalent of some of the lovely whitewashed villages of the Greek Isles. Here, among the

narrow, hilly, cobblestone streets, young, colorfully clad skiers and snowboarders are juxtaposed with elderly Greek women in their traditional black garb.

The next morning, most of the 24-kilometer road that separated us from the skiing was covered in Bing Crosby's favorite color, but this was Easter, for God's sake. It was not Christmas, and we were in southern Greece! I kept our car in second gear and crept slowly upward. Snowchains are not standard equipment in rental cars in Greece. At an elevation of 1750 meters, we pulled into the parking lot of the ski center, where the snow banks were about 2 meters high.

ALL OUR PRECONCEPTIONS ABOUT SKIING in Greece were being shattered minute by minute. Apollo is the god of the sun, but he was definitely out to lunch. Snow was falling steadily and above us stood a massive mountain covered in pure virgin powder. The Mt. Parnassos ski area is made up of fourteen lifts spread out across a broad, treeless area between the elevations of 1600 and 2260 meters.

Much of the resort was closed due to the storm, but we found our way onto some short, steep slopes between rock cliffs on the lower section of mountain. As usual, when skiing in a country where the sport is not so developed, we had these powder slopes all to ourselves. About 15 centimeters of new snow covered the slopes—deep enough to throw up some spray and leave a nice track in the wake of each run.

In the afternoon, I noticed an incongruous sight—a tall, gangling Greek man, about 2 meters in height, on a pair of very short touring skis. As comical as he may have looked, people who do randonnée usually have a good knowledge of the mountains, and I struck up a conversation. I was not mistaken. Vassilis Katsonis told us of fascinating tours that could be made on Mt. Parnassos down to old monasteries on the back side of the mountain.

For the time being, in the poor visibility, Vassilis had another suggestion. He could guide us down a steep off-piste slope, if somebody could pick us all up in a car. Minna became the sacrificial lamb who "volunteered" for the task, and she drove to the parking lot of the Fterolaka section of the ski area.

The Fterolaka half of the lift system has most of the advanced terrain, and was closed due to the poor visibility. The fog was no problem, however, with our local guide in the lead. Christer, Vassilis and I dropped over the ridge that divided Fterolaka from the Kellaria part of the mountain. Smoothly, we laid three tracks into a huge virgin valley. Minna was waiting at the predetermined meeting point, and after thanking Vassilis, we drove back to Arahova.

»...a wonderful place to mix skiing, swimming and culture...«

For the next couple of days, Apollo warred with the clouds, the snow and the fog, sometimes winning a battle, as Mt. Parnassos appeared in all its glory above a sea of clouds, but also losing many fights, as we skied back down into the pea soup. The lack of visibility was not so problematic, as the mountain was smooth, without many obstacles. On slope after slope, we left our mark in 10–15 centimeters of fresh snow. The only drawback was that we were not often able to look back and admire our tracks.

Our third morning, Plastiras Efthimios, the director of the ski area, was kind enough to guide us around, opening up closed lifts at the wave of his magic hand. When the sun peeked through, we saw vast fields of snow as far as the eye could see, without any bare spots, even though it was April. Plastiras explained that there is usually enough snow to ski in Parnassos well into June, but the lifts generally close in mid-April, as the Greek people are mentally heading into the archipelago by that time.

GREECE IS A WONDERFUL PLACE to mix skiing, swimming and culture, and we made the best of the opportunities. We visited Athens for a look at the dramatic Parthenon, on the Acropolis overlooking the city. As we drove north toward Macedonia, the sun poked its head out, and we stopped for a swim in Maliakos Bay, by the village of Stilida.

When we arrived at our next ski destination, Tria-pente Pigadia, it was snowing—no longer a surprise by now. Skiing here was completely different from the treeless slopes of Mt. Parnassos. This small ski area had basically two runs of about 650 vertical meters, each cut out of a forest of oak, chestnut and beech trees. We alternated between the red and the black run, getting a good workout in the soft moguls, and later we had our after-ski, soothing our muscles in some local hot springs near the town of Aridea.

Our next stop was, in various ways, typical of the Greek ski experience. On Mt. Vermio, the host-mountain to Tria-pente Pigadia, also lies the old ski resort of Seli. We arrived about six o'clock Friday evening and the village looked like a ghost town. Almost every house was shuttered and closed up. The eateries and hotels at the base of the lifts were padlocked. One open tavern and two cars were the only signs of life in the resort. It looked certain that Seli was closed for the season.

I followed a sign pointing to Hotel Seli, a lodge that apparently was situated a little outside the center. There were two more cars, and Thomas Tourountzas, who worked at the hotel, invited us in. Thomas explained that the hotel was closed, as the heating system had been damaged by the previous night's storm. He assured us, however, that the ghost-town appearance of the ski area was because Seli was a locals' mountain with almost no midweek overnight guests. He assured us that the lifts would be operating the next day.

THOMAS AND TWO FRIENDS were about to eat dinner, and he insisted that we warm up by the fire and join them. He was apparently the incarnation of Bacchus, the Greek god of wine, for no sooner had we sat down than an endless supply of retsina passed before us. The beverage was accompanied by copious amounts of chops, liver, tomatoes and onions. Greeks are famous for their hospitality, and this feast for strangers was an example of Greek friendliness and generosity at its very finest. Thomas apologized that the cold rooms were not fit for use, and we found lodging 20 kilometers down the mountain in Naoussa.

The next morning, Zeus must have intervened to aid Apollo, for the sun shone brightly. The snow line was at 600 meters. I again cursed the absence of chains to go with our rental car. I quite like first tracks on the slopes, but I can live without them on the roads. The one advantage of first tracks on the road was that there were no Greek drivers ahead of me to get stuck and block the way.

Shortly after nine o'clock, we were on the peak. About 50 kilometers in the distance, the Bay of Thermaikos appeared as a shimmering golden mirror under the morning sun, but here, about 1900 meters up Mt. Vermio, it was –5 degrees centigrade, a brisk wind chilled the air, and 10 centimeters of cold winter powder awaited us.

Although Seli is lower than Tria-pente Pigadia, it is a moonscape of smooth, shallow slopes devoid of vegetation. It was too late in the season to attract a big weekend crowd, so we shared the lifts with a handful of children and a few Greek tourists. We shared the off-piste with nobody. We etched track after track, side by side in the fresh powder, until it was time to leave.

Mt. Olympus, the highest mountain in Greece and home of Zeus, king of the gods, also has a small ski area. Despite our knowledge that foreigners needed permits (obtainable in Athens) to ski in this military zone, we set course for Zeus's abode. In the end, we were thwarted, not by the military, but by the world's worst road signs.

LEFT PAGE
LEFT: Rocky seaside in Korfu. MIDDLE: Minna Gynther descends into the Former Yugoslavian
Republic of Macedonia. In the background is a chapel situated atop the Vorras ski resort.
RIGHT: With our tracks etched into the powder in the background, Minna starts her hike bike
back up to Vorras.

THIS PAGE
Rafi Betschart flies past one of the beautiful robola trees of Vasilitsa on a recent visit to Greece.

THIS PAGE: Minna attempts to get directions from a local woman. There must have been a communication failure, as we never did find the road to the Mt. Olympus ski area.
RIGHT PAGE: The beautiful cliffs of Meteora and one of the ancient monasteries that are perched atop these cliffs.

The first sign that steered us wrong ended at what looked to be an abandoned old building. Two odd-looking characters, looking not unlike the backwoods products of incest in the film *Deliverance*, appeared in the doorway. We pointed to the skis on the roof of the car, and the one Greek hillbilly genuflected in a telemark motion to indicate that he knew what skiing was. Nevertheless, he still did not know where the skiing on his mountain existed.

We backtracked and tried an alternate route. This road changed from asphalt to gravel after a few kilometers. Then came a segment of road where huge boulders and landslides had covered half the street. Soon after, the road degenerated from gravel to dirt and narrowed appreciably. When the next transformation came, from dirt to mud, we once again turned around. Our third attempted route, which I do believe to have been correct, had to be abandoned when the surface switched from dirt to snow.

Driven into retreat by the apparent will of Zeus, Christer and I consulted our map and found a small icon of a schussing skier next to the dot indicating Vasilitsa, a location almost due east of Mt. Olympus. It was too late for any skiing that day, so we stopped on the way at Meteora, certainly one of the most fascinating spots in the world.

THE VILLAGE OF KALAMBAKA IS BUILT in the foothills of Meteora, a 3-square-kilometer region of huge and bizarre rock formations that rise over 400 vertical meters straight up from the village. Ancient monasteries are precariously perched atop six of these perpendicular rock walls, the oldest of which dates to the 12th century.

The early monks placed beams into cracks and spaces in the cliffs, and built scaffolding onto these beams to attain the tops. For centuries, the monks hauled people and supplies up in nets or by using long rope ladders. In the last hundred years or so, sets of stairs have been cut into the cliffs to make these retreats more accessible.

From Meteora, snow-covered mountains could be seen glistening in the sun. That did not last for long. I am not sure who the Greek god of snow is, but he had already figured prominently in our spring sojourn through this land of mythology, and as we drove, he once again reared his head. What had begun as a sunny morning turned into a snowstorm by the time we reached the slopes.

It was Sunday, and a cacophony of sound attacked us at the base of the mountain. Hard rock blared from two huge speakers situated in front of one of the small restaurants, Greek pop music emanated from the neighboring hut, and Greek Orthodox church-music droned through the speakers hanging from each lift tower. Fortunately, the snow was better than the music.

Through the storm, we could make out the contours of unusually beautiful trees flanking the piste. *Robola*, as this tree is called in Greece, is a very large species of pine, which grows in odd, asymmetrical shapes between 1600 and 2200 meters. The wood from these trees is often used to make special wine barrels, which give a very distinct taste to the wines; but here, their snow-laden branches bowed down into the powder and served to give a fairytale look to the landscape. We wove our way between

the *robolas*, played amidst some small rocks and cliffs, and left our tracks in 40 centimeters of fresh snow all over the mountain.

At lunch, the proprietor of one of the restaurants recognized me as a foreigner and invited me to four rounds of grappa. Local hospitality didn't stop there. After the lifts had closed, we were given a ride with a snow cat to try one more off-piste route, one that we had not had time for during the ordinary operating hours. It was almost dark when we loaded the car and headed toward our final destination in Greece.

The last target of our trip was a relatively newly built ski area (1995) called Vorras, situated on the third-highest mountain in the country. Can you imagine a Greek ski resort, with primarily south-facing pistes, that has plenty of snow in May? It sounds like another page of mythology, but it is true.

Even in ski destinations in latitudes far north of Greece, rarely is a ski resort built with most of its slopes facing the sun. It defies all logic. But Vorras is situated on the border with the Former Yugoslav Republic of Macedonia, and only the southern half of the mountain is Greek. Since these two Balkan neighbors are not always the best of friends, no lifts exist on the north side.

We didn't mind. The sun was finally shining on us, and by ten o'clock, we were cruising on perfect corn snow. It was midweek, and as is quite often the case in Greece, only one of the ski lifts was open to service the 30 to 40 skiers. From the pistes, we could gaze out over a lovely panorama that included Lake Vegoriti below, the Seli and the Tria-pente Pigadia ski areas to the south, and even Mt. Olympus, 100 kilometers in the distance.

From the top of the lift, it is a short walk to the peak (2524 m), where a small chapel commemorates thousands of people who died on this mountain during both the Balkan Wars and World War I. While looking at the church, we could not help but notice inviting fields of powder stretching down the north face into the Former Yugoslav Republic of Macedonia.

THE SIGHT WAS TOO MUCH FOR US to resist. In spite of the late hour, we hurried down to our room and gathered our touring equipment together. Soon, we were putting powder tracks into what the Yugoslavs now call Macedonia. The slope was relatively steep, making it all the more enjoyable—on the way *down*.

It was not long, however, before we stood at the snow line, with a long, steep and arduous hike back up awaiting us. We watched a beautiful red sunset, but this took place, unfortunately, before we re-attained the summit. That meant eventually skiing the piste back to our hotel by radar. The piste was not difficult, but each time a ski hit a chunk of refrozen corn snow, invisible in the dark, one of us went flying. At 8:30 in the evening, in the pitch dark of night, our Greek ski odyssey finally came to a close.

During our ten days in Greece, we learned to discern mythology from reality. That there is no skiing or no good skiing in this rugged, ancient land is a myth. That one should expect warm weather and spring conditions is another myth. That Greece is so far south that it has a short or uncertain ski season is still one more myth.

The reality is that Greece is a country with many ski centers, historical sites and beach resorts all in close proximity to each other. The water is still cold in early spring, but so is the snow, and one can easily swim and ski on the same day. Be prepared for any and all kinds of weather. Pack warm clothes, shorts, strong sun cream and an umbrella…and by all means, don't forget a good set of tire chains.

Chapter 12. CYPRUS

SKI AND BEACH

At the far eastern end of the Mediterranean Sea lies the small island country of Cyprus. It is a country that suffers from schizophrenia. Throughout its long and storied history, many empires have ruled Cyprus. Among the various rulers who have left their stamp on the nation, the Greeks, the Turks and the British still play a very important role today.

Like so many of its neighbors in the Middle East, Cypriots have not been able to get along with each other for many years. Since 1974, when many people were uprooted from their homes and killed, the island has been divided into a Greek and Turkish sector. Since that time, Cyprus has remained peaceful and tourism has flourished (especially in the Greek sector), but the problems that divide the country have not been resolved.

The British officially relinquished control of Cyprus in 1960, but their influence is still pervasive today. If the ruins that are visited all over the island are the remnants of the Greek and Roman periods in Cyprus, then the myriad of pubs that abound in each major city are proof that the British "cultural" heritage has outlasted its legal jurisdiction.

Another institution introduced by the British to Cyprus is skiing. Cyprus seems like an unlikely place to have ski slopes, but to the surprise of all but the most knowledgeable skiers, Mt. Troodos, situated in the middle of the Greek part of the island, is home to four ski lifts.

To be sure, skiing on Cyprus is a novelty. The lifts and slopes are short and nobody short of a total fanatic would come to Cyprus for the sole purpose of skiing. Cyprus is, after all, a summer resort with its focus on beaches and sunshine. Nevertheless, an off-season visitor to the country can experience the diversity of skiing and swimming in the sea on the same day. The mercury on a typical day in February might reach 20 degrees centigrade or more on the coast, while an hour's drive can bring visitors to a winter scenario.

The ski runs are situated amidst a beautiful forest of cypress trees, and the views from the peak (1950 m) stretch out over green farmland to the sea. Despite the shortness of the pistes, some of the terrain is relatively steep, and one can even ski off-piste in the forest.

An off-season visit to Cyprus offers the opportunity to visit the prettiest beaches, famous monasteries, Byzantine churches and other historical sites without the crowds. It is also a time of year when one can get to know the friendly local people, when they are not caught up in the entrapments of their high season. If one decides to visit Cyprus during the winter months, then by all means, a day on the slopes of Mt. Troodos is a must for any skier.

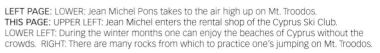
LEFT PAGE: LOWER: Jean Michel Pons takes to the air high up on Mt. Troodos.
THIS PAGE: UPPER LEFT: Jean Michel enters the rental shop of the Cyprus Ski Club.
LOWER LEFT: During the winter months one can enjoy the beaches of Cyprus without the crowds. RIGHT: There are many rocks from which to practice one's jumping on Mt. Troodos.

Europe – The Mediterranean in a Nutshell

LOCATION	NEAREST TOWN	NEAREST AIRPORT	SEASON	PEAK ELEVATION	VERTICAL DROP	SIZE	SNOW	BEAUTY	VILLAGE	NOVICE	INTERMEDIATE	ADVANCED	OFF-PISTE	NIGHTLIFE	RATING AVERAGE	WEB SITE
ANDORRA																
Arcalis	Ordino	Barcelona	December–April	2600 m	660 m	2	2	3	3	4	4	4	3	4	3	3.2	www.arcalis.andorramania.com
Grandvalira	Canillo	Barcelona	late November–mid April	2640 m	850 m	3	5	3	2	2	5	5	3	2	2	3.2	www.grandvalira.com
Pal-Arinsal	Andorra la Vella	Barcelona	December–April	2560 m	1110 m	3	4	3	3	3	4	3	2	3	3	3.1	www.arinsal_pal.andorramania.com
CYPRUS																
Troodos	Limassol	Larnaka	mid January–mid March [1]	1920 m	125 m	1	1	1	3	1	2	1	1	1	1	1.3	www.skicyprus.com
GREECE																
Parnassos	Arahova	Athens	December–April	2280 m	660 m	2	2	4	3	4	3	4	2	3	2	2.9	www.parnassos-eot.gr
Seli	Naoussa	Thessaloniki	December–March	1874 m	275 m	1	1	3	3	2	3	2	2	2	1	2	www.seli-ski.gr
Tria-pente Pigadia	Veroia	Thessaloniki	December–March	2005 m	585 m	2	1	2	2	2	2	2	2	1	1	1.7	www.3-5pigadia.gr
Vasilitsa	Grevena	Thessaloniki	December–April	2100 m	450 m	2	1	4	4	3	3	3	2	3	2	2.7	www.vasilitsa.com
Voras	Agios Athanasios	Thessaloniki	November–May	2480 m	430 m	2	1	3	4	4	3	3	1	2	2	2.5	www.kaimaktsalan.gr
SPAIN																
Astún	Jaca	Toulouse	December–April	2324 m	674 m	2	2	3	5	1	3	4	3	5	2	3	www.astun.com
Baqueira Beret	Veilha	Toulouse	Dec.–early April	2510 m	1000 m	3	4	3	3	2	4	5	3	5	3	3.5	www.baqueira.es
Boi Taüll	Veilha	Toulouse	December–April	2783 m	762 m	2	2	3	3	2	3	4	3	3	2	2.7	www.boitaullresort.es
Candanchú	Jaca	Toulouse	December–April	2400 m	900 m	3	3	3	5	2 [2]	2	3	5	4	3	3.3	www.candanchu.com
El Formigal	Jaca	Barcelona	December–April	2415 m	915 m	3	3	3	3	1	4	4	4	3	3	3.1	www.aramon.es
La Molina/Masella	Puidcerdà	Barcelona	December–April	2537 m	935 m	3	3	3	4	2 [2]	5	5	4	4	2 [2]	3.5	www.lamolina.com
Port Ainé	Rialp	Barcelona/Toulouse	December–April	2440 m	790 m	2	1	3	3	2	5	3	2	2	1	2.3	www.port-aine.com
Sierra Nevadas	Granada	Malaga	December–April	3300 m	1200 m	3	3	3	4	1	5	5	2	3	2	3.1	www.sierranevadaski.com

(1) The ski season here can vary quite a bit from year to year.
(2) These ratings would improve by one point if one stayed in the nearest town instead of in the actual resort.

EUROPE – THE NORTH IV

PREVIOUS PAGES: Thomas Heisig appears as if he might ski straight into the blue waters of Storfjord as he descends off-piste from the Roaldshorn to Stranda.
RIGHT PAGE: The moon is up, but the sun is still shining on Ketil Singstad as he telemarks through the powder at 9 p.m. on a ski tour close to his home in Narvik.

CHAPTER 13. NORWAY

Norway is a small country of between four and five million people, which boasts one of the most spectacular coastlines in the world. Her western seaboard is lined with a labyrinth of long fjords, giving Norway an amazing 21,300 kilometers of shoreline. Many of these long arms of the sea stretch inland for well over a hundred kilometers, and every centimeter is worth seeing.

The fjords are generally flanked by granite walls that often reach 1000 meters above the water and are decorated by endless waterfalls cascading down every nook and cranny of these cliffs. They are sure to keep a tourist in awe for every second of his journey through Norway. Around each bend in the road awaits another surprise—a new arm of the waterway, a surge of spring meltwater rushing down the valley from a hanging glacier, or a picturesque village squeezed into a small meadow at the end of a fjord.

Norway is an appropriate place to begin a ski tour of northern Europe, for this is where it all started thousands of years ago. While skiing was primarily a form of transportation for many centuries, the Norwegians are given credit for starting and developing it as a sport as well. Immigrants from Norway spread skiing to the United States in the mid-1800s. Later, the Alpine countries started importing Norwegian ski instructors at the beginning of the 20th century to teach people the telemark turn.

Of the countries of northern Europe, Norway is also the only location to have hosted the Winter Olympic Games. It has done so twice, with the 1952 games held in Oslo and the 1994 events taking place in Lillehammer. The alpine skiing events for the Oslo games took place in Norefjell, which has Norway's greatest vertical drop (1003 m), while Kvitfjell and Hafjell became famous during the '94 Olympics. These venues were used because of their easy access and infrastructure, but they do not really represent what is best, unique and most interesting about Norwegian skiing.

Other well-known and popular Norwegian resorts include Hemsedal, Geilo and Trysil, but they also owe much of their success to their proximity to the major population centers. The skiing that best typifies Norway, however, lies a bit further afield.

The remote villages of Narvik and Stranda are locations where a skier can combine excellent skiing with sea views and landscapes that are uniquely Norwegian. Oppdal, one of the largest ski areas in Norway, is an excellent location for open, above-tree-line skiing. It offers a combination of many pistes, a large amount of backcountry territory and a robust après-ski life. Finally, Stryn is where winter meets summer. This glacial area opens about a month after most other Norwegian ski resorts close, and it provides a juxtaposition of the seasons where glacial snow coexists with green summer grass in beautiful counterpoint.

NARVIK — SKIING AT THE END OF THE WORLD

If Narvik is not the end of the world, you can certainly see it from atop the Fagernesfjell, which rises 1272 meters directly up behind this remote Norwegian village. At 68.5 degrees north latitude, Narvik is situated about 250 kilometers north of the Arctic Circle, putting it on line with such other outposts of civilization as Quasigiannguit, Greenland and Norilsk, Siberia.

If it were not for the Gulf Stream, only seals and polar bears would inhabit northern Norway. Instead, this mountainous promontory that juts spectacularly into the sea between Rombaksfjord and Ofotfjord is filled with the colorful homes of about 18,000 Norwegians. With the exception of a few very knowledgeable freeriders, these 18,000 people are the only ones privy to the information that right behind their house is the best skiers' mountain in all of Scandinavia.

The skiing experience in Narvik is quite unusual in the world of skiing. Imagine having a private mountain with around 900 vertical meters of skiing in your backyard. Pretend that the mountain has three T-bars, a chair lift and a gondola, offers good pistes and exciting off-piste skiing and is primarily at the disposal of you and your best ski cronies.

Now, come to Narvik and meet Ketil Singstad, the marketing director for Narvik Ski Center. He is the man with the keys to all the rides in this magnificent Nordic playground. He is also the leader of a pack of 20–30 crazy telemark skiers and snowboarders whose Viking ancestry is well documented by their devil-may-care abandon for life and limb.

I arrived here around eight o'clock on a pleasant evening in late April. Despite the late hour, the sun shone brightly on the northwest-facing bowls on the back side of Fagernesfjell. The snow was still a meter deep in many backyards in town. As I approached the mountain, I noticed that the lifts were still running. Halfway through my late evening meal in the Norlandia Narvik Hotell at the base of the mountain, I watched the skiers making their final descent of the day. It was 9:15 p.m. and the last rays of light shed a pinkish glow over the landscape.

NARVIK'S REMOTE NORTHERLY LOCATION makes for operating hours that are quite different from conventional ski resorts. During the deep of winter, the operating hours in Narvik are limited by the harsh conditions and long Arctic nights. After mid-February, however, the lifts are open from 1–9 p.m. on weekdays and 10-5 on weekends and during Easter week. These times suit the schedules of the local school children and the working inhabitants of the town.

The following afternoon, I met Ketil and a few of his pals shortly after

THIS PAGE
LEFT: Fagernesfjell offers views of the fjords around Narvik from almost every vantage point. The skier is Trond Olssen.
MIDDLE: Fagernesfjell as seen from Narvik at around 9 p.m. on a late April evening.
RIGHT: Ketil Singstad leaps off the cornice into Mørkhåla.

RIGHT PAGE
The granite cliff that flanks the couloir and the fjord below make Gangnesaksla one of the most dramatic descents I have ever skied. The skier is Leif Betten.

the lifts opened. As we rode up the lift, Ketil filled me in on a bit of local history.

Narvik is a working-class town that owes its existence to the railroad line, built in 1902 to link the iron-ore mines in Kiruna, Sweden with the deep-sea harbor here. The first gondola to serve skiers was built in 1956, and for the next 30 years, that gondola and a few T-bars served the community's skiing needs.

Then, from 1986–1991, an infusion of about 50 million Norwegian kroner built a few new lifts, including a double chair lift. Not only did that lift add 350 vertical meters to the skiing here, it opened up a whole world of off-piste skiing and single-handedly transformed Fagernesfjell into a world-class ski center. Northern Norway, however, does not have the population to support a destination ski area, and marketing, according to Ketil, was an expression relatively unknown to this little community at the edge of the world. Into this scenario stepped Ketil in 1995, to become the ski center's first marketing man.

By the time we got to this juncture in Ketil's story, we had arrived at the summit, from where stunning views of the surrounding fjords were coming into clear focus, and I began to doubt Ketil's explanation that these backwards locals had never heard of marketing. The sun glistened on Rombaksfjord below, untouched powder waited patiently, and I understood perfectly that the indigenous skiers were not into sharing their paradise with the rest of the world.

Ketil swung his skis into the fall line and began to etch first tracks onto the spacious north face of Fagernesfjell. He did not stop to wait for me until 450 vertical meters below, when he reached the top of the tree line.

> **» My heart had already been in my throat entering the bowl from the previous peak...«**

"From here, you have to follow me more closely," he said with a grin, as he again peeled off and snaked a path through the birch forest that now separated us from the village. I had no chance to keep pace with my leader, but his tracks were easy to follow in the fresh snow, and we soon headed back up for another go.

AT THE TOP, KETIL AND HIS BUDDIES exchanged a few words, and I knew I was in for something special when a slightly mischievous grin began to spread across Ketil's face.

"You don't mind a little walk, do you?" he asked cheerily.

I assured him that I didn't, and a half-dozen of us slung our skis onto our shoulders and began a half-hour hike. About 250 vertical meters later, we arrived at a cornice, which hung ominously out over the steep entry to a huge, untouched bowl. The surrounding rocks were plastered with a thick coat of rime. Before I could even get my camera unpacked, the first of Ketil's faithful followers had leapt out over the edge, landed 5 meters below and was busily planting telemark turns into the steep upper slope.

"This is Mørkhåla (Dark Hole)," Ketil stated succinctly, as a kind of epithet to the second telemark lunatic lurching over the precipice into an uncertain future. We all cut fresh tracks into the bowl and picked our way through the birch forest until we arrived back in town. By early evening, my host had some work to attend to, but he left me with his henchmen.

Einar Sund, one of the linchpins of the gang, took me under his wing and asked, "Have you been in the *real* Mørkhåla yet?"

"What do you mean 'the *real* Mørkhåla'?" I asked. "What the hell was that we just skied? Wasn't that Mørkhåla?"

"Uhh, yes and no," Einar answered deliberately. "That was the Mørkhåla for tourists," he explained. "I'll show you the more difficult variation!" he finished, and he began to lead us toward what the locals call the Tredje Toppen (Third Peak).

"More difficult, indeed!" I muttered under my breath.

My heart had already been in my throat entering the bowl from the

previous peak, and I wondered, with some trepidation, what the extra 10-minute walk to the Tredje Toppen would reveal.

Instead of the daunting cornice-topped bowl, I now looked down a long precipitous slope of windblown powder. There were numerous rocky outcrops below, which, with a bit of luck, could be avoided. On the other hand, one definitely did not want to cross a tip. This was a spot where one could make some money with one of those machines that sell on-the-spot life-insurance policies.

It was again about eight o'clock in the evening. The sun had transformed the fjord to gold, but I had little time to dwell on the beauty of the nature just then. Each turn required my full concentration. I traversed out past the worst of the rocks, and gingerly began my descent. I began by jumping one or two turns at a time, apprehensive of a possible slab avalanche. The snow seemed stable, and about 100 meters down from the summit, I began to relax and enjoy the skiing and the view. The last hour of sunlight, which illuminated the fjord so brilliantly, immersed the whole mountain in an orange glow, as we put the last touches on an unforgettable ski day.

That night, clouds blew in, and by morning it was snowing lightly. The lifts officially open at 1 p.m., but at 4:30, when I arrived at the base of the mountain, they were still idle.

I greeted Johnny, the lift operator, and asked, "What's the matter? Is the lift broken?"

"No," he replied with a groan, "You're our first skier of the day. No idea for me to waste electricity, you know. But I'll warn you right now—I'm not staying here all day if you're our only guest!"

I AM NOT ACCUSTOMED TO HOPING that the pistes will get more crowded, but in this case, I had to make an exception. I gave a silent cheer for each new skier who arrived that afternoon. By six o'clock, four more skiers had joined me. Five guests satisfied Johnny and he kept the T-bars in operation for the entire evening. (Ketil reports that the operation has become

more professional since my visit, and the lifts will keep to their operating timetable even if *nobody* is skiing!)

I skied perfectly groomed pistes until hunger struck and I met Ketil for a pizza. After dinner, he asked if I had touring equipment, and I answered in the affirmative.

"Good. I'll pick you up at ten tomorrow morning," he said. "I have a little surprise for you." Almost as an afterthought, he added with a wink, "Get a good night's sleep," and then he left.

I wondered during breakfast what kind of surprise Ketil could possibly still have in store for me after a stay that had already offered a whole series of revelations. I did not have to ponder for too long. Soon, Ketil and a platoon of his band of demented, balls-to-the-wall disciples arrived for me. I could see in their deranged grins that some sort of hair-raising happening awaited us.

I hopped in the car, and we drove 48 kilometers to nearby Skjomen Fjord. They all began to attach their skins under their telemark skis, and I got my touring skis ready for action. We then began a 4-hour ascent from the fjord to the top of Gangnesaksla (1318 m).

To say that the hike took 4 hours is not quite accurate. It took me 4 hours, while Ketil and most of his merry men made it in 3 hours. Then, there was Lars Thomas Nordkild, one of the locals who hikes the 900 vertical meters in Narvik in less than an hour. He sometimes hikes that route three times a day just for fun, because he doesn't feel the skiing alone gives him enough exercise. I don't know what Lars Thomas's hiking time was, but suffice it to say that he started well behind me, passed me by early on and was probably back in Narvik doing an afternoon hike before I sat down to lunch.

The summit of Gangnesaksla was completely flat, and my anticipation built as we took in a little nourishment before our descent. After eating, we glided slowly across the horizontal landscape until I found myself suddenly looking straight down a 1200-vertical-meter ribbon of snow that ended in a huge pile of avalanche rubble where the mountain met the fjord. My skis were perched precariously on the edge of the abyss, with only the questionable strength of the cornice keeping me from dropping involuntarily into the chute. I backed up.

The corridor was shaped like a funnel, narrowing to 4 or 5 meters approximately halfway down. It had an average gradient of 35–40 degrees and was flanked by snow-covered rocks on the right and a sheer granite wall on the left. The granite was spectacularly decorated by an imposing frozen waterfall. Way below, the reflection of the dark, murky sky turned the fjord an ominous midnight blue.

Ketil jumped in first. The landing was firm and the avalanche danger seemed minimal. He dug a hole to get a snow profile anyway, just to be on the safe side. The profile verified the lack of danger, and soon, we were hopping around like kangaroos.

The avalanche, which had cleared all of the soft snow out of the gully a few days earlier, left a very hard layer of snow for us to ski. Therefore, we worked our way down in sets of tight jump turns to keep our speed to a minimum. The edges gripped nicely, and I could once again immerse myself in this stunning nature experience.

Between the black sea below and the wall of rock above, I felt like a dwarf. I almost expected Grieg's "Hall of the Mountain King" to begin echoing among the cliffs. It did not. Instead, the sound of scraping ski edges biting into the hard surface provided the soundtrack to this unforgettable run. The day concluded with an arduous walk along the shoreline back to the car and celebratory steaks for the famished group.

That night, I sat in front of my laptop and pondered the paradoxical nature of my occupation. My peculiar profession at times entails reporting honestly about an obscure paradise like Narvik. In so doing, I bring a degree of publicity to the location, and in the process, I sometimes advance the destruction of the very qualities of tranquility and solitude that make that location special.

I thought about Einar and Lars Thomas and the others who so kindly guided me around to their favorite powder stashes, knowing full well that I would reveal their secrets in print. They are generous, friendly people, and it is in their nature to share.

I imagined the usual chain reaction. My article would bring a number of new tourists and a handful of other ski writers and photographers to Narvik. They would publish their material. The following season, there would be still more skiers, and the snowball would continue to roll. Would I return here sometime in the future to find this heretofore undiscovered skiers' utopia overrun by tourists? I shuddered.

Maybe, it would not happen that way. After all, Narvik is so remote. Perhaps, only a few curious adventurers and powder fanatics will be added to the list of ski patrons. Maybe, the non-commercial grassroots charm of this ski area and the spontaneous friendliness of its inhabitants will remain unaffected. Anyway, it is my job to write about my ski experiences. I began to work the keyboard with mixed emotions. I felt like one feels when writing a private, personal diary—compelled to put down the truth but hoping that nobody will read it.

EASTER IN OPPDAL

Norway's small towns and villages are steeped in religious tradition. Picturesque wooden churches are the focal point of fishing and farming villages that are spread out through the wild terrain of this long, narrow Scandinavian land. In keeping with their Lutheran heritage, the Norwegian people have always held a particular reverence for Easter.

There is, however, much more to Easter in Norway than religion. These Norsemen, who must endure a long, cold, dark winter, are great sun worshipers, and Easter falls at that time of year when winter is passé, spring is in the air, and the people are full of the joy and anticipation of the summer to come. By Easter time, the sky above Oppdal is still light well past 9 p.m., and the Norwegians are looking forward to the long summer nights when it never gets completely dark.

Now, they can begin to stock up on the sunshine they have missed for the past half-year. It is a time when winter truly meets summer with a short, fond caress, and the local people embrace this holiday week with the exultation and celebration more often reserved for some pagan sun god than with the religious fervor usually associated with one of Christianity's high holy days. The Norwegians' love of the mountains and skiing and their yearning for the long, warm days of summer converge during the Easter vacation in a burst of energy.

Anders Karlsson, Jonas Nilsson, Ken Jensen and I went to experience

this annual spring metamorphosis at the little Norwegian ski town of Oppdal, arriving the Thursday before Easter. Our host was Per Erik Gulliksen, who had been born on his grandfather's farm, smack dab in the middle of the pistes here. I suspect that his mother must have had rather a lot of pain giving birth, as Per Erik indubitably had his telemark skis strapped onto his little feet as he emerged from the womb.

AS WE BEGAN TO UNPACK OUR JEEP upon our arrival in Oppdal, I thought we had packed all the necessary equipment—skis, poles, boots, goggles, sunglasses, ski clothes, backpacks, etc., but I soon became aware that there had been a major omission in our organization.

Per Erik called my attention to my error when he asked simply, "Where's the beer?"

The religious roots in Norway run deep, and the state-owned Vinmonopolet (liquor monopoly) has its doors shut for five consecutive days surrounding Easter. In addition, the high Norwegian tax on spirits makes the cost of a mixed drink in a pub or restaurant here prohibitively expensive. Hence, the Norwegians arrive for such a holiday weekend well stocked with a supply of alcohol from home. We remained unperturbed. We came here to ski, and we were well equipped for that purpose at least.

Per Erik's grandfather had owned much of the land that makes up the Oppdal ski area and had helped with the development of Oppdal for the purpose of skiing. In 1952, he had played an instrumental role in the building of one of Norway's first lifts. It is not strange, therefore, that Per Erik knew every stone, tree and cornice on these mountains. Fortunately, he was happy to share his knowledge with us.

The ski area stretches out over a huge expanse of mountain, approximately 20 kilometers wide. The terrain around Oppdal is typical of most of the Norwegian *fjäll*—ancient, rounded mountains, often rather flat near the tops, and gradually getting steeper on the lower slopes. The snow-laden *fjäll* are bare of vegetation down to an altitude of about 900 meters, at which point they begin to become populated with birch forests. The great breadth of the ski system in Oppdal lends itself well to off-piste skiing, for one can easily access a large area by cutting across the flat tops.

Per Erik began by guiding us around the pistes for a few hours. There

supposedly were 7000 skiers and boarders in Oppdal for Easter, but one hardly noticed them on the pistes. All weekend long, queues were virtually nonexistent among the sixteen lifts. Easter in Oppdal seemed to be about sun, sex and rock-'n'-roll immersed in a solution of beer and booze, with snowsports taking a distinctive back seat and Jesus nowhere in sight.

A LARGE CONGREGATION OF PEOPLE spent most of the day listening to a live band at Ådalen, a valley in the middle of the lift system. Others sat or lay in the sun in small groups all over the landscape, while some people had built small half-igloos, where they sat lazily for a good part of the day with a book and a large thermos of coffee.

At one o'clock, weather permitting, large snow cats embark from two spots on the mountain and use long ropes to pull visitors up to the very top of Blåøret (1605 m), about 300 vertical meters above the highest point in the lift system. This 15-minute ride left us gazing out over vast expanses of pristine corn snow.

We followed Per Erik over the gently rolling terrain. I felt like Fred Astaire in his best tap-dancing shoes, with the largest dance floor in the world under my feet. Anders headed down in wide swoops on his carving skis.

> » I felt like Fred Astaire in his best tap-dancing shoes, with the largest dance floor in the world under my feet.«

Jonas seemed to be counting turns as he linked tight arcs together to see how many he could grind out before lactic acid would get the upper hand. Finally, the two Norwegians, Per Erik and Ken, gleefully cruised on their telemark skis.

Per Erik led us into a little valley known as Isfossen, where he knew that a huge overhanging cornice, a picturesque frozen waterfall and a fistful of extremely steep turns awaited us, before the terrain once again mellowed out. Per Erik and Jonas performed masterful jumps out from the cornice, while the rest of us demurred and chose a somewhat easier route.

I have seen some happening après-ski bars in my day, but none of them could top the revelry at the Rockoss Pub during this Easter weekend. It was packed to the rafters by the time the band started playing, and most

of the people were standing on the tables and benches singing and swaying. The beer flowed hard and heavy, but nobody could fall on their face as long as they stood amongst the shoulder-to-shoulder wall of people in the Rockoss.

The party finally began to wane when the band packed it in at about 7:30 p.m. It was now that our failure to come here with a trunk load of six-packs came into play. The Norwegian way to party is to spend a few hours at a *vorspiel* or BYOB (bring your own booze) pre-party. From there, the drinking moves to one of the discos or clubs from about eleven o'clock until two or three in the morning. Finally, everybody finishes the evening at a BYOB *nachspiel* or post-party.

We met back at the hotel for a shower and a quick meal. Eating does not seem to be as high a priority as drinking at the Norwegian Easter festivities. I made no protestations, for after all, who am I to say what actually was consumed at the Last Supper. Anyway, when in Norway, do as the Norwegians do.

We devoured a plateful of spaghetti and meat sauce and then proceeded to a *vorspiel* organized by some of Per Erik's friends. It took place in a very special traditional building called a *gamme*—a large, round, wooden structure with a roof that slopes upward to a point in the middle, similar to the shape of a circus tent. We had to walk for 15 minutes through heavy slush to get to the *gamme*, but it was worthwhile. We dried out our feet by the fire roaring in the center of the building, and we warmed our insides thoroughly with a form of potato moonshine mixed with hot coffee, which the locals call *karsk*.

The *vorspiel* itself was enough to lay less practiced drinkers under the table, and indeed, I am quite sure that a number of the participants never completed stage two of the evening's activities. The heartier of the revelers continued to one of Oppdal's nightspots such as the Hotel Nor, the George Pub or even the more laid-back bar at the Hotel Sletvold.

WE FINALLY MANAGED to drag ourselves homeward around 3 a.m., skipping whatever some private *nachspiel* might have had to offer in deference to getting at least half our quota of sleep and a reasonably early start the following morning.

At Per Erik's suggestion, we began the next day by leaving one of our cars at a pickup point a few kilometers past Stølen, the easternmost part of the lift system. From the top of Aurhøa (1280 m), we pushed our way across a mountain called Kinnpiken. After a 10-minute walk, the plateau

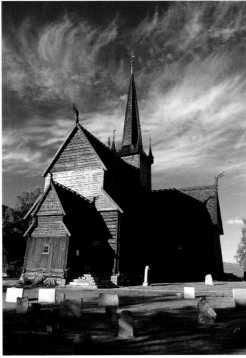

abruptly ceased, and a moderately steep valley of untouched corn snow lay before us.

There are many acres of unpisted territory in Oppdal, but there is a definite difference between the wide areas of open terrain that lie between the pistes and the territory that stretches out beyond the perimeter of the ski area proper. The inner areas had been skied regularly, while the slopes beyond the lifts were almost devoid of tracks, even though there had been no recent snowfall.

Similar to our run from Blåøret the day before, we could sweep down Kinnpiken in an uninhibited fashion, as the open slopes allowed us total freedom of movement—that is, until we reached the tree line.

The last part of each off-piste run in Oppdal is a birch slalom that necessitates precision. To make the process all the more challenging, the snow on these lower slopes was deep spring slush, rendering concisely cut turns close to impossible. At one point, an inexact change of direction among the tightly set trees almost left my manhood impaled upon a passing branch. I slowed my pace, intensified my focus, and negotiated the rest of the birches without calamity.

WE CONTINUED TO CAVORT IN THE CORN on runs called Vestsida (West Side) and Flesklia, and repeated our snow-cat rope tow up to Blåøret. From the top, our host pointed to a mountain across the valley called Almannberget.

"We could hike up there tomorrow, or perhaps organize a few friends with snowmobiles to take us up and ski the north side. It has some really nice descents," said Per Erik.

I gazed across the valley at Almannberget, which did not, by any stretch of the imagination, resemble the smooth, rounded *fjäll* upon which the lift system was built. In fact, it was a face of granite with but a few threads of snow nestled into some ominous-looking couloirs on the north face.

My retort lacked enthusiasm, to which Per Erik replied, "They are not as bad as they look. They're only about 45 degrees, and we could start with the short one on the left. It's much easier than the one under the radio mast, at least once you clear the cornice."

I pondered Per Erik's reckless abandon as he had fearlessly thrust himself out over cornices the day before, and I was not sure that his definition of "easy" was the equivalent of my own. I suggested cautiously that we wait and see what the weather would be like the following day.

By the next morning, Per Erik had fallen victim to the Norwegian Easter malady known as the hangover, so we began to reconnoiter and explore on our own. We decided to try a few runs even further west than the day before. We did laps in corn snow, each time hitchhiking back to the lifts. After our first run, we passed the church on our way back, and the parking lot was quite full of cars—many more than in the lot by the ski lift. Still, most people seemed to be "celebrating" Easter Sunday in bed.

WE GLIDED BACK TO THE ROAD after our final run, quite satisfied with our day's activity, and a local couple picked us up. They asked what we were doing with full ski gear in the middle of nowhere, and we explained that we had been skiing off-piste.

"Oh, if you like off-piste, you should perhaps try the couloirs on the other side," said our driver, and he pointed at Almannberget. "One of our friends did the 'Radio Antenna Couloir' on telemark skis yesterday and said it was excellent."

I had almost forgotten the narrow chutes that Per Erik had pointed out the day before, and I had quite frankly written the idea off as the delusional idea of a lunatic. Having Per Erik's suggestion corroborated by an independent source kindled my curiosity. As we packed the skis onto our car and got ready to leave Oppdal, I pulled out my zoom lens and focused on the main couloir. The chutes still looked quite daunting, but they were indeed skiable.

As I peered through my lens, I traced the route down with my eyes, and it almost hypnotized me. I could imagine myself on some future visit, heart in my throat looking straight down at Oppdal from under the radio mast. Steep couloirs are somewhat of a drug for me, I must admit.

Karl Marx stated, "Religion…is the opium of the people." In Oppdal, many forms of opium could be found in abundance. The fundamentalists had their five days when the alcohol stores were off-limits, and they filled the pews of the picturesque, white, steepled country church on Sunday. The pagan sun-worshipers tanned their bodies and had their official kickoff to the season of light. The hedonists could certainly get their fill of sex, booze and rock-'n'-roll.

As for the pantheists among us, who find God in the many elements of nature—we had, perhaps, the best time of all. The serene rolling *fjäll*, the birch forests, the dramatic cornices and the marvelous corn snow that allowed us to glide through this delightful landscape gave us a religious experience as well. It was an Easter that we would not soon forget.

STRANDA — THE WORLD'S MOST BEAUTIFUL UNKNOWN SKI RESORT

Stranda is not as far north as Narvik, but its location in the fjord country of western Norway makes it every bit as spectacular. My friend Anders Karlsson sat beside me as I guided my Jeep along the serpentine roads of this panoramic landscape in mid-April, en route to check out this little-known spot. Anders sat nervously fidgeting with his safety belt, as my eyes, fascinated by the surrounding scenery, were focused everywhere but on the dotted line. I heard a sigh of relief as we finally pulled safely to a halt at our destination, a village of approximately 3500 people situated on the southern side of 100-kilometer-long Storfjord.

The Stranda ski area is about a 10-minute drive from the village, in a valley called Hevsdalen. At this time of year, as one travels the 450 vertical meters from sea level to the base of the lifts, spring turns into winter in a matter of minutes. We left the green grass along the shoreline, and by the time we passed the last houses at the outskirts of town, the snow was almost a meter deep in people's gardens. A few minutes later, at the base of the lifts, the snow depth was up to two meters, and atop 1230-meter-high Roaldshorn, there was certainly enough white stuff to last weeks into the summer.

Our first morning, Anders and I went down for breakfast in the 75-seat dining room of Stranda's only hotel and sat alone. We were Stranda Hotel's sole guests. A huge Norwegian smorgasbord was laid out for us, including five kinds of herring filets, mackerel, smoked trout, caviar, liver paté, ham, three kinds of salamis, various cheeses and cereals, hard boiled eggs with shrimps and mayonnaise, and numerous yogurts and juices.

A few minutes later, we were met at the hotel by my friend, Thomas Heisig, a German expatriate from Garmisch-Partenkirchen. Thomas had discovered this little corner of the world a few years earlier, immigrated to Norway and never looked back. It was on Thomas's recommendation that we now found ourselves in Stranda, and he would be our guide here.

STRANDA MAY WELL BE the most beautiful spot you have never skied, with the most spectacular views and vistas you have never seen. In fact, almost nobody has ever skied in Stranda with the exception of the local inhabitants and a small following of skiers from some of the "major metropolises" of western Norway such as Ålesund, Sykkylven, Hellesylt and Liabygda.

Thomas Heisig enjoys the view while skiing off-piste on the Roaldshorn.

Skiing came to Stranda way back in 1957, in the form of one of Norway's first lifts, powered by a four-speed Volkswagen Beetle 1200 engine. Nevertheless, Stranda's remoteness has guarantied its obscurity even well over 40 years after that first lift was put into place.

In spite of its astounding beauty, so few people ski in Stranda that the ski center is only fully open on weekends and holidays. In addition to that, a couple of lifts open a few evenings a week under floodlights, and one lift is put into service twice a week for a few hours to accommodate the high school physical education classes. It is a classic example of a locals' ski area—a small lift system that caters to the skiing needs of a regional constituency rather than fitting into the habits of tourists and travelers.

There is, however, an addendum to the normal operating hours, according to Gutthorn Wundgraben, the mountain manager. "If there is a group who wants to ski when we are ordinarily closed, they must only contact me the day before, and we will try to accommodate them. If the group is too small to justify opening the lifts, perhaps we will take them up the mountain a few times with the snow cat, but we try to satisfy all our guests."

I must admit that I was somewhat leery as to the efficiency of this system, but my curiosity to see how this concept functioned in practice would

have to wait. It was Easter Monday, and all four lifts were in full swing.

We spent most of the day riding to the top of Roaldshorn and diving into a large off-piste bowl called Blådalen (Blue Valley). The bowl has a southerly exposure, and at this time of year, that translates into corn snow. The mountains in much of Norway are old, rounded and rather flat peaks, with gentle, rolling slopes. This is not so in the fjordlands of the west. The terrain in Stranda has enough steeps to keep any good rider interested, and Blådalen was no exception. The upper slopes were about 35 degrees, and we started spraying corn snow in all directions like buckshot on the opening day of hunting season.

A little more than halfway down, the slope began to mellow out, and we were glad it did, for that was the level of the tree line. The birches provided a challenging slalom on the lower mountain, but Thomas seemed to know every glen in the woods and we just followed.

STRANDA'S SKI MAP WAS A JOKE! The Roaldshorn side of the ski area showed one black, two red, one blue and two green (very easy) runs. It was clear that the creator of this fiction was either unintelligent or colorblind. There was nothing on this mountain that even vaguely resembled a green piste.

Mr. Wundgraben gave a slightly different explanation. "Yes, it is a problem," he said succinctly, "but we cannot call all the runs black or nobody would come here."

I must admit that I admired his logic. In fact, the Roaldshorn has a few black and a few red runs, but at least 75 percent of the mountain is one great off-piste bonanza. We had so far only seen the tip of the iceberg.

Thomas now led us around to the back side of the mountain, where an enormous expanse of snow-clad territory lay before us. It was our second big smorgasbord of the day. We dropped off a cornice into a steep, shady bowl, with the fjord looming ever closer in front of us. The descent known as Alperittløypa took us 5 kilometers and 1000 vertical meters down to the village, where we finished the run by skiing through the backyard of somebody's home onto one of the residential streets of Stranda.

THE NIGHTLIFE IN STRANDA is as unimpressive as the skiing is memorable. Actually, nonexistent is a better description than unimpressive. Even in the evening, Mother Nature provided the best of the nocturnal entertainment with a rose-colored sunset to light up the mountains and fjord. It is advisable to bring a deck of cards or a lover if you want any entertainment after the lifts close in Stranda. We had neither, so we got an early night's sleep.

Mountain manager Gutthorn Wundgraben was true to his word. For the next couple of days, the mountain was literally ours—four lifts for three skiers! Of course, we had to pitch in and help a bit. I carried a 20-liter can of diesel halfway up the

» We cannot call all the runs black, or nobody would come here.«

Roaldshorn to start the upper lift. We also went through a crash course in pushing the correct buttons to turn off the various lifts after we had finished skiing that part of the mountain. It was tough work but we sacrificed ourselves! (This visit to Stranda took place a few years ago. The tourist office reports that today there is a higher quota of people necessary for the lift company to run lifts outside its published operating hours.)

We began our second day by exploring the Langdalsegga side of the road. Stranda has a tremendous amount of variety for such a small ski area, and we skied various north faces up-valley from the lifts. Then we took a long, steep run all the way to the road, where we began to cross-country ski the few kilometers back to the lifts.

Fifteen minutes passed, and a man appeared in view a few hundred meters ahead. As we neared, he greeted us.

"Are you the journalists?" queried Nils Saetre. When we gave a surprised affirmative nod, he continued, "I'm from the local newspaper, and wonder if I might be allowed to take a few photos of you and interview you, when you have time. You see, this is real news for a little place like Stranda that a ski journalist would come from abroad to visit us."

I had to chuckle at the paradox of a journalist being news, and we agreed to meet him later. We headed back up the Langdalsegga and

THIS PAGE
LEFT: Since we were the only skiers on the mountain that morning, the Stranda mountain manager gave us the responsibility to turn off the lifts after we were finished skiing.
RIGHT: Anders and I enjoy a solitary après-ski, sitting alone in the ski center parking lot near Stranda.

RIGHT PAGE
Many skiers at Stryn's Summer Ski Center try their luck at water-skiing when the opportunity arises.

began a series of runs down the wide fields of snow on the west face toward the pizza factory, one of Stranda's main industries. There were no tracks, the slope was gentle and the corn snow was ripe to perfection. Our turns emerged effortlessly as if our skis were self-propelled. It was like scraping a butter knife over a cube of margarine. No thought, no force and no energy were required. I churned out close to 300 turns, and I don't believe I burned a calorie.

VIRGIN CORN SNOW, LIKE POWDER, is a precious commodity for a skier. One often feels stressed and rushes to get a couple of runs in the untouched snow before the masses come and decimate the slope. Stress and Stranda begin with the same two letters, but that is where the similarity ends. Ultimate calm and harmony describe the feeling of skiing a virgin slope knowing that you are the only skiers on the mountain. Nobody was going to disturb the purity of that snow until it came time for us to carve our next line a few meters to the right or left of our previous tracks.

What is a ski day without an après-ski? We were prepared for that as well. We pulled a few beers out of the trunk of the car, plopped ourselves down in front of the closed rental shop and enjoyed the afternoon sun. Our view was of the empty parking lot and the Langdalsegga side of our private ski resort. We took our skis off at 6:30 p.m., one of my longest ski days ever, and headed back to the hotel to meet the reporter for the interview.

Shortly after returning home, I received in the mail a copy of the April 29 edition of the *Sunnmøringen*, the twelve-page newspaper that is published in Stranda twice a week. Anders and I smiled out of the front page. The headline stated, "American Journalist Has No Doubts: Hevsdalen is World Class". I read on in the sub-heading that "Hevsdalen actually has the world's most beautiful off-piste run."

Now, I don't usually believe everything I read in the newspaper, and I am prone to regard small regional journals as a propaganda arm of local chambers of commerce. In passing judgment on what one reads, however, one should always consider the source. In this case, I am rather well acquainted with the American journalist in question, and I believe him to be indisputably well-qualified to make such a statement.

Everyone, however, must be his or her own judge, for beauty is in the eye of the beholder. Make a trip to Stranda and see for yourself. Maybe, the most beautiful ski resort you have never seen will become the most beautiful resort you have ever seen. And perhaps the next time I'm in Stranda I may have to share the corn snow with a few more skiers, but then again, the après-ski is bound to be a little more exciting too.

STRYN — FOR THOSE WHO JUST CAN´T GET ENOUGH

Many skiers and snowboarders are also windsurfers, golfers, mountain bikers, tennis players or sailors. In other words, there exist snowsports enthusiasts who are normal people. They are happy to live in a world with four seasons, and they enjoy lying on the beach and relaxing during the summer months. Basically, these are people who have a life beyond snow.

Then there are those among us who go kicking and screaming into the spring, fighting tooth and nail against nature's inevitable metamorphosis from white to green. *They* are the true fanatics of the slopes—the riders who have no adrenaline substitute for the thrill of sending billows of powder dust skyward or setting a crisp line of corn kernels into motion, cascading down some steep pitch. These psychological cripples cringe at the thought of letting their skis or board gather dust in some dingy cellar for eight months without seeing the light of day. These are the true snow freaks who just can't get enough, and it is to these addicts that Stryn offers salvation.

LIKE ALL ADDICTIONS, SNOWSPORTS ARE NOT cheap, and if your dependency is so great that the mere thought of a full summer without the white stuff has you clawing the walls, you are burdened with a very expensive habit. The snowfields of South America, Australia and New Zealand are not cheap to get to from the Northern Hemisphere. The alternative is to head to one of the glaciers in the Alps, but many of them are not steep enough to give an adrenaline rush to a rank beginner. Are there other options?

My friend Jonas Nilsson is a ski junkie. His skis were hardly dry after his Alpine season ended in early May, when he called me.

His voice betrayed urgency, and he initiated our conversation with, "I gotta go skiing! You wanna join me?"

It was mid-May, and as a fellow addict, I was two to three weeks into withdrawal myself and open to any and all suggestions.

"What do you think about the *Midsommar* weekend in Stryn?" Jonas queried imploringly.

I quickly agreed and all was settled but the waiting. After all, the summer solstice, which is always celebrated with great reverence in the Nordic countries, was still five weeks away. We survived the long interim of abstinence, and by departure time our ranks had grown with the addition of Carl and Marcus, two similarly dependent snowboarders, and Ken, a diehard telemark skier.

Stryn is not only a lot closer and cheaper to get to than Argentina for those living in Europe, but at less than $10 per person to cram us into a 16-square-meter cabin at Strynsvatn Camping, the accommodation was not about to break anybody's bankroll.

Situated in the fjord country of western Norway between Bergen and Trondheim, Stryn is a sleepy little village near the end of Nordfjord. It is set in the midst of a stunning landscape of dark, murky fjords, emerald green lakes, hanging glaciers, perpendicular granite precipices, and more waterfalls than the average person sees in a lifetime. The raw, naked beauty in this region makes the area a cinch candidate for *National Geographic* playmate of the year. To top it all off, just 40 minutes from the village is the summer solution for snow junkies—Stryn Summer Ski Center.

The two lifts on the Tystig Glacier open in early June, shortly after most traditional ski resorts close up shop for the season, and they offer medicinal help for hooked snow addicts through August. Green transformed to white as we drove east from Stryn, and by the time we reached the lifts, the embankment of snow along the road dwarfed the parked cars.

Mogul fields on either side of the lifts were being carved up by many of the best telemark skiers I had ever seen. Some of them proved to be the national telemark team in training, but many others were ordinary Norwegian skiers. I could hardly tell the difference. In Norway, even the average Olav telemarks like he was born on these loosely attached boards.

The snowboarders looked like they were also in seventh heaven, with a huge halfpipe on the east side of the lift and a jump that gave monster air to the west. Near the middle station was an icy, light-green pool of glacial meltwater, which enticed boarders and skiers alike to try to aqua-plane over the surface, while lunch visitors and sunbathers at the nearby Glacier Cafe applauded and laughed at the ongoing show.

Any doubts we had about the quality of skiing in Stryn were quickly alleviated. While one has to be careful of crevasses here, as on any glacier, the cracks do very little to inhibit the off-piste possibilities in Stryn. There is, in fact, perhaps more danger from some of the steep slopes and exposed rocks than from the crevasses.

We wasted no time in getting ourselves acquainted with the area. One quick warmup in the moguls had us ready for some off-piste adventures, and Stryn offers an abundance of them, including routes known as the Edge (Egga), Speedski, Guts (Tarmen), Mannefallet, Lada, Videseter and the Short and Long Backside.

Much of the off-piste skiing in Stryn consists of traversing and walking out to the east of the upper lift and eventually finding a route down between the rocks. It is important to check and analyze, from below, where one intends to ski, carefully noting landmarks that will make the

Tarmen, perhaps the steepest skiing that Stryn has to offer. The gradient increases the further down one skis, and the convex nature of the slope obscures the lower portion of the run. Looking down, one can discern virtually nothing between one's skis and the creek snaking along in the flats at the base of the mountain.

Halfway down, we ran into a group of Finns who had evidently failed to do the mandatory preliminary reconnaissance work. Ola Eriksson was the lead skier of the Finnish entourage, and he cut left where an outcrop divided the slope into two passages. Bad choice!

Ola shouted for us to go the other way, and stood now literally between a rock and a hard place. The snow had virtually ended above some rocks and cliffs, save for a meter-wide, diagonal passage of white that extended about 30 meters to the left, reconnecting with the slope after threading between the cliffs both above and below him. Ola was standing on the steepest part of Tarmen, faced with a very unenviable choice. One possibility was to take off his skis at this precarious point and walk back up the 40-degree slope, a task that would be somewhat dangerous and quite arduous. His alternate option was to try and thread the needle with an angled, edged schuss, a choice which was almost suicidal, albeit not the least bit strenuous.

I thought the choice was a no-brainer and perhaps it was, but Ola turned in the opposite direction than I had expected.

"Oh my God!" I gasped.

This looked like Russian roulette with five bullets and only one chamber empty. Before I had time to think any more, and certainly before Ola had had time to think, he was standing coolly on the opposite side awaiting the rest of us.

Even the correct route was hair-raising. We cut numerous turns above the cliffs, sending millions of marbles of ice careening down over the rocks. A poorly negotiated turn here would have been like a jump into a meat grinder. The snow, however, was excellent. The surface was smooth and totally virgin. Typical of summer snow, the surface was also somewhat slow, allowing us to keep our speed well in check, even on such a steep pitch. By the time we were back on the lift, everyone's adrenaline supply had been replenished, and we felt justified to take a pause to watch the fun by the pond of meltwater.

FOLLOWING OUR DAY OF SKIING, it was just as exhilarating to drive from winter back into summer as it had been to do the converse earlier in the day. The contrast of the two seasons bordered on the surreal. The dramatic, snow-covered peaks were mirrored in the turquoise water of the lake by our cabin, and the hills and meadows were awash in the rich, warm green of June.

That evening, we went into town to check out the nightlife, which consists of a cozy pub called Base Camp and a disco under the Stryn Hotel. It was at Base Camp, over some billiards and beer, that I met Thomas Heisig for the first time. Thomas lived in Stryn and knew the nearby backcountry better than anybody. Before the evening was over, he promised to guide us around the next day and to show us a little something special.

As we had spent most of the previous day skiing east of the lifts, Thomas took us around the western side of Strynfjellet. We began with a run down the Edge, probably Stryn's most skied off-piste run. Soon, Thomas led us just a few steps over the summit, where we entered a *long* off-piste run ironically named Short Backside. As with much of the skiing the day before, this descent begins with a long, rather flat section. Just as one is being lulled into a sense of false security, the bottom drops out. The run steepens dramatically and offers various paths between the rocks that all end up on the road, a short walk from the ski center. We enjoyed a few variations of the Short and Long Backside, before Thomas decided that we were ready for the day's *coup de grâce*.

Thomas asked me to follow him in my car, and we drove about 40 minutes toward the famous Geirangerfjord. We wound down a series of hairpin curves toward the spectacular 100-kilometer-long fjord until Thomas stopped and instructed me to park. Then we all drove back up the moun-

descent easy to find from above. Sometimes that proved to be easier said than done.

THE TRAVERSE ACROSS THE TOP of the mountain is followed by a flat plateau from where one can see various openings between the rocks, with very little clue of what lies beyond. It is often only once one has passed the point of no return that the nature of the descent reveals itself in its entirety, and many of the routes are definitely not for the faint of heart. Some descents are narrow, exposed, and 35–40 degrees steep in places. In addition, early morning corn snow after a cold night is not the easiest condition in which to quickly arrest a slide following a fall.

We first tried Speedski, a rather wide route with small moguls. Now we were ready for some of the steeper fare, and we opted for

THIS PAGE
LEFT: The Seven Sisters Waterfall pours into Geirangerfjord.
MIDDLE: Thomas Heisig cools off in the spray of the Briksdal Waterfall.
RIGHT: While skiing the descent from Dalsnibba, Kristin Sandven skis past a waterfall.

RIGHT PAGE
In western Norway, there is another spectacular view around every corner. This view is from Strynsvatn, between the town of Stryn and the ski center.

tain in his car, ending at Dalsnibba (1500 m), a scenic lookout point with magnificent views of the fjord and its surroundings. We took in the panorama from the edge of a cliff, wondering what on Earth our new friend had in store for us.

Soon, Thomas slung his boards onto his shoulder and led us over to a north face of white. The spring snow shimmered in the afternoon sun. What followed was about 1000 vertical meters of the most visually spectacular skiing of anyone's life. I tried to concentrate on the skiing, but I could not take my eyes off the scenery.

A huge cruise ship pulled into the end of Geirangerfjord far below and was slowly coming about. To the left we could see the many bends of the serpentine road we had just ascended. Halfway down to the right were a dark mountain lake and a waterfall.

We had to get our minds back on the skiing, for the route was becoming increasingly difficult the further down we skied. Our path steepened and narrowed as we passed between some rocks.

Thomas told us to wait, took off his skis and proceeded to the edge of a cliff to scout the next section of the run. We all followed him across 60 or 70 meters of grass and moss, until we remounted our boards atop a steep avalanche gully. Our route had swung around to the west, exposing it to more sunlight, and the ravine we were skiing was flanked by green on both sides. Far below, my car looked like a toy. The roar of water could be heard, and suddenly, we passed right next to a large waterfall, spewing out meltwater at full force.

ALL TOO SOON, OUR MAGIC RIDE from winter into summer was over. We ran out of snow entirely and walked the last 5 minutes to the car. We then continued down the road, further and further into summer, until we arrived in the little village of Geiranger itself.

During the summer, Norway's long days allow people to pack a whole week of activities into a long weekend, and we did just that. For the next few days, we combined our skiing with a sightseeing boat ride in Geirangerfjord, a few games of beach volleyball at the campground, a short swim in the icy waters of Strynsvatn and a short hike to the Briksdal Glacier.

It is with good reason that Geiranger is the most visited spot in Norway. Waterfalls abound around every bend of the cruise, climaxed by the famous Seven Sisters group. The tour guide pointed out unbelievable farms situated on narrow ledges hundreds of meters straight up from the water. In some cases, when these farms were active in the first half of the 1900s, families had to keep both animals and children on carefully measured leashes to keep them from falling to their deaths.

Prior to this visit, I never realized how many different colors water has. Oh? Water has no color you say. Perhaps not when it comes out of your kitchen tap in San Francisco, London or Copenhagen, but in western Norway, the colors of water are almost infinite. The fjord water ranges among shades of black, navy-blue and forest green. The lakes display every possible hue between blue and green, changing from moment to moment as the sun plays hide-and-go-seek with the cumulus clouds. We even saw many nuances of white water among the many waterfalls and rushing streams.

In the end, Stryn turned out to be not only a reprieve for snow addicts from the blight of summer, but also a possible salvation from their helpless dependency. Here, where snow enthusiasts can combine a ski holiday with a variety of outdoor summer activities and a sightseeing experience nonpareil, snow junkies can go through detox. In this rarest of locations, where winter lives parallel to summer in the most beautiful of settings, addicts can slowly wean themselves off skiing and boarding, gradually replacing snow with the kind of summer experiences that enrich the lives of normal people.

Or might it, God forbid, turn out contrarily? Is Stryn the devil's playground, where snow mainliners will introduce their habit-forming sports to unsuspecting tourists coming here for a simple dose of Norwegian landscapes? Might evil, incorrigible ski maniacs and board freaks tempt innocent children away from their parents during a fishing, biking or boating holiday, and lure them onto the exciting snowfields of Stryn Ski Center, from where they will never again be able to return to a normal existence?

Only one thing is certain. Whether it is skiing, boarding, spectacular scenery or any one of a dozen summer outdoor activities that gets a person's adrenaline pumping, Stryn is a place where an adrenaline rush becomes a mundane, everyday occurrence.

Chapter 14. SWEDEN

Sweden, like Norway, has a rich tradition in downhill skiing. The old, still functional funicular at Åre provided the first uphill transport for skiers as early as 1910.

Although alpine skiing is rooted so far back in Sweden, it did not begin its heyday until Ingemar Stenmark's enormous success on the World Cup circuit in the 1970s prompted the Swedes to take to the downhill slopes en masse.

The Åre-Duved ski area is still today the best ski resort in Sweden, with over 40 lifts and 880 vertical meters of skiing. Other large ski areas in Sweden include Sälen, Sweden's largest ski center, Funäsdalen and Idre Fjäll. Nevertheless, the best area in Sweden for good skiers, besides

Åre, is the tiny Arctic outpost of Riksgränsen.

This unique ski resort, with only a handful of lifts and less than 500 meters of vertical, has also been providing thrills and spills for skiers since the very early days. Because of its location above the Arctic Circle, Riksgränsen's season covers the unusual period from February to June. As one of the few areas which is open so late in the season, it annually attracts some of the world's top skiers during the late spring, who are attracted by the wide range of off-piste possibilities. In addition, the resort caters to the experts with such arrangements as heliskiing and guided ski tours under the midnight sun.

In Riksgränsen, the spring months offer the possibility of skiing under the golden light of the midnight sun. Here, Peter Sandberg skis down the Nordalsfjell in the middle of May. Photo by Lars Thulin.

RIKSGRÄNSEN — SKIING UNDER THE MIDNIGHT SUN

Årromsadje is a Lapp word that translates as "the land where I want to be and live". There are innumerable spots in Lapland to which this expression could apply, but the small Swedish ski resort of Riksgränsen must certainly be among them. With six ski lifts overlooking lovely Lake Vassijaure as well as a panorama of low-growing birch trees and rounded mountain tops, Riksgränsen is vintage Lapland.

From February, when there is finally enough light for the lift system to open, until April, the slopes are covered with powder snow, and a deep winter landscape reigns. By mid-May, most of the lake is still frozen, the snow has generally transformed into spring corn, and the midnight sun has become a part of daily life.

By the middle of June, dozens of smaller lakes and ponds have begun to appear amidst a patchwork design of earth and snow, while large chunks of ice still drift aimlessly with the wind on the surface of Lake Vassijaure, a reminder of the long, hard winter that was. The season of darkness is now but a memory, the slopes are covered with crystalline summer snow, and the valleys below are in full bloom.

Riksgränsen is virtually on the border with Norway, some 200 kilometers north of the Arctic Circle. It may be much easier to get to Innsbruck or Aspen, but it is Riksgränsen's remoteness and extreme northerly location that give this ski resort its charm and unique beauty. Additionally, its northerly location gives the ski area a high season between the first of May and mid-June, a period of the year in which it has a near-monopoly on snowsports. It is not so strange, therefore, that some of the top skiers and snowboarders in the world converge on this isolated spot during the spring to elongate their season.

It is not only skiers and boarders who have been attracted to the long winter and barren beauty of this sparsely populated part of the world. The unique evening light of springtime, with its warm glow and long shadows, has also attracted a number of photographers through the years. Nature and ski photographer Lars Thulin, extreme skier and ski photographer Jonas Abrahamsson, and nature photographer Arne Eriksson all use Riksgränsen as their base of operations; but the photographic tradition here dates back to 1940, when the late Sven Hörnell settled down here.

FOR MORE THAN HALF a century, the famous Swedish nature photographer made this wilderness outpost his home. Riksgränsen has been a ski resort since the 1930s, but when Sven Hörnell chose this spot as a home base for his photography, he was the first year-round resident. In the ensuing years, while Hörnell took advantage of the isolated nature of his home to capture the solitude of Lapland with his lens, Riksgränsen grew slowly to its present size, now boasting a population of about 40 full-time residents.

Until the mid-1980s, there was not even a road to the ski area, and the only regular transport through here was the train from Kiruna, Sweden to Narvik, across the border in Norway. Despite the building of a highway in 1984, one can still say in all honesty that Riksgränsen lies on the crossroads between nowhere and places even more remote.

My friend Martin Söderqvist and I arrived at Hotel Riksgränsen early one Wednesday evening in late spring. As we disembarked from the bus, the air was filled with the unmistakable aroma of roasting meat. A quick scouting mission revealed three reindeer being roasted in a nearby Lapp

ABOVE: Eva Sjöqvist Wenzer hikes up under Riksgränsen's midnight sun.

tent. There was still an hour until the reindeer would be ready to be carved, so we continued our exploration to Grönan, the hotel bar. There, we soon learned that the indigenous drink in these parts was a Lapp aperitif called a *vargtass* (wolf's paw), a painless but potent concoction of cranberry juice and vodka. A couple of *vargtass* and three portions of reindeer put us in perfect condition for the evening's activity—skiing.

Every Wednesday and Friday, the lifts reopen from 10 p.m. to 12:30 a.m., so that guests can ski under the midnight sun. As we reached the top, I wondered if this magic place might be the first fueling stop for Santa on his annual sojourn south. "Santa might have a bit of difficulty putting together a foursome for bridge," I mused to myself, but Dasher, Dancer and company would certainly not get lonely here where the reindeer far outnumber the people, even in the height of the ski season.

Santa never seemed too far away in this Nordic fairyland, and I am quite sure that I heard his elves frolicking in the many nooks and crannies of the mountainside. As I began my descent, I was almost sure that I saw some small groups of elves dancing, playing and skiing amidst the rocks in the orange light. Yet they were as elusive as the aurora borealis.

Whenever I carved my skis around a rock with my camera lens open, hoping to capture one of these Lapland pygmies on celluloid, they vanished without a trace. I could still hear them murmuring faintly in the distance, not unlike the lapping of the waves of Lake Vassijaure, but there was nothing to be seen. The midnight sun cast its horizontal rays of light on another skier on a ridge in the distance and the lake shimmered below, but the elves had done a Houdini act. Oh well, there was enough of beauty to be photographed here, even if Santa's helpers did not cooperate.

RIKSGRÄNSEN IS A RESORT THAT APPEALS to both intermediate and advanced skiers. There are enough easy runs here to make Riksgränsen a suitable spot for intermediates, but despite its short vertical drop of only 460 meters, it is very popular among expert skiers and boarders.

The absence of trees on the slopes allows for almost unlimited off-piste skiing, as one can descend wherever a passage of snow exists between the rocks. In addition, expert riders will enjoy the steepness of the terrain and the numerous cornices and small cliffs suitable for jumping. The resort is a natural terrain park.

Riders who are very fond of steeps can walk 30 minutes from the summit of the upper chair lift, which will bring them to the top of Nordal's Branten. *Brant* is Swedish for steep, and steep, in this case, means sheer—up to 55 degrees in places, according to the locals. Although I did not bring my protractor up to Nordal's Branten, I will testify that someone who skis with good angulation might be well-advised to wear elbow pads, for he could scrape up his arms here without even falling.

Similar to the conditions in Valdez, Alaska, the proximity of the ocean allows for good stability in the snowpack here, somewhat reducing the risk of avalanche danger on such steep slopes. The lessened danger of slides compared to the Alps does not, however, make a run down Nordal's Branten particularly easy or completely safe. In springtime, the steepest section is interspersed with a number of big chunks of granite, making a fall inadvisable.

While the avalanche risk in the soft spring slush was minimal, sloughs of heavy slush were invariably set into motion the moment that I initiated a turn. This phenomenon, in turn, caused two problems. First of all, as I pushed off the snow to initiate a jump turn, the snow slid away and did not give me the necessary resistance. It felt as if the rug was being pulled out from under me. Secondly, the weight of the snow gliding slow-

LEFT PAGE
Martin Söderqvist enjoys the powder while heliskiing in Riksgränsen.

THIS PAGE
The beautiful light in the spring and summer months have attracted nature photographers to Riksgränsen for many years. Here are two more photos by Lars Thulin, who has spent many years in and around this ski resort.
UPPER: UPPER: Anders Hagman enjoys the midnight sun on Kårsachokka at 2 a.m. on a June morning.
LOWER: Midnight fun in Riksgränsen.

THIS PAGE: Martin Söderqvist skiing above the Hotel Riksgränsen.
RIGHT PAGE: Pelle Lindh heads down a piste toward Åre Lake.

ly downward was more than enough to disturb my balance if I stayed in the same line.

Nevertheless, I battled my way down, happy that nobody was pointing a camera my way to memorialize my style for posterity. At best, my run could be described as survival technique, but I still felt a touch of satisfaction standing amidst the debris of many spring sloughs, looking back up at the sheer face I had just negotiated.

Riksgränsen offers a few other bonuses for experienced riders. From mid-March until early June, heliskiing is available at some of the cheapest rates in the world. A week before our arrival, a group had done eighteen flights and 13,000 vertical meters—and that was heliskiing from 10 a.m. until 5 p.m. Imagine what they could have done if they had wanted ed to make use of the midnight sun! With a rucksack full

»...the lifts reopen from 10 p.m. to 12:30 a.m., so that guests can ski under the midnight sun.«

of Red Bull and a reservation for a full body massage the day after at Riksgränsen's new spa, they might have vied for a place in Guinness's record book.

Martin and I were eager to try the heliskiing, and we were not disappointed. Our guide, Pette Halme, who spends his winters in Verbier, showed us that the springtime here could offer powder on the north slopes and corn snow on the southerly exposures. The terrain was as varied as the snow, including mellow cruising as well as slopes steep enough to get a chamois's adrenaline pumping.

The touring and off-piste possibilities in and around Riksgränsen are limited only by the boundaries of a person's imagination. From the top of the lifts at Riksgränsen's peak, Gatternjunni, one can also ski off-piste all the way down to the sea, a tour organized by the hotel each week, weather permitting.

While the best snow can be found in Riksgränsen in the early part of the season, I would definitely advocate a visit in the late season to enjoy the novelty of night skiing and boarding under natural light. Another lure of a late season visit is the possibility of seeing a lovely blend of winter and spring. While Riksgränsen is still clad in her winter white in June, one can hike down into the green of springtime at the bottom of Rombaksfjord in just a few hours.

Riksgränsen's first resident, Sven Hörnell, has described the spring thus:

Spring in the mountains. Melting water spreads while snow vanishes. Humus and ferric oxide push through crevasses, coloring the ice.

The redwing has arrived and seems never to rest.

The constant light of the Arctic summer night allows a short, but intense, blooming. Purple saxifrage is the first flower of spring.

We have reached that period of the year when the power of the sun increases every day. It is felt much stronger here in the North than further south. There is an explosive development of the nature.

From my window in Riksgränsen, I can see the sun from May 31 to July 15 over the horizon continuously. The light of the night seems warmer, more red, than during the day. Astonishingly, a new day starts without there having been a 'night' before it.

Nature is as much a part of snowsports as the skis or the board. Similarly, the love of nature is as much a part of a rider as his love of cold, fresh powder snow sprinkling his face and caking on his goggles as he tries to negotiate powder turns by radar. A rider can hardly feel any closer to the mountains and the nature that are his home than he can feel amidst the Arctic splendor and the remote tranquility of Riksgränsen.

ÅRE — IT´S ALL ABOUT LIFESTYLE

At the beginning of the last century, Carl-Olaf Rahm visited the Swiss ski resort of Davos, saw the famed Parsenn train, one of the world's first ski lifts, and brought the idea back to his home in the little Swedish village of Åre. Soon after, his concept became a reality. The Åre Bergbanan made its inaugural 193-vertical-meter climb up to Fjällgården, making Rahm's hometown the first ski resort in Scandinavia. At first, it was more about sledding than skiing, as most of Åre's winter visitors used the cogwheel train to access the bobsled run.

It wasn't until Åre hosted the Alpine World Championships in 1954 that skiing really became its claim to fame. Since then, Åre's ascent into a world-class destination for skiers has continued unabated. The development of the nearby village of Duved as a ski area in 1966 was followed by the addition of Åre's 853-vertical-meter cable car ten years later and the construction of dozens of additional lifts in the ensuing years.

Today, Åre continues to grow and develop. At last count there were over 30 bona fide ski lifts and another dozen short tows for beginners. More fame for Sweden's oldest resort is just around the corner, as Åre has been accepted to host the World Championships of Skiing once more, in 2007.

I RECENTLY WENT with a few friends for a late April visit to Sweden's premiere ski resort. The atmosphere was mellow, the slopes were not crowded, and we cruised happily around in the soft corn snow.

Åre, which gets its share of winter powder and can test the hardiness of the toughest skiers with extremely cold temperatures in January, was definitely in the process of shedding its winter white. Åreskutan, the 1430-meter-high peak that is the linchpin of the resort, was a patchwork quilt of snow, rock and earth; and Åresjön, the long, narrow lake at the base of the village, was now only half-frozen.

The weather can change abruptly in Åre, and our spring fever was suddenly doused with a snowstorm. The wind howled and the upper mountain was closed. My friend, Pelle Lindh, and I practiced our slalom technique in the tight birch trees on the lower mountain. We picked our way through a few of the Vinkelrännorna (Angle Gullies). The brief reminder of winter, with 10 centimeters of new snow to soften the pack under our boards, was a pleasant complement to the spring corn that had so far prevailed during our stay.

Then, as quickly as it had come, the storm abated and we awoke to bright sunshine. We got up early and were met by Emil Magnusson, a racer and freeride freak who lives in Åre. Having a local to guide one around is advantageous anywhere, but it is indispensable here.

Åreskutan is one huge rock quarry. The upper mountain appears at first glance to be covered in boulders everywhere, and there do not seem to be any skiable routes through the stony landscape. This is actually not very far from the truth. In fact, the so-called high zone of the mountain ordinarily does not even open until February, because it needs so much snow to make any part of it skiable. Until that time, visitors satisfy themselves by skiing within the lower zone, consisting of the trails that are below the tree line.

Emil met Pelle and me at the top station of the cable car and decided to show us his favorite off-piste descent.

"It starts with a traverse around to the east," explained Emil. "Then after making a few turns, we arrive at Mårtens Brant (Mårten's Steep). Later, we traverse again, descend Östra Ravinen (East Ravine), and end up skiing out in Susabäcken. Most of the off-piste skiing here in Åre," Emil went on to explain, "is made up of a series of rather short lines connected by various traverses. It's necessary because of the rocky terrain. We don't have any top-to-bottom lines on Åreskutan."

AS WE BEGAN OUR FIRST TRAVERSE, around a quarter of the mountain, I did not see one place where we could have linked two turns together. Without guiding, I never would have imagined that if I went far enough around the peak, a skiable slope would appear; but of course, we eventually reached pay dirt.

We skied the first slope, and headed for Mårtens Brant. It could just as well have been named Mårtens cliff as far as I was concerned. The entry was guarded by a huge cornice, which immediately told me that I would choose an alternate route. I am not into descents with mandatory air. Although my choice was appreciably more gentle, my second turn set off a nasty slab avalanche. The fresh snow had definitely not bonded with the previous layer. Slab slides are not at all unusual for Åre, whose upper slopes are very prone to hard winds.

I cautioned Emil, as he stood perched atop a rock face, ready to leap

in. It was like warning Kitzbühel local Tony Sailer to watch out for the infamous Mousetrap on the Hahnenkamm. Emil was not deterred. Emil competes in extreme competitions and this was his home mountain.

"Yeah, it'll probably go," he said calmly.

Then he flew high in the air, started the new snow sliding immediately with his landing and cut hard right to avoid the brunt of the slough.

Enormous cornices hung over the entry of almost every steep section of Åreskutan. These wind-created overhangs seem to mark each local rite of passage like a double-diamond sign would do in North America.

Östra Ravinen was no different. The snow was more stable here on the lower mountain, as it was not as deep and the wind had not been as strong. But even Emil had to admit that the huge cornice atop Östra Ravinen was something to be avoided this late in spring, when the warm weather had weakened the overhang to the extent that the weight of a skier could send a few tons of snow careening into the gully.

This time, we all carefully circumvented the cornice and made an easy entry. The thin layer of new powder over old corn snow made for enjoyable skiing, but the new snow was rather uneven. Wherever the powder was a bit thicker, my upper body lurched forward in a herky-jerky style reminiscent of a teenager making his first attempt at driving with a stick shift.

Susabäcken is the name of a small creek that winds down the mountain at the base of Östra Ravinen, and our trip ended trying to tightrope ski the narrow path that switched from one side of this creek to the other.

SOME OFF-PISTE VENTURES in Åre are attainable by hiking about 30 minutes from the cable car station to the actual peak of the mountain. Emil next led us on one of these routes. The classic run down the back side of the mountain is aptly named Baksidan, but this was obviously too tame for Emil. Instead, Emil once again led us on a traverse/hike around to the east.

Soon, Pelle and I found ourselves looking down an elevator shaft of wind slab. Anyone who wishes to become an expert at skiing wind-packed snow should spend a season in Åre. Taking into consideration the earlier slides, we carefully considered where the safest entry would be. It was not

an easy decision, but Mother Nature solved it for us. Our first few turns on the gentle ridge above created strong enough vibrations to break off another large avalanche on the steep slope below.

Now the pitch was safe, at least from snowslides. From this point onward, "skier slides" became the more worrisome issue. The first slope was not long, but it was around 50 degrees and the snow that remained after the avalanche was very firm. I didn't want to end up in a heap at the bottom of the slope, so I skied very cautiously.

We soon met the Baksidan descent, skied over Lillskutan, and finished our run on some relatively untouched pistes on the far side of the ski area, which was already closed at this late date. The wind-packed snow changed to sun crust, and we finished in some wet powder. Thank God for the invention of wide-bodied, all-terrain skis! A few years ago, this combination of snows would have made for a nightmare day, but with all-terrain skis it was all challenging but quite skiable.

ÅRE'S DEVELOPMENT IN THE TOURIST FIELD has paralleled that of many top ski resorts in the world, which began as spas and summer destinations, and years later came up with skiing as a winter option to try to give their area the advantage of year-round tourism. Lake Louise in Canada, Badgastein in Austria, and Engelberg in Switzerland are but a few of the ski resorts that also fit this profile.

In Åre's case, people started visiting the area in the late 1800s for hunting and fresh air. After 1954, however, Åre suddenly was almost entirely about skiing. Now, however, at the dawning of the new century, the pendulum has swung back in the other direction. Åre again, like many other longtime ski resorts, now has mostly winter guests, and has begun to develop a myriad of off-season activities to inspire summer tourism. In so doing, Sweden's long time ski Mecca is becoming more and more of a place that attracts people in search of a year-round lifestyle alternative to the hustle and bustle of city life.

In the '80s, the whole Western world seemed to be obsessed, even more than usual, with making money. While money making has not exactly gone out of fashion since then, by the mid-'90s, so much currency

LEFT PAGE
Emil Magnusson sprays spring powder into the air high up on Åreskutan.

THIS PAGE
LEFT: The cable car climbs up to Åreskutan high above the town of Åre.
RIGHT: Pelle cruises on the lower slopes of Åre.

had already been accumulated by many individuals that the focus of many people shifted from cash to lifestyle. Åre has for a long time been part of whatever is trendy in Sweden, so it should come as no surprise that this picturesque village would also be part of the new focus on lifestyle.

I had tasted Åre, the ski resort; now I wanted to try Åre, the year-round outdoor activity center. I returned in the autumn with my friend, Karin Edlund. On our first evening, we ended up chatting with the owner of one of the local bars.

"I came here for the skiing, and I stayed for the lifestyle," Frasse Johansson told me succinctly. "Taking over this restaurant is merely a way of allowing me to stay."

The lifestyle that Frasse spoke of and so many people search for is a combination of many factors. It is about a slower pace with less stress in a safe environment, and it is about good people and fresh air. It is also about a variety of healthy, wholesome and often rather adventurous activities—biking, hiking, river rafting, riding and paragliding, to name a few.

KARIN AND I DOVE HEADFIRST into the Åre lifestyle on our first day. We drove about half an hour south to the tiny community of Ottsjö to meet Karl-Erik Duvdahl, who, for many years, has been guiding visitors into the local mountains on Icelandic horses.

We mounted our steeds, and headed out single file behind Karl-Erik on a narrow path through thick forest. Mother Nature was decked out in her most spectacular fall fashions. The leaves still clinging to the birch and aspen trees were various shades of yellow and rust, while a smattering of mountain ash trees added dashes of bright red to the landscape. In the forest, lime-green ferns almost seemed to glow, and thousands of small, white butterflies fluttered merrily amidst the thick foliage.

As we gradually gained elevation, the forest gave way to a few dwarf pines and dwarf birches, and we rode through fields of purple heather and large areas of blueberry bushes with tiny reddened leaves. Without the forest to obstruct our view, a 360-degree panorama unfolded, revealing ancient, rolling mountains as far as the eye could see.

We dismounted and Karl-Erik started to brew some coffee over a small fire. The sun shone down on Ottsjön, the long, narrow body of water below us, turning it into a shimmering surface of silver. Thousands of acres of forests lay before us, with but a few isolated clearings sporting a lonely farmhouse and barn as the only evidence of man's intrusion into this vast wilderness. With that sole exception, the land appeared before our eyes more or less as it had looked since long before time began being recorded.

As we sipped our coffee, our eyes drank in large quantities of the serene surroundings. I gazed out over everything and nothing, and the vast expanses of raw forests, streams, waterfalls and rounded mountains gave me a sense of well-being. The feeling of physical and mental confinement that today's metropolitan living imposes on us disappeared from my consciousness. Gone, too, was that city sense of intense competition with my neighbors for the few remaining resources in a finite world growing smaller by the second, as population density grows unabated.

Here, the wide, open spaces translated somehow into a sense of timelessness and plenty, and any stress that I might still have had inside me upon arrival was magically zapped from my body and soul. I was immensely enjoying my lesson in Åre lifestyle.

» I came here for the skiing, and I stayed for the lifestyle.«

The following day, Karin and I were taken out to sample the mountain biking by a local bike enthusiast named Ulf Olofsson. I immediately understood that Ulf was another worshiper of the Åre lifestyle, when he parked his rusty 1982 Volvo 245 and gingerly pulled a $4500 Scott mountain bike out of the trunk of the car. I don't know too many people in the city who have a bicycle worth ten times the value of their car, but for some reason, here in Åre it was no longer even a surprise. Ulf didn't give a damn about keeping up with the Jones or the Janssons in the usual status-filled rat race to see who has more money idly sitting in a big hunk of metal in the driveway. On the other hand, he definitely wanted the best that money could buy under him when he was two-wheeling down from Åreskutan.

In 1999, Åre hosted the Mountain Bike World Championships, and since then, Åre residents started getting into this fast-growing sport at an even faster pace then before. Not only has mountain biking been gaining new converts among the locals, but the World Championships also demonstrated for longtime cyclists the unlimited possibilities that exist in this sport. On the death-defying downhill route from Hummelleden, bikers from around the world pushed the limits of what is humanly possible to do on two wheels. They got more air than Hermann Maier gets on a downhill and inspired many of Åre's younger generation to turn off MTV during the off-season and get back onto the mountain.

I could immediately decipher that I had best make clear to Ulf, in no uncertain terms, the limited amount of experience that a city boy like me has had on a mountain bike. After a bit of convincing, Ulf took Karin and me for a ride to a defunct copper mine near Fröå, on the back side of Åreskutan. This was a lovely two-hour ride, once again taking us through colorful fall foliage, and was proof that there were, in fact, ample trails for neophytes to the Åre way of life.

Later in our stay, Karin and I embarked on a hike on Åreskutan. There, we observed mountain bikers on Skutleden. This black-diamond route from the top station back down to the start of the downhill course is described in Åre's cycling guide as "a fantastic experience on a tough

THIS PAGE
UPPER LEFT: My feet dangle below my camera as I enjoy a tandem paraglider ride above Åre Lake in the off-season. UPPER RIGHT: Autumn colors decorate the countryside near Duved. LOWER LEFT: Karin Edlund gazes out over the desolate landscape that surrounds Åreskutan. LOWER RIGHT: The sun breaks through the clouds to light up part of Åre Lake.

RIGHT PAGE
Entering Ånn Lake with inflatable rafts to begin a river-rafting trip on the Tångbole Stream.

and steep trail that demands good skills from the rider especially in wet conditions."

There are a few misleading parts of this description. First of all, the conditions on this mountain are almost always wet. That's just a fact of life in Sweden.

Second, the description takes very great liberties with the word "trail". Åreskutan is a rather barren block of granite, in which a "trail", be it for walking or biking, is not much more than the least intimidating route down. If this "trail" were for skiing, it would be off-piste. The path looked troublesome for hikers and suicidal for a bicyclist, but in defiance of anything that my mind would consider reasonable, numerous locals went flying down the mountain in a manner that could well have put their next ski season in great jeopardy.

AFTER WATCHING THE MOUNTAIN BIKERS for a while, we began a short walk from the cable car station to the peak. With each step of gained elevation, a wider view stretched out before us. The desolate panorama of rocks and boulders sprinkled with dozens of bodies of water—large slinking lakes, mountain ponds of snowmelt, and everything in between—offered a barren beauty quite different from the multi-colored autumn scenery which flourished a mere 10-minute cable car ride below.

The region around Åre actually has hikes and treks of all shapes and sizes, from the kind of 2-hour round-trip sampler that we were enjoying to long, multi-day backpacking tours deep into the wilds. There are very short walks to some of the local waterfalls like Tännforsen and Handöls

Waterfall. Tännforsen is known as Sweden's Niagara, and while the two can't really be compared, Tännforsen is, nevertheless, an impressive sight well worth a visit. Alternatively, a visit to Rista Falls can be combined with a pleasant stroll for a couple of kilometers along the Indals River.

For the people who have the time that the Åre lifestyle dictates as a prerequisite to local residency, one of the multi-day hikes is perhaps more appropriate. Many possibilities begin at Storulvån Fjällstation, including various treks ranging from 24 to 104 kilometers in distance.

Karin and I had now tested three different land-based activities, and it was time to take to the water. From late spring, when the local rivers rage with meltwater, until early autumn, river rafting and kayaking are two other local activities which keep the Åre residents active during the off-season. The nearby rivers offer everything from lazy, mellow stretches suitable for first timers and families, to Class IV rapids for those who have an overactive testosterone gland.

Jonas Persson is another local hedonist who is a mountain guide in the winter and has his own river rafting company during the warmer months. Our group was made up of people of completely mixed abilities, and Jonas had an appropriate mode of transport for all. The faint of heart went downstream in stable, six-man, self-bailing rafts, the most experienced "river rats" traveled in kayaks, and Karin and I opted for a two-man, inflatable raft known as a rubber duck.

WE BEGAN ON A BEAUTIFUL LAKE called Ånnsjön on a crystal clear, windless morning. The lake empties into Tångbole Stream, which has Class III rapids in the spring but was quite mellow at this time of year. The current changed its velocity from time to time, and some white water suitable for first-timers appeared now and then. Following a coffee break, the mood of the river changed somewhat. Karin and I had been lulled into a false sense of security. We could see a long stretch of river ahead with lots of protruding rocks and swirling water.

Once the thought of getting stuck entered my mind, we were doomed. A mossy rock snagged us, allowing the other boats all to pass us by.

As some consolation, we managed to shift our weight back and forth and dislodge ourselves in time to see one of our guides get thrown into the river when his raft also stopped short on a rock.

THE FOLLOWING DAY, OUR EXPERIMENT in alternative lifestyles took to the air. Lars Hedström is the head of Skysport, a company offering an activity that is equally attractive during all four seasons. Paragliding is dependent on weather rather than season, and once again, good fortune was with us. The wind was ideal for a tandem flight with an instructor.

All the mental preparation in the world cannot really ready a person for the sprint of faith necessary to get a paraglider airborne. Taking to the air requires that one do the one thing which is psychologically most intimidating—sprint at full tilt down a steep mountainside until the parachute catches the wind. Granted, the process does not take very long, and the wind resistance soon makes it feel as if one is running in place. Nevertheless, I felt as if I were an albatross hurling myself off a cliff for the very first time, trusting in nothing more than a promise that my wings would take care of me the moment my feet leave the ground.

At the urging of my instructor, Patrik, I kept pin-wheeling my legs and pushing forward despite my instincts to the contrary, and within a few seconds I was gazing down at the village between my dangling feet. We flowed free and easy on the wings of the breeze, and for a brief moment I did feel more like an eagle than an albatross.

Then my air chauffeur, not wanting me to get bored (as if that could happen), asked if I would like to try a spiral dive. This is a maneuver in which one makes the paraglider lose altitude much more quickly. By having both people simultaneously shift their weight from side to side, they prompt the paraglider into a spin.

Almost before I got the words "I'll try anything once!" out of my mouth, we were rocking our way into gear. Within a few moments, the desired result was achieved, and the centrifugal force made me feel like a green rookie on his first day of astronaut school. We were not only quickly losing altitude, but I was soon going to lose my lunch if we didn't put

a halt to our dive. No problem. The moment I begged off, Patrik put us back into the cruise mode, and we soon drifted in for a soft touchdown.

All our experiences in Åre went beyond the activities in which we participated. There was a wholeness to our stay in this peaceful, low-key spot at a time of year when most tourists were elsewhere and the locals have time to live. Whether I was riding a horse, paddling a raft, riding a bike, flying or walking, one thing was constant—a sense of space and time. The two went hand in hand. Each time I looked around and drank in the vast amount of raw, untouched land that surrounded me, I understood that time does not really matter much at all.

Time rules our lives, confines our freedom and dictates our every action in the city, where all around us is the evidence of how fast life changes. It seems as if we will be trampled by the march of progress if we don't keep up with the pace.

But here, where the rivers flow in the same direction as they did a thousand years ago, and the forests, lakes and mountains look the same as when the Vikings first laid eyes upon them, there is evidence to the contrary. Time is insignificant. A millennium and more can come and go, and the land is still here for the taking.

Of course, the truth lies somewhere in between the two realities. While certain parts of our Earth remain as timeless as the sod we walk on, other locations have changed immensely over the years. Both worlds are real, and as we stand at the entry into a new millennium, we can mix and match.

Our forefathers had primitive tools to deal with a wild world. The pioneers and farmers who first tried to tame the land did so with crude hoes, sharp axes and a horse. The virgin land was as beautiful then as now, but our forefathers had much less time to enjoy the land, as they were so busy trying to conquer it.

We come today into the wilderness with a laptop, a mobile phone and a car, meeting the wilds on our terms. There are many suitable places in the world to do so, but Åre is one of the best. That is what the Åre lifestyle is truly about.

Chapter 15. FINLAND

SPEED, SAUNA AND SISU

As one moves further east in the Nordic countries, the terrain gets decidedly more horizontal, and the landscape of Finland is more appropriate for cross-country skiing than alpine skiing. Nevertheless, there are a few ski resorts that can still keep an alpine skier in shape. The top resorts in Finland include Ruka, Levi, Pallas, Pyhä and Ylläs, of which Ruka is the most popular, and Levi has the largest number of ski lifts. Ylläs, however, has the greatest vertical with a full 463 meters of skiing, and Pyhä attracts the best skiers because of its somewhat more difficult terrain.

I flew from Helsinki to Rovaniemi, on the Arctic Circle, for a few days of skiing in Finnish Lapland. This was my first visit to ski in Lapland, and I gazed out over kilometer upon kilometer of frozen lakes, forests and swampland—white on white as far as the eye could see. Every now and then a low mound would rise slightly above the pancake-flat landscape surrounding it. The Finns call them mountains, but they know that the two-billion-year-old protrusions of snow in Lapland are really nothing more than hills.

The local people joke lovingly of "Finnish powder" as well, but they also are well aware that the winter winds that sweep at will over their treeless "mountain" tops usually compact the new fallen snow to the extent that it has a character all its own. The Finns have a character all their own too, and as I flew over this vast, desolate winter landscape, it was not difficult to understand the conditions that molded their character.

A rugged, hardy people, the Finns describe themselves as having *sisu*—a combination of guts and determination that gives them a gritty grin-and-bear-it outlook toward any inconvenience that Mother Nature or fate could throw in their path. *Sisu* seems to be an ever-present part of the Finnish psyche and has penetrated deep into the soul of Finnish skiers as well.

In the 1960s, Kalevi Häkkinen set a standard for *sisu* in the Finnish skiing world, when he set the world speed-skiing record, and ever since that day, Finnish skiers have had a passion for velocity. Häkkinen persevered with his speed skiing into his retirement years. In his mid-sixties, he still punched the clock at 200 kilometers per hour. During my stay in Finland, I found out that many of his countrymen are constantly trying to emulate his example.

Upon my arrival in Lapland, my friend Mika Salokangas picked me up in his new Saab at Rovaniemi airport, and we drove 150 kilometers to the ski resort of Yllas. As we drove, Mika's speed was kept in check by reindeer, which wandered into the road periodically throughout our journey.

Fog encompassed the mountain in the early hours of the day, until about eleven o'clock, when the spring sun burnt through the clouds. With the veil lifted, the sun revealed an all-around winter sports area, with more than 1000 kilometers of cross-country tracks and 600 kilometers of snowmobile trails, as well as 21 ski lifts. The runs in Yllas are extremely well-groomed and not very difficult. Runs labeled as black are more like red runs in the Alps, and the green runs look more like cross-country tracks.

The black and red runs were perfect for setting the skis into overdrive and churning out high-speed giant slalom turns. The snow was winter powder in late April, and the pistes and lifts were almost empty. With those conditions, it did not take long to cruise through the entire selection of runs and set our sights on the off-piste terrain.

The mountain is more or less round, and most of the skiing is above the tree line. Therefore, one can ski down anywhere, 360 degrees around the mountain. Mika and I spent the rest of the day carving fresh tracks into the thin layer of powder on every face and exposure, before heading back for the all-important climax of every ski day in Finland, the sauna.

Most people know that the sauna is a Finnish invention, but unless one has visited here, one cannot imagine to what extent the sauna is a part of the Finnish way of life. A visit to the sauna is an almost daily ritual that takes on aspects of religious fanaticism. It is a bar, a business conference center, a social club, a bathtub and a sanctuary from the pressures and tensions of daily life. One imbibes alcohol here and purges it from the pores all in the same go.

In most countries, a sauna is a prelude to a Jacuzzi and a swim, but in Finland, it is an event unto itself, often lasting a couple of hours. Numerous visits into the heat are generally interspersed with intervals for drinking beer and chatting in a neighboring room, not to mention a few obligatory rolls in the snow to cool off.

After our sauna, Mika and I dressed for a traditional Lapland dinner at the Äkäs Hotel. We entered the huge dining salon, where many of the guests were dancing to a live band that was playing a repertoire of Finnish dance music.

Lapland offers some extraordinary culinary specialties. We began with an aperitif—a *poronpotku* or "reindeer's kicks"—consisting of gin, tonic and cranberry liqueur. This was followed by cream of salmon soup, sautéed reindeer with mashed potatoes and cranberries, and Lapp bread-cheese covered with cloudberries and cream.

THE NEXT MORNING, WE MET Jukka-Pekka Joensuu, a fifth-generation reindeer herder and at that time, the manager of the hotel and ski area. It soon became clear that he was suffering from an overdose of *sisu* and a Häkkinen complex. He drove us to the lifts as if he were competing with another Häkkinen, two-time Formula One World Champion driver Mika. We skidded and slid around every curve of the snow-covered road, and he finally parked by default, sliding sideways into a ditch near the lifts.

Jukka-Pekka stepped out of his car and into a pair of telemark skis. Soon we were at the top, and even sooner, our host was back at the bottom. It was as if my skis were set in cement compared to Jukka-Pekka, as he nearly flew down the mountain. I was not surprised to hear later that he had been a forerunner at a recent speed-skiing competition, and had clocked in at upwards of 120 kilometers per hour on his telemark skis.

That afternoon, we hopped into a helicopter, and Jukka-Pekka showed us that he was equally adept at negotiating some tricky off-piste spring crud on his telemark boards. To top off the day, our guide once again put his passion for speed on parade as he led us on a 30-kilometer snowmobile safari.

I sped over the trail at breakneck speed, trying to no avail to keep sight of our leader, as the bumps in the path bounced me constantly high off my seat like a Brahma bull at a Wyoming rodeo. The therapeutic heat of the sauna soothing my muscles was a very welcome conclusion to a day

THIS PAGE
LEFT: Antti-Pekka Auvinen telemarks down one of the black runs in Pyhä.
UPPER RIGHT: Finland has excellent terrain for cross-country skiing.
LOWER RIGHT: Many people grill hot dogs over an open fire at lunchtime in Pyhä.

RIGHT PAGE
Frozen lakes, low hills and endless forests make up the typical landscape around the Finnish ski centers. The skier is Petri Lehikoinen.

of trying to keep pace with a Lapp who apparently quenches his thirst gulping reindeer adrenaline.

On a more recent tour of Lapland, my friend Marja Salokangas organized for the two of us to visit both Ruka and Pyhä. With eighteen lifts and 28 pistes, Ruka is one of Finland's largest ski areas and also was the host resort for the 2005 Freestyle World Championships. Finnish alpine skiing has come a long way from the days when speed skiing was its only claim to fame, and the honor of hosting the ultimate freestyle competition is not the only evidence of that fact.

It is not so strange that this event should be held in Finland, as they have proven themselves more than worthy of the honor what with Mikko Ronkainen winning the Freestyle Mogul World Championships in 2001 and 2003, and Janne Lahtela capturing the 2002 Olympic gold medal.

In fact, recent years have seen the Finns come from nowhere to prove themselves in many top categories of alpine skiing. Besides the freestyle stars, Kalle Palander has emerged as one of the best slalom and giant slalom skiers in the world, winning the slalom World Champion title in 1999. In addition, Tanja Poutiainen captured the Women's World Cup titles in both the slalom and giant slalom in 2005.

> **»Even as simple a thing as a pizza can be a unique experience in Lapland.«**

In snowboarding, the Finnish *sisu* has also taken them to new heights, with Risto Mattila and Antti Autti finishing one–two in the world in the halfpipe in 2004. Ten Finns finished among the top 30 "Big Air" specialists the same year, and Autti swept the FIS Halfpipe World Championship and the Winter X Games a year later. Our host in Ruka, Antti-Pekka Auvinen, was even more proof of Finland's snowsports prowess, having won the title of Telemark Giant Slalom World Champion in 2001.

"We have fun here," explained Antti-Pekka, as he guided us around the short slopes of Ruka, "but Ruka's slopes have only 200 vertical meters. One needs some challenges to keep the skiing interesting if one is going

to spend a whole season in one of our small Finnish resorts. That is probably why we Finns get into all sorts of odd tangents of skiing like telemarking, freestyle, speed skiing and so on."

It was a beautiful, warm spring morning, and small mountain or not, the view from the top of Ruka was inspiring. I gazed out over a panorama of forests and frozen lakes that stretched to the horizon in all directions. Here and there a small rise in the flat landscape was evidence of another Lapp "peak" and one more ski resort. To the east, one could see the mountains called Nuorunen across the border in Russia. Similar to many Finnish resorts, Ruka has pistes that descend on all faces, so it is simple in springtime to begin the day on the sun-drenched south- and east-facing slopes, and move to the west and north faces as the snow gets softer.

AFTER A WHILE, ANTTI-PEKKA SKIED over to the black mogul run, where a few members of the freestyle team were training. I watched as a young freestyler pumped his legs at lightning speed like the pistons of a well-oiled Porsche, guiding his skis through the troughs of the monster moguls. Then Antti-Pekka also showed the bumps who was boss on his free-heeled skis, and I understood that he had not quit the telemark circuit because of old age or disability.

Late that afternoon, Antti-Pekka drove us 170 kilometers north to the 540-meter-high mound of snow known as Pyhä Tunturi or Holy Hill. Pyhä is linked by a common lift pass to the smaller ski resort of Luosto, about 20 kilometers away. While Luosto appeals primarily to intermediates and beginners, Pyhä has a reputation for being the Finnish ski center for "real skiers", and that translates into a gathering place for Finnish crazies with an overactive *sisu* gland.

Hungry after our drive, I ordered a pizza in the hotel restaurant. Even as simple a thing as a pizza can be a unique experience in Lapland. I was served a frutti di Pyhä made up of reindeer, salmon and cloudberry toppings. This was definitely not a pizza that could be replicated in Italy!

Almost the moment I sat down in the restaurant, I ran into Ari Heinilä, the founder and former editor of the Finnish ski magazine *Skimbaaja* and an accomplished speed skier. At one time, Ari held the record for having fallen at the highest speed in history, a 208-kilometer-per-hour slide into the record book in Les Arcs in 1988. He described that incident for me as we rode up the lift together.

"I knew I was gonna burn," explained Ari. "But I didn't try to stop myself. That's how you get hurt. I just kept my limbs up and said to myself, 'Let it burn.'"

"Afterwards, I was totally black from my ass all the way up my back. Ordinarily I would have taken it easy that evening," continued Ari, "but my girlfriend at that time, Tarja, broke the world speed record for women that same day. So I went to the celebration and had some champagne. It was odd because I felt queasy after only two glasses. [This is quite unusual with respect to the normal Finnish capacity for alcohol consumption.] I got the explanation the following day, when the doctor explained to me that my black posterior was due to a loss of about one and a half liters of blood!" Finnish *sisu*!

By now, we were at the top, and Ari started to show me around the primarily intermediate slopes of Pyhä. The foggy weather kept Ari's speed down to a minimum, and still I had trouble keeping up. During the day, we made use of all of Pyhä's lifts, and Ari guided me among the two blue, three red and two black runs. After trying to keep up with him for a day, I collapsed once more into the sauna, fearing what the pace might be like if the fog lifted and Ari could see where he was going.

VISITS TO LAPLAND CAN DIFFER greatly depending on the time of year. During the winter months, the days are very short, the sun never gets far above the horizon and one finishes the ski day carving under floodlights. A clear night during January or February often includes a presentation put on by the aurora borealis. Spring provides a very different experience. During my stay, the days were about 20 hours long, and the sky never seemed to get completely dark

My first evening in Pyhä, I learned that Finnish nightlife can be somewhat confusing in April. If one quaffs too much lager during the evening sauna, one can tend to lose track of time. Sunset and sunrise are not many hours apart, and as the evening wears on, you can never be quite

sure which direction the sun is actually moving. I believe it was, in fact, the pink and orange hues of the sunrise that I photographed sometime during the Lapp night. When I tried to ski the following day, the lack of response from my thigh and calf muscles assured me that it had indeed been the sunrise.

Ari had headed home after our day of skiing, so I hoped for a lazy day on the slopes, but it was not to be. I ran into Uffe Tollet, the former trainer of the Finnish freestyle team, and he promised to show me some of the off-piste skiing that Pyhä had to offer.

Uffe is another one of those loonies who suffers from an overabundance of testosterone, and spends the day trying to invent new methods of burning it off. He, too, has taken *sisu* to new limits. One of Uffe's favorite pastimes is practicing various disciplines of skiing with the wrong kind of ski. On numerous occasions, for example, he has skied off 90-meter ski jump ramps wearing regular alpine skis. Just the day before, he had spent the whole day skiing the pistes of Pyhä (including the black mogul run) on cross-country skis. Uffe calls this "creative craziness", although other phrases, such as "sheer insanity" or "instant suicide" come more quickly to my mind.

The fog had disappeared by the next morning, and as we rode up the Polar T-bar, three reindeer rested lazily under a tree about 5 meters from the lift. The skiers on the mountain outnumbered the reindeer slightly, but the difference was negligible.

Late April is a great time to ski in Finland. The interest of most Finns has turned to their sailboats or their summerhouses, and the slopes are almost devoid of skiers. We cruised around at max speed for a few runs without a worry of another skier disturbing our lines.

After our warmup, Uffe led me on a corn-snow plunge down a rather steep funnel called Isokuru or Big Ravine. Uffe pointed out a frozen pond and a waterfall off to the right, where the Lapps had performed christening ceremonies in the 1600s. The ravine narrowed drastically with each turn, until it finally spit us out into a small valley at the bottom.

From the valley floor, we began what should have been a steep 30-minute walk up the next hill, Ukonhattu. The east-facing slope had

already received too much sun, however, and every four or five steps, we found ourselves breaking through the corn snow and standing in a meter-deep hole.

This condition boded not so well for the descent to follow, but the law of Finnish *sisu* apparently forbade backtracking on a goal once the initial step had been taken. That the downhill part of our excursion would be deep, heavy spring crud rather than smooth, firm corn snow was all the more reason to continue with our quest. An hour later, we stood at the top, and I pondered the best technique to avoid serious injury in this bone-breaking spring slush.

"It's no problem," proclaimed Uffe. "High speed is the answer!"

Of course! I should have known. High speed always seemed to be the answer in Finland. In fact, I knew he was right. If I went fast enough, my weight would be displaced over a large enough area so that I could avoid breaking through the weak crust. Of course, if I skied just slightly slower than "fast enough", I would turn about two dozen cartwheels and shred myself into hamburger meat on the rocks below.

Uffe's words were still cavorting around in my cerebrum, when I peered down to see him waving from the bottom. My technique was markedly more conservative, which seemed to work about three turns out of every four. I was very happy that nobody had a video camera to record my less-than-graceful survival technique.

We replenished lost fluids with a large beer at the lodge and headed off-piste to a ravine called Aittokuru. This time, we were joined by half a dozen gung-ho employees with an apparent death wish. We began skiing in rather good corn snow on a west face, but just as the slope took us to the edge of a steep pitch, we once again were breaking through the old mush down to the crocus buds. This minor detail made no difference to Uffe. He pushed on relentlessly down a route that most of us would not have ventured into in the best of conditions. Meanwhile, the rest of us floundered around in the porridge until we found a slope that held more firmly underfoot.

No sooner were we down than the troops did an about face and began marching back up. I stayed in the valley and watched as they punched thigh-deep holes in the snow in quest of an ominous looking wind cornice which the mysterious Lapp god of *sisu* had presumably deemed a sacrificial offering place for young Finnish jumping enthusiasts. Despite a close call or two, the *sisu* god's lust for young blood was thwarted, and we soon found ourselves back at the bottom of the Pohjoisrinteet Lift.

THE DAY'S FINAL TEST OF SISU came in the bar, where many Finnish skiers perform incredible feats nearly equal to their exploits on the slopes. Our proud leader, Uffe, was once again the man to show the way.

There is a special drink known only among a handful of Pyhä regulars. This drink is nothing you would ever order for yourself. It is more of a dare drink to be ordered for others, testing the intestinal fortitude of those who consider themselves to be hardy drinkers. The rules of the game determine that if someone buys you a *Karpaattien nero*, you must take off your shirt and down it or, of course, lose face. In many cases, it is a matter of lose-face or lose-lunch.

Shortly after we had sat down in the hotel bar, Uffe was presented with a glass with a salted rim. The glass held two centiliters of aquavit, two centiliters of Fernet-Branca and a raw egg yolk, while hanging over the edge of the glass was a small, raw fish to be devoured in the same swallow.

Uffe did not bat an eye. He stood bare to the waist, placed the raw fish gingerly in his mouth, poured the rest of the concoction in and ingested it all in one gulp. The god of *sisu* was undoubtedly pleased, and Uffe had proven, to nobody in particular, that he was a completely well-rounded skier—in the true Finnish sense.

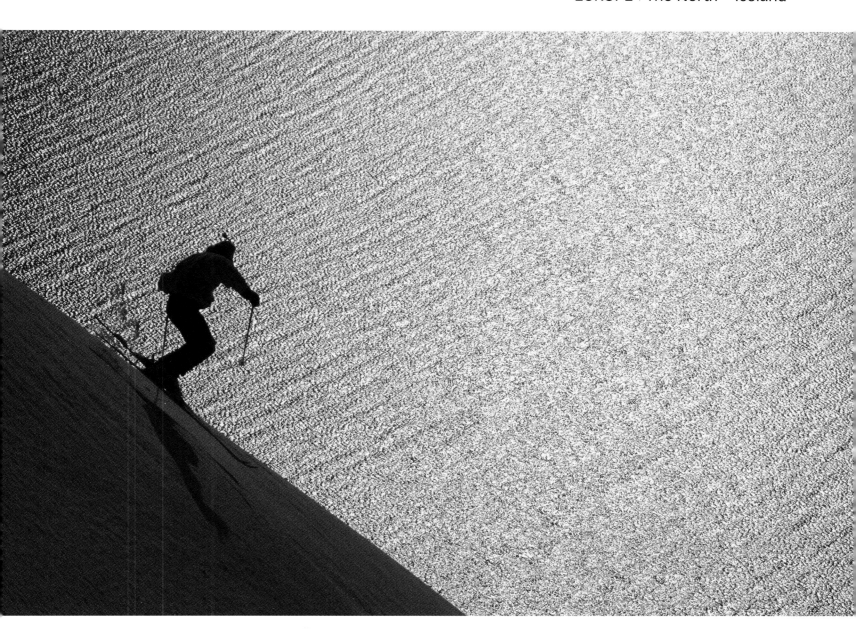

Chapter 16. ICELAND
A GUIDE TO SKIING IN THE GREENHOUSE AGE

It came to pass in one of the abominable winters that have plagued the Alps and the Rockies on-and-off in recent years. The morning paper featured an article about the greenhouse effect, and I began to seriously worry about the future of my favorite sport. I felt the need to find a safe haven from a potential 365-day summer. I wanted to feel secure that I could ski into my retirement years without worrying about global warming.

Because of its name, Iceland seemed like a logical place to start my research. My handy "Junior Woodchuck Manual" informed me that glaciers cover 11.5 percent of Iceland, and that the mean annual temperature in approximately 75 percent of the country is 2 degrees centigrade or less. Those statistics spurred me into action. If the greenhouse effect lives up to the ominous forecasts of the scientists, this land, covered almost from shore to shore with mountains, may become the last bastion for skiers in a world taken over by the beachwear industry.

I lost no time. Within minutes, I had Icelandair on the phone. Then, I called my old skiing crony, Caspar Möller, who fortunately had nothing more pressing on his social calendar than the quest to find a skier's refuge from global warming.

A FEW DAYS LATER, I WOKE UP in Reykjavik to the smell of somebody cooking eggs for breakfast. But the smell was only Caspar in the geothermally heated shower. Iceland, with all its volcanoes, has great geothermal resources, which provide showers with a touch of sulfur. Feeling fresh as a three-egg omelet, we caught a morning flight for Ísafjördur, a small fishing village in the northwestern part of the island.

Downhill skiing began in Ísafjördur around 1960 with a homemade tow pulled by an old Buick motor with three gears.

"It wasn't much of a lift," explained one of the lift attendants, "but that sucker could give you quite a ride when you threw her into third."

Since those days, the old Buick has been replaced by more modern machinery, and Ísafjördur now has three lifts, 3500 residents, and no winter tourists. These figures give one a little insight into Icelandic skiing—it is a nonprofit organization.

Iceland, with a total population of about 300,000 inhabitants, is not really a country; it is a neighborhood. Everybody seems to know each other here—an entire nation of people on a first-name basis. In fact, with the patronymic system of names that is used here, Icelanders literally have no last names. When Stefan has a daughter, Hildur, she is known as Hildur Stefansdottir, (Stefan's daughter) while his son, Thor, is called Thor Stefansson. There is also almost no crime in this society of friends and acquaintances, and a great trust and faith in the honesty of their fellow man exists among the inhabitants.

Skiing in Iceland reflects the same friendly familiarity. Here, skiing is not a business; it is an organized community activity. Almost every ski area in the country annually runs a deficit. Each local municipality assumes the loss, as the sport is considered an indispensable source of recreation for the local people. How refreshing to escape all of the industry hype, and get back to the grass roots of skiing, where the whole ski experience revolves around a love for the sport without an inkling of the profit motive involved.

Caspar and I got the feel of the Icelandic ski atmosphere immediately. There was nobody to check our tickets on the self-service lower lift, which operated strictly on the honor system. We rode up amidst a handful of school children who were polishing up their racing technique.

The slopes were covered with about 5 centimeters of fresh snow over a corn-snow base, and we continued to the top of the upper lift. After a few runs, it became evident that there were no more than four of us who were interested in using this lift. Once that fact had been established, the lift operator introduced himself as Finn, and he joined us for the entire afternoon. Each run, he would load us, ride up behind us, turn off the lift at the top and follow us down in the powder. As the five of us carved fresh tracks run after run, I couldn't help but think that the greenhouse age may yet be years away, but Ísafjördur could be today's answer to the lift-line blight that is the bane of much of the ski world.

THE VILLAGE OF ÍSAFJÖRDUR is situated on a small peninsula that juts out into a fjord of the same name. It is flanked on both sides by steep mountains that rise about 800 meters from the sea, with plateau-like tops, typical of glacially carved mountains. Hundreds of steep couloirs run between rocky ridges from the plateau down to the fjord. As we yo-yoed up and down the little lifts of Ísafjördur, we often found our eyes riveted to those untouched chutes. They were about 45–50 degrees at the top and all emptied out onto the road.

Once back in town, Caspar and I inquired if anybody had ever skied these chutes, and were told that one man, Halfdan Ingolfsson, regarded by some of the town's inhabitants to be the local lunatic, had made some such descents. We immediately called Halfdan, and spoke with his brother Hördur.

"Yes, they are very nice, these couloirs," said Hördur. "My two brothers, Halfdan and Örn, and I, we have a small plane which we have built, and we customized some skis and attached them onto the plane for landing on snow. I can fly you up there if we have some good weather."

The weather, however, is always a big "if" in Iceland. Some local people claim that Iceland has no weather, only samples of weather, as the conditions change so quickly, often providing samples of sunshine, overcast, rain and snow on the same day. The following day offered only samples of overcast and snow, so Caspar and I skied within the lift system. When the third morning looked no better, we headed back to Reykjavik with a promise that we would ring Hördur periodically to check on the weather.

THE FOLLOWING DAY, WE DROVE half an hour from the capital through ancient lava fields to the ski area of Bláfjöll (the Blue Mountains). With eleven lifts, Bláfjöll is the largest ski complex in Iceland. The sky was blue and a "spring zephyr" was wafting in from Greenland at about 80 kilometers per hour. It was what the locals call "window weather"—nice skies to look at from behind a closed window. We were lucky, however, that the ski area was open at all, a fact that one cannot take for granted at Bláfjöll. Of all the ski areas in Iceland, Bláfjöll is the most susceptible to the whims of the elements, and in a good season, the area is only operable about 60 percent of the time.

On this particular day, the wind chill factor was such that we really forgot our worries about global warming altogether. Yet, one of the locals informed us proudly, with no hint of irony, that this day, April 25, was a holiday celebrating the first day of summer (presumably, in accordance with some archaic Viking calendar).

A few days later, we were back in the north, and we called Hördur for a weather report from the northwest. We were advised that the conditions were more promising in other parts of the country. We set our sights, instead, on Dalvik, a small northern town of 1500 people with two lifts run by the local ski club. We phoned Jon Halldorsson, one of the ski club's officers, who informed us that because of a race in nearby Akureyri, almost all the local skiers had gone there for the day. Hence, they had not intended to open the lifts at all.

"But, it's such a nice spring day," continued Jon. "So why don't you come over, and we can open the lifts anyway. It is really no problem."

We grabbed our gear, headed down to the main road, and put out our thumbs. Hitchhiking is a conventional and convenient form of travel in Iceland. The friendly nature of the people and the lack of crime on the island make it quite easy to get a lift. If the first passing car does not pick up a hitchhiker in Iceland, his Porsche already has six passengers or he is traveling in the opposite direction. After a few minutes, we were moving west.

"Oh, yes, I know Jon," said our driver, and 30 kilometers later we were dropped off on his doorstep.

If you ever dreamed about owning your own private mountain and ski lifts and operating them solely for your friends, Iceland is the closest you can come to realizing that dream. We climbed into the back of Jon's van, and 3 minutes from his driveway, literally in his backyard, was the ski area. Jon took the keys out of his pocket, started up the lift with a turn of his wrist and we entered the very private world of Dalvik skiing. With stunning views of the village and fjord below, we spent the next 3 hours making first tracks in spring snow and sunshine. In a part of the world where "lift line" certainly has no place in the vocabulary, skiing in Dalvik was still one notch better. Sundance, Utah may be much larger, but owner Robert Redford still has to share first tracks with a lot of strangers.

JON GAVE US A RIDE late that afternoon to Ólafsfjördur. We thanked him profusely and bid him farewell. The lone local lift was closed by the time we arrived, but there is more than one way to get up a mountain in Iceland.

Snowmobiles are an ingrained part of the Icelandic psyche, and it was not long before we had organized a lift with a group of locals with snowmobiles. My driver looked dubiously young, and I inquired how old one had to be to get such a license in Iceland. He told me that fifteen was the minimum age and I scrutinized him carefully.

"And how old are you?" I asked.

"Thirteen," he shot back. "But you'll be okay. I've been driving these since I was six."

With that reassurance, he threw me a rope, and we headed out over an iced-over section of fjord. His last words of "Hold on tight, I like to go fast!" almost got drowned out by the revving of his engine. I swung out to the side like a water skier, and we headed out over the frozen water. As we got up to 70 kilometers per hour, it became difficult to stay out to the side, and I skied back into place directly in the wake of the snowmobile.

At 85 kilometers per hour, the slush off the lake was spurting back in large chunks, and I deeply regretted not having my goggles on. I also was a little sorry that we were doing this at 9:30 p.m. Dusk was definitely upon us, and I was having a lot of trouble discerning the many irregularities in the surface. "I would hate to catch an edge on a heavy clump of half-frozen slush at this speed," I thought. At 100 kilometers per hour, sanity briefly took over, and I wisely let go of the rope.

I loaded the skis on the back of the snowmobile, hopped on, and we rode together up the valley to a pass from where we could watch the last pink shades of sunset over the fjords. By the time we started down on our skis in the last rays of twilight, the snow had turned to breakable crust and Caspar and I gingerly negotiated our way downward.

Once again, we were at a juncture of our travels where hitchhiking was the necessary mode of transportation. Even far to the other side of midnight, we found people willing to pick up two weary hitchhikers in full ski regalia. In keeping with the usual Icelandic hospitality, we were left right at the doorstep of our hotel at about 1 a.m.

The following day was spent skiing under sunny skies in Akureyri, the second largest ski area in the country. Like so many of the ski hills in this beautiful land, it, too, offered views out over one of the many fjords.

Late that afternoon, Caspar and I flew out to the tiny south coast enclave of Höfn and Europe's largest glacier, Vatnajökull. This is not

Hördur lands his papier-mâché homemade flying sardine can atop one of the flat peaks near Ísafjördur.

only a big glacier, it is larger than all the glaciers on the European mainland combined. This massive desert of ice and snow covers an area of 8400 square kilometers and is up to 1000 meters thick in places. Around Höfn, various arms of this immense chunk of ice creep imperceptibly toward the sea, and we arrived there in time to watch a spectacular sunset over one of those arms.

There were no lifts on Vatnajökull, but there were companies that offered snowmobile tours on this mammoth mountain of ice. By now we were experienced in the fine art of snowmobile transport. Once again, we looped a rope around our ski poles and were whiplashed into motion.

With snowmobile skiing, it is a tossup whether it is more fun riding up or skiing down, but the uphill phase is certainly more frightening and more tiresome. There were choices however. When my arms were exhausted from hanging on for dear life at 80 kilometers per hour, I could just pack my skis on my shoulder and sit down behind my chauffeur.

Our day on Vatnajökull involved not only skiing and snowmobiling, but also included stunning views of the sea as well as of glacial crevasses and seracs. Additionally, we got a glimpse of Hvannadalshnukur (2119 m), the highest mountain in Iceland, and made a visit to Jökulsárlón, where icebergs break off the glacier into a dark-green lagoon. (While there are still companies who offer snowmobile adventures on Vatnajökull, none of them currently take people skiing in this manner. There are, however, mountain guides available who take people ski touring on the glacier.)

NOW IT WAS TIME TO CHECK IN once again with Hördur for a weather update from the northwest. This time, he said the conditions were good, so we caught an afternoon plane back to Ísafjördur, a nineteen-seat Twin Otter. This aircraft seemed like a 747 Boeing when Hördur met us at the airport with his homemade papier-mâché flying sardine can known as an Avid Flyer. The whole plane weighed less than 200 kilos, and the word "EXPERIMENTAL" was printed in bold black letters under the door.

I was beginning to have second thoughts. Hördur had to cram me into my seat and pry me back out, as my ski boots made it almost impossible to get through the small doorway without assistance. The first thing I noticed on the interior of the plane was a small sign that read: "Passenger Warning: This aircraft is amateur built and does not comply with the federal safety regulations for standard aircraft."

I could already feel a severe migraine coming on, and then Hördur

THIS PAGE
The famous Blue Lagoon geothermal spa near Reykjavik.

RIGHT PAGE
UPPER: At about 9:30 p.m. under threatening skies, I began to ski down the first of three first descents that we accomplished high above the little village of Ísafjördur.
Photo by Caspar Möller.
LOWER LEFT: Heimaey, the only inhabited island of the Westman Islands off the southern coast of Iceland, had a major volcanic eruption in 1973. Over 400 buildings were destroyed where the dark lava is visible in the photo. After the eruption, the inhabitants returned and rebuilt the village directly adjacent to where their previous homes had been destroyed.
LOWER RIGHT: Reykjavik.

pointed to a small button strategically placed mere millimeters from my left ski boot.

"Make sure not to accidentally push your foot against that button," he advised, "because that causes the motor to stall."

Instantly, I moved my foot as far away as possible from the button, so now leg cramps were added to my migraine.

All my consternation proved to be unnecessary. It took no more than 100 meters of runway for us to become airborne. We soared like a seagull, putt-putting at about 80 kilometers per hour—a bit slower than my snowmobile ride. Just 5 minutes later, we touched down softly on the plateau above the couloirs with the altimeter indicating an elevation of just under 800 meters. Hördur went back to pick Caspar up and we were soon ready for our descent.

Forty-five degrees looks much steeper from the top looking down than the other way around. We located a corridor that did not have a cornice and dropped deliberately off the rim. We tested the snow for avalanche danger with short hops and tried to get a handle on what kind of snow we would be skiing.

At the top, it was compressed, crusty and inconsistent. Some of my jump turns broke through the crust and others did not. The upper section was the steepest, and we took the turns one at a time. As we descended, the snow began to change to heavy spring snow. Jump turns were still the most effective technique, but now we could link a series of hops together, as the snow was less variable.

A few hundred kangaroo steps below, Hördur picked us up in his car. It was 9:30 p.m. by the time our friend whisked us away to a local restaurant for a celebratory dinner.

The weather held stable, and we dragged ourselves from bed at five o'clock the following morning to a view of rose-colored peaks. By seven, we were back at 800 meters above the sea, looking straight down a gunbarrel couloir at the morning sun shimmering on the fjord below. To our delight, the sun had already softened the Icelandic elevator shaft into perfect corn snow. The capricious local weather held steady even long enough for yet a second morning plunge into another of Isafjördur's nameless corridors. The corn kernels scraped loose under our skis and raced us down to the fjord. We made a couple of attempts at still another landing, but the wind was picking up, and Hördur deemed touching down as too dangerous in his flying matchbox.

"I'm sorry," he apologized. "Maybe tomorrow..."

"Don't worry," Caspar replied. "This has been fantastic. We've got all the information and photos we need now for our 'Skier's Guide to the Greenhouse Age', and we really have to be getting back home. How much do we owe your for everything?"

"I always accept payment only for the gas when I fly people," he answered. "That comes to about $25."

"You're kidding, right?" asked Caspar.

"No. The Avid Flyer doesn't consume much more fuel than a Volkswagen. Anyway, I love to fly as much as you guys love to ski, so that works out about right. Give me $25 and put my name in your article. Maybe a few more good skiers will turn up. That would be fun."

"A few more!" I almost shouted. "Man, Hördur, you don't realize how crazy skiers are. They'll come from all over for an experience like this. I'll do it, but just promise to keep a few days free for me next Easter. I'm canceling my heliskiing in Canada!"

*   *   *   *   *   *   *   *

Hördur Ingolfsson has since moved to Reykjavik, while his brothers Halfdan and Örn keep the Avid Flyer airborne over Ísafjördur as often as possible.

Chapter 17.
GREENLAND

FAR FROM THE MADDING CROWD

Do the crowded streets, packed subways and grocery store queues of the big city get on your nerves after a while? Do you sometimes long for the wide, open spaces where you have a bit of elbowroom? Welcome to Greenland. This is a country of 56,000 people sharing 2,175,600 square kilometers of land! That is a population density of almost 39 square kilometers per person. Greenland has a national park that is larger than any country in Europe, and the municipality of Ittoqqortoormiit is larger than Great Britain.

Anyone who can vaguely understand a map can figure out that "Greenland" is a rather inappropriate name for the world's largest island. It is the equivalent of attaching the nickname "Tiny" to Shaq O'Neal, or calling Attila the Hun "The Great Peacemaker". The name, however, was no mistake—merely a marketing ploy concocted by the Viking Eric the Red to attract immigration to this mass of snow and ice which he discovered over a thousand years ago. Some people followed Eric, but eventually, the Nordic settlement mysteriously disappeared without a trace.

Nowadays, Eric would not need his false marketing to attract visitors. There are plenty of us for whom limitless untracked powder snow and a low population of skiers per square kilometer is a very attractive statistic.

MOST SKI CENTERS IN COUNTRIES as remote as Greenland bear very little similarity to ski areas in the more populated parts of the planet. That is to say that one can hardly call these places "ski resorts". There do exist some ski lifts sporadically placed around the country for the entertainment and use of the local population, but no tourist infrastructure is in place around the ski lifts. In addition, the hours of operation are generally based upon the leisure-time habits and customs of the local villagers.

Be that as it may, Greenland is a fabulous country in which to enjoy skiing, be it with the use of normal ski lifts, with the expensive aid of a helicopter or by the traditional means of skins and touring skis. Then, there are also special Greenland options of uphill transportation such as snowmobile or dogsled.

The Quassussuaq area near the Nuuk airport has two lifts, and the villages of Sisimiut, Tasiilaq, Maniitsoq, Narsaq, Ammassalik and Qasigiannguit all have a lift as well. The largest of these ski centers is the one near Nuuk, which has 300 vertical meters of skiing and a run that is a full kilometer long.

The season of operation of the lifts varies from location to location. The lifts in Nuuk are generally running from January into May, whereas those in Sisimiut have a shorter season, running only between February and April. In actual fact, this can all vary from season to season, so that anybody hoping to make lift-accessed skiing a key component of his visit to Greenland is well advised to call the local tourist office of that village.

It is far more likely that a skier might take advantage of some of the so-called summer ski centers, located in Disko Island, Kangerluarsunnguaq, and Apussuit. These areas are on glaciers and generally have no lifts, but rather are locations where the terrain is suitable for downhill skiing and the location is reasonably accessible.

"Reasonably accessible" is a very relative term. According to the Lonely Planet book on Iceland, Greenland and the Faroe Islands, the summer ski center of Kangerluarsunnguaq is a four-day hike from Nuuk, with overnight possibilities at huts along the way as well as at the ski center itself. Some skiers might not consider four days of trekking to be very reasonable or very accessible, while ski touring enthusiasts would certainly delight at such an arrangement.

In the end, Greenland has so much ice and snow that skiing, in one form or another, is possible almost everywhere. One's possibilities are limited, however, to locations where the villages and mountains lie close to each other. Population centers in Greenland exist only along the seacoast, and are connected by boat rather than by road. Therefore, any skiing short of a major expedition onto the inland ice must be done in close proximity to a village. Perhaps the best location for adventure skiing is in the Apussuit Adventure Camp, close to the village of Maniitsoq.

WITH THAT IN MIND, Papi Tuomala, Tatu Lehmuskallio and I flew from Copenhagen to Maniitsoq in mid-May in search of adventure and powder snow. We continued our journey with an hour's boat ride and were dropped on a distant shore of the Kangerdluarssuk fjord. There, we were picked up by Adam Lyberth, Levi Levisen and Ludvig Kreutzmann, our

gear was placed in snowmobile trailers and we were whisked 900 vertical meters up to a small ski center atop the Apussuit Glacier.

Did I say small? I meant tiny. Miniscule is perhaps a more appropriate word. There are six rudimentary buildings and no ski lifts! Greenland is a different kind of country and it demands different kinds of solutions. Apussuit's solution to skiing is snowmobiles with drivers. The resort has a capacity of 24 people.

I have skied in many small and remote ski areas in the world—in Dardha, Albania; Rio Turbio, Argentina; Kashka-Suu, Kyrgyzstan; and Stranda, Norway, among others. In Rio Turbio, I arrived at 3 p.m. and was the first skier of the day, and in Stranda, my friend Anders and I were the only skiers of the day. In Apussuit, however, we were the only skiers of the season! Now we are talking remote.

You want to make fresh tracks every day? This is the place. Apussuit's

THIS PAGE
UPPER: In Greenland, snowmobiles are much more practical than cars.
MIDDLE LEFT: A couple of turns lower down, I fell. That is a good way to end up wet, cold and dead. Photo by Papi Tuomala.
MIDDLE RIGHT: This sign in the Kangerlussuaq airport indicates that we are now closer to the North Pole than to Copenhagen.
LOWER: A fishing boat chugs past some of the colossal icebergs of the Ilulissat Ice Fjord.

RIGHT PAGE
UPPER LEFT: This is not a place to rock the boat. Tipping your kayak in these waters brings your life expectancy down to about 5 minutes.
UPPER RIGHT: Greenland has only had its own flag since 1985.
LOWER LEFT: Greenlanders still today acquire 70 percent of their food by hunting and fishing. To this end, their dog sleds are essential to carrying them to the best locations.
LOWER RIGHT: Adam proudly displays his Apussuit logo by turning his back to us.

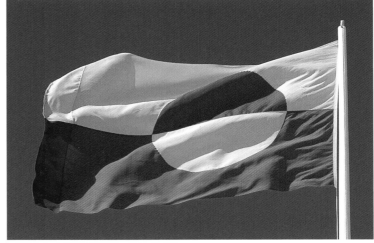

skiable terrain covers about 1200 square kilometers of snow. With the three of us to share this area, that works out to a population density of one skier per 400 square kilometers. Whistler Blackcomb, North America's largest ski area, by comparison, has a lift system spread out over approximately 29 square kilometers and averages 16,000 skiers a day. That works out to a population density of 552 skiers per square kilometer—almost 221,000 times the density in Apussuit!

Apussuit's existence and functionality is very much dependent on two men—Poul Therkelsen and Adam Lyberth. Poul, a transplanted Dane with a toothy grin and a funny-looking wide-brimmed hat, has become a sort of one-man tourist office for Maniitsoq. He organizes heliskiing as well as the snowmobile skiing, not to mention deep-sea fishing, kayaking and almost any other adventure activity that one could imagine to do in this region.

ADAM IS AN EVEN MORE CRITICAL PART of the daily workings of Apussuit. He is a Greenlander who knows the huge expanse of territory on the Apussuit Glacier better than the local polar bears and whose guiding skills are instrumental in the day-to-day ski activities here. He is a short, stocky man with muscles on his muscles. After only a short chat with Adam, one comes to realize that he not only knows the backcountry around his native Maniitsoq, but he also has a pride and love for that backcountry. He is soft-spoken and well educated and at the same time, rugged and powerful. Looking at Adam, I got the feeling that he could meet a wolf, a whale or a walrus on its own turf and walk away the victor.

In most ski areas, powder enthusiasts need a guide to lead them to the untracked snow. Here, a guide is also indispensable for steering clear of crevasses and of the many icefalls where the glaciers end. In addition, one comes to Greenland, in part, to observe the scenery, and Adam led us to some truly spectacular spots.

Our first dawn in Apussuit revealed a remarkable view of the coastline to the west and of the fjord with its thousands of skerries. To the north stood a ridge of jagged peaks, while the huge, flat plateau of the glacier lay to the east.

After a hearty breakfast in the communal kitchen, Adam led our small snowmobile convoy to the South Top, 10 minutes away. There, we began our day with a few warmup runs on some gentle slopes that pointed towards the Søndre Isortoqfjord. It was –8 degrees centigrade, and the 10 centimeters of new snow was feather-light. We slid down through the fresh powder, and the fjord's murky water below was an ever-present reminder of where we were.

In a season with heavy snowfall, Adam explained, one could ski all the way down to the sea at this time of year. This year, however, had been very mild, and the snow cover was now 4–5 meters below normal. We were satisfied with the 500 vertical meters of skiing that was available. After all, with snowmobiles at our beck and call, it made little difference whether we skied the entire slope once or the upper half twice.

By noon, we moved over to the Chip's Bowl area. We skied a run where we glided in the shadow of some magnificent seracs. Little did I realize that these stunning ice formations were only a small sample of things to come.

At lunchtime, we sat in the midday sun gazing out over a 20-meter-high icefall that periodically deposited huge ice cubes into a large Greenlandic drink called Lake 530. With mountains, lakes, fjords, glaciers and other features of nature that outnumber people by an enormous ratio, it is perhaps not so odd that many of those features are numbered instead of named. In many cases, they are totally nameless.

After lunch, Adam and his cohorts transported us up to the top of one of those no-name peaks, where we hoped to ski down between two sectors of exposed ice cliffs, on an area of the glacier that seemed skiable. This was not the easiest task.

There is a lack of qualified mountain men in Greenland, because its people have generally turned to the sea rather than to the inland ice and mountains. Hence, Adam must double as both the ski guide and the snowmobile guide. This meant that we had no leader once we were on skis.

The particular type of terrain here also complicated matters. Even the experienced Adam was not sure what the correct starting point was for this descent, as the flat, featureless top of the so-called mountain possessed absolutely no reference point. There was not a stone, a bush or a bump to show us where we actually were on the mountain.

Adam, of course, knew the solution. He gave us a walkie-talkie, zipped back down to the lake and talked us to the starting point, which was only discernible from below. Then, they lined up the three snowmobiles to indicate the route we should follow. This was absolutely necessary until we put down the first set of tracks as a reference point.

» In Apussuit...we were the only skiers of the season! Now we are talking remote.«

Glaciers are generally convex, and they steepen continually until the ice abruptly ends. If one chooses the wrong line, the run ends in a cliff that is not visible until you are airborne. There is an additional hazard. As the slope steepens, there is less and less surface snow to cover the ice, because the snow sloughs off soon after every snowfall.

Our run began with a soft, easy rollover. Powder flew and we merrily danced our way down toward the line of vehicles. As the slope got steeper, the spectacular icefall to the left came into view. Beyond it, one could see a kilometer-long cliff of ice that met the lakeshore.

To the skier's right was the steepest sector, but it was also more difficult to figure. We enjoyed the steep face, but we never knew at what point one of us might hit the blue ice underneath and be sent into a treacherous slide—the kind of slide one did not want to make on an exposed slope.

Far to the right, of course, the icefall lay in wait like a patient assassin, in case somebody might try something foolish.

We played it safe and kept to the middle on our first run. It was an excellent run, and we repeated it on into the late afternoon. Adam mentioned that there was an alternative route down the mountain further to the west that had never been skied—a first descent. But we were having too much fun where we were. After all, it was our first day and it was getting late. We would leave that for another day.

As the evening wore on, we were getting more daring—perhaps too daring. On our last run, Tatu and I stayed far to our right, directly above the icefall, while Papi skied our usual route. While I took photos of Tatu, I heard his ski edges scrape loudly on the glacial ice. He regained his balance and we traversed a ways to the left.

"I think we can do a few more turns here," announced Tatu.

The pitch was close to 45 degrees at this point and getting steeper with every turn. Then Papi shouted from the lake below that it was time to cease and desist, and we dutifully followed orders. When we arrived at the lake from where we could see our tracks, it was quite scary to see how close we had been to an unplanned "mandatory" (a necessary jump to complete the descent).

We mounted our "Greenland horses" for the day's last ride. Adam drives a snowmobile as if he was behind the wheel of a Porsche on an empty Autobahn. I held on for dear life as we bounced back to camp at 100 kilometers an hour. It was 8:30 p.m., and we had been skiing for almost 12 hours. There definitely were some advantages to skiing Greenland style.

The weather can change in a heartbeat in Greenland and often does. The fog rolls in and out and moves up and down simultaneously, and the wind shifts direction like a fickle girlfriend, keeping the weather service usually a step behind in its forecasts.

LEFT PAGE
The midnight sun shines down on icebergs floating aimlessly in the sea off the coast of Ilulissat.

THIS PAGE
UPPER: Papi's face reveals a shocked expression at the steepness of the slope directly adjacent to the icefall. MIDDLE: Musk oxen grazing near Kangerlussuaq.
LOWER: Local women show off their traditional outfits.

We watched a beautiful sunset before turning in shortly after ten o'clock, but before we even got to sleep, the south wind was howling. The following morning, we were engulfed in fog, and snow was falling. Skiing was impossible amidst the featureless milky white that surrounded us. Our day's activity was to join Adam on a mission to replenish the water supply. This involved drilling a hole through a 2.5-meter layer of ice, and sucking out lake water with a hose. Then, we transported the water back to base camp in big 100-liter barrels.

The storm left us about 30 centimeters of fresh snow to play in when the sun reemerged the following day. The upper slopes were wind-packed powder but quite skiable with big-mountain skis. As we dropped into the lee of the wind on the north face just below the base camp, the snow became more powdery and the Kangerdluarssuk Fjord came into view. The lower we skied on each run, the better the snow quality got.

We began the morning skiing gentle lines that would definitely be secure from avalanches. With each run we tried steeper lines, gradually working our way across to a beautiful 35-degree face called Moment of Truth. We laid track after track on that slope, content in the knowledge that the lines we had not yet skied would not be gobbled up by others. The runs were short—about 350 vertical meters—but as we found out on our first day, the many hours of daylight gave us plenty of skiing before the sun set.

In business, the Peter Principle warns that people in an organization rise to the level of their incompetence. It makes sense. As people succeed at a job, they are promoted until they reach a level where they no longer perform well, and there they often stay.

This principle could well have a ski corollary, which is very applicable on an avalanche-prone day. "Powder skiers will invariably test and try progressively steeper slopes during the course of a powder day until they start an avalanche." Every success inspires them to turn it up a notch. It is a formula destined for ultimate disaster.

We fell into this trap. Buoyed by the apparent stability of the snow on

Moment of Truth, we ventured onto another nearby slope simply known as North Face. Situated between a rocky section of mountain on one side and one of the many icefalls of the glacier on the other, this lovely slope rolls over slowly to reach a pitch of about 40 degrees.

On this day, it lay basking naked in the sun, flaunting its virginity. And the three of us—educated, experienced, middle-aged skiers—fell for this temptress as if she were Lolita herself.

We did our best to feign caution, but our prurient desire was obvious. We entered slowly and did many solitary turns, pushing hard while stopping to see if she would slide. Nothing—no movement. But the moment the first of us linked three consecutive turns on the steepest pitch, the snow gave way. In no time, all the powder was resting in a pile in the flats, and Tatu was close to the pile of snow nursing a torn ligament. We had pressed our luck too far, so we packed it in. It was close to 8 p.m. and we had put in another 10-hour ski day.

NO SOONER DID WE GET BACK to our quarters than the wind again started whistling outside and Apussuit once again was inundated by fog. By morning, the wind had subsided but the fog remained.

Tatu was grounded of course, but Papi and I attempted a run down the easy west-facing flank of the mountain from base camp. This is the slope most often used by less experienced groups of skiers who come here for a taste of Greenlandic skiing. Today, it was not so easy. We hoped that we would soon get beneath the cloud layer but that was not to be.

We tried a second run, this time skiing the route from base camp down toward the boat dock. This is a long, gentle slope marked by sticks set into the snow every 50 meters or so. We could not see the sticks until we nearly hit them. Instead, we could only follow the snowmobile track for guidance.

There are various styles of skiing, what with old school, New School, carving turns, racing turns and so on, but today I developed a new style—the Helen Keller turn. This is a hesitant, tentative turn with the weight back, unsure of whether one is going uphill or downhill—not to be recommended. The title of Procol Harum's famous hit, "Whiter Shade of Pale", gives an accurate description of the visibility that day.

Adam laughed when we arrived at the snowmobile for pickup.

"The fog is not so bad today," he said. "Sometimes, we cannot see the 50 meters from the sleeping cabins to the main house. The wind is blowing so hard, and the snow and fog are so dense that we must hang ropes between the buildings to keep us from getting lost."

In spite of the knowledge that it could get worse, we decided that our two runs would suffice for this day's outdoor exercise.

Our leader had hoped to take us to a section of steep mountains about a 3-hour snowmobile ride from our quarters. He pointed out Adam's Peak on the map, as we plotted and planned for the next days. There were some steep and interesting lines there, he promised.

"How did the peak get its name?" wondered Tatu, noticing that it bore the same title as our leader.

Tatu's suspicions were correct. The peak was named after Adam, who had made a first descent there. I suddenly realized that skiing here was different than even in Alaska. Both Alaska and Greenland are full of first descents and unnamed mountains, but here in Greenland, we were skiing with the guy who makes the maps! This was truly Adam's domain. Nobody knew these mountains better than he, and no one was better qualified to chart the territory. There were no-name mountains all around us just waiting to be labeled Tatu's Top or Petterson Peak on some future map of Greenland. It was like sailing around with Amerigo Vespucci.

WE NEVER GOT ANOTHER CHANCE. The low clouds and unstable weather made even an easy first descent too dangerous in an area so riddled with glaciers. For the final two days of our stay, we had to settle for many sets of first tracks instead of first descents. There is no fun or honor, of course, in naming a mountain without achieving something.

It didn't really matter. Greenland is not a place where the first descents will disappear and the mountains will all be christened before we get the chance to ski with Adam again.

I sometimes rush about this shrinking globe of ours, attempting to

LEFT PAGE
Papi gazes out over the skerries and the fjord from the Apússuit ski center.

THIS PAGE
A vodka tonic here may taste the same as back home, but you can't fill the glass with five-million-year-old ice cubes in Oslo or London.

experience things as quickly as possible, afraid that a few years from now those experiences will no longer be there for the taking. How long will it be before the Bushmen of Africa or the tribesmen of New Guinea all wear blue jeans? For how long will the giraffe and the cheetah lope free on the shrinking plains of Africa? And will we still be able to see whales on their annual migration twenty years from now?

Here in the vastness of a land that looked as if the Ice Age never receded, I felt a great sense of peace and harmony. The population of Greenland really hasn't grown very much since the days of Eric the Red, when 5000 Vikings inhabited the island along with the native Inuits. With all this knowledge, I felt calm in the prospect that not only I but also my great-grandchildren could someday ski first descents and christen unnamed peaks in Greenland. We would just have to stay in touch with Adam's descendants.

Europe – The North in a Nutshell

LOCATION	NEAREST TOWN	NEAREST AIRPORT	SEASON	PEAK ELEVATION	VERTICAL DROP	SIZE	SNOW	BEAUTY	VILLAGE	NOVICE	INTERMEDIATE	ADVANCED	OFF-PISTE	NIGHTLIFE	RATING AVERAGE	WEB SITE
NORWAY																
Narvik	Narvik	Evenes	early December–May [1]	1002 m	877 m	3	1	4	5	4	2	3	4	5	3.4	www.narvikinfo.no
Oppdal	Oppdal	Trondheim	December–late April	1350 m	1145 m [2]	3	2	4	3	4	4	4	2	4	3.5	www.oppdal.com
Strandafjellet	Stranda	Ålesund	mid November–late April	1230 m	1000 m	3	1	4	5	3	2	3	4	5	1	3.1	www.strandafjellet.no
Strynfjellet	Stryn	Ålesund	early June–early August	1600 m	540 m	2	1	3	5	4	1	2	4	4	4	3.0	www.strynefjellet.com
SWEDEN																
Riksgränsen	Abisko	Kiruna	February–late June	910 m	410 m	2	1	4	3	2	3	3	3	3	3	2.7	www.riksgransen.nu
Åre	Åre	Östersund	December–early May	1274 m	880 m	3	5	4	4	4	4	4	4	3	5	3.9	www.skistar.com/are
FINLAND																
Pyhä-Luosto	Pelkoseniemi	Rovaniemi	early Oct.–early May	540 m	280 m	1	2	4	3	2	4	3	3	3	2.8	www.phya.fi
Ruka	Kuusamo	Kuusamo	mid Oct.–mid May [3]	492 m	201 m	1	2	4	3	2	5	2	2	1	4	2.6	www.ruka.fi
Ylläs	Kittilä	Kittilä	mid Feb. –early May	718 m	463 m	2	3	4	3	2	5	3	2	3	3	3.0	www.yllas.fi
ICELAND																
Hlídarfjall	Akureyri	Akureyri	mid Dec.–end of April	971 m	491 m	2	1	4	4	3	3	3	2	2	4	2.8	www.eyjafjordur.is/special/hlidarfjall
Bláfjöll	Reykjavik	Reykjavik	mid November–April	700 m	220 m	1	2	3	3	1	3	2	1	1	5 [4]	2.2	www.skidasvaedi.is
Böggvisstadafjall	Dalvik	Akureyri	December–April	320 m	275 m	1	1	4	5	3	3	2	2	2	1	2.4	www/skidalvik.is/area.php
Tungudal	Isafjördur	Isafjördur	mid December–late April	510 m	410 m	2	1	4	5	3	3	2	3	3	1	2.7	www.travelnet.is/JKL/journey/sv_vf/isafjordur.htm
GREENLAND																
Apussuit	Maniitsoq	Maniitsoq	mid March–mid June	931 m	850 m	3	1	5	5	1	1	1	1	5	1	2.4	www.greenland-guide.gl/maniitsoq-tourist/apussuit-camp.htm

(1) Upper lift opens in early March.
(2) 790 vertical meters if skiing is lift-accessed. The additional 355 meters is a result of a snowcat service that brings skiers twice a day to the peak of Blåøret.

(3) Ruka also offers summer skiing on one slope of artificial snow in June.
(4) This refers to the nightlife in Reykjavik.

EASTERN EUROPE V

EASTERN EUROPE

"East is East, and West is West, and never the twain shall meet." Rudyard Kipling did not have Eastern Europe in mind when he wrote this sentence. I also do not believe that Kipling was a skier, but his words certainly hold true in describing the breach between a ski holiday in the West and a vacation in some of the former members of the East Bloc.

In the years that have passed since the iron hand of Soviet rule removed its shadow from half the continent, Eastern Europe's ski resorts have shown mixed results. Some areas have benefited from a major investment of capital, while other resorts have merely grown older and more outdated.

One of the problems has been that more Eastern Europeans have been taking their ski vacations in Western Europe than the other way around. There have recently been some signs that a more balanced exchange of winter tourism is beginning to emerge, and that can only bode well for the East.

In Bulgaria, Borovets has for years been entertaining low-budget West European skiers, and there are currently plans in the works for a €100–150-million upgrade that would, among other things, add 80 kilometers of pistes to the existing area. Not that far away, in the little resort of Bansko, they are already beyond the planning stage. In the last few years, they have added five lifts, extensive snow-making equipment, and a dozen snow cats to keep the mountain well groomed.

The nations of former Yugoslavia are also finally getting back to more positive endeavors following more than a decade of bloodshed. The ski areas around the Olympic city of Sarajevo have cleared the pistes of land mines and are back in business, and the Serbian resort of Kapaonik is receiving British charter tourists once again for the first time since the early '90s.

Georgia is another country where the ski infrastructure is relatively good. The Gudauri ski area was updated with new Dopplmayer lifts at the very beginning of the post-Soviet era thanks to a large input of Austrian money. Gudauri offers a combination of traditional ski lifts and an experienced heliski operation.

On the other hand, there are many ski locations in Eastern Europe where the problems of poor infrastructure, low maintenance and long lift lines are still the order of the day. In Brezovica, Kosovo, we stayed in a hotel where one hardly noticed a difference between the temperature inside and outside. In Slovakia, Mt. Chopok's most important lift can no longer pass the safety inspection, but no new lift has been built to replace it. And in Zakopane, Poland, the queues for the cable car are reminiscent of the old breadline days.

Let this not discourage you. Remember that the steady march of progress is a two-edged sword. With improved infrastructure come major marketing, more good skiers, and a homogenization of the ski and cultural experience that will ultimately blur the distinction between East and West.

Mt. Elbrus and Mt. Cheget in Russia suffer from long queues, but the freeride skiing is world class, and there is still plenty to go around. Popova Sapka in Macedonia can hardly muster the quorum necessary to get the lifts open, but when they are running, skiers will not be disappointed. The rooms were cold in Brezovica, but we only had to share the powder with about twenty other skiers. The infrastructure of Sinaia in Rumania won't match that in Val Thorens, but you can't get a room for under $10 in Val Thorens.

So it goes. The changes will eventually come, and they will indubitably be for better and for worse. In case Kipling erred and the twain someday do meet, it would be advisable to enjoy the unique flavor of Eastern Europe before that comes to pass. That is where the adventure lies, and after all, skiing is an adventure sport.

Chapter 18. RUSSIA

RUSSIAN ROULETTE

Russia is a land that potentially offers many possibilities for skiing, as there are mountains in various regions of the country. In the Caucasus are the resorts of Dombai and Krasnay Polyana, of which the latter is becoming increasingly popular among freeriders. Ski lifts also exist in parts of the Urals, the Kola Peninsula, the Kamchatka Peninsula and other regions. Nevertheless, one must say that Russia is pretty much an untapped resource when it comes to skiing.

Many mountainous sections of Siberia are too far from major population centers to merit any investment in winter sports, and the many years of Communist rule were not very conducive to the development of decadent leisure-time activities.

Since the fall of Communism in the early 1990s, numerous republics that were home to some of the most prominent ski areas of the former Soviet Union have become independent. Hence, the ski resort of Gudauri is in the independent country of Georgia, Chimbulak ski area is part of Kazakhstan, the ski lifts of Beldersay now fall into the realm of the republic of Uzbekistan and Issyk-Kul ski area is part of Kyrgyzstan.

The wilderness area of Kamchatka, still part of Russia, has achieved some notoriety for heliskiing in recent years. Here, a whirlybird gives access to a myriad of stunning volcanic peaks that are only easily accessible from the air. Conventional skiing in this region exists near the city of Petropavlovsk-Kamchatsky, where Moroznaya offers skiing on two lifts, and Krasnaya Sopka has a lone lift that transports skiers up 600 vertical meters. While these lifts offer an option to heliskiers during down time, they hardly merit a visit to distant Kamchatka in their own right.

Among the various possibilities, however, there are two Russian ski resorts, situated side by side in the Caucasus Mountains, that are a must for avid freeriders—Mt. Cheget and Mt. Elbrus.

WHEN I WAS GROWING UP, Mont Blanc was considered the highest mountain in Europe. I never heard any theory postulated to the contrary. Its gleaming glaciers towered high over the Alps, and at 4807 meters, it was without question head and shoulders above any of its neighbors. Today, visitors to Courmayeur on the Italian side or to Chamonix on the French

side will certainly still read the promotional material referring to Mont Blanc as the roof of Europe.

Something has changed, however, somewhere between my childhood and the present day—the world has gotten smaller and Europe has gotten bigger. The shrinking of the Earth is, of course, a figurative occurrence, brought about by the communications revolution and globalization, while the growing of Europe is a literal fact, caused in part by the disintegration of the Soviet Union.

One of the results of all this is that Mt. Elbrus, the 5642-meter-high, dormant volcano situated in the Caucasus Mountains of southwestern Russia, is now considered by many to be the highest mountain in Europe. The French, the Italians and the Russians all have a partisan interest, but the world of alpinists has basically given the nod to Mt. Elbrus. Dick Bass and Frank Wells set the benchmark for the elite "Seven Summits" group of mountaineers who have climbed the highest peak of each continent, when they made Elbrus their first joint climb way back in 1981. That is good enough for me.

MONT BLANC AND CHAMONIX HAVE BEEN household words among skiers almost since the infancy of the sport. A train took skiers and other sightseers part way up the mountain from St. Gervais as early as 1913, and the famous Aiguille du Midi cable car and Vallée Blanche descent have been legendary since the construction of this unique *téléphérique* in 1954.

Skiing on Elbrus, however, did not get started until the '70s, and even then, the rift between the communist and capitalist world that existed at the time did not really allow the word to get to very many skiers beyond the Iron Curtain. But that has all changed by now...or has it? Not really.

While Mont Blanc remains the world's foremost mountaineering Mecca, Mt. Elbrus lives on in relative obscurity. A few of us have an interest in the obscure, however, and last spring Rafael Betschart, Christoph Bichsel and I decided that we would like to ski on Europe's highest mountain.

From the very outset, it was not easy. In Russia, very little goes according to plan. Air connections were poor to begin with, and then our flight to nearby Mineralny Vody was canceled, as the airport was closed for renovations.

Not all the breaches between East and West have been bridged yet, despite many years of capitalism in Russia; and our Western travel agent could not purchase air tickets for us from Moscow to any other local cities. We got ourselves a travel agent in Russia. She arranged a flight from Moscow to Stavropol. She also organized a young snowboarder to pick us up in Moscow's Sheremetyevo-2 Airport at six in the morning, deliver our internal flight tickets, and drive us in his old Lada to the Domodedova Airport on the other side of town.

Instead of a 2-hour bus transfer from Mineralny Vody, we now faced a 6-hour mini-bus ride to Mt. Elbrus, but that was the best available alternative. We were not deterred. Skiing on Europe's highest mountain must be worth a few difficulties. Late in the evening, more than 24 hours after our journey began, our taxi pulled into the Wolfram Hotel in the village of Terskol.

Terskol is not really the idyll of a mountain village. It will never replace Chamonix in terms of charm, coziness and mountain atmosphere. It is a combination of large high-rise buildings, constructed in typical communist-era block-like shapes, and small shacks that primarily house grocery stores and small restaurants. There are also numerous half-built structures—the never-to-be-finished remains of projects that died along with Communist rule in Russia.

Terskol lies between the lifts that bring skiers up Mt. Elbrus and another set of lifts that rise up Mt. Cheget, on the opposite side of the valley.

These are both unusual mountains. They are both monsters. They are gigantic—larger than life—and they are frightening mountains in the best of times. There are a few unprepared pistes at each ski area, and the rest of the territory is covered by rugged, wild terrain, full of gorges, waterfalls and massive rock faces.

Elbrus is Russia's answer to La Grave in France or Alagna in Italy. Its high top station gives freeriders access to an enormous amount of terrain, but there is a catch. Enter at your own risk! Avalanche danger, cliffs, crevasses and risky couloirs are all around.

Despite the danger, Elbrus has a magnetic allure. Once a freerider sets his eyes on this temptress, he falls in love. It is the Lorelei in spades. It is an aphrodisiac to powder hounds and nature lovers alike. It is an opium den full of naked Chinese concubines. Skiing here can be a game of Russian roulette in its purest form. Each time one enters one of Elbrus's windloaded slopes, one pulls the trigger on a revolver that has a bullet in one chamber.

> » Each time one enters, one pulls the trigger on a revolver that has a bullet in one chamber.«

This is where Liza Pahl came into the picture. She is the travel agent who saved our trip, but just as Elbrus is no ordinary mountain, Liza is no ordinary travel agent. Liza is a young German woman who fell in love in the early '90s with a Russian man, Sasha, and a Russian mountain. She is a snowboarder who has twice won the Russian Extreme Championships. Along with her Sasha, she guides and protects people on the two local giants. This aspect of her services, we were soon to find out, was an absolute necessity.

A trip up Mt. Elbrus begins with two cable cars, which bring skiers from approximately 2200 meters to 3500 meters. They were constructed in 1969 and 1977 respectively. The upper tram had its cable restrung recently, with the usual Russian penchant for exactness. When we arrived at the top station, the loaded cable car was too heavy, and the first patrons had to step 70–80 centimeters up to the platform to unload!

From 3500 meters, a rickety, single chair lift continues up to 3800 meters. This lift was certainly already outdated when it was installed in 1982, but it is one of the highest lifts in the world, ranking in the top ten in this category. Elbrus, however, does not really settle for second fiddle in the uphill transportation competition either. From 3800 meters to the lofty heights of 4200 meters, a piste machine provides the service of bringing skiers even higher.

THE CABLE CARS HAVE A MEAGER capacity of 27 people, a figure that did not foresee the end of communism and a growing middle class of Russians who can afford to go skiing. The lift line in the morning was not pretty, but fortunately for us, the rules of privilege die hard in this country. An influential friend within the system leads certain skiers to the back door of the cable car building, circumventing the lift line, and Liza seemed to have many friends. We moved into the cable car directly.

It was the last week of March, but Mt. Elbrus was apparently unaware of the calendar. We arrived to winter powder and –15 degrees centigrade, but the sun was shining and we could enjoy the magnificent scenery immediately.

The twin peaks of Elbrus rose high into the deep blue sky, surrounded by glaciers baring their icy teeth. It almost appeared as if the old volcano was waking from her deep slumber, as her peaks played hide-and-go-seek behind a wispy cloud that looked like a plume of smoke.

Liza led us on a warmup run among the sharp volcanic boulders under the chair lift. Now we were ready for a full guided tour, which began with a descent down the Garabashi Gorge (knows as "Ushelye" among Russian freeriders).

Liza led us safely along a ridgeline, but I deviated from the path, choosing a juicy slope between two ridges. I calculated the possible danger, but the slope was no more than about 30 degrees, and I dove in. Three turns into the powder, a slab avalanche broke loose, sending me on a very straight schuss off to the left. The snowslide was limited to about 50 meters in length, but I decided very quickly to follow Liza much more closely the rest of the day.

Rafi, a freerider who generally makes three turns where I make twenty, commented, "Jimmy, I think this is a New-School mountain!"

He was right. My shorter, more bouncy, old-school turns were more likely to set off a slide in the wind-loaded powder, and were also less likely to get me quickly out of the line of fire.

Soon, however, Rafi proved that even he was not immune. He, too, deviated from Liza's lead and traversed high as we entered the steep-sided gorge that gives its name to the run we were now skiing. It was one more round of Russian roulette, and another small slide broke loose. It was no more than 20 meters long, but it was enough to gobble up one of Rafi's skis. The slide debris was a meter deep, and we unpacked our shovels and began digging, with no success. Liza used her probe pole and soon found the missing ski.

At the end of the run, we snaked our way alongside a stream of snowmelt, gazing up at the vertical basalt walls of the gorge, which rose hundreds of meters straight up above us. Ultimately, we emerged on the road between Terskol and the lifts and walked 10 minutes back to the cable car.

IN THE AFTERNOON, LIZA LED US on another route from top to bottom. As with many mountains, the slopes of Elbrus are shallower at the higher elevations and steepen as one descends. This makes it very difficult to ski without a guide, as one does not know what kind of exit one will have until long past the point of no return. This time we wove our way between the rocks into a very steep couloir of south-facing sun crust.

» Three turns into the powder, a slab avalanche broke loose...«

Rafi and Christian screamed down the 40-degree chute in their New-School style, and Liza, with her snowboard, also had no problem with the crust. Meanwhile, I huffed and puffed in the high altitude, breaking through the crust on every turn in a series of old-school jump turns. "There really are a few advantages to this New School," I thought to myself, as I tried to catch my breath.

We finished the day with a run on the piste and a beer and pastry at one of the many small cafes at the base of the cable car. Before ten o'clock, we were as deep in sleep as Elbrus itself.

A new day brings new adventure, and the unexpected began already at breakfast every morning at the Hotel Wolfram. This day, our morning offering was fried chicken with Russian salad!

After "breakfast", we rode a taxi a couple of kilometers down the road to the Cheget ski area. Our taxi passed the wide north face, and we could see how the broad, open slopes of the upper mountain funneled into a series of avalanche gullies. Most of the gullies had already slid, and avalanche debris spread out below each ravine like an alluvial fan.

Cheget's lift system consists of a single and a double chair lift which go up to the middle station, a single chair that continues from there, and a short drag lift at the top.

There was nothing in sight that even vaguely resembled a blue piste, and only the short upper lift that could, perhaps, be considered a red run. This ski area was as black as they come. Various descents full of moguls were visible on both sides of the lifts, and there was a huge expanse of no-man's-land on either side.

I was amazed at how many Russian skiers were good enough to make use of this terrain, and their equipment was state of the art as well. When I visited the Soviet Union for skiing in the early '90s, most of the local patrons slid around on Bulgarian-made Mladost skis or old hand-me-downs from the West. Now, we saw the locals skiing on the latest that Fischer, Salomon and Atomic had to offer. They wore the trendiest parkas, helmets and backpacks with shovels.

LIZA LED US DIRECTLY to the north face. We began with a 5-minute walk above the lifts to give us a few more vertical meters of powder. There were many more entries further up Mt. Cheget, but they were still too dangerous.

We were joined today by Sasha and Ludka, one of his freeride clients from Moscow. The wide upper mountain still offered some good lines of powder with minimal tracks, and we skied one by one.

We all watched from below as Ludka descended. Halfway down the first pitch, she dug a tip, did an elegant double somersault and hiked back up to gather her gear.

"I see," she must have thought to herself, "Za weight shoult be a leettle more back."

She then proceeded to shoot down the rest of the slope in what first seemed to be a gigantic freeride turn. It was only as she approached the four of us without the slightest decrease in speed that I realized that her weight was on her haunches and she was totally out of control. It was "bowling for rubles", and we were the bowling pins. Rafi and I attempted a quick last second two-step to either side, as she came hurtling directly into our midst like a Russian rocket gone awry.

As her head reemerged from one of the classic face-plants I have ever seen, she must have been thinking, "Maybe za weight shoult *not* be so-o-o-o far back."

She smiled and shook the snow out of her hair like a sheepdog that had just come out of the water, and we were ready to press on.

We continued down through powder for much of the way, but the exit-couloir was completely packed, as all the off-piste skiers had to exit by way of a handful of narrow corridors. The days when the few foreign visitors were the only ones to defile the sanctity of Russian powder are a thing of the past. The new wave of middle- and upper-class Russian skiers that has recently developed, has grown into the sport hand in hand with the freeride fad, with all its accompanying gear, marketing and hoopla.

A skier-packed trail led us back to the lifts, and we proceeded with round two. This time, we followed our leader onto the large eastern slope of Mt. Cheget. Here, one can traverse out until one's left leg gets too tired or until one wants to descend, whichever comes first. The slope is quite steep and according to Liza, it is very avalanche-prone in deep powder. We had no incidents, however, and finished the run in a valley that led us back to the lift.

Unfortunately, by the time we arrived at the middle station again, a fog as thick as Russian borscht had encompassed the mountain. We followed very closely as our guide led us from the middle station directly into an extremely tight birch forest.

Liza had some difficulties on her long snowboard, Rafi and Christoph thought it was fun, and I felt like an American prisoner of the Cold War, being put through some Soviet torture. The snow was quite heavy, there were a few old tracks, and the birch trees left as much space between them as the Minnesota Vikings' front line. I broke a dozen branches and had one major confrontation with a birch trunk before I finally emerged from the forest, vanquished.

With the fog came fresh snow, and by the following morning we were back in the sunshine. We had hoped to use the snow cat that is supposed to take skiers above the chair lift of Mt. Elbrus, but it was out of commission, an unsurprising occurrence in Russia. Liza, however, was used to accommodating for the inefficiencies of the Russian system.

We began a 15-minute hike past odd-looking dormitories for summer climbers, situated at 3850 meters. They looked like an oversized six-pack laid out side by side—a row of large cylinders of corrugated steel. It was a mountain refuge that only a Russian could appreciate.

Soon we embarked on a spectacular run over the Small Azau Glacier. It was an easy descent, but full of stunning views of glacial seracs and crevasses. Liza enjoyed sharing with us the world that she had fallen in love with a decade earlier.

The day ended with the best powder of our visit. Despite the fact that most of the slopes of Elbrus face south or east, the cold weather had preserved the powder. I had packed away my camera for the day, and Rafi and Christoph were elated. They careened down the guts of a 35-degree face like two fire trucks on their way to a four-alarm blaze.

By now, we had recovered from our long journey enough to take in an evening of the local nightlife. We checked out a few night spots and found that the bar under the Hotel Cheget was definitely the place to be. The vodka flowed like water (it usually does in Russia) and I, for one, woke up the next morning with a head the size of the Kremlin and repeated my biannual vow to give up drinking. I know the Cold War is long over, but there are still more dangers lurking in Russia than meet the eye.

LIZA WENT INTO MOTION ONCE AGAIN to outdo herself. A long traverse and a 30-minute hike to the east brought us beyond the mountain observatory and into a whole new valley. Here, we skied alongside the Terskol Glacier, a chunk of ice even larger and more spectacular than the Small Azau Glacier from the day before. The descent ultimately took us through a gargantuan glacial valley back to the road.

As usual, this route was hazardous. Besides the fact that Elbrus is an avalanche-prone mountain at any time of year, the extreme changes in temperature that are characteristic on all mountains during the spring added extra danger in late March.

As on the first day, Liza showed us the safe route, but sometimes we deviated. Numerous of our variations were poorly chosen. Christoph did a jump for the camera into a slope that Liza warned would probably set the snow into motion—another game of Russian roulette. The whole slope broke loose upon his landing but Christoph, fortunately, skied out to the side.

No more than 20 minutes later, I lay in the snow to photograph another small cliff jump. Deja vu! Christoph's impact again started a small slab moving all around me.

It reminded me once again, "Listen to Liza! Think with your brain and not your camera! Pay attention to Liza!"

WE FINISHED THE DAY back on the north face of Cheget. A hundred turns down the mountain (or eight turns for Rafi and Christoph), we entered a different exit-couloir than on our previous day—400 vertical meters, 5 meters wide and 45 degrees steep. That was okay. Unfortunately, there was a slight problem in the middle of the chute. It narrowed to less than 2 meters, and there were a few bare rocks. It was what they call a "mandatory".

Rafi jumped it. Christoph circumvented it with an even more difficult route. Jimmy, unfortunately, hummed, hawed and hesitated. Should I jump, should I kick turn, should I take off my skis and try to walk down? Murphy's law came immediately into play. Whatever decision you make will be wrong!

I lost my edge above the rocks and performed an ignominious slide over them on my butt. One ski ended up 100 meters below me. It was an inopportune location for a "yard sale", but the only thing hurt was my pride. All things considered, it was really just another empty chamber in our daily game of Russian roulette.

Another day of our Elbrus adventure had come to a close, and we were all intact. Liza had again been our secret defense—our *Star-Wars* shield—

protecting us against the forces of evil among these untamed giants of the Caucasus.

We woke up on our last day to another sparkling morning and embarked on a ski tour. We followed our intrepid leader on a 2-hour hike across vast fields of snow-covered ice—another one of Elbrus's 77 glaciers. Mt. Elbrus is covered by 145 square kilometers of glaciers and some are up to 400 meters thick.

The hiking was relatively flat. After a pause for an apple and a candy bar, we enjoyed another beautiful run on this most versatile of mountains. Late in the day, we separated. Liza and I decided to have a late lunch, while Rafi and Christoph tried to get as much skiing in as they could before the lifts closed.

When Liza and I returned to the base of the mountain at five o'clock, the cable car was still open, but surprisingly, Rafi and Christoph were sitting at one of the après-ski restaurants and had called it a day. Knowing of their boundless energy for skiing, I was mystified.

Then Rafi sheepishly told me that he had unleashed yet another snowslide high above a couloir. Fortunately, he had again managed to ski out to the side unscathed. Now, the premature end of their ski day made more sense. It was the fifth avalanche of our stay. We had so far dodged the bullet, but after all, a revolver has only six chambers.

Chapter 19. GEORGIA

GEORGIA ON MY MIND

"Well the Ukraine girls really knock me out, they leave the West behind, and Moscow girls make me sing and shout, that Georgia's always on my mi-mi-mi-mi-mind." So sang John Lennon back in 1968, and these were about the first positive words out of the West to be said about the Soviet Union since another Lenin initiated the whole proletariat movement in Mother Russia.

Since the breakup of the Soviet Union, however, the changes have been coming fast and furious in the last great colonial empire. One of those changes has been the development of a top heliski destination and four-star hotel in the heart of the Caucasus Mountains of Georgia. With the advent of Glasnost at the beginning of the '90s, the government of Georgia immediately traded its copy of the Communist Manifesto for a few back issues of *Powder Magazine*, and simultaneously figured out what to do with some of its unemployed helicopter pilots recently returned from Afghanistan.

In the heart of this 1200-kilometer-long range of snow-covered mountains, which stretches from the Black Sea to the Caspian Sea, lies the small ski resort of Gudauri. In 1987, Gudauri consisted of three antiquated lifts and a village that resembled a half-built shantytown. But since then, Western money and the state of Georgia have jointly transformed Gudauri with the addition of four Dopplmayer lifts, a 200-bed hotel and a small fleet of Aeroflot helicopters. The village itself still looks like something scourged by the Nazis in World War II, but the Austrian-built hotel, 4 kilometers away, is regal enough for a czar to set up court.

The hotel offers every convenience, including tennis courts, billiard tables, bowling alleys, a video room, swimming pool, sauna, fitness room, Jacuzzi, and massage room, as well as two restaurants and two bars. With all its amenities, it is the height of Western decadence and certainly has comrades Stalin, Trotsky, and company doing convulsive pirouettes in their graves.

I WAS JOINED ON THIS TRIP by two friends, Arne Bredow and Keith Johnston. Our Aeroflot flight had just taken off from Munich when it became clear that we were, indeed, headed for some Eastern European destination where vodka is the equivalent of water.

No sooner had the fasten-your-seat-belt sign flashed off, when a man in the first row, who was probably too obese even to use a seat belt, removed a bottle from his private stash and began filling water glasses with straight vodka. He passed the glasses around indiscriminately to all the passengers in his vicinity. Within a short time, the front of the plane (hopefully with the exception of the cockpit) was immersed in a very jovial atmosphere.

Soon, our rotund host, who turned out to be Georgia's Minister of Finance, passed the vodka bottle back through the plane so that the rest of us could also partake in the aerial party, Georgia style. The afterglow of the vodka kept us in reasonably good spirits through our 2-hour wait for baggage and customs in Tbilisi and helped us sleep on the 3-hour bus ride to Gudauri.

Once we hit the pistes, it did not take long to notice that we were light-years away from the Alpine ski environment. At the middle station, Georgian peasants peddled apples, apricot fruit leather and Cossack socks, instead of the usual *Würstel* and *Gulaschsuppe* that we were accustomed to.

It was also quite easy to distinguish the Soviet skiers from the foreigners.

It was the sunscreen protection system that most clearly separated East from West. Gudauri is situated around the same latitude as Rome, so it is quite understandable that the sun is intense, especially in late March. I began my holiday with factor five cream, progressed quickly to factor nine on the second day, applied factor twelve on day three, and finished my holiday smearing gobs of factor 25 into my reddened cheeks.

The locals had developed a simpler and cheaper system. Some Soviet skiers covered all but their eyes with a bandana, while others took their sun protection a step further and covered their heads with pillowcases with small holes cut out for their eyes and mouth. Even the local skiers who stripped down to shorts and bikinis to catch some rays at the middle station kept their hoods and scarves in place over their faces. It never became clear whether sun lotion was unavailable in Georgia or merely too expensive, but with nobody revealing their faces, the scene resembled a Ku Klux Klan meeting in Alabama.

The local skiers confined themselves primarily to the prepared pistes, while we took advantage of the treeless slopes and spent the afternoon exploring the off-piste possibilities. We skied a number of runs in very good corn snow and ended up on the hotel verandah at 5:30, just in time to partake in a *shashlik* (Georgian shish kebab) barbecue, hosted by our Soviet helicopter pilots. These pilots turned out to be virtual jacks of all trades, who could not only fly and cook but later entertained us with a guitar and a variety of Georgian songs as well.

ON OUR SECOND MORNING, the sunrise turned the nearby peaks a bright pink, and by 8:15, four guides and eighteen of us had climbed aboard a bright orange whirlybird. As we elevated, an aerial view of the Caucasus displayed that they were ideal skiing mountains—relatively rounded, with much fewer rock faces and jagged pinnacles than the Alps. Most peaks seemed to be skiable in all directions, without the obstacles of cliffs and thick forests, which render many Alpine faces inaccessible.

The snow glistened invitingly in the morning sun, and we managed to carve up seven corn-snow faces before heading back to the hotel for lunch at about 1:30. After lunch, we explored the lift system and also descended off-piste to the village of Gudauri.

One of the highlights of our trip was the morning we began skiing above the tiny peasant village of Tschutta, a mountain community of about 200 people. The night had been cold and the crust was still solid and smooth as a baby's bottom when we started skiing. One of our guides, Roland Beeler, led us down the mountain, churning out sweeping giant slalom turns as if he were training for the World Cup circuit.

Just 50 meters above Tschutta, we came across one of the villagers attempting to practice his skiing technique on some rather suspect equipment. He wore cross-country skis, one blue and one red, apparently the two remaining skis of separate pairs. His ski poles differed about 20 centimeters in length, and a pair of rudimentary cross-country bindings kept his black rain boots attached to his skis.

"Our helicopter's not full," called out one of the guides. "Let's give him a thrill."

One of our Georgian guides spoke briefly to the man, and 5 minutes

LEFT PAGE
UPPER LEFT: Arne Bredow skis some of the off-piste terrain accessible from Gudauri's ski lifts.
LOWER LEFT: Georgian kids on their homemade sleds get ready for the ride of their life after the helicopter dropped them high above their village. Do you think helisledding will ever catch on big time?
RIGHT: This Georgia native joined our heliski entourage on some equipment that I would be afraid to use on a rope tow for beginners.

THIS PAGE
LEFT: Once the Russians bailed out of Afghanistan, these choppers got put to a much more pleasant use—heliskiing.
RIGHT: This Georgian skier is either preparing to rob a bank or got extremely sunburnt earlier on his holiday.

later, he landed with the rest of us 800 vertical meters above Tschutta. His style on his descent was not exactly vintage Ingemar Stenmark, but it was certainly better than any of us could have done on his equipment.

We decided to ski the same mountain a third run, and this time, four local boys with homemade sleds as well as our friend with the "downhill rain boots" joined us in the chopper. The primitive sleds were no more than 50 centimeters long, not exactly built for stability. Nonetheless, before we could even get into our bindings at the top, the four kids had shot down the mountain. Within a few minutes, they had completed a descent that, by comparison, made the famous Cresta Run in St. Moritz look like an amusement park ride for underage tots.

We eventually departed from our newly acquired Georgian acquaintances and followed the sun on to other corn-snow slopes, once again heading back to the hotel about two o'clock, having completed ten descents.

Near the end of the week, I mentioned to our Georgian guide, Sukchi, that it would be interesting to get away from the hotel and go to a local restaurant, to get a better sampling of the Georgian way of life. Half an hour later, four of us were heading down the valley in a borrowed Lada to a nearby village. We decided to let our Georgian host do the ordering.

We were soon served a first course of sliced cucumbers, cabbage, parsley, radishes, onions and cold meat in aspic. This was followed up by a main course of fried pork with a very spicy sauce and home-cut French fried potatoes. The dinner was accompanied by the obligatory liter bottle of vodka and a pitcher of pear juice with which to dilute the spirits. The meal was simple but edible, and the price would not have put a large dent in a Western McDonald's employee's hourly wage. We made a reasonable assault on the vodka, but considering that we were still planning to ski the following day, we reluctantly left about one third of the bottle's contents behind and returned to the hotel.

My tale of East meets West is not complete without the following story, told to us by a young lady skier from Moscow, whom we met on the chair lift.

"I was eenvited last year from a friend een West to ski een Italy. He sent me a plane ticket and peeck me up een Milano. When we come to ski resort, I begin to cry. The mountains are green, there ees almost no snow, and one hour to wait with thousand peoples to come up zee mountain. I say my friend, 'You come to Gudauri. We always have snow and never have lift lines.' Next time, I go for shopping trip to West, and ski vacation in Soviet."

Chapter 20. SLOVAKIA

THE TRUTH, THE WHOLE TRUTH…

Anders Karlsson, Andreas Thelander and I packed my car full of ski gear and headed east, out of the Alps, toward the Tatra Mountains of Slovakia and Poland. Our first destination was the ski resort of Jasna, in the Low Tatras, near the town of Liptovsky Mikulas. En route to Jasna and Mt. Chopok, Anders began teasing me about the practices of ski journalists.

"I think it is very odd," he related, "how in every article I have ever read in a ski magazine, some journalist has discovered some formerly unknown ski village, where his arrival just happens to coincide with a meter of fresh powder. On his first morning in Snowyodel, Austria or Pastapowder, Italy, through some stroke of good fortune, he rides up the lift with some local yokel who turns out to be a combination of Jeremy Nobis and Hermann Maier. The local hero, out of the goodness of his heart, then proceeds, over the next three or four days, to reveal to our snorkel-bearing Shakespeare every secret powder stash on his whole mountain! Now, does that sound believable?"

I laughed. I had also, at times, wondered about my own credibility when I wrote about conditions that were too good to be true.

"It's just the ski writer's prerogative to use poetic license," I answered.

I must admit that he did get me thinking. So in the interest of truth in the media, and so as not to further sully the already tarnished reputation of my journalistic brethren, I promise here to relate the story exactly as it really happened. May God strike me down in my ski tracks or may Anders write a scathing letter to the publisher if I divert one iota from reality.

A day's drive after leaving the Alps, we pulled into Jasna and checked into the Druzba Hotel. At dinner, we noticed that the cutlery at the Druzba still bore the engraved "IH" of the former state-owned chain, Inter-Hotel, but the Druzba had been in private hands for quite a few years already. The only other remnant of the old Warsaw Pact was our rather cute waitress who seemed to be under police orders not to smile. Then again, maybe it was something I said.

In any case, everyone else was friendly and the food was excellent. We occupied a clean room with a TV and a bath, and the price tag was suitable for a ski bum.

DURING THE DAYS OF COMMUNISM, the East Bloc countries built up a bureaucracy that was something to be reckoned with, and in the years since the Iron Curtain was drawn aside, that bureaucracy has far from crumbled. As a ski journalist, it is normal practice to be given a complimentary lift ticket. Early our first morning, I drove down to Liptovsky Mikulas and found the local tourist office, ordinarily the organization in charge of such matters. They were nice, apologized that it was really not within their jurisdiction, and sent me back to Jasna.

I spent the next hour visiting various lackeys of the lift company, until I reached the office where sat the manager and assistant manager of the lifts. They, too, evidently did not feel that they had the proper credentials for doling out a few cheap lift passes. Therefore, the assistant manager, Robert Gejdas, was given the task of introducing me to the director of the company that owned the lifts and a number of major hotels. This man was, of course, occupied with more pressing matters, and a couple of hours after we started, we were back to square one.

By this time, Robert and I had spent enough time together to become rather chummy, and in view of the circumstances, he resourcefully offered an alternative solution—escorting us personally through the lifts for the next few days. This, of course, was a stroke of genius that only someone well steeped in the art of bureaucracy could fathom, but the solution was really rather obvious.

If Robert was fearful of dishing out lift passes without the okay of his superiors, then it logically follows that all the lift attendants would capitulate to his authority, when at each lift, he told them to let us go through without a ticket. Now that everything was settled, Anders, Andreas and I had our own private guide for the next few days, who also was not averse to cutting lift lines (a rather necessary sin in Slovakia). He even was able to open lifts for us that were officially closed. I realize that it seems an unlikely coincidence that we should get involved with this helpful patron of journalistic causes, but I swear, as Anders is my witness, it is true.

Robert first introduced us to the Koliesko-Lukova Lift, a side-winding, two-seat chair lift with an odd–looking, steel umbrella above each chair to protect people from the elements. The upper section of the lift was closed due to high winds, but with a few strongly put words from Robert, the wheels creaked into motion and we found ourselves riding past snow-encrusted lift pylons to the top station of Mt. Chopok at 2024 meters. (This lift has since been permanently closed for safety reasons. Without the use of this critical lift, Mt. Chopok is effectively divided into two separate ski areas—Chopok North and Chopok South. While there are plans to build a new link, the usual Eastern European question marks apply to the timetable.)

The building atop Mt. Chopok was a combination lift station, meteor-ological station and mountaintop restaurant. It was encased in a thick layer of rime and looked like a cross between Ice Station Zebra and Santa's workshop. From here, we had access to Chopok South, a set of five lifts and a few hotels on the open south faces of the ski area. From the peak, we also looked out over some excellent off-piste bowls and couloirs, easily reachable along both flanks of the top station.

AT THIS JUNCTURE, I WOULD LIKE to write how we glided effortlessly over the open fields of sparkling corn snow for the rest of the morning, wolfed down a quick lunch, and spent the afternoon leaving our signature on a series of yet-to-be-named Slovakian couloirs.

I cannot. I must defer to my pact with Anders. No, as often happens in real life, our trip did not coincide with optimal conditions. We in fact sank up to our ankles in the spring slush on the south slopes, and our skis glided through the porridge with the silky smooth agility of an albatross taking to the air. We gulped down a cheap beer at the top station and

LEFT PAGE
Rime-encrusted building atop Mt. Chopok.

THIS PAGE
UPPER LEFT: The Tatra Mountains provide a picturesque backdrop to this Slovakian village.
LOWER LEFT: A small cable car has been taking sightseers from Skalnate Pleso to Lomnicky Stit since December 19, 1941. There is no skiing from the top.
RIGHT: Andreas and Anders ride the rime-covered upper section of the now defunct Koliesko-Lukova Lift on Mt. Chopok.

found that even the north-facing, off-piste slopes were too soft and avalanche dangerous to ski.

For the next three days, Robert was the perfect host, guiding us around the lift system, cutting us in front of lift lines and ordering his subordinates to allow us on the lifts without a ticket. In addition, he introduced us to two rather pretty, female ski racers, arranged a nice après-ski in the cozy Koliesko Hut, and organized an evening out for the six of us at the nightclub of the Junior Hotel.

Armed with a small English-Slovak dictionary and enough money to keep the wine flowing, Andreas tried hard to bridge the gap between East and West. It took him 8 full hours to discover that her name was Janna, she liked to dance and she did not wish to have an intimate relationship with a Swedish ski bum who is heading home in a few days. Oh well, nothing ventured, nothing gained.

OUR GRACIOUS GUIDE WAS HEADING out of town for a few days, and Andreas had decided that the language barrier would most likely thwart another day of his best efforts, so we headed east to the High Tatras. The High Tatras have been called the smallest big mountains in the world and that is probably true. The range is a mere 27 kilometers long, but jagged peaks such as Gerlachovsky Stit (2654 m) and Lomnicky Stit (2632 m) create a craggy, rugged skyline reminiscent of the French Alps. This small crest of peaks rises precipitously out of the flat farmland of the Demänova, Rackova and Ziarska Valleys.

Our first stop in the High Tatras was Strbske Pleso, a small but popular ski area with a few lifts, even fewer runs, and no piste much steeper than Denmark. Nevertheless, we found a very steep, narrow ravine between the cliffs that fell away to the east of the main piste. We managed an early morning descent in very respectable corn snow, walked 15 minutes back to the piste, and felt justified to move on to bigger and better things.

Bigger and better was exactly what we found just half an hour away, in Tatranska Lomnica, where the lifts rise from the valley floor (850 m) all the way to the top of Lomnicky Stit (2632 m). But in Slovakia, what you see is not necessarily what you get.

An antiquated cable car stretched from the village to a midpoint on the mountain called Skalnate Pleso. The lift had a capacity of about 30 people (25, if they were well-fed Westerners). As we approached this relic of a bygone era, we noticed a man walking up the mountain with his skis slung over his shoulder.

"Either he's an exercise freak, or we're in for a problem here!" I mumbled to nobody in particular.

Sure enough, a short visit to the ticket booth substantiated my suspicions—the tickets for the cable car were sold out for the entire day! A short chat with a local added some information. Up until a few years earlier, an almost equally outmoded gondola augmented this ancient, low-capacity apparatus. Then, however, one of the gondolas found its way off the cable, killing its occupants, and the government closed the killer lift.

After the accident, the skiing at Tatranska Lomnica began to involve a rather inconvenient procedure. The bad news was that the lift office opened at 6 a.m., and it was advisable to arrive well in advance of that time so as to ensure a reservation at a good time of the morning. The good news was that one person could buy tickets for all his or her family and friends, while the others could stay cozy and warm under their down comforters. (More good news is that this gondola has been rebuilt since the time of our visit.)

ALL THIS INFORMATION WAS IRRELEVANT to our situation. We needed to get up the mountain *now*. I thought of the story a Finnish lawyer friend, Ilka Malka, once told me about how things worked in Eastern Europe. He and an associate were trying to catch a plane from Moscow to Leningrad. They arrived in time for the flight, but the plane was completely full.

Ilka flashed a fistful of cash and threw around some heavyweight credentials until the Aeroflot employee asked the two lawyers to follow him. Ilka and his companion followed the civil servant to the plane, which was about to take off.

The man from Aeroflot then pointed at two Russian passengers and said curtly, "You and you, go home!"

Ski journalists do not usually have so much money to impress with, but we are not short of credentials. A few moments of negotiations landed us three tickets on the next tram. I was very happy, and I must say that I tried not to let my conscience bother me about who might have had to go home on account of us.

Our day of surprises was by no means over. From the middle station of Skalnate Pleso (1751 m), an even smaller cable car continued to the peak, while a double chair lift took skiers up to Lomnicke Sedlo (2189 m). A line of people waited for the tiny cable car, but a bearded ski patrolman, who smelled like he had consumed a fifth of vodka on his corn flakes for breakfast, grumbled vaguely about the upper lift being only for sightseers. All things considered, we opted for the chair lift. The terrain was steep and open, and the local heroes had not made too much of a dent in the 15 centimeters of fresh powder that lay around begging to be skied.

IT DID NOT TAKE MORE THAN ONE RUN to get us into trouble. We cut into an untouched bowl east of the main piste. We enjoyed it immensely, but the lift personnel did not get the same joy from our descent.

Upon our return to the chair, we were met by a surly lift attendant who began ranting, "No go! No go! No go!"

We tried to decipher what the problem was, for there had certainly not been any avalanche danger, nor did any signs prohibit entry to the area we had skied.

Each of our lucid observations was met by the same clear response of "No go! No go!" to which our friend added in his best school English, "You go, you pay!"

At that point our lift tickets were temporarily confiscated to ensure obedience.

"Well guys, what do you say we try the other side of the piste instead?"

It did not really matter much. The powder was just as good to the west of the piste, and the views were fabulous everywhere. As we skied, we looked out over a checkerboard of flat, green fields juxtaposed incongruously with the sheer, snow-clad Tatras. If the Matterhorn were situated in the middle of Iowa, it would look something like the High Tatras.

We could have anticipated our next problem, had we been thinking. But, you know how it is on a powder day—not much energy left over for thought. We had forgotten to consider the old truism: "What goes up, must come down." In this case, I am referring to people.

DUE TO THE LACK OF SNOW in the valley in April, most of the skiers were planning on descending from the mountain by the same inefficient lift that had brought them up. At this point, none of us was in the mood for a 2-hour wait to get off the mountain. While my press card might have turned the trick one more time, I did not want to incite a riot in a country that had supposedly shed the shackles of a system based on privilege. Instead, snow or no snow, we decided to see how far we could get on the 8-kilometer-long piste back to town.

We had to walk the last half-hour and built up a reasonable appetite, so we stopped for dinner in the Grand Hotel at the nearby village of Stary Smokovec. While cable cars from a bygone era might prove to be inconvenient, the stately grandeur of a hundred-year-old hotel brings back the regal atmosphere that pervaded much of Europe at the turn of the 19th century. Here, we could sample the grandiose style that also exists at the likes of the Palace Hotel in St. Moritz or the Hospiz in St. Christoph, but at a fraction of the price. We stuffed ourselves silly on a multi-course dinner, paid about what the tip would amount to in St. Moritz and headed off to slumber land. The next morning we would continue our road-trip into Poland.

Chapter 21. POLAND

...AND NOTHING BUT THE TRUTH

The Tatras extend into Poland, and Anders, Andreas and I crossed the border and headed for Zakopane, on the northern side of the range. Zakopane is a picturesque but very spread-out town. It is interspersed with large, beautiful homes from the early 1900s, and it is surrounded with unconnected lifts, which lie helter-skelter in all possible directions from the center.

We headed directly for another medieval-looking cable car, which accesses the main ski area of Kasprowy Wierch (2000 m). We had learned our lesson the day before. We walked straight past a huge queue of people and entered the lift house via a side door. There, my press credentials once more served us well, and we soon found ourselves on top. On each side of the peak was a large, open bowl, and at the base of each bowl was a dilapidated chair lift, returning skiers to the top station.

At lunch, we befriended some of the local ski patrol, and I am sure

LEFT PAGE: Hillside castle near the Slovakian capital of Bratislava.
THIS PAGE: Andreas Thelander skiing the powder down from Lomnicke Sedlo in the Tatranska Lomnica ski area of Slovakia. The High Tatras rise high above the surrounding farmland.

Anders Karlsson will once again corroborate my story when I tell you that they became invaluable guides for us. I admit, none of them looked like Glen Plake, nor did any of them ski like the Herminator—but no matter. They invited us into the patrol house for a drink and promised that one of them would guide us down an "interesting descent" into national-park area where it was officially forbidden to ski. It was easy to see, once again, that the dogma of privilege dies hard in the East—be it party privilege or ski-patrol privilege. We were, in any case, with the empowered, and we were not about to turn down the opportunity.

GOD'S FINGER IS A STEEP COULOIR situated directly under the cable car and in the shadow of a precipitous spire that gives the chute its name. It is a forbidding sight in the best of weather, but by the time we finished our mid-afternoon alcoholic refreshment, the fog had rolled in. The pinnacle finger was completely gone from view and we could see at best 10 meters down the guts of the chute.

For reasons beyond my knowledge, it was decided that a beer-bellied, unfit-looking patrolman, who appeared to be in his mid-fifties, would lead us down the now invisible couloir. The decision may have been based on the fact that he had consumed the most alcohol during our post-lunch session, but I cannot be sure that this was their reasoning. I can be sure, on the other hand, that he *had* imbibed the largest amount of spirits.

Our guide, whom I will refer to by the pseudonym of Juric (changing his name to protect the guilty), chortled a bit at the sight of the fog, or should I say, the lack of sight in the fog. He then belched out a deep, gaseous, vodka-based burp and asked if we were certain that we wanted to ski God's Finger.

We were not at all certain, but of course we said we were. He laughed once more, and with a series of three double-pole-plant jump turns, of which I could see two-and-a-half, he disappeared into oblivion. I knew we could not exactly lose our way in the ravine, but I nevertheless did not wish to lose sight of Juric for too long. So I leapt into action behind him with Anders and Andreas in hot pursuit.

I am not sure whether the lack of visibility made God's Finger more daunting or less so than if we had skied it in sunshine. Suffice it to say that it gave me a distinctly eerie feeling to ski this precipitous chute in a kind of void, with only the scratchy sounds of turning skis ahead of me and behind me to give some sort of auditory perspective to the whole experience.

Once out of the couloir, Juric guided us to the middle station of the old tram, where he suggested that enough payola for a bottle of vodka would be a suitable remuneration for the lift lackey to arrange for the cable car to pick up a few unexpected passengers. I followed his suggestion.

It was further implied that our guide would also not be averse to a similar token of our esteem once we were safely back in the patrol room. We purchased a fifth at the restaurant, Juric mixed up some of the local version of Jägertee, and it did not take much longer than 45 minutes for Juric, his two ski-patrol buddies, and the three of us to finish the bottle.

BY NOW, THE LIFTS WERE CLOSING, and it was time for the patrol to sweep the mountain. This was a sweep to be remembered. Where I come from, the patrol is supposed to come down last, making certain that everyone has safely gotten off the slopes and aiding any stragglers. We were, however, definitely *not* where I come from.

Juric and company swept down in the fog like Superman on his way to a fire. I would like to say that they took the whole mountain like a tribute to Franz Klammer, but I cannot, in all honesty, say that for sure. After they went into a tuck near the top, they disappeared into the fog, and I didn't see them again until I arrived, totally out of breath, at the bottom. By this time, they had changed clothes and were well into their second rubber of bridge—or was it their third bottle of vodka?

I swear, that is exactly how it happened—the truth, the whole truth and nothing but the truth, so help me God. No poetic license, no hyperbole and no exaggeration—just the facts. To verify any doubts about truth and honesty in the content of this story, one can contact Anders Karlsson at anders@farghusetohamn.se.

Chapter 22. ROMANIA
EAST IS EAST AND WEST IS WEST...

My comrade in arms for my next couple of adventures in Eastern Europe was Christer Henning. Christer and I pointed my Jeep east out of Vienna in March and cruised across Hungary. We soon exchanged the smooth freeway of the Magyar Republic for the potholes of Romania. Our pace slowed considerably, but we managed to reach our first destination, the ski resort of Poiana Brasov, late that night.

Poiana Brasov is a purpose-built resort, just 13 kilometers from the beautiful medieval town of Brasov. It has two cable cars, a gondola, and a handful of shorter lifts, and Christer and I headed up the mountain on a gray, dreary day to explore the area. All the lifts access exactly the same terrain, giving a skier the option among a blue, a red and a black run, which descend about 700 vertical meters back to the base. The runs are all trails cut out of the trees, with few places where a skier can dive into the woods for a handful of off-piste turns before running out of elbow-room. Basically, Poiana Brasov has about as much diversity as a communist-era menu.

Much more interesting than the one-dimensional skiing and the rather ugly resort is the proximity of Bran Castle. Just a short drive from the skiing, this old stronghold is thought to be the former home of Vlad Tepes the Impaler, the horrible 14th-century ghoul who became known as Dracula.

The dark, brooding skies were not the ideal greeting to our Transylvania ski holiday, but they created a suitable backdrop to this evil-looking fortress. The north side of the dwelling continues directly up from a steep cliff, and the castle also has a hidden dungeon and a spooky narrow back stairway. If this was not Dracula's home, it should have been.

MOST OF THE SKIING in Romania is situated in the Carpathian Mountains that flank both sides of the Prahova Valley south of Brasov. In fast order, one passes the ski areas of Predeal, Azuga, Busteni and Sinaia.

The most interesting of these regions is Sinaia, an enchanting village, where picturesque old houses are situated around every corner. The crown jewel of these relics from the 1800s is Peles Castle, King Carol's summer residence, erected in 1870. Even some of the hotels, such as the Palace and the Paltinis, give off the aura of another day and age. Christer and I checked into a suite at the Paltinis, a spa hotel which boasts only two stars, but whose high ceilings and old-fashioned style emit a nostalgic flavor of the past.

To quote prices would be rather useless as they change from year to year, but suffice it to say that the prices in Romania were microscopic. I am a ski bum and do not generally spend money on superfluous extras. In Romania, I could afford to add an hour-long massage to my after-ski itinerary.

SINAIA'S CABLE CAR TAKES SKIERS in two stages from the village to Cota 2000. From there, most people ski on the back of the mountain, among a choice of easy and intermediate slopes, which end up in a basin from where two lifts take them back to higher ground. The front face of the tram, on the other hand, is the domain of experienced skiers. Here, challenging mogul runs and various off-piste descents can take skiers back to the middle station, or more than 1000 vertical meters down to the valley floor.

It sounds pretty good so far, right? An extremely inexpensive, cozy village and decent skiing for all ability groups—who could ask for more?

There is, however, a downside. The lift infrastructure is quite inadequate. The low-capacity cable car, which carries 35 people on the lower leg and 28 people from the middle station, can translate into a 2-hour wait in peak season.

Fortunately, we were not visiting in high season, but we soon discovered other drawbacks. We enjoyed our first day cruising around the pistes and getting a good idea of the lay of the land. It was on day two that our problems started.

Our second day in Sinaia was a Monday and the valley station of the cable car was suspiciously inactive. We soon found out that Monday is "maintenance day" in Romania, because the law mandates all trams in the land to be closed every Monday for service. A day of sightseeing was substituted into our schedule.

Tuesday, the cable car was again closed, this time because of wind. We quickly put plan B into effect, which was to try one of the small ski centers in the area. Plan B was thwarted by the "quota system". A gray, windy, low-season Tuesday is not a busy day in the world of Romanian skiing, and both Predeal and Azuga would not open the lifts unless they had a minimum of twenty skiers who were poised and ready to purchase a day pass. Christer and I understood that it was time to move on.

We left without having really solved the Romanian dilemma. If the lifts are too crowded to be fun on weekends and in the high season, too sparsely visited to open in low season, and closed on Mondays for maintenance, when exactly should one go skiing in Romania?

THIS PAGE
LEFT: The cozy former home of Vlad the Impaler aka Dracula.
RIGHT: The gondola in Poiana Brasov.

RIGHT PAGE
Lothar, our East German pal, guides us down through untouched powder on the back side of the resort in Bansko.

Chapter 23. BULGARIA
...AND NEVER THE TWAIN SHALL MEET

While Romania and Bulgaria share some similarities in being neighbors and former satellites of the Soviet Union set adrift in space at approximately the same time, there are marked differences between the two countries as well. Christer and I found communication and organization to take a drastic turn for the worse once we crossed the border into Bulgaria.

It is said that we live today in the information age, but Bulgaria has not yet reached maturity in this new epoch. This seemed to be, rather, the land of disinformation, misinformation and lack of information. Whether the blame for the communication failures should be laid on Christer and me or on the Bulgarians is certainly a debatable point. Suffice it to say that the two of us were in a bit of a fog from the moment we crossed the Danube into the Bulgarian town of Ruse.

The border crossing itself was a confusing, trying and expensive experience that took well over an hour. We had to stop at more than half a dozen checkpoints to show our passport, and to pay a road tax, an ecological tax, an automobile disinfection fee and a supplementary automobile insurance.

Our communication gap emerged immediately after our arrival, as we pulled over to give a ride to a female hitchhiker. When we stopped the car, she opened the door, gave her miniskirt a little hitch, and sat on my lap. With that less-than-subtle gesture, our first misunderstanding became apparent—she wanted to give me a ride, rather than the other way around. We cleared up the mistake, placed the young lady strategically back on the highway and moved on. After that incident, we noticed

that scantily clad women were advertising their wares every kilometer or two on this stretch of open road.

Once the prostitute parade waned, we picked up speed, and that also proved to be a mistake. Bulgarian traffic police with radar guns had situated themselves in the bushes of every other village, and before our first day in Bulgaria had drawn to a close, we had been stopped no less than five times for two routine checks and three speeding violations of debatable seriousness. After our third speeding incident, we finally adjusted to the situation. We drove the rest of the way to Sofia so slowly that even the potholes no longer bothered us. We ultimately reached our destination long after dark and even longer after our projected arrival time.

Our first dinner in Bulgaria was further proof of the information gap. While the food was good, the English translation on the menu often did not make it completely evident what one was ordering. During our stay, menus included such interesting fare as "tongue in earth", "faggots pane", "minced meat rool (nervous)" and "boned cock"!

Sofia is situated at the foot of Mt. Vitosha, a broad mountain made up of numerous sub-peaks and covering a full 278 square kilometers. This massif, which dominates the capital, played a prominent role in the Bulgarian plans when Sofia bid for the Olympics in the early '90s.

The ski resort on Vitosha includes a long gondola that climbs 1100 vertical meters from Simeonovo, a village in the outskirts of town, to Aleko, the ski center (1810 m). From that point, a handful of chair lifts, platter-pulls and T-bars extend both above and below the gondola station.

Christer and I had begun our tour of Bulgaria in a mental fog, and that now extended into the realm of climatic reality. A thick layer of low clouds encompassed everything above the tree line in a white soup on our first day in Vitosha. The poor visibility just intensified the problems innate to this land of no information, for our eyes could no longer compensate for the knowledge we failed to get elsewhere.

Bulgaria uses the Cyrillic alphabet, so to begin with, signs are not of very much assistance to a foreigner. This fact was rather irrelevant, as the ski area did not provide any helpful signs anyway. Nowhere was it posted which lifts or runs were open or closed; piste markers were inadequate, and small trail maps were unavailable. Our confusion was multiplied exponentially by the fact that Vitosha is also guilty of the ultimate in mountain management incompetence—separate lift systems within the same ski area.

» There are always Eastern European solutions to Eastern European problems.«

Christer and I began by purchasing a round-trip ticket on the gondola, a lift used basically for access. Ski lift tickets were not available there. Once we arrived at Aleko, the ski center, we skied down to the Romanski Chair Lift, where we bought a day pass and boarded the lift. We soon found ourselves inside a cloud, high above the tree line.

We skied by radar, staying close to some poles, which appeared in the mist periodically but were nearly covered by the snowpack. It did not take long for us to lose sight of the piste markers, and the only thing left to guide us was a piste machine track that was 3 meters wide. The visibility was approximately 1.7 meters, so I could just manage to make out this track, if my knees were adequately bent.

When we had finally felt our way down below the tree line, a local skier was kind enough to guide us down to a decent run that was entirely below the fog. It proved to be the case, however, that the lift that serviced this run belonged to the Vitosha Lale lift system, a different enterprise, and we once again were forced to open our wallets.

The lower slopes salvaged our day to some degree, and we eventually ended up overindulging ourselves on Bulgarian specialties at an excellent local restaurant. We started with *shopska* salad, the Bulgarian version of Greek salad, followed by stuffed mushrooms baked with a cheese topping. Theses courses were followed by *tarator*, a cold soup made of yogurt and cucumber, and *kavarma*, a stew of diced meat and vegetables served in a terra cotta pot. It all washed down nicely with a liter of very good local wine. The meal was so inexpensive that the bill provoked a rare argument between two ski bums who both wanted to pick up the tab!

WE BOTH HOPED FOR BETTER communication with the sun god in the days to come, but a cursory glance at our guidebook was not promising. According to the statistics in our pamphlet, Vitosha averages 117 snowy days per year. (That is in addition to 76 rainy days!) It did not take a math major to calculate that the odds of sunshine were not in our favor.

We are not quitters. We persisted through the next three foggy days with a steady menu of sightseeing, Braille skiing, cheap eating and overdrinking. One advantage of skiing in Vitosha is its nearness to Sofia. The

Bulgarian capital has good nightlife, including a number of night spots with excellent live music. In addition, contrary to popular stereotypes, Bulgarian females do not resemble beefy weight lifters, but actually rival some of the most beautiful women in the world.

On day five our stick-to-itiveness paid off, and the sun showed its elusive face to the mountain. Vitosha proved to have some very interesting terrain worth waiting for. The main ski area of Aleko primarily offers poorly groomed novice and intermediate skiing, featuring a 4-kilometer-long run along the western perimeter of the ski area. The Vitosha Lale Chair Lift, however, delivers off-piste specialists to the demanding section of mountain known ominously as the Lavina (avalanche) area. The Lavina region, with its steep slopes situated on the eastern flank of Vitosha, stands in stark contrast to the rest of the mountain.

We traversed out from the Lale triple chair, and found ourselves looking down a selection of 35–40-degree couloirs, the likes of which would compare with anything the French or Austrian Alps could offer, albeit not as long.

This was heaven, and we slashed down through the spring slush with a vengeance. Small balls of wet snow, set into motion by our skis, built up into large snow wheels that trailed us down the gullies, but we did not mind. We enjoyed the views of the city below, we relished our first day of sunshine, and we were happy to be skiing some tough terrain. I could see routes that could be skied all the way to the suburbs of Sofia earlier in the season, when snow covers the lower elevations of the mountain as well.

THE ENTRENCHED FOG AND stubborn low clouds that had plagued our first week in the Balkans now seemed a thing of the past, and Christer and I went into the heart of Sofia for a celebratory dinner.

On the way into the restaurant, after parking my Jeep Cherokee in the middle of a long row of old Ladas, I jokingly remarked, "Which of these cars is most likely to get stolen?"

Ninety minutes later, we giddily emerged from our meal to see that my good joke had turned into a bad dream. The car was gone, and with it much of the the ski equipment and many other possessions as well.

For the next two long days, the sun shone its spring beams on the Balkans, but we spent our precious time waiting in administrative queues, filing reports and getting official stamps in dusty, dingy police offices and government buildings. Our remaining energy was expended on organizing air travel home and mobilizing a rental car. The task was not made easier by a bureaucratic tradition inherited from the communist era and a language gap between the police and us that necessitated finding an interpreter.

There emerged, however, a silver lining in the ever-darkening clouds that had by now permeated our Balkan travels. First, Georgi, the owner of the private house where we were renting a room, took 3 hours out of his Sunday to translate for the police. He asked for no compensation for this imposition and only reluctantly accepted some money that we insisted he take for his help.

The following day was a workday, and we needed a new interpreter. I found a university student who was willing to help. For 5 hours, Toni Pimpireva led us around Sofia to acquire the necessary stamps, seals and signatures. In between the drudgery, she even fixed us lunch in her home.

Because of our plight, we were acutely aware every time the squeal of a car alarm pierced the air.

"Bulgarian music," Toni commented sardonically, and the thought occurred to me that she and her countrymen had to live with the fear and anxiety of such lawlessness on a daily basis.

After our second full day of pavement pounding to attain ink insignias of questionable necessity, I felt that Bulgaria had truly developed incompetence into an art form. Imagine my shock and disbelief when, at two o'clock in the morning, the police woke our landlord to report that they had recovered our vehicle, albeit minus much of our gear.

Our poor host now spent the hours between 2 and 5:30 a.m. once again at the police station. Toni had wanted no money for her long afternoon with us and Georgi again refused to accept anything for a disturbed night's sleep and a long, early morning of translating. I pondered where else in the world that sort of kindness and generosity would be bestowed on a couple of strangers, and I was left with grave doubts whether anybody in the West would give so freely of life's most valuable commodity—time.

REJUVENATED BY THE RETURN of our car and the kindness of our newly found friends, Christer and I got back to the business of skiing. This time, our destination was Borovets, Bulgaria's most popular ski resort, situated just 72 kilometers south of Sofia.

Borovets is a bizarre juxtaposition of large, fancy, four-star hotels and small, wooden structures that line a muddy main street. The nice hotels cater to the Sofia upper class, who pack the village every weekend, and a mixed international clientele who come to enjoy the pleasures of four Bulgarian stars at prices that are in tune with low-budget travel for a skier from Western Europe. Meanwhile, the other buildings, which house small shops and restaurants, give the village the appearance of an old Western mining town. All the while, horse-drawn wagons ferry skiers around among the lifts and hotels here, adding to the gold-rush atmosphere that permeates the resort.

An interesting aspect of the skiing in Borovets is the fact that there are different prices for Bulgarians and international tourists. (This is actually true of all Bulgarian ski resorts, but we first found out about it here.) A foreigner is charged about double the locals' price for a ski pass.

On the other hand, there are always Eastern European solutions to

Eastern European problems. One of these solutions is bribery. On our second day, I skied up to the Sitnyakovo Lift and asked the old lift attendant where to buy a ski pass, and he pointed out the ticket office. He also offered that I could pay an appreciably lower sum of money directly into his pocket, for which I could ride his lift all day. The communist system dies hard.

I am always looking for a bargain, but I was not really sure that I wanted to limit myself to one lift for my day's activities, so we tried plan B—getting a Bulgarian to buy half-price lift passes for us. There was a definite risk with this method that our state-of-the-art ski equipment would give us away, but ski bums are not loath to taking chances. We spent the day in the Sitnyamovo and Martinovi Baraki ski regions, where the runs basically consist of narrow trails below the tree line. We did not get nailed for using ski passes for Bulgarian citizens.

THE FOLLOWING DAY, WE TOOK a 30-minute ride up the gondola, taking us 1000 vertical meters above the village to the Markoudjik sector of the resort. There, one can choose to ski among a few T-bars that are all above the tree line. The slopes are quite gentle in this section of Borovets, but there is somewhat more variety than among the trails of the Sitnykovo area. Here, one can choose among skiing the pistes, traversing off the piste into the wide, open spaces, or cutting a very tight slalom among some dwarf pines. One can even don some touring gear and hike up to Mt. Moussala. At 2925 meters, the peak is Bulgaria's highest point and offers some good slopes just a stone's throw from the ski area.

Christer and I explored as much of the upper slopes of Borovets as time allowed. We completed our day with a very respectable run of 1250 vertical meters from the top of the Markoudjik area back to the village, and we were ready to hit the road.

Borovets is one of the Eastern European destinations that has been changing dramatically in recent years, and the modernization is scheduled to accelerate. As recently as the end of the 1990s, there were still rickety, old single chair lifts in service, while today all the chair lifts are quads. By 2009, the new investment plan expects to have at least seven new lifts and nineteen new pistes in place in addition to a massive construction of new hotels.

We now traveled further south into the Pirin Mountains, the location of the picturesque village of Bansko. After the tacky atmosphere of the purpose-built resort of Borovets, it was a breath of fresh air to arrive in a real mountain village. Narrow cobblestone streets, old stone buildings and goat-herding peasants characterized Bansko, and it was all in the shadow of Mt. Vihren (2914 m) and a whole range of snow-clad tops.

It got even better. A short drive from town brought us to the ski area. A trip to the summit provided lovely panoramas of flat, green fields drenched in spring sunlight and the Rila Mountains in the distance to the north. The upper lifts top out at 2560 meters, so there is a goodly amount of skiing above the tree line.

Bansko is another location where recent investment has transformed the ski area into a very modern resort. Among other things, the most recent expansion now gives Bansko a 16-kilometer run that drops over 1600 vertical meters.

I used one of my usual methods to find the best skiing. I asked a local instructor about the off-piste possibilities.

He pointed to three or four areas and concluded by waving his finger ominously toward a couple of tantalizing steep faces and warned, "Don't go there—very dangerous!"

His advice could have been taken seriously had there been avalanche-prone powder on the 35-degree slopes he so kindly pointed out, but with crisp corn snow sparkling in the spring sun, we headed directly for the forbidden fruit. Our edges carved up the virgin corn with S's as easily as a saber slicing the air. Halfway down the hill, we skied through the forest to the piste, and cruised to the bottom of the chair lift.

By noon, we had investigated all angles of the mountain except the western flank. We traversed a mere hundred meters or so from the top of the Todorka Chair Lift, and got the day's biggest surprise. Fanned out below us was a series of juicy, steep couloirs and ridges that plunged about 800 vertical meters into a valley far below. Best of all, there were a handful of tracks to be seen, which indicated that the slope quite possibly led somehow back to the lifts. On the other hand, the tracks could have been made by people on touring skis.

As tempting as this descent looked, we had to be sure, and to find decipherable answers in the land of misinformation seemed like a formidable task. That day, however, luck was with us. Just getting off the lift was a snowboarder with a rucksack and collapsible ski poles attached to his pack. I skied over to ask if he was familiar with the area. Pay dirt! Lothar, who had been born and raised in East Germany, not only knew the mountain, he had also, in fact, sculpted the tracks we had just seen. Within moments, our newfound guide was sharing with us the pleasures that he and his friends had discovered a year earlier—pleasures so sweet that it had tempted them back for a two-month stay in Bansko the following season.

THE NORTHWEST SIDE OF THE RAVINE was still old powder, while the southwest shank was covered in corn snow. I unleashed 40 turns in the powder, and then stopped to watch Christer across the ravine, spraying up corn kernels. Then we crossed over, and tasted a candy of a different flavor. Meanwhile, our boarding buddy shot halfway down the slope in six or seven large swoops.

As we continued down, the ravine narrowed, both sides were corn, and one could stay in the guts of the gully. One could bank off each flank, almost like in a halfpipe, or ride the ridges that separated the various chutes. I moved up on one of the ridges, and darted in and out of some well-spaced trees. Ultimately, the couloir ended on a road from where we slid 15 minutes back to the ski area parking lot.

As we pushed our way back to civilization, I glanced constantly up to my right, where a whole array of chutes and ridges revealed themselves to us. This had been Lothar's private domain for the last five or six weeks, and while Chris and I were a bit envious, we were very grateful to our new friend for having shared his secret stash with a couple of skiers from the West.

Our Balkan holiday was almost over, and one thing was certain—we needed a holiday. For ten days, Christer and I had battled fog, misinformation, bureaucracy, crime, inefficiency, incompetence, language barriers, poor roads and traffic police. We were ready for a rest.

While much of our ski equipment has probably been auctioned off in some Sofia yard long ago, we did not come home from Bulgaria empty-handed. We had discovered some excellent skiing in the Lavina section of Vitosha and in Lothar's couloirs in Bansko. We are also much wiser as to the dos and don'ts of how to have a successful ski vacation in Bulgaria the second time around.

Perhaps most important, we had been enriched by the kindness of people who gave unselfishly of their time to foreign strangers. It may still take years before a trip through Bulgaria will glide as effortlessly as travel in Western Europe, but in the realm of personal communications, East truly did meet West. Many thanks to Georgi, Toni and Lothar for bridging that gap with us.

THIS PAGE: A view of central Sofia.
RIGHT PAGE: Christer Henning glides through the corn snow in one of the off-piste couloirs of Bansko.

ABOVE: The Chain Bridge brightens the Budapest night.

Chapter 24. HUNGARY

FOR SKIAHOLICS ONLY

Just in case you happened to be curious…yes, one can ski in the relatively horizontal country of Hungary. There are a few hills scattered here and there among the flatlands that make up most of the Magyar Republic. This, of course, is information that is not particularly relevant to anyone less than a full-blown skiaholic—an addict who often wakes up in a cold sweat from a nightmare of being stranded somewhere where a ski slope is not within close reach.

Just such a fanatic might not even dare to venture to such a beautiful land as Hungary for fear of going through traumatic withdrawal symptoms. In an attempt to guarantee the peace of mind of such diehard skiers, I recently took on the task of investigating the skiing possibilities here.

Very few people can lay claim to having put the first tracks of the season on the slope of Galyatetö, Hungary—because the lift there has not been in existence for very many years. I had that opportunity since my visit preceded the annual opening of the ski lift. I might add that not only did I make the first tracks of the season on this approximately 150-vertical-meter "monolith", but all 75 turns (I counted them, of course) were in 50 centimeters of powder!

Hungarian powder, of course, is not the equivalent of Utah powder; but then again, Hungary is not famous for its powder, but for its goulash. This is not to say that the powder was like goulash—it was much tastier!

Following my perfect season-opening run, I celebrated with a beer at the Grand Hotel, situated near the top of the lift, and decided that my mission was not yet complete. I could not just write a self-indulgent piece about my achievement, without turning it into a more fully researched and relevant article for the benefit of skiaholics everywhere.

WHILE SIPPING MY BEER, I pored over a map of Hungary, locating her highest peak, Mt. Kékes, a 1015-meter monster only a short drive away. I deemed that a personal account of the ski possibilities there would certainly enhance the usefulness of this report.

Upon my arrival, I was disappointed to find out that the longest drag lift on Mt. Kékes was broken. This fact, however, turned out to be insignificant, as the lift on Mt. Kékes is quite irrelevant. In fact, the ski run is longer than the lift, and even when the machinery is operational, skiers can get a much longer descent by skiing further down and transporting themselves by minibus back to the peak.

A handful of real Hungarian snow enthusiasts were doing laps in this manner and I joined them. The expense of this mode of uphill transportation was only about $0.60 per lift, as the driver was cramming 13–15 passengers per ride into his vehicle, making the process affordable for us and profitable for him.

The weather was foggy and grim, but one could hardly get lost, as the piste was a trail that was cut out of thick forest on either side. It ran for 1.8 kilometers and boasted a robust 310 vertical meters or so. The readers who are proficient at mathematics can probably deduce that those figures add up to a very flat ski run. Nevertheless, it was skiing, and the section of snow bordering the forest was relatively untouched—perfect for a powder freak like myself. Getting enough speed to make a turn in the untracked snow, however, took a rather major effort.

To be fair to the Hungarians, there are actually over 30 different so-called ski areas in the country, with the largest one at Bánkút having eight lifts and 580 vertical meters of skiing. The fact that the ski area peaks out at 930 meters and the runs descend to 350 meters, however, does not promise a very long ski season, and the local ski industry is not presently preparing for an onslaught of skiers from the rest of the world.

HUNGARY IS, HOWEVER, ready, willing and able to host hordes of tourists who come to discover the magnificence and charm of Budapest. Skiaholics will be happy to hear that they can visit the Hungarian capital during the winter while still being within a reasonable distance of the ski slopes.

The Danube River divides the hills of Buda from the flat Pest section of the city, and all along the riverside are enough sights of interest to keep a visitor busy for many days. Sights worth visiting on Buda's side of the city include the Castle Palace, the Matthias Church and the Fisherman's Bastion.

Buda is dominated by Castle Hill, where an enclave of baroque-style houses surrounds the gigantic Castle Palace. The hill has been the home of one castle or another since the middle of the 13th century, but Budapest's stormy history has seen these different fortifications and palaces destroyed periodically through the years. It will come as a complete shock to visitors that the palace and surrounding baroque buildings that line the cobblestone streets today are the product of a total and brilliant restoration after being demolished by the retreating Nazis in 1945.

Not far from Castle Palace is the beautiful Matthias Church (built 1255–1269) and the unusual looking Fisherman's Bastion, built as recently as 1905 but looking much older due to its neo-Gothic style. This architectural tribute to the fishermen who defended Buda in medieval times is a great spot for panoramic views of the city.

From here one can look out over the lovely Chain Bridge, as well as numerous other bridges that connect the two halves of the city. Almost directly across the river, one sees the huge, domed Parliament Building, yet another neo-Gothic structure, reminiscent of Westminster Abbey in London. The Parliament has close to 700 rooms, and its 268-meter-long riverside facade makes it one of the true jewels of Budapest.

Attractions and landmarks on the Pest side of the city are prevalent in and around the large City Park. Here, among other things, one can get some winter exercise at a lovely outdoor ice skating rink. The rink looks out over one of the most astonishing buildings in Budapest, Vajdahunyadvár, constructed in conjunction with Budapest's millennium celebration in 1896. Architect Ignác's creation makes use of 22 different buildings as models for this bizarre work. Much of the building is a replica of a Romanian castle, but Vajdahunyadvár also makes use of Gothic, Romanesque and baroque architecture.

NEAR THE NORTHWEST CORNER of the park is Hero's Square, which features the archangel Gabriel, perched atop a 36-meter-high pillar. The pillar, known as the Millennial Monument, is surrounded by various statues of Hungarian nobles and statesmen who stand in a semicircle around the Tomb of the Unknown Soldier.

For some additional physical activity in the City Park, one can also visit the enormous Széchenyi Gyógyturdö baths, built in 1909. These indoor and outdoor baths, still among the largest such spas in Europe, are a time-machine trip back to the days of Art Nouveau.

Spas and mineral baths are as ingrained in the Hungarian culture as the sauna is a part of the Finnish way of life, and no tourist should visit

Hungary without a visit or two to some of the wide assortment of spas. Another bathhouse of particular note is the Rudasfûrdö Baths, a magnificent Turkish construction dating back to the 16th century. Perhaps the most stylish of the local spas is the unique Gellert Baths, part of the elegant Art Nouveau Hotel Gellert.

The baths are among many features of Budapest that thrust visitors into the atmosphere of a bygone era. This romantic city on the Danube has numerous cafes and pastry shops whose ambiance is strictly pre-World War I Austro-Hungarian Empire. The Gerbeaud, the Lukas *pâtisserie*, the Cafe Mürész, the Hungária and the Ruszwurm, full of its Biedermeier furniture, all take visitors back into the regal atmosphere that existed a hundred years ago.

A trip to Budapest should also include a visit to the Nagycsarnok (Market Hall), a monstrous building with hundreds of stands offering a full assortment of fruits, vegetables, fish, meat and sausages, as well as souvenirs. There are numerous such halls but the largest one is at Tolbuhin Körút.

The aforementioned suggestions are only the tip of the iceberg of what there is to see and do in Budapest, but one may not have time for much more, especially with Hungarian skiing so high on the agenda! Anyone arriving as early as November might even get the opportunity to be added to the growing list of people who have put first tracks in the snows of Galyatetö.

UPPER: The House of Parliament dominates the shoreline on the Pest side of the Danube.
LOWER LEFT: When the gradient of the slope is less than 5 degrees, one can always build a small jump—but watch out for the flat landing.
MIDDLE RIGHT: Ice skaters enjoy the ambiance of Budapest by night.
LOWER RIGHT: The view from the top of the ski run on Hungary's highest mountain, Mt. Kékes. The slope is only slightly steeper than the ice skating rink.

Chapter 25.
THE CZECH REPUBLIC
CITY AND SKI

There are not many places where one can easily combine a ski holiday with a visit to one of the great cities of the world. Paris, London, New York, Rome, Florence, San Francisco, Rio de Janeiro, St. Petersburg, Hong Kong—they are all a bit too far removed from the ski fields. Even Vienna is too far away from Austria's mountains to make for a convenient commute. While Hungary is one place where this possibility exists, few people would realistically travel to Hungary specifically for its snowsports. The Czech Republic, on the other hand, with around 200 ski areas, is a different story.

The landscape of the northern part of the country, the home of the Krkonose or Giant Mountains, is full of ski resorts, although many of them are very small, with less than 200 vertical meters of skiing. One well-known ski area in the region is Pec Pod Snezkou, home of the Czech Republic's highest mountain, Snezka (1602 m). Unfortunately, the historic side-winding double chair lift that rises to the peak of Snezka accesses no pistes, and skiing is officially prohibited. The actual ski area, a few kilometers away, offers a more limited vertical of 385 meters on the slopes of Javor (1215 m).

During my visit to the Czech Republic, I visited Spindleruv Mlyn, the nation's largest ski resort, situated only 130 kilometers from Prague. Here,

a combination of cheap prices and adequate slopes legitimately attracts homegrown riders as well as enthusiasts from other nearby countries.

Spindleruv Mlyn has 23 lifts and about 25 kilometers of pistes. Two separate ski areas are situated in the mountains around the village, at Medvedin and at Svaty Petr, with Svaty Petr being the larger of the two with 495 vertical meters of skiing and sixteen lifts. The skiing in Spindleruv Mlyn reaches to 1310 meters, barely topping the Hungarian ski areas. Nevertheless, there is usually adequate snow cover well into April.

THE TERRAIN IS STRICTLY FOR LEARNING and intermediate cruising, and off-piste skiing is not much to think about in these lowlands where most of the pistes are trails with thick forests along both flanks. Nevertheless, the prices for lodging, skiing, food and drink are low, making Spindleruv Mlyn a decent alternative for families with young children as well as for skiers in the early stages of development.

Hotel prices start from €10–20 per night, and the accommodation is generally clean and comfortable, even in the lower price range. While one can get housing for less than half of what it costs in the West, one saves even more money on beer—and after all, the Czechs are more renowned for their beer than their ski slopes.

On my way from Spindleruv Mlyn back to Prague, I pulled into the microbrewery at the Hotel Pivovarská Basta for an après-ski. After enjoying a pint of their home-brewed product, I continued toward the city for a stroll around the town center and a taste of the Prague nightlife.

Prague, to the delight of anyone who has ever visited here, was spared the devastation that destroyed so many European cities during World War II.

Franz Kafka, a native, once said of his hometown, "Prague does not let go, either of you or of me. The little mother has claws…"

I could not imagine how Kafka could have known this about me, but as I looked out at the Vltava River, I knew already that he was right. At night, the reflection of the Prague Castle and the floodlit Karluv Most (Charles Bridge) shimmered in the river.

The Charles Bridge can well be a tour unto itself. It was constructed

for Charles IV, under the guiding hand of Peter Parler, between 1357 and 1387. The bridge is flanked by towers on both ends and houses 30 baroque statues, added between 1683 and 1714, now turned black by about 300 years of soot. Much of the bridge's attraction, however, is a 21st century aura provided by a multitude of artists, street performers, vendors and tourists.

I stopped for a while to watch a jazz band, moved on to enjoy a puppet show, and finally left for the Lesser Quarter, west of the river, firmly convinced that the Charles Bridge could have kept me entertained for my entire stay in Prague.

Almost immediately after crossing west of the Vltava, one comes to the St. Nicholas Church of the Lesser Quarter, considered the most exquisite baroque church in the city. From there, cobblestone streets lined with interesting shops and medieval bars and restaurants wind their way up Hradcany Hill. As one nears Prague Castle, the atmosphere changes, as the small shops give way to baroque and Renaissance mini-palaces, like the Archbishop's Palace in Hradcany Square.

The crown jewel of the hill is, of course, Prague Castle, which features the Gothic masterpiece, St. Vitus Cathedral. Despite the large courtyard alongside the southern wall of this enormous piece of architecture, I had to wedge myself into the furthest corner of the square to be able to fit the whole building into a photograph—even with a wide-angle lens.

Probably the best example of Gothic architecture in central Europe, St. Vitus was started in 1344. While it has undergone numerous additions and alterations along the way, and the last stone was not laid until the 1920s, most of the masterpiece can, like the Charles Bridge, be attributed to Peter Parler.

The most salient features of the cathedral were built during various periods. A mosaic, known as the Golden Portal, was part of Parler's original work while the 6500-pipe organ was constructed in 1757 and the gargantuan, stained-glass window, called *The Creation of the World*, was one of the last additions to St. Vitus, in 1928. Despite these interesting details, St. Vitus is perhaps most impressive for its ornate Gothic facades and its sheer size.

EVENINGS IN PRAGUE are easy to fill. In addition to all the atmospheric localities to drink a half-liter of Bohemian brew, the Czech capital is one of the cultural centers of Europe, with a wide variety of concerts, operas and plays to choose from.

LEFT PAGE
UPPER: The Czech Republic is famous for its beer, and Prague has many atmospheric localities to sample the local brew.
LOWER LEFT: Far in the distance behind the Vltava River, the top of St. Vitus Cathedral is visible high above the surrounding buildings.
LOWER RIGHT: The world famous Astronomical Clock of the Old Town Hall in Prague.

THIS PAGE
Most of the ski terrain in the Czech Republic is below the tree line.

The following day, I set out for the former Jewish ghetto, which includes the unusual Old Jewish Cemetery. For many years, the graveyard was not allowed to expand outwards, and therefore it houses bodies nine layers deep, with commemorative stones placed in a disorderly fashion almost on top of one another.

I then proceeded to Old Town Square, another location that can keep a person occupied for great lengths of time. Here again, the mixture of Gothic and baroque architecture gives the square a unique look. There are innumerable landmarks of note all around this part of Prague, including the Storch House, the Kinsky Palace, and the House at the Minute. Many of the buildings are painted with cheerful pastels, while others display murals on the outer walls.

The square's distinctive character is largely derived from the medieval spires of the Tyn Church and the Old Town Hall and Astronomical Clock Tower, additional Gothic structures. Hundreds of visitors gather hourly under the Clock Tower to watch a procession of small wooden figures going through a ritual march. Carved figures, representing the specter of death, Jesus, all of his Apostles, and various other people, appear in small openings in the tower at the stroke of each hour.

In a typical, if twisted, bit of medieval gratitude, the man who was primarily responsible for creating this work of art in 1490 had his eyes put out so that he could not recreate his masterpiece for anyone else.

There are, in fact, so many artistic wonders in Prague that it is doubtful they could ever be duplicated here or anywhere else. In addition, the architectural jewels of the city combine with a vibrant and dynamic atmosphere, rendering Prague a unique place to visit.

Whether it be Prague or Budapest that seems most alluring, ski addicts should rest easy in the knowledge that a winter visit to either of these interesting and beautiful cities can easily be combined with available skiing, only a short distance away.

Chapter 26.
BOSNIA-HERZEGOVINA
POWDER LINES AND LAND MINES

My Swiss buddy, Rafael Betschart, packed his Volkswagen van with the precision of a Swiss watchmaker adjusting and calibrating the moving parts of a Rolex. Rucksacks were placed in a neat row and an elastic band was run through the loops of each pack to keep them standing upright on the journey. My luggage was packed all in the same area for easy access from the back door. Road maps, pen, note pad and organizer were neatly situated in a homemade box between the driver's and the front passenger's seat. Five pairs of skis and a snowboard were packed in along the inside panel of the van, and ski boots were lined up near the warm air vents for obvious reasons.

Frenchman Jean Michel Pons and I observed with amazement as Rafi worked. Once he had finished his meticulous packing, we were ready to travel into the former domain of Marshal Josip Broz Tito. Yugoslavia, held together for 35 years by Tito's iron leadership, disintegrated and imploded shortly after his death. Regional quibbling and religious differences have seen this beautiful country destroyed by wars and separated into a handful of separate lands during the 1990s.

Some of the areas were harder hit than others, and Sarajevo, the Bosnian site of the 1984 Winter Olympics, was unfortunately a center of wartime activity. Here, the inhabitants of the city valiantly withstood a three-year siege at the hands of the Serbs. Surrounded by Serb forces,

they built an amazing 1.5-meter-wide tunnel that acted as a lifeline to the outside world, and they endured thousands of their civilian citizenry being picked off one-by-one by Serb snipers.

As always, however, out of the dust comes a process of rebuilding and rebirth, and we had come to discover the Bosnia of today—a region that has remained almost devoid of ski tourism in recent years.

The tone for the trip was set at the border crossing into Bosnia and Herzegovina. While one border guard scrutinized our passports, matching each one with a face, another guard opened the back door of the van, revealing our whole array of ski equipment.

She then asked the lucid question, "Vhat do you plan to do here?"

Indeed, in a region where the people are self-consciously aware of the devastation that they have brought upon themselves, they are still not used to the fact that anybody would want to come here to enjoy the pleasures that their country has to offer.

AS WE DROVE INTO SARAJEVO, bullet marks and large holes in the plaster facades of the apartment buildings remained as clear evidence of the period from 1992 to 1995, when about 278,000 people perished in the country's civil strife. Yet, a walk through Sarajevo's Old Town revealed a charming labyrinth of stone walking streets, picturesque shops and cozy restaurants.

Twenty kilometers south of the city is Bjelasnica Mountain, site of most of the Olympic ski competitions. The ski resort had also been devastated by the war, and reminders of that black period were everywhere. Empty shells of buildings were in evidence all around the resort. Where once had stood a group of modern hotels, only the Hotel Marsal remained, and 80 percent of it had been rebuilt after the cease-fire.

A couple of NATO trucks displaying small German flags were parked at the base of the lifts, and German soldiers informed us that there were still well over 1000 peace-keeping troops here.

We entered the restaurant at the base of the lifts. Directly across from the doorway hung a map of the ski area. It was, however, not the normal colorful drawing depicting lifts, ski runs and restaurants. It was a contour map entitled "Mine Contamination Map", and the only colorful markings were small red dots depicting spots where mines remained.

THERE WERE NONE MARKED within the confines of the existing ski area. We asked a nice gentleman who worked at the base of the mountain about mines. He assured us that there was nothing to worry about.

"There are still some mines in the forest behind the mountain, over there," he advised, with a sweep of his hand, "but now there is so much snow, so it is no problem there either!"

We were not completely convinced. This was not a region where we freeride fans felt like exploring beyond the ski area boundary.

Despite masses of snow all over the region, the uppermost lift, which accessed the open slopes above the tree line, was closed for lack of snow.

The wind had apparently mishandled the powder at the higher elevations. Forests, however, surrounded the lower slopes. There, we found endless lines in the trees that had not been previously touched by man or wind. Even in the trees, the knowledge of the mines left us with an uneasy feeling—similar to the nagging doubt one sometimes gets when skiing an avalanche-prone slope in questionable conditions.

We took time away from the powder to test the Olympic Downhill and to try a few of the other pistes, but the descents in the trees kept beckoning us back for more.

A few kilometers down the road from Bjelasnica is Igman, where one can find one additional lift and piste, both included on the same lift pass. It was the site of the Olympic ski jumping events in 1984.

> **» There are still some mines, but now there is so much snow, so it is no problem...«**

At the top of the lift, Jean Michel immediately noticed a skull-and-crossbones symbol on a bright red sign, again warning of possible mines in the forest. On the surface, there did not seem like much for a freerider to do in Igman, but Rafi is always full of energy and suffers from an overactive imagination. He first led us on an interesting plunge in the powder directly under the chair lift.

Two-thirds of the way down, he veered left. Before I could catch my breath, Rafi was halfway up the staircase in the war-damaged ski jump tower. While Rafi's jumping skills are limited to rocks and small cliffs, he had noticed that the jump was covered with about 30 centimeters of powder. After all, this was the closest thing to a fun park that existed in Bosnia, and anyway, skiing down a narrow ski jump ramp is not that different from putting tight turns into a narrow couloir.

In Switzerland, a crazy stunt like this would probably have brought

out the National Guard and landed Rafi with a mandatory stay in the local penitentiary. But, here in Bosnia, nobody but his two friends paid any attention to a loony Swiss freerider bouncing powder turns down the Olympic ski jump.

"Hey, at least there were no mines!" exclaimed Rafi, in vague justification for his actions.

The landing of the jump provided another steep pitch that was also covered with a generous layer of powder, and it was more than enough to keep us busy until the lift closed.

Late in the day, we met Melissa, a young local snowboarder, and her friend, Adele. They offered to show us around Sarajevo that evening. The Old Town was beautiful by night, as illuminated minarets and church towers harmonized to create a warm ambiance. The girls also spoke of harmony in the years since the fighting had ceased. They told us that the war was history and the hatred was now forgotten.

"People have moved on with their lives," explained Melissa.

I sensed, however, that somewhere beneath the surface, like the mines that remain hidden under the snow, there are lingering aftereffects, which cannot be blotted out as easily as people would like.

The two girls had very different stories. Melissa, along with her mother and siblings, had temporarily moved to New York during the war, while her father stayed behind. She now longs to live in America, and her life will certainly never be the same. Adele did not have the opportunity to escape the battlefield. She spent the years of the war living in the cellar of her home, going sporadically to school when the situation allowed.

They took us to a bustling pub in the middle of town called the City Bar. Even here, so many years after, the evidence of the war years was clear, as the bar was frequented by an overabundance of females.

"Yes," admitted Melissa, "there are about 10 percent more women than men in Sarajevo today."

Melissa joined us the following day, as we went to visit the other ski resort in the outskirts of Sarajevo—Jahorina. The pistes of Jahorina do not offer as many vertical meters as those in Bjelasnica, but Jahorina is a larger ski center with more lifts and runs and better infrastructure. It had clearly not suffered as heavily during the fighting.

There were quite a few hotels and private houses near the base of the lifts in Jahorina, and numerous small restaurants were scattered around the slopes. Melissa had almost never been here, she explained, because

it is a "Serbian ski resort." She and all her Bosnian friends frequent Bjelasnica exclusively. I wondered if she remembered telling me that people had moved on with their lives.

Much of the upper mountain in Jahorina was made up of open slopes, and on the lower mountain, the trees were spaced even wider apart than in Bjelasnica. Rafi, Jean Michel and I sniffed out fresh powder in every clump of trees. No new snow had come for quite a while, but the slopes were all north facing and the –15-degree (centigrade) weather had preserved the powder.

At the end of the day, we traversed far out to the east of the resort to reach some virgin territory above the tree line. Ultimately, we continued giddily into some glades in the trees, and before we knew it, we had gobbled up 1000 vertical meters of powder, and we were on a road far below the lifts. By then the lifts had closed, and we were on the wrong side of the mountain.

The three of us were fortunate to have Melissa with us, as the situation necessitated emergency measures. We skied down the road to a farmhouse, where our new Bosnian friend negotiated a deal with the resident farmer.

A few minutes later, we were riding in a rusty, unregistered 1986 Lada, chugging up a back mountain road in first gear. Our chauffeur could not take us directly to our car, as his lack of license plates would have made a meeting with the local *policija* quite inopportune.

We were more than satisfied, and left him with almost enough "taxi fare" to get his car registered again. He gave us a toothless grin, a handshake and a big wave goodbye, and the only question remaining was whether the farmer or we found the experience to be funnier.

As he drove away, I could see him shaking his head and chuckling, and we were doing the same. "Crazy skiers," he was probably saying to himself, while Melissa laughed and said, "Funny farmer." None of us wondered if he was a Serb or a Bosnian, a Christian or a Muslim. Nobody cared.

It will take some more time for the deepest sores to mend, but I now knew that the healing would come. It would come when people would identify each other by their profession or their hobbies, and not by their ethnicity or their religion. The demographics of snowboarders and skiers may differ radically, but to this date, there has never been a war between the two groups. After all, they both pay homage to the God of snow. Amen.

THIS PAGE
Jean Michel Pons flies through the trees on the lower mountain in Zare Lazarevski.

RIGHT PAGE
UPPER: This local car, parked along the road outside a Macedonian farmhouse, has seen better days.
LOWER: Rafi never ran out of energy. Here he partakes in a bit of skijoring behind his VW bus.

Chapter 27. MACEDONIA

WEEKEND-SKIER SYNDROME

Macedonia is a small, mountainous, landlocked country in the southernmost part of what used to be known as Yugoslavia. In fact, the official name of the country is the Former Yugoslavian Republic of Macedonia (FYROM), a cumbersome title forced upon the country by its Greek neighbors. The Greeks are very proud of their northernmost province, called Macedonia, birthplace of Alexander the Great, and wanted there to be no confusion between their region and the newly formed country.

Former Yugoslavian Macedonia not only has had problems over its name with its neighbors to the south, the people have also had difficulties getting along with just about everybody in the region, including themselves. There is obviously no love lost between the Macedonians and the Serbs to the north, from whom they split to form their own nation. Then, in 2001, civil war broke out between the ethnic Albanian population within the country and the rest of the citizenry.

While all this bickering, squabbling and fighting is more or less par for the course anywhere in the Balkans, it has quite understandably had an adverse effect on the local ski industry. Warring countries that don't get along with their neighbors have difficulty building up a skier population base large enough to support ski resorts. Therefore, the ski areas in Former Yugoslavian Macedonia suffer from "weekend-skier syndrome".

"Weekend-skier syndrome" is a malady common among many poorer countries whose ski lifts are frequented almost exclusively by the indigenous population. I had already come across this problem in Romania and various other places in my travels. Saturdays and Sundays, when the locals have the possibility to ski, are characterized by long lines, as the lift capacity is not adequate to take care of the crowds. Weekdays, on the other hand, provide so few skiers that the ski areas often open only a few of their lifts in an effort to save money. Sometimes, they keep the lifts entirely shut.

It did not take long for my friends, Rafi and Jean Michel, and me to fall victim to the "weekend-skier syndrome". We entered the country from the south and drove to Pelistar on a Monday morning to begin our adventure in Former Yugoslavian Macedonia. It was a false start. Upon arrival, we were told that the lone ski lift in Pelistar is always closed on Mondays due to lack of skier interest.

We improvised an alternate plan—a visit to the summer resort of nearby Lake Ohrid. The city of Ohrid, situated on the shores of the large lake of the same name, has a beautiful Old Town with narrow cobblestone streets that climb up a hillside to the 1000-year-old fortification, Tsar Samoil's Citadel. There is a pedestrian street lined with shops and restaurants, and picturesque Greek Orthodox churches are scattered around the town to add local color.

STILL, WE DID NOT COME HERE to enjoy summer tourism—our purpose was to ski. Having been thwarted in Pelistar, we eliminated Macedonia's other two small ski areas—Krushevo and Oteshevo—from our list, and decided that our midweek timing necessitated that we concentrate on the larger resorts. We drove to Zare Lazarevski, a ski center by the village of Mavrovo, near the shores of Lake Mavrovo.

We arrived at dusk and my two friends were bursting with unreleased ski energy. The road passed over a large dam with a low-grade, terraced incline. Rafi slammed on the brakes, and before I could mumble, "What the hell are you up to?" he and Jean Michel were spraying powder off the dam.

Zare Lazarevski has eleven ski lifts. It was Tuesday and four were in operation. Admittedly, the upper lifts were closed due to high winds, while only a few of the lower lifts were inactive as a result of the small skier turnout. In any case, we were able to experience a good deal of the ski area with the operating machinery.

The infrastructure was good, with an international-standard hotel at the base of the lifts, various smaller hotels and pensions in the village, and a variety of small restaurants to choose from. The pistes were very well-groomed and alongside the runs, a few snow cannons gave additional evidence that the resort had definitely entered the new millennium. The snow cannons were superfluous, as there was plenty of natural white stuff covering all the pistes and more was falling out of the heavens.

The lower section of the mountain has very good runs for intermediate and advanced skiers, while the upper mountain is flatter, providing excellent terrain for beginners and low intermediates. This particular day did not offer much value for freeriders. The open upper slopes were wind-packed while the snow lower down was very heavy.

We did the best we could under the circumstances. We raced down the perfectly prepared pistes during the morning hours, enjoying the almost empty slopes. Later, we kept ourselves occupied with a few lines in tight trees adjacent to the lower trails and some short sections of untouched snow on various parts of the mountain.

LEFT PAGE
Rafi flies down a 40-degree slope far from the pistes of Mt. Ceripasina in Popova Sapka.

THIS PAGE
Jean Michel heads down the front face in Popova Sapka.

The three of us like to collect decals or sew-on patches from some of the unusual locations we ski, and at the end of the ski day, we attempted to find such souvenirs. Nothing like that was available. Jean Michel asked the ski school if he could buy a ski instructor insignia patch, but that was also not possible.

We drove north. Driving through the country, a couple of things became painfully clear. If potholes and litter were dollars and cents, Macedonia would be the richest country in the world. The truth of the matter is that the poor roads keep one's speed down to a crawl, so that one has the opportunity to very clearly view tons of garbage strewn randomly all along what would otherwise be a very pretty countryside. To be frank, much of the country looked like a big garbage dump!

At least our journey was short. After an hour we arrived in the city of Tetovo, the base of the Popova Sapka ski resort—at least it *used to be* the

base. Up until 2001, skiers could begin their day by riding a small gondola directly from the city up to the ski area. That lift was damaged beyond repair during the civil war.

There are plans to rebuild the gondola in the very near future, but in a land that does not seem to have the financial wherewithal to take care of its roads and garbage, one wonders how realistic those plans are. For the time being, one must drive from Tetovo up to the small group of mountain hotels that now serve as the base of the resort.

Again it was snowing hard, and fog clad the mountain. Popova Sapka has a half-dozen lifts, but only two short T-bars for beginners were open. That seemed to be more than enough to take care of a unit of soldiers who were more or less the only guests that day. The soldiers were decked out in camouflage white, but if Macedonia's next war was to be fought on the snow, their outfits were not going to be enough to save this group of

LEFT PAGE
Rafi finds a stash of deep powder on the lower slopes of Popova Sapka.

THIS PAGE
UPPER: Jean Michel poses for a photo in the war-damaged gondola that used to bring visitors from the town of Tetovo to the ski resort of Popova Sapka.
LOWER LEFT: Many of the slopes of Zare Lazarevski offer views of Lake Mavrovo.
LOWER RIGHT: The town of Tetovo.

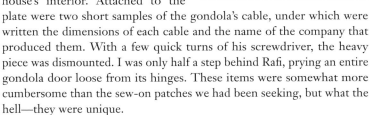

warriors. They were fighting a losing battle against the horizontal terrain. They did, however, provide a short respite of entertainment on a day that had very little for us to do.

Again, Rafi and Jean Michel inquired at every hotel about souvenir emblems or stickers, but the result was the same as in Zare Lazarevski—no luck.

Off the slopes, weekdays in Macedonia are also a far cry from Manhattan or "Gay Paree". All bars, restaurants and other assorted night-spots are mandated to close by midnight. Our short ski day was followed by an early night and a little prayer for better weather or luck.

Our prayer was answered. Blue skies the following morning revealed an old, double chair lift that climbed up Mt. Ceripasina (2510 m) to just a hundred vertical meters or so below its peak—and it was moving! A Balkan slalom race was going on, making for more than enough skiers to render a profit on a weekday, and the lack of wind allowed the decrepit piece of machinery to function with a minimum of danger.

We began a 22-minute ride up Mt. Ceripasina. The long, slow journey afforded us plenty of time to examine a beautiful freeride mountain. It was also a dream location for ski touring. There were possible descents in various directions, even including routes down to villages in Kosovo.

While the lower runs had been prepared adequately for the novices, only one track had been groomed from the top. The remainder of the mountain and its possible descents were left to the fantasy of each skier.

Skiers who ski down the wall of a dam have a rather active imagination, so it was not long before the three of us were exploring as many routes as time allowed. The upper slopes were firm wind pack that turned into powder part way down. It was all very inviting, but we were certain that Popova Sapka had no ski patrol to blast potentially dangerous slopes. Rafi almost straight-lined a 40-degree pitch, and we did not make too many turns on any of the steeper slopes.

There were a number of couloirs near the top, and a few lovely groves of pine trees on the lower mountain. We won some time by skipping lunch, but it all ended too soon. The local slalom finished at 2:30 and 10 minutes later the chair lift ceased operation. We complained, argued and quarreled with the lift operator like true Balkan people, but it was to no avail.

There were still a few vertical meters available—a run under the old defunct gondola to the middle station between the resort and Tetovo. This involved hitchhiking back up the mountain to our car, but we had plenty of time. The narrow path looked as if it had been a piste in the pre-war days, but now, ours were the only tracks of the day.

At the middle station, we rummaged around the ruins of what had been an active ski lift only a few years earlier. One gondola lay flat on the cement floor of the lift house, while the others hung motionless on the old cable, slowly rusting away. Broken plastic and glass were strewn about amidst the dust and cobwebs of the building. Jean Michel climbed into one of the small red and yellow cabins and posed for a photo. That would have to suffice as a unique souvenir of our Macedonia ski trip—or would it?

Suddenly, Rafi pulled out his Swiss army knife as he eyed a heavy, metal plate fastened to the wall of the lift house's interior. Attached to the plate were two short samples of the gondola's cable, under which were written the dimensions of each cable and the name of the company that produced them. With a few quick turns of his screwdriver, the heavy piece was dismounted. I was only half a step behind Rafi, prying an entire gondola door loose from its hinges. These items were somewhat more cumbersome than the sew-on patches we had been seeking, but what the hell—they were unique.

Rafi caught a lift up to his van, and we soon loaded our scavenged artifacts into the vehicle. Were they souvenirs or spoils of war? One thing is certain. Our mementos would be an ever-present reminder to us of a great freeride day on a mountain that deserves a better fate.

*   *   *   *   *   *   *   *

Less than a month later, I was visiting one of the top Alpine resorts with my son Erik during the Easter holidays. Everything there stood in marked contrast to my recent tour through Macedonia. The lift system was made up of numerous six-seat, high-speed detachable chairs and eight-person gondolas, and there was no uncertainty, of course, about whether they would be operating or not, regardless of the number of people who might ski on any particular day.

As we reached the top of one of these state-of-the-art lifts the first morning, Erik asked whether we would be skiing on the marked slopes or off-piste. I told him that the snow conditions would keep us relegated to the groomed runs.

"I won't need my helmet today then, right dad?" my son inquired.

I looked around me, observing a crowd of around 100 people all putting their skis on simultaneously. Beyond them, I could see the slopes looking like a swarming anthill. The day would certainly consist of an 8-hour people-slalom.

"No," I finally answered, "you *will* need your helmet today. But next year, I might take you to Popova Sapka, and there you can ski without a helmet if you wish, whether we are on or off the pistes."

Chapter 28. CROATIA
IN THE SKI TRACKS OF THE "CROATIAN SENSATION"

Croatia is famous for its long seacoast full of stunning beaches—a haven for sailors, swimmers and sunbathers during its long summer. Its Dalmatian coastline runs down the Adriatic Sea paralleling Italy's shoreline on the opposite side. Other tourist attractions include the Old Towns of Dubrovnik and Split, picturesque and quaint historical cities, both of which have UNESCO World Heritage status.

Ski resorts and mountains, however, are two categories for which Croatia has no claim to fame. If it weren't for the fact that Janica Kostelic, long known in ski racing circles as the "Croatian Sensation", and her brother Ivica, two of the world's top ski racers, both hail from this beach paradise, nobody would know that there was any skiing at all in Croatia.

There are, indeed, a few tiny ski areas in the country, including Platak and Sljeme, but the largest is Bjelolasica. Sure enough, both Janica and Ivica started their skiing careers on the humble slopes of this little resort.

At the base of Bjelolasica Mountain stands one lone hotel, and that sums up the housing facilities of what is known in Croatia as the Olympic Training Center.

Boasting a grand total of five lifts and 767 vertical meters of skiing, Bjelolasica is not going to make anyone forgot Val d'Isère, Innsbruck or any of the other locations that one usual equates with the words "Olympic Center". On the other hand, since Janica became the first alpine skier to take four medals in a single Olympic Games (2002), an avalanche of aspiring racers may want to train in Bjelolasica in the near future.

Rafi, Jean Michel and I felt it would be an injustice to pass through Croatia without at least sampling what Bjelolasica had to offer. Shortly after our arrival, we mounted a slow-moving double chair lift that rose up the lower mountain. The lift carried us over a long, steep, mogul-covered piste that revealed numerous rocks and bare spots. At the top of the chair, four shorter lifts fanned out.

We had expected spring-like weather in a ski area that is less than 25 kilometers from the Adriatic as the crow flies, but that turned out to be a total miscalculation. All fears of global warming dissipated into the frosty air as the mercury hovered around –15 degrees centigrade.

We found the upper slopes were covered with good, packed powder. Even better, light powder lay untouched in the thick forest, and we played around, skiing short lines in or near the trees. The lower mountain offered a longer and steeper run, but the poor snow coverage kept us away until the end of the day. It was then that I noticed that the entry to the descent was roped off, and the run was closed. I approached the ski patrol.

"There is not so much snow on the lower run," explained one man. "The snow is not good now. It is too cold, so it does not stick to the ground. The snow is better when it is about plus 4 degrees."

Although his logic was flawed, I understood what he meant. All good skiers, of course, dream of the kind of light snow that falls during cold weather, but this excellent powder was easily blown away and did not serve well as a base.

Good base or not, tradition mandated that we should ski down. No real ski bum would ever ride down on a lift if it were even vaguely possible to descend on skis. We tap-danced between the obstacles, and our skis were not too much the worse for wear when we arrived back at the car.

LEFT PAGE
Jean Michel Pons wears a homemade fur mask on his face to protect him from the Arctic weather in Bjelolasica. He made the mask during a long adventure on the Kamchatka Peninsula of Russia.

THIS PAGE
UPPER: A storm is brewing over Dubrovnik.
LOWER LEFT: The Old Town of Dubrovnik.
LOWER MIDDLE: Sign indicates that we are approaching Bjelolasica.
LOWER RIGHT: Jean Michel enjoys a short pitch in the trees of Bjelolasica.

During the day, the slopes had been occupied by no more than a handful of skiers. It was evident that the Kostelic siblings notwithstanding, the Croatians were not heavily into the sport. I suppose that many Croatian ski enthusiasts were in nearby Austria or elsewhere, but one place they were not was in Bjelolasica.

The Kostelic siblings have by now outgrown the small Olympic Training Center in their home country, and after our ski day, we too opted for whiter pastures and headed south. We drove along the panoramic coastline, making worthwhile stops in the living museums of Split and Dubrovnik. Our next ski destination was to be in the country now called Serbia and Montenegro, another part of the former Yugoslavia and one where the mountains are more prominent than in Croatia.

283

Chapter 29.
SERBIA AND MONTENEGRO
FREERIDE MOUNTAIN FOR SALE

Over the past few years, the European Union has turned border crossings into convenient non-events. This is not so in the various parts of what used to be called Yugoslavia. In fact, there was very little of what happened to Rafi Betschart, Jean Michel Pons and me in Serbia and Montenegro that was a non-event.

At the frontier to Montenegro, curious guards inspected the contents of our vehicle and wondered why *three* skiers would be traveling with *five* pairs of top-of-the-line skis and a snowboard. This abundance of state-of-the-art equipment seemed to be reasonable evidence of a possible ski-theft and smuggling ring. They wanted to see purchase receipts for our gear.

I am an experienced traveler. I speak four languages, I can read a road map, and I know how to pack my toilet kit. I have never forgotten my passport, credit card, cash or any other necessity on a trip. But I do not generally carry receipts of my possessions with me on the road.

It was fortunate that Jean Michel, the linguist of our entourage, possessed a fluency in English, German, Spanish and Russian in addition to his native French. In this case, it was his Russian in addition to his penchant for diplomacy that was adequate to explain to the border patrol that our collection of equipment was not entirely out of the ordinary among decadent Westerners. After a rather lengthy discussion, our road-trip was allowed to continue into Montenegro.

RAFI, MY OTHER COMPANION on this trip, is one of the best and most daring skiers I know. There is nary a couloir or cliff jump that can make him flinch. He jumps in first and thinks later. For better or worse, he drives a car just like he skis.

We had a long drive to Durmitor, our first destination in Montenegro, and we had lost time during our extended border stop. The mountain roads were snow covered and narrow to begin with, and the massive amounts of snow that the plows had piled alongside the road rendered the highway most suitable to one-way traffic. Rafi nevertheless tried to make up for lost time. He raced along the windy path like a rally driver taking his wife to the hospital.

Jean Michel rode shotgun and read the maps, and I lay in the back of the van, trying to find a way to keep my seatbelt fastened while finding a comfortable reclining position—mission impossible. The centrifugal

force of the curves in the road sent my body careening from side to side. Sometimes Rafi slammed on the brakes, as he noticed—too late—that the curve was sharper than he had anticipated. Each time he attempted to decelerate, my body lurched forward, straining against the seatbelt which kept me from rolling onto the floor. I dozed intermittently, only to be startled out of my slumber every few minutes by the inconsistencies in the road.

Finally I did fall asleep. I'm not sure how long I was out, but the next time I woke up, it was bright light and a wave of laughter from my comrades that brought me back to consciousness. I blinked my eyes open to find Rafi driving among the turbines inside a massive power plant. It was a scene right out of a James Bond film, except that Rafi's VW was no match for Bond's usual set of wheels. I expected Ernst Blofeld or some other arch-villain to appear any moment high on a walkway on the upper level of the hangar-sized interior of the plant, shouting down, "You won't get away from me this time, Bond!"

We had obviously made a wrong turn somewhere, but rarely has a missed road sign landed me in such bizarre surroundings. How we were able to simply drive right into the plant will always remain a mystery to me. There was no sign of human life, and we soon hightailed it back out of the monstrous building. Above us was a massive dam rising about 200 meters straight up the breach in a narrow gorge.

We were soon back on the road, and I returned to slumber land as if the whole experience had been a bad dream. I did not wake up again until Rafi missed a sharp turn and drove our chariot into a snowbank a few kilometers from Zabljak.

ZABLJAK IS A PICTURESQUE VILLAGE nestled at the base of the highest mountains in Montenegro. The ski area, Durmitor, has no more than five lifts, but the upper chair lift is one of the steepest in the world, rising into a domain of limestone cliffs reminiscent of the Dolomites.

A black, ungroomed piste descends down a large valley in the shadow of some of those rock walls, and we took a few runs down that piste, finding a handful of powder turns along the way. The best freeride domain, however, required a 15-minute hike above the lift. The walk circumvented more cliffs and accessed a wide east face that descended 800 vertical meters back to the base of the resort. The wind had unfortunately done

LEFT PAGE
LEFT: The border between Montenegro and Kosovo is not a very friendly-looking place.
RIGHT: Local graveyard in Kolasin, close to the ski center of Bjelasica in Montenegro.

THIS PAGE
UPPER: The highest mountains in Montenegro lord over the picturesque village of Zabljak.
LOWER: Jean Michel and Rafi hike up toward the peak of Savin Kuk, high above the ski resort of Durmitor.

irreparable damage to the snow, and we struggled down without finding much consistency.

Near the end of the day, we hiked once more above the top lift to the peak of Savin Kuk (2313 m). We had observed a mammoth valley to the north of the mountain on our first run, and a local snowboarder had told us that there was an entry couloir. Rafi was determined to find it.

We walked along a wind cornice in search of the entry, but all we found were sheer cliffs that plunged 400 meters straight down. At 4:30, with the sun already below the horizon, Rafi called out that he had discovered the gateway—but it was too late for any such endeavor.

"Ahh, zee snow vill also be vind packed zere," said Jean Michel with a shrug of indifference and a touch of "sour grapes" in his voice. For better or worse, the back side of Savin Kuk would have to wait for another visit.

Rafi was frustrated and still full of energy. There was good powder all along the road outside of Zabljak, and my Swiss pal hates to see such a commodity go to waste, even if it is lying horizontally. He hooked up 10 meters of climbing rope onto the back of his van, and we spent an hour skijoring until it was pitch dark.

» I blinked my eyes open to find Rafi driving among the turbines inside a massive power plant. «

THE NEXT MORNING, WE PACKED OUR CAR and headed on toward the village of Kolasin and the Bjelasica ski resort. This also did not proceed without event. Not more than a few kilometers out of Zabljak, the road began winding down the mountain. A few isolated, hillside farmhouses were interspersed amidst the winter landscape of snow-covered haystacks and fields. The snow glistened in the morning sunlight, and we couldn't resist a few road-runs.

One of us drove the car, as the other two took turns skiing past a surprised but friendly farmer at work. It was not a first descent reminiscent of anything in the Chugach Mountains of Alaska, but I suspect it was a first descent nevertheless. My runs were no more than about 120 vertical meters, but they were 60 turns of perfect powder.

An hour later, we were back on our way. It was not yet ten in the morning and our day was already made. We followed a serpentine path through the stunning Moraca Canyon, whose limestone walls rose dramatically skyward on both sides of the road.

After many days of Arctic temperatures, the sun was strong, and the snow clinging precariously to the surrounding rocks was beginning to get heavy. Rafi drove quickly and nervously, looking up all the while. He knew that avalanche danger is not limited to ski slopes and that Montenegro was not the kind of place where the road service was likely to pay much attention to any such potential peril.

Just a few kilometers before reaching our destination, and only a hundred meters in front of us, the anticipated danger proved to be real. Powder snow cascaded down a narrow ravine, blocking the road. While a queue of cars began to build behind our van, Rafi, Jean Michel and I removed our avalanche shovels from our packs and began doing roadwork. Numerous locals pitched in and took turns helping us. Moments before we had a passage cleared, a snowplow arrived and finished the job, and we were able to continue to Bjelasica.

Another small ski center for local weekenders, Bjelasica offers 500 vertical meters of skiing, half of which is above the tree line. The director of the ski area gave us complimentary lift tickets and cut us into line ahead of the Sunday crowd. The presence of a foreign ski journalist in Bjelasica was obviously not an every day occurrence, and by lunchtime I was doing a TV interview for the evening news.

After lunch, we sought out the powder. A few locals had already ventured beyond the safe confines of the piste on the open upper slopes, but it was still easy to find fresh lines. Once in the forest, however, the snow got even better, and not a track was to be seen—well, soon there were three tracks…then there were six…then…we were on the road again.

We drove out of Montenegro and into Serbia to visit Kopaonik, whose twenty ski lifts make it by far the largest ski resort in the country. Kapaonik is nirvana for beginners. If Durmitor possesses one of the steepest chair lifts in the world, Kopaonik has a number of chairs that can vie for the honor of the flattest on Earth. The Karaman Greben Lift,

for example, rises an imperceptible 165 meters over a length of almost 1.5-kilometers, and many of the lifts here have similar statistics.

If you want to have a reasonable chance of getting to know this resort, by all means, *avoid* picking up a copy of the small brochure that provides a map with facts and figures. The facts and figures list the vertical drop as 521 meters instead of 821 meters and describe the longest slope as 35 kilometers long instead of 3.5 kilometers. The diagram of pistes and lifts is also certain to get any visitor hopelessly lost. In addition, the brochure proudly depicts the Krcmar Lift rising to 2017 meters, the highest point in the lift system. Unfortunately, this lift has been closed since the end of the last century because of land mines.

SATURDAYS AND SUNDAYS ARE BAD NEWS in this part of the ski world, as the lift capacity has trouble keeping pace with weekend traffic. It was Sunday, and two-thirds of the lifts were closed due to high winds or poor management, depending on whose story you believe. Pardon my cynicism, but

Jean Michel powers through some difficult snow on Savin Kuk as if it were perfect powder.

it is hard for me to fathom why one lift is open and a different lift that rises to the same altitude a few hundred meters away must be closed on account of wind.

Rafi, Jean Michel and I battled our way forward as best we could in the lift lines. Sometimes, we sneaked into the special queue for the ski school. In between standing in queues, we managed to ski down a few steep pitches in the trees, but poor visibility and minimal snow cover off-piste confined us to the marked runs for most of the day. A local suggested that if we would like some steeper skiing that we should visit Brezovica in Kosovo.

"I'm afraid to go to Kosovo since the war," he explained, "but I spent much time there before, and it is an excellent area for good skiers."

Kopaonik was proof positive that bigger does not mean better, and we headed south. The border-crossing point into Kosovo was quite different in appearance than the others we had passed through. There was a low lookout post surrounded by protective sandbags, coils of barbed wire and

numerous military vehicles. While we went through the usual formalities, the car in front of us removed his Serbian license plate and replaced it with a local one that he pulled out of his trunk. Fear and mistrust were clearly still a part of daily life here.

KOSOVO IS A LAND IN LIMBO since the end of the 1999 hostilities. It is officially still part of Serbia but governed independently, and it seems to be run, controlled and financed to some degree by a combination of bureaucracies including the European Union, NATO, the United Nations and the United States.

Brezovica was, at one time, the best ski resort in Yugoslavia, according to many locals, and it was easy for us to see why. Nine lifts were spread out over a beautiful mountain, apparently offering over 800 vertical meters of skiing. It had what a ski resort should have—terrain suitable for all abilities and a large expanse of off-piste territory. Unfortunately, Brezovica also had a number of characteristics that a ski resort should not have—government ownership, incompetent management and dilapidated lifts. "Infrastructure" does not translate well into Serbian.

The resort is in a state of limbo similar to that plaguing Kosovo as a whole. During the reign of Milosevic, the ownership of the resort was transferred fraudulently from the state to Milosevic's brother-in-law. During the time it has taken the courts to return the resort to the state, of course, Brezovica's status has remained uncertain. Since the war, the nearby Serbs who used to frequent the resort in large numbers are afraid even to enter Kosovo, and the ski area cannot generate much income.

We checked into the Sara Hotel at the base of one of the lifts—one that, it turned out, was not operating. The hotel has 110 beds, and we were three of seven guests. The rooms were inexpensive, the personnel were friendly and helpful, the water was cold and the rooms were colder. Breakfast was tasty, but one had to eat it wearing one's full ski apparel. No problem—we had not traveled to Brezovica expecting Gstaad.

It snowed during the night, and the three of us were champing at the bit to get on the slopes the next morning. In this part of the world, patience is definitely a virtue. The lifts were due to open at nine o'clock, and we were ready and waiting, as were numerous other skiers—but the lift personnel were not. About an hour later, a short T-bar for beginners slowly ground into motion. That left eight lifts to go.

We inquired at the ticket office and got some vague noises about wind. I wanted to speak to the manager, but 10 a.m. was apparently a bit early to disturb the head honcho. He had not yet arrived. At 11:45, one double chair lift was finally opened. According to those in the know, that was the

most that could be expected on a slow Monday, and we ought to be very grateful for that. We were.

LITERALLY NOBODY IN KOSOVO ventures off the piste, and for good reason. Judging by the show the locals put on underneath the chair lift, they definitely had their hands full skiing on the groomed slopes. In fact, I suspect that the piste could be a more dangerous place to be than the off-piste terrain, what with the local kamikazes. Either way, we were happy to have a private powder playground.

We did not come close to a piste all day. We spent most of our time in a steep freeride haven called Lavlja Vrata (Lion's Neck). One could enter through a series of couloirs or from a steep, open slope. The terrain included numerous small cliffs and glades of trees. Late in the day, we dropped off the back of the mountain into Durlov Potok, a large back valley that ends up on the road a few hundred meters below the resort. It was better than Gstaad—steeper too.

By day's end, we were more than satisfied. The skiing had far exceeded our expectations, and we could only imagine the bounty available to skiers if the rest of the lifts would be operational. That would add 300 vertical meters to the ski area as well as many more acres of terrain.

We sought explanations as to the true reason why most of the lifts stood idle, and we got many answers. Parts from some of the lifts had been stolen during the war, rendering the lifts unusable, explained one local. The upper lift, even in the best of times, had only been used for FIS races, related another longtime patron of the resort. A third explanation

LEFT PAGE
LEFT: Rafi sprays up a shield of powder in the Lavlja Vrata section of Brezovica. UPPER RIGHT: Jean Michel gets some tips on his powder technique from a local farmer, while skiing across his farm close to Zabljak. LOWER RIGHT: The upper chair lift in Durmitor is one of the steepest I have seen.

THIS PAGE: Jean Michel lays down a track on a mellow road-run close to Zabljak.

was that all the lifts but the two we had used had been deemed unsafe by a recent Austrian inspection. Many people, however, concurred that a simple, shortsighted philosophy of the management was the primary culprit—why open many lifts for few skiers?

We were hungry and found a few small cozy restaurants to choose from. They each had a warm fire crackling in the fireplace and offered some local specialties.

During the night, the snowfall increased and the wind howled. Over half a meter of new snow covered the parking lot and the road when we awoke at seven o'clock. People in this part of Europe are accustomed to and seem satisfied with the answer, "I don't know." This was the only answer we received to the inquiry of when we might be able to leave. Around nine o'clock, a procession of resort workers arrived trudging up the road, but there was not yet any sign of a snowplow.

THERE MIGHT BE WORSE PLACES to get snowed in than Brezovica, but I cannot think of any off the top of my head. The lifts were bound to stay shut all day, and alternate activities were very limited.

On the more positive side, being snowed in gave us more time for investigative research. I spoke for a while with Kirk Adams, the Deputy Director of Privatization for the Kosovo Trust Agency, an American organization in charge of privatizing state-operated entities. He explained that his organization would soon put the resort up for sale. According to Adams, Vail Resorts had already expressed an interest in the ski area.

I discovered another positive aspect to being snowed-in in Kosovo. The personnel and patrons of the hotel began drinking straight vodka at 9 a.m., and I was invited to join. Morning vodka brings a lucidity that borders on clairvoyance.

In a perfect world, an investor will be found to turn Brezovica back into the kind of ski resort that the mountain deserves. The lifts will be updated and return to action, and a policy will be established to keep all lifts operating whenever possible.

The infrastructure and hotel standard will improve, but not to the extent that the local people will be priced out of the market. Small, locally owned restaurants will still prevail. The standardization that so often goes hand in hand with large, international investment will not homogenize the end product so that Brezovica ends up looking like Vail East.

I DOWNED ANOTHER SHOT of vodka. What else was necessary for the Hollywood happy ending? Ahh, yes! The residual fears and apprehensions about visiting Kosovo will dissipate with time, and Serbs will return to this excellent mountain along with an international community of skiers who will discover it for the first time.

I pondered for a moment. One more thing—the new improved Brezovica will be marketed to families, to piste-bashers, and to partygoers in search of cheap alcohol. Somehow, the powder hounds and freeriders of the world will remain oblivious to Brezovica.

My friends and I will return sometime in the next decade to a warm room and full lift service to the top of the best freeride mountain in former Yugoslavia, and we will enjoy the same solitude in the powder that we experienced on this visit. Now that is a happy ending!

Any potential investors, who feel they can fulfill these guidelines for a development and marketing strategy, please contact kirk.adams@eumik.org.

It was noon, and the plow was clearing the parking lot…one more shot of vodka…"*Na zdravlje.*"

LEFT PAGE: Bled Castle, perched on a cliff about 100 meters above Bled Lake, used to be the summer residence of the Yugoslav royal family.
THIS PAGE: Jonas Nilsson finds a patch of snow amidst the dwarf-pines of Krvavec.

Chapter 30. SLOVENIA
IT´S THE LITTLE THINGS THAT COUNT

Imagine a raw and underdeveloped Austria, like Austria itself was about 50 years ago—poorer, cheaper and with only a few-odd ski lifts to dot the landscape here and there. Picture it with pristine lakes and jagged mountains, but the peaks are not quite as high. The country is smaller—one-fourth the size with one-fourth the population. There is little infrastructure in place for mass tourism, most of the skiers are local weekenders from the surrounding towns, and the friendliness of the people is genuine and unrelated to their quest for tourist dollars.

Wave the magic wand...abracadabra...poof...Slovenia! This tiny nation is proof that good things do come in small packages. To begin with, it is the only part of former Yugoslavia to break away from the federation with almost no violence. A country of about 20,000 square kilometers, Slovenia is home to about two million people, and the Slovenians have a skiing tradition every bit as rich as that of their neighbors to the north, without all the hoopla, fanfare and media hype. The people here have been skiing for over 300 years, and there are around 50 ski areas in the country. They too are small, as only a few have more than ten lifts and more than half of them have only three lifts or fewer.

Slovenia is perhaps too small to put together a full-fledged Olympic bid by herself, but together with Italy and the Austrian province of Carinthia, Slovenia was part of the first multi-nation bid for the Winter Games, an event they had offered to host jointly in 2006. That fact alone was enough to intrigue my friend Jonas Nilsson and me into visiting this rugged little land to see what it had to offer skiers.

Two Italian border guards, who were apparently frontal-lobotomy victims, thumbed inexplicably through our passports, cross-checking the numbers against a moth-eaten, multi-thousand-page document, that might have been anything from a list of World War I casualties to a telephone directory of Tokyo. They checked the passport photos against our faces a dozen times. Then they stared at our credentials for a while, as if they had never seen a passport before. After 20 minutes of this tedium, they waved us on. The Slovenian border attendant, by contrast, shined us a friendly smile, did not even look in our little blue books, and said simply, "Welcome to Slovenia."

The route by which we entered Slovenia passes directly into Triglav National Park, a fairytale land of dark, enchanted forests, majestic, craggy, snow-covered peaks, and Hansel-and-Gretel houses. Only the witches, trolls and forest nymphs were missing from this fantasyland, and perhaps they could be seen as well, if we looked hard enough.

We wound our way through this charming landscape until we arrived in Bovec, a picturesque village nestled in a valley of the Julian Alps. The Julian Alps form the eastern extension of the Dolomites, and are every bit as impressive as the Italian section of this chain of limestone precipices. On the outskirts of Bovec is the ski resort of Kanin, where a four-person gondola rises about 1700 vertical meters into the heart of these peaks.

JONAS AND I TOOK THE HALF-HOUR RIDE to the top station of the gondola, from where a handful of short lifts take skiers to an elevation of just under 2300 meters. At first glance, the skiing looked somewhat limited, best for beginners and intermediates. There is one piste that drops about 700 vertical meters to one of the intermediate stations of the gondola. One can pursue a few off-piste variations to the main run, but the soft limestone here creates a landscape with many small cliffs, rises, bluffs and other obstacles to off-piste skiing. In addition, spectacular cliffs on both sides hem in the ski area.

As is often the case, there is more to Kanin than at first meets the eye. On a hunch, Jonas and I rode the highest lift and looked over the back of the mountain. Stretched out below us was a valley the size of some small countries, with steep slopes in the shade of a sheer wall. There was no piste, but there were tracks. Not wanting to go astray in this vast off-piste province, we sought out the head of the ski school. Ljubo Bizjak confirmed that it was easy to get lost in the Krnica area and apologized that he had no instructors available to guide us.

"Please come back to me in an hour, and I will see what I can do to help you," said Ljubo.

When we returned, Ljubo pointed to a snowboarder sitting in the sun near the top of the mountain.

"Tomaz, there, is a professional boarder who competes on the international circuit. He has already gone down in Krnica three times this morning and would be happy to show you around," explained Ljubo.

We were quickly being made to feel very welcome in Slovenia. Tomaz introduced himself with a friendly smile and glided into the lead. The snow was spring-like, and we hopped around in our newly discovered playground like Easter bunnies, until we finally ran out of open spaces. Tight forest now combined with overly mushy and patchy spring snow to create a hazardous route back to civilization.

Our guide threaded neatly through the obstacle course like a fox slithering through a hillside of brambles. Meanwhile, we sweated, stumbled, hip-checked and kick-turned our way down the lower slopes until we emerged on a road, which eventually brought us around to an even lower gondola station than the one we had skied to on the piste.

After our ski day, Jonas had a personal mission. He obsessively collects sew-on patches from every ski destination he visits, and it was imperative to get one from his first visit to Slovenia. I tried to help, and we split up to cover more ground. It was to no avail. By shop-closing time, a disappointed Jonas and I returned to the hotel empty-handed.

At dinner, we made a new discovery. Portions of food in Slovenia are gargantuan—even more than the average hungry skier can force down. A sum of money that would barely dent a ski bum's budget bought a large beer, a first course, a mixed salad that was a meal in itself, and a trout that would have been a prize for any angler.

After our overindulgence, it was time to dance off the extra kilos we had just forced on ourselves, and we headed to the local disco, the Elvis Club. The good news was that it was open on a Monday night in low

season. The bad news was that we had to rouse the bartender from what was, no doubt, an engrossing novel, to serve a beer to his first and possibly only customers of the night. While a weekend here would certainly be somewhat livelier, we could safely surmise that Bovec would not soon replace St. Anton or Zell am See on the après-ski and nightlife circuit.

On our second morning, I noticed a contour map outside our hotel, which depicted lifts connecting Kanin with the little Italian ski area of Sella Nevea. I asked the hotel receptionist about these lifts, and he explained that they were projected for a future link between the countries.

His answer begged the question of "When do they expect to have the project finished?"

The answer to this question gave a clear insight into Slovenia. "The project has already been on the map for twenty years or so," was the retort.

The financial catalyst necessary to transfer idea into reality has often been lacking in Slovenia, regardless of whether a socialistic or capitalistic mentality has dominated the country. It was clear that Jonas and I might not live long enough to see this dream come true, so we tucked our passports neatly into our rucksacks and prepared to take matters into our own hands.

AS WE READIED OURSELVES for our little adventure, we ran into Ljubo once again. Jonas asked if he knew where we could purchase the kind of patch he was seeking. Ljubo laughed and explained that a little Slovenian ski area like Kanin does not yet have such a developed marketing concept as to have such souvenirs available.

"But, not to worry," our new friend added. "I have a few extra patches like these which I can give you," he said, pointing to the official Slovenian ski instructor emblem attached to his parka. "What hotel do you stay at? I will leave them there."

Jonas beamed as he told the ski school director the name of our local headquarters, and I could see that his trip had been saved. As we rode the top lift to take us into Italy, I thought that Ljubo was actually quite

wrong. Slovenia had the excellent marketing technique of genuine friendliness, kindness and generosity.

Soon, we dropped once again over the back of the mountain and hung a hard left turn where we had cut right the day before. We were now in the area known as Prevala. After some wide carves in early-morning corn snow, we approached a little sign proclaiming the border with Italy. We skied in the basin of a wide valley until we eventually reached the first Italian lifts.

Sella Nevea, like Kanin, has a few short lifts for beginners, but the cornerstone of this tiny ski area is a cable car and a 700-vertical-meter descent, which splits into two runs about halfway down the mountain. This north-facing piste was perfectly manicured, and in a ski resort that even most Italians have never heard of, it was also almost devoid of people. The lack of other skiers allowed Jonas and me the liberty to shift into high gear, and we spent the rest of the day cruising Italian corduroy. Sometimes, we passed no more than one or two people on an entire run.

The small size and lack of major patronage at Sella Nevea, however, eventually posed a negative side as well, for we had to return to Bovec, and we were not exactly on a major transportation artery. We soon discovered that with a series of buses it would take us many hours to get back to our starting point.

The solution to our problem turned out to be relatively simple nevertheless. We walked through the sparsely populated parking lot at closing time trying to bum a lift. We soon came upon a Hungarian couple who gave us a ride, offered us a couple of soft drinks and even drove a few kilometers out of their way to leave us right at the border. A Slovenian couple, who arrived at the border simultaneously with us, then gave us a ride directly to our car in the Kanin parking lot. Once again, a few helpful individuals turned an ordinary ski day into a fond memory of kind and obliging people.

A strap on my rucksack had broken during the day, and that evening I tried to find a tailor to repair it. I couldn't locate the place, and asked a local man for directions. The communication gap was too great, so he jumped in his car and led me to the tailor. It was one more small gesture

of people going out of their way to be helpful, and I must say that I was not even surprised anymore.

The local kindness had still not run out. In many poorer countries, a Westerner might expect to get gouged for an abnormally high fee for certain items or services. In Slovenia, I was beginning to expect the opposite, and not without reason. A couple of hours after leaving my rucksack with the local tailor, I returned to pick it up. The tailor informed me that the job was so little work, that he would not accept any payment whatsoever!

THE NEXT LOCATION on our Slovenian menu was Kranjska Gora. The prominent men's slalom and giant slalom races which have been held here for many years and the nearby Planica ski jumping venue have made Kranjska Gora, without question, the most well-known ski village in Slovenia. Its proximity to the Austrian and Italian borders also makes it the ski resort most easily accessible to Western Europe. Despite its familiar name among Westerners, however, any Slovenian will tell you immediately that Kranjska Gora certainly is not the best of their ski areas. The village is picturesquely nestled into a valley dominated by Mt. Razor (2601 m) and Mt. Prisank (2547 m), but the ski slopes that rise to only 1570 meters up Mt. Vitrane are rather disappointing.

The ski center boasts twenty lifts, but this is misleading as well, since most of the lifts are short T-bars that access identical and rather boring slopes and trails cut out of the forest on the lower section of the mountain. Only the old single chair lift to the top rises above 1300 meters, so it is understandable that Kranjska Gora has a relatively short season. Off-piste skiing is virtually nonexistent here, as the thick forests that separate the pistes are not conducive to being skied by anyone who is not equipped with a chain saw.

Jonas and I did not stay long in Kranjska Gora, but circumvented Triglav National Park and entered the beautiful reserve again near the village of Bled. Mother Nature and man have combined quite admirably in creating the storybook scenery in and around Bled.

The village is situated on the shores of Lake Bled, and is dominated by

snow-covered peaks to the north. Man has added to the natural surroundings by building a castle on the cliffs above the water and a church on a tiny island in the middle of the lake. Just seeing this picture-perfect, hundred-year-old resort makes a trip to Slovenia worthwhile. Bled, however, is also the gateway to the lovely Bohinj Valley, home to the ski resorts of Vogel and Kobla. These two ski centers are built near the shores of yet another emerald of Triglav Park, Lake Bohinj.

JONAS AND I BOARDED VOGEL'S cable car, which took us straight up to a mountaintop hotel. The north-facing bedrooms of the Hotel Vogel not only offer a panorama over the entire lake, but they also look out over Mt. Triglav itself. Climbing Triglav, the highest peak in Slovenia at 2864 meters, is a kind of ritual pilgrimage for the natives, who consider conquering the peak at least once in a lifetime to be a mark of national identity. Triglav seems a worthy god, as it stands head and shoulders above the surrounding peaks and towers above the lake and basin, which the Triglav Glacier carved out many millenniums ago.

Mt. Triglav is a prominent part of the landscape as one skis around the slopes of Vogel as well. Most of the runs here are short, easy pistes that fan out from a plateau behind the Hotel Vogel. In addition, a long descent of over 1200 vertical meters is also possible, taking skiers from atop the uppermost lift back to the base of the cable car. Freeriders willing to hike for an hour can also enjoy a peak to valley off-piste descent, in the opposite direction from the lifts.

After a couple of runs from top to bottom, Jonas and I were quite hungry. The perfect lunch spot at Vogel is the cozy Pri Merjascu, which specializes in wild boar. As always in Slovenia, we certainly ate our fill. Even after a full afternoon of skiing, we had not really worked off our lunch and sought some extra exercise. With the spring sun having melted off much of the snow at the lower elevations, we extended our day's activities with a hike to the Savica Falls at the end of the valley.

The same lift ticket is good at either Vogel or Kobla, and the following day, we visited the latter resort, situated just a short drive away, above the village of Bohinjska Bistrica. Although the altitude figures here are not

THIS PAGE
UPPER: The Old Town of Ljubljana.
LOWER: Mt. Triglav towers above the Hotel Vogel.

RIGHT PAGE
I enjoy a moment of sunshine and powder above the tiny village of Dardha, Albania.
Photo by Ronald Naar.

The skiing has a fair amount of variety for intermediate skiers with most of the area being made up of wide slopes, a number of which are full of moguls. Nevertheless, most runs are quite short, there is not much to challenge an advanced skier, and off-piste possibilities are quite limited.

As with many of the Slovenian resorts, a close look at a map of the ski area here revealed a plethora of dotted lines (nine to be exact) indicating future lift projects. These future lifts could eventually extend the skiing onto new peaks and open up an area almost twice as large as the existing one. These projects have perhaps, as in Kanin, also been in the works for some time, but there is a difference. The nearness of Krvavec to the main population centers of Slovenia give this mountain a stable customer base, perhaps allowing for the realization of some of these dreams in the not-too-distant future.

For foreign tourists, Krvavec's short distance from Ljubljana provides the interesting opportunity of combining a ski visit with a cultural aspect, as the Old Town of Ljubljana is a must for any visitor to Slovenia. In the same way as Slovenia's mountain villages and forests conjure up images of 19th century fairies, giants and dwarfs, the Old Town of Ljubljana is the epitome of baroque central Europe.

The Old Town is surrounded by the Ljubljanica River and dominated by a large hill, topped by an old castle. In between is a maze of picturesque, cobblestone streets lined with lovely old buildings from centuries past. It does not take much imagination to visualize the streets bustling with horse-drawn carriages, lords and ladies, and proud tradesmen tending their shops.

OUR SKI VISIT TO SLOVENIA WAS TRULY a special experience—revealing a composite of qualities borrowed from different eras to create a unique blend that is Slovenia. The natural beauty of the Julian Alps was timeless and eternal. The skiing, meanwhile, had a distinctive laid-back atmosphere that characterized skiing in the West 50 years ago, before it was a huge industry. The prices, too, seemed from years gone by. The architecture in Ljubljana added a flavor from the 19th century and even earlier. And the memorable friendliness of the people was definitely left over from a past age, before the "me first" generation began to set the standards of normalcy in the West.

While the landscape will certainly maintain its beauty unscathed long into the new millennium, some of the other aspects of a ski holiday in Slovenia are very susceptible to change. It is well worth a visit to this charming land before those alterations take place.

very impressive, with the lifts rising from 540 to 1480 meters, we were surprised to see that one could still use the full vertical of the resort, even in mid-March. The runs are all trails flanked on both sides by forest, and the few skiers who were using the ski area at this time of year seemed to be more interested in working on their tans than on their technique. Jonas and I could carve up the empty slopes at full speed without putting anyone at risk.

Our final ski destination in Slovenia was Krvavec, whose twelve lifts, spread out over three rounded peaks, make it one of the largest ski areas in the land. Rising to just under 2000 meters, it is also the second-highest ski resort in the country, giving it a season that goes well into April. This ski area is in a section of mountains called the Kamnik Alps, situated a mere 32 kilometers from the capital city of Ljubljana.

Krvavec's proximity to Ljubljana plays a distinctive role in the atmosphere here. There is far more activity here than in the other Slovenian resorts, with a bit of a party atmosphere on weekends, as the young people from both the capital and the nearby city of Kranj fill the pistes. The action, however, is primarily on the slopes, as the locals retreat back to their home cities after the skiing is finished.

Chapter 31. ALBANIA

BACK TO THE ROOTS

This story began as far back as June 2000, when my cousin, Gina Schaar, decided to quit her high-paying position as a Washington, D.C. lawyer, and become part of a voluntary, non-profit, American-sponsored program to help the government of Albania democratize its judicial system.

Gina's e-mails to her friends and family were brimming with interesting and amazing facts and anecdotes.

Regarding the driving skills of the locals, she explained that "since no one was allowed to own a car before 1992, and cars have become common only in the last few years, all drivers have the experience and judgment of teenage drivers...in the U.S."

Gina was reluctant to buy meat or poultry in her new home country because "many shops don't refrigerate at all—the carcasses hang in the window or open air to be carved up on request."

When monitoring a local election, Gina also noted what she called some "minor problems". For example, many people did not know where to vote, because many areas of Tirana have no street addresses! Some people who did manage to find their way to the polls used "family voting," where "whole families would go behind the screen with their ballots, while father told everyone else how to fill them in."

The current situation in Albania was well summed up by a message written on a blackboard in the Albanian Magistrates' School, which read, "God grant me the Serenity to accept the things I cannot change, Courage to change the things I can, and Wisdom to know the difference."

The more I read of Gina's letters, the more interested I became to visit this backward island that is situated in one of the most progressive and successful parts of the world.

Gina also wrote us about Enver Hoxha, who had ruled with an iron fist for the 40-year, post-World War II period. Hoxha's brand of Marxism was more stringent and austere than any other such system, and *fun* and *entertainment* seemed to have been exorcised from the Albanian lexicon. Other words, such as *infrastructure*, were also left by the wayside in Hoxha's bizarre quest for a pure form of self-sufficient Marxism.

Whereas the Romans built roads and the Americans introduced skyscrapers, Hoxha's construction legacy is bunkers. The countryside is today littered with about two million such concrete structures, a tribute to the longtime leader's xenophobia.

GINA ALSO DESCRIBED A COUNTRY full of beautiful scenery and lovely mountain ranges. As a skier, I was fascinated by the possibility of visiting Albania to practice my favorite pastime. Albania, however, was different from the other poor countries in which I had skied. Even the likes of Bolivia, Kyrgyzstan, Uzbekistan, India and Romania were the proud benefactors of some rudimentary form of ski lifts—not Albania. It had no time for such excesses under Hoxha's rule, and this land, 70 percent of whose surface is covered by mountains, has not a single ski lift. My interest was piqued even more.

Gina began to investigate for me, but information did not come easily. Skiers were a little hard to come by, but Gina persevered. She met Helmut Obermoser, a transplanted Austrian who had been working in Albania for four years and knew the mountains of the country very well, at least in summer. She also found a couple of locals, Maqo and Mandi, two among very few Albanian ski enthusiasts.

She gathered information. Albania has many areas with snow-covered mountains. In the north, along the border with Serbia and Montenegro, are the spectacular Dinaric or Albanian Alps, a range of dramatic, cliff-laden, limestone peaks. Mt. Jezerca, at 2693 meters, is the highest mountain in this range. To the east, along the Macedonian border, lies the Korabi Range

and Albania's highest peak, Mt. Korabi (2751 m); and in the south, near Korca, are the Morava Mountains. The latter region had various places where one could ski, according to her local contacts.

This was enough information to set me into motion. Dutch adventurer Ronald Naar joined me, and we arrived in Albania's capital, Tirana, in January.

To think that there are no "ski resorts" in Albania is wrong, but the Albanian ski locations were not what we in the West think of today as a ski resort. Rather, they are more like what existed in the Alps about 80 years ago—a village in the mountains where one can go skiing. After all, this is the way skiing began. We were going back to the roots—we just didn't know quite how far back we were going.

Merely to get to the mountain villages of Albania during the winter is

a labor of love. Road building was not Hoxha's forte. On the best high-ways in the country, provided they are clear of snow, a passenger vehicle can expect to average 35 kilometers per hour! That is the speed we would have achieved on our drive from Tirana to Korca if the landscape had not been so beautiful.

Our six-person entourage departed from Tirana in Helmut's four-wheel-drive Mitsubishi and a rented Land Rover. We drove over the mountains southeast of Tirana and down toward the city of Elbasan. The Shkumbini River snaked its way along the wide valley floor, shimmering in the morning sun. In the distance, Mt. Tomori towered majestically over the valley in the sun haze. Incongruously, the lovely landscape was marred by the still-functioning, gargantuan steel mill of Elbasan, another relic of the Communist era.

We were very impressed with the scenery throughout Albania. Here, Mt. Tomori rises majestically in the morning sun above a sea of hills close to the city of Elbasan.

We continued over another mountain pass. This time, the summit revealed vistas of beautiful Lake Ohrid with a backdrop of the snow-covered mountains of Macedonia. Our trip continued past tranquil meadows where shepherds minded their flocks, and mountain villages with picturesque churches and mosques.

Finally, we reached Korca. Here we met up with Maqo and were introduced to an Albanian ritual, which would be repeated time and again before our short visit was finished. Our trip could not continue without a taste of Albanian hospitality. These proud Balkan people are famous for their friendliness, and it is close to a capital offense to deny an Albanian the opportunity to invite newcomers into his home for some food and drink. The food we were served when breaking bread with the locals varied, but raki, the Albanian national drink, was never missing.

Now came the time to push into the true mountains and our first destination, the tiny village of Dardha. We left asphalt behind us. The road had been plowed, but there was plenty of snow still covering the surface. The dizzying speed of 35 kilometers per hour now plummeted to about 5 kilometers per hour and eventually dropped to zero. Even our four-wheel-drive SUVs could not make it over the pass without chains, and we had none.

IN ALBANIA, IT IS CRITICAL always to have a plan B in reserve, and our leaders were prepared. They were hardly fazed by our failure to achieve the desired goal (perhaps they had expected it), and we headed back down and to the mountain "resort" of Voskopoja.

We arrived late and tired at our destination. The hotel restaurant

THIS PAGE
UPPER: Helmut Obermoser is a few steps ahead of me as we head up into uncharted terrain near Dardha. LOWER: What goes up, must come down, and I must admit that the powder was pretty good.

RIGHT PAGE
Helmut finds a nice cut in the woods near Dardha.
All photos by Ronald Naar.

provided a surprise. There, our Albanian friends laid out a spread of food they had bought at the local market, and we bought only beverages from the house bar. This is apparently common practice in this poor country, where people often cannot afford to buy restaurant meals.

Similar to some of the Alpine countries, it is common practice in Albania for local schools to bring large groups of teenagers to the mountains for a ski week. That is where the similarity ends. Albanian students generally do not own any equipment. The schools rely on hand-me-downs sent to the Albanian Ski Federation by charitable organizations in Austria and elsewhere. In the morning, we watched as a few teachers assembled such a school group in the courtyard of the hotel. It was a misfit army of happy-looking teenagers proudly holding skis that were a sundry variation of relics from two decades ago.

Some lucky students also wore ski boots. Others wore rubber rain boots, while some were only equipped with tennis shoes! The teachers led the school group on a 30-minute morning march toward the "slopes". We watched the group trudge over snow, dirt and mud to a few slightly graded meadows sugar-coated with a meager layer of snow.

While Albania is full of stunning mountains steep enough to put the heart of any skier into his throat, the slopes here in Voskopoja resembled the ski terrain in Denmark or Belgium, and we convinced our Albanian colleagues that we would like to make a second attempt at reaching Dardha.

We regrouped in Korca, where the fifth or sixth auto supply store we went to managed to outfit Helmut with some tire chains that fit his 4x4. Meanwhile, we arranged to pay a local villager with a four-wheel-drive vehicle to cart the rest of us to our destination.

Dardha is a picturesque village of old stone houses dominated by an Orthodox church. It is situated at approximately 1400 meters and is surrounded by a mixed forest of birch, Balkan pine and other trees. Communication here is at the same level as the transportation. There are no land telephone lines in the village, mobile phones have no coverage and even the ordinary post usually does not reach Dardha. E-mail? Forget it! You are in the wrong century! There were two hotels and no stores. The rest of the town was made up of private houses, many of which had long ago been abandoned and were falling apart.

Mandi gave me an explanation for the village's odd state. The town had a population of around 500 people in the 1920s, at which time a major migration to the United States took place. Most of the immigrants found a better life in America and never returned. Many homes were just left to the elements, and now there were no more than about 40 people left.

WE WERE IMMEDIATELY INVITED into the home of one of the locals, and once again we indulged in clinking glasses of raki together, drinking tea and eating chocolates.

Our accommodation the first night was a private home belonging to one of Maqo's friends. The house consisted of a living room, a kitchen and four bedrooms. There was neither a toilet nor an outhouse. The great outdoors would have to suffice for relieving oneself.

The house was heated by firewood, and that meant that we spent the evening huddled around the old, wood-burning iron stove in the kitchen. The bedrooms did not have the benefit of heat, and my room had a temperature of 3 degrees centigrade—at least it was plus degrees! As it turned out, it didn't matter at all. My bed was covered with seven thick, woolen

blankets and quilts, the combined weight of which was certainly in the neighborhood of 15 kilos. I cuddled with a hot water bottle between my legs under my seven heavy layers of Albanian wool, and I felt as warm and secure as an unborn baby in its mother's womb.

The following morning, the time had finally come to do what we had come here for—skiing. But I was somewhat mystified as to where our local friends had intended to take us for our ski tour. Surrounded by forest as we were, I saw nothing that really resembled touring terrain. I asked Mandi.

He pointed enthusiastically to a couple of clearings in the woods, each of which provided about a 50-meter vertical drop, and crowed happily, "It is very good, eh? And look at that road. It is covered with snow, and we can also ski there."

I tried not to reveal my shock or disappointment and nodded my approval. It was at this moment that the truth finally dawned on me.

Words like democracy, independence and capitalism are most often misunderstood or meaningless to people that have never experienced them firsthand. What I had not realized until now was that "skiing" was

another concept whose Albanian definition bore little resemblance to the 21st-century version of the word.

We knew there were no lifts, but our local friends had obviously not really understood our explanation of "ski touring". They did not know that we expected a particular grade for the skiing to be interesting. They were equally ignorant of the fact that we were accustomed to skiing at least 700 to 1000 vertical meters to make for a respectable ski tour.

I began to realize another thing. The problem was not only conceptual but logistical as well. The poor roads in Albania, which are barely passable in summer, make it extremely difficult in winter to get close enough to good touring terrain, despite the abundance of mountains that cover this country.

Early alpine skiing, before the age of lifts, was most often accessed by the brilliantly constructed railroads which brought people to the likes of Zermatt, Andermatt, St. Anton and other pioneer ski villages. Hoxha, however, had been equally negligent of railroad construction as he was of road building.

Upon my realization of the truth of the situation, I consulted with

Ronald, Helmut and Gina. They too had come to similar conclusions. We were, however, determined to do some skiing, whether it be by Albanian definition or our own. We had not come this far only to drink raki.

THE WEATHER WAS NOT being helpful to our mission. It was snowing hard, and the visibility was poor. We would use this day to reconnoiter. We skinned our way up a road toward one of the "ski slopes" which Mandi had pointed out. We did not hike very far before we came to a saddle.

The fog lifted briefly, and we saw that we had two choices for a semblance of "real" skiing. If the following day's weather was good, we could start very early and skin for 3–4 hours, which would bring us to the base of a mountain that would provide a proper ski tour. We could get high above the tree line and ski in open terrain. It would be a long, 10–12-hour day, but it was doable. If the weather was poor the following day, we could serpentine our way up a small mountain, where the trees were more widely spaced, and satisfy ourselves with a bit of tree-skiing.

Soon, the fog dropped its blanket back over us. Our activity for the day had included 45 minutes of skinning up a road, a long schuss in powder on one of Mandi's "ski slopes", which had too gentle a gradient to make a turn in deep snow, and a ski back down the road to the village. It had been a true Albanian ski day.

Our host for our first evening, Maqo, had to leave to bring his children to a ski race in Macedonia, so that evening we moved into the Hotel Turist Batelli, one of the local hotels. Our host, 68-year-old Pandi Batelli, proudly informed us through Mandi, our translator, that he had three times in his youth been the Albanian ski champion. Exactly what that amounted to was anybody's guess, but by now I had a rough idea, as I was getting more and more familiar with the Albanian definition of skiing.

During dinner, our host found out that I was American. Then, he left the room and returned with the biggest surprise of a trip full of the unexpected. He showed me his American passport. He had been an American citizen since birth! He could not speak a word of English, but he was a fellow American nevertheless. I almost fell off my chair. In this remote outpost deep in the back woods of Albania, this was not exactly what I had expected.

Pandi's father, who had been among the wave of immigrants to the U.S. in the 1920s, returned to Albania during the Depression. Pandi, being the son of a naturalized American citizen, had his own U.S. citizenship conferred upon him at birth.

By the time Pandi became a teenager, Hoxha already had a stranglehold on the country, and our host never had the chance to take advantage of his citizenship. Finally, in October 2000, at the age of 65, he made his first trip to America, and now he was hoping to immigrate there.

The following day brought a continuation of the unstable weather, so a very long ski tour was out of the question. Instead, we continued higher and further into the mountains than on our first day. The trees started thinning out, and the new powder gave us a reasonable cover for the many obstacles that dotted the wooded mountains. After a few hours of skinning, we were ready for a proper Albanian ski run, short though it might be. In any case, it was real powder, and the Lord knows that many a ski tour has been consummated in less favorable snow conditions.

THAT RUN WOULD BE THE CLIMAX of our Albanian ski holiday. It was time for our slow, step-by-step return to Tirana and beyond. What we had missed in physical activity, we had gained in new knowledge, and while the Dardha area did seem to pose obstacles to a successful future ski tour, we had learned a lot.

If we wished to return to Dardha, we should bring a tent and camping equipment. But what of the Dinaric Alps in the North or the Korabi range in the east? There was much left to discover among the snow-covered mountains of Albania. All endeavors begin with one small step, and we had taken it. With the publishing of this information, I am quite certain that some adventurous souls will be inspired to take the next step or steps, if Ronald and I do not take them first.

It is a rare opportunity to be involved in a small way with skiing in a country such as Albania, where the sport is still almost nonexistent. It is the possibility to be a pioneer—an experience that the 21st-century planet Earth does not dish out in great abundance as it once did. For all the would-be Daniel Boones of the ski world, Albania offers a unique chance for adventure.

The most revered pioneers in history, from Marco Polo to Lewis and Clark, came bearing gifts and not guns. Ronald and I traveled to Albania with some used ski jackets, ski caps and other equipment, which we left behind for the locals. It was a fitting return for the hospitality we received. Rarely have I seen gifts so appreciated by their recipients.

I am currently trying to organize shipments of old equipment from Austrian rental shops to be transferred to the Albanian Ski Federation. All contributions are very helpful. So, fellow pioneers, travel forth heavy and return home light.

Along with an essay like this, I often leave the name, address, telephone number and web site of a tourist office where interested parties can get further information on visiting the area described. In this case, that would serve no purpose. As a pioneer, although my experience is limited, I become a primary source of "further information". Therefore, for the first time in my many ski travels, I am obliged to say: For further information on ski touring in Albania, contact Jimmy Petterson at skibum@telia.com For information about donations to the Albanian Ski Federation, contact Shkëlqim Mema at sh_mema@yahoo.com.

LEFT PAGE
UPPER: Two fishermen on Lake Ohrid, with the snow-clad peaks of Macedonia in the background.
LOWER LEFT: Shepherd minds his flock in the meadows. All the while, nobody is taking advantage of the snow-drenched mountains behind him.
LOWER RIGHT: Hoxha's pride and joy—one of the two million bunkers that dot the Albanian landscape.

THIS PAGE
Daily life in the Albanian countryside is hard work for most of the inhabitants.

UPPER: The mountains of northern Albania as seen from the plane.
MIDDLE LEFT: Proud student shows off some of the skis available to their school class.
MIDDLE CENTER: With the temperature hovering around zero in our borrowed house in Dardha, you can be sure that I slept with my ski cap on.
MIDDLE RIGHT: Gina Schaar cooking some fish we bought from a young boy on the street.
LOWER LEFT: Most everything in Albania was old, but this snowplow was a true collector's item.
LOWER RIGHT: Fellow Americans, Pandi and I.

Eastern Europe in a Nutshell

LOCATION	NEAREST TOWN	NEAREST AIRPORT	SEASON	PEAK ELEVATION	VERTICAL DROP	SIZE	SNOW	BEAUTY	VILLAGE	NOVICE	INTERMEDIATE	ADVANCED	OFF-PISTE	NIGHTLIFE	RATING AVERAGE	WEB SITE
ALBANIA																
Dardha	Korca	Tirana	December–March	touring [1]	touring [1]	2	1	3	3	4	1	1	1	2	1.9	Are you kidding?
BOSNIA-HERZEGOVINA																
Bjelasnica and Igman	Sarajevo	Sarajevo	December–April	2067 m	803 m	3	1	4	3	4	3	2	3	4 [2]	2.9	www.skijanje.co.yu/Ski_Centri/BiH/bjelasnica.htm
Jahorina	Sarajevo	Sarajevo	December–April	1916 m	616 m	2	2	4	3	4	4	4	2	4 [2]	3.2	www.jahorina.co.yu
BULGARIA																
Bansko	Bansko	Sofia	December–late April	2560 m	1610 m	5	2	4	3	4	3	4	2	2	3.2	www.banskoski.com
Borovets	Samokov	Sofia	December–late April	2550 m	1233 m	4	2	3	2	3	3	2	1	5	2.8	www.borovets-bg.com
Vitosha	Simeonovo	Sofia	December–April	2115 m	1295 m	4 [3]	2	3	3 [4]	2	4	3	3	5 [4]	3.2	www.travel-bulgaria.com/content/vitosha_resort.shtml
CROATIA																
Bjelolasica	Ogulin	Zagreb	January–March	1392 m	773 m	2	1	2	2	1	2	2	1	1	1.5	www.bjelolasica.hr
CZECH REPUBLIC																
Pec Pod Snezkou	Pec Pod Snezkou	Prague	November–April	1215 m [5]	385 m	1	2	2	2	3	4	3	1	3	2.2	www.pecpodsnezkou.cz
Spindleruv Mlyn	Spindleruv Mlyn	Prague	December–April	1310 m	495 m	2	2	2	2	3	4	3	1	3	2.3	www.spindleruv.mlyn.cz
GEORGIA																
Gudauri	Gudauri	Tbilisi	December–April	3000 m	1000 m	3	1	4	3	1	3	3	3	2	2.5 [6]	www.gudauri.ge
HUNGARY																
Galyatetö	Gyöngyös	Budapest	November–March	950 m	150 m	1	1	2	1	2	1	1	1	1	1.3	www.sielok.hu/Galyateto.htm
Mt. Kékes	Gyöngyös	Budapest	January–March	1015 m	310 m	1	1	2	1	2	1	1	1	1	1.3	www.kekesteto.com
MACEDONIA																
Popova Sapka	Tetovo	Skopje	mid Dec.–mid March [7]	2400 m	700 m	2	1	3	3	1	3	2	4	2	2.4	www.popovashapka.com
Zare Lazarevski	Mavrova	Skopje	late Nov.–early April	1860 m	605 m	2	2	3	4	2	4	3	3	2	2.7	www.zarelaz.com
POLAND																
Zakopane	Zakopane	Krakow	December–March	1960 m	929 m	3	5	3	3	5	3	3	2	3	3.2	www.zakopane.pl
ROMANIA																
Poiana Brasov	Brasov	Bucharest	mid Dec.–March	1770 m	775 m	2	2	2	1 [8]	2	2	1	1	3	1.8	www.poiana-brasov.com
Sinaia	Sinaia	Bucharest	December–March	2030 m	1030 m	2	2	2	3	3	3	5	3	3	3.0	www.sinaia.8k.com
RUSSIA																
Mt. Elbrus	Terskol	Mineralnye Vody	early Nov.–mid May [9]	3800 m [10]	1600 m	5	1	4	4	1	2	3	5	1	3.0	www.go-elbrus.com
Mt. Tcheget	Terskol	Mineralnye Vody	December–late April	3040 m	1000 m	3	1	5	4	1	1	1	5	2	2.7	www.go-elbrus.com
SERBIA & MONTENEGRO																
Bjelasica	Kolasin	Belgrade	mid Nov.–early May	1970 m	500 m	2	1	4	3	3	4	4	1	3	2.8	www.bjelasica.com
Brezovica (Kosovo) [11]	Shtrpce	Skopje	Christmas–late April	2202 m	482 m	2	1	4	3	1	2	1	4	1	2.1	www.kosovayellowpages.com/html/sq_version/ski.htm
Durmitor	Zabljak	Belgrade	mid Dec.–late March	2200 m	800 m	3	1	3	4	3	4	2	4	3	3.1	www.durmitorcg.com
Kopaonik	Raska	Belgrade	mid Dec.–late March	2017 m	821 m	3	2	2	2	5	2	1	2	3	2.5	www.kopaonik.net
SLOVAKIA																
Jasná	Liptovsky Mikulas	Krakow, Poland	mid December–mid April	2000 m	809 m	3	2	3	1	3	3	3	4	2	2.7	www.jasna.sk
Strbské Pleso	Strbské Pleso	Krakow, Poland	December–April	1815 m	430 m	2	2	3	3	2	3	2	1	2	2.1	www.parksnow.sk/tatry/index.php
Tatranská Lomnica	Tatranská Lomnica	Krakow, Poland	late December–late April	2180 m	1284 m	4	2	3	2	1	1	2	2	2	2.2	www.tldtatry.sk
SLOVENIA																
Kanin	Bovec	Ljubljana/Klagenfurt	early Dec.–mid April	2289 m	700 m	2	1	3	3	4	3	2	3	1	2.4	www.bovec.net/kanin
Kobla	Bohinjska Bistrica	Ljubljana/Klagenfurt	mid Dec.–late March	1480 m	940 m	2	1	4	3	3	2	1	1	2	2.1	www.bohinj.si/kobla
Kranjska Gora	Jesenice	Ljubljana/Klagenfurt	mid Dec.–late March	1570 m	761 m	2	1	3	3	3	2	1	1	3	2.1	www.kranjska-gora.si
Krvavec	Kranj	Ljubljana	early Dec.–mid April	1971 m	521 m	2	2	3	4 [11]	5	4	2	1	4 [12]	3.0	www.rtc-krvavec.si
Vogel	Bohinjska Bistrica	Ljubljana/Klagenfurt	December–Easter	1800 m	1231 m	4	1	5	3	4	3	1	2	2	2.8	www.bohinj.si/vogel

(1) The maximum elevation depends on how far from the village one is willing to go. Good touring terrain is quite a distance away.

(2) This rating is for staying in the city of Sarajevo.

(3) This amount of vertical is only attainable when there is heavy snow cover. Much of the time, the maximum vertical drop is around 600 meters.

(4) This point total is a rating for Sofia. There is no separate ski village.

(5) Lifts go up to 1602 meters on Snezka, the Czech Republic's highest peak, but there are no pistes, and skiing is officially prohibited.

(6) This point total rates the actual lift system. As a heli-ski destination, Gudauri scores higher on vertical drop and off-piste skiing and lower as a resort for novices.

(7) This is the official season, but the true length of the season can be much longer, sometimes extending from late October to the end of April.

(8) This rating refers to the purpose-built resort at the base of the lifts. The atmosphere in the nearby village of Brasov rates 4 points.

(9) Skiing and boarding is possible on the upper lift all year round.

(10) There is also often a snow-cat service to bring skiers up to 4200 meters.

(11) The ratings for vertical drop, novice, intermediate and advanced would be higher if the entire lift system were operational. The scores above reflect the fact that only two lifts are currently operational.

(12) As there is no proper village for Krvavec, the village and nightlife rating is for Ljubljana, 32 kilometers away.

PREVIOUS PAGES: Antti-Pekka Auvinen glides down the Antuco volcano through perfect corn snow toward the Laguna del Laja.
THIS PAGE: Alpacas grazing on the Chilean *altiplano*.
RIGHT PAGE: Antti-Pekka starts down in the powder of Valle Nevado.

Chapter 32. CHILE

No country has been more meaningful to my many years as a ski journalist than Chile, for it was there that my career in ski writing and photography began back in 1985. I had planned an adventure trip to ski in Chile, and I came upon a ski-bum scheme to help me save money on lift tickets. A friend of a friend of mine, who happened to be the editor of the Finnish ski magazine, *Skimbaaja*, helped me realize my sneaky plan. Ari Heinilä wrote a to-whom-it-may-concern letter, introducing me as a ski journalist. I carried this document with me throughout my travels, hoping that it would be my passport to free skiing all around Chile.

In actual fact, I had never written an article about skiing or anything else, nor had I ever had any kind of photograph published, and I had no intention of doing any journalism. I was a poser—an impostor—an unscrupulous, conscienceless ski bum planning to scam the South Americans.

A funny thing happened. At a few of my stops, the local people were even more gullible or generous than I had ever expected. I not only scored free lift passes but the locals gave me complimentary hotel rooms and meals to boot. Confronted by this kindness, I found that I actually had a conscience after all, and I felt compelled to try to return the favor.

There was somewhat of a stumbling block to my new plan. I was traveling around with a hand-me-down, Russian-built Zorki 10 camera, not really the dream camera for a budding young photojournalist. It had a fixed 45-millimeter lens, I had never used it before, and I had also never used slide film in my life. Nevertheless, I decided that I did not want to be a cheat and a liar after all.

I loaded some slide film into my Zorki, shot some photos and wrote a few articles. When I returned to the Northern Hemisphere, I submitted my "work", and to my surprise, both articles and photographs were published—not only in Finland, but in Norway, Sweden and Denmark as well. I was a ski journalist!

Recently, nearly a generation later, I returned to where it had all started for me. I traveled around Chile with a fistful of bona fide credentials, a proper camera and a laptop, and the local people were still as generous and kind to me as they had been so many years ago, when my accreditation was one big bluff. In the years that have passed since my first trip, many parts of Chile's ski world have changed dramatically, while in other ski centers, time has virtually stood still.

Certain large ski areas like Portillo and other tiny locals' areas such as Cerro Mirador and Antillanca have not changed too much since my first visit. On the other hand, brand new ski resorts such as Valle Nevado have sprung up from nothing, and the ski center at Chillán has grown from a tiny, one-hotel locals' ski area to a destination resort with two large hotels, four condominium structures and a fistful of ski lifts.

Chile has more geological diversity than almost any country in the world, and her ski resorts reflect this variety. Chile extends 4329 kilometers from the Atacama Desert—the most arid spot on Earth—in the north to Tierra del Fuego in the south. En route, one finds one of the world's longest seacoasts; the *altiplano*, rich with llamas, alpacas and a myriad of other wild animals; rich vineyards and farmland; volcanoes towering over pristine lakes; and the wild glaciers, fjords and peaks of Patagonia. Chile has all of this, and then it also has the Andes, the second-highest mountain range on the planet.

For skiers, a smorgasbord of types and sizes of ski areas stretches from close to Santiago down to the Straits of Magellan. Northernmost on the Chilean ski map is Portillo, one of South America's oldest ski resorts and still one of its best. Slightly further south are Valle Nevado, La Parva and El Colorado, a cluster of loosely interconnected ski areas situated about an hour of hair-raising hairpin curves east of Santiago.

Continuing south, skiers arrive among some of the most spectacular volcanoes in the world, many of which have ski lifts. The volcanoes of Chillán, Villarica, Antillanca, Antuco, Lonquimay, Llaima and Osorno all offer skiing, some of them with a plume of smoke rising high above the powder. The little non-volcanic ski area of Los Arenales is also situated amidst this setting of the pyramid peaks and icy blue lakes of central Chile. Finally, at the southern tip of the country, near the city of Punta Arenas, is the little one-lift ski center, Cerro Mirador, which overlooks the Straits of Magellan.

While reading the descriptions of the skiing in Chile, keep an important fact in mind. Everything is upside-down in this part of the world. What I mean to say is that one of the basic principles applicable to skiers is topsy-turvy. Specifically, in the Southern Hemisphere, a south face is a shady, powdery slope, while the north-facing slopes are the sun-drenched sides of the mountain, optimal for corn-snow skiing when the conditions are right.

PORTILLO — AMBIANCE IN THE ANDES

The age when one luxurious, self-sufficient ski lodge could accommodate the entire skiing public of a particular resort is a page from a bygone era in most parts of the world. It is a concept born of the time when skiing was a small, elitist sport enjoyed by the upper class, who all stayed together in a large but cozy mountain hotel. They skied together, ate their meals together and played together after skiing, and if this small group did not already know each other before they arrived, they certainly had become friends by the time of their departure.

For a ski-lodge kind of resort to develop, it is necessary for the area to be relatively isolated, so that there is no convenient nearby local village for skiers to stay in. It is also imperative for the ski area to be small, for no large, modern-day ski resort can sustain itself financially on income from the guests of a single hotel.

This concept has never existed in the Alps. The development of skiing in Austria, Switzerland, Italy and Germany took place in existing villages as they gradually discovered "white gold", and traded in their rakes, hoes and tractors for skis, poles and a Mercedes. In France, some *stations de ski* have been developed in isolated mountain locations, but the local skiing market was already so large at the time of their conception, that entire villages were built at once.

In the 1940s, when American skiing was in its infancy, the lodge concept, with all its charm and intimacy, flourished for a while in resorts like Sun Valley and Alta. But as the skiing population grew, the ski areas naturally built more lifts, and more hotels were constructed hand-in-hand with the new lifts. In this age of a huge ski industry, nobody conceiving of a new ski resort thinks in terms of the ski-lodge system, because it is inadequate for the ever-growing snowsports public.

Nevertheless, a few of these friendly old dinosaurs still survive—gilt-edged museum pieces in today's modern ski world. In one of these lovely relics, you can transpose yourself back to a time when skiing was the exclusive pastime of a small clique of elitist mountaineers, and a ski lodge was a fraternity of friends, similar to the tennis or yacht club.

High in the Andes of Chile stands one of these stately edifices of that bygone, more personal era of skiing, the Hotel Portillo. This grand duchess, along with a couple of auxiliary buildings, houses 450 guests at a time, and is the only place to stay if you come to this Andean hideaway.

I DISCOVERED THE OLD-FASHIONED CHARM of Portillo in the 1980s, and a return visit with my friend, Antti-Pekka Auvinen, twenty years later proved that fortunately little had changed. The capacity of the lodge was the same, and the intimacy and laid-back atmosphere were both intact.

Completed in 1949, the Hotel Portillo rests on one of the most spectacular ski sites imaginable. Near a pass over the Andes once used by the Incas that links Santiago, Chile with Mendoza, Argentina, the hotel is situated on the shores of a lovely mountain lake called Laguna del Inca. It is surrounded by steep snowfields gradually giving way to rugged cliffs and glaciers, which continue to rise interminably into the deep-blue Andean sky. Less than 30 minutes' drive from the hotel, the road winds its way past Mt. Aconcagua, at 6956 meters the highest point in the Western Hemisphere.

Chile, like most South American countries, is divided into classes. It has a small minority of wealthy citizens, who all can afford to ski and prefer to do so in a luxurious manner; a large population too poor to even think about such pleasant diversions; and too small a middle class in between. With this kind of market, a small, luxurious ski resort that caters very meticulously to every need of its clientele is very much in keeping with

South American economic and social realities. Most ski resorts in Europe and North America, by comparison, are not so exclusive, as their clientele nowadays consists largely of middle-class patrons.

Portillo is destined to keep its special character long into the future, not merely because its market is limited, but also because its location confines expansion. Lifts have been well placed in this narrow valley to make good use of just about all the skiable terrain. So there will never be a need to increase the lodging capacity either.

Nor is there any desire to expand. American owner Henry Purcell does not wish to compete with other kinds of ski resorts. He recognizes his ski area as a small resort, with a special friendly and personal atmosphere that only such a small operation could offer, and he wishes to maintain that charm. In fact, Henry has consciously omitted putting televisions in the rooms in order to stimulate guests to get out into the communal areas and meet each other.

THE LAYOUT OF THE HOTEL PROBABLY HELPS the special ambiance develop as well. The outdoor spa and swimming pool, which overlook the lake, and the friendly bar and sitting room, often with fires glowing in the fireplaces, create an atmosphere where new acquaintances and friendships are readily cultivated. You also might make new friends in the sauna, card room, recreation room, discotheque or restaurant, or even on the outdoor ice skating rink and basketball court. But perhaps the greatest reason for the intimacy here is that whomever you meet on the ski slopes during the day is almost certainly staying in the same hotel as you.

The joint ownership of the hotel and ski lifts by the same company offers advantages to the hotel guests over and above the hotel's ambiance. A good example is provided during snow-poor winters. When there is a lack of snow all over the Andes, Portillo is known to take out ads in the Santiago newspapers announcing that lift tickets are temporarily not available to the general public. By this method, Portillo preserves the existing snow for the hotel guests.

Over the years, this combination of special personal attention, amiable atmosphere and diversity of ski terrain have helped build up a following of Portillo fans who come back year after year. Usually, the guests come here during the same period each season, so they can have an annual reunion with the ski friends they have cultivated over the years. Besides the Chileans, many guests come from Brazil, the United States and England, although you are likely to meet some of the high society from the other South American countries as well.

THE SKIING IN PORTILLO PROVIDES SOMETHING for everybody. For beginners, there are five small Poma lifts and a multi-lingual international ski school. Intermediates and advanced skiers will spend their time on two chair lifts and a couple of very odd *va et vient* (come and go) lifts to get to the highest reaches of the ski area at 3350 meters.

Antti and I arrived to a picture-per-

» **Whomever you meet on the ski slopes...is almost certainly staying in the same hotel as you.«**

fect day, and followed the pattern of the majority of the guests, who spend their mornings bathed in early morning sunshine on the east-facing slopes of the resort. This side of the ski area includes the famous Roca Jack *va et vient* lift, a bizarre French invention which has five Poma platters connected together. Five skiers, therefore, are pulled up 340 vertical meters side by side—if all goes well. The whole system functions without benefit of a lift tower, a design necessary because frequent avalanches on the steep slope would otherwise constantly destroy the towers.

The *va et vient* was conceivably originated during the French Inquisition as an instrument of torture to deal with religious heretics. Riding up the precarious Roca Jack, which is over 30 degrees steep, with your well-being dependent on the ability of yourself and four others to maintain balance on this contraption, is an experience every bit as exciting and adventurous as skiing the steep slope back down.

THIS PAGE
Antti-Pekka up to his chest in powder in Valle Nevado.

RIGHT PAGE
Okay, there is also a down side to powder—but it is definitely worth it.

For added thrills, the lift track rises over numerous moguls and inconsistencies in the terrain. During the ascent, a multi-lingual conversation is usually necessary to organize the order of disembarkation. The preferred method of releasing the platters on such a steep slope is to slide off backwards into a reverse snowplow, but if all five perform this maneuver simultaneously, the invariable result is a tangle of skis, poles and bodies gliding en masse back toward the original point of departure.

Once the disembarkation has been successfully negotiated, one can ski an 800-vertical-meter piste to the bottom of the Juncalillo Chair Lift or take a high traverse to reach a series of off-piste powder chutes. One of the chutes off the Roca Jack was used as the site of the Flying Kilometer speed-skiing championships back in the 1970s.

Antti and I hiked the 150-odd steps from the top of the Roca Jack to reach the rather treacherous high traverse. Despite the fact that it had not snowed for a few days, the slopes were rife with untracked powder. The traverse crosses over four major ridges, with steep lines inviting freeriders between the rocks. We traversed past the last ridge, where wide fields of white were still completely virgin.

Antti dove in and bounced merrily on his telemark skis until he was a mere speck in the distance, as I watched and shared his exhilaration.

When I finally caught up to him, he grinned and said, "It has been a long trip to get here, but it is already worth it!"

The weather was hot, and the high traverse usually closes at noon because of avalanche danger during warm weather. A morning on the Roca Jack side of the mountain is usually followed by a leisurely,

three-course lunch back at the hotel. Who were we to buck tradition?

After lunch, most skiers follow the afternoon sun over to the west-facing Plateau Chair Lift and Condor *va et vient*. These lifts provide suitable terrain for both intermediates and advanced skiers. Among the runs on the west faces is the notorious Garganta (the Throat) run, used for the giant slalom in the 1966 Skiing World Championships. Incredibly, the giant slalom course went right through a narrow passage between rock cliffs, from which the run gets its name—a route that challenges expert skiers even at low speeds.

Many of the descents on this side of the mountain offer beautiful views of the lake, which was not yet frozen. High above us, condors floated. Below, the Andes reflected in the lake's indigo waters, and in between heaven and earth, Antti and I glided downward, firm in the knowledge that we had definitely arrived in South America.

We whiled away the afternoon hours skiing the western slopes until the lifts closed. Now, as a few isolated cumulus clouds turned pink above us, we began to mingle with other Portillo visitors in the huge outdoor spa overlooking the lake.

If you are making a trip through this exotic and fascinating continent, Portillo is the perfect jumping-off point. For one thing, it is conveniently close to Santiago, which has regular flights from most parts of the world. Even more importantly, with its friendly lodge atmosphere, by the time you have completed a visit here, you are very likely to possess an address book full of new friends to visit on the rest of your journey through South America.

VALLE NEVADO, LA PARVA, EL COLORADO — THE STEPSISTERS

Portillo has the name and the history. There is no question about that. It is also unique with its bright-yellow hotel standing in solitary glory along the shores of Laguna del Inca. Just a short distance away, however, are three interlinked resorts which are higher, possess more than three times the number of lifts, and have 25 times as many hectares of terrain.

I don't want to take anything away from Portillo, an interesting and excellent ski resort in its own right, but certainly the poor stepsisters of Valle Nevado, La Parva and El Colorado are also worth a look if one happens to be in the vicinity.

Following a few spring-like days in Portillo, my friend Antti-Pekka and I woke to a bleak gray shrouding the nearby peaks, and snow drifting lightly downward. The road between Santiago and Portillo is extremely sensitive to snowy weather, and the police are given to closing it down at a moment's notice once the snow starts flying. While there are much worse places to be snowed-in than Portillo's cozy lodge, we had an imposing itinerary in front of us, and the local weather service had predicted a rather large storm. It was time to move.

I GUIDED OUR RENTAL CAR on the serpentine road back to Santiago, and Antti had the honor of driving up to South America's highest ski resort (3670 m) and one of the highest in the world, Valle Nevado. Antti got the short end of the stick. Storms move in fast in the Andes, and 10 centimeters of snow covered the last of the 60-odd hairpin curves when we finally pulled into the resort. The snowplow had been active in front of us, but some of the snow which it had pushed off the road started small sloughs onto the portion of road below, leaving Antti the task of trying to negotiate our car, in some places, through more than 30 centimeters of powder.

Sometimes, one has to be lucky. The snow gods had not been kind to the Andes up to that point of the winter, and our arrival at the beginning of August (the equivalent of February in the Northern Hemisphere) found a number of the Andean resorts with very little snow cover. By our first morning in Valle Nevado this was no longer true. Lifts that had so far been closed all season for lack of snow were now closed because of the heavy storm, and the terrain that was open offered 70 centimeters of light white and still counting.

Valle Nevado consists primarily of gentle terrain—mellow valleys with somewhat steeper sides. This is fine for the Brazilians who make up 40–45 percent of the visitors, but for a few of us, it was difficult to find steep enough slopes for the depth of snow we were now confronted with. The fog and dense snowfall made matters even more difficult, but

we managed adequately. All day long, we discovered short pitches of 15–20 turns of heaven. In between the powder pitches, we schussed long stretches to bring us to the next steep slope.

The snowfall continued all night, and in the morning the Andes Lift, closed the day before, opened, adding some more terrain to the resort's repertoire. In addition, it looked as if the sun was going to win the day. We could actually see where we were going—at least until a series of face shots once again obscured everything from view. *That*, however, is the sort of blindness that powder hounds long for.

The sun was short-lived, but we were already used to skiing by Braille from the day before, and after all, a meter of fresh powder covers a broad range of inconsistencies in the terrain.

Shortly after noon, another brief glimpse of sunlight allowed us to ski down into the La Parva ski area, a very different ski resort from Valle Nevado. While Valle Nevado lives off an international clientele of Brazilians, Americans and many other nationalities with the noticeable absence of Chileans, La Parva is so dominated by the local upper class that it does not even have a hotel! Tourists must stay in nearby Farellones, while the entire village of La Parva consists of private houses and apartments.

The Chilean upper class are apparently not heavily into skiing extremely deep snow in pea-soup fog, for there seemed to be well under 100 skiers on the entire mountain. Antti and I managed to find a couple of very friendly ski patrolmen, who, perhaps in consideration of the lack of visitors, deemed it appropriate to give us some one-to-one service and act as our Seeing Eye dogs for the rest of the day.

Similar to Valle Nevado, the upper mountain was closed due to the storm, but our newly found guides had no problem leading us to a long, steep pitch called Loma Vega where we did laps for the rest of the day. We soon understood that the village of La Parva might well be owned by the rich folks of Santiago, but the slopes were "owned" by the local ski patrol. Even in South America, there are a few realities that manage to level the playing field between the classes.

The ski patrol must do some real work sometimes. When our new friends departed for duty around four o'clock, we hitchhiked back to Valle Nevado, since the upper lifts of La Parva that ordinarily connect the resorts were closed.

AUGUST 5 WAS ONE OF THOSE magic days that skiers live for. Three days of heavy snowfall had covered the Andes in a meter-thick coat of white, and we awoke to a windless morning of crystalline blue. It was a little-boy-in-the-candy-store kind of day. We didn't know where to go first; deep powder called to us from all directions. We began by laying tracks in a large off-piste valley just west of the Andes Express Lift, known as Valle Olimpico. This took us to the Cono Este Lift, a T-bar that serves the steepest sector of the El Colorado ski area. Four virgin laps were all that time allowed before the entire face was decimated. The east-facing snow was getting heavy anyway.

The west-facing slopes out past the Avion piste toward the El Colorado area boundary were still untouched—three more laps. There was so much more around, but time was not on our side. No matter how hard we tried, we could not use up all the powder. Oh well, some people refer to the Spanish-speaking regions of the world as "*mañana* countries", and we could certainly wait until *mañana* to continue our "work".

Jimmy Ackerson, the general manager of Valle Nevado made an interesting point while describing Valle Nevado.

"This may be the highest resort in South America," he said, "but look at this map here. We are literally only in the foothills of the Andes."

Sure enough, El Plomo, the southernmost point of the old Inca Trail, situated just behind the highest lifts, stands proudly at 5430 meters. Not far behind stands Mt. Juncal (6110 m), Mt. Tupungato (6570 m) and a host of other monsters that line the border between Chile and Argentina.

If one wants to explore the territory that is beyond the limits of the conventional resort, one can do so—with the help of a helicopter. The following morning, Antti and I did just that. Our guide, Nelson, led us down steep pitches of powder into the Ballicas Canyon behind the base of the ski area. At the end of our run, I huddled close to the ground as the chopper approached, whipping snow around like an Arctic storm.

Antti left his face exposed to the snow-blasting blades, and as we boarded, he quipped, "Feels just like a typical spring day skiing in Finland."

When one begins the day heliskiing in 60 centimeters of powder, whatever one might try to do as a follow-up seems doomed to be an anticlimax. This was not the case. Powder still abounded all around the La Parva area. We skied fresh lines into La Parva from Valle Nevado. Then, staying as high as we could, we traversed out west of the Manatiales Norte run, beyond the area boundary. A couple hundred powder turns later, we traversed back to the lifts, having completed an afternoon of heliskiing without the chopper.

THE VOLCANO COUNTRY OF CHILE
DREAMERS, FOOLS OR VISIONARIES

Throughout the 19th century, droves of Americans and immigrants from around the world moved out into the American frontier. They pushed to the fringe of law and order in search of gold, land, furs, freedom, a new start and for a myriad of other reasons. They were probably all dreamers of a sort, many were fools and a few were visionaries. Some died as a result of Indian attacks, lawlessness and the harsh elements. Others eked out a bare existence, and a handful of the chosen became American success stories. Whatever their fate, there was no doubt that they were in the land of opportunity.

Today, in the early years of the 21st century, on the western fringe of a different continent, Chile has a flavor of those Wild West days of opportunity, and the volcanic ski centers of central Chile share in this entrepreneurial atmosphere. The Purcell family struck white gold in the internationally known resort of Portillo many years ago, a story that began when they purchased the hotel and lifts from the Chilean government back in 1962. But Portillo is only a 2-hour drive from the major population center and international airport in Santiago and has a long-standing track record of good weather during the ski season. Likewise,

LEFT PAGE
LEFT: Antti-Pekka enjoys the backcountry of El Colorado beyond the Avion piste.
RIGHT: Right behind the Hotel Tres Puntas is the steep Ballicas Canyon. We skied into the gorge and came back out with the helicopter.

THIS PAGE
UPPER: Bruno Visconti leaps off the ridge under the last rays of light in Los Arenales.
LOWER: Antti-Pekka was not the only telemark skier in El Colorado. This unidentified freerider flies down through the fresh snow near the Cono Este Lift.

Valle Nevado, El Colorado and La Parva, all 45–60 kilometers from the capital, also do a thriving business.

Further south, however, it is a very different proposition to make a go of it in the ski industry. "Industry" is perhaps the operative word here, because the little resorts that decorate many of the volcanoes of Chile can hardly be termed an "industry". Rather, they bring to mind a picture of the ski scene in the United States directly after World War II. Each little ski center is almost vacant on weekdays, attracts 100–200 locals on sunny weekends, and struggles to survive financially on a daily basis.

THEY DO NOT HAVE THE ADVANTAGE of a strong local population base, as most Chileans outside Santiago cannot afford to ski. In addition, they are too small and remote to attract an international clientele of destination guests. A third problem is Mother Nature. The warm El Puelche wind often sweeps off the pampas of Argentina into Chile's volcano country with gale force, closing lifts on a regular basis, and decimating good powder with a vengeance. Sometimes the ski centers have been completely destroyed by volcanic eruptions, only to reappear in one form or another after the dust has cleared.

What these little centers do have are some of the most spectacular panoramas on the planet. Several of these giant smokestacks belch out white puffs of smoke, and the volcanoes are surrounded by a prehistoric world of large, pristine lakes, ancient oak forests, monkey-puzzle-tree groves and tropical rain forest. Gazing out over the scenery, one seems more likely to see a herd of dinosaurs than a busload of Chilean skiers.

These ski areas also often have a dreamer/fool/visionary at the helm. The entrepreneurs who steer the small Chilean ski areas do have some justification for their hopes, plans and visions, for there is a model of success amidst them—Termas de Chillán.

TERMAS DE CHILLAN

When I first visited Chile in 1985, I found a handful of tiny family ski areas situated in this most majestic setting of volcanoes, stretching from Termas de Chillán in the north to Osorno in the south.

Chillán is the volcano resort closest to Santiago, about 480 kilometers south of the capital. On the occasion of my first visit, it was not much different from any of the other volcano resorts, other than that it had a swimming pool behind the base lodge that was filled with hot water from the nearby sulfur springs.

Since that time, however, a five-star hotel, a three-star hotel, two new swimming pools, a handful of condominium buildings and half a dozen new lifts have turned Chillán into a destination resort and another success story. It has risen from obscurity and matured into a world-class resort. When we arrived, members of the American and Canadian national teams were training on the upper slopes.

The Chillán volcano actually has two cones, and the mountain is a sprawling massif of lava ridges and gullies that fan out to the west and south. East of the ski lifts is a huge, out-of-bounds bowl that funnels into a narrow canyon. This area, known as Pirigallo, is an enter-at-your-own-risk proposition and rightfully so. A more dangerous terrain trap would be hard to find.

Naturally, the Pirigallo area was that which immediately piqued the interest of Antti and me. We were blessed with corn snow conditions, so the potential avalanche danger did not apply on that day. Between the rocks and cliffs, we discovered various east faces into the canyon, all of which were steep, steeper or steepest. We did see a track or two, but did not see another soul skiing in this area during our stay. Each run ended with a 5-minute walk from the base of the canyon past *fumaroles* (small volcanic holes puffing out smoke) back to the lifts.

The corn conditions did not hold for long. By the end of the ski day, a storm had blown in and we soothed our bodies in the thermal springs while snowflakes drifted gently from the sky. Thirty centimeters of powder covered the mountain the next morning. The low clouds made the skiing difficult, but we set fresh lines into various bowls on either side of the old Don Otto Lift during the morning.

By afternoon, the clouds had lifted, and a few patches of blue were evident, allowing for a bit more experimentation. We found numerous variations on either side of the long Tres Maria run. These routes provid-

ed a few steep pitches, but were generally mellow skiing. There are other hazards of volcanic terrain, however, and we learned a few lessons from our afternoon of putting first tracks in some uncharted valleys.

One lesson was that the valleys usually narrowed into gullies, with steep walls making it difficult to exit. In addition, certain ravines had creeks running under the snow, and the lower terrain necessitated numerous crossings over snow bridges of dubious strength.

Our second lesson was geometric and geological in nature. It had two corollaries. First of all, on a volcano, a traverse near the peak translates into a mu-u-u-ch longer traverse back near the base. Second, traversing on a lava volcano, laden with lava ridges divided by deep gullies and canyons, is no easy proposition!

We traversed a few hundred meters west after exiting the El Condor Lift and found lots of virgin faces and gullies. We were heading down the huge massif, however, at approximately a two-o'clock angle, and the base of the lifts was at twelve-o'clock. When the conventional run is a full 14 kilometers long, even a rider who flunked math could probably tell you that the further you euphorically pump powder willy-nilly, the more energy you had better save for the way back. Needless to say, we spent an extra hour in the sulfur baths that evening.

LOS ARENALES

The volcano ski centers south of Chillán offer a potpourri of dreams and nightmares, plans and projects, successes, failures and question marks. For the entrepreneur involved, each ski center amounts to a major investment of hard work and cash, but for a skier and traveler, the small ski areas comprise a real-life amusement park of adventure.

Los Arenales, for example, is one of the smallest ski centers in South America, consisting of no more than a beginners tow, a platter-pull lift, and a short T-bar. Even the tiniest ski areas, however, have a story, and a short one-day visit here offers a tale as well.

Los Arenales is situated about a half-hour drive from Lonquimay, amidst a beautiful forest of monkey-puzzle trees, an unusual looking plant that is, in and of itself, worth the trip up to the mountain. The monkey-puzzle tree, known in Spanish as the *araucaria*, is an unusual species of evergreen tree indigenous to only a few countries. Instead of pine needles, the branches are laden with cactus-like foliage.

Barnabas Kovacs is a Hungarian entrepreneur who came to Chile in the late '90s to train racers. He somehow stumbled upon and became enchanted with this little corner of the Earth, and in 1999, he inaugurated

a new ski area. A few years into the project now, Barnabas admits that he has a few infrastructure problems. For example, the *refugio* at the base of the lifts has twenty beds. After housing himself, a few of his children and a staff of eight people, the eight remaining beds are hardly enough to support a ski area!

This is apparently not the only long-shot investment that Mr. Kovacs is involved with. His ski rental shop is equipped with Explosiv skis, a brand produced by his own ski company. He and his partners sell these skis primarily in Russia, Eastern Europe and Italy, but of course, it can't hurt to have introduced them to the South American market as well.

On a Monday in August, we shared the slopes of Los Arenales with about twenty Chilean soldiers (who primarily floundered on the rope tow), Barnabas and his son, two Dutch tourists, and about eight loco French freeriders. It perhaps comes as no surprise that Los Arenales does not turn a profit, but that is not necessarily due to any lack of quality.

The south-facing slopes had plenty of untouched powder adjacent to the piste, and a 10-minute walk to the east accessed some lovely descents

down to the road. The open upper slopes began with a short, steep pitch that mellowed as the rider entered the forest. The Frenchmen left a pick-up truck on the road to taxi us back to the lifts, and we did powder laps for much of the day.

In the late afternoon, one of the hospitable employees offered the whole group a ride on the company's snow cat to a slightly higher mountain behind the lifts, free of charge. A classic pink and orange sunset lit up the Chilean sky at around 5:30, and we had to avoid the day's last few monkey-puzzle trees in the dark. It was a truly unforgettable experience and yet a mere typical day of Chilean skiing. A return visit might be in order in a decade or two to discover what has evolved out of Mr. Kovacs' dream.

CORRALCO

In the meantime, Antti and I traveled to Corralco. Ski lifts have existed here on the Lonquimay volcano since the mid-1980s, when the Chilean government built a couple of beginners rope tows and one drag lift as part of a development project for various volcanoes in Southern Chile.

The ski area was known as Nevados de Curacautin until 2003, when private investors built a 300-vertical-meter double chair lift and changed the name of the resort to Corralco. In addition, the old refugio at the base of the lifts has already been converted into a small, cozy hotel with gourmet food. This is only the beginning, as many additional beds are planned at the base of the volcano.

As in Los Arenales, the road to Corralco winds through an amazing grove of *araucaria* trees, many of which are over 1000 years old. There is much more. Just as the grove ends, a moonscape of smooth, barren, rounded hills appears, lorded over by Lonquimay. Lonquimay is an ash volcano, making for a surface that is almost devoid of rocks and inconsistencies.

ANTTI AND I DISCOVERED IMMEDIATELY that the lift here is situated perfectly to give the possibility of both corn- and powder-snow skiing, as it accesses east- and south-facing slopes. We warmed up for a few runs on the well prepared pistes, but soon we ventured further afield.

We traversed a few minutes to the west, reaching a very steep pitch that emptied into a large canyon. Firm, wind-packed powder on the south face turned into soft spring snow as the sun exposure shifted. We spent our day alternating between the two types of snow.

A bit of hiking accesses an ever-increasing amount of terrain. In fact, Lonquimay is one of the easiest and most popular ascents among Chile's volcanoes, and we spent part of the afternoon hiking for a longer and steeper descent. The solitude we enjoyed may not be around for too long. The double-edged sword of progress is forever moving, and additional lifts extending higher are currently envisioned by the new ownership.

We finished the day in the hot tub on the hotel deck looking directly out over the volcano. Could there be a better way to end a ski day than soaking in a soothing Jacuzzi as moonlight glows on the mountain?

LAS ARAUCARIAS

Into every life a little rain must fall. The wet stuff hit us on the Llaima volcano at the little Las Araucarias Ski Center. As its name suggests, this is another ski area that features the beauty of these unusual trees. Before the rain and fog beat us into submission, we did manage to discern a few basic facts about the ski area. The volcano is a broad, smooth ash volcano with a lot of open terrain fanning out on either side of the main T-bar. There are also wide natural halfpipes beyond the pistes on each side and a short, steep pitch down the back, from where one can swing back around the mountain to return to the lifts.

VILLARICA

Next on the agenda was the Villarica volcano just outside the town of Pucón, one of Chile's top summer resorts. Villarica is rather active and a 1984 eruption destroyed the entire ski area. Once the smoke had cleared, it was all built up from scratch once again, and today it is one of the most popular ski areas in the country.

Villarica's peak can be reached with about a 4-hour hike from the top lift, and skiers can get the added thrill of looking down into the bubbling cauldron in the crater. Any ambitions we might have had to make such a tour were thwarted by wind and fog, two conditions that are more prevalent here than at most of the Chilean resorts. The limited visibility kept the upper lifts closed during the entire three days of our visit.

The bad weather, however, did not prevent us from meeting a different kind of entrepreneur. While inquiring in a local bar about a room for the night, we were introduced to Brad Newton, a recent immigrant from Zimbabwe. Not so long ago, Brad had met and fallen in love with Vivi Delgadillo, a local girl. The two of them had recently finished building a home on her parents' land, a job that they did almost entirely themselves. They built a number of extra bedrooms for backpackers and call it Hostel Monkey Puzzle. For about $5 a night, we slept comfortably and enjoyed the company of the young couple. Always happy to do my small part for dreamers and young lovers, I might add that travelers can contact Brad at bradbehavior@yahoo.co.uk.

ANTILLANCA

Antillanca differs from most of the other volcanoes in this region in that it is extinct. Otherwise, it bears many similarities to its neighbors. The 40-minute drive from Lake Puyehue up the mountain to the base of the lifts winds through thickly-vegetated rain forest, and the peak affords lovely views of three lakes and various nearby volcanoes. Like Corralco, it is an ash volcano, so that the snow covers a surface of volcanic sand.

If the skier who first said, "If God had wanted man to ski moguls, he would have made snow fall in piles," ever discovers Antillanca, he will probably think he has died and gone to heaven. Here, he can easily ski into the years of his old-age pension without worry of moguls doing premature damage to his aging knees. With no rocks or vegetation, this mountain has absolutely no natural bumps. The few skiers who populate the slopes also pose no major threat of creating many moguls.

THIS PAGE
UPPER: Deep in the Andes of Chile, one still comes across an oxcart now and then.
LOWER: A thin layer of morning fog adds to the majesty of Osorno.

RIGHT PAGE
With its panorama of Laguna del Laja, Antuco is one of the most beautiful ski centers in the world.

During our visit to Antillanca, we enjoyed one of the greatest days of corn-snow skiing I have ever experienced. The relatively low elevation of just over 1000 meters makes the area quite susceptible to rain. This is not necessarily a bad thing. Although one is not likely to find light powder here very often, a small dose of rain can hasten the development of corn snow. After the clouds have passed, a cold night turns the mountain into an icy crust, and the next morning, as the sun starts to caress the slopes with her gentle rays, lo and behold—perfect, untouched corn.

An additional delight in Antillanca is that this rounded dome of a mountain offers descents to the north, west and south, so that one can follow the clock and ski on the perfect consistency of spring snow all day long. We were still leaving shiny snail tracks on the mountain at 5:30, when a stunning sunset turned the sky and lakes below to gold, providing a suitable climax to a perfect day.

OSORNO

Everything is not always what it appears to be. Upon our arrival in Chile, Antti and I purchased a road map from a gas station. Quite conveniently, this map indicated all the ski centers of the country with a small icon of a skier. When we reached Osorno, as at our previous destinations, we followed the road toward where the icon was marked on the map. Only this time, we did not fare so well.

After quite a few kilometers of dirt road headed toward the north side of the volcano, our path met a boulder-strewn riverbed that hardly seemed negotiable. It would have been very risky at best, and since we had already experienced a flat tire earlier that morning, our margin for error was limited. We turned back defeated, but perplexed as to how a ski center could survive with such an obstacle to travelers.

Through a lucky fluke, we passed a mountain biker, the only other person using this road, and I decided to ask him about the ski area. He looked at our map and laughed.

"That ski center marked on your map was destroyed in an earthquake in the 1960s," he informed us. "The new Osorno ski area is on the south side of the mountain!"

With renewed hope, we redirected ourselves, but this endeavor did not go that much better. As we emerged from yet another rain forest onto the exposed part of road that approached the lifts, El Puelche, the dreaded prairie wind, was howling. We had already mounted chains, but they were not sufficient to get us to our destination. The wind had created large snowdrifts that were impassable without a four-wheel-drive vehicle. Before we could even plot a strategy, however, a pickup truck from the resort arrived to give us a lift the rest of the way.

They certainly aimed to please at the new Osorno ski resort. In fact, the owner and primary investor, who also happened to own Chilean Travel Services, one of the largest travel agencies in the country, was personally on hand to work on the mountain.

The ski area was no less than spectacular. Looking up, we gazed across the glacier-filled south face of the volcano, while below us, it seemed as if one could ski right into the deep, blue waters of Lago Llanquihue. There were good pistes and miles of open spaces for freeriders.

The wind prevented the upper lift from operating, but it didn't matter. Floran Schaack, a vagabond French mountain man, was grooming the upper mountain for the following day, and he was more than happy

to give us a ride. Over the din of the diesel motor, the obligatory discussion ensued.

"How the heck did you end up in this obscure corner of the Earth?" I asked.

Frenchmen are lovers by nature, so Floran's answer was only partially a surprise.

I had half expected that he had fallen for some lovely Chilean *señorita*, but instead, he explained, "I fell in love with the mountain. I also love to create, and I have been here for three years helping to build this ski center."

During that time, Floran had spent many hours exploring Osorno on his randonnée skis, but now that the ski center had opened and the work was almost done, he felt that he would soon move on.

Floran was a dreamer of a different sort. He did not come to Chile with dollar signs in his eyes, hoping to make his fortune or to start a new life. He was the skiing equivalent of a Wild West fur trapper—an adventurer and a drifter, seeking to stay on the perimeter of civilization where he could maintain a sense of freedom.

I couldn't help but think of the old movie, *Paint your Wagon*, that depicted the wild days of the California Gold Rush. On a gray, snowy morning, Ben Rumson (played by actor Lee Marvin) was riding out of town when he met another old-timer.

The other man said something to the effect of, "Well, Ben, the way I figures it, some people's a goin' places and some's a stayin' places, and I'm a stayin'."

Ben replies, "There's two kinds of people, them goin' somewhere and them goin' nowhere…"

At this point in the musical, Marvin breaks into his classic, gruff, bass ode to man's restless nature, "Wanderin' Star". I supposed that Floran Schaak and I could well have joined Mr. Marvin and sung the song as a trio.

Now that the Osorno resort was up and running, an ever-increasing number of skiers would certainly arrive, and Floran would drift even further to the edge of ski civilization. Maybe he would end up in Antuco.

ANTUCO

The north-facing ski center of Antuco had an entirely different flavor than Osorno and many of the other volcano areas we visited. To begin with, the dirt and gravel path from "civilization" to the ski center was quite a bit longer than most of the other access roads that we experienced. It was no less beautiful, as the perfect cone-shaped mountain loomed nearer with each bend in the road.

In addition, here were no entrepreneurs and investors. So many of the resorts we had visited gave us trail maps with projected lifts indicated by dotted lines. There were no dotted lines on the Antuco map—in fact, they had no map. Antuco is a tiny locals' area—two lifts, a handful of primitive buildings with corrugated steel roofs, families learning to ski or playing in the snow, and kids practicing racing technique. A healthy 490-vertical-meter drop, however, makes Antuco very attractive to advanced skiers.

The grooming was poor or nonexistent, but left and right of the piste were fields of perfect corn snow. To the west, the slopes were gentle cruising terrain, with lots of rises, gullies and ridges to keep things interesting. East of the lift, the slopes were steeper, with ridges, ravines and natural halfpipes, all typical of a lava volcano. We sprayed spring kernels off our edges in all directions and enjoyed the views of the lapping waters of Laguna del Laja below, all the while we skied. The higher one got on the mountain, the better the view. Had we been blessed with more time, a ski tour from the top of Antuco would have been a must.

Sometimes it is interesting and exciting to revisit a place many years later and observe all the changes, as I did in Chillán. On the other hand, it can be wonderful and reassuring to return to a location after many years and find that time has stood still. I hope that I can return to Antuco some day to experience the latter.

Chapter 33. ARGENTINA
THE LORD GIVETH AND THE LORD TAKETH AWAY

I first discovered the joys and trials of Argentine skiing on an extended visit in 1985. An experience in the village of Rio Turbio characterized skiing on this continent at that time. Today, the ski area, situated a few kilometers from Rio Turbio, is called Valdelén, and it is still relatively obscure, even by South American standards. My short visit at this tiny ski area so long ago taught me that one does not need a lot of lifts or record-breaking vertical to enjoy a good day of skiing. In a way, that day was a kind of inspiration for this book, for it began a long sojourn in search of remote and little-known ski centers.

To begin with, making my way to Rio Turbio was not the easiest task I have ever undertaken. I had heard from vaguely reliable sources that there did exist a ski center in Rio Turbio, and I located the village on the map. It lies far into the southernmost regions of Patagonia, not far from the Straits of Magellan. This is about as remote as one can get in the ski world, short of a visit to Antarctica.

I flew to Punta Arenas, Chile, a somewhat redundant flight, since it took me 250 kilometers further south than my destination, but it was an easier connection than any that went through Argentina. From there, I backtracked 4 hours north by bus to Puerto Natales, a beautiful Chilean village of 18,000 inhabitants situated in the midst of the Patagonian fjord country.

The ski center is located exactly on the border between Chile and Argentina, officially in Argentina, 20 kilometers from Puerto Natales. Being so close to my destination, I decided to get a little information before embarking on the last leg of my journey. That was the South American version of *Mission Impossible*.

I asked many people from the village, and they had not heard of Rio Turbio. Local mountain guides did not know that a ski area even existed. Eventually, I found a travel agent who assured me that the ski area did exist, but she had no idea of the number of lifts, the altitude, the vertical drop or most important, whether or not the ski area was open! I suggested that a phone call might help, but that proved to be impossible as well.

The only solution was the usual third-world remedy—go to the source. The bus traveled over dirt roads covered with 30 centimeters of snow, and the trip went about as well as could be expected. That is to say that approximately halfway between the two towns, our bus skidded off the road. Numerous efforts using "passenger power" finally put us back on track. At the tiny border station, officials from both countries inspected and stamped my passport, and I walked the hundred meters to the lifts.

I WAS EXTREMELY LATE. THE BUS RIDE had taken an hour longer than expected, and there was also an hour's time difference between the two countries, of which the travel agent had neglected to inform me. The ski area had opened at ten o'clock and I did not arrive before three o'clock.

In a small shack with a wood-burning stove, I found a lone man huddled over the fire. I inquired about skiing, and he slowly walked me over to a small booth and sold me a ticket. I then followed him 50 meters further to a small rope tow. He pressed the starter button, and the apparatus ground into motion. It was 5 hours into the ski day, 30 centimeters of fresh powder covered the hill, and I was the first customer.

The lift pulled me up a slope that had a vertical rise of about 150 meters. Translated into powder turns, that is about 60 tight turns—not

exactly Mt. Blanc, but on the other hand, here I was pumping powder all by myself.

After half an hour, I was joined by another ambitious soul. He introduced himself as Horacio, the proprietor of the bar and restaurant. He explained that as there was not an overabundance of business, he thought he would ski a while. He went on to say that if I wanted a coffee or a bite to eat, I should just let him know and we would go in together.

Horacio was also a wealth of local information, explaining to me that the base of the ski area was about 600 meters high, and that there was in fact an upper rope tow as well. It was currently in disrepair, but when in operation, it would almost double the vertical rise of the ski area. He also pointed out the coal mine across the valley, which provided the livelihood for the entire village of Rio Turbio.

Within an hour or so, three more enthusiasts arrived. Irritated by this onslaught of mass tourism, Horacio and I departed for his warming hut. Once inside, my host apologized that due to the irregularity of guests, all items on the menu except the ham-and-cheese toast were unavailable. I did have a toast as well as a hot chocolate with rum, a Grand Marnier, and an Irish coffee at various intervals in my skiing. My gracious host insisted on inviting me for all of my consumption.

About the time of my second stop for refreshments, I noticed that the ski center actually had lights and offered night skiing. It was in fact the first ski lift in South America to have night skiing. The lift usually closed at 10 p.m., but since the skies had cleared, Horacio kept it open half an hour longer for his solitary guest. The other three patrons had long since departed. I finished the day under starry skies, still making tracks in virgin powder—all alone. Then I boarded a minibus filled with miners, and headed back across the border.

The information available on the area had been nonexistent, the infrastructure had been equally lacking, and the ski center itself was tiny with not much more vertical than a high diving board. But my reception had been friendly and personal, and the experience had been unique. It had been a typical day skiing in the Third World, and one I would recall long after many of my ordinary ski days in the Alps had faded from my memory.

During that same first visit, an Argentine man good-naturedly told me a joke poking fun at himself and his countrymen.

"When God was creating the Earth," he related, "he was discussing with St. Peter all the while. When it came time to create Argentina, God built a beautiful country that had everything. He made a long, lovely seacoast rich with fish and the beautiful Andes Mountains. He created the pampas and the cattle that graze there—considered by many to give the best quality beef in the world. He threw in pristine lakes, rich farmland and all kinds of mineral wealth.

"At the same time, God created some countries like Bolivia that, by comparison, had few of the same advantages. Bolivia is landlocked and covered with austere terrain, making it difficult for the poor Indians to eke out an existence. Upon observing the gross inequality, St. Peter remarked to God about it. 'Oh, don't worry,' replied God to St. Peter, 'I'll even things out—I will also create the Argentine people!'"

This self-mocking story points out the trouble that Argentina has had with turning its God-given resources into a successful country. A large

LEFT PAGE
The Argentine flag wafts in the breeze in front of the peak named Las Leñas.

THIS PAGE
Cerro Bayo, on the shores of Lake Nahuel Huapi, offers some of the finest panoramas anywhere in the ski world. The skier is Antti-Pekka Auvinen.

THIS PAGE: The lights of Bariloche on the shores of Lake Nahuel Huapi.

RIGHT PAGE
UPPER: Antti-Pekka cruises down in the off-piste Laguna section of the Cerro Catedral ski area.
LOWER: The La Hoya ski center is the proud owner of this bizarre lift which has both T-bars and single chairs on the same cable.

part of the problem has been an iniquitous class system that has seen a high percentage of the land consolidated in the hands of very few people, while the middle class has been too small and weak to support healthy economic growth. Throw in a bit of old-fashioned government corruption, and one can well understand why modern Argentine history has been fraught with political and economic instability.

With predictable regularity, the economy falters, often resulting in major inflation and a devaluation of the peso. This can, however, work to the advantage of skiers and other tourists. During a recent road-trip through the top Argentine resorts, my friend Antti-Pekka Auvinen and I enjoyed prices that were about 70 percent lower than what they are in many other ski resorts in the world.

Numerous times during our visit, however, I couldn't help but think back to this joke as we experienced the Argentine ski scene firsthand. The people were extremely helpful, kind and friendly wherever we went, but the planning and organization were not always stellar.

THE JOKE CERTAINLY SEEMED RELEVANT during our visit to the ski center of Cerro Catedral, Argentina's oldest and largest ski area. Similar to the joke, nature and geography seem to have given Cerro Catedral every advantage. It is situated about 15 kilometers from the lakeside summer resort of San Carlos de Bariloche, giving it a strong population base, a nearby airport and a ready-made infrastructure of hotels, restaurants and nightlife. In addition, the pistes offer spectacular vistas of Lake Nahuel Huapi.

The rest of the story of Cerro Catedral, however, does not flow as smoothly. It could have been bad luck or bad timing, but the resort's early beginnings saw the owners order a cable car from Italy in 1939, which didn't arrive until ten years later, as Italy's involvement in World War II prevented the timely delivery of the merchandise.

To follow this ignominious start, two separate companies built lifts on the mountain and feuded with each other for half a century. The result has been that, with the exception of a short period of conciliation, Cerro Catedral's patrons could only use one half or the other half of the ski lifts during their winter holiday here. This situation was not ultimately resolved until 2004!

To add to all this, the large, lovely lake, while providing such a great background to the skiing, also has a negative effect, creating much humidity which, in turn, affects snow quality. Because of this and other factors, even in a good season, Cerro Catedral is usually only skiable to the bottom for about four to five weeks each winter.

ANTTI AND I DID NOT VISIT during the short period in which Mother Nature provides snow to the base. There was, however, ample snow on the upper slopes, and even some good powder in the off-piste Laguna section of the mountain.

We began our day riding halfway up on the Sextuple Express Lift. Mysteriously, the connecting lift, the Punta Nevada Chair, was closed, so we had to ski down over rocks and stones and wait in a rather long queue to reach the top. I inquired why this important lift was out of service. A snowboard instructor informed me that a chair had broken loose from the cable and slid backwards into the next chair two weeks earlier. All in all, three chairs in succession detached and glided down the cable. Miraculously, the accident resulted in no more than a few broken legs.

Maintenance does not seem to hold a high priority in Argentina. Meanwhile, I checked my area map and tried to plan as much of our ski day as possible on T-bars and drag lifts.

We rode up the Princesa III Lift and began a 20-minute hike to access the Laguna area. It was a lovely mix of bowls, steep faces and gullies with spectacular views of yet one more body of water, Lago Gutiérrez. Fresh lines abounded.

Argentine organization came back into view, however, once we traversed back to the piste. Lo and behold, the lift that should have brought us back up the mountain had been disassembled prior to the start of the season in anticipation of a new and more modern lift that should have replaced it. The only problem was that the new lift's construction had been delayed for one season. The lack of snow on the lower slopes did not allow us to ski down, and the result was an hour-long walk to the nearest functioning lift.

Cerro Catedral is not alone among Argentine ski areas with stunning scenery. The so-called Lake District is also the home to Cerro Chapulco

and Cerro Bayo near the villages of San Martin de Los Andes and Angostura, respectively. Skiers in Chapulco can view Lago Lacar from the mountain, while Cerro Bayo skiers almost seem as if they will ski into the waters of Nahuel Huapi as they cruise around the upper mountain.

Each of these resorts also has some interesting sections for freeriders. In Cerro Bayo, Antti and I hiked 15 minutes above the Lenga Lift to reach some virgin terrain on the back of the mountain. In Chapulco, the local freeriders dive into the steep, south-facing bowl behind the ski area for an adrenaline rush, but it requires a rather long hike back out. Alternatively, the steep La Pala region can satiate top skiers' lust for challenging terrain without the accompanying hike.

Some of the best and most easily accessed off-piste terrain in Argentina can be found in the little-known ski center of La Hoya, just outside the town of Esquel. Whereas San Carlos de Bariloche, San Martin de Los Andes, and Angostura are all summer and winter resort towns, Esquel is an ordinary village.

La Hoya, on the other hand, is no ordinary locals' ski resort. The 850 vertical meters of skiing is quite substantial for a small ski center, and the primarily south-facing slopes preserve the dry snow that generally falls in this region. High above the base are a handful of steep couloirs and faces that not only keep the powder but also do not get skied out so quickly by the local riders.

THE ELDORADO OF ARGENTINE SKIING is one of the country's northernmost resorts, Las Leñas. To drive from the ski centers of the Lake District to Las Leñas is a true study in contrasts. One is transported from a landscape of lush, green pine forests and crystalline-blue waters through 1000 kilometers of austere prairie, where nary a tree is to be seen and the desert

wind blows the tumbleweed hither and yon at will. All the while, the eastern slope of the Andes looms alluringly on the driver's side of the car.

The highway often withers like the desert vegetation. First the dividing line disappears, and soon thereafter, potholes appear ever more frequently in the asphalt, until it too vanishes entirely, and the road degenerates into a primitive path of dirt and rocks. Make sure your spare tire is in good order.

The road is punctuated by small, grim enclaves of houses, which appear to be large towns on the map but prove to be hardly more than pony-express outposts when one drives through. Even these meager villages are few and far between and so are the gas stations. Bring an extra canister of gasoline with your spare tire. One day we were relegated to coasting downhill for many kilometers to avoid running out of gas, and on another occasion, we were lucky to be able to buy 5 liters of petrol from the general store, as the village had no gas station.

There is one skiers' oasis between San Martin de Los Andes and Las Leñas—the Volcano Copahue. The existing lifts are primarily suited for beginners and intermediates, with a few good powder turns to be made by off-piste skiers on either side of the uppermost pistes. Here too, however, there is more of interest than the intermediate slopes.

The village of Caviahue lies along the shores of a horseshoe-shaped lake bearing the same name. On the other side of town is a beautiful grove of monkey-puzzle trees that work their way right up the slopes, and behind the pistes towers Mt. Copahue (2900 m). A snow cat provides the service of taking freeriders and sightseers up to within a couple of hundred vertical meters of the summit. The scenery is magical, and it gets better the closer one comes to the top.

The ride down was also memorable. The wind was howling, but at least it was a tail wind, and Antti and I found long pockets full of blown-in powder.

The map of slopes depicted five planned lifts—part of a development project that should greatly increase the skiable terrain over the next five years—if it comes to fruition. The projected lifts would ultimately bring skiers almost to the top of the volcano.

There is a catch. The wind we experienced is apparently a fairly regular part of the local scene, which would seem to put the viability of that plan in question. Then again, this *is* Argentina. Good sense and planning do not always play a very important role here.

THE GRANDIOSE PLANS REMINDED ME of my first visit to Argentina's best ski resort, Las Leñas. The area was only a couple of years old when I interviewed Ernesto "Tito" Lowenstein, the Argentine entrepreneur who envisioned and created his dream resort in the early 1980s.

Lowenstein explained that careful meteorological studies of snow, sun, temperature and wind had been made of the area to find the best location for a ski resort. This particular valley was chosen because it was blessed with 80 percent clear and sunny days, and yet it still averaged over 6 meters of snowfall at the base of the mountain each year. He also explained that the entire project had been put together without having to resort to borrowing money from a bank.

"If you have to work for the bank," explained Lowenstein, "I prefer to own the bank."

Unfortunately, the fable did not have a happy ending. The true number of sunny days in the early years was closer to 65 percent, and while 6 meters of snow is a nice average, it is exactly that—an average. Some years had appreciably more snow, while certain seasons were almost bare. In addition, further development of Las Leñas required more money than Lowenstein could bankroll by himself and he did have to borrow money. Eventually, as so often is the case in Argentina, Tito's dreams were derailed by the instability of the Argentine economy and various other factors, and the banks assumed ownership of the resort.

Only recently has a large investment group taken over Las Leñas with the promise of a long-range plan to improve and expand the ski area. Today, the ski center has thirteen lifts and 3400 beds, with a plan to renovate some old lifts, build three new ones, and add about 400 new beds per year over the next three or four years.

Despite the unraveling of Lowenstein's grand scheme, he is still a sort of hero for local skiers, for he did succeed in creating the best skiers' mountain in the Southern Hemisphere. It would be the last stop on our road-trip, and Antti and I drove through the Valle de Las Leñas full of anticipation.

We turned east at the drab desert town of Malargüe, and headed through 70 kilometers of desolate prairie toward the eastern slope of the Andes. The harsh, barren lifelessness of the surrounding nature was relentless. Then, rounding the final bend in the road, into view came an isolated cluster of modern buildings and numerous ski lifts making their way up the sides of 3400-meter-high, rocky Cerro Los Fosiles.

> » *Brazilianos mucho loco.* Try ski everywhere...So we keep closed sign all season.«

To a person who understands Spanish, this lifeless landscape is even more peculiar, for Las Leñas means "firewood". There is nothing even closely resembling a tree for many kilometers around in any direction of this isolated resort. In fact, the name comes from the Indian name for a flammable bush that grows in the valley.

The remoteness of Las Leñas perhaps best comes to light, if one knows that the resort is only about 50 kilometers from the spot where the plane carrying the Uruguayan rugby team crashed in the early 1970s. The story of their harrowing ordeal to survive in this desolate corner of the world, including the necessity to resort to eating the remains of their compatriots, was made famous in Piers Paul Read's book, *Alive*.

CERRO LOS FOSILES REALLY OFFERS something for everybody. The slopes are very well-groomed, and the long blue and red runs from the top provide not only good skiing for intermediates but also excellent cruising for advanced skiers. The latter of these two runs, in fact, was used for a World Cup downhill back in 1985.

It is with the freeride crowd, however, that Las Leñas has really made its mark. The Marte Chair Lift has one of the greatest vertical rises in the world (786 m) among chair lifts, and it is one of the steepest chairs in the world as well. Directly underneath the lift, a black run descends the entire way back to the base of the lift.

Chris Lizza, author of the *South America Ski Guide*, describes the infamous lift as follows:

"Marte. The chair lift of every skier's dreams. It's a silly place for a chair lift, really. Ascending over the throat of a 1500-meter-long (5000 ft)

double chute, it was destroyed by a midnight avalanche in 1987. New control and defense systems should prevent a similar occurrence in the future, but they won't. Who cares anyway, as long as they keep rebuilding it?

"Marte. Forget the rest of Las Leñas. No skier could ever find—let alone ski—all the possibilities presented by this chair lift. Marte. World Cup racers can't complete a non-stop from the top. Marte. With a compass full of exposures, all conditions are always available somewhere. Marte. Marte defines extreme. Thanks, Tito."

As Lizza describes, this one lift brings skiers not only to the Marte run, but also to a whole host of couloirs and corridors, the likes of which have lured off-piste fans here from all over the world in recent years. In addition, it accesses the snow-cat service called Snowbus. This service takes skiers about 800 vertical meters into the backcountry to the base of a spine of rocky pinnacles called Torrecillas, accessing even more terrain.

UNFORTUNATELY, THERE IS A CHINK in the armor of the ski area. Despite Lowenstein's intensive research, the Marte Chair was constructed in a location where a crosswind keeps it closed about 40 percent of the time. This seems like poor planning and it is, but the story gets even worse. Another lift, the Juno Chair, was closed so much of the time during the early years that it was actually dismantled in the 1990s and resituated onto the lower mountain, *eliminating* about 30 percent of the lift-accessed ski area!

When the Marte Lift is inoperable, Las Leñas' vertical is cut in half and most of the good freeride terrain is inaccessible. The new ownership has plans to resolve this problem when they build new lifts, but until then, visitors can be subjected to a fair amount of frustration.

IT HAS TAKEN A LONG TIME for Las Leñas to develop a policy to deal with the large amount of extreme terrain within its domain. The first time I ever skied here, the closed sign was posted at the entry to the Marte run, although there did not seem to be any avalanche danger. I asked a ski patrolman why it was closed, and if it was possible for me to ski it.

"Where do you come from?" he asked me in Spanish.

When I answered that I was from the United States, he replied, "No problemo, you ski. Marte run closed all season for *Brazilianos*." When the patrolman saw the perplexed look on my face, he elaborated in broken English. "You see, Brazil no have snow, and *Brazilianos* no can ski. But *Brazilianos mucho loco*. Try ski everywhere. They try ski Marte run. We must rescue. So we keep closed sign all season."

Nowadays, these rather extreme double-diamond descents are part of the off-piste domain and are strictly an enter-at-your-own-risk affair. In fact, the modern trail maps make no mention of the Marte run, Mercurio 2, Cenidor 1 and 2, Paraiso, or Juno 3, all descents that used to be clearly marked on the maps. Freeriders or overly optimistic *Brazilianos* alike

THIS PAGE
LEFT: Las Leñas attracts freeriders from all over the world, and for good reason—awesome terrain.
RIGHT: The village of Caviahue is mirrored in the glassy waters of Lake Caviahue.

RIGHT PAGE
UPPER: The corn snow high up on the Mercurio descent in Las Leñas contrasts with the dry prairie in the valley.
LOWER: Argentine gaucho rides toward the horizon.

can now attempt the Marte run or any other off-piste area by signing a waiver. In the document, they are informed of the off-piste rescue costs and given a little armband to signify that they have released the ski area of any liability. Many of us wish it were as easy in the litigation-giddy United States.

Antti and I gladly signed away all our rights in exchange for total freedom. But the Marte Lift had already been closed for a few days because of wind problems, and our first day was the same. It had been a few weeks since the last snowfall, and the cover was thin. Nevertheless, we enjoyed a few corn-snow descents down the steep Cenidor 1 and a nearby couloir that required a short hike. We had a good day in the spring-like sunshine.

We whiled away the evening hours in the Wine Bar, exchanging half-truths with other adventurers under the influence of some excellent Argentine wine. The local freeriders were not only hoping for the winds to subside to allow the Marte Lift to open, but were also talking a great deal about the annual Santa Rosa storm. It was late August, and according to the "regulars", every year at the very end of the month, Santa Rosa brings a bounty of powder to Las Leñas. It sounded a bit farfetched, but who was I to argue with local folklore.

NO STORM CLOUDS WERE IN SIGHT the following day. The wind, however, had subsided somewhat, and the powers that be ordained that Marte was safe. We boarded full of anticipation. Halfway up the mountain, the lift stopped for a few minutes—enough time to allow us patrons to sway in the "breeze" for a little while. I contemplated the poor maintenance in Bariloche that had caused the accident a few weeks earlier. I also thought about the fact that Henry Purcell, the longtime owner of the Portillo ski resort in Chile, refuses to ride the Marte Lift, because, he claims, they do not do adequate maintenance.

Soon, the lift continued its upward movement, and my thoughts drifted elsewhere. A few minutes later, we were at the summit. The corn snow had thawed to perfection on the steep, east-facing Mercurio descent. We hurriedly indulged in two quick runs, for one never knew how long the Marte Lift would stay open. We did a couple more runs on Cenidor 1 and a 7-kilometer-long leg-burner on the Jupiter run, until my thighs begged for mercy.

A full day of hard skiing invokes a night of deep sleep, and I was pumping out turns in my dreams when I was roused by a knock on our door at 4:45 a.m. My Spanish is poor, but the hotel's night porter was trying

to explain something about our car and a bus. At first, I thought he wanted ed me to move my car, because it was parked where a bus was supposed to be.

Unfortunately, this was not the case. The truth was that one of the Las Leñas company buses, parked on a hill above the hotel, had malfunctioned. The emergency brake had apparently broken in the middle of the night, and the bus had come hurtling down the hill, crashing into three or four vehicles, including our rental car. Fortunately nobody had been injured, but our car was a wreck.

Suddenly, I no longer cared whether the Marte Lift would open the next day. Even the prospect of Santa Rosa appearing any day was not enough to keep me in Las Leñas any longer. As soon as we dispensed with the accident-report bureaucracy, Antti and I left the resort as quickly as we could.

Argentina's God-given resources, however, are too plentiful to keep me away for long. The magnificent views from the mountains of the Lake District and the thrilling descents in La Hoya, Las Leñas and Copahue have left an indelible memory. I will just have to take out a good insurance policy before my return. And the next time I sign a freeride waiver in Argentina, I will check the small print to see what it says about runaway buses, poorly maintained lifts, and other manmade mountain hazards. If I am to meet my fate in the mountains, I much prefer it to be at the hands of Mother Nature.

Chapter 34. BOLIVIA

CHACALTAYA — THE WORLD'S HIGHEST "SKY" RESORT?

Toward the end of the film *Butch Cassidy and the Sundance Kid*, the two protagonists head optimistically to rob banks in Bolivia, because the banks had not progressed past the use of very primitive safes that could easily be cracked. Upon their arrival, however, they discovered to their dismay that the safes were not the only things that were utterly basic. Ultimately, they met their fate in a desolate pueblo which made some of the loosely thrown-together gold-rush towns of the Wild West seem like midtown Manhattan. Suffice it to say that Bolivia has not made too much progress since those late 1800s.

Despite the primitive state of almost all parts of life in Bolivia, the country is a lovely place to visit as a result of, among other things, an array of spectacular glacial peaks, some of which tower in the neighborhood of 6500 meters above sea level. La Paz, at 3640 meters the world's highest capital city, is surrounded by such giants, and among them, only 90 minutes' drive from the city center, is Chacaltaya, the oldest ski area in South America.

Ski trivia buffs will also know that, more importantly, Chacaltaya has for years laid claim to the status of the highest ski resort in the world. Despite this fact, it has always been a bit of a mystery as to the true height of the summit. Credit Bolivia's total disregard for detail. Normally, one would think that a location proclaimed to be the highest would proudly announce its exact elevation on signs, maps and marketing literature—not so in Bolivia!

During a visit I made to Chacaltaya, a large sign in the dining room of the *refugio* (below the summit) proclaimed the spot to be 5270 meters high, while in the adjoining room, a plaque announced an elevation of 5300 meters. The peak itself bore no such marking whatsoever. One of the local employees said that the top was 5600 meters high, and a member of Club Andino, who was with us on our day trip, put the peak's height at 5370 meters. The president of Club Andino had no idea.

My edition of the *South American Handbook*, known as "the bible" to most *gringos* who travel on this continent, listed the elevation as 5570

meters, and *The World Ski and Snowboarding Guide*, compiled by ski trivia's supreme commander, Patrick Thorne, pegs it at 5421 meters!

Patrick's figure sounds reasonable, but for a brief time in 2004, accuracy became irrelevant. In an 80-page treatise entitled *The World's Highest Lifts*, Patrick dethroned Chacaltaya from its honored position atop the ski world.

Patrick wrote, "Although reports are patchy, several trekkers and climbers in the area have reported that the surface tow—popularly reported as the world's fastest, most dangerous and difficult to ride as well as the highest—has disappeared. The glacier terrain which it served has also largely thawed away."

In fact, like Bolivia as a whole, Chacaltaya has a history that is the prototype of inefficiency, and it would seem that this recent situation was just one new chapter in that long story. At the best of times, the ancient rope tow that was placed here in 1938 was likely to be inoperable for more reasons than even a vivid imagination could dream up.

My friend Papi Tuomala made a visit in the early 1980s, and the lift was not running. Upon inquiry as to the reason, he was informed that the man with the keys to start the motor had unfortunately stumbled over a precipice a few hours earlier and plummeted to an untimely death.

The prone body of the former employee, although quite accessible, was still in repose in its landing place, with the keys to the lift in his pocket.

ABOVE: In spite of the lifts being non-operational (as usual), Anders Nilsson rented some equipment from the rental shop and did some skiing from the top of Chacaltaya on a recent visit to Bolivia. He reports that the old lift house had recently received a new coat of red and white paint—if that is of any help to skiers. Photo by Caspar Möller.

Apparently, nobody had made any attempt to either remove the body or recover the lone set of keys to open the ski lift. Having come all the way from Finland, and not wishing to be thwarted in his quest to ski the highest ski run in the world, Papi energetically organized a group to retrieve the corpse. They subsequently removed the keys from his pocket and opened the ski area themselves at about three o'clock in the afternoon.

Some years later, I visited Chacaltaya, meeting a similar but different fate. Upon my arrival in La Paz, literally every tourist agency in town offered trips to the highest "sky" resort in the world. The pun brought about by this misspelling was hardly intended.

Since the time of Papi's visit, the lift operator had with time been replaced, but unfortunately, the lift had not. The old automobile motor that, on its cooperative days, had had the capacity to pull eight skiers simultaneously up the mountain had broken down about two weeks previously. We were told that the lift would again be operable in another week or so.

The simple explanation for the reason why the lift was currently at a standstill was "*falta plata*" (no money).

In a paradox of blind optimism in the face of economic reality, the mountain manager showed me plans for a projected second lift, which, he explained, they hoped to have completed sometime the following year.

Not wanting to miss my chance to ski the highest run in the world, I hiked up the approximately 200-vertical-meter ski run. My companion on my visit, my then-girlfriend, Eva Sjöqvist, was not so lucky as to have ski equipment along and therefore had to rely on the resources of the local rental shop. Since she was the only person renting equipment due to the disrepair of the lift, she did manage to get the cream of the crop, a pair of 15-year-old Rossignols with bindings of a similar vintage.

Many of the skis on display in the rental shop looked as if they had been salvaged from some dump, where they most likely had previously been discarded by the ski-trooper division of the Bolivian armed forces after about 30 years of heavy usage.

Finally outfitted, we started our hike. If you have ever trekked wearing ski boots at elevations of over 5000 meters, you know that the progress is snail-like. Before beginning our ascent, we had prepared for this endeavor at the mountain restaurant with a few cups of coca tea. Prepared from the same coca plant from which Bolivia's more famous "snow" is derived, coca tea is an excellent aid to altitude acclimatization. Thus fortified, we did eventually reach the summit and complete one run for posterity.

The most recent downgrading of Chacaltaya's longtime status as the world's highest ski lift was, according to hearsay, the result of foul play by a former employee of the resort, a disgruntled Austrian. After not having received his pay, the European villain vengefully stole parts of the motor. Sometime after that, with the motor still out of service, the rope was apparently removed.

Despite these negative reports from not so long ago, skiers can again breathe a collective sigh of relief. Patrick Thorne's most recent update on Bolivia's mythical ski center has the lift back in operation, albeit only on weekends and often only once a week.

Even if one has the good fortune to show up at Chacaltaya on a day when the whims of the old automobile engine allow you an opportunity to ride the lift, the uphill transportation provides challenges of its own. A metal hook and a wooden stick are attached to opposite ends of a piece of rope, and to ride the contraption, one is required to attach the hook to the moving rope tow while simultaneously placing the stick between one's legs. In the end, many skiers and boarders may find the hike up in the rarified air to be less arduous than riding the rope tow.

Regardless of whether the lift is running or not, any skier who has made it as far as La Paz ought to head up the winding dirt road to Chacaltaya. Bring along your own ski equipment, a perfunctory awareness of the Bolivian way of life, and a good sense of humor, and you will certainly have a memorable day at the highest "sky" resort in the world.

South America in a Nutshell

LOCATION	NEAREST TOWN	NEAREST AIRPORT	SEASON	PEAK ELEVATION	VERTICAL DROP	SIZE	SNOW	BEAUTY	VILLAGE	NOVICE	INTERMEDIATE	ADVANCED	OFF-PISTE	NIGHTLIFE	RATING AVERAGE	WEB SITE
ARGENTINA																
Copahue	Caviahue	Neuquén	July–September	2151 m	405 m	2	1	2	4	2	4	3	1	2	1	2.2	www.caviahue.com
Cerro Bayo	Villa La Angostura	Bariloche	July–September	1752 m	732 m	2	2	2	5	3	2	3	2	2	2	2.5	www.cerrobayoweb.com
Cerro Castor	Ushuaia	Ushuaia	June–October	967 m	792 m	2	1	3	4	3	2	3	3	4	2	2.7	www.cerrocastor.com
Cerro Catedral	Bariloche	Bariloche	July–September	2000 m	970 m	3	3	2	4	3	2	3	3	2	3	2.8	www.catedralaltapatagonia.com
Cerro Chapelco	San Martin de los Andes	Bariloche	July–September	1980 m	720 m	2	2	2	3	4	3	3	2	2	3	2.6	www.chapelco.org
La Hoya	Esquel	Bariloche	July–September	2150 m	800 m	2	1	3	3	1	3	3	4	4	1	2.5	www.camlahoya.com.ar
Las Leñas	Los Molles	Malargüe	June–October	3430 m	1230 m	4	2	3	3	1	4	4	4	4	2	3.1	www.laslenas.com
Valdelén	Rio Turbio	Julia Dufour, Arg./ Punta Arenas, Chile	July–September	830 m	250 m	1	1	3	3	2	2	2	1	1	1	1.7	www.valle-mina1.com.ar
BOLIVIA																
Chacaltaya	La Paz	La Paz	November–March [1]	5421 m	200 m	1	1	3	4	1	1	2	3	3	1	2.0	www.goski.com/bolivia.htm
CHILE																
Antillanca	Termas de Puyehue	Osorno	July–mid September	1600 m	530 m	2	1	2	5	3	2	3	2	3	1	2.4	www.skiantillanca.cl
Antuco	Antuco	Los Angeles	July–September	1835 m	490 m	2	1	3	5	2	1	2	2	3	1	2.2	www.chileanski.com
Cerro Mirador	Punta Arenas	Punta Arenas	July–early October	450 m	350 m	1	1	1	3	3	1	2	1	1	1	1.5	www.clubandino.cl
Corralco	Malalcahuello	Temuco	July–mid October	1920 m	300 m	1	1	3	4	2	2	3	2	3	2	2.3	www.corralco.com
El Colorado	Farellones	Santiago	late June–mid Oct.	3333 m	903 m	3	4	4 [2]	3	2	4	3	2	3	2	3.0	www.elcolorado.cl
La Parva	Farellones	Santiago	late June–early Oct.	3630 m	960 m	3	4	4 [2]	3	2	2	3	3	4	2	3.0	www.laparva.cl
Los Arenales	Lonquimay	Temuco	mid June–mid Oct.	1760 m	270 m	1	1	3	3	2	2	1	1	2	1	1.7	www.gochile.cl
Las Araucarias	Cherquenco	Temuco	July–mid October	1942 m	382 m	1	1	3	3	2	2	2	2	2	1	1.9	www.skiaraucarias.cl
Osorno	Puerto Varas	Puerto Montt	mid June–mid Sept.	1760 m	613 m	2	1	2	5	4	2	3	2	3	2	2.6	www.volcanosorno.com
Portillo	Juncal	Santiago	late June–early Oct.	3310 m	812 m	3	2	3	4	3	2	3	3	4	3	3.0	www.skiportillo.com
Termas de Chillán	Las Trancas	Chillan	late June–early Oct.	2700 m	1120 m	3	2	3	3	3	3	3	3	3	2	2.8	www.skichillan.cl
Valle Nevado	Farellones	Santiago	mid June–mid Oct.	3670 m	661 m	2	4	4 [2]	3	2	4	4	2	3	2	3.0	www.vallenevado.com
Villarica	Pucón	Pucon	July–November	1800 m	600 m	2	1	2	4	4	3	3	2	2	3	2.6	www.skipucon.cl

(1) Lift operates irregularly on weekends only.   (2) Combination of lifts in linked area of Colorado, La Parva and Valle Nevado.

ASIA VII

PREVIOUS PAGES
The view from the cockpit of a Kazak helicopter depicts the stunning Tien Shan Mountains, with 7000-meter-high Khan Tengri's pyramid-shaped top visible through the second window from the left. Khan Tengri is sometimes listed as 6995 meters high and alternately attributed an elevation of 7010 meters. The former figure is the highest point of solid rock, while the latter figure is based on the elevation of a cornice of snow atop the peak.

LEFT PAGE
Ortwin Eckert breaking the law by skiing off-piste in Shiga Kogen.

Chapter 35. JAPAN

LICE, ORYMPICS AND FLEELIDE

John Jay, the official U.S. cinematographer for three Winter Olympic Games and a predecessor to the filmmaker, Warren Miller, used to tour the United States each autumn and winter, personally narrating his latest ski film. It was he who introduced me to Japanese skiing and Japanese skiers. Sometime in the late '50s, he included some film footage of this Far East wannabe ski nation that left the 2000 spectators in the Wilshire Ebell Theater in stitches.

We laughed until it hurt, as we watched hundreds of neophyte Japanese skiers crisscrossing a small crowded slope like out-of-control kamikazes. There were numerous broadside and head-on collisions, as the masses slid helter-skelter in some vague attempt to do snowplow turns. Some skiers were hunched over with their backs parallel to the slope, others came hurtling down with their weight so far back that only Providence could control where they would land, and the crashes that were narrowly avoided were a matter of sheer luck or divine intervention. We in the audience doubled over with laughter as Mr. Jay showed the sequence again at a higher speed. The spectators were rolling in the aisles as he then ran the film footage backwards. It looked like an anthill in a state of total anarchy.

Japanese skiing has come a long way since then. This workaholic nation, which has risen from the ashes of World War II and transformed itself into one of the world's economic powerhouses, has taken to skiing with the same dedication and zeal that is so characteristic of everything the Japanese people do.

Between 1970 and 2006, only two countries have had the honor of hosting the Winter Olympic Games on two separate occasions—the United States and Japan. Japan hosted the 1972 Games in Sapporo and the 1998 Olympics in Nagano. Many Westerners might feel that the reason for this is simple politics—that the Olympic Committee feels it necessary to award the Games periodically to different sectors of the world.

In fact, Japan has earned the right to host this respected event with credentials that could hardly be better.

This rather small nation of islands, which is known for her overcrowded cities, has such a high population density in its urban areas because 72 percent of her land is covered by mountains. Mountains alone do not qualify a country for hosting winter sports' most prestigious competition, but in the years since I laughed so heartily at the expense of Japanese skiers, the industrious inhabitants of this small nation have covered their landscape with ski resorts and lifts. The "Land of the Rising Sun" is now fourth in the world in number of ski lifts and first in number of chair lifts.

Mother Nature has also pitched in. Snowstorms breeze into the Japanese mountains almost unabatedly from December until late March. The cold, stormy fronts blow in from Siberia, picking up extra moisture as they cross the Sea of Japan. They then dump enormous amounts of white fluff all along the western side of Japan. A number of the Japanese resorts rank among the most snow-rich ski areas in the world.

Even armed with this kind of background information, Anders Karlsson, Christer Henning and I did not really know what to expect of this enigmatic country upon our arrival in Tokyo's Narita Airport. This is a nation of contrasts. What should we make of a land where an American import like baseball can flourish as a national pastime side by side with sumo wrestling? What should we deduce about people who are in love with 21st century high-tech gadgetry and are simultaneously steeped in the traditional values that have been handed down to them by their forefathers?

From the moment we disembarked in Tokyo, we were bombarded with an array of new impressions of Japanese skiing, its culture, its people and their habits.

NOZAWA ONSEN

Japan has over 400 ski resorts, so it is not so easy to plot an itinerary for a two-week ski vacation. We started our sojourn in Nozawa Onsen, on the island of Honshu. This was an appropriate beginning, for it was here that Hannes Schneider, the legendary Austrian father of modern ski technique, visited in the 1920s to spread the gospel of the religion of skiing. Large posters of Herr Schneider can still be seen everywhere, including the tourist office, some slopeside restaurants, and various pensions and hotels. Nozawa Onsen is one of Japan's oldest resorts, and has managed to maintain the cozy kind of atmosphere that once was a given when it came to skiing.

Many of modern-day Japan's top ski areas are purpose-built resorts, but Nozawa shows no capitulation whatsoever to this trend. The village is made up of narrow streets lined with private houses, small pensions and intimate bars and restaurants. We checked into one of those cozy pensions, known in Japan as a *minshuku*.

THE MOMENT WE CROSSED THE THRESHOLD of Minshuku Takasaka (known in English as the Apple Inn), we walked into the heart of what a ski vacation in Japan is all about—a cultural experience. We were greeted warmly by the smiling proprietress, Satuki Takasaka, who began our first course of instruction in Japanese living.

In halting english and with a small dictionary always handy, Satuki showed us to place our shoes on a shelf by the front door, and to put on a pair of slippers. There was a choice of about 40 pairs, all of which would have been a perfect fit for anybody with a girl's size-35 shoe. Otherwise, you found yourself walking around with the back 8–10 centimeters of your heel dragging along the floor. The solution was easy—we wore the slippers. We were in Japan, and were determined to fit into the culture as best we could.

Each room we entered was an adventure in its own right. Satuki showed us to our sleeping quarters, a traditional Japanese-style bedroom with straw *tatami* mats on the floor situated around a small, 30-centimeter-high, square table covered by a quilt. Three *yukatas* (Japanese light, cotton dressing gowns) were laid out for us. We slipped out of our dirty, well-traveled blue jeans, complemented our tiny slippers with *yukatas*, and our new wardrobe was complete.

We were now instructed to sit on the floor around the little table and to place our crossed legs under the quilt that lay over it. Thus began our first look into the fascinating world of Japanese gadgetry. A heating lamp was attached to the underside of the table, and by the time Satuki placed some rice balls wrapped in seaweed in front of us, we were extremely warm and cozy.

Our rice-ball midnight snack was the first of 45 consecutive meals that included rice as the staple ingredient. Everywhere we traveled, rice paddies surrounded the ski resorts, and we soon found out that rice was an integral part of every day life. If this important Japanese foodstuff had been a little more slippery, I am sure they would have used it as artificial snow as well.

After our meal, Satuki removed three futons (thin Japanese mattresses) from the closet and rolled them out on the floor. I crawled under a heavy quilt, laid my head down on a rice-filled pillow, and drifted gently into a dream about big rice flakes falling gingerly over the local mountains.

Breakfast the next morning was also Japanese style, once again sitting cross-legged on a pillow on the floor of the dining room. Soon, a delightful array of Japanese breakfast specialties was staring us in the face. Misu soup, cold scrambled eggs rolled into a pancake, fish and meat balls wrapped in dough, sashimi (raw fish), Nozawa pickles, yogurt with fresh strawberries, rolls with very sweet butter and jam, a big pot of rice with dried seaweed strips, and of course, tea, were all part of the morning meal.

LEFT PAGE: Christer Henning enters a top-to-bottom tree run in Nozawa Onsen.

THIS PAGE: Local woman cooks her vegetables in the hot spring known as Ogama (the Kitchen), in the center of Nozawa Onsen.

By the time we left our *minshuku*, we were well energized for our first day on the slopes. Nozawa Onsen is one of many ski resorts belonging to Nagano Prefecture, and the Nagano Tourist Bureau was kind enough to lend us a rare, if not unique, commodity—a Japanese-speaking Austrian ski instructor. For the next few days of our travels around the various top resorts of Nagano Prefecture, Ortwin Eckert became our interpreter, ski guide, chauffeur and cultural guru, helping us decipher and understand the many intricacies of this new and foreign culture.

We walked to the slopes the first morning really wondering what to expect. It was April 2, Nozawa Village lies 560 meters high, and the lifts top out at 1650 meters. In addition, Nozawa is at the same latitude as Morocco. What would you expect?

Forget that! Throw conventional wisdom out the window. The snow base was about 4–5 meters deep, and there was fresh snow. This is not the least bit unusual for Nozawa, which we soon found out averages 14.5 meters of snowfall per season. According to *The World Ski and Snowboarding Guide*, this puts Nozawa second to only Mt. Alyeska, Alaska (15.25 meters per year) in the category of annual average snowfall among ski resorts worldwide.

THE SKI RUNS IN NOZAWA ARE CUT OUT of forests of larch, birch and cherry trees, with a few other species thrown in for good measure. On the upper mountain, the trees are very well spaced, and it is simple to dive off the runs virtually anywhere to ski the fresh snow in the forest. It is easy, that is, except for one major hindrance—off-piste skiing or "fleeliding" is *officially* prohibited everywhere in Japan. Japanese ski resorts have more "KEEP OUT" and "CLOSED AREA" signs than a nuclear power plant, and almost every centimeter of piste is cordoned off on both sides with rope, to make sure that no mistakes can be made.

Ortwin explained that the Japanese ski patrol is not really well enough educated in avalanche safety or first aid to deal with the ramifications

of opening and closing off-piste areas in accordance with the prevailing conditions. Therefore, the matter is simplified by barring off-piste skiing entirely. There are mountain guides available who can take tourists off-piste, but they usually use the lifts to access the backcountry, and then go beyond the ski area, rather than diving in and out of the ropes.

The conditions on this particular day were not dangerous, so Ortwin, a certified instructor in his home country, ducked under the nylon cord and led us into the forest. We poached powder in the trees between the two upper lifts for a while until it was time to go big-game hunting.

We now followed Ortwin past the skull-and-crossbones symbol into a lovely canyon decorated with well spaced trees. We plunged in greedily, spraying a layer of spring powder off our skis with each turn. The ravine wound its way almost the full vertical drop of the ski area, until we skied past a huge avalanche barricade that protected one of the beginners slopes from any possible damage that this gully could cause under more dangerous snow conditions.

During the rest of the day, Ortwin led us around, giving us an excellent overview of what Nozawa Onsen had to offer. We cruised along the well manicured intermediate runs, and bashed through an array of soft spring moguls on Schneider Course and a couple other black pistes.

When the lifts finally ground to a half, Ortwin introduced us to a Nozawa-style après-ski. *Onsen* is the Japanese word for "hot spring", and Nozawa Onsen's name is well-deserved. Thirteen bathhouses filled with hot-springs water are located in the center of town, and bathing in the springs is the local substitute for drenching oneself in beer and schnapps

> » **Our rice-ball midnight snack was the first of 45 consecutive meals that included rice as the staple ingredient.**«

after a day on the slopes. It is not at all uncommon to see Japanese visitors walking the narrow streets of Nozawa in their slippers and *yukatas*, as they go from their hotel to the nearest *onsen*.

In addition, Nozawa has a very special *onsen*, near the base of the lifts, known as Ogama (the Kitchen). The Kitchen is made up of a few hot pools that are close to the source of the spring, and close to boiling. Many locals use them as a kitchen cauldron and come here each morning to boil their eggs and cook their vegetables.

Communal bathing is part of the Japanese culture, and every *onsen* we visited was well patronized by locals, who all religiously wash and rinse their bodies thoroughly before entering the communal spring water. The first *onsen* we tried was called Oyu, and Ortwin warned us that it was special. We had no great difficulty getting accustomed to the odor of sulfur that accompanied a bath in any of the local hot springs, but it was not quite as easy to get used to the heat. Oyu *onsen* had two pools—extremely hot and even hotter.

Anders dipped his big toe into the more amenable of the pools and gave up immediately, while Chris and I took a good 10 minutes to ease our way—body part by body part—into the less extreme of the two. A few elderly Japanese men chuckled at us as they slid easily into the scalding water of the hotter pool without so much as a grimace, and we understood that we were overmatched.

Most of the *onsens* in Nozawa are indoor pools, but one can also enjoy a beautiful outdoor spring just a short drive outside town at Maguse Onsen. Here, one can ease the aches and pains of a tough ski day in 43-degree spring water, while watching the last rays of sunlight over the slopes of the nearby Kijimadaira ski area.

FOLLOWING OUR APRÈS-SKI *onsen* came dinner. This was also an unforgettable experience, in which a continuous flow of different dishes were paraded in and placed before us. Beginning the procession was noodle soup with mushrooms and green onions. To make sure we stayed healthy, I suppose, Satuki served tofu, turnips, mushrooms, green salad, glass noodles and *chawamushi*—an egg-based pudding mixed with chicken and vegetables. The rest of the table was filled with sashimi of scallops, squid and tuna; an octopus and cucumber salad; shrimp, fish and vegetable tempura; and *sukiyaki*—a typical Japanese dish made up of thinly sliced beef. Of course there was also rice.

I decided to skip dessert and wondered how the Japanese managed to all stay so slim.

SHIGA KOGEN

I was still full when we drove the following morning to Shiga Kogen, site of both the slalom and giant slalom races in the 1998 Olympics, and with 72 lifts, the largest ski area in Japan. The Americans built the first lift here in 1946, during the post-war occupation of Japan, but by 1950, a Japanese firm had taken over the operation, and they added on from there.

The vertical is no more than 600 meters on any of the mountains, but we had no complaints. This is another spot that gets close to 15 meters of snowfall per year, and we were lucky enough to have the sun shining on a light dusting of fresh snow.

Grab your camera quickly when the sun shines, for it might be next month before you see it again. The Japanese don't mind. White is beautiful to the Japanese, and that refers to skin as well as snow. People do not want a tan. Quite possibly, this preference for light skin is rooted in olden times when darker skins were equated with working-class people who labored long hours under the sun.

In any case, the local aversion to tanning is quite obvious, as many Japanese wear face masks on warm, sunny days to avoid any semblance of color. Outdoor terraces do not exist at the lunch restaurants, so one has to carry tables and chairs outside if one wishes to bask in the spring warmth.

AS IN NOZAWA, ALMOST ALL the off-piste skiing in Shiga Kogen was in the trees. That was just as well, because the first time we emerged from the forest to ski a few *open* slopes away from the piste, we were reprimanded by the nearest lift operator.

"Avaranche Dangel," he repeated a few times with perfect clarity.

We tried to explain that the 10 centimeters of new snow on the slopes did not really pose much of a threat, but it was to no avail.

"Back into the trees, boys!"

The Japanese are very law-abiding by nature, and we were the only trespassers on the mountain. At least in the forest our violations were not quite as flagrant.

The runs in the trees were always very short, but they were beautiful. The mixture of pine, larch, birch and wild cherry trees, generally decorated by some bamboo shrubs, made for a unique ski setting. We finished the day with a nice run under one of the lifts, and ended up in a birch forest that was so tight that I longed for a pair of snowblades.

That evening, we went to dinner at a sushi restaurant called Kappa. We sat at the counter, where a narrow conveyor belt presented us with a movable feast, offering up various types of sushi and other dishes. We could just take whatever suited our fancy from the rolling band, and at the end of the meal, the waitress counted the plates to figure out the bill.

On our second day at Shiga Kogen, we had our après-ski at a different type of hot spring. Near one of the lifts is a hot spring and pool which is always full of wild macaques (snow monkeys). Hundreds of the playful creatures were in the trees, running around in the snow or relaxing in the hot baths. These baths, however, did not seem very inviting. The monkeys had not learned the Japanese tradition of cleaning themselves thoroughly before entering the pool, so this time we opted to be mere spectators.

HAKUBA

The next morning we drove to Hakuba, a ski village that is surrounded by seven separate ski areas, the best of which are Happo-one and Goryu-Toomi. We started the morning in Happo-one, doing laps on the slope that had been used for the 1998 Olympic Downhill. The spring snow was perfect, it was midweek and the resort was empty. We carved sweeping GS turns on the beautifully prepared piste, and we still found untouched corduroy at noon.

Hakuba had a very different appearance from both Nozawa and Shiga Kogen, as the mountains surrounding the village are more rugged and Alpine in nature. The lower pistes were primarily trails as in the previous

resorts, but from the peak, both flanks of the mountain revealed a series of long, steep valleys, completely devoid of trees, and with what seemed to be easy access back to civilization.

I crossed under a rope merely to take a photo, but I was immediately chased away by the ski patrol. Somebody told me that Glen Plake and Scott Schmidt had spent a fair amount of time playing around in the back bowls here a few years earlier, but after four snowboarders died in an avalanche, the ski area has become much more strict about off-piste skiing.

IN THE AFTERNOON, WE MOVED OVER to Goryu-Toomi, one of Japan's most popular destinations among snowboarders. We could see why. The pistes were steeper than in most Japanese areas, and beyond the prohibitive ropes, there seemed to be lots of interesting gullies and ridges that disappeared in all directions into the trees. We detected a handful of tracks in the forbidden areas, proving that at least a few powder poachers existed even in Japan.

By the time we began exploring here, the spring snow was much too soft to even think of leaving the groomed areas. We had to satisfy ourselves with imagining could-have-beens, and planning for a longer stay in Hakuba on our next trip to Japan.

MT. FUJI

Our stay on Honshu, Japan's largest island, could not have been complete without a visit to Mt. Fuji (3800 m). Japan's highest mountain can be seen from Tokyo on a clear day, but one must come much closer to feel a real sense of her majesty. By mid-April, the flowers are starting to bloom in and around Tokyo, and the combination of cherry-blossom pink against the winter white of Japan's sacred mountain is one of the island nation's most spectacular scenes.

Although the flowers are in bloom, one can still ski at a couple of small resorts at the base of Mt. Fuji, and we opted for the tiny Fuji Tenjinyama

resort. The pistes were almost horizontal and there were only a few lifts, but the views alone kept us happy for a couple of hours.

The Japanese prohibition of off-piste skiing extends to Mt. Fuji as well. The access road that takes cars to 2500 meters, a good starting point for a trek up the volcano, is closed during the entire winter, and a sign warns that violators might be subject to a $1000 fine or six months in prison. Yet, as we cruised the ultra-tame slopes of Fuji Tenjinyama, I couldn't help but gaze up at her lofty peak and mentally plot out possible routes.

EVERYONE HEARS HORROR STORIES about the prices in Japan, but with a little preparation and knowledge one can avoid getting ripped off. The sushi bars are quite inexpensive and one can always pick up a cheap meal in a convenience store. Sometimes, I had the impression that the entire country was not much more than a huge chain of such outlets. They are everywhere, and almost always open.

If you want to save money on hotel costs, there are many youth hostels, or try a "love hotel". "Love hotels" cater to the prurient desires of young couples who need a place to rendezvous in this conservative society, where offspring often live with their parents well into their twenties. Rooms are rented in such places by the hour, but after about 10 p.m. one can often rent such an accommodation for the rest of the night.

Because of the nature of this business, complete discretion is necessary, and the hotel personnel are not to know who the guests are. Hence,

a gang of ski bums can camp out in such a room that is actually intended for only two people. This can be an inexpensive way to spend a night on the road, as long as one does not buy any of the sex toys available for purchase from a special menu in the room!

NISEKO

Our visit on Honshu was drawing to a close, and it was time to visit Hokkaido, the northernmost large island of the country. We flew into Sapporo and traveled by train to the beautiful Niseko ski area. This ski resort is at about the latitude of Rome, but the skiing is even lower than near Nagano. The village is situated at an elevation of only 300 meters, and the top of Niseko Annupuri is a meager 1300 meters high. Again, any doubts we had about lack of snow in mid-April were dispelled immediately upon our arrival. The snowpack was still 1–2 meters deep in the village!

Similar to most ski resorts in Japan, a variety of ski lift companies coexist side by side on Niseko Annupuri, and it is quite easy to end up at the base of a lift for which your ski pass does not provide access. It took us less than half an hour to find ourselves in that situation. Either the lift attendants were understanding, or perhaps it was that they did not understand us, but a short amount of small talk and double-talk got us headed back in the right direction without having to pay a surcharge.

From every vantage point on the mountain, one can look out over Mt. Yotei, a perfectly shaped volcano a few kilometers away. The lifts in Niseko do not quite reach the top, but a 20-minute hike beyond the top lift to the actual peak is a worthwhile endeavor. From there one can see the ocean on a clear day, and one can also gain access to the backcountry. We could see some hot springs at the bottom of the back side of the mountain and I mulled over the idea of an off-piste descent. Skiing such backcountry terrain is not prohibited, but it is quite advisable to use a guide.

The backcountry, however, was not our only option. There was also a huge, untracked bowl down the front face that met back up with the piste, and I was certain that we could not get lost there. The corn snow was just the right consistency, and we felt good about having done a small off-piste experiment. It left me wanting more, and at the end of the ski day, I went to visit Ross Carty, owner and operator of Niseko Adventure Centre.

IWANAI

Ross, a former ski patrolman from Australia turned entrepreneur, had founded his adventure company a few years earlier. He told me that he guides many people each year down to the hot springs we had seen. We discussed various possibilities, and it was he who suggested that the nearby ski area of Iwanai, situated only a few kilometers from the Sea of Japan, provided even better views than Niseko.

The Iwanai area was closed for the season, but Ross assured us that it was for lack of interest and not for lack of snow. Anders, Christer and I all had skins and touring inserts with us, so the next day's activity was decided.

That evening, Anders and Christer fell victim to a longstanding ski bum tradition—excessive drinking. The following morning, Christer claimed he had a bad back, and I presumed that in Sweden, where he comes from, *back* is spelled h-e-a-d. He bailed out of the program before we started. Anders, on the other hand, tried to show some Viking spirit and joined me in the van when Toru Takikawa, our guide and chauffeur, picked us up at 7 a.m.

Each day in Japan was filled with new impressions, and this day was no exception. We stopped to buy gas and I went to use the restroom. Not only was the floor clean enough to eat off, but small vases with real roses added an additional touch of cleanliness to this roadside urinal.

At this early hour, the department store adjacent to the gas station was already open for business. The night before, when we visited the local

tourist office, quite a few people were still in front of their computers at seven in the evening.

Doesn't anybody ever sleep around here? The answer is yes. One can find Japanese people napping at every lunch restaurant on the mountain. This nation of workaholics skis almost exclusively on weekends. After working late on Friday, they hop in the car and still drive quite a few hours to the mountains. Next morning they are up early, waiting in line for the lifts to open. By lunchtime, it has all caught up with them, and Japanese lunch patrons often lay their heads on the restaurant tables and nod off for an hour or so right after their meal.

ANDERS REALLY GAVE IT the old college try, sweating out alcohol for 2 hours, as he ploddingly gained 600 vertical meters. Nevertheless, an hour or so from the peak, he succumbed to the previous evening's overindulgence, and gave in to the temptation to lie in the sun for a while. Toru and I continued alone. Finally, we arrived at the top (1085 m) and sat down for a well-deserved rest.

The north face of the mountain is a big bowl looking out over the sea, no more than 5 kilometers away. At least we didn't have to worry about breaking the rules in Iwanai. With the lifts already closed for the season, there was nobody to reprimand us for going beyond the ropes.

Toru and I dove into the bowl hungrily. It did not matter whether we were in the untouched bowl or on the piste. With the lifts closed, virgin corn snow awaited us everywhere, and there was nobody around to inhibit our speed, our line or our feeling of ultimate freedom.

FURANO

The time had come for us to travel on to the final destination of our Japanese ski odyssey, Furano. Furano has traditionally hosted World Cup events, and is yet another region where various ski lift companies share

one mountain. Here we stayed at the luxurious Prince Hotel, directly adjacent to the pistes. The uppermost lift provided a short area of excellent off-piste skiing in the trees, while the majority of the mountain was made up of easy cruising runs. Far in the distance, one could make out plumes of smoke rising from the volcano, Tokachidake.

While many of the Japanese chair lifts at Furano and elsewhere are quads, Japan still has many ancient single chairs in operation. Furano's top lift was one such relic, and Japanese single chairs are unlike any others I have seen. They have no bar to pull in front of you and no rail on either side. Even the backrest is no more than about 10 centimeters high. Basically, they look like small, flat stools and nothing more, and are horrifying at first glance. Neil Armstrong, John Glenn and other astronauts might not think twice about riding these lifts, but most Westerners would be reluctant to mount one of these primitive contraptions.

The temptation of good tree-skiing, however, has often lured me to forgo prudence, and after all, the locals were lining up for the lift without trepidation. I reluctantly slid in front of my first "stool lift". Once airborne, it was really no problem, but I was glad the wind was not blowing! Fresh lines in some late-season powder in the birch trees helped me to forget my reticence, and we spent most of the day doing laps on the old "stool lift".

Like everywhere in Japan, our days in Furano were a mix of good skiing and interesting culture—sushi, sashimi, rice and tea mixed with spring powder and April corduroy on empty pistes. There was much more—volcanoes, hot springs, tree-skiing, sukiyaki, Olympic ski runs, ultra-polite people, raiding closed runs, sake, *yukatas* and public transportation that always arrived on the minute. Every day was a kaleidoscope of new impressions.

It was our last day, and the sun was setting over the "Land of the Rising Sun". The last rays of light shifted the shadows of the trees almost fast enough to see them moving, and we slithered between the birches and

larches one last time before catching our train back to Sapporo.

On the train, I sat back with a last bottle of Kirin beer and tried to make sense of it all. I thought of the horrific footage I had once seen of the atomic bomb and a Japan left much in ruins at the end of World War II. How quickly this country had raised itself from the ashes to become a world economic power. I thought back again to those old John Jay films and those funny, impossible skiers. They had used their sense of discipline and their work ethic to persevere and excel at this sport and turn much of their country into a ski playground.

A little over 50 years earlier, the conquering Americans had built Shiga Kogen's first lift to provide some recreation for their occupying troops. By now, Shiga Kogen has not only hosted the Winter Olympics, but little Japan possesses as many ski resorts as North America.

JAPAN REMAINS A NATION of contrasts, and they are as obvious in the ski areas as anywhere else in the society. The pistes are often empty during the week and overcrowded on weekends. Traditional *minshukus* and *ryokans* (inns) stand side by side with Western-style high-rise hotels. A calm, relaxing après-ski in a hot spring contrasts with a drunken, giggly night out at a Karaoke bar. A plethora of antiquated single chair lifts are juxtaposed with modern floodlights for night skiing.

Old-fashioned, conservative family values battle with a severely demanding work ethic and a love of modern gadgetry. A person might still boil his vegetables in the local hot spring, but his toilet seat is electrically heated, and the toilet can clean his posterior with water and blow dry it at the touch of a button.

I took a long swig of my beer, and continued my pondering. Perhaps the greatest contrast of all was the built-in paradox of Japanese skiing itself. A sport whose attraction is rooted in a sense of freedom meets a regimented society of strict adherence to rules, regulations, traditions and laws. The result is a skiing culture that has constricted the innate freedom of the sport with an endless array of ropes and signs.

Everything in the world changes quickly in this day and age, however, and so it is in the snowsports industry. In recent years, we have seen the explosion of snowboarding, the invention of parabolic skis, and the redefining of off-piste skiing as freeriding, but on equipment much more suitable to wild terrain than ever before.

Japan has some of the best snow in the world for freeriding, and in huge quantities. I suspect that with time there will be pressure to change some of Japan's ski rules and regulations. Where the likes of Glen Plake and Scott Schmidt have come seeking, more will follow.

I HOPE ONE DAY TO RETURN to Japan. I will enjoy her contrasts and contradictions as I did this time. I will visit the likes of Nozawa Onsen, Hakuba, Niseko, Furano and Shiga Kogen in the height of winter. Blankets of fresh snow will cover the ground and will give a white outline to the intricate latticework of tree branches.

One characteristic will be different. I will comb the trees for a good opening, but there will be no rope or sign to block me from the perfect line. I won't have to poach, sneak or hide. I will dive into Japan's wonderful world of white with a good conscience, and I will enjoy her boundless resource of powder without recrimination. After skiing, I will again gorge myself on her unique cuisine. Then I will curl up on a futon and fall into the sound sleep of the innocent.

LEFT PAGE
Ortwin takes to the air while heading down the piste toward Nozawa Onsen.

THIS PAGE
LEFT: Christer, Anders, Ortwin and a few Japanese skiers enjoy the sunset while relaxing in the Maguse Onsen.
UPPER RIGHT: A fisherman provides a picturesque foreground to majestic Mt. Fuji.
LOWER RIGHT: Some people might be reluctant to ride up the mountain in Furano on this old single chair lift.

Chapter 36. KYRGYZSTAN

PIONEERING THE LAST FRONTIER

In 1938, my mother left her native Austria and immigrated to the United States. She brought with her to America a love for the mountains, an ability to ski and not much else. In the years that followed, she and many of her transplanted countrymen became pioneers in the nascent sport of skiing. She instructed skiing and worked in bars and restaurants in a number of one- or two-lift resorts, which were often on the verge of bankruptcy, as the ski lovers tried, slowly but surely, to market their favorite sport to enough people to develop skiing into a viable business.

This page out of the glossy scrapbook of the current multi-billion-dollar ski industry is a yellowing piece of black-and-white nostalgia, extremely far removed from the chic, trendy sport of the 21st century. Those pioneer days—before grooming and lift lines, when the patrons of the sport all knew each other—are as extinct as the covered wagon or the horse and carriage. This is what I had thought, at least, until Minna Gynther and I boarded an Aeroflot time machine that carried us to Central Asia, taking us 50 years back in time in the process.

Our first stop was Kyrgyzstan, a small, landlocked former member of the Soviet Union, in which 70 percent of the land is over 3000 meters high! In this infant nation, not only skiing but also the society as a whole is in the pioneer stage of development. We found few hotels and restaurants, not much of a credit or banking system, and many roads where four-wheel drive is mandatory for all vehicles, but horses are still the more common mode of transportation.

In his book, *Central Asia*, author Giles Whittell quotes one of Gorbachev's aides in 1991, at a time when the Soviet Union was beginning to unravel at the seams. According to Whittell, when asked about travel regulations by a visiting journalist, "the aide grinned, sighed, and replied, 'Gentlemen, there are no rules here any more!'"

This bit of wisdom was still applicable when we traveled in Kyrgyzstan. With the KGB and the long, strong arm of Russia no longer on the scene, life here resembled Dodge City without Wyatt Earp. Don't plan past today with any sense of security, expect the unexpected, and go with the flow.

Upon our arrival in Kyrgyzstan, a Lada jeep transported Minna and me *almost* the entire 30 kilometers from the capital, Bishkek, to the "ski resort" of Kashka-Suu. Forty centimeters of snow on the road and the lack of local snowplows dictated that the last 45 minutes of our journey was on foot!

Kashka-Suu has only two lifts, an old rope tow and a double chair lift. The bad news was that only the rope tow was operating, offering about 250 vertical meters of skiing. The good news was that there were only ten other skiers to share the powder with us. Even with only one lift working, that translated into two days of fresh tracks.

The power inexplicably shut down between two and four o'clock on the second day, and I asked our guide, Genia, for an explanation. His simple answer helped us reorient our frame of reference for the rest of our trip.

He just shrugged his shoulders and said, "This is Asia!"

»... a former member of the Soviet Union, in which 70 percent of the land is over 3000 meters high!«

No more explanation is ever necessary to account for the curious, the unreasonable or the bizarre in this corner of the world.

During the following days, we enjoyed the same wonderful, light powder in the likes of Kizil-Beles and Oru-Sai, just a few kilometers from Kashka-Suu. We laughed until we almost cried at some of the primitive lift arrangements. When using the local rope tows, instead of a lift ticket, one received a 25-centimeter-long stick attached to a nylon cord with a hook at the end. The stick was to be placed between one's legs, the hook was meant to hang over the wire cable of the lift, and with a lot of practice, we eventually learned how to reach the top without the hook falling off.

Even more amusing than the rope tows was the Russian-built platter-pull lift in Oru-Sai. The disk that we placed between our legs was somewhat larger than that of a French Poma lift, and the springs were a bit older. Otherwise, the contraption seemed quite like its Western counterpart—until our skis left the ground! All of a sudden, we found ourselves dangling 3–4 meters in the air, as if we were riding on some strange Asian amusement-park attraction.

The pioneer spirit again came over me. What a joy it was to get down to the grassroots of skiing, far from the crowds, the hype and the commercialism.

PIONEERS ARE ALWAYS ON THE MOVE, and we soon headed further east, along the shore of Lake Issyk-Kul. One of the largest and deepest sweetwater lakes in the world, Issyk-Kul covers 6200 square kilometers, and despite the harsh cold here, it never freezes. The locals claim that the 700-meter-deep lake is warmed by the Earth's core.

We circumvented this giant swimming pool, and drove to the town of Karakol and a nearby ski center of the same name. It had been touted as the best ski region in the country, with about 900 vertical meters of skiing.

As usual, things did not turn out quite as expected. The motors of the two upper lifts had recently been stolen to sell copper parts to nearby China. This cut the vertical drop down to 500 meters. The lower lift was also out of service for some reason known only to God and the ghost of Joseph Stalin. The one remaining lift was in the process of being repaired, and would be operational again at about 1:30 in the afternoon. This was not our lucky day!

The good news was that the sun was shining, and by that time we had grown accustomed to the fact that, as Genia had pointed out earlier, this was Asia. Ultimately, we managed to ski for 3 hours in the afternoon.

That evening, we were taken to dinner by the local director of tourism, but we did not fare much better than at the ski area. The first three restaurants to which he chose to take us were all closed. When we finally got a meal at his fourth choice, he apologized and explained sheepishly that of the approximately 400 tourists who come here annually, only about ten foreigners a year visit during the winter!

THIS PAGE
UPPER: Local skier observes Minna as she arrives at the top of the rope tow in Kashka-Suu.
LOWER: One of the highlights of a trip along the old Silk Road is the Ark in Bukhara, Uzbekistan.

RIGHT PAGE
These locals in the town of Karakol show that the horse is still the most popular way to get around in the eastern part of Kyrgyzstan.

Chapter 37. UZBEKISTAN
SKIING THE OLD SILK ROAD

With the wisdom of Mr. Whittell and Genia in mind, Minna and I now headed on to the neighboring country of Uzbekistan. In contrast to the infant democracy in agrarian Kyrgyzstan, Uzbekistan is an authoritarian, communist stronghold with a mix of industry and agriculture.

The Tien Shan and Pamir Mountains in the east give way to large deserts in the central and western parts of the nation. Here lie some of the major watering holes of the old Silk Road, for over 2000 years the major artery connecting Europe with China. The Uzbek cities of Samarkand, Bukhara and Khiva are fascinating, living proof of these bygone days when caravans and conquerors blazed a trail of trade and terror along this route.

The best skiing in Uzbekistan, perhaps in all of Central Asia, is a little area about 80 kilometers from Tashkent called Beldersay. As usual, the infrastructure was lacking here. There was no public transport to the skiing, there was no hotel at the base of the mountain, and it was definitely a bring-your-own-lunch type of place. The absence of infrastructure, however, stood in marked contrast to the double chair lift, the Doppelmayr T-bar, the 800-meter vertical drop, and the immense amount of off-piste skiing.

As in most of Central Asia (and parts of Eastern Europe), the lifts here operate on a kind of quorum system—they open if and when there have arrived a sufficient number of guests to make the day's work a viable economic proposition. On our first morning, we arrived at the supposed opening time of nine o'clock, and the chair lift began operating at 10:30. It didn't matter. The gods had smiled upon us again with a dump of fresh snow, and either way, we were in position for first tracks.

There were a number of rather steep ravines and ridges on the upper mountain, and we satisfied ourselves with decorating the hill with snake tracks all morning long.

At 2:30, the quorum method went back into effect. The weather was cloudy, it had begun to snow again, and many of the 30–40 paying customers had headed for home. The visibility was still adequate, there was plenty of untouched powder left, and we were not ready to sit by the hearth.

My intuition told me that corruption was the answer to this problem. I was right. A small bribe did the trick and kept the lifts open for another hour of powder skiing.

The extra time we had "bought" proved to be profitable. We met Alexander Chopikov, a local mountain man who had built a house on the slopes and was a kind of de facto one-man ski school, mountain-guide service, and ski patrol. He kindly led us to a few additional powder-filled gullies, and pointed out a long off-piste route that led almost all the way to the bottom of the mountain. He had given us enough fodder to keep us busy for a few days.

AFTER GETTING OUR FILL of Uzbek skiing, it came time to move from our newly found powder routes to the ancient Silk Route. Our rented van descended from the Zerafshan Mountains and took us westward toward Samarkand.

Alexander the Great passed this way in 329 B.C. and stated, "Everything I have heard about the beauty of Samarkand is true—except that it is even more beautiful than I could have imagined."

The ruthless Genghis Khan razed much of the city and massacred most of its inhabitants in the 1200s, and the equally evil Tamarlane made it the capital of his bloody empire a century later.

The center of modern day Samarkand is Registan Square, surrounded on three sides by *madrasahs* (Islamic seminaries) and minarets, the earliest of which dates back to the early 15th century. These grandiose structures are covered by intricate mosaic patterns of midnight blue, turquoise, white and other colors mixed in a work of art and architecture which makes the Taj Majal pale by comparison. Registan Square is the most impressive of many beautiful relics of the Silk Route, including Gur Emir Mausoleum (Tamarlane's tomb) and the Bibi Khanym Mosque, also in Samarkand.

Not too far away from Samarkand is Bukhara, where the remains of years gone by are highlighted by the 2000-year-old fortification known as the Ark, and the Kalyan Minaret, possibly the tallest manmade structure in the world when it was erected around 900 years ago. Even Genghis Khan did not have the heart to topple this tower when he destroyed the rest of Bukhara.

Skiers may not travel the distance or brave the uncertainties of a vacation in Uzbekistan merely for the opportunity to ski in Beldersay. Nevertheless, the combination of a fabled history, so well-preserved in the towns and cities of the old Silk Road, and the good skiing at this little Asian ski resort make a combined ski and sightseeing trip to this region very worthwhile.

THIS PAGE
LEFT: Proud Uzbek man in Bukhara still wears his war medals.
MIDDLE: Sign advertising Beldersay (most common spelling is with a "y"), with the mountain just behind. There is some very good off-piste skiing on the mountain.
RIGHT: Lift operators work on the broken lift in Beldersay. We were back in action after no more than 30–40 minutes.

RIGHT PAGE
Sher Dor *madrasah* (1619-1635), designed by architect Abdujabor, one of three magnificent *madrasah*s that adorn Registan Square in Samarkand.

Chapter 38. KAZAKHSTAN

HELISKIING THE HEAVENS

While Kyrgyzstan and Uzbekistan are relatively small countries, Kazakhstan is a huge nation, covering an area the size of Western Europe. It is also the fourth largest nuclear power in the world. Ninety percent of the country is grassland, but in the southeastern section, near the capital of Almaty, lies the northern slope of the Tien Shan Mountains. The peaks rise majestically on the outskirts of the city in this corner of Kazakhstan and fill the region to the Chinese border and beyond.

Fitzroy Maclean, diplomat and writer, arrived by train in Almaty in the late 1930s, and described his first impressions thus: "Far to the south, dimly seen in the remote distance, towering high above the desert, rose a mighty range of mountains, their lower slopes veiled in cloud and vapors, their snow-clad peaks glittering in the sunlight, suspended between earth and sky...The tree-covered foothills of the Tien Shan rose steeply toward the snow-covered peaks behind them. I was in Central Asia."

The green, tree-clad mounds of earth that Maclean called "foothills" are actually mountains in their own right, attaining elevations of 3000 meters. Yet, they appear to be mere hills compared to the towering Tien Shan or "Celestial Mountains", which stretch up to the heavens behind them. The "foothills" are but a staircase to the white world of glaciated six- and seven-thousand-meter monsters that lie beyond.

Here in Kazakhstan, from atop a wide choice of nameless peaks, there are spectacular views over Kyrgyzstan, Kazakhstan and China. In the blink of an eye one can behold the world's two northernmost 7000-meter peaks, a glacier which is over 50 kilometers long, and a lake full of icebergs which does a Houdini act every August and vanishes, only to reappear again the following year. If all this is not enough to get the adrenaline flowing, there is skiing to be had amidst the seracs of eternal ice almost in the shadow of these 7000-meter monoliths.

900-vertical-meter runs where generations of Soviet ski teams had trained and raced over the years.

The following day we were greeted by 30 centimeters of fresh powder and a healthy Saturday-morning turnout of skiers. Whilst the locals stayed on the piste, Minna and I spent the morning cutting up the fresh snow.

At lunch, we met Ian de Renzie Duncan, an immigrant ski pioneer, not unlike my mother, but about 60 years later and half a world away. Renzie, as he is called, came to Almaty from Australia to work as a lawyer for a multinational firm. A former member of the Australian National Team, he spent many of his weekends in Chimbulak. The ski area had no ski school at the time, and when Renzie's legal work dried up, a 3-minute chat with the director of the ski center got him the okay to start one.

Again, a sense of the Wild West was evident. Gone were the days of the tedious legal roadblocks of Soviet bureaucracy, having been replaced by an entrepreneurial climate, in which the only thing that stood between a new idea and its realization was the elbow grease to make it happen. After getting his permission, Renzie rolled up his sleeves and built a small shack at the base of the lifts, and his new ski school was born.

After lunch, Renzie cut us in front of the lift line, and told me a bit more about his pioneering effort.

"On the weekends, we have some pretty horrific queues here, and I wondered to myself, 'How am I gonna cut line all winter?' Beginning a ski school was the answer. They really need it, as you can see, looking at some of our protégés. Now, we have two Americans, two Frenchmen, a Kazakh and nine Russian instructors, in addition to myself. We haven't made any money to speak of yet, but it really doesn't matter."

By now, we had reached the top of the lift, and Renzie led us into a small valley on the western side of the ski area. Virgin powder beat a rhythmic melody against our chests all the way down to the base of the lift. I could understand why the money didn't really matter. What mattered was making first tracks in a virgin valley, cutting lift lines, and being part of the small and cozy community of skiers who greeted Renzie wherever he went. Renzie felt a sense of belonging and contributing to an infant sport in a newborn country, a pioneer at the edge of a new frontier. Such an opportunity is hard to find in this day and age, and *that* was what really mattered.

KAN TENGRI MOUNTAIN SERVICE

While Chimbulak is the only bona fide ski resort in the country, the wonderful world of helicopters turns the Tien Shan mountains into a kind of fantasyland for skiers. Later that year, in August, an Aeroflot jet returned me to Almaty, so that I could attempt to enter that dream world.

At the airport, I was picked up by Kan Tengri Mountain Service, which transported me in an old Russian military transport vehicle for 5 hours into ever more desolate terrain. Every now and then, a nomad's yurt could be seen alone amidst the vast, hilly grasslands, like a small boat in the Pacific, with no other sign of human life from horizon to horizon. In early evening, I was deposited at Karkara Base Camp, a small enclave of about 30 tents, situated in a beautiful mountain meadow, 2200 meters above sea level.

The grassy slopes around were covered with wildflowers. Edelweiss, so rare in the Alps, blanketed the fields as daisies might do at home, and pine forests dotted the surrounding slopes for about 500 vertical meters. Above that point, the trees ceased, but the mountains continued upward. These were the "foothills" referred to by Maclean, and to the south, a few snow-covered tops were visible.

My tent looked down on the green Karkara River that marks the border between Kazakhstan and Kyrgyzstan, and a small cluster of Kyrgyz farmhouses were sprinkled along the opposite bank of the river. Tomorrow, a helicopter would transport us into a region that had been off limits, even to the local people, for most of the 20th century. I stood silently by my tent, here at the perimeter of one of the highest mountain ranges in the world and pondered my good fortune.

Very few people on Earth have ever set eyes on this astonishing corner of the world, and still fewer can call themselves familiar with the area. One person who falls into the latter category is Kazbek Valiev, Kazakh

CHIMBULAK

The only ski resort in Kazakhstan, Chimbulak, lies a convenient half-hour from Almaty. There was no bus service all the way from town to the ski area, and as we drove up, we noticed a number of dedicated but clearly less-than-wealthy skiers walking the last hour of road to get to the lifts. On the other hand, the parking lot displayed a showroom selection of spanking new Pajeros, Chevy vans, and Grand Cherokee four-by-fours.

Evidence of the new capitalist wave was everywhere. In the lunch restaurant, the Marlboro cowboy and the Camel man tried to out-stare each other from opposite walls. Signs and ads of all sizes, preaching the merits of Absolut vodka, Snickers and Lange ski boots were displayed in abundance. While the ads were all brand new, one could not say the same for the ski facilities. Nevertheless, with a handful of lifts, two restaurants, a hotel and a ski school, Chimbulak is blessed with the best infrastructure of any ski area in Central Asia.

Minna and I arrived on a Friday, and we had very little company as we rode the lifts to the strains of Western pop music wailing through speakers hanging from every lift tower. We skied almost alone down the

climber supreme, who has conquered Mt. Khan Tengri (7010 m) and Pik Pobedy (7439 m) here in the Tien Shan, as well as Mt. Everest and nineteen other mountains of 7000 meters or more. Valiev now operates Kan Tengri Mountain Service, a company that gives climbers and trekkers as well as skiers the chance to experience this region that is so dear to his heart. For skiers, Kazbek has put together probably the most unusual heliskiing program in the world. It is a summer program, which, weather permitting, climaxes with a descent from the dizzying top of Mt. Semyonov at 5816 meters.

This is no ordinary mountain playground, and the people who visit here are, understandably, not your average tourists. During our first dinner at the base camp restaurant, there were guests from as far afield as Austria, Switzerland, France, Germany, Italy, Spain, Russia, Japan, America and Australia. Many lively stories were exchanged over a traditional Russian meal of *shashlik* as we all got to know one another.

I spoke with an elderly Italian man who told me of having skied from the top of Mustagh Ata, a Chinese colossus of 7546 meters. This is quite a feat in itself, but he had done it at the age of 60! I turned to my left and chatted a bit with a young lady who was just returning from a trekking adventure. She was Petra Kronberger, Austrian Olympic skiing gold medalist.

The group with whom I would ski was interesting as well. More than half of them had worked as ski instructors or mountain guides in the Alps. I was also surprised to meet 60-year-old Hilde Braun of Germany and her husband, 69-year-old Peter. This was definitely not the age group I had expected on a ski adventure in the rarified atmosphere above 5000 meters, but in spite of their age, they were probably more qualified than I for the endeavor we were soon to embark upon.

Hilde had been on the German National Ski Team. In 1953, she had

swept the board with gold medals in the slalom, giant slalom and downhill at the Student Skiing World Championships. As for Peter, our upcoming adventure would probably seem as tame to him as a Sunday walk in the park. He had been a part of history's first expedition to conquer Mt. Dhaulagiri in Nepal in 1953. Among the hardships his team had encountered was a 20-kilometer stretch of thick jungle that took a full sixteen days to hack through. While they did not attain the summit, they did reach the lofty height of 7700 meters.

So we had a good lineup of participants for such a specialized skiing adventure, possessing an abundance of mountain knowledge among us as well as a proper understanding that this was a far cry from ordinary skiing. The rewards as well as the perils on a ski trip like this are more similar to those usually found in mountain climbing, and the people comprising our group were well aware of that fact.

The following morning, we piled our skis and ourselves into an orange monster which had the faded words "Kazakhstan Airlines" barely legible in blue lettering on the side. The Mi-8 MTB was an important part of the ill-fated Soviet campaign in the mountains of Afghanistan, for it is specially suited for high-altitude flying. Used for skiing, this chopper can carry ten skiers and their gear as high as 6000 meters! Compared to the sleek, four-passenger Lama whirlybirds used for heliskiing in nearby India, the Mi-8 MTB looks like a pterodactyl, but it is a very capable beast.

HALF AN HOUR AFTER LIFT-OFF, we were set down on a peak of approximately the elevation of Mt. Blanc. I asked Kazbek the name of this mountain, and he explained that this top was so low (4700 m) that nobody had bothered to name it! The peak may well have been anonymous, but my lungs and head told me that it definitely wasn't "low". My head was light, and my breathing was heavy, even before I started to exert myself skiing. Here, I required a rest after simply buckling my boots.

What breath I had was taken away by the surrounding scenery. Kazakhstan has 2700 glaciers, and it seemed as if we could see all of them from here. Seracs glistened in the sun all around us, and a minefield of crevasses yawned lazily like giant Venus flytraps waiting for an unsuspecting victim to venture too close.

It was not the visible crevasses that worried me, it was the ones I could

not see that gnawed on my brain. We were all outfitted not only with avalanche transceivers, but also with harnesses bearing carabiners, a precaution necessitated by the largely unexplored glacial terrain.

"Follow the guide's tracks closely, stay constantly alert, and by all means, don't fall," I thought to myself. This was a preferable plan to testing the harness. Here, a fall which, under ordinary circumstances, might carry a skier on a harmless 10-meter slide, could be fatal. Our margin for error was often much less than 10 meters.

We began our descent along the ridge of the mountain. To the right, the ice dropped off in a blue cliff. It was the middle of summer, but at this elevation, it snows often and we skied in 15 centimeters of powder. On the ridge, however, the snow was wind packed.

The imperative goal of not falling weighed heavily on my mind, and I negotiated each turn on the windblown ridge with trepidation. Suddenly

my tips crossed, and I went head over heels down the slope for a short distance. I was okay, but Roland, our Swiss guide, immediately warned me what I already knew.

"Jimmy, don't fall!" he shouted succinctly.

We continued to thread our way between the obstacles, holding closely to the tracks of Oleg, our Kazakh guide. Soon we arrived at a slope with a much wider area of safety, and Oleg told us that we could spread out and enjoy making first tracks in the fresh snow. The slope had been protected from the wind, and the snow was perfect, but I still did not have much stamina. Ten turns were easy, but by turn twenty, I was laboring, and after 30 turns, a lactic-acid attack ground me to a halt. I lurched to a stop, accompanied by a soundtrack of heavy breathing right out of a porno film.

Our day continued like this, with wind crust on the upper slopes and

powder lower down. We skied five more descents averaging 600 vertical meters per run, and everybody was drained by the time we headed home. It had been both exhilarating and exhausting. As I relaxed in my tent back in Karkara, I felt as if I had completed the first day of boot camp in the marines. The day had offered sections of skiing that were sensational and others that were mere self-preservation, and I wondered with great anticipation what the morrow would bring.

For the next two days, overcast skies covered Karkara, and snow fell in the high mountains. Our "whirlybeast" was grounded, and we had a chance to go horseback riding instead. Throughout history, the Kazakh people have been renowned horsemen, and in this part of the country, the horse is without question the main means of transportation.

One of the locals brought some horses to the camp, and we headed up into the high meadows above the tree line. From there, the vastness of Central Asia could really be appreciated. Lush, green, empty land stretched as far as the eye could see. We could ride to the horizon ten times in each direction, and still look out over a landscape almost devoid of human trespassers. It was a staggering thought. The face of this huge expanse of land had not changed for a thousand years and more.

I gazed out over the countryside and visualized an immense cloud of dust rising skyward, many kilometers away. The dust rose higher in the sky, and I could hear the soft thunder of thousands of horses' hooves pounding the turf in unison. This continuous din became ever louder until it was almost unbearable. Genghis Khan led his Mongol hordes straight into my imagination, as I sat silently surveying the land that he once ruled. We were perhaps the fifth group ever to ski in this region, so it was not so strange that a sense of history easily swept into my mind amidst the grandeur of the surroundings.

DAY FOUR WAS CRYSTAL CLEAR, new snow was sprinkled even on the tops of the foothills, and our air taxi was back in action. The panorama from the helicopter was spectacular. All of us bounced from one side of the chop-

LEFT PAGE
The heliskiing in Kazakhstan included some fantastically steep terrain.

THIS PAGE
UPPER LEFT: Merzbacher Lake, named after German explorer Gottfried Merzbacher, who discovered the lake in 1903. Every summer, an ice plug melts and the water of the lake drains out under the tongue of the North Inylchek Glacier.
UPPER RIGHT: Part of the Inylchek Glacier and Khan Tengri, on the right side of the glacier.
LOWER LEFT: Market place in Almaty—anybody interested in a nice horse-head dinner tonight?
LOWER RIGHT: One can still see a lone yurt tent here and there among the grasslands and mountains of Kazakhstan.

per to the other like Ping-Pong balls in a wind tunnel, trying not to miss a view from either side.

We passed over high plateaus and immense river valleys where the water was a silver snake, shimmering in the sun. Soon, the landscape became entirely white. Below us were enormous glacial cirques and hanging glaciers, while up ahead, looming ever closer, were Khan Tengri and Pik Pobedy. The altimeter showed 5230 meters as we touched down atop still another no-name peak.

"This is only a warmup!" said Kazbek, with a grin. "You can ski some named summits later!"

As on our first day, the upper exposed slopes were windblown, and the lower sections were good powder. We were now higher and the runs were longer than the day before, and I was still breathing like a dinosaur in heat. What we were doing bore little resemblance to ordinary skiing, and was actually a far cry from heliskiing elsewhere in the world. Here, one did not worry about style, but rather skied a technique of function and safety. Conserve energy and avoid falling.

There is one danger, however, that even the most careful technique cannot always avoid. Shortly after beginning our second run, Oleg, who was leading the group, broke off a large slab avalanche. As we looked on in horror, he was carried down the mountain and out of our sight. The avalanche cascaded down amidst a sea of glacial ice, and we hoped to God

Enormous glacial seracs tower above the skiers heliskiing in Kazakhstan.

that he had not been buried or swept into a crevasse.

In a chaotic descent, we tried incongruously to combine speed with caution. As quickly as possible, we followed in the wake of the avalanche, but still it took quite a few minutes to reach the next hump in the glacier from where we could see Oleg's fate. Everyone breathed a heavy sigh of relief to see our guide standing, shaken and without his skis, but nevertheless in one piece. It had been a shocking reminder that this was, in fact, a skiing expedition, and not a day of pleasure skiing.

The afternoon did not pass without event either. We landed atop Pik Ignatiev, at 5488 meters the highest elevation most of us had ever reached. After skiing just a few hundred meters, one of the Austrians was close to blacking out. He was feeling sick and scared, and he began to hyperventilate. Fortunately, Peter Braun was not only an experienced mountaineer, but a doctor as well. He gave our disabled companion a tablet to relax him along with some calming words, and we were soon able to negotiate Pik Ignatiev successfully.

> **» Just like a giant bathtub, the lake drains out under the North Inylchek Glacier…«**

Following yet another storm came our final ski day. The additional new snow in conjunction with the avalanche earlier in the trip left me with grave doubts about the prudence of attempting to ski a run from the summit of Pik Semyonov (5816 m). I considered the avalanche danger and took the difficult decision not join the group.

Ultimately, the Pik Semyonov descent was called off after yet another avalanche had been set off by one of the guides. Discretion is often the better part of valor, and I believe that I sensed, among the group, a slight feeling of relief, rather than disappointment, in the decision not to press on to our original goal. The last snowfall had brought the powder on the wind-protected slopes to a depth of 30–40 centimeters and our entourage satisfied itself with some excellent powder on the lower slopes.

MY FINAL DAY WAS CLIMAXED by an afternoon journey with the helicopter into the climbers' base camps for Khan Tengri, Pik Pobedy and Mramornaya. First, we flew over the magical Lake Merzbacher. Here, each August, an ice plug melts. Just like a giant bathtub, the lake drains out under the North Inylchek Glacier, creating geyser-like fountains that spew out water through holes in the ice further down the glacier. Three days later, the lake is empty.

Next, we landed at the base camp for Pik Pobedy, situated right on the South Inylchek Glacier. This is the second largest ice flow in the CIS (Commonwealth of Independent States) countries, a veritable river of ice more than a kilometer wide that winds for over 50 kilometers between two immense ridges of the Tien Shan.

Soon after, we landed near the foot of Khan Tengri, the pyramidal peak whose northern wall is made up of yellow marble, and which many climbers consider to be the most beautiful mountain in the world. In fact, when the sun's last rays shine on the marble of the upper mountain, the crimson color that often appears has inspired legends and sagas for hundreds of years. My whistle-stop tour of these base camps provided one high point after another, a fitting finale to a journey that had had its share of highs and lows, exhilaration and exhaustion, risks and rewards.

After the sun had set on our final evening in Karkara, I had five hours of bumpy road to Almaty during which to contemplate and internalize our entire experience. I had experienced skiing as I had never done before—high altitude skiing—where certain risks unavoidably go with the territory.

The reward was not the usual exhilaration of having powder explode in one's face at the nadir of every turn, or the sensation of effortlessly floating down a slope of bottomless fluff. Instead, the skiing was often a struggle through difficult snow along with a constant battle for oxygen. Hence, the compensation here was different.

One of the payoffs was the sense of being awed and mesmerized by the unique scenery around us. Another reward was the sense of achievement, skiing in a region where very few people had ever ventured and at altitudes at which only a handful of humans had ever skied. Perhaps the ultimate payoff, however, was the one that goes hand in hand with the element of risk. It is a reward well-know to the climber, but not so often familiar to the skier—the feeling of survival.

THIS PAGE: Sunset over the Taj Mahal.
RIGHT PAGE: UPPER: Sylvain Saudan coordinating his heliski operation in Kashmir. Perhaps he is speaking with a yeti. LOWER: Uwe Bauer follows very closely behind guide Pierrick Colin as they weave through a field of crevasses.

Chapter 39. INDIA

Mark Twain once said, "India is a land all men long to see, and having had a glimpse, would not trade for all the world's sights." Mr. Twain was certainly close to the "mark", so to speak, but the experience of India is not only visual. One sees, hears, tastes, smells and feels India with every part of one's body, for better and for worse, 24 hours a day. Skiing in many parts of the world is strictly a ski experience. In India, however, you cannot divorce the skiing from the country, and that is certainly part of the adventure.

The smells of India inundate a visitor from all sides. One passes by a spice shop and the essence of turmeric powder, chili and ginger fill one's nostrils. In the mountain villages, the smoky smell of burning coal and pine wafts through the streets, as people start building small fires to stave off the evening chill. The pungent odor of human and animal excrement drift periodically up from the side of the road, and the sharp, distinct smell of incense of various sorts permeates the air as one walks past small temples and mosques.

Add to this the sounds of the market place, the taste of a lamb curry or tandoori chicken, and the contrasting effects that the humid heat of Bombay and the dry cold of the Himalaya Mountains have on one's body, and you have India in a nutshell.

Few countries have more mountains than India, and no nation can really claim to have a more spectacular range than the Himalayas. Yet the skiing possibilities here are somewhat limited because of the lack of infrastructure.

Just a short drive from Srinigar, at an elevation of 2730 meters, lies Gulmarg, the only bona fide ski resort in India. For many years, Gulmarg's slopes were suitable primarily for novices, with one short chair lift and a few rope tows and T-bars providing the uphill transportation. An ambitious project to build a gondola to the top of Mt. Afarwat (4390 m) was set into motion in 1990, but work was halted by the years of civil strife in Kashmir.

Since 2003, the political situation has been improving dramatically and the hotels and restaurants of Srinigar are again bustling with tourists from all over India and the rest of the world. In the spring of 2005, after 15 years of waiting, the Mt. Afarwat gondola project was finally completed, giving Gulmarg one of the highest ski lifts in the world and a world-class 1660 vertical meters of skiing.

Ski touring is another way for expert skiers to enjoy the Himalayas. Aside from Gulmarg, there are also good touring possibilities in the Sangla Valley and various other areas of India.

Those advanced skiers who are not willing to break trail and break a sweat can turn to one of the heliskiing operations here to get a true taste of what India's Himalayas have to offer. They can choose from Sylvain Saudan's heliskiing trips based in Srinigar or Roddy Mackenzie's Himachal Heliski operation near Manali. Either option offers the adventure of a lifetime.

KASHMIR — IN SEARCH OF THE YETI WITH SYLVAIN SAUDAN

In Nepal, the people know what you are talking about if you ask about the yeti. In the Himalayas of Pakistan, he is called the "snowman", and in Kashmir, the local people know him as *von muhnue*, which means "forest man". His name may vary from place to place, but wherever Himalayan villages appear at the upper end of isolated mountain valleys, he has a name. A few of the village elders often have tales about the yeti, but the younger generation is most often very reluctant to believe in anything that they have never seen.

In the West, the reluctance is the same. Every now and then, a story about the yeti appears in one of the rather disreputable tabloids, accompanied by a gorilla photo that has been retouched. Such a picture is likely to appear next to similarly tampered photos of the Loch Ness monster and a report that Elvis is alive, living as a Buddhist monk in Tibet. These kinds of reports tend to discredit rather than confirm the existence of the yeti. Nevertheless, the sightings and incidents involving this mysterious animal continue to occur periodically, and the myth (or is it a myth?) persists.

In 1988, the legendary father of extreme skiing, Sylvain Saudan, almost a myth himself, began running a helicopter skiing operation in the Himalayas of Kashmir. Since then, Sylvain has been guiding people down countless slopes, gullies, ridges and valleys of Kashmir, whenever the civil strife in the region has allowed. Not too long ago, Sylvain discovered something to add to the yeti lore.

I had not seen Sylvain since my first visit to ski with him in Kashmir, and I phoned his home in Chamonix to hear what was new. With Sylvain Saudan, you can bet there is always something new, and this was no exception.

"Allo, Jeemmy," he said, "Eet 'as been a long time seence you 'ave veesit me in Kashmir. A lot has been going on here seence zat time. Not so long ago, I saw zee tracks of zee yeti. I 'ave taken zee photographs," he reported excitedly. "But you must come and see for yourself 'ow eet ees

now. Can you not come and veezit me in Kashmir zees winter?"

I thanked Sylvain for the invitation and said I would love to come if I had the time.

A few months later, my friend Papi and I arrived in Kashmir's capital, Srinigar. As we drove to Sylvain's headquarters in the Hotel Centaur, the splendor of Srinigar came into full view. The city is built on the shores of Daal Lake and surrounded by the snow-covered Himalayas. On the lake float many hundreds of houseboats—some primitive ones which house local families and many luxurious ones which cater to both Western and Indian tourists.

Many of the houseboats are decorated with ornate woodcarvings and furnished with exquisite Kashmir rugs and hand-carved furniture. Along the shoreline, the apple and almond trees were full of the white blossoms of spring, and all over the lake, gondola-like boats called *shikaras* added to the local color, as they ferried goods and passengers to and from the shops and houseboats.

But Srinigar appeared immediately different from five years earlier, when I had previously visited this exotic location. The evidence of the insurgent independence movement was everywhere. Armed Indian soldiers could be seen patrolling the main streets every 50 meters or so, and tourists seemed to be as scarce as a snowstorm in July. Many hotels and restaurants were closed for lack of business, and the lovely houseboats lay idly in the water with nobody to appreciate their unique charm. (This is no longer the case today. Since the time of my last visit, hostilities have officially ceased, and Kashmir is back on the tourist map.)

Our taxi pulled up to the gates of the Hotel Centaur, where soldiers, protected behind bunkers of sandbags, checked our papers. The once-proud Centaur, which had boasted five stars a few years earlier, hardly resembled its former self. There was nobody at the front desk, and the hotel bar no longer existed. I saw not a soul in a hotel uniform. Two large army tents were set up in the courtyard, and a couple dozen soldiers stood at ease, listening to their commander.

Our group of heliskiers made up the Centaur's only true guests, sharing the accommodation with about 75 Indian government functionaries. The rest of the hotel's 250 beds remained empty. Sylvain seemed to run a small hotel within the Centaur, with a hand-picked staff. Rassol, one of Sylvain's staff, led us down what had once been a stately hallway.

Thirty-four ceiling lamps hung in place to light this long passageway, but only a lone light bulb functioned, casting a ghostly aura over the scene. Some of the windows that overlook the courtyard were broken and the carpeting underfoot looked as if it had spent some time at the murky bottom of Daal Lake. Rassol led us to our suite at the end of the hall. Inside the suite, the rooms were warm and friendly, and our balcony offered a stunning view of the lake and the Himalayas.

"Come, I will take you to Sylvain," said Rassol, and he led us out to the hotel garden.

"Allo, Jeemy! *Ça va*?" greeted my ears, and our host greeted me with a handshake and hug. Srinigar seemed different and the Hotel Centaur was very different, but I was happy to see that Sylvain had not changed much since I had last seen him. He still looked like he could sling his skis and rucksack onto his back and head up 8068-meter-high Hidden Peak with no trouble at all. His face looked healthy and well tanned, and his boyish grin and hearty laugh told me immediately that this man's lust for life was every bit as intense as when we had first met.

"How is the yeti?" I grinned back at Sylvain.

"I zink he is okay. We start zee search tomorrow," he retorted, "but I hope we find zee female. She is much more fun!" he laughed.

Breakfast was at seven o'clock, and our Heli Union Lama helicopter took the first group up at 7:30 a.m. April, according to Sylvain, was the ideal time to find yeti tracks. The powder snow of winter gets blown around by the wind, destroying any possible tracks, while the corn snow of April is more likely to keep the tracks intact for a longer time.

We found no sign of the yeti our first day, but we did locate some very nice spring snow. The day was cloudy, allowing us to ski corn snow until three o'clock before it got too soft.

Directly after skiing, Sylvain left us briefly to prepare *Glühwein* for our après-ski. After an hour or so, our host disappeared again, and at dinner, we were treated to pasta à la Sylvain. In between his guiding, cooking and organizing, Sylvain kept everybody well entertained with a seemingly endless stream of amazing and humorous anecdotes.

Morning number two was crystal clear. The rising sun set the snow-covered mountains in the distance ablaze with light long before it appeared over the horizon, and the lake was mirror calm. We headed for higher ground in search of powder and of course the yeti. As Sylvain conferred with the pilot, he acted like a little boy in a candy store.

"Look out zere!" he exclaimed. "Zee possibilities are endless. We could ski here zee rest of our lives, and 'ave new places to try every day!"

Our leader guided us from a myriad of towering peaks, over ancient glaciers and through anonymous valleys. On our third run, he casually mentioned, "Zis is za first time we ski on zees place."

Suddenly, an awing thought came over me. Here, in the highest mountain range on Earth, we were standing where no person had previously set foot. I was about to leave my signature in the powder where no pair of boards had ever before cut a track into the snow.

It was a very special sensation, reaching beyond skiing and transporting me into a different realm of reality. I felt minute and insignificant amidst the tens of thousands of unnamed peaks and valleys. Yet, in the same instant, I felt unique and kingly, standing on the throne of Mother Nature's kingdom, on a small piece of real estate which was solely my own in all the annals of time.

I could savor my place in history only briefly, for soon we pushed

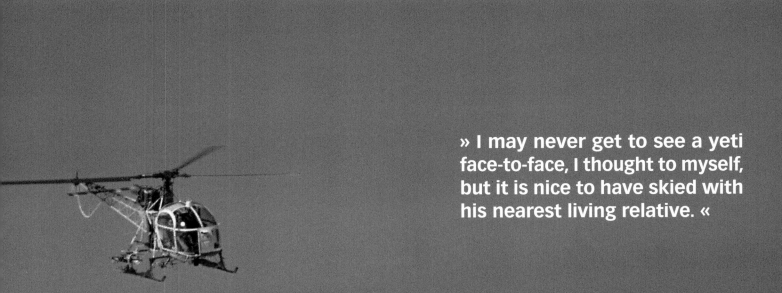

» I may never get to see a yeti face-to-face, I thought to myself, but it is nice to have skied with his nearest living relative. «

gently off into 30 centimeters of powder and 1000 vertical meters of virgin territory—virgin to man at least, but perhaps not to the yeti.

At lunch, I was able to hear more about Sylvain's yeti experience.

"At first, I zought eet was za track of zee man," he related. "I zink it 'as been a climber up here, for zee length ees similar. But, I notice zee width of zee foot ees quite a beet larger. Of course, zen we see zee shape ees no footprint of man.

"We closely follow zee prints and find zat whoever 'as made zees marks 'as climbed up from quite a sheer cleef. Zen, eet 'as walked through za snow around zee peak and made zee descent on zee ozer side, again down za almost vertical wall. We take many photographs of zee prints. I zend zee photos to laboratories in London and Parees, and zee National Geographic Society, and we get zee same reply from all three—'animal track—species unknown.'

"We abandoned skiing for zee day, and we search wiz zee 'elicopter for 2 hours, but we find nozzing more. But, I am quite sure eet ees zee yeti. In seven years 'ere, I 'ave never seen zee snow leopard, but I know he exist. I 'ave spoken weeth [world-famous mountain climber Reinhold] Messner, and he is also quite sure zee yeti ees real. Za older people in za villages, zey tell stories, but nobody believe."

SYLVAIN'S UNFLINCHING LOVE for the mountains and skiing is totally intertwined with his love of freedom. This fact gives Sylvain's heliski operation a style uniquely its own. He wants his guests also to enjoy the freedom that is the essence of skiing. Papi and I got a taste of that freedom at lunchtime.

"Jeemy," Sylvain said, "If you want a short lunch, you and Papi and zee German are zee competent skiers. Zee pilot can take you up on your own

There is no doubt that a helicopter is the best way to get around in the Himalayas of Kashmir.

LEFT PAGE
The heliskiing in Kashmir includes many dramatic runs on glaciers. Pierrick Colin leads us on this beautiful descent.

THIS PAGE
LEFT: In spring of 2005, the French project to build a gondola to the top of Mt. Afarwat in Gulmarg was finally completed after 15 years of snail-like progress. This photo depicts the state of affairs in 1994, at which time the project had been halted by the civil war in Kashmir, and gondolas lay around rusting away in the snow. Photo by Papi Tuomala.
RIGHT: The aftermath of the avalanche that almost killed our whole group.

a few times if you like, and you ski back each time to zee base camp 'ere."

A few minutes later, our threesome arrived back at the top. I kept my eyes peeled for any sign of the yeti but to no avail. The only tracks to be seen were our own. I must admit that my concentration on our elusive furry friend was soon distracted by the thrill of putting more tracks in the fresh powder. Four more afternoon runs, and we were ready for a cold beer on the hotel verandah.

As we enjoyed the afternoon sun, I queried Sylvain about the difficulty of keeping his operation running and profitable despite the extraordinary circumstances of civil strife and heavy military occupation.

"Oh, zees ees not bad at all, now," said Sylvain. "Eet ees quite calm now. Some years ago—zat was very treeky. We 'ad much trouble getting food. The bank was closed for zree weeks. You 'ave to be well organized to make zings work. My organization is Swiss, you know," he laughed, "and my laugh is French. Zere 'ave been deefficulties, but most of my guests are repeat customers because za skiing in Kashmir is very special, you know."

AN EQUALLY IMPORTANT FACT is that Sylvain Saudan is very special. His eternal optimism and nothing-is-impossible attitude is inspiring, his sense of humor is entertaining, and his charisma is magnetic.

That evening, a storm moved in, and like everything else in the Himalayas, it was larger than life. For the next days it poured in Srinigar, the wind whipped white-capped waves around the lake, and the skies dumped billions of tons of snow on the nearby mountains. Any possible yeti tracks that might have existed were once again obscured forever. Then, when we awoke on Thursday morning, as fast as it had appeared, the storm was gone.

All morning, we bounced gleefully through the powder. The uppermost segment was wide open and somewhat crusted, but only a hundred meters down, the crust dissipated entirely. I felt my skis really sinking into the powder…face shots…30 turns…my legs begged for mercy…40…my brain wanted more…50…lactic acid overdose…I had to stop…just for a minute…deep breaths. I bounced back into action…50 more undulations…and 50 more.

I approached the forest. Large birch trees grow about 300 meters higher than the pines here, and I started picking a path between the widely spaced birches. Then, before I knew it, I was back at the helicopter, ready for another lift to the top.

It was about noon, and we had just completed about our sixth run. I removed my skis and tied them in a bundle with the skis of the other skiers who were awaiting the next lift.

All of a sudden, our pilot's voice came through Sylvain's walkie-talkie, "*Attention*, Sylvain, *une avalanche grande*."

Ten of us looked up in horror to see the entire mountainside bearing down on us. A huge snow cloud was billowing 100 meters into the sky, and Sylvain shouted, "Quickly, everybody to za trees!"

I tried to run for the cover of the pines about 40 meters away, but the snow was deep and soft, and I was sinking in to my thighs. I crawled and groped. My ski boots felt like lead.

"Quickly, quickly!" I heard Sylvain again shouting to the group. I had no time to pause and look up, and yet as I clawed my way slowly forward, I could not help but glance up at the advancing monster. It was mesmerizing. The cloud of snow was now hundreds of meters high.

> **» I was still panting heavily from the longest 40 meters of my life.«**

I murmured out loud the only thought in my mind, "I'm dead!" Yet of course, I did not give up. I crept forward as fast as I could, like a World War I soldier slithering between two trenches. Every second was an eternity. Suddenly, I was there, huddled behind a huge pine tree trunk, gasping for air. Again I looked up at the massive snow cloud that now was almost upon us.

I wanted to hold my breath, but I had no breath to hold. I was still panting heavily from the longest 40 meters of my life. I prepared for the worst, and then I saw the snow cloud begin to disintegrate into thin air. I watched in silent terror as a massive wall of snow pushed slowly, relentlessly forward, just a stone's throw away from us. Within moments, it ground to a halt—a contorted, twisted pile of ice and snow, 8 meters high.

We surveyed the scene afterwards from the air, and saw that the avalanche had torn loose almost at the top of the mountain. The fracture line was about 1.5 meters deep and 300–400 meters wide. The avalanche had filled two valleys with snow and had tumbled and slid approximately 2000 vertical meters.

THAT EVENING, EVERYONE WAS GLAD to be alive, and there were many stories—Himalayan adventures, avalanche stories and tales of the yeti of course. Sylvain and his fellow guide, Jean Pierre, recounted their expedition to Hidden Peak. An earthquake had set off avalanches all over the range.

"Za mountains were coming down all around me," related Sylvain, "but for some reason, za place I stand did not slide. Our base camp was spared as well. Za avalanches were so large zat zee snow cloud fill zee air for 2 hours. Zere ees always some risk in za 'igh mountains. We try to minimize za risk, but we need to be lucky also," added Sylvain with the twinkle of a man who realized that he had more lives than a cat.

Then, one of the locals told of *rantas*, a female yeti, whom he described as having large breasts and hair all over her face and body. He had heard

THIS PAGE
UPPER: Sunrise over Daal Lake. A shikara waits along the shore to carry passengers to one of the houseboats visible in the background.
LOWER: Sunset on the lake.

RIGHT PAGE
Local man with his morning paper and his water pipe. Note that between his legs he has a "winter wife". A "winter wife" is a small pot of burning coals. Kashmiri men place the "winter wife" under their pheran (gown) to keep them warm. A woman's version is called a "winter husband".

from one of the old people in the town of Baramulla how *rantas* had kidnapped a man about 50 years earlier, forced him to have children with her and held him captive for many years. After fifteen years, the man escaped back to the town, and every night, *rantas* came to the village searching for him. Finally, the townspeople built a ring of fire around the entire community each night until *rantas* was forced to give up.

Our remaining days in Kashmir were filled with powder and corn snow, sometimes even on the same run, but not a sign of the wily yeti, and all too soon our stay was drawing to a close.

I spoke one more time to our host about the yeti before we departed.

"You know," said Sylvain, "he 'as managed for so long to avoid man's attempts at definitively proving hees existence. He 'as remained 'alf-myth,

'alf-mystery. Eet would almost be a shame for zat to change—but if someone will someday verify his being, I would prefer eet to be me."

"One last question, Sylvain," I said. "What if you saw the yeti, your camera malfunctioned, and you had a tranquilizer gun at your disposal? Would you..."

I could not finish my question before Sylvain interrupted, and the man whose love of freedom is so acute did not disappoint.

"Oh no, never," blurted Sylvain, and a strong sense of kinship became evident in his voice and eyes. "To photograph ees okay, but I would never take heem away from zee mountains."

I may never get to see a yeti face-to-face, I thought to myself, but it is nice to have skied with his nearest living relative.

THIS PAGE
UPPER: When I saw this stunning formation of glacial ice a couple hundred meters from where we were skiing, I asked our guide Pierrick if it was safe to ski in front of it so that I could get a photo. He answered, "I don't know. We have never skied zere, but it is okay for me. You are za photographer—you must ski first."
LOWER LEFT: Fruit salesman in Srinigar. LOWER RIGHT: During the time of our visit, sentries

guarded the Hotel Centaur because of the civil strife in Kashmir. Today, Kashmir is seeing a renaissance of tourism as a result of the improved political situation.

RIGHT PAGE
Papi Tuomala sprays up some corn snow among the birch trees, while heliskiing in Himachal Pradesh. In some parts of the Himalayas, trees can grow above 4000 meters.

HIMACHAL PRADESH — INDIAN POWDER

In the 1960s, the pioneers who were testing the outer limits of skiing went off with Hans Gmoser to Canada, stayed in a converted mining camp, and flew all over the Bugaboo Mountains in a helicopter, discovering first descents. Today, Canadian Mountain Holidays is a multi-million-dollar business, with over a dozen destinations, most of which have modern ski lodges with all the comforts of home and then some. Each destination has marked landing places that have been tried and tested hundreds of times, the first descent is as extinct as the dodo bird, and the whole organization runs like a Swiss clock.

Where, then, does the skier of the new millennium go to be on the frontier of the ski world? How about joining an eccentric Australian mountain climber for heliskiing in the Himalayas of India? Roddy Mackenzie's heliski operation in the Himachal Pradesh province of India is ski adventure at its best, where a skier rightfully feels like a trailblazer.

After our adventures in Kashmir, Papi and I continued to our next destination, Manali—base camp for Himachal Heliski. The drive from the airport to the resort was also a far cry from Canada. Indian traffic seems to be governed by some mysterious law of organized chaos. Indians drive exclusively with their horn and rarely use their brakes. Shock absorbers do not seem to have been invented. Cars in both directions straddle the center divider most of the time, and the overtaking of vehicles is like a game of "chicken" following Darwin's rule of survival of the fittest, where the biggest vehicle wins.

We did manage to survive the traffic jungle, and Roddy met us at the hotel and told us a bit about his life's journey. He first came to India in 1984, as a raw youth of 22, to climb Mt. Everest. He eventually reached the summit on a subsequent attempt in 1989, but while he was in the area, his adventurous mind saw the potential for heliskiing in India.

He began to set the wheels into motion, but going up against Indian bureaucracy is no lightweight task. According to *Lonely Planet India: A Travel Survival Kit*, an Indian man "in 1966, won a court case which had been filed by his ancestor 761 years earlier—the Indian bureaucracy in full swing!"

Roddy's journey through the maze of Indian paperwork was not that long, but he did need three years in the bureaucratic mill and another three years of research and analysis to find the best possible location for heliskiing.

"In a two-month period, I spent over 450 hours on buses between Delhi and Himachal Pradesh," Roddy related.

Most of that time was spent sleeping on the roofs of night buses, an illegal practice, but a necessary part of his *modus operandi*, so that he would be available during the daylight hours to hassle and haggle with the Indian paper pushers.

BY THE TIME PAPI AND I arrived at the hotel, we had spent a week in India, but our intestinal tracts still had not adjusted to our new Indian diet. The unusual foods and spices were fascinating and delicious, but we had come to understand that when skiing in India, the "runs" does not always refer to the ski descents. In fact, the hotel food was excellent and caused no stomach problems for the guests who did not go astray as I had done, eating street-market snacks.

In our hotel bathroom, a 20-liter bucket and a half-liter pail stood to the left of the toilet. This is standard inventory in an Indian toilet, where the local people customarily clean themselves with water rather than paper.

The right side of the toilet was apparently the tourist side, because there hung a roll of paper as well as a wall telephone, the latter item presumably strategically situated where a Western tourist was likely to spend much of his time. On the slopes, a roll of toilet paper became standard equipment in my rucksack alongside ski goggles, an extra sweater, and factor 500 sun-protection cream.

Manali is situated at about the same latitude as San Diego or Marrakech, and hence, one has to go quite high for the skiing. On our first day, we landed on peaks of between 3800 and 4000 meters. At those altitudes, you do not want to forget your sun cream or by day two you will feel like you are the main course at a barbecue.

It had snowed a bit the night before, and we spent most of the day

LEFT PAGE
Papi is dwarfed by a huge wall—everything in the Himalayas is king-size.

THIS PAGE
LEFT: Street vendor in Manali.
RIGHT: Native woman at her loom.

gliding merrily through 5–10 centimeters of powder. The runs began along open ridges and bowls, and we usually finished on rather steep pitches, often picking a route among widely spaced birch trees. The altitude took its toll on the energy level of a bunch of flatlanders, and nobody complained when Trevor, our guide, decided to head back at about four o'clock.

In the afternoon, we took a short look around Manali. We visited the Tibetan monastery, walked through the bazaar, and wound our way through small side streets where shopkeepers of every kind take care of business in their 10 square meters of real estate.

It snowed again during the night, and the next morning, Patrick, the pilot of our Air Zermatt Lama helicopter, was taking us to somewhat higher ground, usually landing at about 4300 meters. The higher we landed, the deeper was the powder, but our guides wisely did not try to take us too high all at once. The terrain on our second day was glacial. We silently wove a pattern of ski tracks into huge, prehistoric moraines. Often, the runs finished with us skiing among boulders the size of houses, which some long forgotten glacier had deposited sometime in the last Ice Age.

Our après-ski event on Monday came as a result of a tip from one of our guides. A Canadian guide name Pablo had loaned his local Manali barber $500 to help him move from a chair that had been literally on the street, into a small shop of his own. So, on Pablo's recommendation, Papi and I visited "Unique Hair Dresser".

There, Nanak Chand gave me the nicest, closest shave of my life. He spent about 5 minutes softening my beard with lather as thick as the whipped cream on a Viennese pastry. He then shaved me twice, so that my cheeks and chin were left as hairless as a baby's bottom. He gave me a half-hour head massage to boot, and the whole procedure set me back no more than 20 rupees ($0.40).

OUR THIRD DAY AGAIN PROVIDED cloudless skies and fresh powder. Since the group was slowly getting used to the altitude, and the weather was stable, Patrick was now moving us higher into the stratosphere, with landings at 4500 and 4600 meters.

We began most runs on steep north faces. The 40 centimeters of powder was just the right amount for the slope, so that we did not really have to exert any energy. Gravity played its part, and the powder provided just the right amount of resistance so that no work was required to break our speed. As we descended, the new snow gradually tapered off to about 15 centimeters.

Eventually, we swung around to some west-facing slopes, and lo and behold, winter powder magically transformed into spring snow. No problem. I pressed the button to the GS mode, and I continued in long, fast arcs until, 1300–1400 meters below our starting point, Patrick was waiting patiently to return us to outer space.

Our third afternoon provided still another view of the local color. India is full of *sadhus* and *babas*—mediators and sages, who have renounced the material world in quest of truth, salvation or liberation. High up on the hillside, above the hotel, lived such a *baba*. We took an afternoon hike to visit this hermit, who lived in a small stone house by a cave. This particular recluse was a devotee of Shiva, the Hindu god of destruction. People come to the *baba* with problems, and with the help of ceremonial prayers and offerings to Shiva, as well as by smoking an enormous amount of hashish, he attempts to get Shiva to destroy the bad things which are troubling visitors.

THE BABA MUST HAVE CHANTED some productive incantations on our behalf, for the skiing was just getting better and better. On Thursday morning, Patrick landed us at 5000 meters. Words cannot do justice to the view—a virtual ocean of mountains all around us, some rising as high as 6500 meters. Massive seas of blue-gray glacial ice surrounded us, while 1000-meter-high, sheer granite faces rose straight up, like Mother Nature's church steeples.

The skiing was equally inspiring. Trevor led us down a steep powder bowl, and my adrenaline started pumping just looking at the slope. I bounced up and down 70 times, and caught my breath as I watched Papi do the same. Papi enjoys skiing as much as anyone I have ever met, and to hear him whooping and see his wide grin as he skied, I could literally enjoy this slope a second time.

As we descended further, the powder gradually gave way, once again, to steep ravines and ridges of spring snow. We racked up vertical meters in abundance until a storm moved in and curtailed the day's skiing.

The afternoon offered another ramble around the narrow pathways of Old Manali. The ancient wooden houses with hand-carved doors and stone roofs, surrounded by snow-capped peaks, made the village look from a distance like Zermatt must have looked in the 19th century.

Upon closer inspection, the community was most decidedly Indian. I passed old, wrinkled women whose faces were adorned by fifteen to twenty earrings and a nose ring for good measure. At every other house, women worked busily at weaving looms, and around town, the men squatted peacefully in that familiar position which is comfortable only to somebody born and raised in Asia.

It was snowing on our final morning, and the cloud cover limited where

Patrick could fly. The skiing was not bad, but almost anything would have been anti-climactic after the previous day.

In the bar that last evening, Patrick said how sorry he was for the bad weather.

"If the weather had permitted," he explained, "I had planned to land you on a peak of 6000 meters today! We have never landed that high before, but I tried it out while you were skiing yesterday, and it was not a problem. I discussed the idea with Roddy and the guides, and they were all in agreement," he finished, with a touch of disappointment in his voice.

It was then that it struck me how our experience here in the Himalayas was not only an adventure for us tourists, but also for the pilot and guides.

THIS PAGE
LEFT: A woman in Chitkul doles out a portion of rice at a communal dinner in the town square.
UPPER RIGHT: Local boy.
LOWER RIGHT: Boys in Chitkul have a skylight in their room!

RIGHT PAGE
The road into the Sangla Valley weaves precariously, high above the valley.

I thought again how a 6000-meter landing was something that would be completely inconceivable in Canada, and how special it was to heliski in the highest mountain range in the world.

"Aw, it doesn't matter so much," I finally replied to Patrick. "You'll be back here next year, won't you?"

SANGLA VALLEY — SKI TOURING IN SHANGRI-LA

During our visit in Himachal Pradesh, Roddy Mackenzie tipped us off about the Sangla Valley, an isolated and little-visited enclave of villages deep in the district of Kinnaur, near the Tibetan border. When someone of Roddy's stature speaks about the mountains of India, you listen.

"The mountains are stunning," he related. "There is some excellent touring terrain, and best of all, one can finish the touring day by staying overnight in picturesque mountain villages, the likes of which you have certainly never seen. The people are beautiful and very friendly. It truly is a little paradise."

Roddy's description sold us almost immediately. We gleaned as much

information from our Australian friend as possible, thanked him and set out to organize our trip. It took a day or so to gather together an Indian-made Jeep with a driver, a week's worth of supplies and an all-purpose helper who could act as a cook and translator. The next morning we were ready to embark.

Some genius once said, "Getting there is half the fun." Had he been in India, he might well have added, "...and takes up three-quarters of the time." Four-fifths of the time might even be more accurate, but it was, indeed, fun, so who's counting?

On our map, the distance from Simla, in the foothills of the Himalayas, to the Sangla Valley did not really look so far. The Hindustan-Tibet Highway, however, bears no similarity to the German Autobahn or any other highway in the world. "Highway" is certainly a misnomer for this narrow road which weaves precariously 500–700 meters above the Satluj River for a good portion of the way between Simla and Sangla. The road makes even the worst roller coaster in the world seem like a Sunday buggy ride in the park. We gasped, gaped, oohed and aahed, as Ducha, our driver, calmly drove with one hand on the steering wheel and the other on the horn for much of the next two days.

EVENTUALLY, OUR JEEP ARRIVED in a realm where the automobile plays an almost nonexistent role. A full moon was just rising over the Himalayas as we entered the village of Sangla (2680 m), and Papi and I made a moonlight reconnaissance mission, while Kurmu, our cook, prepared our evening ration of *tarkari* and *dal bhat* (vegetable curry, lentils and rice). The curved rooftops of the homes had a distinctive Oriental look about them, and the scene seemed somewhat surrealistic in the glow of the full moon.

The following morning, we drove 14 kilometers to Rakcham (3050 m), where the snow line met the road level. This village gives access to good touring, but we were headed even higher. It was time to exchange our jeep for our skis and skins, and we skinned the last 10 kilometers of road to the village at the end of the valley, Chitkul (3450 m).

I do not suppose that James Hilton had ever visited Chitkul prior to describing the paradise of Shangri-la in his book *Lost Horizon*. How could he have? Up to but a few years ago, the Sangla Valley was one of those sensitive zones of India that had been kept off limits to foreigners since forever. As if the protective walls of the Himalayas were not enough to keep this isolated paradise of pure mountain culture insulated from the evil influences of the outside world, the Indian government had made completely sure that the valley would remain untarnished by the West. But the Indian bureaucracy works in mysterious ways. Each year, with very little rhyme or reason, the powers that be randomly open some previously restricted regions. This happened to the Sangla Valley in the early 1990s.

It was late afternoon as we entered Chitkul, and the low sun, which had over scores of years etched a reddish-brown color into the wood of the local houses, illuminated those houses handsomely. At the end of the valley, a Matterhorn-shaped peak towered over the village from a perch of well over 6000 meters.

The paths between the houses were narrow and muddy from the spring thaw, and the local people greeted us with the same warmth as the afternoon sun. We were invited in for tea to so many houses that, had we accepted all the invitations, we would probably have metamorphosed into Englishmen.

Kurmu had organized for us to stay in the government building of the Department of Water and Power. This was fine, but at the same time, it was somewhat disappointing, for I am sure we would have been welcome in any one of many villager's homes.

The nightlife was rather sparse in Chitkul, so we got to bed early and woke up equally early the following morning. We crossed a bridge over the Baspa River and began our ski tour up a side valley. Our path wound along a small creek for part of the morning. The north faces offered powder, while some of the other exposures had transformed into corn snow. As the valley began to widen out, we chose a steep slope for the day's downhill activity.

We paused for a short lunch, a long drink, and a little meditation. I thought of various ski tours I had done in the past, but never had I sat with the absolute certainty that no other human being would cross my path that day. Snow leopards, perhaps; even a yeti would be a more likely visitor that another human being. This was true solitude, and it was a good feeling. It is, really, what touring is all about.

Lunch and meditation behind us, we stepped into our bindings, and one at a time carved a track into the pure Himalayan powder. I was at one with the universe.

If my tête-à-tête with nature gave me a feeling of harmony, that sensation only increased as we returned from the wilds to civilization. Chitkul is the kind of place, of course, where life comes down to the basics. The useless trimmings and superfluous accoutrements that are so much an integral part of modern day Western society are nonexistent, and the apparent inner harmony of the natives seems to validate the simple life.

As I strolled back through the village following our tour, I passed by the town square. It was about five o'clock, and many of the townspeople were gathered to eat what appeared to be a communal meal. Women tended enormous vats of rice and lentils, while others were passing out tea to the rest of the villagers. I was met by a sea of warm smiles, and was invited to join them for their dinner. I politely declined the first half-dozen offers, but it was to no avail. Tea and food were soon brought before me in spite of my protestations, and I must admit that I had no problem putting away a few portions after our day's tour.

JAMES HILTON'S HEROES WERE STRANDED in Shangri-la, and when the chance finally came to leave, most of them opted for the peace and harmony that they had found in their lost world, and declined a return to so-called civilization. My young son, Erik, would not have been very happy, had I exercised that option.

Inner peace and harmony are, however, virtually priceless commodities in today's world. Papi and I gathered in deep breaths of both these valuable possessions before our departure, and brought as much home as was allowed under our airline overweight restrictions. Our supply will probably not last forever—no matter. I keep a map to the Sangla Valley hidden in a safe place, and I will certainly return whenever my soul needs to replenish its supply of the essence of life.

Chapter 40. SOUTH KOREA

"MADE IN SOUTH KOREA"

In the 1950s, "Made in Japan" was synonymous with a cheap, poor quality imitation of a Western product, and "Made in Korea" did not really exist for us in Europe and North America. Twenty-five years later, "Made in Japan" had become a guarantee of high quality, and Korean products were known as cheap, lower-quality Japanese copies. The Koreans, however, like the Japanese, are industrious people, and they have made large strides since that time. Their products are still less expensive than their Japanese counterparts, but the quality of their work has been catching up by leaps and bounds.

In the world of skiing, their ingenuity and hard work can be seen as well. They have achieved something that no other country has ever done—created ski areas literally out of thin air. I don't mean that they have built a bunch of ski-domes—not at all. The Koreans have taken a land of hills that are too low and too thickly forested for skiing and a climate that is too dry, and they have, nevertheless, constructed...ski resorts. They have clearly observed their neighbors in Japan, sent spies to the United States, and borrowed consultants and ideas from the Alps. The end result is a product that is classic Korea in its attempts to copy, combine and inculcate the best ideas and concepts from the various major ski countries of the world.

THE KOREAN SKI RESORTS ARE NO LESS of an achievement than the Dutchmen's famous reclamation of land from the sea. The thick forests that cover much of the Korean landscape have been cleared to create pistes, and the land has been bulldozed and shaped with no less preci-

sion than a road engineer would use to create a highway. This is not so unusual, in and of itself.

The more interesting part of the story is that Korea has a monsoon kind of weather pattern—heavy precipitation in the summer months and extremely dry during the winter. Seoul, the Korean capital, averages less than 10 centimeters of rain for the combined months of December, January and February, and the Korean ski resorts have similar precipitation patterns. The mid-winter temperatures are cold in Korea, however, and in this day and age of "instant everything", it has been no problem for the Koreans to come up with some pre-packaged powder.

MY FRIENDS, CHRISTOPH BICHSEL, PASCAL KELLER AND I visited this land of artificial ski resorts in February. We were amazed at the Koreans' ability to play God and create a winter playground that the good Lord had never intended them to have. Nevertheless, in the end, it was the friendly nature of the people and not their industriousness that ultimately left us with the most vivid memories of our visit.

We had to wait no longer than the first evening of our stay to be introduced to the hospitality that is such a large part of the Korean nature. We arrived at the Yong Pyong ski area just in time to get a taste of the local nightlife.

Anywhere in this country, a big part of the evening scene is the karaoke bar. One can get by in a karaoke club without breaking the bank by sticking to beer and crooning a few songs, but this is not the usual Korean way of doing things. They generally fill the table with various plates of snacks, buy extremely expensive bottles of seventeen-year-old Scotch, and drink and sing themselves into oblivion. The less affluent may substitute the local poison, a rice-based alcohol called *soju*, for the whiskey, but the result is invariably the same.

We sat at the bar sucking on our $4 beers, and observed a company gathering of about twenty locals who were already well on their way to a colossal group hangover. It did not take more than a few minutes before a few of the Koreans were pulling us over to their tables, asking us questions with great curiosity and pouring us generous shots of whiskey.

For the next couple of hours we ate, drank and sang (perhaps wailed is a better word) together, until the CEO of the company clapped his hands together, and the group dutifully filed out of the club like children on a field trip.

We stayed in an *ondol*-style accommodation, a room where one sleeps on mattresses rolled out onto the floor. Most Korean buildings use floor heating, and as the winters are very cold, the floors are, in turn, extremely warm. The combination of the thin mattress laid out over the heated floor resulted in my pillow being drenched with sweat the next morning.

WITH ONLY A SLIGHT HANGOVER for our troubles, we were now ready for our first taste of Korean skiing. Some Americans say that what a skier from Colorado calls "ice" is "powder" for a New Englander. In that case, Colorado ice is probably *deep* powder to a Korean. Leave your freeride skis at home, bring your carvers, and make sure your edges are razor sharp. The Korean pistes are what might euphemistically be referred to as "hard pack" and there is no off-piste skiing at all here.

While all three of us consider ourselves to be freeriders, Christoph, at least, had spent a number of seasons training young racers. Even Pascal

had had some experience racing. The closest that I have ever come to skiing gates has been bobbing through a deep-powder tree-slalom. This is to say that my style left something to be desired on the advanced runs of Yong Pyong.

My Swiss friends furrowed their brow with determination, set a hard edge, and cut up the slopes of Rainbow (the most challenging part of the lift system) with the precision of Zorro. Meanwhile, it often took me 50 vertical meters to complete a turn, and most of the time, it merely looked as if I were sideslipping.

The following day, we went for a hike and some sightseeing in nearby Seoraksan (Snowy Crags Mountains) National Park. This is considered by many people to be the most beautiful park in Korea, and it is only a stone's throw from Yong Pyong. I fastened some crampons under my tennis shoes and was giddy merely to have some traction for the first time since I arrived.

Yong Pyong is situated a mere half-hour from the eastern seaboard, and we couldn't resist the temptation to drive down to the coast for a sea-food dinner. After all, in Korea, where off-piste skiing is nonexistent, the food culture becomes a main ingredient of the adventure.

Adventure it truly was, especially to a couple of conservative Swiss. Christoph and Pascal feel no pangs of fear about leaping over rock faces or slithering between glacial seracs in their native country, but they both looked rather queasy when a selection of underwater creatures straight out of Jacques Cousteau's aquarium were placed on the dinner table. Sea urchin, seaweed, sea slugs and various other bizarre looking forms of aquatic life now seemed much more dangerous than an oncoming avalanche.

The next morning, we drove north from Yong Pyong to another of Korea's top ski resorts, Alps. Along the way, we passed a location for ice climbers. To my surprise, the ice that covered the rocks was every bit as

artificial as the surface we had been skiing on. The ingenious Koreans had created the ice wall by merely piping water in and hosing it over the cliff's edge. The only question in my mind was whether I would have an easier time trying to set an edge on the ice wall than I had had carving a turn on the slopes the previous day.

There are various reasons for the lack of off-piste skiing in Korea. The main reason is the lack of natural snow, but even had God suddenly changed the world's weather pattern, the thick forests that line the trails would be a rather strong deterrent to venturing off-piste. Then there are the fences. As most Koreans are not very good skiers and tend to attempt more than their ability allows, net fences with padded plastic poles line every centimeter of slope, to keep the locals from crashing into the woods.

If all these facts were not enough to keep avid freeriders from leaving the prepared slopes, the local ski patrol is ready and able to be the last line of defense. These guys should be stationed along the border with North Korea. Their style was reminiscent of the Gestapo.

» **Muju's lifts open at 6:30 a.m. on weekends and holidays for those who want to get the most out of their ski day...«**

During our day at Alps, I stopped for a moment to get a photo, and suddenly the shrill whistle of the patrol pierced the morning air. I was told to move on—no stopping allowed. A bit later, Christoph stood on the perimeter of the piste, where the snow had not been packed by the groomer. He was warned not to ski there. We had the audacity to step over a fence, and the patrol was again on us like flies on feces before we could negotiate a single turn on the other side of the fence.

We satisfied ourselves by cruising around the pistes, staying out of the way of the ski patrol for the rest of the day and saving our love of adventure for the dinner table once again.

That night we treated ourselves to a pork barbecue. In traditional Korean style, we sat on the floor secluded in our own little booth, where a small grill was placed on the table. In addition to the meat, about fifteen small dishes were placed around the table. The spiced cabbage that is the national dish was complemented by pickled radishes, bean sprouts, salads, garlic, mushrooms and various other spiced vegetables.

THE FOLLOWING MORNING, WE WERE on the road again. All over the country, the highways are excellent and the road signs are in English as well as Korean. In addition, the country is small, so in less than half a day, we traveled from the far northeastern corner of the country to Muju in south central Korea.

Rise and shine in Muju—another typical Korean winter day: blue skies, sunshine and more artificial snow. Nowhere in the country is the evidence of the Korean penchant for copying more clearly seen than at the base of the Muju Resort, where the five-star Hotel Tirol looks out over the pistes.

An Austrian architect designed this tribute to his home country. The interior is done almost entirely in pinewood paneling, and Austrian antiques and murals decorate the lobby and halls. Outside on the front facade is an exact facsimile of Emperor Maximilian I's royal box in Innsbruck. Only the famous golden roof is missing from this replica. Meanwhile, cute Korean girls bustle around the lobby clad incongruously in Austrian *dirndls*.

AUSTRIAN SNOW IS MORE DIFFICULT to replicate. Muju, like the other Korean resorts, gets a small amount of natural snow but must supplement nature's bounty with the manmade variety. The quality of snow created by snow cannons may not be the best, but skiers looking for a fair-weather ski holiday probably have a better chance in Korea than anywhere else in the world.

The locals do not seem to be deterred at all by the "firm" snow conditions. In fact, this is definitely a country for skiers who can't get enough of their favorite sport. The Crazy Daisy pub in Zell Am See, Austria sells T-shirts that claim, "You can't ski all night!" That may be true, but the Koreans may one day eclipse that notion. Not only do all of the Korean resorts offer night skiing, but some ski areas even have an early morning session for insomniacs and whoever else might espouse the adage that the early bird gets the worm.

Muju's lifts open at 6:30 a.m. on weekends and holidays for those who want to get the most out of their ski day and beat the crowds. This dawn session does not come for free, mind you. You must pay extra for each part of the day that you ski. The skier who wishes to take advantage of a true full day of his favorite pastime, however, gets a reduced rate and must fork over a "mere" $66 to carve from 6:30 a.m. to 10 p.m.

This may all sound crazy to a Westerner, but the Koreans are very fanatical about their skiing, and put in long, hard hours to improve their technique. They did not build a modern society out of the ashes of the civil war without determination and an overzealous work ethic. They take their skiing seriously too, and seem to go about it as a skill to be learned rather than a hobby full of thrills and adventure.

Solchonbong Peak in Muju offered much more vertical, longer runs and better skiing than the Mansonbong Peak, and it was here in the gondola that we again made some new friends. Jung Jun Tak and Won Goan Sic are good examples of ambitious young Korean skiers with a passion for improvement. Already excellent skiers, they immediately latched onto my two ski-instructing buddies, eager to get some pointers in the latest trends and techniques being taught in Switzerland. Their English was negligible, but with the help of some demonstrations and the Korean ability to copy, they were soon adapting some Swiss style into their technique.

We opted against the night skiing and instead spent a soothing après-ski

LEFT PAGE
LEFT, MIDDLE AND RIGHT: Very many Korean winter activities seemed to involve artificial ice. That includes, from the left, ice climbing on artificial ice, ice carving, and "ice sledding" on an artificial lake.

THIS PAGE
UPPER LEFT: The five-star Hotel Tirol is situated at the base of Muju's pistes, but you better bring your platinum credit card for a stay here.
UPPER RIGHT: Local snowboarder
LOWER: So as not to mislead anybody, I must point out that this photo of Christoph Bichsel making a turn in Korean powder is an extremely rare photo. There really is no off-piste skiing in South Korea.

at the local hot springs. Similar to Japan, almost all the Korean ski resorts have nearby thermal activity, and Muju has some of the best springs.

Our reward for our teaching assistance during the day was an invitation to dinner, followed by an evening of *soju* at a karaoke bar. Just as the demonstrations of skiing technique bridged the language gap during the day, the introduction of Korea's favorite alcoholic beverage made for lucid understanding between cultures after the sun went down.

By the time we hit our pillows, we had not only sung a good percentage of the tunes in the karaoke book, but we had developed a brilliant plan for reuniting the two Koreas as well. It was not so difficult really. After all, they even speak the same language. The ski slopes have always been a location for making new friends, and we had already discovered that there was no better place for this than Korea. One could only wish that the leaders of North and South could get together for a weekend of sliding, *soju* and singing, and perhaps some inroads could be made in resolving the many years of conflict between the two parties.

THIS PAGE
Despite China's recent economic shift to the right, Mao is still a great hero there.

RIGHT PAGE
UPPER: This is the photo of Lake Tian Chi that I saw in a coffee-table book in Beijing.
It inspired me to traverse the globe to visit and ski on this mountain.
LOWER: I guess we arrived a few months too late or too early to see the deep blue waters
of Lake Tian Chi. This is the way the lake looked when we arrived in the month of February.
Pascal Keller admires the view.

Chapter 41. CHINA

SKIING — THE NEW CULTURAL REVOLUTION

This tale begins in a travel agency in Beijing where I came across a spectacular photograph of a volcano with a huge lake at the bottom of the crater. Snow covered much of the landscape, but the lake in the photograph was an unfrozen blue. Then and there, I determined that I wanted to stand atop the rim of that crater someday with my skis on.

A series of questions to the travel-agency personnel and a fair amount of subsequent research produced the following results: Changbai Shan (2691 m), the volcano in the photo, is situated directly on the border between China and North Korea, and the Koreans consider it to be a holy mountain. There are actually sixteen peaks that surround the lake, the highest of which is Baitou Shan (2744 m). The name of the lake is Tian Chi (Heavenly Pool), and at 2189 meters, it is the highest crater lake in the world. The region is also the home of the Siberian tiger, a fact that might be of relevant interest to backcountry skiers.

My research piqued my interest even more. Now I needed somebody with whom to make such a trip, but that was a tough order to fill.

Four years later, two half-demented Swiss comrades, Christoph Bichsel and Pascal Keller, were ready to travel to a remote corner of China based on vague and tentative hearsay to check out Changbai Shan and whatever else we could find out about Chinese skiing. In the meantime I had done a lot more research— enough to find out that skiing, which basically did not even exist in China in 1990, was now booming albeit on a very primitive level.

When Chairman Mao's 40-year reign of power came to an end with his death in 1976, nobody in the world's most heavily populated country would have had the money, let alone the time, for this relatively expensive leisure-time pursuit. Day-to-day survival was still pretty much a full-time activity for the Chinese. In addition, considering Mao's rigid adherence to Communist dogma, skiing would certainly have fallen under the category of superfluous and decadent Western customs.

Mao's reign of power was succeeded by approximately twenty years with Deng Xiaoping at the helm, and the face of China changed to the extent that it is today unrecognizable to anyone who might have visited the country during its previous epoch. Deng slowly introduced his land to capitalism. Since then, this country, which for 30 years harbored some of the most dogmatic Marxists in the world, although still under central control, has definitely moved West.

WHAT HAS ALL THIS TO DO with skiing? Quite a lot, in fact. The move toward a market economy has created a fast-growing middle class, and the acceptance of Western values has suddenly made skiing as popular as rice. As recently as the beginning of the 1990s, there were still no true ski resorts in China. Yet today, there are well over 200 small ski areas, with new ones popping up every year.

Despite, and perhaps also because of, all the changes in recent years, China remains the same enigma and paradox that it has always been, albeit wearing a different suit of clothes. One of China's paradoxes can immediately be applied to skiing. This huge land which has dramatic mountains in almost every province and corner is actually ill-suited to the sport.

The southern sections of the country are far too warm to accommodate skiing at "normal" elevations. Yunnan Province, for example, is home to some of China's most spectacular peaks. Kunming, the provincial capital, lies at 2000 meters, but the average temperature in January is 20 degrees centigrade. Hence, although one can find skiing in Yunnan, one has to approach altitudes where even the mountain goats need oxygen.

The colossal peaks of Tibet and far-western China are suitable for only the top echelon of ski mountaineers. Mustagh Ata (7546 m), in the western part of Xinjiang province, is considered the most skiable 7000-meter peak in the world. The lone giant rises at a steady incline of about 25 degrees from the high plateau, and is the highest mountain in the world that is not a technical climb. Nevertheless, this is not really relevant for the average skier, let alone a new generation of Chinese who are strapping a pair of boards onto their feet for the first time.

Northeastern China is ultimately the only region of the country in which skiing in its conventional format is possible. It is cold enough and it is relatively close to the population center of Beijing, but this part of the country has another problem—lack of precipitation. Beijing, with its monsoon climate, receives an average of only one meager centimeter of rainfall for the 3-month period from December through February! This slight inconvenience has not stopped the Chinese. A handful of small ski areas have been built within an hour or so of the capital, relying entirely on artificial snow.

Christoph, Pascal and I began our Chinese ski research in one of these local ski resorts, about an hour's drive from Beijing, shortly after stepping off the plane. Huaibei International Ski Resort does not really seem very international in nature, but its advertising material, which boldly announces, "Ski the Great Wall," is not far from the truth. This seven-lift operation, situated very close to the Mutianyu section of the Wall, offers skiing that is almost in the shadow of China's most renowned tourist attraction.

We come from regions of the world where artificial snow generally is used merely to augment Mother Nature's bounty. We found it therefore to be an incongruous sight, indeed, to see strips of white amid dry, arid mountains that appeared to have been baked by a summer heat wave. Towers of the Great Wall were visible against the blue skyline on both sides of the lifts, and I'm sure Mao was shuddering in his grave.

While the one piste suitable for intermediate skiers and the hardly staggering 238 vertical meters offered by Huaibei Resort are not features likely to get Europeans to abandon the Alps, the area is well suited for the indigenous population, who are entering the ski world for the first time. The rental shop is prepared for an onslaught of locals, as 5000 pairs of skis of debatable quality are ready and waiting for Beijing weekenders.

We warmed up our muscles with a few hours of cruising on the upper piste. We then rode a taxi for about 15 minutes to a gondola that took us up onto the Wall itself. By dark, our taxi had returned us to Beijing's airport, from where we flew north.

Fifty-six kilometers from Jilin is the ski resort of Beida Hu Hua Xue Chang (better known as merely Beidahu), built in 1994. It is a privately financed operation, complete with six lifts, a full-scale ski jump, and a 600-bed hotel. The 900 vertical meters of skiing offered here would do any Western ski area proud, and the 700-vertical-meter black run is also world class. The snow here, while not prevalent in great abundance, is natural. The trails have been cut out of thick forest, giving Beidahu an aura of New England.

Unfortunately, a few other details did not function quite up to snuff. Some of the hotel walls were so covered with mildew that they seemed to have spent some time underwater. Most of the personnel in the hotel were walking around in down parkas, an indication that the heating system was also not up to snuff. In addition, hot water seemed to be inconsistent at best. As a result, many guests to Beidahu stay in nearby Jilin, and drive up for the day.

There was another problem. Upon our arrival, only one short

T-bar was open. Although the area advertises that it has snow cover from November through April, it is actually only open from December until the end of February. In addition, we were informed that the high season in China consisted of the short period between Christmas and late January. At that time, one could find enough lifts open to access all the slopes. In low season, however, there were not enough skiers, and especially not enough good skiers, to justify the operation of more than this one lift.

Having traveled quite a few thousand kilometers to check out Chinese skiing, we were not that easily deterred. A chat with the director of operations, Mr. Lin, was fruitful. He opened the lift that accesses the black piste for a couple of hours and personally took us over and skied a few runs with us.

During the afternoon, we cruised repeatedly down the T-bar run, enjoying the children who watched our every move. They asked politely if they could ride the lift with me, and they greeted us constantly on the slopes. Many of them would also have been ready for the black piste, but it didn't seem to matter that it was closed. They were having a wonderful time on the one open slope. They built small jumps to train on, swooped down the mountain like budding racers, and could not get enough of this new Chinese sport.

Now the time had come for our visit to the location whose beauty had originally lured me to this faraway land—Changbai Shan. We flew to Yanji and were driven for 5 hours to our hotel in the nature reserve.

When we arrived in Changbai Shan, it did not exactly look like the original photo that had fascinated me. The skies were misty, the temperature was –25 centigrade, and the howling wind swirled the snow around and brought the chill factor to about –40 degrees. It was early afternoon, and we decided, despite the conditions, to spend a couple of hours skinning our way up the road toward the peak. The road was quite flat, and we did not gain altitude in a hurry. The lake above us may well have been

LEFT PAGE
UPPER: Pascal Keller skis down from Changbai Shan. The name means always (*chang*) white (*bai*) mountain (*shan*). The lake is about 13 square kilometers in size and is 373 meters deep.
MIDDLE: One can clearly see the volcanic nature of the rock in the Changbai Shan region.
LOWER: Pascal finds a path through a maze of birch trees on the lower section of Changbai Shan.

THIS PAGE
Chrisoph Bichsel skis one of the couliors high up near the peak of Changbai Shan.

"heavenly" as its name promised, but our route up seemed like the road to hell. To add to our troubles, the extreme cold left our skis about as slippery as sandpaper.

Fortunately, the next morning was sunny and windless, and we had found out about a snow cat that took people up the 11-kilometer road to the peak. I am no purist! Snow-cat skiing is quite respectable as far as I am concerned. I was happy enough to part with a few of my hard-earned yuan in exchange for skipping a 5-hour hike in polar weather.

At 10:30 a.m. we stood atop Changbai Shan and gazed down at the frozen waters of Lake Tien Chi, surrounded by a circle of jagged, volcanic pinnacles. In the other three directions, virgin forests were visible to the horizon, under a totally cloudless sky.

Christoph, apparently not accustomed to taking the easy way up the mountain, had far too much adrenaline or testosterone in his body, and decided to ski a short but treacherous couloir. The entire chute was no more than a dozen short turns, but the windswept snow was hellish, and an array of rough, volcanic rock lay in wait below, like the teeth of the Siberian tiger. Fortunately, he has the skiing skills to survive his overactive testosterone production, and all went well.

Soon, it was time to descend. The snow was patchy, having been blown into gullies and onto lee faces by the wind. We walked across the barren upper mountain for 10 minutes until we found a snow-filled ravine. We followed this path of white as far as we could, skied along sections of the road, took off our skis a time or two, and ultimately arrived atop an old, out-of-service ski lift. Some powder turns in the birch forest below the tree line and another stretch of road brought us back to the bottom.

One could hardly brag about the snow conditions or the skiing. We made a few good tracks, of course. I am always pleased when I can string together twenty good turns in changeable wind pack. But, there had not been enough snow, and the rocky mountain was far from optimal ski terrain. The run was not steep or exciting.

It made little difference to me. Not every ski run is going to be dream powder. Not every descent can be the perfect 35–45 degrees that gets my heart pounding a little faster and my adrenaline flowing a bit quicker. If we are only after the most perfect descent, we are relegated to forever staying in one of the tried and true ski areas that we already know. I was on the Chinese–North Korean border skiing down an ancient volcano, and that was more than enough for me. I suspect that I will go the rest of my life without ever meeting another person who has skied on Changbai Shan. I was satisfied.

Another area about which reliable information was virtually impossible to come by was Yulong Xue Shan (Jade Dragon Snow Mountain). This 5596-meter-high peak is a stunning, jagged, glacier-covered precipice that rises up to the heavens behind the southern city of Lijiang. Before our journey, I had received a brochure from the Chinese Tourist Office about the relatively new gondola that had been built there, spanning the distance between 3356 meters and 4506 meters.

The information in the pamphlet, however, was very ambiguous with regard to skiing. On the one hand, the gondola was advertised as a "sight-

seeing ropeway", while at the same time, there were two photos of skiers in the brochure. The brochure states, "It is one of the best places for skiing and snow-enjoyment in our country." Further inquiry via telephone and e-mail to tourist offices in China, however, provided the answer that there was no skiing available on Yulong Xue Shan for skiers of higher ability.

There was only one way to discover the truth—go to the source. A visit to Lijiang would be a worthwhile endeavor regardless of whether or not one could ski on Jade Dragon Mountain. Lijiang is the capital of the

Naxi Kingdom, a fascinating ethnic minority that migrated from Tibet more than 1000 years ago.

The Old Town of Lijiang, known as Dayan, is on the UNESCO World Heritage List, and for good reason. The narrow cobblestone streets are only open to pedestrian traffic, and these roads are full of Naxi people, all clad in their colorful, traditional native costumes. The beautiful Naxi homes, each built around a courtyard garden, are still another interesting feature of Dayan. In addition, the Old Town is full of old stone bridges and channels of running water where the locals wash their vegetables, dishes and clothes. Cozy teahouses and restaurants add to the daily pleasures of Dayan, and one can easily meander around here for days or even weeks without getting bored.

The city is built on a plateau about 2500 meters above sea level, and is dominated by Jade Dragon Mountain, which seems to be visible from all parts of town. With the snowy peak beckoning to us from around every corner, it was not long before we packed our skis into a taxi in an effort to answer another question that had brought us so far from home.

Riding up the world's highest gondola, our three sets of eyes peered curiously down, surveying the viability of a descent. The snow was a bit sparse in the forest, but there was no doubt in our minds that there was a skiable route. We were also sure that a descent would not go down without some problems, and we were right.

The sightseeing and snow play area atop the gondola was all cordoned off and decorated with signs prohibiting visitors from venturing beyond the ropes. We had planned a quick dash under the cords, but it was to no avail. We were immediately stopped by a security guard. Christoph and Pascal whipped out their Swiss ski instructor licenses, which were about as legible to our uniformed friend as the Dead Sea Scrolls, but the situation really did not need an explanation. It was crystal clear what we wanted to do.

ing toward us, and we feared the worst. Prepared to attempt a getaway, we noticed a pleasant smile on the man's face and we held our ground. We were greeted cordially and brought to the restaurant where the mountain manager and a translator were waiting for us.

To our surprise, we were heralded as mini-celebrities, as we had apparently just completed the premiere descent of the full length of the gondola. We were invited for beer, lunch and whatever else our hearts desired, while the mountain manager and his translator queried us on the feasibility of building ski lifts on the upper part of the mountain. Our every word was translated and jotted down, as if we were the wisest of ski-resort planning consultants. That might not be a bad idea at all as a way of financing a return trip to the world's fastest growing ski country!

OUR FINAL CHINESE SKI DESTINATION was Yabuli, situated about a 3-hour drive from the northern city of Harbin. In 1993, Yabuli became China's first bona fide ski resort. Our arrival was lucky enough to coincide with a visit by the primary investor in the resort, Dr. Tian Yuan, chairman of the China International Futures Company. Because of his investment in skiing here, Dr. Tian was introduced to me as the founder of Chinese skiing.

He related his story for me. Before 1993, China had only a handful of scattered ski lifts, which were not open to the public but used exclusively as training sites for competitive skiers. Yabuli had one of these lifts and two small buildings to house the athletes. There was no hotel, no hot water, no telephone service, etc. In a word, there was no infrastructure whatsoever.

Yabuli was chosen as the site for the Third Asia Winter Games, at which time Dr. Tien came into the picture with an investment of $40,000,000. That amount was enough to build a hotel complex, three lifts, about a dozen ski runs, and the accompanying infrastructure for a "tourist ski resort" alongside the existing training site for athletes. One year later, skiing as a Chinese leisure-time activity was born.

Today, the Yabuli tourist resort coexists alongside the athletes' training site, whose longer vertical drop and steeper runs are still not open to the public. While the small artificial-snow operations close to Beijing turn a good profit, Dr. Tien's contribution to China's fast-evolving lifestyle revolution is still losing $2,000,000 a year. Nevertheless, his investment in skiing was a very large impetus to the blooming industry that has exploded in recent years.

I asked Dr. Tien if he had regrets or felt that he was ten years too early with his investment. His answer couldn't have been more fitting for a founding father.

"It was too early for making money, but it was the right time for China," he told me succinctly. "I want to see the habits and customs change in my country, and there is a need for winter-sports activity."

Dr. Tien seemed satisfied to wait out the necessary time for the success of his destination resort. I asked the doctor about the future. He informed me that he was exploring the idea of combining his resort with the state-operated lifts to create a much larger ski experience.

"To cut through the Chinese government bureaucracy, however, is not easy," explained Dr. Tien, "and it is too early to know what will come of this idea."

Christoph, Pascal and I sampled the various runs. We cruised the popular, 3-kilometer-long intermediate run #6 a few times. Then we tackled the zigzag cut in the woods that the map calls #10 and bombed down

The guard got on his cell phone and exchanged a few words with some unseen higher authority. Moments later, he smiled, lifted up the cord for us to pass under it, and waved goodbye. The biggest hurdle—Chinese bureaucracy—had apparently been defeated, and now we only had to conquer the mountain as well.

The beginning of our descent consisted of 25-degree slopes of corn snow. Soon, a different exposure brought us to a long, steep bowl of old powder. Eventually the bowl narrowed into a steep but rather wide couloir of hard snow.

When we reached the tree line, it was necessary to hike up for about 20 minutes before negotiating our way carefully through the forest. The trees were quite thick and the snow cover in the lower elevations was minimal, so we basically transported ourselves through the final leg of our journey by skiing down a hiking trail.

As we emerged from the forest, we saw another man in uniform com-the black #6 a few times. But I was interested in more fodder about the future.

We took a taxi to the athletes' ski area, which did have a couple of small beginner's lifts open to the public, to have a talk with the director, Mr. Dong Linmo. He explained that a gondola intended for the future use of the general public had already been built, but the Chinese people were not yet ready for such difficult slopes as those accessed by this gondola. His answers were somewhat vague and noncommittal, but he seemed to think that training athletes to win medals was a higher priority than extending facilities for the general public. In addition, he seemed to be of the opinion that the public sector's ability to ski at the level of the pistes here was still quite a few years away.

He was kind enough, however, to open the old, made-in-Japan single chair used by the athletes to allow us one run on the big mountain. We were honored. It was snowing and blowing hard as we skied off the top and followed our guide into the woods to sample some Chinese powder, known here as "wild snow". We followed the cut under the lift for a ways, and continued in about 15 centimeters of "wild snow" alongside the piste for as long as we could.

ALL TOO SOON, OUR RUN WAS OVER, and we headed back to the "tamer" snow of the tourist pistes. By late afternoon, the wind had picked up the tempo a few notches, and the mercury had dropped down to around −20 degrees. Most of the Chinese skiers, however, were still out brav-

THIS PAGE
UPPER LEFT: Jade Dragon Mountain towers high above the surrounding plains.
LOWER LEFT: The gondola up Jade Dragon Mountain is the highest gondola in the world.
RIGHT: Pascal entering the top of the couloir on our descent from Jade Dragon Mountain.

RIGHT PAGE
LEFT: From the top of Moon Hill, near Yangshuo, one can look out over the amazing karst peaks of Guilin Province.
RIGHT: Christoph still has many powder turns in front of him atop this long slope on Jade Dragon Mountain.

ing the elements. As I took my last ride up, two snowboarders appeared below the chair lift, cutting up the "wild snow" in a rather narrow and difficult piece of territory.

I pondered something I had heard the night before from Michael Pettis, an American professor who teaches at Tsinghua University. He had told me that "most of the government's ten-year plans nowadays are completed in three years!"

I watched the snowboarders below me and thought about our morning meeting with Mr. Dong. I surmised that he may be in for a big surprise someday soon. Like China as a whole, the snowsports industry in the world's most populous country still has a long way to go, but it is moving fast. The country, the economy, and the Chinese ski industry have done some amazing things in the last ten years, and I believe the young generation of Chinese enthusiasts will be churning up snow alongside the professional athletes before you can say "bourgeoisie." May Mao rest in peace.

Asia in a Nutshell

LOCATION	NEAREST TOWN	NEAREST AIRPORT	SEASON	PEAK ELEVATION	VERTICAL DROP	SIZE	SNOW	BEAUTY	VILLAGE	NOVICE	INTERMEDIATE	ADVANCED	OFF-PISTE	NIGHTLIFE	RATING AVERAGE	WEB SITE
CHINA																
Beidahu	Jilin	Jilin	December–February	1400 m	900 m	3	1	3	3	1	3	2	3 (1)	1	1	2.1	www.chinahighlights.com/travelguide/ski/beidahu.htm
Changbai Shan	Baihe	Yanji	November–early May	2691 m (2)	1000 m	3	1	3	5	2	1	1	1	2	1	2.0	www.4panda.com/special/ski/changbaishanski.htm
Huaibei Resort	Beijing	Beijing	late Nov.–early Mar.	380 m	238 m	1	1	2	3	5	4	2	1	1	3 (3)	2.3	www.hbski.com
Jade Dragon Mt.	Lijiang	Lijiang	Not a conventional ski resort	4506 m	1150 m	3	1	4	5	5	1	1	1	3	4	2.8	www.travelchinaguide.com/attraction/yunnan/lijiang/jade_dragon.htm
Yabuli	Yabuli	Harbin	November–mid April	1000 m (4)	600 m (4)	2	1	3	2	3	2	3	2	1	2	2.1	www.yabuli.com
INDIA																
Himachal Heliski	Manali	Kullu	late Jan.–mid April	5200 m	2550 m	5	5 (5)	5	5	5	1	1	5	5	3	4.0	www.himachal.com
Gulmarg	Srinigar	Sriningar	late Dec.–late April	4390 m	1660 m	5	1	5	4	2	4	2	3	5	2	3.3	www.skihimalaya.com/site/gulmarg
Kashmir Heliski	Srinigar	Srinigar	February–May	4500 m	2200 m	5	5 (5)	5	5	5	1	2 (6)	5	5	3	4.1	www.himalaya-heliski-cachemire.com
JAPAN																
Fuji Tenjinyama	Kawaguchiko	Tokyo	December–mid April	1480 m	200 m	1	1	3	5	3	5	3	1	1	1	2.4	www.fujiten.net
Furano	Furano	Sapporo	November–April	1209 m	974 m	3	2	4	3	3	3	4	2	2 (7)	1	2.7	www.furano.ne.jp/kankou/english
Hakuba	Hakuba	Nagano	December–May	1831 m	1071 m	3	5	4	4	3	5	5	3	5 (7)	3	4.0	www.japanspecialists.com/files/hakuba_resorts.html
Niseko	Niseko	Sapporo	November–May	1200 m	920 m	3	4	5	4	4	4	5	3	5 (8)	3	4.0	www.niseko-hirafu.com
Nozawa Onsen	Togari Nozauaonsen	Nagano	December–May	1650 m	1090 m	3	3	5	4	5	4	3	4	3 (7)	3	3.6	www.vill.nozawaonsen.nagano.jp/info/english/resort.htm
Shiga Kogen	Yudanaka	Nagano	mid Nov.–mid May	2305 m	980 m	3	5	4	4	3	5	5	3	2 (7)	2	3.6	www.japanspecialists.com/files/shiga_guide.html
KAZAKHSTAN																
Chimbulak	Almaty	Almaty	December–April	3163 m	960 m	3	1	4	4	4	3	3	2	3	3	3.0	www.chimbulak.kz/en/about/
Kan Tengri Heliski	Almaty	Almaty	July–August	5816 m	1800 m	5	5 (5)	4	5	4	1	1	5	5	2	3.7	www.kantengri.kz/heliski_prog_01.htm
KOREA																
Alps	Sokcho	Yangyang	early Dec.–late March	852 m	252 m	1	1	2	3	2	2	1	1	2	1.7	www.alpsresort.co.kr
Muju	Yeongdong	Daegu	December–March	1510 m	787 m	2	2	1	3	3	3	2	2	1	3	2.2	www.mujuresort.com
Yong Pyong	Gangneung	Yangyang	Nov. 20–mid April	1458 m	700 m	2	2	1	3	2	2	2	2	1	3	2.0	www.yongpyong.co.kr
KYRGYZSTAN																
Karakol	Karakol	Bishkek	late Oct.–late April	2950 m	650 m	2	1	3	3	2	2	2	2	1	2.0	www.opt.web.kg/en/skialpin/basa.php?m=1
Kashka-Suu	Bishkek	Bishkek	mid November–April	2270 m	400 m	2	1	3	3	2	2	2	2	1	2.0	www.opt.web.kg/en/skialpin/basa.php?m=2
UZBEKISTAN																
Beldersay	Chimgan	Tashkent	January–May	2880 m	765 m	2	1	3	3	1	1	2	3	4	1	2.1	www.sport.uz/eng/belder.htm

(1) If lifts are open.
(2) With snow cat.
(3) in Beijing.
(4) This is the peak of the conventional ski area. The peak elevation of the training site for athletes is 1374 meters. It naturally has an accordingly larger vertical drop as well.

(5) There are no lifts, but having a helicopter at your disposal rates five points.
(6) This rating improves to a 3 during spring when corn snow conditions are prevalent.
(7) Off-piste skiing is officially illegal. These ratings reflect the off-piste skiing if one breaks the law.
(8) Off-piste skiing is accepted here.

AFRICA AND THE MIDDLE EAST VIII

Chapter 42. MOROCCO

INSHALLAH

More than 25 years ago, a fellow traveler told me of a location deep in the Himalayas of India where one was transported up the mountains by mule in order to make ski descents. I pictured the scene in my mind's eye, and it fascinated me. I visualized villagers in some remote back valley guiding me up on their mules to ski some rarely visited peaks. It took a long time for that dream to reach fruition, but not so long ago, I finally rode that mule with a second one in tow to carry skis, boots and other equipment. In the end, it did not take place in the Himalayas at all but in the High Atlas Mountains of Morocco.

There is something other-worldly about Morocco. You notice it the first day. It is a most remarkable land of contrasts and contradictions. It is a hot country with blistering deserts and it is a cold land with towering citadels of ice and snow. The streets and the *souqs* are a bustle of chaotic energy, while inside the sanctuary of one's pension, hotel or home, it is tranquil.

Morocco is no longer Europe, but it is not typical Africa. The French were there for a long time, and they have left their mark on the culture, but it is most decidedly not French. It is truly a world unto itself—a mystical, enchanted, harmonious place, where for many Moroccans, life is harsh, and yet the people seem happy and satisfied.

TO BEGIN TO UNDERSTAND MOROCCO and its people, one should start by learning and understanding the word *inshallah*. This is an Arabic expression which means "if God wills", and it is one of the most commonly used expressions in all Arabic countries. Whereas we in the West might answer the farewell "see you later" with a simple "okay" or "goodbye",

PREVIOUS PAGES
When traveling to the Sahara, one should come prepared. The dromedaries are already there, but bring your own skis and boots, as the rental equipment is not always state of the art. You also never know when a guitar might come in handy at an après-ski event.
LEFT: Papi Tuomala skiing down the front face in Oukaïmeden.

recovery of my ski equipment in the hands of the airline personnel, but it was clear that this important task was to be left to a higher power.

We went to get the rental car, which we had ordered with a roof rack, but the rack had been omitted. It seemed that Allah was really out to lunch that day. There was no alternative but to cram our skis into the tiny Fiat, and hope to deal with the problem in the morning.

We drove the few minutes from the airport to the Medina, as the old part of town is called, and we checked into Dar Chaumissa. A *dar* is the Moroccan equivalent of a small pension—a private home with four or five rooms to rent. Then we walked to Place Djemaa el-Fna, a large square where at least 50 street stands were set up side by side, peddling a colorful taste explosion of Moroccan specialties.

We ate small kebabs, fresh shrimp boiled in oil, fried fish, eggplant, green peppers, black and green olives, red beets and a variety of small salads. There were also two kinds of sauce to add zest to what was already a spice orgy. We washed it all down with copious amounts of hot mint tea. This beverage was as soothing as the food was hot and fiery. While Marrakech has many excellent up-market restaurants, the food there could hardly be better than in the street market, where an entire meal costs a pittance.

THE FOLLOWING MORNING, WE MANAGED eventually, with great effort and lost time, to obtain a rack for our skis, and to drive the 75 kilometers of winding mountain road to the ski resort of Oukaïmeden. Allah was again of little help. Cold hard cash, about four times the actual value of the ski rack, is what turned the trick.

The route to Oukaïmeden takes one from an elevation of about 500 meters up to 2600 meters. We drove past picturesque mountain villages, and near the end of the journey, a deep gorge began to develop out of the rocky terrain along the left side of the road. The cliffs were of a purple-pinkish color. Not surprisingly, the brick houses of the villages bore the exact same hue. Over the next week, we were to discover that wherever we traveled in Morocco, the color of the adobe houses exactly matched the many shades of red, orange, pink and brown of the nearby sediment.

As we rose higher and higher into the High Atlas, we expected to see snow, but what little we saw was only a sugar coating sprinkled gently between the rocks—nothing skiable. Perhaps Allah had not been informed of our mission.

Finally, we rounded the last curve in the road. A small lake appeared, surrounded by green grass. Off to the right were a number of hotels, vacation homes and various other buildings—also surrounded by grass. But looming directly in front of us was a lone mountain rising about 600 vertical meters above the meadows. The rocky ridges were bare but the valleys, bowls and gullies in between were white.

"Allah be praised!" I announced, but I was premature. The chair lift, which rose to the top of the mountain, was idle. A quick inquiry informed us that it was closed due to excessive wind.

I was beginning to think that Allah was not a skier. He had, in any case, not been smiling on *our* endeavor.

Papi and I decided to make the best of the situation and skinned partway up the mountain. We needed a bit of training anyway for the ski tour that we intended to do later on our trip.

That evening, I said a little prayer to Allah for better weather, but once again my prayers went unheeded. The satellite picture for the High Atlas was not so promising for the coming days, and we pointed the Fiat instead over the Tizi-n-ticka Pass (2280 m) and into the Sahara Desert. Our destination was the village of Merzouga, where we planned to do some sand-dune skiing. No rain had fallen here in over two years, and we surmised that even God's will would be hard pressed to thwart our plans.

Once we had passed onto the south side of the High Atlas, the terrain became extremely barren and dry. Nevertheless, the arid scenery was sporadically decorated by an oasis, around which a town had sprung up. The streets of the desert villages were lined with trees and often had plots of

a Moroccan would reply, "*Inshallah.*" By this, he really means, "We will see each other later, if God wills it."

Inshallah reflects the fatalistic philosophy that is part and parcel of the Muslim religion, and it helps Morocco maintain a pleasant, ambling pace of life, for after all, there can never be any reason to get upset, stressed or overworked, because the future is out of our hands anyway. I personally have never been much of a fatalist, but on my visit here, I too became a believer.

My friend Papi and I departed from Lyon in early March, leaving behind the world of the French Alps, where the mountain men answer to the names of Jean-Claude, Pierre and Henri. We soon landed in a milieu where we would be assisted for the next ten days by the likes of Abdullah, Mohammed and Azdour. Our jet touched down in Marrakech shortly after the sun passed behind the Atlas Mountains. There was still a yellow afterglow behind the peaks that turned the entire range into a jagged, purple silhouette.

Our flight was on time but my luggage was not on it. I reported the missing baggage and asked when I might expect it.

The answer was a shrug of the shoulders, and of course, "*Inshallah.*"

I personally would have preferred to put the responsibility of a speedy

land where date palms were cultivated. All the while, the clean desert air kept the snow-capped Irhil M'Goun (4071 m) and the surrounding mountains in clear view, and Papi eyed them longingly.

Upon our arrival in the northern Sahara, we were taken under the wing of 20-year-old Atman Batrchi, who along with his family organizes desert excursions. We learned from him that the desert sand has different qualities, similar to the snow we are more used to skiing on.

"There is the black desert, the white desert and the dunes, and only the latter has sand of a quality high enough to ski," explained our new friend.

This information was, however, as far as he could help us with sand-skiing tips, as he was not a skier himself. The rest remained for us to discover and learn through trial and error.

Near the center of Merzouga, Mohammed Karraoui and his family have a shop that sells carpets and souvenirs, and rents a few pairs of skis on the side. We decided to check it out before subjecting our own skis

and bindings to the wear and tear that can be caused by sand. Outside Mohammed's store, with their colors faded from years of desert sun, were pairs of Rossignol, Elan and Fischer skis from the mid-1980s, as well as a couple pairs of water skis. Alongside this potpourri of fine memorabilia were two or three pairs of ski boots, which looked as if they had most recently been rented by a camel. We opted to use our own gear.

The best way to get to the largest sand dune in the neighborhood was to ride from our hotel for 2 hours on a dromedary. My mule ride would have to wait. Our equipment was loaded on one "desert ship" while Papi and I did our skier's variation of a Lawrence of Arabia imitation.

We learned many lessons about skiing on sand, not to mention hiking on sand. Our first lesson, learned on the upward route, was that skins are not necessary. Sand is not a fast, slippery surface like snow. If it is not very steep, you can hike uphill with your skis on. In spite of this revelation, we carried our skis, as sections of the dune *were* quite steep.

Secondly, I can reveal that it is not great fun to hike in sand with ski boots on. With or without ski boots, the sand slides down as one attempts to hike up steeper slopes, translating into a simple mathematical equation of one step up equals half a step back down.

Ultimately we did reach the summit of Ergchibe or La Grande Dune, and we were ready for a 120-vertical-meter descent. As we had already discovered, sand is much slower than snow. Therefore, it is necessary to seek the steepest slope, and choose a good, direct line. We stayed in the fall line for a rather long time to gain speed. Once a reasonable speed was attained, we could make short, incomplete turns. To complete a turn on sand is not advisable, as it would arrest one's speed too much.

I also must report that the New School big-turn technique will inevitably be doomed to failure in the Sahara. Swooping freeride turns require a higher speed than is normally attainable on sand.

It took a bit of practice, but by our third run, we had adjusted pretty well to sand skiing, and by keeping the turns small, we gained enough speed to make the whole experience lots of fun.

The accommodations available to Sahara skiers are also quite different from sleeping quarters in the Alps. Once night fell, the lack of electricity made for one of the most beautiful starry nights I can remember. We lay under heaven's light show for a while, but the desert nights can also get cold, and we ultimately slept under many kilos of thick woolen blankets in a Bedouin tent.

Desert scenery consists of much more than sand dunes, and for the next couple of days, Papi and I explored two remarkable gorges. They

LEFT PAGE
UPPER: En route from Marrakech to Oukaïmeden, the green valley contrasts dramatically with the Atlas Mountains.
LOWER LEFT: Papi, a large Finn, is hardly phased when a small Moroccan beginner nearly crashes into him in Oukaïmeden.
LOWER RIGHT: Fulfilling a dream, I ride a mule up toward snowfields in the High Atlas Mountains.

THIS PAGE
UPPER: Papi skis down from our ski tour on the Toubkal Massif.
LOWER LEFT: Dar Chaumissa, where we stayed for a few days in Marrakech, displays typical Moroccan architecture. *Dars* are generally rather inexpensive. Marrakech is also home to some beautiful *riads*, which also exhibit typical Moroccan architecture. A *riad*, by definition, is a large, old, extravagant Moroccan villa. A number of *riads* have been converted in recent years from private homes into unique guesthouses. These are a more expensive accommodation that the *dars*.
LOWER MIDDLE: In early March, the lake and meadows in Oukaïmeden were already free of snow, but there was still enough snow on the mountain for some good spring skiing.
LOWER RIGHT: Local women.

were rich in all shades of red and orange, and were full of rock formations that looked as if Walt Disney had created them. We hiked past nomad camps and passed a woman grazing her dromedaries high in the mountains that rise above the Todra Gorge.

Even more interesting was a hike we made in the Dadés Gorge, where we found a canyon within the canyon! We hiked through a cleft in the rocks, so narrow that we simultaneously scraped our shoulders on both sides in some places. Elsewhere on the hike, we had to clamber up steep walls until we ultimately arrived at a small oasis. Amidst the dry desert landscape, we suddenly stood in a patch of green grass. Around us were

THIS PAGE: Not many rental shops give you a choice of snow skis or water skis!
RIGHT PAGE: Papi swoops down La Grande Dune to the little enclave of tents where we spent the night. This is definitely a good destination for fair-weather skiers, and the sand does no major damage to one's skis.

apple trees in full bloom, grazing goats and one primitive stone house, which stood incongruously in the middle of this stunning red-rock landscape.

We could have spent many days hiking, climbing and exploring the gorges, but Papi and I still had snow skiing on our agenda. We returned to Oukaïmeden, and this time Allah was smiling on the High Atlas Mountains. There was not a cloud in the sky as we rode the double chair lift to the top.

We took a few warmup runs on a T-bar on the top of the mountain, as we waited for the African sun to thaw the front face into corn snow. The view was magnificent and again emphasized this land of contrast. As we skied across fields of white, we gazed out over the red-rock hills and canyon to the east and the brown and green plains to the north that separate Oukaïmeden from Marrakech.

We skied the one black piste and numerous off-piste ravines on the front of the mountain. A steep gully filled with over-ripe corn snow provided a fitting climax to the day.

WITH THE OFF-PISTE SNOW now getting too soft, we headed back to Marrakech for an afternoon of wandering through the labyrinth of *souqs*. These narrow alleyways that dominate the Medina are a world unto themselves. Thousands of tiny shops sell all imaginable types of clothes, foods, souvenirs, art, antiques, shoes and a hundred other items in the Moroccan equivalent of a shopping mall. The tiny stands coexist amidst an amazing network of narrow corridors in an obscure pattern with no rhyme nor reason. I think that even Daniel Boone would have gotten lost in this Moroccan maze, although perhaps not as lost as I!

Getting lost did not take any of the pleasure out of my wandering. A journey through the *souqs* is an assault on the senses. The festive colors of the cloth and clothing in the shops is so bright that sunglasses are almost obligatory, and around each corner one is inundated by the aromas of fried food, fresh fruit or any one of a thousand exotic spices.

I could not help but stop periodically to buy some nuts, dates, fried fish, kebab or some other scrumptious snack. The shopkeepers bantered and pleaded incessantly for me to enter their shop for "just a look," and all the while I found myself further from home and more lost with every step forward. Miraculously, I ultimately found my way back to our hotel. This feat was surely Allah's will, for it is certain that my navigational skills played a very insignificant part in my eventual arrival back at our *dar*.

The last activity on our heavy schedule was to spend a couple of days ski touring on the Toubkal Massif. We began with a short drive to Imlil (1800 m), a mountain village that serves as a base for activities in this region. It straddles a narrow valley full of small terraces of cultivated land, whose bright green color, even in February, stands out in marked juxtaposition to the desolate rocky landscape all around.

We spent the night in one of the dormitory rooms of Azdour Lahen Ben Houssa, who organizes excursions into the mountains. The next morning, we were met by Abdullah, our mountain guide. With him were a few mules and their tenders. Moroccan saddles, with huge bags for carrying things, were slung over the pack animals, and our leaders began piling food, backpacks, ski boots and other odds and ends into these bags. Skis and poles were roped onto one of the beasts of burden as well, while one of the other animals had the misfortune of receiving a heavier load—me.

My mule wore no stirrups, so I mounted him from a nearby rock and placed myself gingerly in front of the full saddlebags, so that my legs and feet would have some place to dangle.

For the next few hours, Papi and I rode upward. Only a short ways out of Imlil, we turned a corner, and Toubkal, Morocco's highest peak (4167 m), loomed forbiddingly in front of us. Her windswept ridges were bare while her ravines and couloirs were filled with snow.

The trail wound its way upward with only a smattering of small trees and low shrubs to add a touch of green to the otherwise barren landscape. At around 2200 meters, the last of the trees were behind us, and we passed through Sidi Chamharouch, the last enclave of houses before civilization totally petered out.

As I rode, I thought back to that long-ago beach in Bali, where "Ski Bum Charlie" had first told me of riding pack mules to go skiing. So many years had passed since then, and so much had changed in our fast-moving world, but still there was a magic place where one could ride mules to reach remote ski slopes. How wonderful it was.

The trail got progressively narrower, and the valley receded far below into the distance. The mountainside was steep, but my "travel partner" was surefooted, and I felt secure.

At around 2900 meters we met the snow line and snow began falling as well. Here we parted ways with our helpers. Our mule tenders headed back down with their charges, and we finally had to load our gear onto our own backs. Another hour and 300 vertical meters brought us to the Refuge du Toubkal and none too soon. By this time, it was snowing hard, the wind was howling and a heavy mist had engulfed us entirely.

THE REFUGE LOOKED LIKE A SMALL Moorish castle, visible as a vague and ghostly silhouette in the fog. It was a welcome sight. The building sleeps 80 people, and it was already relatively full, so we quickly claimed a couple of empty bunks and went downstairs to the dining room. Following a hearty meal of couscous, lamb and an assortment of vegetables, I drifted into a deep sleep.

The next morning was cloudy and gray, but the wind had subsided. Papi and I followed Abdullah up the valley that separated Toubkal from another 4000-meter peak named Ouanoukrim (4088 m). Our plan had been to skin to the top of Ouanoukrim, but the night's storm had blown

the snow along the last section of our route into drifted contortions that were insurmountable with our equipment. *Inshallah*!

We had to settle for reaching the 3750-meter-high saddle between the two peaks. In spite of this slight setback, things were looking up. The sun began to peek through the clouds, giving us much better light for our descent. The night's storm had brought more wind than snow, but the few centimeters of new powder made for a pleasant run back down.

Now our arrival procedure was reversed. The mule tenders had returned with their animals to meet us at the snow line, and we began to ride back down. At dusk, I looked back at Mt. Toubkal whose snowfields gave off a pink glow in the setting sun. We paused for a moment to watch the last rays of light turn her from pink to crimson.

Again, my mind drifted back to that tale of adventure that had filled my ear and piqued my fantasy long ago. Our lives are full of hopes, dreams and ideas that develop from early childhood until very late in life. They are large and small, important and insignificant, childlike and serious. They will stir us from the backs of our minds, and keep us motivated to new and different endeavors throughout our lifetimes. Some will come to fruition, while others will remain unfulfilled forever. As I sat silently on my mule, I felt a sense of closure. *Mashallah*—this is what God has willed.

Chapter 43. IRAN
COLD POWDER AND WARM PEOPLE

I was riding up the old double chair lift, the noonday sun warming my face, as I gazed out at the tracks that I had just etched into the powder to the east. A young man next to me introduced himself and we began to chat. He explained that he lived in Los Angeles, where I was born and raised, and he told me that his ski holiday last season had been spent in Aspen.

"But you know," he said, "I got to thinking that I can go *home* and ski for an entire season for the same amount of money that I paid for ten days in Colorado! So that's what I did this year."

I did some quick calculating in my head. A lift pass here cost about $5 a day, plus an extra buck on weekends. A hundred-square-meter apartment could be rented here for about $175 a month. I've often seen a half-dozen ski bums crammed into 30 square meters in the French Alps, so a large Iranian apartment would be a luxury by comparison and cost no more than $30 per person per month. Restaurant dinners cost about $5, throw in another fiver for breakfast and lunch, and a 120-day season comes to a grand total of $1800. Welcome to Shemshak, Iran.

Okay, the price is not the only difference between Iranian and American skiing. Shemshak has only seven lifts and 550 vertical meters of skiing, but on the other hand, the powder lies untouched for days, even weeks. In addition, 5 minutes away is the little one-lift ski area of Darbandsar, and another 20-minute drive brings Iranian skiers to Dizin, the country's largest ski resort.

ANDERS KARLSSON, HENRIK WESTELIUS AND I came to Iran not only to experience Iranian skiing, but in the hopes of learning about the country's history, its culture and its people. It was not a difficult task. The spectacular, snow-covered mountains were literally in our face from the moment we landed in Tehran, and in cities like Esfahan, we stumbled over the history and culture on every street corner. And the people—we didn't have to search or strive to make contact at all; the locals reached out to make us welcome as if we were long-lost relatives.

I must admit that we stood out in a crowd. If our light hair was not enough to label us immediately as foreigners, our red, orange and yel-

ABOVE
As I skied down to the middle station in Tochal, I met this elderly gentleman on his way up. Music was being emitted from his mobile phone, which was neatly tucked into the fold of his Diesel cap.

RIGHT
Skiing down the piste between the top gondola station and the third station at Tochal.

low ski jackets were highly visible in a country where almost everybody is clad in black.

"Hello! Welcome to Iran. Where you come from? Ruski? German?" We heard these phrases constantly during our stay. But the openness of the local people went far beyond mere curiosity.

When I answered, "American," I was invariably met with the reaction, "Oh, America, very good." It is a strange reply considering the many negative ways in which the American government has meddled in Iran's affairs in the last 50 years. Not only did the CIA oust the popularly elected President Mossadegh in 1953 to install the Shah of Iran on the throne, but during the bitter war between Iraq and Iran in the 1980s, the American government supported the hated regime of Saddam Hussein. Nevertheless, the positive reaction to me as an American was consistent throughout my stay.

I have traveled in about 60 countries, and I have not experienced any people who outshone the Iranians in warmth and hospitality. I stopped to photograph a fruit salesman with his wares and he gave me a banana. I hiked to the top of the Fire Temple, outside Esfahan, and a stranger gave me a glass of tea from his thermos and some candies.

One of our first days, we rode the ski lift with a local man, and before we reached the top, my friends and I had all been invited to a party at his apartment. Two nights later, we found ourselves drinking the local moonshine, a date-and-raisin-based alcohol known as *aragh*, singing and partying until 2 a.m. Behind closed doors, explained our host, many people in Iran live a life not too far removed from how we live in the West. In public, however, the truth is hidden behind a veil, similar to that worn by the more devout women in the country.

On another occasion, I paid for pizza and kebab at a local snack shop, and I exchanged a few words with the cashier. At 10:30 p.m., when he got off work, he approached our table and invited us out to a tearoom. Every day, someone new surprised us with a gesture of warmth and kindness. But I am getting ahead of myself. Allow me to go back to the beginning.

Our first morning in Tehran, we woke up to the call-to-prayer that wails from every minaret shortly after dawn. Sleepily, I peered out my hotel window. The sun began to turn the sky a bright orange behind the snow-covered mountains to the east of the city. Soon the sun was above the ridge, lighting up the rest of the Alborz range to the north. Visible far to the east was the pyramid-shaped volcano, Mt. Damavand (5671 meters), Iran's highest peak; and close enough to touch lay Mt. Tochal (3950 m), a ski area that is reachable directly from the outskirts of Tehran.

The mountains that surround Tehran are the nicest feature of the city, but once the morning traffic gets into full swing, they often become obscured by the thick layer of smog created by the city's many automobiles. We attempted an early escape, but it was not early enough to avoid the morning rush hour.

We learned our first lesson about Iran from the inside of our taxicab. Darwin would have been right at home here, because survival of the fittest is the only rule of the road in Iran. The horn is much more important than the brakes, traffic lights are ignored and one-way traffic arrows are disrespected. The dotted line that is supposed to separate lanes becomes an additional lane for the local automobile kamikazes in their small Iranian-made Paykans.

Our taxi trip through town was the ride from hell. All drivers seemed to leave so little space between vehicles that you could light a cigarette for or pick the pocket of the guy in the car next to you. Ski racks are not standard equipment on the cabs of Tehran, and our boards jutted out

about 40 centimeters sideways from the trunk. This packing job made our skis odds-on to arrive at our destination broken. Henrik immediately donned his ski helmet, Anders began some incantations to Allah, and I merely closed my eyes as our chauffeur wove through the rush-hour traffic like a slalom skier on hallucinogenic drugs.

MIRACULOUSLY, OUR SKIS AND BODIES arrived at the bottom station of the Tochal ski area unscathed. The Tochal gondola is a four-stage, six-seat lift that takes sightseers and skiers on a magnificent trip almost 2000 vertical meters above the traffic and the city. At the top of the mountain are two short lifts well suited for intermediate skiers. Two additional chair lifts in the higher reaches of the resort were out of service, one possibly for lack of snow and the other most probably for lack of good management. The locals didn't complain. They are certainly used to poor management.

In any case, the Iranians have more important things to worry about than a few closed ski lifts, such as a closed society. On the other hand, they also have much to be thankful for, because things are much more liberal on the ski slopes than they were just a few years ago.

For a time, men and women were required to ski on separate pistes and the black chador was mandatory ski garb for women, but both of those practices have fallen by the wayside. The rule requiring separate lift queues is the one remnant of the old policy, and we were quite happy for that fact as we entered the Tochal lift station. A local girl's school was having an excursion that day, and we quite legally walked past a couple of hundred giggling, chattering schoolgirls and immediately entered the gondola, as there was nobody ahead of us in the male lift line.

We spent an hour or so puttering around on the upper lifts, by which time we were ready for a run on the 850-vertical-meter slope that divided the top station from the third station of the gondola. We had an inkling that we might not be in accordance with the wishes of the authorities after we noticed a small barrier partially blocking the entry to the descent. The slope had plenty of snow; however, there was no avalanche danger, and the skiing looked more interesting here than on the upper slopes. We were ready for a plunge into the great unknown, whatever the rules might be.

I quickly circumvented the barrier, but my partners lagged behind and were thwarted by a number of lift attendants ranting and raving in Farsi. At the bottom of my descent, I found a lift attendant who spoke a smattering of English. Fully aware that I had broken the rules, with typical Iranian cordiality and hospitality, he rewarded my outlaw run by allowing me to return up the closed gondola. He also informed me that after 2:30, the run *is* open, so I was very welcome to ski it again! Most Iranian rules and laws defy logic, so this was par for the course.

By the end of the day, we had seen and skied all that was available in Tochal. It was time to gather our belongings and travel to Dizen, 120 kilometers away. The Iranian penchant for hospitality and generosity again played a large part in our story there.

Machmed Abrishamchi is an Iranian acquaintance of mine. We know each other through an annual conference that we both attend. My arrival in Tehran unfortunately found Machmed in Dubai on business. Nevertheless, he told me over the phone that upon arrival in Dizen, I should ask for a man named Kayvin.

WHEN WE CLIMBED OUT OF OUR TAXI in Dizin, Kayvin was waiting for us with the keys to Machmed's two-bedroom chalet at the base of the ski slopes. He then spoke briefly with the restaurant staff and told us that all our meals would go on Machmed's tab.

He was still not finished. We were introduced to Ahmad, the ski-school director's son. He was an excellent skier who spoke English almost entirely in one-word sentences. Kayvin explained that Ahmad would provide lift tickets for us, guide us around the ski area, and help us cut ahead of the lift queues if necessary. The hospitality wagon didn't stop there either. Ahmad arrived at the chalet with soft drinks. We went to play billiards— paid for. Telephone bill—paid for.

Machmed later returned to Iran in time to wine and dine us on our last evening in Tehran and give us a proper send-off. The red carpet had not been longer or wider when the Ayatollah himself returned to the country.

Then came the skiing. Our first day offered about 15 centimeters of powder on top, half as much at the base and crystalline blue skies. It was late January and the powder was light. Poor Ahmad! In charge of three

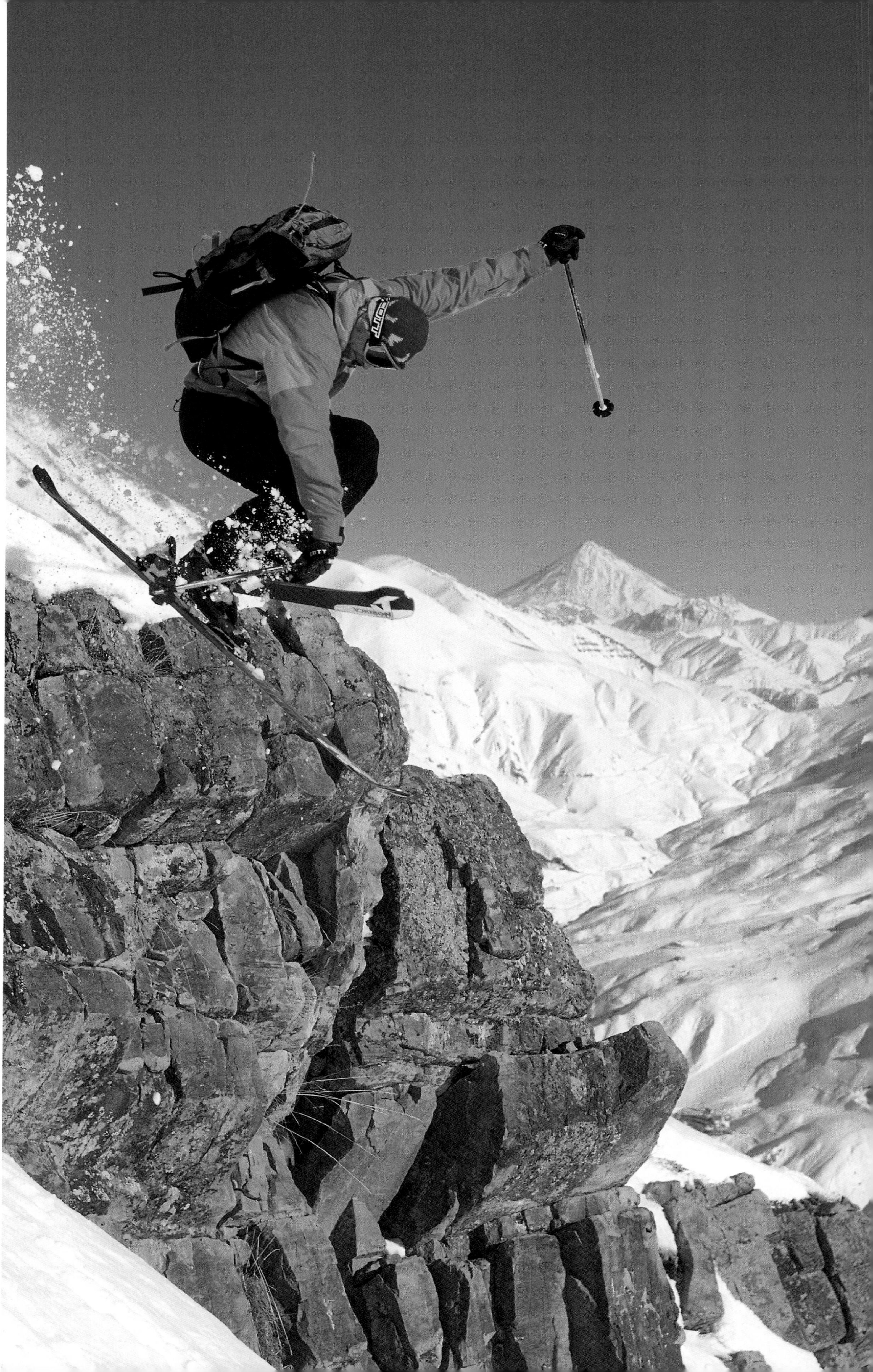

LEFT PAGE
Henrik Westelius needs no help from Allah to land his leap while skiing off-piste between Dizin and Darbandsar. Mt. Damavand is visible in the background.

THIS PAGE
UPPER: Anders Karlsson and Henrik Westelius have a pretty large area of fresh powder to themselves in Dizin.
LOWER: The long gondola up to Mt. Tochal rises right out of the outskirts of Tehran.

Henrik leaves a cloud of snow in his wake as he heads off-piste from Dizin. Mt. Damavand can be seen in the distance.

powder-crazed Western skiers who knew more about avalanches than he. At least we thought we knew more.

Our first morning was full of short discussions.

Ahmad pointed to a tantalizing slope and said, "Danger!"

One of us said, "There is not enough new snow to make that dangerous."

Someone else added, "That is not steep enough to be dangerous."

"Okay, okay," answered our leader with a wince, and we headed off in the direction of the so-called dangerous slope.

We cut fresh tracks all day. For the most part, the terrain was interesting but not extremely difficult. Dizin is an excellent area for skiers to learn to ski powder, and there was more than enough fluff to keep us veterans interested as well.

The area is a playground of ridges and gullies. Twenty-five-degree pitches gradually flatten out and end on a crest before dipping into a

new slope. There are some steeper pitches as well. We enjoyed a juicy 35-degree slope to the far west of the lift system. Dizen is also a paradise for lift-accessed backcountry. With touring skis and skins, one can reach all kinds of spectacular skiing terrain.

SOMETIMES WE DID DEFER TO Ahmad's better knowledge of the area. Henrik pointed longingly to a much steeper slope than those we had been skiing, but Ahmad explained in his most loquacious rhetoric, "Morning—okay; afternoon—danger!" We acquiesced to his opinion.

The hotels in Dizen were almost entirely devoid of guests. Most of the skiers here are denizens of Tehran who drive up for the day. Dancing and alcohol are among many Western evils that are illegal in Iran, so the nightlife here consists of cards and billiards. On the positive side, they did play Western music in the billiard room, and Westerners who are feeling pangs of alcohol withdrawal can purchase some alcohol-free beer. Suffice

some weather for it the following day. From the top of Dizin, we began an hour-long hike along a ridge toward Darbandsar. Ahmad was busy that day, but we needed no guide with good visibility. He had instructed us to merely proceed the entire way in the direction of Mt. Damavand.

As we hiked, we gazed out over ridge after ridge of snow-glazed peaks. Dry powder, very few cliffs, and enormous expanses of above-tree-line skiing are ingredients that make Iran a backcountry-skier's paradise. The steep slopes of Mt. Damavand are perhaps the ultimate prizes for a ski-touring fan, but there are enough other mountains to keep adventurous skiers busy for years.

Soon we stood perched high above a long, broad, pristine slope that began our descent. There were endless possibilities, and I must admit we got a bit carried away, or at least Henrik did. He swooped down in big-mountain turns, until he realized that he had skied too far into a side valley, and needed a half-hour hike to meet Anders and me at the top of the Darbandsar lift system. This was a rather inopportune time for such a mistake. It was a bit past three o'clock, Darbandsar's lifts had closed for the day, and a lone ski patrolman was waiting for us so that he could sweep the mountain.

It is easy to imagine the reaction of a Western ski-patrolman if some clueless tourist had wandered astray, and kept him away from his hot toddy or *glühwein* for an extra half-hour. Life is different in Iran. Here, Mohammed waited patiently, followed us down without a word, and then invited us to join him and his colleagues in the patrol shack. He called a taxi for us, and boiled a pot of tea to keep us warm while we waited. It was yet one more instance of Iranian hospitality.

OUR FINAL DAY OF SKIING brought us to Shemshak. The pistes were much steeper here, with lots of moguls under the lift. But outside the piste, stretching up the valley were steep ridges and gullies of powder where we warmed up with a few runs.

After lunch, we were in search of new adventure—and we found it. On the Darbandsar side of the mountain was a long, steep descent down to the road, with various slopes all emptying into the same ravine. This was a definite avalanche trap—not a place to ski right after a snowfall. The snow had had a day to settle, however, and we spent still one more afternoon taking advantage of one of Iran's major legal pleasures—virgin powder.

Henrik was using his wide boards and flew down the ravine at high speed. Anders and I pumped out classic short powder turns. At the bottom we had to negotiate our way around four loose dogs which were snarling angrily and baring their teeth. Our answer was to show them our Colgate smiles but keep our ski poles handy. We christened the descent "Angry Dog Valley".

Hitchhiking back to the lifts, we were immediately picked up by a couple of young men blasting hip-hop from their CD player. It was clear that this kind of music was among the many forbidden fruits in Iran, but in the Internet age, many laws that are legislated cannot be enforced. Our driver verified that he had downloaded the music from the web.

We skied a few more runs down "Angry Dog Valley" to finish our day, each time avoiding our yapping enemies and each time being assisted back to the lifts by friendly Iranians.

On my last ride up the chair lift, I met yet one more local skier. For the umpteenth time I answered the standard question, telling him that I was American. He told me that I was not the first American he had met and that he liked American people. Then he tied the knot on our Iranian visit with one simple statement.

"It is too bad," he said, "that our governments have had so much trouble with each other for many years, but we are people, and we can be friends regardless of government policy."

it to say that one usually gets a long night's sleep here and awakes fresh for the morning powder.

Indeed, the next day provided more new snow. The clear skies of the night before had again given way to snow drifting lightly from the heavens. The visibility was poor on the upper mountain, but we were in luck. The Iranian National Team was doing some slalom training with their French coach, and one of the upper Poma lifts was open for that purpose, despite the snowy conditions. None of the other locals ventured off-piste, so we shared the Poma all morning with the racers and a half-dozen Scandinavian skiers—one more day of fresh tracks on every run.

It was easy to see why the Iranian team might have some difficulty competing against their European counterparts. Slalom training in Iranian powder does not really get a racer ready for the salted-down, icy slalom courses of the racing circuit.

We wanted to see the other ski areas in the vicinity, and we finally got

THIS PAGE
All of the slopes of Palandöken are above the tree line.

RIGHT PAGE
Local villager and his son are on their way home along this trail high up in the Palandöken ski area.

Chapter 44. TURKEY

COLD TURKEY

I must admit that my friend Arne Bredow and I got some peculiar looks from the Viennese when we boarded the plane to Istanbul with ski boots as hand luggage. On the other hand, none of the Turks looked twice upon our arrival. Few Turks ski, but they all seem to know that their country is full of snow-covered mountains each winter.

Our first stop was Erzurum, a bleak-looking city, where gray is the brightest color to be seen. This place is so drab that you could let a gang from East L.A. loose with a few dozen cans of spray paint, and it would improve the appearance of the city. Only 6 kilometers up the road from Erzurum, however, is the ski area of Palandöken, which offers the services of one rather short T-bar, a few chair lifts, and a gondola. This transportation network brings skiers to an elevation of over 3000 meters, with descents up to 7 kilometers long.

IT WAS SPRING, AND THE ENTIRE MOUNTAIN was covered in corn snow. The open, treeless slopes afford a skier the opportunity to ski almost anywhere, and Arne and I tried many variations between the pistes on our first day. We were all alone the moment we diverted from the marked trails, and we enjoyed our solitude.

Late in the afternoon, a savvy German skier who had been living in Turkey for a while taught us a little trick to help us with our excessive appetite for skiing. At closing time, he glided up to a lift operator with a small bottle of scotch, and presto, the lift stayed open for an extra hour. That was the first of various surprises during our stay in Turkey.

The following morning I realized that it was not only skiers who made use of the ski facilities. Ahead of us on the lift were two peasants, transporting themselves home from Erzurum, where they had sold some of their wares.

After they disembarked, they wrapped plastic bags around their old shoes, and began a 2-kilometer walk through the snow to their mountain village. We skipped the plastic bags, stepped instead into our skis and followed them a little ways. Eventually, we parted from our "guides" and headed down a long off-piste canyon. We passed a peasant village on the way and finally arrived at a very strange community at the end of a cul-de-sac.

What looked to be a small town from the distance began to resemble a concentration camp as we skied closer. The community was composed of five or six rows of gray, barracks-like structures. Walls topped with barbed wire surrounded the buildings, and a guard protected the entrance.

"Could it be a prison?" I asked Arne.

The sight became even more bizarre and incongruous as we noticed about twenty taxis waiting outside this odd compound.

"The taxis can't be waiting to take prisoners home, and they certainly aren't standing here anticipating throngs of Turkish off-piste skiers," said Arne sarcastically.

It was not long before we realized that we had inadvertently stumbled upon a large-scale brothel. It was later explained to us that prostitution is legal in Turkey, but the strict Muslim town of Erzurum had decided to clean their community of such vile elements. Hence, the government built this unique compound at the end of a canyon to nowhere, and women of ill repute could rent rooms inside this mountainside sin center. It was further explained that the barbed wire and other security measures were in place to protect the women from irate family members who might want to do away with them to save the family honor. The whole setup was a rather interesting après-ski alternative, but Arne and I are very traditional, and we did not dally before returning by taxi to the ski area.

Those who are surprised to read that skiing exists at all in Turkey will be even more astonished to learn that the ski season in Palandöken is generally 150 days long, stretching from November into May. It is advisable, however, to visit from February to April, as the early season can be brutally cold, with harsh winds and temperatures between –15 and –20 degrees centigrade.

AFTER A FEW MORE DAYS at Palandöken, we packed our gear on a night bus and headed for Kayseri and the extinct volcano, Mt. Erciyes (3917 m). Communication with the locals was often a problem in Turkey, and on this occasion, we were shaken to consciousness at 5:30 a.m. and deposited on the highway in the middle of nowhere. Our bus had overshot Kayseri by 15 kilometers, and no decipherable explanation was ever given as to why we were not put off at the Kayseri bus terminal.

Eventually, we caught a cab to Mt. Erciyes, but in Turkey, the early bird does not always get the proverbial worm. The lifts here were meant to open at 9:30 a.m., but this was low season, and there were not enough

guests to justify opening even one lift. The necessary quorum was deemed to be five people, but it was not before 1:30 p.m. that Arne and I were joined by a German and two Australians. At that point a local lackey was sent from the hotel to open one old chair lift.

Two o'clock is not an ideal starting time for skiing spring snow. Where we could have been gliding spryly across fields of perfect corn at 10 a.m., we instead found ourselves slugging through thick porridge in mid-afternoon.

With the benefit of our experience, we set our sights on a ski tour for the following day. The night's freeze was good, and the sun also complied.

By eleven o'clock, we had gained enough altitude for a very respectable descent. We paused briefly for a snack. An ordinary orange after our 3-hour hike tasted like a tropical fruit salad fresh from Tahiti.

Now, the ripe spring snow awaited us. There is something very special about touring—the solitude, the sweat and the sense of having justly earned the descent.

By the time we arrived back at the base of the lifts, it was 11:30 and the lifts were all still motionless. We felt satisfied with the day, however, and ready to press on.

Any visitor to this area should make a side trip to see Cappadocia and view a landscape unique in the world. This part of Central Anatolia looks like something from another galaxy. Massive volcanic eruptions from both Mt. Erciyes and nearby Mt. Hasandag deposited enormous amounts of soft volcanic ash all over this region. Subsequent erosion has created thousands of odd cone- and mushroom-shaped formations. Adding still another dimension to this already bizarre natural phenomenon, various ancient civilizations chiseled cave dwellings out of these "fairy castles", so that the surroundings look as if Fred Flintstone had constructed a city on Mars.

We took a couple of days to explore Cappadocia before continuing our ski adventures in Saklikent. This tiny area, a mere 50 kilometers from

the Mediterranean Sea, has only a couple of relatively short T-bars, but it is surrounded by 3000-meter-high peaks. The stunning juxtaposition of the azure waters around Antalya and the lush, green Mediterranean vegetation against the backdrop of snow-covered Mt. Gömlekdag, Mt. Kizlarsivrisi and Mt. Oyuklutepe is in itself worth the trip. In addition, a springtime visit in March offers the opportunity to go skiing in the morning and take an afternoon dip in the Mediterranean, one of the few places in the world where this possibility exists.

By the time we arrived in Saklikent, the season was over, the lifts were closed and the village of vacation homes was deserted. The ridges were bare, but there was still a wide enough streak of white in some protected gullies to practice a long string of short turns. In addition, a light dusting of snow the night before gave our edges just enough to bite into.

OUR FINAL DESTINATION in Turkey was Uludag. This is where the jet set of Turkey go to ski, and while the terrain in Erzurum is more interesting for an expert skier, Uludag is the only spot in Turkey that has all the accoutrements of a full-scale ski resort.

We were cruising around the rather bland intermediate slopes, when suddenly the subdued morning atmosphere was broken by an obtrusive but familiar and friendly noise. The whop-whop-whop-whop that pierced the morning air brought back found memories of Canada, and a glance upward revealed a chopper heading for the peak of nearby Mt. Zirve. Heliskiers could enjoy an 800-meter-descent from that peak.

A lift with a helicopter would have been a welcome change after a few days of ski touring, but the price of a chopper lift is not very compatible with the going wage of a ski journalist. I looked around for the marketing department, but when nobody offered us a freebie, we finished our day on the normal pistes.

A few of the T-bars in Uludag have lighting for night skiing, but a skier will definitely not be at a loss for nocturnal activities. Among the many

LEFT PAGE
Approaching the ski resort of Saklikent, we traveled from the green valleys of the Turkish spring toward a range of jagged snow-covered peaks.

THIS PAGE
UPPER LEFT: Turkey in springtime was a paradise of corn snow, but in winter, one can also find plenty of powder.
UPPER RIGHT: Snow-capped mountains provide a beautiful background to the Turkish coast near Antalya.
LOWER LEFT: Peasants heading home in the Palandöken area.
LOWER RIGHT: Local woman stands among some of the "fairy castles" of Cappadocia.

hotels, there are two ice-skating rinks, two swimming pools, gymnasiums, saunas, Jacuzzis and Turkish massages. There are also a handful of discos, where one can dance and drink *raki* (the anise-flavored national drink) with the very chic Turkish high society.

Whereas the other ski areas have good but relatively basic food, in Uludag one can also take advantage of the excellent Turkish cuisine, and gorge oneself on the various well-seasoned kebabs that Turkey is famous for as well as an array of seafood from the nearby Sea of Marmara. *Mezes* (hors d'oeuvres) are the trademark of a Turkish dinner, and they accompany every meal in Turkey. Almost more important than the main course, these starters include such items as calamari, eggplant specialties, spicy chopped tomato salad, dolmas, and light cheese- or meat-filled pastries known as *börek*. After a full sampling of *mezes* and a main course, one needs about 4 hours at the disco to work it all off again.

Back in Istanbul, with a few hours to kill before our return flight, I caught a cab to a 300-year-old Turkish steam bath. As a small Turkish man with hands like Hercules gave my back the S & M version of what is normally called a massage, I contemplated the past two weeks. It had been mellow, touring Turkey in springtime. The corn snow and sunshine had been perfect for a first visit.

But one of these days, I'm going to head back to Palandöken at the time of year when the snow falls hard and cold. I'll leave the regiments of freeriders in the popular Alpine and North American destinations to their trench-war battles over a few hundred square meters of powder-covered land. I'll share the lift once again with the peasants of Eastern Turkey. My backpack will be full of Johnny Walker, the lift operators will let us ski powder until the stars come out, and the only tracks I'll cross all day will be footprints made by shoes wrapped in plastic bags.

Chapter 45. LEBANON
THE CALM AFTER THE STORM

Skiing in Lebanon is much more than a matter of snow and mountains. It is also a story of history and archaeology, of tragedy and rejuvenation, and above all, of people.

For almost twenty years, from 1975 until 1992, almost the only printed words in the Western press about Lebanon were about their long and debilitating civil war. All previous realities about Beirut being the Paris of the Middle East and the playground of the rich and famous had been obliterated. The image of Beirut as a cosmopolitan and stunningly beautiful hub where East meets West had been purged from the Western consciousness by the many years of TV images depicting bombs and AK-47s.

In the post-war years, the Lebanese have done a remarkable job of rebuilding from the ashes and debris. To be sure, some bullet holes can still be seen in old walls here and there, and the blackened shell of a bombed building is also still visible in places. Most of the city, however, has been completely renovated, but the memories die hard. This has been especially true among foreigners.

It has taken a long time to get the word out that Lebanon is again a safe place to visit and its people are every bit as warm and hospitable as before. Slowly, tourists have begun to return. First, it was visitors from their neighbors in the Middle East, and now, gradually, more adventurous Westerners have started visiting Lebanon as well. The Lebanese put their best foot forward as they try to build up the booming tourist trade that once was, but it does not happen over night.

NOT SO LONG AGO, I WAS the lucky beneficiary of the kind of hospitality that has given the Lebanese their well-earned reputation as warm and generous people. Tony Haswany, a former member of the Lebanese ski team, is the man who taught me the Lebanese manner of treating guests.

Tony is an acquaintance of an acquaintance. What we had in common before my arrival in his country was one mutual acquaintance, one phone call and a love of skiing.

Tony greeted my friend Christer Henning and me at Beirut airport on a day in late March with the news that we could not drive to the Faraya ski resort this first evening as planned, for the road was closed because of snow. Instead, Tony drove us to his home for a couple of drinks. Then, he invited us for a delicious dinner of Lebanese specialties and refused to let us pay a cent.

Early the next morning, Tony headed his car out of Beirut toward the mountains, and an hour later we were already buckling on our boots at the 1850-meter base of Faraya-Mzaar. The Dome du Mzaar rises an additional 615 vertical meters above the sea, which appears to be close enough to dive into from the peak.

This day, the upper mountain was fogged-in and windy, so our skiing was limited to the lower slopes. Only three of ten lifts were open, but on the other hand, only 20–30 skiers were on hand to enjoy the fresh snow. The Lebanese are notorious fair-weather skiers, explained Tony, and suffice it to say that all the space to either side of the pistes was virtually our private mountain. We engraved track after track in the fresh, soft snow. After we had left enough of our marks on the slopes to satisfy our egos, Tony deposited us in his vacation home.

"You can stay here as long as you like," he announced, turning over the keys to us. "I must work tomorrow, but we'll stay in touch."

For the next two days, a blizzard raged and all the lifts were closed.

Still, there was more than enough to occupy our time. Tony's friend, Nadim, picked us up and showed us around the beach-resort city of Jounieh, 20 kilometers north of Beirut. We also gambled at the Casino du Liban. While the snow was dumping on the Dome, 20 crow kilometers away, it was sunny on the coast, and we went swimming in the outskirts of Byblos, the oldest city in the world. There, one can rummage through the ruins of seventeen civilizations, the oldest of which dates back to 5000 B.C.

When we finally returned to Faraya, a meter of new snow was blocking the doorway to Tony's apartment. The treeless mountains resembled a moonscape, drenched in a thick, new coat of white, and the deep blue of the sea and the sky almost blended into a horizonless backdrop to this unusual panorama.

The wind had howled mercilessly during the storm, but to our surprise, the slopes were not rutted, uneven and unskiable wind crust. Instead, the combination of wind and humid sea air had created a kind of compressed powder that made for excellent skiing. It was not deep powder, for one only sank into the upper 5–10 centimeters, but there was still enough to savor and enjoy its virgin qualities.

In spite of the cloudless skies, it was midweek, so the slopes were empty. We had a free pass to Disneyland and all the other kids were at school! We didn't know which untracked slope to violate first.

Besides the fresh snow and empty slopes, the friendly people left a deep impression on us. In the morning, I rode up the lift with Nayef Kassatly, a local skier who took the time to show us a few off-piste routes. Around lunchtime, we ran into Christian Rizk, the administrative director of Faraya. He apologized that the uppermost lift was closed, as winds of up to 150 kilometers per hour had blown the lift cable down. He quickly organized snowmobiles to transport us to a higher point on the mountain and still more first tracks.

Late in the day, we decided to try an off-piste descent from Faraya to the nearby resort of Faqra. Of course, we had no lift ticket for Faqra—no problem.

"Oh, you are here from America and Sweden? Welcome. Do you like Lebanon? I am glad. Please take the lift up."

From the top of Faqra, we spied the lone lift of the Qanat Bakiche ski area, also within striking distance. To ski three areas in one day would be a feather in our cap, we thought, and we began a long traverse. Unfortunately, we ran out of vertical a good 20-minute walk from our destination. At that very moment, two youths playing on snowmo-

» **Lifts stretched up into a horseshoe-shaped bowl, half the size of Alaska.«**

biles came zooming over a knoll, and 2 minutes later, we were whisking our way to the lift on two impromptu, free-of-charge snow taxis.

It was too late, for the lift had already closed. This was also no hindrance.

"You have come from so far away to ski here in Lebanon? How nice. Of course, we can allow you to have one run also in Bakiche."

Like magic, the lift was reopened.

Sick of almost two decades of war and international isolation, each person we met was so happy to meet a foreigner that their joy seemed to emerge from every pore. Young people were full of curiosity to meet foreigners. Older people were glad, for each tourist reaffirmed a slow return to normalcy.

Each person we encountered was extremely concerned about what we thought of Lebanon and how we liked it. It is a nation with a complex—like a divorced person back in the singles market after twenty years of marriage—psychologically scarred and physically aged and worn, insecure and unsure if he or she is still attractive enough or has anything to offer to somebody new.

Early Friday morning, we left Tony's Faraya apartment and headed north, driving up the southern flank of the spectacular Kadisha Valley, where old mountain villages like Hasroun, Hadchit and Bécharré are built along the cliffs of the canyon. From Bécharré, we crept along the winding and poorly maintained road to the Cedars ski resort, named for a grove of these famous, ancient trees situated near the ski area. These trees, so much a part of the Lebanese history and psyche that they are featured on its flag, were exported all over the known world back in the days of King Solomon, until the country was deforested. A few groves of these beautiful trees still survive; some of the cedars are more than 1000 years old.

Whereas Faraya is a relatively modern ski resort that caters to the sophisticated Beirut crowd, the Cedars resort has much of the local color that one might expect to find in a Middle Eastern ski area. A group of Muslim teenagers were frolicking in the snow at the base of the lift. A hundred pairs of pre-civil war ski boots were spread out on the parking lot flanked by skis of a similar vintage—a kind of makeshift rental shop. Across the parking lot stood Lebanon's oldest lift, a single chair lift from the early '50s deemed obsolete about twenty years earlier, but still standing, a nostalgic reminder of the pioneer days of Lebanese skiing.

This relic, as well as the newer lifts, stretched up into a horseshoe-shaped bowl, half the size of Alaska. A person with a pair of telemark skis and skins could spend most of his life skiing different descents from end to end of this enormous bowl.

Like most Lebanese ski areas, Cedars operated under the same set of principles that I had found in so much of the more undeveloped ski world. Namely, they open a number of lifts commensurate with the skier turnout of the day. But Hassib Fakhry, the elderly owner of the lifts, like every other Lebanese we had met, aimed to please. While we took a few runs on the one operating lift, he sent one employee to open a higher T-bar for us to try. He even dispatched another of his personnel to dig out the upper lift, so that his foreign visitors could sample the full variety of slopes.

WHEN THE NEXT BLIZZARD BLEW IN off the Mediterranean Sea the following day, Christer and I retreated down the valley to the picturesque village of Bécharré, birthplace of the painter, poet and prophet, Khalil Gibran. We visited the Gibran museum and the beautiful St. Antoine Monastery a little further down the valley.

Then we headed south to see the Roman ruins at Baalbek, an absolute must for any visitor to Lebanon. A person may have seen the Acropolis in Athens or the Roman Colosseum, but they cannot outshine the remains of the Temple of Jupiter and the Temple of Bacchus in Baalbek. The sheer size of the structures, the amount of what is still intact, and the lack of tourists with which one has to share this archaeological wonder combine to create a unique experience. The six remaining pillars of Jupiter's Temple are 22 meters high, the world's tallest, and some of the blocks of stone used at this site are also among the largest in the world. In the old Roman quarry nearby is one stone, almost ready for use in some future project, which weighs approximately 1000 tons and would take 40,000 men to move into place.

We returned to Beirut that evening for a final night on the town with

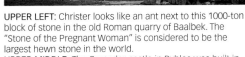

UPPER LEFT: Christer looks like an ant next to this 1000-ton block of stone in the old Roman quarry of Baalbek. The "Stone of the Pregnant Woman" is considered to be the largest hewn stone in the world.
UPPER MIDDLE: The Crusader castle in Byblos was built in the 12th century.
UPPER RIGHT: With nineteen of its 42 Corinthian pillars still standing, the Temple of Bacchus in Baalbek is one of the best-preserved Roman temples in the world.
LOWER LEFT: With the skiing only an hour's drive from the coast, in spring one can swim in the sea and ski on the same day.
LOWER RIGHT: The shadows of some clouds looked like small islands on the golden surface of the Mediterranean Sea, as we drove from Faraya back to Beirut at sunset.

Close to the Cedars ski center is one of the few locations in Lebanon where the famous cedar trees still exist.

Tony and Nadim. They took us to dinner at an up-market Tex-Mex place called the Lone Star Cafe, and we stopped into a few other bars along the way.

Each time I tried to pay something, Tony or Nadim stepped in, grabbed my hand, and chided, "No, you are in Lebanon now!"

We had a half-day left on this journey already so filled with diverse impressions. We wandered through a slum district of Beirut where the devastation of the war was still evident. Some of the shells of destroyed houses were still inhabited.

It was not with despair, however, that we observed the wreckage of the war, for the strife was over, and had been for some years now. The center of Beirut has undergone a multi-billion-dollar facelift, the Baalbek Music Festival, founded in 1955, is again an annual event after a 25-year hiatus, and the world-famous Lebanese wine production is back in full swing. In the Cedars resort, an infusion of capital is currently being used to update all the lifts. Lebanon is back on the tourist map and the skiers' map as well.

I looked at the few remaining ruins through my camera lens as I had peered at the remnants of seventeen civilizations in Byblos. The war was a closed page of history, no less than the ancient ruins nearby. The snowy mountains and the shimmering sea, in such stunning proximity, will beckon more international skiers and sunbathers every year, as in days of yore. And the warmhearted Lebanese people, prevented for so many years from showering their hospitality on outsiders, will meet more and more recipients for their kindness and generosity. This is a time of renaissance and rejuvenation.

Africa and The Middle East in a Nutshell

LOCATION	NEAREST TOWN	NEAREST AIRPORT	SEASON	PEAK ELEVATION	VERTICAL DROP	SIZE	SNOW	BEAUTY	VILLAGE	NOVICE	INTERMEDIATE	ADVANCED	OFF-PISTE	NIGHTLIFE	RATING AVERAGE	WEB SITE
IRAN																
Dizin	Gajereh	Tehran	late November–late May	3550 m	850 m	3	2	5	3	2	3	4	2	4	1	2.9	www.skifed.ir
Shemshak	Shemshak	Tehran	late November–early April	2850 m	550 m	2	1	5	3	3	1	2	4	4	2	2.7	www.skifed.ir
Tochal	Tehran	Tehran	December–April	3850 m	850 m	3	1	5	4	2	3	3	2	2	2	2.7	www.goski.com/rira/tochal.htm
LEBANON																
Cedars	Bécharré	Tripoli	November–late April	2700 m	550 m	2	1	3	4	2	3	4	2	2	2	2.5	www.skileb.com
Faraya	Hrajel	Beirut	late December–April	2465 m	615 m	2	2	3	4	3	4	4	2	3	3	3.0	www.skileb.com
MOROCCO																
Oukaïmeden	Tahanaout	Marrakech	January–mid March	3258 m	663 m	2	1	3	4	2	2	2	3	3	1	2.3	www.snow-forecast.com/resorts/Oukaimeden.html
TURKEY																
Mt. Erciyes	Kayseri	Kayseri	late November–late April	2774 m	559 m	2	1	3	3	2	2	3	2	3	1	2.2	www.guidetoturkey.com/ski_centers
Palandöken	Erzurum	Erzurum	early Dec.–early May	3100 m	900 m	3	1	4	3	1	3	3	4	4	1	2.7	www.adiyamanli.org/winter_sports_turkey.htm
Saklikent	Elmali	Antalya	late December–mid April	2130 m	240 m	1	1	2	4	2	3	3	2	2	1	2.1	www.saklikent.com.tr
Uludag	Bursa	Istanbul	late December–late March	2232 m	467 m	2	2	3	2	3	5	3	1	2	3	2.4	www.guidetoturkey.com/ski_centers

OCEANIA IX

PREVIOUS PAGES: Lake Coleridge, behind the Porter Heights ski center, provides a classic New Zealand panorama.
THIS PAGE: A four-wheel-drive vehicle was not enough to conquer the Mt. Olympus road without the help of a Bulldozer. Driving down was somewhat easier.
RIGHT PAGE: Tuomas Uotila picks a path through the seracs, crevasses and ice caves of the Tasman Glacier.

Chapter 46. NEW ZEALAND

ONLY THE STRONG SURVIVE

Skiing in New Zealand is a decidedly different experience than skiing in most other parts of the world. To understand the differences, one must begin with special definitions for a few words as they are commonly used in New Zealand.

kiwi: an indigenous bird; *Kiwi*: a person from New Zealand. In this essay it is the human Kiwi who is most relevant.

Powder snow: wind slab, wind crust, or wind-packed snow. Americans and Europeans define the word *powder* as a light, fluffy, fresh-fallen snow. Most Kiwis have never seen this kind of powder.

Mission: a very difficult task, usually involving danger as well as great effort to accomplish.

Two words that are *not* part of the local lexicon are *comfort* and *convenience*. In the world of *Kiwis*, it is quite a *mission* to go skiing in *powder snow*. In fact, all of the rules, customs and habits that have traditionally defined the manner in which one organizes a ski holiday can be thrown out the window in New Zealand. Press delete and start with a new frame of reference.

Kiwis are a tough bunch, and they have to be, especially the skiers. In this strange, upside-down country, every part of skiing is an adventure: getting to the ski slopes, riding the infamous "nutcracker" rope tows, and surviving the often brutal and fickle weather conditions. But the skiing can be a wonderful adventure and a stunning nature experience that makes it all worthwhile.

To begin with, a fair number of New Zealand's so-called ski resorts are "club fields"—low-budget ski areas operated by local ski clubs. These ski centers generally have dirt access roads where four-wheel drive, chains or both are almost always mandatory. Even many of the commercial areas fall into this category. Many of these club fields are dominated by long rope tows the likes of which have not been seen for half a century or more in the rest of the ski world. Visitors often stay in inexpensive clubhouses where everybody shares in kitchen duties and other chores. This is not something for the Gstaad or Deer Valley crowd.

Even if one has skied in Eastern Europe or Asia, one has not really experienced primitive infrastructure until one visits the club fields of New Zealand. Visitors to Temple Basin, for example, must hike for an hour between the parking lot and the ski lifts for a morning warmup!

New Zealand is a nation obsessed with weather, and for good reason—it has some of the most fickle conditions on the planet. Whether one is a sheep farmer or a skier, weather is extremely important, and the country is regularly exposed to heavy rains and gale-force winds, which can come and go at a moment's notice.

It is not at all abnormal here for 80 percent or more of the ski areas to be entirely closed on any given day because of high winds or impassable roads. The access roads to most of the ski fields seem to have been designed and engineered by the same folks who create the latest amusement-park roller coasters—but the New Zealand roads have left out the safety features.

Vehicles often must drive up steep grades above cliffs, and there are never any guardrails. The access to Mt. Hutt, one of the South Island's premiere resorts, is so exposed that numerous automobiles have blown off the road over the years. And the largest ski resort in the country sometimes misses a full season due to volcanic eruptions.

Despite all these problems, on any given day, the Maori Gods can smile down and bestow an epic day upon the local riders. The trick is merely to hit as many of those memorable days as possible and have a good book with which to while away the down days.

One's plans must be loose and one needs a car for spontaneous flexibility. Many of the ski resorts in New Zealand are clustered into a few different areas, and an early-morning Internet visit might reveal that one of the nearby resorts is open while all the others are not functioning for a variety of reasons. Alternatively, the orientation of one ski field might render the snow quality poor, while another area right around the corner could have much better conditions. Skiing New Zealand is a research project in progress.

THIS PAGE

UPPER: Tuomas drops from a small cornice in Treble Cone, with Lake Wanaka in the background. The New Zealand scenery looks quite unusual as a result of major deforestation that began with the early Polynesian settlers and continued during the period of European colonization and settlement. MIDDLE LEFT: The North Island is famous for its geysers. New Zealand has the third-largest number of active geysers in the world, behind the United States and Russia. MIDDLE RIGHT: At Hot Water Beach on the North Island, one can dig out one's own private hot tub during low tide. One must mix cold sea

water with hot thermal water to create a temperature to suit one's fancy.
LOWER LEFT: Not every activity in New Zealand is extreme. Lawn bowling is very popular with New Zealand's older generation. The Rotorua Museum of Art and History provides an Old World background to the lawn bowling at Government Gardens.
LOWER RIGHT: Tuomas prepares to abseil into the Ruakuri Cave on the North Island.

RIGHT PAGE

A snowboarder enjoys one of the natural halfpipes in the Whakapapa ski area.

MT. RUAPEHU

My friend Tuomas Uotila and I began our visit to New Zealand on the North Island, where the main source of skiing is Mt. Ruapehu, a very active volcano that is home to the ski fields of Whakapapa, Turoa and Tukino. Skiing here is unique. Most skiers know about the dangers of avalanches and crevasses, but *lahar* is not generally a part of our vocabulary. New Zealand skiers, however, generally know that a *lahar* is a mud flow from a volcano.

Upon arrival at the Whakapapa ski resort, along with a trail map we received a brochure entitled "Volcanic Hazards at Whakapapa Mt. Ruapehu". It explained about the dangers of gas, flying rocks and particularly *lahars*, which can glide down the mountain gullies at about 100 kilometers per hour. This information could come in quite handy, as the winter seasons of 1995 and 1996 were both abruptly terminated by eruptions.

The brochure tells about an "Eruption Detection System" that has been improved since the last outbursts. It automatically initiates a warning siren and loudspeaker announcement in case of any unusual volcanic activity. This system can, according to the pamphlet, "give more than a minute of warning to skiers on even the highest runs."

"Gosh, a whole minute," I thought to myself. "That really puts me at ease!"

As it turned out, what we really needed in Whakapapa was an ice warning system. I noticed that the ski patrol carried crampons and an ice ax as standard equipment, and I seriously began to contemplate whether I could somehow affix crampons to my skis to get a better grip on the slopes. Eruptions only come about every decade or so, but ice is a much more regular part of life on Mt. Ruapehu.

In fact, the pistes on the mountain are very well-groomed, and not that icy. It was the off-piste sections of the mountain that were more suitable for hockey than skiing. Interestingly enough, Mt. Ruapehu is not only subject to extremes of wind and weather, but the weather conditions can differ greatly between the various ski areas on the same mountain.

THE FOLLOWING DAY, WE TESTED the slopes at Turoa, on the opposite side of the volcano. Merely driving up on the south side was a completely different experience than the day before's. The landscape approaching Whakapapa had consisted of a flat plateau with no trees, while to reach Turoa, we wound our way through thick beech forest, mixed with a blend of ferns, palms and various other plant life.

On this, the shady side of the mountain, the handicraft of the strong New Zealand westerly wind was very visible. Everything from the rock faces to the mid-station restaurant was covered in a thick layer of rime. As I surveyed the scene, I prepared for the worst.

I was pleasantly surprised. There was no wind that day, and the views stretched over rain forest, farmland and rolling hills all the way to the horizon. Turoa had received about 10 centimeters of snow that had evaded Whakapapa. The bowls and gullies on the eastern side of the mountain were superb, with fresh tracks to be made in a variety of protected places.

A fair number of riders could be observed making the 75-minute hike to the peak for an extra-long ride in the soft snow. The peak holds an additional attraction—Crater Lake. This is a sight that is difficult to describe, as it changes appearance almost as quickly as the weather.

The lake used to be a spectacular green color, providing a dramatic subject for numerous postcards. People even used to swim it its warm water. Then for quite some time after the most recent eruptions, it was a steaming, bubbling cauldron of hot water.

Nowadays, Crater Lake is a murky brownish-gray color and large amounts of sulfur render it unfit for swimming. Tomorrow? Who knows? Crater Lake, like the wind and weather on Mt. Ruapehu, is a fickle friend, changing constantly. If skiing is a dynamic sport, it certainly becomes more so in a spot where the mountain is dynamic as well.

THE NEXT MORNING THE DYNAMICS changed drastically. The weather report read, "Cloudy with rain developing during the afternoon and northwesterlies rising to 100 kilometers per hour with gusts of 150 kilometers per hour about the tops. Freezing level rising to 2000 meters." It was definitely time to bring out the good book reserved for such days.

Alternatively, some resourceful locals have developed a different kind of adventure ride not too far away, in the Ruakuri Cave. Marketed as "Black Water Rafting", the caves offer a treat that adrenaline junkies almost can't afford to pass up. The excitement begins by abseiling about 50 meters into the caves, followed by making a leap of faith into the river, and tubing in a sub-terrestrial stream under a glowworm-studded ceiling. The

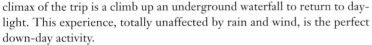

climax of the trip is a climb up an underground waterfall to return to daylight. This experience, totally unaffected by rain and wind, is the perfect down-day activity.

The caves can save skiers from boredom for the first down day, but the weather service had promised about four such days. I thought it prudent to move to the South Island.

MT. HUTT

Mt. Hutt is one of the best and most popular ski fields in New Zealand. It is situated a half-hour's drive from Methvyn, an archetypal New Zealand village. Known to its detractors as "Mt. Shut" because of the tendency for wind to close the access road, Mt. Hutt nevertheless has many fans, owing to the fact that it is the highest ski field and has the most vertical of any resort on the South Island. On a clear day, one can gaze out over the green patchwork quilt of the Canterbury Plains all the way to the sea.

At Mt. Hutt, like many of the New Zealand ski fields, there are numer-

ous variables that have to fall into place to allow for the optimal ski experience. The first question is whether the road is open. A 7 a.m. check on the Web told us it was, but the upper lifts were on "wind hold". Once again, that translates into a day for good skiers to find an alternative activity.

THE FOLLOWING MORNING, the road and all lifts were operating, and we headed up. Unfortunately, the day didn't pass the third criterion. All of the black runs were closed due to ice, and the backcountry was equally firm. Tuomas, a former racer for whom ice is a way of life, enjoyed the morning hours, but I prefer my ice in a gin and tonic.

By 11 a.m., the whimsical weather had changed. The fog had rolled in, it began snowing and lightning struck one of the chair lifts, closing it temporarily. We went in for an early lunch. By early afternoon, all lifts were back in operation, and a few inches of powder cushioned the previously bone-hard surface. It was all just one more four-course menu of N.Z. weather.

THE LAKES AND THE SOUTHERN ALPS

The resorts of the Southern Alps have the most hospitable skiing in New Zealand, and some of the most beautiful ski resorts in the world. Treble Cone offers tremendous views of Lake Wanaka, while Coronet Peak, Cardrona and The Remarkables all look out over Lake Wakatipu. Wind is generally less of a problem in this region of the country, and all four mountains are commercial areas where rope tows have disappeared long ago.

For better or worse, one of the idiosyncrasies of New Zealand skiing is that the accommodation is usually in a town or village in the valley, between 20 and 60 minutes' drive from the ski field. While this sort of inconvenience does not sit well with the French, who are accustomed to skiing from their door to the lifts, it does mean that visitors here generally live in a snow-free environment. Therefore, it is quite possible to alternate skiing with various activities not usually equated with winter.

If one wants to take a day off from skiing because of weather or other reasons, one is never at a loss for something to do in and around nearby Queenstown. This is a town that caters to adrenaline junkies. It was here, from the Kawarau Bridge, that A. J. Hackett started the bungee-jumping craze back in 1988, and it is still going strong. In addition to that lunacy, one can also try paragliding, hang-gliding, sky diving, aerobatic biplane rides, jetboating, whitewater rafting, and a few New Zealand inventions that defy description. For tourists without a death wish, there is also hot-air ballooning, horseback riding, fly fishing, golfing and hiking.

Despite the fact that New Zealand is chock full of a myriad of extreme sports, perhaps the most dangerous activity of all for a tourist (at least a non-British Commonwealth tourist) is to drive his rental car around in this backwards, right-hand-drive country. On a couple of occasions, I found myself starting the morning in the wrong lane of traffic on a collision course with an oncoming car, before I quickly veered off the road in utter shock.

It was in exactly this fashion that Tuomas and I began our drive up to Treble Cone, perhaps the best skier's mountain in the country. The

Lake Wakatipu costars with Tuomas in this photo from The Remarkables.

pistes here are excellent cruisers, on which some of the European national teams come to train, but most of the mountain is an open playground of freeride terrain. It is full of ridges, gullies, cliff jumps and a handful of very steep chutes west of the Saddle T-bar. On most of the mountain, it looks as if one will ski right into Lake Wanaka below.

An hour further south is a resort called The Remarkables. They got their name because the range runs due north and south. While this may seem unusual to some people, the views here are even more remarkable, and the skiing is also worth mentioning. The Remarkables are ideally suited for spring skiing, with a large expanse of east-facing freeride terrain for the morning, and the west-facing hike-accessed Toilet Bowl for afternoon corn snow. Both of these options take riders down to the road, where a shuttle bus does a regular pickup. For the extreme skiers, a 20–40 minute hike accesses a series of south-facing chutes that drop down to the frozen Lake Alta.

Just as some of the most interesting skiing is not that obvious, neither are the views, as they too are not visible without a short walk. A five-minute hike from the top of the Shadow Basin Lift, however, is all that is necessary to attain one of the best panoramas anywhere.

Coronet Peak also has lovely scenery, albeit at a greater distance from Lake Wakatipu. There is nothing here that is as steep as the chutes down to Lake Alta, but off-piste road-runs are possible and the pistes are more abundant and more varied than at The Remarkables. This is an excellent resort for intermediate skiers but is enjoyable for all ability groups.

The last resort in this region, Cardrona, has great cruising runs and one of the best terrain parks in the country. In addition, the Arcadia Chutes section of the mountain has some relatively steep descents between the rocks that will keep advanced skiers interested.

THE MACKENZIE REGION

A few hours north of Queenstown are the ski fields of the MacKenzie region of New Zealand, including Mt. Dobson, Fox Peak, Round Hill and Ohau. The atmosphere is entirely different here than in the Lake District. The hype and bustle dissipate the further north one drives, and one suddenly finds oneself in an area of desolate beauty, where a ski field is accompanied by two or three lodges in the valley and not much else.

Ohau is just such a place. It is a commercial resort with a club field atmosphere. Tuomas and I checked into the Lake Ohau Lodge, a cozy accommodation with two hot tubs and stunning lake views, and we proceeded 10 kilometers up one of the usual hair-raising mountain roads that typify New Zealand skiing.

Like many of the small New Zealand fields, Ohau's skiing is centered on a couple of lifts that go straight up the middle of a large basin. Most of the skiing is rather steep, and one can traverse far out to either side to reach a wide array of slopes. In addition, 30–60-minute hikes along the ridge behind the upper lift bring skiers to new bowls and chutes in the backcountry.

We began with a morning hike along the ridge. Lake Ohau's turquoise waters of glacial silt seemed close enough to touch. After a 45-minute walk, we dove into the spring snow on Hemi's, a lovely run down to the access road.

We had ambitious plans for a descent of one of the couloirs known as the Northeast Bluffs in the afternoon, but it was not to be—at least not as anticipated. A 30-minute hike took us to a wide choice of steep slopes down a back bowl east of the resort. We swooped down in long arcs toward a traverse that would access the couloirs.

The east-facing traverse, however, was isothermal, and our plan had to be abandoned. The avalanche risk was too great. Instead of finishing our day with a long, lovely chute, we plodded back up the same steep pitch we had just descended. With our backs to the valley, we couldn't even enjoy the lake view any longer.

I could take solace in only one thing. The extra hiking would serve as a good warmup for the days to come. We were heading for the club fields of Arthur's Pass, and hiking is the name of the game in all these little ski fields. We had just done a day of basic training.

ARTHUR'S PASS

I walked into the Springfield Pub to get a bit of information about the various ski fields that lie a short distance up Arthur's Pass from Springfield. Soon, I was chatting with David Vallet, a South African working as a ski instructor at Porter Heights.

With David's help, Tuomas and I moved into an empty room in the Springfield Holiday Lodge, an accommodation otherwise occupied almost entirely by the Porter Heights Ski School. The next morning was one of those New Zealand days that one hopes for—new snow, blue sky, and no wind.

It was here, however, that I had my first encounter with another one of the dangerous aspects of New Zealand skiing. The kea, the world's only alpine parrot, is a bird indigenous exclusively to New Zealand's South Island. They are mischievous beasts who relish in pecking the rubber out of windshield wipers or absconding with any item left loose by some unwary tourist. They can be found plotting trouble in all of the southern ski fields. My left ski glove became victim to one of their evil deeds.

PORTER HEIGHTS HAS A FEW short pistes and two steep, off-piste faces known as Big Mama and Bluff Face. Tuomas and I made first tracks on Big Mama, and went into the Dome Restaurant for a bite of breakfast. The Dome is a bizarre, igloo-shaped building with portholes for windows. It looks as if it had been designed by Captain Nemo.

Sitting dejectedly with a cup of coffee was David. The director of the ski school had sent him home because he was not clean-shaven, and David was unsure of his fate and future in Porter Heights.

One person's misfortune is often another's good luck. We suddenly found ourselves with a new playmate, and a knowledgeable one at that.

We cut some fresh tracks on Bluff Face, and David showed us the panorama of Lake Coleridge behind the resort.

Then he pointed out Crystal Valley, a vast bowl funneling into a river valley that eventually ran out of snow a short walk from the road. David had never skied it, but he knew the way. The untouched snow told us that nobody else had skied it since the last snowfall. Steep, wind-blown powder slopes near the entry gave way to a rare substance almost akin to "real" powder in the guts of the valley. It was the perfect finish to the day.

The following morning, David showed up at the ski school with no trace of stubble and all was forgiven. Meanwhile, we pointed our car toward Mt. Olympus and our first encounter with the dreaded "nutcrackers". To add to the challenges of the Kiwi rope-tow torture, the route to this club field is one of the most atrocious mountain roads in the country. It is sometimes said that getting there is half the fun, and in the case of the club fields, getting there is also half the adventure. The Kiwis succinctly say, "It's a mission!"

We had been warned that one could not reach the ski field without a four-wheel-drive vehicle, so we parked our rental Holden and hitched a ride from a brave local woman in a four-by-four Honda. It, too, proved to be inadequate to conquer the 30-centimeter-deep mud ruts that filled the lower road. Ultimately, a bulldozer towed us through the worst section, and we arrived at the lifts a mere hour behind schedule.

We never found out if the bulldozer service was standard procedure at Mt. Olympus or a fortuitous happenstance. One thing did become clear upon our drive down, however, when we observed another four-wheel-drive vehicle that had been abandoned, barely clinging to the side of the road at a 45-degree angle. Not everybody had been as lucky as we had.

Having attained the parking lot, we were really only half done. We still

UPPER LEFT: Part of a traditional Maori war dance involves male dancers sticking out their tongues, rolling their eyes, and making grimaces. Maoris traditionally had tattoos to scare their enemies. A bone chisel was used in what was an extremely long and painful process.
UPPER RIGHT: Cathedral Cove in the Coromandel region of the North Island.
LOWER LEFT: With about 47 million sheep, New Zealand's sheep population is more than ten times greater than the human population. Fortunately, none of the sheep are skiers.
LOWER RIGHT: Two Keas up to their usual mischief, pecking at the rubber around the windows of this car.

had to reach the mountain summit. First of all, we needed some special equipment, beginning with a "nutcracker". This is a device shaped like the ordinary tool for cracking nuts. It hangs from some twine attached to a belt that skiers wear around their waists and clamps onto the fast-moving rope tows.

The veterans of the area often attach the device to a climbing harness to avoid putting all the strain of the tow ride on their lower back. A harness is not really standard equipment in my backpack, so I had to make do with the ordinary belt apparatus that is available at the club fields. Another necessary piece of equipment is a pair of glove protectors, for sale at the fields. Without them one can discard one's hand gear in the rubbish bin at the end of the day or earlier.

Once properly equipped, "nutcracker" lessons are mandatory. A friendly ski patrolman demonstrated how I should take firm hold of the rope with my inside hand, while quickly flipping the medieval instrument of torture over the rope with a flick of the wrist. The process must be completed quickly, before the rope reaches the first pulley wheel, where survival dictates that you must release your inside hand from the rope or have your hand crushed. The *click-clack* noise as the rope passes over or through the pulley wheels indicates that all has gone well, whereas the *squish-squash* sound should be avoided.

UNFORTUNATELY, THE QUICK FLIP does not always function smoothly. To his credit, the ski patrolman showed an abundance of patience and gave me repeated instruction as I misfired numerous times before ultimately completing my first successful mission. Perhaps I should say "semi-successful". While holding the "nutcracker", one's fingers come extremely close to the dreaded pulley wheels at each small tower. I cringed and closed my eyes at each critical moment and invariably pulled the rope off the wheel. By the time I reached the top, the entire towrope was dragging on the snow.

Tuomas did not fare better. Our teacher forgot to mention the neces-

sity of an Elvis hip swivel to the outside while passing the pulley wheels. These rope tows eat GORE-TEX, and Tuomas arrived at the top with a 10-centimeter bite taken out of his ski pants.

We marveled at the local women and children who completed the whole procedure perfectly without batting an eye. Our only consolation was that the ordeal was even more torturous for snowboarders.

The Mt. Olympus road and the "nutcracker" turned out to be the main adventures of the day. A light rain was falling on the ski slopes, and the snowpack was isothermal, eliminating any thought of off-piste adventures. The skiing was as bad as the previous day had been good. Steep and dramatic-looking slopes tantalized our imagination from all sides, but we could only fantasize.

BY NOW WE HAD BEEN in New Zealand long enough to notice that this country has a higher percentage of snowboarders than anywhere else in the world, and I was beginning to understand why. The boarders were having no trouble in the thick, wet snow, just as they glide through wind pack as if it were powder. They were having fun even in the rain, while we skiers were relegated to pushing through the porridge and hoping for better times.

It is in the club fields that one understands the historical roots of New Zealand skiing and also comprehends the innate toughness of its inhabitants. Our visit to Broken River, where the club members had built the road themselves with a homemade bulldozer, was another example of this. Here our ordeal began with the mounting of chains where the highway meets the dirt road. A 15-minute drive through a thick forest of mountain beech trees brought us to the parking lot.

We now threw our skis and packs onto a "goods lift" that took them to the lodge, while we hiked for 20 minutes. The lodge was an interim stop. Pick up the gear, buy a lift ticket, and walk 10 minutes further to the Rugby Lift, so named because its first motor was taken from a 1920s Rugby car.

LEFT PAGE
One of Broken River's rope tows.

THIS PAGE
UPPER LEFT: The turquoise water of Lake Ohau is close enough to touch as Tuomas enjoys an off-piste run down Hemi's in the Ohau ski area.
UPPER RIGHT: Cardrona farmer John Lee collects and displays bras on his fence alongside the highway that passes by his farm. Some women strip down right by the fence and leave their undergarments, but Mr. Lee even gets bras sent in the mail.
LOWER LEFT: Our plane trip to the Tasman Glacier afforded us stunning views of the glacial scenery around Mt. Cook.
LOWER RIGHT: Tuomas cruises among the seracs of the Tasman Glacier.

This was day two of our "Nutcracker Ballet", but I had not yet achieved Nureyev status. The rope tow track was no piece of cake here, as it was steep, uneven, icy and sloped down to the left. On one occasion, it took me a dozen false starts before finally making it past the first pulley.

Once one has managed to get to the top at Broken River, coming back down is not much easier. The slopes are skier-groomed, since there is no way of getting a snow cat up the mountain to do modern grooming. This means that even the beginners tow is riddled with uneven terrain.

To a freerider, of course, the absence of prepared pistes is a blessing, as it leaves more area than usual on which to make first tracks. To either side of the main bowl at Broken River are short, steep pitches running down side valleys. We skied both Avalanche and Allan's Basin a few times, and ultimately finished the day by skiing the latter valley all the way down to the parking lot. This was by far the best and longest run of the day, and saved me the effort of hiking back down, something I was truly not ready for after six hours of struggling with the "nutcrackers".

ONE VALLEY NORTH OF BROKEN RIVER is Craigieburn, acre for acre the most difficult ski area in the world. Cragieburn offers no quarter for the weak and no rest for the weary. Three consecutive "nutcrackers" are required to reach the top, and then one has a choice of single-, double-, and even triple-diamond descents. The trail map defines these three categories as "expert," "tricky" and "suicidal." The intermediate runs here are un-groomed 30-degree slopes, and there are not many.

The morning snow report promised 15 centimeters of powder. Most of that powder was on the road, where even four-by-fours needed chains. We hitched a ride up with a local, and his chains fell off three times on the steepest pitches.

By the time we reached the lifts, the fluffy stuff was gone. The slopes were covered with "NZ powder"—breakable wind slab on the south faces and heavy, wet snow on the eastern slope. The wind at the top was strong enough to blow anybody lighter than a rugby player right off the ridge—just another run-of-the-mill ski day in New Zealand.

Tuomas, a former top junior racer, went into his GS mode and aggressively powered his way down. Meanwhile, I tried powder technique, piste style, old-school jump turns, New-School big-mountain turns, and a number of fusion techniques, all to no avail. It was mortal combat.

The terrain was spectacular. We skied Siberia Basin, and a couple of runs down Hamilton Face. Then we dropped into one of the multi-diamond chutes. It emptied into Middle Basin, and left us on the road, a 15-minute walk from the lower lift.

At lunch, I gazed up at the chutes with my trail map in hand, trying to figure out whether we had skied a double-diamond or triple-diamond couloir, but I was quickly deflated by one of the local club members.

"Those diamonds aren't very relevant right now," he said. "This is the most snow we've had in ten years. The chutes are all too easy now. Try coming back in early season in a bad winter. Then, those diamonds have some meaning!"

After lunch, I had enough energy left for one more struggle with the nutcrackers and one last run down Hamilton, and I was ready for a session with my chiropractor and an hour in the Jacuzzi. I usually consider skiing to be fun. This day had been more like a marathon workout at the gym.

THE TASMAN GLACIER

When Hans Gmoser invented heliskiing in the mid-1960s, he was actually a few years behind the New Zealanders with regard to accessing ski terrain by air; but in the Southern Hemisphere, it all started with ski planes on the Tasman Glacier. In September 1955, the first such landing was made, and shortly thereafter, skiers began being dropped onto the glacier by the small planes. Five decades later, things have changed somewhat, but the planes are still offering skiers the opportunity to ski amidst some of the most spectacular scenery in the world.

In the early '60s, as a youngster, I viewed a ski film depicting Stein Eriksson bounding among the seracs and crevasses of the Tasman, and I determined that this was a location that I must visit some day. It took a long time, but I finally made it. As a culmination of our visit to New

Zealand, Tuomas and I joined Trevor Streat of Alpine Heliguides on a perfect, cloudless day for two descents in this winter wonderland.

The Tasman has not changed much since those early beginnings five decades earlier, but the ski world has. Since the advent of heliskiing two generations ago, skiers have regularly been dropped onto much more difficult slopes than those where a ski plane can deposit them. In addition, since the beginning of the '90s, the extreme-skiing rage has annually pushed the envelope, as ever steeper terrain is being accessed by air in Alaska, the Himalayas and other spots around the globe.

The rather flat skiing of the Tasman, an experience for the ski elite of 50 years ago, is now far too tame to attract today's generation of thrill seekers. Instead, it services an entirely different clientele. This is a location where even low intermediates can ski fresh snow and enjoy a unique nature experience.

Rather than sharing the slopes with the helmet-and-transceiver crowd, we were joined on this excursion by a host of Japanese skiers who stemmed and snowplowed their way over the glacier. After putting my

survival skills to the test in the likes of Craigieburn, Broken River and Mt. Ohau, the tame, mellow descents suited me fine. Compared with the club field mode of uphill transportation, our little Cessna 185 was like a Rolls Royce limo. And the snow was not wind pack, sun crust or wet cement.

Here, on the Tasman, we glided through miles of true powder. Gigantic fields of seracs rose above us to the west on Mt. Cook, Mt. Tasman, and a host of New Zealand's highest peaks. We slithered between crevasses and explored ice caves. Best of all, there was not a "nutcracker" in site.

THIS PAGE
UPPER: Landing atop the Tasman Glacier.
LOWER LEFT: There are many ice caves to discover amidst the fairytale world of the Tasman Glacier.
LOWER RIGHT: Our guide, Trevor Streat, leads Tuomas down the Tasman in gentle fields of powder.

RIGHT PAGE
Trevor skis among the giant seracs of the Tasman Glacier.

THIS PAGE
Tuomas Uotila carves through the snowgums in Perisher Blue.

RIGHT PAGE
LEFT: Talangatta is not the epicenter of Australian tourism. Maybe they close the gas pumps early to keep a few visitors around—at least for one night.
RIGHT: The village of Falls Creek can be seen at the base of the Summit Chair.

Chapter 47. AUSTRALIA

AUSTRALIAN ROAD-TRIP OR THE LIFE OF A SKI JOURNALIST

Many skiers believe that I have the ideal job, and I must admit that I have no complaints. I travel around the world with my laptop and camera, exploring the best and the most exotic ski destinations on Earth. It is a wonderful life and I am grateful for it.

Even on a bad-weather day, as the wind and snow are abusing my exposed face on some mountaintop, I often say to whomever is on the chair lift next to me, "It still beats going to the office."

Or as ski hall-of-famer and powder guru Alf Engen once told me as we stood upon one of Alta's peaks, "Look around. This is my office. I am the luckiest man in the world."

There is another side of the story of course. In the interest of trying to prevent passionate skiers who work desk jobs from committing suicide out of sheer envy or quitting their secure occupation to compete with me as snowsports journalists, I feel it is necessary to allow the whole truth to be documented.

It is 5:30 in the morning, and I am in front of my laptop at Mt. Buller, Australia, writing my first draft of a road-trip story. This road-trip has taken me for 58 days through 34 ski areas in Chile, Argentina, New Zealand and Australia. My travels included 40 days of skiing, three or four down days because wind kept the lifts closed, a handful of days for sightseeing, and many days of flying and driving.

This kind of itinerary is hardly what one could call a vacation—quite the contrary. I now *need* a vacation. I am up before dawn because this is the only viable time to do some writing on such a trip. The distances are often rather long between ski resorts, and after a hard day of skiing, we often must drive three or four hours to get to our next destination. Then we are in a rush to get a quick shower and find a bite to eat before the local restaurants close. By the time we have finished dinner, it is about 10:30; I am exhausted and fall into bed in a heap.

IN SPITE OF THESE MINOR complaints, I have come to Australia of my own free will. It was not so with the first white settlers to arrive. King George III of England sent the first boatloads of prisoners and their jailers to Australia in 1788, and the first reports from there suggest that it was not the most hospitable environment around.

Arriving in Sydney Harbor, one of the entourage, Lieutenant Ralph Clark, wrote, "This is the poorest country in the world...overrun with large trees, not one acre of clear ground to be seen."

The Reverend Richard Johnson added, "Scarcely anything is to be seen but rocks or eaten but rats."

Major Ross summed it all up by saying, "I do not scruple to pronounce that in the whole world is not a worse country than what we have seen of this."

The country has come a ways since those beginnings. It is a shame that Ross, Johnson, Clark and company never got the chance to ride the surf at Narrabeen or catch a performance of Aida at the Sydney Opera. They should have stuck a snorkel in their mouth and flapped their fins around the Great Barrier Reef for a while, and I wonder what they would write in their diaries today if they had viewed the 2000 Sydney Olympics.

The trees and rocks that they complained about are abundant enough in the ski resorts of Australia to make for some interesting riding, but there are plenty of open spaces on the upper slopes as well. While Australia is more famous for its sand and surf, there is definitely something worthwhile here for snowsports enthusiasts. In springtime, Australia is an ideal location for a sea and ski holiday.

My partner in Australia was Tuomas Uotila, a former junior racer. Tuomas is a nice young man and an excellent skier. He is a Finn, which means his alter ego is that of a Formula 1 driver. This was evident every time he sat behind the wheel on the curvy Australian mountain roads while I got carsick trying to send text messages with my cell phone.

Tuomas is also 23 years old. That meant that during many long hours on the road, I was "entertained" by a potpourri of Finnish rock, hip-hop, and heavy metal at many decibels over my pain threshold. It is all part of the package as a ski journalist. I suppose it keeps me young as well.

Our visit to Australia began at the early hour of 3:45 a.m., in Auckland, New Zealand, where I drove Tuomas to the airport to catch a six o'clock flight. My own flight was to leave at nine, so I had plenty of time to kill at the airport.

First of all, I spent half an hour guarding Tuomas's hand baggage while he checked in. This is a relatively new task of the ski-bum or ski-journalist lifestyle since the airlines started going on a "screw the customer" campaign after 9/11. Airlines have always had guidelines and rules for baggage, but they were relatively generous, and the limits were not enforced very often. The policy was one of keeping the customer satisfied.

Pre-9/11, skis, poles and boots were considered "sports equipment", and allowed free of charge—over and above the kilo baggage limit. Hand

THIS PAGE
UPPER LEFT: This snowgum shows off its multi-colored bark.
UPPER RIGHT: The koala bear is a nocturnal animal, and you are not likely to see any of these cute creatures any place other than a zoo.
MIDDLE LEFT: Drive carefully on the Australian roads.

MIDDLE RIGHT: Scenery en route to Falls Creek.
LOWER: Sydney Harbour with the Sydney Opera House and the Sydney Harbour Bridge.

RIGHT PAGE
Tuomas catches some air among the snowgums of Threadbo.

baggage was widely overlooked entirely. Nowadays, one is made to put every last item on the scale, and favorable status for ski equipment is often no longer extended.

Tuomas had been hit by Quantas for a US$140 overweight charge on his way to New Zealand for his ski equipment and hoped to avoid that on the way back. Hence, he had repacked his hockey bag, putting all the heaviest items into two backpacks and removing his ski boots as well. These three pieces would now be carry-on luggage, but he could not allow the ticketing personnel to see the excessive hand baggage. Neither could he leave the three pieces alone for fear of some overzealous security guard destroying them as a potential bomb threat.

AFTER MY GUARD DUTY was finished, I alternately worked on my computer and dozed in an uncomfortable airport chair until my departure. Having managed our flights with limited financial damage in the baggage department, our next task was to organize a rental car at Sydney Airport. Avis, Hertz and Budget had no economy cars available. We were about to sign the paperwork with Thrifty, when the girl casually mentioned that the car was not permitted on unpaved roads.

"We are going to ski at your five top resorts, Perisher Blue, Thredbo, Mt. Bullar, Mt. Hotham and Falls Creek," I explained. "Are the roads paved all the way to those areas?"

"You'll have to figure that out for yourself," she retorted, "or alternatively you can pay an extra $250 fee for the week to drive on gravel roads."

Then she smiled that sickeningly insincere the-customer-is always-right smile, and I left the counter to do investigative research. Twenty minutes and a half-dozen phone calls later, I came back to the counter with the information that the roads we needed were all covered with asphalt.

It was a pleasure to get out on the highway and begin our drive through the Australian countryside en route to the Snowy Mountains. The roads are good, but once one leaves the freeway, one must often keep one's speed down because of the various wild animals that abound. Every few kilometers, we passed signs informing us that wombats, kangaroos, koala bears and even emus like to cross the road in our vicinity. The roadkill visible on either side was proof that many drivers had not heeded the warning signs—or perhaps the animals had been negligent about setting up their "car-crossing" signs. We drove slowly in those areas.

One of the perks of being a ski journalist is that ski-resort marketing departments quite often provides you with a complimentary room in addition to free lift passes. The Thredbo people were kind enough to take care of us in the Thredbo Alpine Hotel, adjacent to the slopes.

We took a short siesta following our arrival, and left in search of an evening meal at about nine o'clock. The first ten restaurants we entered

> **» We had not realized how provincial Australia is, outside its major cities.«**

had already closed their kitchens. My frustration was brimming over to anger when we finally found the only open eatery in the entire resort.

No kangaroos had earlier hopped in front of our car, but I soon had a portion of one set on a plate in front of me. After our restaurant search I was famished, and the kangaroo steak was a scrumptious end to our long day.

The morning brought perfect weather and our first chance to ski amidst the famous snowgums of Australia. We could choose between weaving amongst the leafless gums in the Golf Course Bowl, not yet recovered from the major bush fire of 2002, or the fully foliated trees in the remainder of the resort. We enjoyed both. We also found a few small cliffs for jumping and did a few top-to-bottom, non-stop descents to take advantage of Thredbo's 672-meter vertical drop—Australia's longest.

Not far from Thredbo, also situated within Kosciuszko National Park, is Perisher Blue. With 50 lifts, it is Australia's largest ski resort.

We wolfed down a hurried breakfast in Thredbo the next morning, and drove the winding mountain road to Perisher.

It was another idyllic spring day, and we were in cruiser heaven—perfect slopes for intermediates. We cranked it up a notch on the speedometer and did some high-speed turns so that we could see the whole area in the short time we had available. We managed to find a bit of lovely corn snow in a back valley behind Mt. Perisher. We enjoyed a couple of beers on a sun-drenched verandah at lunch, skied until closing time and were back on the road again at 4:30.

NOW WE HAD A LONG drive ahead. We were leaving New South Wales and heading for the Australian Alps of Victoria Province. This route took us through the beautiful eucalyptus forests of the national park and the rolling green farmland beyond the mountains.

We had made a miscalculation. We had not realized how provincial Australia is, outside its major cities. At 8 p.m. we stopped in Tallangatta for gas, only to find that the only gas station in town had closed two hours earlier. Gas pumps that can be paid automatically do not exist, and a few inquiries left no doubt that there was no place nearby where we could purchase fuel until the following morning.

Dinner was a similar problem. This town, which looked like a metropolis on the map, had about half a dozen eateries, all of which were now closed. We could get a beer at the local pub, and for US$7 per person, a rather shoddy room for the night. Oh well, "Early to bed, early to rise..." At least we would get an early start on our way to Falls Creek.

After refueling, we drove through pastures that displayed the bright-green mantle of spring. Soon a peak clad in white appeared on the horizon, and we knew we were approaching Falls Creek.

Falls Creek is a cute little enclave of lodges where one can ski from one's door to the lifts and vice-versa. We checked into the appropriately named Friendly Valley Lodge—a cozy hotel with a big lobby, where families played box games by the fireplace and strangers became friends over après-ski drinks.

It was another day of spring snow. The beginners and intermediates plowed along on the back side of the mountain with picturesque views over the Rocky Valley Reservoir, while the more advanced skiers pumped through fields of moguls on narrow trails like Widow Maker, Zipper and Valley of the Moon. Tuomas and I tried it all. We spent most of the day on the black runs on either side of the Summit Chair Lift. This is a wide

face with a number of rocks, crowns and gullies to keep the skiing interesting.

Not far away from Falls Creek is Mt. Hotham, Australia's freeride capital. More than half a dozen double-diamond chutes, ridges and steep walls are accessible off the Gotcha Lift. Open slopes above the tree line allowed us to acclimatize to the tough terrain before it got narrower and gnarlier with glades of gums and small cliffs lower down.

The ski patrol often keeps the double-diamond playground closed on cold mornings until the snow softens up, and of course, there are days when it remains bone-hard until closing time. I felt happy to be skiing in warm weather, as the soft spring snow kept me from exceeding my speed limit on the steep pitches.

THE "APRÈS-SKI" ON A ROAD TRIP is often a long drive just when one would prefer a beer and a sauna. Four hours of heavy metal later, we began to creep up the mountain road to Mt. Buller in pea-soup fog.

Buller is another resort with a lot of challenging slopes, albeit mostly riddled with bumps. The spring snow was ideal for skiing moguls, and we tried the likes of Fanny's Finish, Powder Keg, Thulke's, Rush Run, Yurredla and Funnel until my legs begged for mercy.

My wannabe young mind can still ski bumps, but my knees most often veto the project. Looking for some smoother, yet steep terrain, Tuomas suggested the chutes beyond Fanny's. They are so steep that they don't get enough skiers to create moguls. It sounded like a good idea, but we were unable to scout them adequately in the misty weather. We started down with more hopes than brains.

The steep grade of the chute caused the upper 5 centimeters of spring slush to slide slowly behind me as I descended. As the slope narrowed between ominous rock walls, it also steepened and became convex. It was impossible to discern whether I could continue. After a morning of moguls, my legs were not particularly fond of hiking back up a 40-degree incline, but that was the most prudent option. Twenty minutes of sweat later, I entered an alternate route that was visible in its entirety. Mission accomplished!

Our last run of the day took us down to the lower elevations, where the short snowgums began to give way to a forest of towering eucalyptus trees. All of a sudden, a wombat jumped out of the bushes in front of us, lest we should forget where we were. From the distance, the wombat looked like a giant rodent and I thought about Reverend Johnson's long-ago remark about eating rats.

Now there was nothing left for this journalistic endeavor but a 10-hour drive to Sydney directly after our full day of hard skiing. No, the life of a ski journalist is not always what it is cracked up to be. On the other hand, I suppose that sailing the seven seas in Her Majesty's Royal Navy seemed like an adventurous job, envied by many in the 1780s, but Major Ross, nevertheless, had a few bones to pick. All things considered, I prefer hitting the road with my skis, camera and laptop.

Oceania in a Nutshell

LOCATION	NEAREST TOWN	NEAREST AIRPORT	SEASON	PEAK ELEVATION	VERTICAL DROP	SIZE	SNOW	BEAUTY	VILLAGE	NOVICE	INTERMEDIATE	ADVANCED	OFF-PISTE	NIGHTLIFE	RATING AVERAGE	WEB SITE
AUSTRALIA																
Falls Creek	Wodonga	Albury	mid June–early Oct.	1842 m	267 m	1	2	3	4	4	4	3	3	2	2	2.8	www.fallscreek.com.au
Mt. Buller	Mansfield	Melbourne	June–October	1804 m	405 m	2	3	2	3	3	3	3	2	3	2	2.6	www.mtbuller.com.au
Mt. Hotham	Wangaratta	Albury	early June–mid Oct.	1850 m	400 m	1	2	3	3	2	2	2	4	3	2	2.4	www.hotham.com.au
Perisher Blue	Jindabyne	Canberra	July–September	2034 m	355 m	1	5	3	3	2	5	5	2	1	2	2.8	www.perisherblue.com.au
Thredbo	Jindabyne	Canberra	early June–mid Oct.	2037 m	672 m	2	2	3	3	3	3	3	3	2	2	2.6	www.thredbo.com.au
NEW ZEALAND																
Broken River	Springfield/Arthur's Pass	Christchurch	late June–October	1820 m	420 m	2	1	2	3	1	1	1	2	3	1	1.7	www.snow.co.nz/brokenriver
Cardrona	Cardrona	Queenstown	late June–October	1894 m	390 m	1	1	3	2	1	3	4	2	2	1	2.0	www.cardrona.com
Coronet Peak	Queenstown	Queenstown	June–October	1649 m	420 m	2	1	3	4	5	3	4	3	2	3	3.0	www.nzski.com
Craigieburn	Springfield/Arthur's Pass	Christchurch	early July–October	1811 m	500 m	2	1	2	3	1	1	1	2	4	1	1.8	www.craigieburn.co.nz
Mt. Hutt	Methven	Christchurch	June–October	2075 m	672 m	2	1	3	3	2	3	3	3	3	2	2.5	www.nzski.com
Mt. Olympus	Springfield/Arthur's Pass	Christchurch	late June–October	1875 m	450 m	2	1	2	2	1	1	1	3	3	1	1.7	www.mtolympus.co.nz
Ohau	Twizel	Queenstown	late June–October	1850 m	400 m	1	3	3	5	2	2	3	4	4	2	2.7	wwwohau.co.nz
Porter Heights	Springfield/Arthur's Pass	Christchurch	late June–October	1980 m	620 m	2	1	3	4	1	2	2	3	4	1	2.3	www.porterheights.co.nz
Remarkables	Frankton	Queenstown	late June–October	1935 m	557 m [1]	2	1	3	5	5	3	3	3	4	3	3.2	www.nzski.com
Tasman Glacier	Aoraki	Queenstown	July–September	2500 m	1000 m	3	1	3	5	1	1	3	5	4	1	2.7	www.skithetasman.co.nz
Treble Cone	Wanaka	Queenstown	late June–early Oct.	1860 m	600 m	2	1	3	5	4	2	4	4	4	3	3.0	www.treblecone.com
Turoa	Ohakune	Palmerston	June–October	2322 m	690 m	2	1	3	3	4	3	3	3	4	3	2.9	www.MtRuapehu.com
Whakapapa	National Park	Taupo	July–November	2300 m	670 m	2	2	3	4	3	3	3	3	3	1	2.7	www.MtRuapehu.com

(1) The lift system itself has a vertical drop of 357 meters, but an additional 200 vertical meters is accessible with a shuttle bus.

The Best Ski Resort in the World

Not too long ago, while discussing ideas for new ski articles with a ski magazine editor, he suggested, "Why don't you write an article about the best ski resort in the world?"

I pondered the idea. This occasion, of course, was not the first time I had mulled over the possibility of writing such an essay—not even the one-hundred-and-first time. Every ski writer has probably fantasized some version of the following telephone conversation:

"Hello, may I speak with Jimmy Petterson, please?"

"Speaking."

"Jimmy, I may call you Jimmy? Yes? Good. This is 'Avalanche' Alf Alpvillage, the editor of *Ski World*, the ski publication with a readership of 100,000,000 skiers. Are you familiar with our magazine, Jimmy? Yes? Great.

"Listen, I happened to come across an article of yours in the October issue of the *Wolf Creek Gazette* while I was sitting in the restroom of the Yellowstone Park forest ranger station. I quite enjoyed your work. Therefore, I'd like to commission you to do an article for us, determining the best ski resort in the world.

"Before you accept this undertaking, I want you to fully realize the immense amount of research that will be necessary. You must have the time available as well as the inclination to take a few years away from all other projects, so you can circle the globe in pursuit of the answer to this universal skier's question. It won't be easy. You'll be forced to visit ski resorts in both hemispheres and log endless hours of arduous powder skiing.

"In addition, you will have to work late nights, checking out the nightlife of each resort. You'll be obliged to gorge yourself on endless four- and five-course meals, so that you can compare the standard of cuisine among the ski areas everywhere on Earth.

"We at *Ski World* realize that this is no cheap undertaking, Jimmy, so if you wish to accept this assignment, we are prepared to send you a retainer of $100,000 to start with. Of course, when you need more, just give us a call..."

About this time, I usually get jolted back to reality by the words, "Back to work, Petterson! Coffee break's over!" or "Honey, can you take out the garbage?"

Truthfully speaking, when a person finds out that I have skied in close to 50 countries, that very question which has dawdled in my daydreams for many years invariably comes up. "So which ski area is the best?" is an inquiry that I have heard more than once. The answer, however, is as complex as the question is simple.

To attempt to choose the best ski area in the world is a surefire way of making new enemies. Half of the readers will be antagonized and alienated because their favorite resort has been omitted. The other half will be equally miffed for fear that their secret powder paradise will be turned into one enormous mogul hill. Recognizing that this answer will not win me any popularity contests, here then, is the conclusion of many years of arduous research.

If there were a resort that really had it all and the price was right, the lift line would go up to the top of the peak and down the other side! It is probably for the best then, that the perfect ski resort does not exist. It can't, because the priorities of most skiers do not often coexist.

Modern facilities cost money, so it will be more expensive to ski in Aspen, Colorado than in Borovets, Bulgaria. Modern ski villages with easy lift access are often less cozy and authentic than traditional mountain villages. Tons of fresh powder and cloudless skies go hand in hand in the movies, but rarely do so in reality. Locations that get frequent dumps of powder don't generally get a lot of sunshine, while the resorts that have a great sunshine record are not famous for powder.

Hence, the best ski area for any individual depends very much upon the skier's priorities. What is important to him or her? Is a skier looking for well-groomed cruisers, monster moguls, or good powder? Does he or she prefer open bowls and valleys, tight tree-skiing, trails, or a variety of terrain? How important is après-ski and nightlife? Does he want a cozy village with ambiance and history, or is it more important that he can step into his bindings at his front door and glide right down to the lift? How much weight does the skier put on modern infrastructure

SKI RESORTS TO MEET THE RICH AND FAMOUS	
Beaver Creek	Colorado, U.S.A.
Cortina	Italy
Courchevel	France
Deer Valley	Utah, U.S.A
Gstaad	Switzerland
Lech	Austria
Megève	France
St. Moritz	Switzerland
Telluride	Colorado, U.S.A.
Zermatt	Switzerland

GOOD RESORTS FOR BEGINNERS AND INTERMEDIATES	
Aspen-Snowmass	Colorado, U.S.A.
Cervinia	Italy
Grandvalira	Andorra
La Plagne	France
La Thuile	Italy
Les Arcs	France
Megève	France
Portes du Soleil	France and Switzerland
Saalbach	Austria
Vail	Colorado, U.S.A.

SKI RESORTS FOR SKI BUMS AND OTHER CHEAPSKATES	
Beldersay	Uzbekistan
Chimbulak	Kazakhstan
Durmitor	Serbia & Montenegro
Dizin	Iran
Elbrus	Russia
Gulmarg	India
Kashka-Suu	Kyrgyzstan
Oukaïmeden	Morocco
Sinaia	Romania
Zare Lazarevski	Macedonia

These skia areas are in alphabetical order. They do *not* have a ranking order.

SKI RESORTS FOR HERMITS AND OTHER LONERS

For the most possible solitude in these resorts, visit midweek, but it might be advisable to make sure that the important lifts are running.

Apussuit	Greenland
Brezovica	Kosovo
Copahue	Argentina
Darbandsar	Iran
Ísafjördur	Iceland
Los Arenales	Chile
Mt. Olympus	New Zealand
Narvik	Norway
Popova Sapka	Macedonia
Stranda	Norway

The table listing resorts with the world's biggest vertical ranks the ski areas in order according to vertical meters. The other tables on these two pages have no ranking order.

and how important is the price tag of the trip? Does he want sunshine or fresh snow?

I personally am most interested in good snow, fresh powder, few people, village ambiance and a variety of ski terrain. Less important to me are sunshine, infrastructure, nightlife and price. As a photographer, I am also impressed with the visual aesthetics of a ski area.

Whatever a person's priorities are, however, a very interesting fact complicates the question even far beyond a skier's different preferences. THE BEST SKI RESORT IN THE WORLD IS NOT A CONSTANT. It is forever changing.

Think of the most fascinating cities in the world—Paris, London, New York, Hong Kong, Berlin, San Francisco, etc. While their attraction may be rather eternal, there still was an optimal time—a period of history—when these cities were the epicenter of world events. This is to say that the dynamics of history determine that certain locations would have been more interesting to visit in some decades than in others.

It would have been extremely exciting to visit New York, for example, during the "Roaring '20s". Europe was in the doldrums after World War I, Wall Street was booming, and the Big Apple was simply the place to be. San Francisco or London, on the other hand, had a heyday in the 1960s, what with the flower-power generation setting up western headquarters in the city by the Bay, while the Beatles and the whole Mercy beat made London the European center of the same phenomenon.

Simply put, the same can be said about skiing. There are certain ski resorts that were among the best in the world in the 1960s, while others flourished in the '80s, and completely different ones would be my choice today.

Sun Valley, Idaho was among the coolest ski resorts in the 1940s. The Sun Valley Lodge was an icon, and Averill Harriman installed the world's first chair lift there in 1936, based on the design of an apparatus that unloaded bananas from ships.

Harriman, Sun Valley's founder and the chairman of the Union Pacific Railroad, also made sure that many film stars and everybody else who was somebody went to Sun Valley during that period. It was the best publicity he could get, and it filled his trains as well as his beds. All this is not to say that Sun Valley is a bad place now. I merely mean that Sun Valley was definitely one of the best places to ski and be during the 1940s.

Alta was a great place to ski in the 1950s and it is my personal choice as the best ski resort to have visited in the '50s. It had some of the best powder in the world, as it still does today. But more important, it had a great staff of instructors who focused on teaching powder technique, while most other resorts did not have this specialty.

If I could choose any one place to have skied in the 1960s, I would choose Chamonix. This beautiful French icon has been a mountain center for so long that even 50 years ago, it was dripping with Old World charm. Nowadays the lift infrastructure of many ski resorts has left Chamonix in the dust, but "Cham" was quite state of the art in the '60s. At that time, the off-piste skiing that has made Chamonix so famous could be enjoyed for a rather long time before it got skied out and one could ski through the magic world of ice on the Vallée Blanche without the masses that frequent this descent today.

I choose Austria's Arlberg as my favorite region of the 1970s. The Rendl side of the valley in St. Anton had been newly developed in the first half of the decade, and its west- and north-facing slopes lay untouched for days while everyone waited in line to ski the famous Valluga. In addition, the Arlberg area had three separate lift passes during the '70s. All the best skiers stayed in St. Anton, but they did not venture to Lech, Zurs or Stuben, where their season pass was not valid. That left endless powder in a large section of the Arlberg to be shared among very few skiers.

Another of my favorite resorts during this decade was the huge Tignes–Val d'Isère area. In a period of time before couloir skiing had become the thing to do, these two resorts had the terrain to do it. My friends and

I often put first tracks into couloirs here five days after a snowfall.

By the 1980s, the resorts most famous for their off-piste pleasures were beginning to get overpopulated. Hence, my favorite resort for this decade is the area that has been my home-away-from-home for so many seasons—Saalbach-Hinterglemm.

While the powder hounds battled for first tracks elsewhere in the ski world, Saalbach and Hinterglemm attracted a combination of beer-guzzlers and families. By this time, the two villages had already built up an excellent après-ski reputation, with an atmosphere that was very genuine. The few powder fans in the Glemmtal enjoyed the best of both worlds with uncrowded, virgin slopes during the day and active, busy nightspots in the evening.

Other favorite resorts of mine during this period include the Trois Vallèes of France and the Dolomites of Italy. Both of these areas already had large and efficient lift systems that had not yet begun to attract the number of guests that they do today.

The pace of life gets forever faster, and the world of skiing was changing faster in the '90s than ever before. Marketing departments were more sophisticated and by the latter part of the decade, the Internet was spreading information at a frenzied pace. Therefore, my favorite ski resort of the '90s was constantly changing.

At the beginning of the decade, La Grave was the whispered secret that gave a unique off-piste experience without the crowds. Eventually, the cat got out of the bag. My top choice moved to Alagna, then to Narvik, and on to Engelberg.

What about the present day? The new millennium has seen an explosion in the popularity of off-piste skiing. It is becoming increasingly difficult to find and ski the perfect run—at least before somebody else has found and skied it.

Strangely enough, in recent years, I have rediscovered Switzerland, a country that is as mainstream as can be. It is a country with skiing possibilities that are very suitable to my personal requirements. During the past few winters, I have revisited both St. Moritz and Zermatt, two of the first Alpine resorts I ever skied. Both these resorts still today

BEST APRÈS-SKI	
Aspen	Colorado, U.S.A.
Bláfjöll	Iceland (Reykjavik)
Borovets	Bulgaria
Chamonix and Val d'Isère	France
Hemsedal and Oppdal	Norway
Ischgl, Kitzbühel, Saalbach, St. Anton and Zell am See	Austria
Sauze d'Oulx	Italy
Verbier	Switzerland
Whistler Blackcomb	Canada
Åre	Sweden

BIGGEST VERTICAL DROP		
1	Chamonix (2807 m)	France
2	Verbier (2509 m) *Off-piste route from Mont Fort to Le Châble*	Switzerland
3	Les Arcs (2276 m) *Off-piste route from Aiguille Rouge to Villaroger*	France
4	Kaprun (2229 m) *Off-piste route from the Kitzsteinhorn to Niedernsill*	Austria
5	Zermatt (2200 m)	Switzerland
6	Mürren (2175 m)	Switzerland
7	La Grave (2150 m)	France
8	Alpe d'Huez (2080 m) *Route to Vaujany*	France
9	Alagna (2069 m)	Italy
10	Davos (2034 m)	Switzerland

LARGEST SKI AREAS

Ski resort size is measured in various ways, including number of lifts, lift capacity, and kilometers of trails. This statistical information is complicated further by the fact that there are lift-linked areas, where one can ski among all the lifts without leaving the slopes, and non-lift-linked regions that are covered by one ski pass.

In some cases, the entire measurement system becomes ridiculous as certain regions call themselves one ski area for marketing purposes despite the fact that there are long distances to be covered by road. In other cases, lifts are built to connect areas strictly for bragging rights, even though the skiing that links the areas is of poor quality, made up primarily of narrow trails and roads.

Therefore, this list of large ski areas is just that—a list of large ski areas. It does not attempt to claim one or the other to be the largest. All of these ski regions are among the largest in the world. I have not included "lift-pass regions" that package many resorts that are a long distance from each other under one lift pass.

Portes du Soleil *Morzine, Avoriaz, Les Gets, etc.*	France and Switzerland
Les Trois Vallées *Val Thorens, Méribel, Courchevel, etc.*	France
The Dolomites Superski Region *Cortina, Val Gardena, Canazei, etc.*	Italy
Verbier and the Four Valleys *Verbier, Bruson, Veysonnaz, etc.*	Switzerland
La Plagne–Les Arcs	France
L'Espace Killy *Tignes–Val d'Isère*	France
The Milky Way *Sestriere, Sauze d'Oulx, San Sicario, etc.*	Italy and France
Salzburger Sportwelt Amadé *Wagrain, Flachau, Zauchensee, etc.*	Austria
The Arlberg *St. Anton, St. Christoph, Lech, Zürs, etc.*	Austria
Super Zillertal *Hintertux, Mayrhofen, Zell am Ziller, Gerlos, etc.*	Austria

FAVORITE DESCENTS

AUSTRIA	A. Bad Gastein – *The north face in Sport Gastein* B. Hinterglemm – *Various routes from Hinterglemm into the Hörndlingergraben to Fieberbrunn.* C. Innsbruck – *The Hafelekar descent* D. Saalbach – *The Amsel from the Bernkogel to the Spielberghaus* E. St. Anton – *The north face of the Rendl* F. Stuben – *The run to Langen from the Maroikopf behind the Albonagrat*
FRANCE	A. La Plagne – *The north face of the Bellecôte* B. Les Arcs – *The north face of the Aiguille Rouge* C. St. Foy – *Descent from Pointe de Fogliettar to Le Miroir*
ICELAND	Ísafjördur – *The unnamed couloirs high above the village*
IRAN	Shemshak – *"Angry Dog Valley"*
ITALY	Dolomites – *Holzer Couloir from the Sella Group (In most years a mandatory rappel is necessary in the middle of the couloir.)*
NORWAY	A. Narvik – *Gagnesaksla near Narvik* B. Narvik – *Mørkhåla* C. Stranda – *Alperittløypa from the Roaldshorn* D. Stryn – *The road-run from Dalsnibba, near Stryn, to the road that goes to Geirangerfjord*
SPAIN	Candanchú – *Zapatilla Couloir*
SWITZER-LAND	A. Davos – *Teufi descent from Jakobshorn* B Engelberg – *Laub* C. Super-St.-Bernard – *South face to Crévacol, Italy*
RUSSIA	Mt. Elbrus – *Garabashi Gorge ("Ushelye")*
UNITED STATES	A. Alta, Utah – *Baldy Chutes* B. Wolf Creek, Colorado – *Waterfall*

MOST BEAUTIFUL RESORTS

Antillanca, Antuco and Osorno	Chile
Bariloche and Cerro Bayo	Argentina
Chamonix	France
The Dolomites (various villages)	Italy
Heavenly and Kirkwood Meadows	California, U.S.A.
Ísafjördur	Iceland
Mt. Bachelor and Mt. Hood	Oregon, U.S.A.
Narvik and Stranda	Norway
Ohau, The Remarkables and Treble Cone	New Zealand
Zermatt	Switzerland

LEFT PAGE
Antti-Pekka Auvinen is all by himself, showing why Copahue in Argentina is a good place to get away from the crowds.

THIS PAGE
LEFT: Austria's Kitzsteinhorn, as seen here from Zell am See, is a good place for summer skiing up on the glacier. During the winter, however, it offers one of the longest vertical descents in the world, down to the village of Niedernsill.
RIGHT: Cerro Bayo, Argentina offers stunning panoramas of Lake Nahuel Huapi.

GREAT SKI TOWNS

Aspen	Colorado, U.S.A.
Banff	Canada
Chamonix	France
Garmisch-Partenkirchen	Germany
Nozawa Onsen	Japan
Queentstown	New Zealand
St. Anton	Austria
Telluride	Colorado, U.S.A.
Zermatt	Switzerland
Åre	Sweden

All tables on these two pages are in alphabetical order and have no ranking order.

offer a fantastic off-piste experience along with excellent infrastructure, great pistes, and especially in the case of Zermatt, superb ambiance. Of course, the reason why the powder does not get skied out immediately in these areas is that the high price tag is prohibitive to most skiers on a limited budget.

Also in Switzerland, the little-known areas of Andermatt, Disentis, and Val d'Anniviers are among my present-day favorites. These Swiss resorts have up until now avoided being overrun by freeriders and powder hounds partly because of their lack of nightlife.

In recent years, I have also gone further afield in search of the ski experience close to my heart. Ski resorts that are small and remote fulfill my quest for a combination of adventure, cultural experience and virgin slopes that I can discover in relative solitude. Mt. Elbrus, Dizen,

Shemshak, Stranda and the volcano resorts of Chile all fall into this category.

Have I left anything out? Not much, I hope—only to add that my research goes on. The ski world is forever changing, and there are innumerable ski areas where I have not yet had the opportunity to visit in my quest to find total ski nirvana.

Every skier certainly has his or her own opinions about the best ski resort, the greatest descent and the most beautiful location to ski. I implore my readers to please send any tips about locations I might have missed to *skibum@telia.com*. The crusade to find perfection in the ski world is a lifelong endeavor, but as I stated at the beginning of this book, somebody has to do it.

Epilogue

Since its inception, skiing's development has followed a long road with many curves, but after all, that is part of the fun of skiing—all the curves and turns along the way. It all began, so long ago, primarily as a means of transportation.

Then, as the 19th century came to a close, the hikers and climbers fastened skis on their feet so that they could enjoy their beloved mountains even in the wintertime, when snow covered the land. They wanted to stay fit during the winter months, and the hike up was, in fact, more important to them in most cases than the glide back down. Quite naturally, however, some of these sportsmen discovered that the actual skiing—the byproduct of touring—was a worthwhile activity in and of itself.

It was at this point that ski lifts of all shapes and sizes started dotting the landscape. Ultimately, there were many more people who preferred skiing down to hiking up. For the rest of the century, ski enthusiasts waited eagerly for the inauguration of new ski resorts with new cogwheel trains, aerial trams, chair lifts, T-bars and the like to spring up. Everybody wanted to try the newest, the biggest and the best. While this is still true to a large extent, skiing's direction has again taken a sweeping giant slalom turn in recent years.

The freeride revolution has taken the sport back to its roots. The new equipment of recent years has allowed ever more riders to enjoy the thrill of descending in powder snow, until even the backcountry around major ski resorts has become filled with more and more tracks. Skiers and boarders have sought new terrain away from the crowds of the conventional ski resorts, where they could replicate the back-to-nature experience that drew the early skiers out into the untamed wilderness.

They have looked to helicopters in many cases to reach less accessible regions of the Chugach, the Caucasus, the Tien Shan and even the Himalayas. Ski touring has increased in popularity as well. In addition, the global village that has developed in recent years has also added to the new direction in skiing. Most of the countries of the world are nowadays easily accessible, and snowsports enthusiasts have begun to use this global village to satisfy their trip back to the roots of the sport. This is exactly what this book has been about.

Skiing Around the World has been a trip through some of the biggest, best and most famous ski resorts in the world, but it has also been a journey to the likes of Iran, Kyrgyzstan, Morocco, Albania and other far-flung ski destinations of the planet. The voyage has visited popular locations that offer a plethora of lifts, activities and nightlife; and it has visited remote, uncrowded mountains where the powder lies untouched for days, and the ski experience that awaits is the kind of grass-roots adventure that one cannot find in the larger resorts.

So, what is left at the end of the day? In fact, a hell of a lot. I have now journeyed through 47 countries, but this is really not the end. There is so much more. To begin with, there are enough ski resorts in the major ski countries to keep a skier busy for this lifetime and a few reincarnations. France alone has over 300 resorts, and I have visited a mere handful in this odyssey. Austria offers skiing in around 600 locations, Switzerland has about 400 ski areas, and 500 more resorts can be found in the United States. I get exhausted just thinking about it.

When it comes to different countries where one can ski, there are numerous other countries not included in this book where ski lifts exist, and still more where snow-covered mountains without lifts call out to the more adventurous skiers of the world.

Right in the middle of Western Europe, there are about a dozen small ski centers in the Ardennes of Belgium, and Scotland offers skiing in the likes of Cairngorm, Glencoe and Ben Nevis, as well as a couple of smaller resorts. Even residents of Portugal can ski at Serra da Estrela-Torre. While the 87-meter vertical drop there won't strike fear in the hearts of many skiers, this is always an option, if you find yourself with a free Sunday on your hands some winter in northern Portugal.

Belarus, Estonia and Lithuania all offer skiing, and could any skier's life be complete without a visit to the longest single chair lift in the former Soviet Union? You can find this 2.7-kilometer-long antique rising up Mt. Trostyan in the Ukrainian resort of Slavsko.

Perhaps of more interest are the slopes of Armenia. This little land has mountains that reach over 4000 meters high, and the ski areas of Tsakhadzor/Tekhenis and Vanadzor/Mymex have lifts in elevations of around 3000 meters.

A bit further south, Israel can offer skiers a very respectable 620 vertical meters of pistes serviced by two lifts that rise up Mt. Hermon in the Golan Heights. Even Algeria, whose political climate is not very favorable to tourism of any kind these days, has some interesting ski areas.

Moving further south in Africa, there are glaciers on Mt. Kenya in Kenya, Mt. Kilimanjaro in Tanzania and Mt. Stanley in Uganda. Skiing is somewhat of an endangered species on Mt. Kilimanjaro, where it is forbidden. Even sneaky skiers who might smuggle a pair of snow blades in their backpack have a limited window of opportunity, as the glacier atop Africa's highest peak is quickly melting away, and will quite probably be gone in the not-too-distant future.

For the less adventurous who would like to ski in Africa, there is the possibility to do so on the 90-vertical-meter slope at Tiffindell, South Africa. Even if Mother Nature does not smile on your endeavor, modern snow-making equipment more or less guarantees a ski experience between May and September. Nearby Lesotho also offers a limited amount of skiing when the conditions are right.

For the skier who also likes sea and sand, and has great patience, sometimes one gets snow on volcanic Pico de Teide on the isle of Tenerife. It often melts the same day, but what the heck. Push your skis into the sand of this Canary Island paradise, hang your hammock between the skis, gather a few good books around you, and wait for your opportunity.

The opposite end of the spectrum from the Canary Islands is the great, untapped snow resource of Antarctica. The Scott Base on Ross Island, owned and operated by the New Zealand government, even has a rope tow to accommodate local skiers! This is a location where you can confidently travel without a snow guarantee from your travel agency, as the snow base is about two kilometers deep! You want more variety? Other

LEFT PAGE
Doug Stoup snowboarding down from the summit of Mt. Mill (735 m) in the Antarctica Peninsula Range. This is close to Mt. Shackleton (1465 m), a bit south of the Lemaire Channel. Photo by Kristoffer Erickson.

THIS PAGE
Two employees of the Tiffendell ski center in South Africa take a break near the top of the slope. Keeping the piste at South Africa's only ski resort maintained probably keeps them plenty busy. Tiffendell has snow-making equipment, and reports on their web site that after a good snowfall, the possibility exists to ski an off-piste run of up to 1.5 kilometers in length. The day this photo was taken was apparently *not* soon after a *good* snowfall. Photo by Ronald Naar.

sectors of Antarctica offer skiing as well—in some cases even night skiing is available for those long, dark winter months. This may be where all skiers gather, a few generations from now, if the current greenhouse effect continues.

In South America, although Peru and Ecuador have no lifts, the rugged mountains of Peru and the volcanoes of Ecuador have long drawn ski adventurers and mountaineers to their slopes. Even Colombia has snow-covered peaks, and at one time, Nevado del Ruiz had a ski lift that dropped people off at the lofty height of 5300 meters!

Patrick Thorne, the guru of ski-resort statistics, reports that the lift, which was originally built in 1956, "was abandoned in the late 1970s or early 1980s due to lack of local interest, global warming, ground shifting making lift towers unstable, and a descending glacier. The volcano erupted in 1985 and whilst the lift structure remains, the cables now feed into a wall of glacial ice."

Of additional interest to avid skiers visiting South America, one could get an opportunity to ski quite close to the equator, in Venezuela, if one has a bit of luck with the weather. Mérida is the home of the longest and highest cable car in the world, rising 3188 vertical meters in four stages to the summit of Pico Espejo (4765 m). This cable car takes adventurers within hiking distance of Pico Bolivar, Venezuela's highest peak (5007 m). While one should not count on anything more than hiking, a bit of lift-accessed ski touring is not out of the question, if the snow gods are smiling.

Asia also has many ski locations to which my ski odyssey has not yet taken me. Taiwan offers skiing above 3000 meters in the tiny ski area of Hohuanshan. Even more surprising is that skiing is also possible in Indonesia. Puncak Jaya, also known as Mount Carstenz, on New Guinea, is skiable. There is even a lift here, but it is not a ski lift and one must cut through a fair amount of bureaucratic red tape to get permission to use it. A few hours' hike from the top of the lift gives skiers access to the best skiing Indonesia has to offer.

In Pakistan, in the heart of the Himalayas, lies the little ski resort of Malam Jabba. A visit here could add a pleasant extra dimension for those who don't mind bringing a pair of boards along as they traverse the Karakorum Highway.

What about skiing in the mountainous countries of Afghanistan, Tajikistan, Mongolia, Tibet and Nepal? The mountains are magnificent and there is more than enough snow. Who knows? One day in the

THIS PAGE
UPPER: Self-portrait of Dutch mountaineer Ronald Naar hiking up Margherita Peak (5109 m), the highest part of Mt. Stanley in Uganda. Ronald reports that it took 7 days of walking through the jungle to reach the snow. The descent was about a kilometer in length but offered only a few hundred meters of vertical. Some people will go to great effort to make a few turns and get away from the crowds. Photo by Ronald Naar.
LOWER: Mt. Dhaulagiri (8167 m) in Nepal as seen from Poon Hill at sunrise.

near future, somebody just might build a ski lift in one of those remote regions. Even Burma has a high-elevation ski resort currently in the planning stages.

In 2003, California adventurer Craig Calonica and a group of adventurous cohorts opened Nepal to heliskiing in the Annapurna region of the country, and they are expanding their operation into new areas year by year.

Skiers are dreamers. That is not so strange. Perhaps it is the exalted view that skiers often experience as they look down on a sea of fluffy cumulus clouds that inspires them to the wildest fantasies. Whether your dream is to heliski in the shadow of Everest in Nepal, swoop down some nameless glacier in Antarctica, or be one of the rare visitors to ski the tropics of Indonesia, your own personal skier's odyssey only comes to a close when you cease to dream.

Good night, and sweet dreams.